Book of Stryj (Ukraine)

Translation of *Sefer Stryj*

The Original Yizkor Book:

Edited by N. Kudish, Tel Aviv,

Published by the Former Residents of Stryj in Israel, 1962

Published by JewishGen

An Affiliate of the Museum of Jewish Heritage - A Living Memorial to the Holocaust

New York

Book of Stryj (Ukraine)
Translation of *Sefer Stryj*

Copyright © 2019 by JewishGen, Inc.
All rights reserved.
First Printing: June 2018, Sivan 5778
Second Printing: March 2019, Adar II 5778

Translation Project Coordinator: Mike Kalt
Translated by Susan Rosin, Yocheved Klausner, Israel Pickholtz, Ganit Eiron, Daniella Heller, and Susannah Juni
Layout: Joel Alpert
Cover Design: Nili Goldman

This book may not be reproduced, in whole or in part, including illustrations in any form (beyond that copying permitted by Sections 107 and 108 of the U.S. Copyright Law and except by reviewers for public press), without written permission from the publisher.

Published by JewishGen, Inc.
An Affiliate of the Museum of Jewish Heritage
A Living Memorial to the Holocaust
36 Battery Place, New York, NY 10280

"JewishGen, Inc. is not responsible for inaccuracies or omissions in the original work and makes no representations regarding the accuracy of this translation. Digital images of the original book's contents can be seen online at the New York Public Library Web site."

The mission of the JewishGen organization is to produce a translation of the original work and we cannot verify the accuracy of statements or alter facts cited.

Printed in the United States of America by Lightning Source, Inc.
Library of Congress Control Number (LCCN): 2018944198
ISBN: 978-1-939561-68-8 (hard cover: 760 pages, alk. paper)

Front Cover: Naphtali Siegel with his daughter Hinda – Ayala. Naftali was one of the first teachers in the "Safa Brura" school in Stryj and one of the founders of the "Ivriya" society. His wife Lubka was the daughter of Avraham Levin – Founder of "Yad Harutzim" society in Stryj. Photo was taken in 1936 before the family immigrated to *Eretz-Yisrael* (Palestine at the time). *Photo courtesy of Nili Goldman*

Back cover image is from a post card on a JewishGen KehilaLinks Stryj page provided by Tomas Wisniewski.

JewishGen and the Yizkor-Books-in-Print Project

This book has been published by the **Yizkor-Books-in-Print Project,** as part of the **Yizkor Book Project** of **JewishGen, Inc**.

JewishGen, Inc. is a non-profit organization founded in 1987 as a resource for Jewish genealogy. Its website [www.jewishgen.org] serves as an international clearinghouse and resource center to assist individuals who are researching the history of their Jewish families and the places where they lived. JewishGen provides databases, facilitates discussion groups, and coordinates projects relating to Jewish genealogy and the history of the Jewish people. In 2003, JewishGen became an affiliate of the **Museum of Jewish Heritage - A Living Memorial to the Holocaust** in New York.

The **JewishGen Yizkor Book Project** was organized to make more widely known the existence of Yizkor (Memorial) Books written by survivors and former residents of various Jewish communities throughout the world. Later, volunteers connected to the different destroyed communities began cooperating to have these books translated from the original language—usually Hebrew or Yiddish—into English, thus enabling a wider audience to have access to the valuable information contained within them. As each chapter of these books was translated, it was posted on the JewishGen website and made available to the general public.

The **Yizkor-Books-in-Print Project** began in 2011 as an initiative to print and publish Yizkor Books that had been fully translated, so that hard copies would be available for purchase by the descendants of these communities and also by scholars, universities, synagogues, libraries, and museums.

These Yizkor books have been produced almost entirely through the volunteer effort of researchers from around the world, assisted by donations from private individuals. The books are printed and sold at near cost, so as to make them as affordable as possible. Our goal is to make this important genre of Jewish literature and history available in English in book form, so that people can have the personal histories of their ancestral towns on their bookshelves for themselves and for their children and grandchildren.

A list of all published translated Yizkor Books in the project with prices and ordering information can be found at:

http://www.jewishgen.org/Yizkor/ybip.html

Lance Ackerfeld, Yizkor Book Project Manager
Joel Alpert, Yizkor-Book-in-Print Project Coordinator

Yizkor Book Project

This book is presented by the
Yizkor Books in Print Project
Project Coordinator: Joel Alpert

Part of the
Yizkor Books Project of JewishGen, Inc.
Project Manager: Lance Ackerfeld

These books have been produced solely through volunteer effort of individuals from around the world. The books are printed and sold at near cost, so as to make them as affordable as possible.

Our goal is to make this history and important genre of Jewish literature available in English in book form so that people can have the near-personal histories of their ancestral towns on their bookshelves for themselves and for their children and grandchildren.

Any donations to the Yizkor Books Project are appreciated.

Please send donations to:
Yizkor Book Project
JewishGen
36 Battery Place
New York, NY 10280

JewishGen, Inc. is an affiliate of the
Museum of Jewish Heritage
A Living Memorial to the Holocaust

Acknowledgements

Special thanks to the National Yiddish Book Center in Amherst, Massachusetts and the New York Public Library for supplying the high resolution images used in this book.

Our sincere appreciation to Uriel Zur Shützer z"l, of the Stryj Landsmannschaft, for permission to use this material.

Brief History of the Jewish Community of Stryj

Stryj is located in Western Ukraine (formerly Eastern Galicia) about 40 miles (65 kilometers) south of L'viv. Variants on its spelling include Stryy, Stryi, Stryia, and Stry.

Jews first appeared in Stryj in the late 1500's. The first synagogue was built in 1660. After Poland was partitioned, Stryj became part of the Austrian Empire in 1772, at which time there were about 440 Jewish families in the town and suburbs. After World War I, Stryj was part of the West Ukrainian People's Republic, a short-lived republic that existed in late 1918 and early 1919 in eastern Galicia. The area later became a part of the Second Polish Republic following the Polish–Ukrainian War. The town had a Jewish population of 10,988 in 1921 and about 12,000 in 1939. According to the Polish census of 1931 its population consisted of 35.6% Jews, 34.5% Poles, 28% Ukrainians and 1.6% Germans.

The Germans occupied Stryj at the end of September 1939. Following the Molotov–Ribbentrop non-aggression agreement, Stryj was under control of the Soviet Union. The Germans ended the agreement by launching an attack on the Soviet positions in Eastern Poland during Operation Barbarossa on June 22, 1941. The Germans occupied Stryj on July 2, 1941, and hundreds of Jews were immediately murdered. Twelve hundred Jews were shot in the Holobotow forest in November 1941. Several deportations to extermination camps took place beginning in September 1942. Between June and August of 1943 the Stryj ghetto and labor camps near the town were liquidated. Only a few Jewish survivors had remained in town when the Soviet army occupied Stryj in August 1944. No Jewish community was re-established.

Translator's Foreword

My mother Sofia (Rosalia) Bardach–Oher was fourteen years old when the Germans invaded Galicia for the first time in September 1939. Following the Molotov–Ribbentrop Pact of non-aggression, the Germans retreated and Stryj passed to the Soviet Union a few weeks later.

The youngest of seven children, my mother had a happy childhood, sharing her time with her five sisters and brother between their spacious home in Stryj and the farm her father Wolf Bardach leased and managed with her mother Czarna (Morgenstern) in the village of Piaseczna, about 17 miles north of town. The family lived in the area for ages and can be traced to an ancestor born in the late 1700's (when Jews in this area of the Austro-Hungarian Empire were required to take on family names).

Everything changed when the Germans broke the Molotov–Ribbentrop Pact of non-aggression, and occupied Stryj on June 22nd, 1941. Murders, deportations and hunger became an everyday occurrence. Miraculously my mother, her sisters and their parents survived the war, but her brother was murdered. Five of the sisters and their families and the parents immigrated to Israel in the 1950's. One sister immigrated in the 1980's.

My mother told us a lot about her childhood before the war and it sounded like an idyllic life, especially her experiences in the village. She did not talk much about the war years until much later in life. My daughter, Sharon Rosin-Meraro wanted to record what happened to her grandmother and the family during the war, and this account can be found at: https://www.drohobycz-boryslaw.org/images/attachments/attachments/families/oher/SofiaOherMemoirs.pdf

A number of years ago I decided to trace my family history. JewishGen was my main tool of discovery and for that I am very grateful. After I created my family tree (still a work in progress) I felt I wanted to do some volunteer work for JewishGen. Being fluent in both Hebrew and English, volunteering for the Yizkor Book Project seemed natural and to work on the Yizkor Book of my mother's town was a perfect combination.

I feel very fortunate to participate in this project. Since my mother was a young girl before the start of the war, she was not aware of the rich cultural and political life of the Stryj Jewish community. Through my work on this project I was able to learn so much about this community and truly feel the tremendous loss suffered by this and the rest of the Jewish communities in the holocaust.

May their Memory be Blessed.

Susan (Irit) Oher–Rosin

Brea, CA

May 2018

Book of Stryj

Cover of the Original Yizkor Book

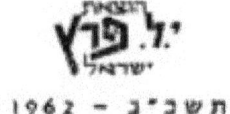

תשכ"ב – 1962

ארגון יוצאי סטרי בישראל
פארבאנד פון סטריער לאנדסלייט

Translation of previous page

Book of Stryj

I. L. Peretz

Publication

Israel

1962

Organization of Former Stryj Residents in Israel

המערכת

ד"ר ג. קודיש * ש. רוונברג * א. רוספלד

הועד להוצאת הספר

ד"ר ע. בר־לב, ד"ר נ. קודיש, מ. קו, ש. רוונברג, א. רוספלד

כתבי־יד ביידיש, בפולנית ובגרמנית תרגם לעברית: ד"ר נ. קודיש

כתבי־יד בעברית תרגם לאנגלית: י. לסק

מפת העיר סטרי שרטט אלפרד וולדמן

הועד להוצאת הספר מביע את תודתו לכל
המשתתפים, שתרמו, הן ברוח והן בחומר,
להוצאת ספר סטרי, יעמדו כלם על הברכה.

Translation of the previous page

Editorial Board:

Dr. N. Kudish   S. Rosenberg   A. Rotfeld

The Book Publication Committee:

Dr. A. Bar-Lev   Dr. N. Kudish   M. Kez   S. Rosenberg   A. Rotfeld

Yiddish, Polish and German Manuscripts were translated into Hebrew by: Dr. N. Kudish

Hebrew Manuscripts were translated into English by: J. Lask

Stryj City Map was drafted by Albert Waldman

The Book Publication Committee expresses its gratitude to all the participants who contributed, both spiritually and in material, to the publication of the Book of Stryj.

Geopolitical Information:

Stryy, Ukraine is located at: 49°15' North Latitude, 23°51' East Longitude

It is 45 miles WNW of Ivano-Frankivsk (Stanisławów) and 40 miles S of L'viv Lwów).

Alternate names for the town are: Stryy [Ukrainian], Stryj [Polish], Stry [Yiddish], Stryi, Stri, Stria, Stryje

Ukrainian: Стрий.   Yiddish: סטרי.   Russian: Стрый.   Hebrew: סְטְרִי

	Town	District	Province	Country
Before World War I (c. 1900):	Stryj	Stryj	Galicia	Austrian Empire
Between the wars (c. 1930):	Stryj	Stryj	Stanisławów	Poland
After World War II (c. 1950):	Stryy	Soviet Union		
Today (c. 2000):	Stryy	Ukraine		

Jewish Population: 6,572 (in 1890), 10,718 (1910)

<u>Nearby Jewish Communities</u>

Lysyatychi 7 miles NE
Sokołów 9 miles ESE
Mizhrichchya 10 miles SSE
Wołoska Wieś 13 miles S
Bolekhiv 13 miles S
Stebnyk 13 miles WNW
Medenychi 13 miles NNW
Hnizdychiv 14 miles ENE
Orov 15 miles WSW
Zhydachiv 16 miles NE
Verkhneye Sinevidnoye 16 miles SW
Truskavets 16 miles W
Drohobych 17 miles WNW
Rozdil 18 miles NNE
Berezdivtsi 19 miles NE
Mykolayiv 19 miles NNE
Zhuravno 20 miles E

Map of the Ukraine with Stryj indicated

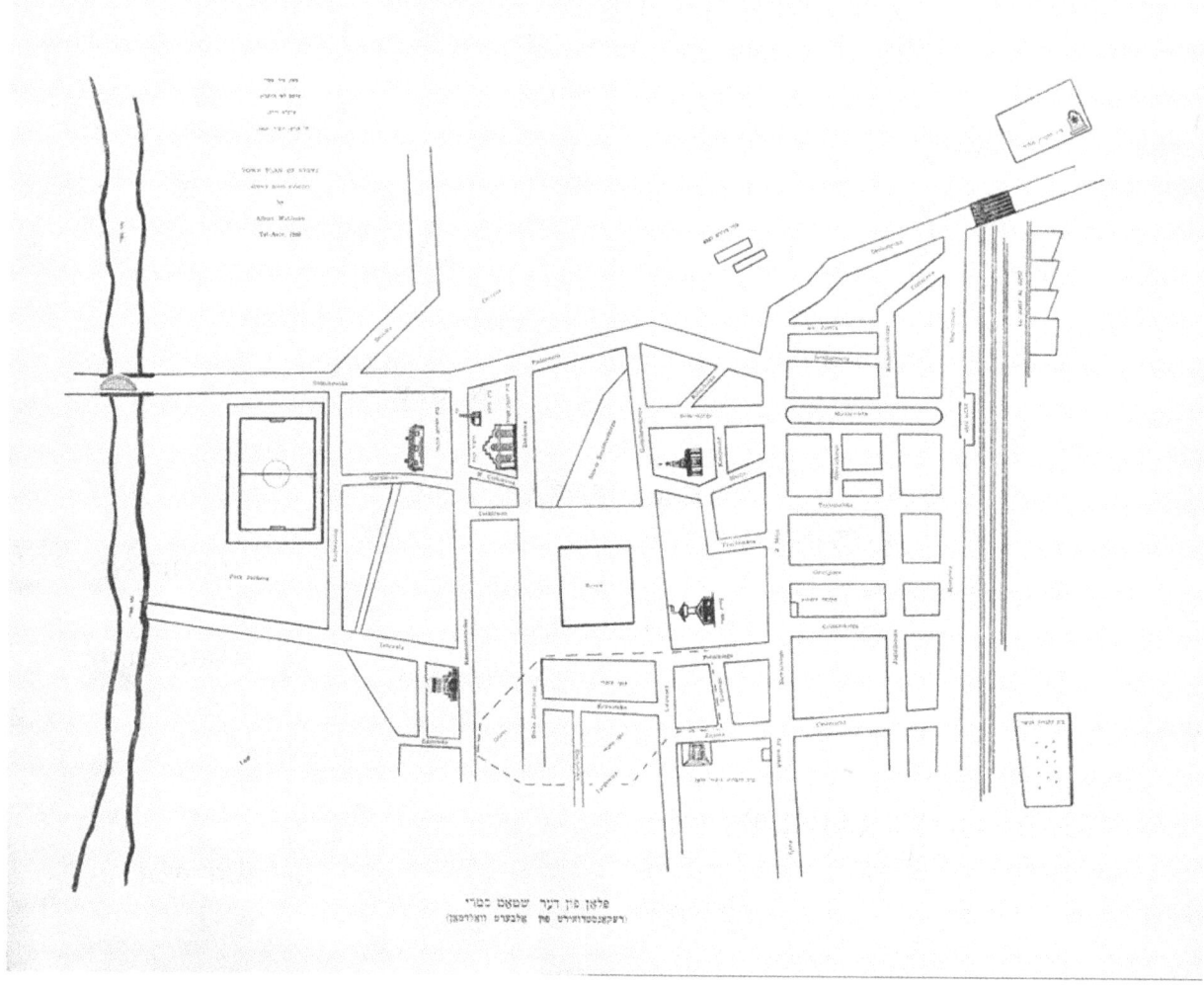

Pre-World War II City Map of Stryj

Notes to the Reader:

We apologize ahead of time for the poor quality of images in the book. Often these images had been scanned from the original Yizkor books which were of poor quality to begin with, being copies of old photographs. Each transfer results in loss of quality. We have done the best we couldm, given the original material and the resources and technology at hand. Even though images often appear of higher quality on computer screens, it does not transfer to high quality images in print. A reader can view the original scans on the web sites listed below.

Within the text the reader will note "[34]" standing ahead of a paragraph. This indicates that the material translated below was on page 34 of the original book. However, when a paragraph was split between two pages in the original book, the marker is placed in this book after the end of the paragraph for ease of reading.

Also please note that all references within the text of the book to page numbers, refer to the page numbers of the original Yizkor Book.

The original book can be seen online at the NY Public Library site:

http://yizkor.nypl.org/index.php?id=2628

or at the Yiddish Book Center web site:

https://www.yiddishbookcenter.org/search/collection/%22NYPL-Yiddish%2520Book%2520Center%2520Yizkor%2520Book%2520Collection%22?search_api_views_fulltext=Stryj&Submit+search=&restrict=

In order to obtain a list of all Shoah victims from Stryj, the reader should access the Yad Vashem web site listed below; one can also search for specific family names using family name option. These lists are continually updated by Yad Vashem, so it is worthwhile to periodically search these lists.

There is much valuable information available on this web site, including the Pages of Testimony, etc.

http://yvng.yadvashem.org

A list of this book and all books available in the Yizkor-Book-In-Print Project along with prices is available at:

http://www.jewishgen.org/Yizkor/ybip.html

Table of Contents

The Community of Stryj Until World War I (1914)

The History of the Jews of Stryj	1
At the End of the Nineteenth Century	82
Beginning of Zionism (Memoirs)	88
From the book "Voices in the Darkness"	93

The First World War (1914-1918)

During the Russian Invasion (1914-1915)	106
The Russian Occupation in Stryj (1914-1915)	107
The Jewish Defense 1918	110
The Jewish Militia in 1918	112
The days of the Ukrainian Rule	116

Institutions and Associations

Stryj Jewish Community between the Two World Wars	112
Synagogues	127
The various minyanim or small prayer groups in our town	157
The Talmud Torah [Torah school for young children]	158
The "Safa Brura" Hebrew School	158
The "Ivriya" Society	163
A Town and its charm	166
The Students' Organizations in Stryj	174
The Academic Society "Emuna"	181
"Kadima"	183
The Academic Society "Hebronia"	184
The Socialist-Zionist Academic Association	186
Bet Ha'am	188
The Orphanage	189
The Jewish Hospital	190
TOZ organization	192
The Jewish Vocational School	192
"The Soup Kitchen"	194

"Ezrat Nashim" (Women's help organization)	195
"Kreuzer Verein Society"	196
The "Gemilut Hesed" (Benevolence) Fund	196
Yad Harutzim Society	197
The "Oseh Tov" Merchants Society	201
Committee for the Rescue of German Jews	202
WIZO	202
The Jewish Economic Society	203
The Jewish "Civic Casino"	204
The Jewish Sport in Stryj	204

Personalities and Public Figures

Rabbi Arie Leib HaKohen Heller	209
Rabbi Asher Enzel Cuzmer	210
The Rabbi of Lissa, the Author of "Havat Da'at" (The Opinion)	211
Rabbi Eliyahu Meir Ben Yaakov HaKohen Rosenblum	216
Rabbi Arie Leibish Horowitz	216
Rabbi Shalom HaKohen Yolles (Der Mościsker)	218
Rabbi Shraga Feivel Hertz (Der Glogover)	219
Rabbi Eliezer Ben Shlomo Ladier	221
Midnight	222
The Dayanim [judges in religious court]	223
Rav R'Asher Yeshayahu Frenkel	223
R'Mordechai (Motel) Druker	224
R'Yitzhak Hauptman Shub (slaughterer and examiner)	226
Dr. Isaac (Isidor) Aaron Bernfeld	228
Dr. Zvi Diesendruk	229
Dr. Naphtali (Tulo) Nussenblatt	231
Jonah Gelernter	233
Yehoshoa Tilleman	234
Dr. Max Bienenstock	236
Dr. Abraham Insler	238
Dr. Zeev Presser	240
Dr. Mordechai Kaufmann	241
Dr. Shlomo Goldberg	242
Dr. Benjamin Millbauer	243

Moshe Aaron Wohlmut	244
Benjamin Klein	246
Dov (Berl) Stern	247
Meir Frankel	248
Dr. Moshe Barlev (Reinhartz)	249
Abraham (Buczi) Apfelgruen	251
Rachel Katz	252
Dr. Malka Leibowitz	255
Aryeh (Leib) Schwamer	256
Dr. Azriel Eisenstein	257
David Zeidman	258
Eliyahu Waldman	259
Aaron Meller	260
Joshua Oberlaender	261
Ben–Zion Garfunkel	261
Abraham Levin	262
Levi Opper	264
Michael (Mechel) Opper	265
Itta Becher	266
The Rossler Brothers	266
Yehoshua Rossler	267
Shlomo Rossler	267
Shlomo Rosenberg	268
Leib Tepper	268
David Seltzer	269
Eliyahu Katz	270
Dr. Joseph Schuster-Shilo	271

Organizations and Parties

General Zionism in Stryj	277
"Arbeitsgemeinschaft" (Working Group – Cooperation Committee)	281
The "Mizrahi" Organization	283
Agudat Israel	284
Poalei Zion	284
Before the Frist World War	285
Poalei Zion Youth	287
The Awakening Behind the Front	288

The Polish Period	297
The Split	297
Elections	299
The Jewish Professional Movement	300
The "Hitahdut"	302
The Unification of "Hitahdut" and "Poalei Zion"	307
Ha'Oved [The Worker]	309
Z.A.S.S. (Zionist Socialist Academic Society)	310
HeHalutz [The Pioneer]	311
Hashomer Hatzair	320
The Women of Stryj	324
The Revisionist Movement	326
The "Betar" Movement	329
"Masada" and the Revisionist HeHalutz	330

Second World War — 332

The Soviet Occupation (1939 – 1941)	338
A Refugee Writes about Stryj's Jews	342
A Stryj Refugee in Russia	344

The Destruction of the Stryj Community — 350

Holocaust Episodes	350
The Destruction of the Stryj Community	395
List of Stryj Martyrs	424

Yiddish Section

Memories, Chronicles, Labor Movement

Memories of the old home	446
The Jewish Militia in Stryj	447
The First Self Defense in Stryj	448
Béla Kun in Stryj	450
The Bloody Wednesday in Stryj	452
The Jewish Labor-Movement in Stryj	455

Po'alei–Zion in Stryj (1900–1914)	457
Z.P.S. – BUND	470
The Jewish Professional Movement	473
The Borochov Library	476
The Soviet Occupation in Stryj	478
A Letter from a Refugee about the Jews of Stryj	484
Stryj Refugees in the Soviet Union	485
The Annihilation of the Jewish Community in Stryj	488

Appendix   257

Former Stryj Residents who died in Israel before 1962 — 502

Index   503
Name Index — 503

English Section   570

The Aftermath of Catastrophe	570
The United Stryjer Young Men's Benevolent Association	573
The History of the Old Independent Stryjer Society in NY	576
The Stryj Community after 1886	580
Between the Two World Wars	601

The Death of a Community

Chapter One: An Established City	638
Chapter Two: In the Throes	645
Chapter Three: Under Soviet Rule	646
Chapter Four: The Destruction of Jewish Stryj	648
Chapter Five: Through the Carpathian Mountains	667
Jews of the Stryjer Community Victims of the Nazi Holocaust as Commemorated by their Relatives in the United States (Necrology)	685

Editorial Board Preface

With great awe, love and compassion we present here to the former residents of Stryj in Israel and the diaspora this memorial book about the community. This book is the result of the hard and relentless work of many individuals for many years.

We did not have archival or historical materials at our disposal about the Jewish life in our town in recent generations. We had no access to resources at the Hebrew University on Mount Scopus[1] and other places. All the rich and diverse material in this book comes from the memories of the former residents of Stryj in Israel and abroad. The only exception is the comprehensive article by Dr. N.M. Gelber about the Jewish History up to the twentieth century.

The material was collected bit by bit, steadily, stubbornly, and with great devotion by several Stryj people. It was accumulated with meager resources and many difficulties.

With the publication of this memorial book we want to show the scroll of Jewish Stryj with its great past and its bitter end. We light a memorial candle to our loved ones who lived, worked and dreamed for many generations. Lovingly we want to memorialize and shed light on the private, public, national, spiritual, religious and economic life of the Stryj Jewish community throughout the generations.

We erect a memorial to our community, famous for its rabbis, authors, intellectuals, and builders who contributed greatly to the Jewish and human culture. To the town's public servants, the people, the pioneers - all of them who added a brick to building the nation and the state of Israel.

---

[1] The Hebrew University on Mount Scopus was under Jordan rule at the time the book was published. Israel gained access to the University in 1967 after the Six Days War

We know we did not achieve perfection. We are aware of the possible omissions in our efforts to paint a complete and full picture of the life and death of Stryj Jewry.

We know that not every value, undertaking, organization, institution, and personality is fully and duly represented here.

We requested all our town's people to contribute for this memorial, but only few were able to respond...

This book is published in agreement with residents of Stryj in the diaspora, mainly in Hebrew with sections in Yiddish and English.

We are grateful to the Stryj organization in New York for their financial support in bringing this book to publication.

We thank all previous residents of the Stryj community who assisted us, encouraged us with advice and guidance in publishing this Yizkor book for the holy community of Stryj.

Once There Was a Community of Stryj

Once there was a Stryj community, an important Jewish town, a lively and vibrant cell in the fabric of the Jewish communities in Poland.

Many generations built it: workers, craftsmen, shopkeepers, merchants, doers and thinkers built the community a layer upon layer for the hundreds years of its existence.

Its beginnings were in the distant past of the middle-ages, hundreds of years ago...and its end was the destruction of Polish Jewry...part of it in the mass graves of the six millions Jews...its place is among the gas chambers...its bones and ashes are spread in the Polish diaspora...

We cannot even express the pain and mourning for the martyrs of Stryj by the Nazis and their many helpers...

Who can count all the leaders, the public servants, all those who performed acts of kindness and charity and all those working for the community and Zion.

Here is Jewish Stryj. A lively and vibrant town. The Jews here are living, working, suffering, believing, preparing and hoping for a better future. With innocent and pure faith in men they adhered to the vision of nations with the belief that humanity and culture will bring salvation to the Jews wherever they are...

And then calamity came suddenly...like a lightning...death came abruptly...

Rich and diverse were the lives of Jews before the holocaust, and such were too the lives of Stryj's Jewry.

Here is the wonderful figure of the Kabbalistic Jew, shrouded in secrecy, just as someone who walked the streets of Toledo or Cordoba in Spain 700 –

800 years ago or 500 years ago in the narrow streets of Tsfat (Safed) in Israel...And here is the enthusiastic Chassid, not much different than the rabbi Israel Baal Shem Tov students 200 years ago...And here is the strong opponent (mitnaged), well versed in the Mishna and Poskim (decisors) and he looks as if transplanted from the times and place of the Vilna Gaon, and here is the Beit HaMidrash student, studying the Gmara, just as did his brethren in the ghettos during the middle ages. There were the learned scholars on the streets of Stryj, just as they were during the days of Peretz Smolenskin, Moshe Leib Lilienblum and Yehudah Leib Gordon 80 – 90 years ago. And outside of these groups were the few assimilationists, renouncing their religion and nation just as did their ancestors about 200 years earlier in the assimilation centers in western Europe...

Here is the national activist trying to convince the community to work for building the nation and the country. And on the other hand the Jewish leaders who believe in the salvation of the Jews wherever they are...

And here are the enthusiastic youth, who enliven the streets with their beauty who realize the Jewish people's destiny with their body and soul by being pioneers thus creating the foundation of the future state of Israel.

It was an accumulation of ideas and personalities, of doers and thinkers, of workers, of multitudes and movements, aspirations and tasks. It was an accumulation of high historical tension that created a crisis in 1939 after which there was only death and destruction...

It is not humanly possible to record and express the martyrology of 1939 – 1945.

The world and the enlightened nations did not want to hear the cries of our tortured brethren before they died, when the "cultured nation" of Germany came with the best tools of destruction to wipe off the earth the eternal nation...

The few survivors from the extermination camps, from the forests, from the caves and the holes and from the hiding places in the cities and the villages live now with their unsettling memories and their pain and agony...they live in the shadows of all those victims who were not brought to a Jewish grave...

May this book speak about our pain and tragedy...hundreds of Stryj Jews who live now in Israel and abroad, every one of them with their own pain and loss, and may this book serve as a memorial – so that we and those who come after us will never forget...

May this book serve as a memorial to the holy community of Stryj, its rise, its glory days and its destruction...

May this book be a humble memorial to the personalities, the sons and daughters, the institutions, the enterprises, the dreams, the faith and vision of the holy community of Stryj...

May this book be a testimony that the ruthless and evil rule is gone and the remnants of the martyrs erected a memorial for this incredible loss.

May this be a prayer book so we can go through its pages and remember our martyrs.

And may this book help us bow our heads and say our mourners' Kaddish...

Nathan Kudish – Yonah Friedler

[Page 17]

The Community of Stryj Until World War I (1914)

The History of the Jews of Stryj
br Dr. M. Gelber

Translated by Susan Rosin

Introduction

The Development of the Town

It is a well-known fact that a catholic house of worship existed in Stryj as early as 1396 therefore it is assumed that a settlement of some sort existed prior to that time. The town had an important function in the trading with Hungary. A customs station and a castle-fortress provided security and control over the surroundings.

At the beginning of the fifteenth century Stryj was the major town in the district and its capital. King Władysław Jagiełło (1386 –1434) granted the entire district and the neighboring districts of Żydaczów and Gródek (present day Horodok, Ukraine) to his brother Bolesław Švitrigaila. Shortly after th at, the districts of Żydaczów and Gródek were given to prince Fedor Lubartowicz and Stryj was returned to the king. Due to the frequent wars, the town was destroyed and only in 1431, the king allowed the nobleman Zaklika (Tarło) to rebuild.

In the middle of the fifteenth century the city was the seat of a land judge (sędzia ziemski) who had jurisdiction over the entire area. He was the subordinate of the elders/seniors (starosta) with jurisdiction authority on all of Rus?' (the lands of Russia and Belarus). Many organizational changes took place during the reign of Władysław Warneńczyk.

From the fifteenth century the town was given the Magdeburg Rights. As we can glean from the October 21st, 1431 privilege bestowed by king Jagiełło thus changing from the Polish and Ruthenian laws to the German laws.

In the first part of the fifteenth century, the town belonged administratively to the Przemyśl region. King Jagiełło established here the Starostwo and the first starosta was Likka Tarło[1].

In 1509 the town was occupied by the armies of the Wojewoda Bohdan from Moldavia and in 1523 it was destroyed by the Tatars. The destruction was so complete that the Sejm decided to exempt the town from paying any type of taxes for eight years.

The town started to improve only during the days of starosta the grand crown hetman Jan Tarnowski. Because of his efforts, many concessions were made for the town's people such as tax exemption in 1549 for fairs held up to 12 miles outside of town.

The town had many craftsmen and merchants who were trading with Hungary. Mainly they brought wine from Hungary that was stored in special warehouses in the center of town and sold salt to the neighboring towns.

During the reign of his son Jan Krzysztof Tarnowski, his administrators oppressed the town's people. But in spite of this situation, the Ruthenian population grew and they had five churches that were under the authority of the Przemyśl – Sambor clergy. In 1650 due to the efforts of Krzysztof Koniecpolski and the influence of the municipality, King Jan Kazimierz (John II Casimir) granted privileges and increased religious rights such as the ability to ring the church bells, exemption from military service for the priests and freedom of worship.

The town's people were merchants, craftsmen and producers of beer. Six "unions" of craftsmen existed in 1635: shoemakers, potters, tailors, furriers, weavers, blacksmiths and metal-workers. In addition there were others that did not have unions of their own such as bakers, barbers and non-professional doctors.

The king Stefan Batory (Stephen Báthory) granted some major privileges to the town in 1578 and on July 8th, 1585. These privileges forced the salt merchants from Dolina to stay in town for three days and give their merchandise to the town's merchants. The privileges also lifted the previous mandatory decree to provide horses for the king and his entourage on their way to Hungary. In the 1585 privilege the king allowed building stores in the town center.

Two very big fires occurred in town in 1592 and in 1605 causing major destruction to such an extent that king Zygmunt III exempted the town and its inhabitants from paying taxes, rents and other obligations for four years.

In 1597, the village Aaplaton was purchased by the town, effectively increasing the town's area.

On March 30th, 1618 the major privileges obtained from the Sejm and king's commissars were ratified by king Zygmunt III. There was a long and hard struggle to obtains these privileges, and they were later ratified by the kings Władysław IV in 1633, Jan II Kazimierz in 1650, Jan Władysław Sobieski in 1861 and Stanisław August Poniatowski on May 22nd, 1766, allowing the town to develop and prosper.

[Page 18]

In the year 1630 the town and its suburbs had six large buildings and 362 homes. In the years 1646 – 1652 during the Cossacks and Tatars wars, 200 of these homes were destroyed. The people suffered greatly from plagues and fires and most of them fled town, leaving more than 100 homes completely vacant and no craftsmen. In 1648 the Belz Wojewoda Andrzej Krakowski defended the town and forced the Cossacks' retreat. In 1657, the leader of the Hungarian revolt, Rákóczi and his staff camped in town. Another fire in 1672 destroyed parts of town and it only recovered during the rule of the starosta Jan Sobieski. During his reign, Serbs who fled from Turkey settled in town, as well as some from Wallachia (a region of historical Romania).

In 1662 the number of inhabitants in the town was 1,477 – 357 Poles, 1040 Ruthenians and 70 Jews. King Jan III Sobieski was very supportive of the town, visited there several times, and authorized the building of many structures as well as enforcing the town's and castles fortifications.[2]

Unfortunately, the calm did not last long. In 1662, the Turks invaded the town, but were defeated by the Polish armies under the command of the wojewoda Stanisław Jan Jabłonowski. In 1677, the town was again invaded by the Turks. These invasions in addition to flooding of the Stryj river and the fires collapsed the economy.

The municipality was governed by a pro-consul and four mayors (Burmistrz) with their assistants who were mostly Ruthenians, because the majority of the inhabitants were of that ethnic origin. Most of the suburbs people were also Ruthenians. The jurisdiction authority was in the hands of the villages' chiefs (wójt) and the municipal court.

Those who lived in suburbs belonging to noblemen were under his jurisdiction and not of the municipality.

Due to the events that took place in town, it owed large amounts of money to the noblemen and therefore had to transfer to them land and buildings. From time to time, the town appealed for relief from taxation.

Until the middle of the seventeenth century, the urban Christians dominated all commerce including money lending. The merchants Maritz Puhacz and his son were known as money-lenders to the nobles. In the second half of the seventeenth century, the Jews dominated most of the commerce and manufacturing of liquor.

The main occupations in the suburbs were agriculture and crafts. The census at the end of the eighteenth century showed 225 homes in town and 470 in the suburbs (those were mainly homes covered in thatch roofs). There were 641 Christian families, and the entire area was more rural than urban.

In 1772 the city became a part of the Austro-Hungary. After the Austrian occupation in 1791, the Starostwo was eliminated and two villages (Dolina and

Grabowiec) and many of the surrounding forests were annexed. Later, Stryj became a district town, and in 1786, the town belonged to Michał Wielhorski, who was an educated nobleman and had a very good library in his palace. In 1785, the Austrian authorities confiscated the Franciscan monastery. A long dispute between the town and the authorities regarding jurisdiction rights and the demand for free elections for the mayor took place during the years 1786 – 1794. In 1788 the town was given the authority for free governance (magistrate) and in 1796 they were allowed free elections for mayor, city council and the establishment of urban governance. The municipal budget was increased from 12,439 to 19,000 florins income and 14,350 expenses. The town owned 12 brandy distilleries and 2 breweries.

In 1783 the first elementary school was established by the Austrian authorities.

The statistics for the population and homes was as follows:

Year	Population	Number of homes
1849	6,000	650
1880	12,625	1,184
1890	16,714	1,400
1900	23,205	1,500
1910	30,942	

In 1853, the first middle school was established that later was expanded to a high school in 1878 and in 1887 was converted to a classical high school.

The town started to develop commercially after the opening of the railway lines of Chyrów–Stryj in 1872, Lvov–Stryj in 1873 and Stryj– Stanisławów in 1875.

[Page 19]

A big fire in 1886 destroyed 970 homes valued at 2,400,000 florins and merchandise valued at 2,000,000 florins.

The town thrived and flourished after the fire. In addition to residences, nice buildings were built for the authorities, public institutions and schools.[3]

1. Ancient Poland

Chapter 1
A. The Jews in Stryj and their struggle to live within the city boundaries

The first Jews settled in town in the middle of the sixteenth century without official permit. The starosta Jan Tarnowski and in 1559 his son Krzysztof Tarnowski allowed the Jews to settle in town asopposed to the privilege. This gesture was done due to their dislike of the urban inhabitants.

In 1567 the Sejm in Piotrkow and the king decided to return the city privileges and the Jews were banned from settling in town. This decision was based in part due to the proximity of the city to the border and the intent to increase fortifications. In 1569, the Sejm in Lublin sent a delegation to investigate the disputes between the starosta and urbanites. On October 10th, 1570, the starosta received explicit orders not to lease to Jews the rights to sell spirits.

On May 6th, 1576 king Zygmunt II August approved the privilege that prohibited Jews from settling in town, purchase homes and land. In 1576 King Stephen Báthory (1576 – 1586) with the support from some senators approved for a number of Jews to settle in town. The municipal courts (Sąd grodzki) in Przemyśl and Żydaczów refused to record this this decree and it was finally recorded in the grad books in Lvov. This permit was given based on the fact that the Jews settled in town illegally earlier and lived there without a license for a long time.

The 1576 privilege mandated that the Jews have to obey all rules and obligations like the rest of the population.

The starosta Mikołaj Sieniawski leased the business of brewing (beer) and selling brandy to the Jews in his efforts to increase the income needed to protect the borders, although it was in contrast to the town privileges. The municipality disputed this decision and the king sent commissars to investigate the situation.

At the end of the investigation, the king ordered on June 23rd, 1578 that the privilege had to be upheld, and prohibited the smuggling of Jews into town. Anyone selling land or home to Jews would be punishable by fines up to 100 grzibani.

To compensate for the loss of income from the Jews, the town was ordered to pay the starosta 17 golden per year. His successor, Andrzej from Tańczyn did not pay too much attention to the prohibitions, causing more complaints from the municipality.

In spite of the prohibitions by the various committees, the 1576 privilege was ratified by king Zygmunt III (1586 – 1632) on April 21st, 1589 with the explicit warning not to harass the Jews.

The urban population in Stryj tried to remove the Jews following the 1576 privilege, stating that in the previous privilege of June 6th, 1567 by king Zygmunt II August (1548 – 1572)[4] the Jews were not allowed to live in town, but that the privilege was circumvented by the starosta and forced the town to lease to the Jews the business of producing and selling brandy, which added a considerable income to the city. In 1569, the town was forced by the starosta's decree to lease the sales of brandy to the Jew Jacob for three years for one hundred tallers. As a response to this and other complaints, the Sejm sent the Kasztelan (Castellan) Nikodem Łekieński, Mikołaj Małachowski and Stanisław Kroczewski to investigate and settle the dispute.

On October 6th, 1570[4a] the commissars cancelled the contract at the insistence of the urban population, and determined that the starosta cannot force the town to lease its income to Jews.

The urban population started to harass the Jews, but they appealed to the king based on the previous privilege to live in town. On October 26th, 1570, the king decreed a prohibition to the urban population to act against the privilege allowing the Jews to live in town, due to their long standing dwelling there.

The urban population refused to comply and they appealed to the court dealing with towns and privileges. In 1580 the court ruled in their favor and the starosta was prohibited from allowing the Jews to live in town. To compensate, the town had to pay 16 golden for his loss of income.[5]

[Page 20]

The Jews did not give up either, and tried to obtain from king Zygmunt III (1587 – 1632) the 1576 privilege from King Stephen Báthory. For all practical matters, their efforts rendered the ruling invalid.

In 1628 a ruling in favor of the Jews was published by representatives of the Sejm, but the urbanites again claimed that they did not base their decision on the previous privileges of Jagiełło in 1431 and the ruling of 1578 by which the Jews were prohibited from living and conduct businesses in town.

It is interesting to note the strange situation in town whereby some of the urbanites had not only business dealings with the Jews, but even friendly and neighborly relationships whereas some others continued to fight and incite against them.

In 1632 with the agreement of the city council and the craftsmen union (cechy) the town leased to the Jews Michal Moskowitz and Wiarszanowitcz in partnership with Isaac the production and selling of brandy for the sum of 1000 zloty. The selling had to take place in one location only, and they had to serve the council members honestly and at decent prices. Sales were not allowed on Sundays and Christian holidays until after church services.

The conditions for the Jews improved considerably under king Władysław IV (1632 – 1648). On October 27th, 1634 the king granted a privilege by which the Jews were allowed to buy land inside and outside of town for a synagogue and a cemetery. A strict warning was given to provide the Jews with all the privileges and freedoms as long as they obeyed the commitments to the starosta and follow the rules regarding the land.

During that time the starosta was Krzysztof Koniecpolski who favored the Jews and provided protection against the urbanites, who were able to obtain a privilege from Jan II Kazimierz (John II Casimir) prohibiting Jews from settling in town. Koniecpolski ignored the privilege and continued in his support of the Jews, whom he felt made important contributions to the economy. He approved the moving the synagogue from a leased land to a land of their own. To stop the incitement against the Jews, he warned that any threats against them would be punishable by fines. He furthered his support by allowing, with agreement from the king, additional Jews to join the community, thus increasing significantly the Jewish population in town. The Jews were afraid that this special treatment would cause agitation and pogroms and therefore the starosta published a special order on April 20th, 1638[6] stating that because of the Jews good behavior, they should be left alone. The Jews on their part tried to keep a low profile and used their privileges carefully and meticulously.

The urbanites still protested against the preferential treatment for the Jews by Koniecpolski. After his death in 1660 the Żydaczów district submitted a claim protesting the fact that the Jews were acting contrary to the king's privilege which prohibits them from living in town, building new homes, and taking over all the commerce and the production of liquor. However, the Jews tried to influence some of the city council, and in 1660 Andrzej Walkowski granted land for a new cemetery that was opened and consecrated on June 4th, 1660.

After they were able to gain support from some in the town council and the starosta, the Jews started brewing beer and grape skin wine and produce and sell liquor although they did not have a license to do so. Some of the urbanites opposed the town council's and starosta policies towards the Jews and they appealed in 1660 claiming that the competition and the sales of alcohol was affecting their livelihood.

[Page 21]

The Jews whose numbers reached 70 in 1662[7] somehow were able to overcome this obstacle and it had not impact on them.

The starosta Jan Sobieski (and future king – Jan III Sobieski) who appreciated the economic value of the Jews showed positive attitudes towards them. In 1663, he approved the privileges that were granted to them by Stefan Batory, that were reaffirmed by Zygmunt III, Władysław IV and Jan II Kazimierz (1648 – 1672) allowing them to engage in all branches of commerce. In addition he tasked the municipality to include two Jewish representatives in all matters concerning municipal taxation. In response to the Jews' concerns about harassment, he decreed that any threats or actions against them will be punished severely ("sub poena arcensi irremissibili" – Google Translate from Latin: under unforgivable penalty).[8]

In 1664, the urbanites complained again about the Jews' trade in alcohol. This time, they raised a new complaint about the establishing of a new synagogue ("Da nova radice" – [Google Translate from Latin: Give fresh roots]), which they were forbidden from doing. The Jews appeared before the court and showed the privileges, and although they won, the urbanites never stopped the complaints against them.

In spite of Sobieski's good intentions and his wishes to keep the peace, conflicts arose during those years regarding taxation that was imposed by the Sejm. The Jews claimed that because they already paid a "poll tax" they should be exempt from the taxation imposed by the national Sejm. When the complaint was submitted, Sobieski organized a committee comprised of Stanisław Jastaszewski (secretary of Halicz region), Paweł Giardziński, Samuel Gorski, Alexander Bidlowski and Jan Krogulecki. This committee came with a verdict on March 8th, 1670 stating that based on the 1667 constitution the Jews should be exempted from these taxes. However, they had to pay national taxes on 11 homes that were built in the previous 18 years as well as a chimney tax (podymne) since they were accepted as the town citizens with equal rights and freedoms. They were allowed to sell alcohol, for which they needed to pay taxes (czopwe) to the royals and other taxes as calculated by the municipality. In this judgment it was emphasized that the town accepted the

Jews "liberalitate et munificnetia" [Google Translate from Latin – generosity and bounty] and they were given land for a synagogue and cemetery. It was further emphasized on March 8th 1678[9] that the Jews will pay chimney taxes on homes that were built in the previous 18 years and they should no longer be bothered about taxes.

After Sobieski became king of Poland (1674 – 1696), the Jews received an important economic privilege on November 24th, 1676. They were allowed to have a market day on Tuesday, and that was in addition to the market day on Saturday in which the Jews were not able to participate.

In 1677 king Sobieski confirmed all the privileges in Stryj and allowed them to benefit from all the privileges that Jews had in royal cities. In addition he allowed them to build a synagogue and establish a cemetery.[10]

In 1662 there was a Jewish street with 10 houses each one of them selling alcohol. There were 115 houses in town in total. Because of economic reasons[10], the Jews wanted to move the market day from Saturday to Friday in addition to the Tuesday market day. The rationale was that the urbanites and their authorities considered the Jews to have equal rights, burdened with the same taxes. Therefore it was unfair to exclude them from the main market day on Saturday, to enable them to buy grain and wood needed for the breweries.

In a letter written on February 19th, 1696, the municipality supported this request with the rationale of collecting taxes from the Jews.

On April 18th, 1696, the king published a note indicating that the two market days from that point on would be on Tuesdays and Fridays.[11]

A minority of three council members objected the decision and claimed that the mayor Jan Baranowski and the other council members supported the Jews against the law.

In 1695, the Jews again complained to the king that they were forced to frequently appear in the municipal courts and they were required to pay unnecessary legal expenses that they felt were unjust and obtained by intrigue.

[Page 22]

On June 24th, 1995, the king decreed from his summer palace in Wilanów that the Jews were subject to the legal system of the starostwo. If the sides were unhappy with the verdict, they could appeal to the manager of the starostwo.

Sobieski's wife Maria Kazimiera, who managed her own estates and farms, also treated the Jews fairly and acted to protect them. When the village chief, Roman Popial did not let the Jew Haim Zildowicz (who was also a customs accountant) to complete the brewery he was building, the queen published an order in Lvov on March 13th, 1698 stating she wanted to see the town being developed, with many buildings, breweries and vineyards to increase the economic base. Therefore, based on the privileges (by her husband the king) granting equal rights to Jews and Christians, she allowed the Jews to improve buildings, establish wineries, breweries for grape skin wines, without interruption and harassment. Her request was from the starwosto authorities to not oppress the Jews.

During that period, the Jews were treated in a friendly and fair manner not only by the starostwo authorities but also by the Catholic Church.

When the Jews were planning to start the building of the synagogue (a wood structure) they applied, as dictated by law to the Przemyśl cardinal Jan Dambeski for a permit. They received a positive response on December 20th, 1689 with conditions that the building would not be taller or more beautiful than the church and that it will not obstruct Christian homes.[11a]

In 1764 the starostwo determined that new taxes (Szarwarki) should be imposed on both the Jews and the Christians for the purpose of public works – to repair mills, fences, sidewalks, roads and to divert the Stryj river.[11b]

In 1766, the last king of Poland Stanisław August Poniatowski approved once again all privileges.

[Page 22]

Chapter 2

The Economic Life

Since the beginning of their settlement in Stryj the Jews made their living by selling spirits, wholesale and retail merchandising, providing tax and customs services for the starosta and banking. In the early years, the Jews were mainly selling spirits.

Stryj received a privilege to produce brandy, beer and grape skin wine. However, the urbanites were unable to produce quality products. The starosta kept pressuring them to improve the quality without much success. The starosta who recognized the Jewish economic talents, pressured the urbanites to lease the spirits production to the Jews. As a result, many conflicts erupted between the urbanites and the starosta as described in the previous chapter leading to law suits and inquiries by various committees and commissars of the Sejms.

In spite of the severe judgments, the Jews continued in the economic activities. The production and sales of spirits was handled mostly by medium sized retail merchants. Since the beginning of the 17th century, some merchants in Stryj consolidated most of the branches of products of the land – salt, wood, oxen, cattle and spirits investing most of their money for safe returns. In addition to trading internally and externally, they also leased salt mines in "stara-sol" for thousands of zloty and consolidated almost all of the export of salt. Among those who leased the salt mines were the brothers Fishel and Josef "members of the holy congregation of Stryj who held salt mines in Lashkavitz. When the lease expired, they were cheated by rabbi Nachman one of the leaders of the Bolechów congregation who made much money".[11c] Another renowned salt merchant was Shmuel Chaimowicz who was able to mine up to 18,000 barrels of salt[12] each year between 1701 and 1704.

Prior to leasing the salt mine, he was the go-between in horse trading where he made a lot of money that he invested in the salt mines.

An important branch of commerce for the Jews was customs leasing. In the middle of the 17th century the Jews were awarded by the authorities the managing of customs revenue. This business – as lessees, sub-lessees, managers and collectors brought about – "nolens volens" (Google translate from Latin "will hear") - many conflicts between the customs lessees and the merchants. Stryj merchants, non-Jews and even the nobles complained that the Jewish customs lessees demanded payments and gifts in addition to the legal rates. The customs agents prohibited the sales of premium wines and caused a collapse of the merchants' businesses.

[Page 23]

In 1677 the urbanites and the nobles complained that the customs lessee Isaac and five others were demanding arbitrary customs rates. Influenced by the complaints, Alexander Koczinski submitted a law suit against Isaac Sakolaski, Josef Moskowitz and Isaac Mojseszowitz stating that they were "stealing from the state". The suit stated that in addition to leasing the customs dues collection, they were also leasing public houses, nobles' estates and factories on those estates, and collecting double taxes from other countries.[13] Conflicts erupted where nobles, urbanites and clergy accused the Jews of cheating, incorrect assessments, unjust customs collection and stealing. There were other accusations as well. The customs lessee Yehuda Nathan and his son were beaten to death when they were accused of insulting the Christian faith and the clergy.

In addition to leasing the customs collections, the Jews were also leasing tax collection. Moshek Subkulaktor was known in 1676 as the city tax collector.

In the 17th and 18th centuries Jews were major players in the trade of oxen and cattle. The merchants Josef Moskowitcz, Gershom Szlomowitcz, Theodor Isakowitcz (was killed in 1617 by the Dobrovlany noble Jan Wiszniaweski[14] on the Lvov-Stryj road) bought herds of oxen and fattened them in the pastures in the mountains. The oxen were bought from the nobles for 80 zloty each or sometimes were traded for German cloths and wine. This trading required much capital that individuals were not able to raise. Partnerships were formed normally with nobles who provided the oxen. The oxen were transported to Silesia where the herds were sold for a profit of 837 ducats.[15] Jewish merchants from Stryj were also the wholesalers of cattle and horses from Hungary.[16]

Trade from Stryj to Hungary started in the 18th century. The military supplier Eliezer Ashkenazy from Karaly in Hungary bought horses for the Austrian army in Stryj from Zvi Hersch, Shimon Maztner and others.[17] The beginning of the horse trading from Stryj to Hungary was documented in Ber Bolichower's memoirs: "The famous officer Eliezer Ashkenazy from Karaly came to Stryj and stayed at the house of wealthy man rabbi Zvi Hersch the son of the late rabbi Mordechai. His brother in law, the officer Mazatner who saw the beautiful horse that he bought in Dolina, ordered me to buy more good horses. I bought three more horses and made a profit of more than three hundred guldens which was considered a large amount in my youth".[18]

The Jews also controlled the trading in grains mostly for export. One of the largest exporters in Stryj was Abraham Shmuelik. This branch of trading also included the maintenance of mills which were mostly in Jewish hands in the Stryj starostvo.

Many Jews were retailers of clothes and haberdashery. Most of the trading was done with Danzig mainly with the merchant David Karwas. However, most of the Jews in retail were trading wines from Hungary.

The authorities ordered that the import of wine from Hungary had to be brought by the route of Jaszlenska-Dukla, Rymanów, Sącz-Biecz, Żmigród, Nowy Targ-Jordanów, Krosno, Sambor-Lisko-Stryj. Whoever brought the wine using a different route lost half of his merchandise to the treasury and half to the informer.

Because of the relatively good transportation routes from Stryj to Hungary, the trade with this country was very important to the Jewish merchants of Stryj.

During the wars of the years 1648 – 1680, the tendency for drinking spirits grew in Poland. The nobles and the urbanites saw great opportunity in this tendency to compensate them for the damages caused by the wars. The Jews, too, saw the economical-opportunities in the production and trading in spirits – brandy, grape skin wine, beer and wine. They dedicated themselves to this branch of trade and obtained licenses to produce spirits.

Most of the peasants preferred drinking brandy, whereas the nobles and urbanites preferred grape skin wine and beer. However, the priests, especially those in higher level preferred wines from Hungary.

[Page 24]

Due to the fact that the main transportation lines passed through Stryj, the Jews of this community understood the importance of this trade. The main merchants and importers of wine from Hungary in Stryj at the beginning of the 18th century were rabbi Zvi Hersch, rabbi Mordechis and Shmuel Chaimowicz who was also the accountant for the starostvo. Because of their connections to the Polish nobles, they had no problems in trading. They bought wine in Miskolcz (Hungary) from the Hungarian wealthy merchants Patay and Karolo Sapasi. Then, they sold the barrels of wine to their partners from Bolechów – Ber Bolechówer and his brother[19], who in turn sold them to the nobles and the clergy in Lvov.

Traders from out of town had large cellars in Stryj[21], where they stored the barrels and distributed them to Lvov and other cities. One of the largest importers was Shmuel Chaimowitcz who also leased the salt mines.

At the end of the 17th century there was already a small group of wealthy Jews who were able to invest in industry, mills and production of beer, grape skin wine and brandy, credit business, leasing of forests[20], estates and even iron mines.

In the years 1680 – 1711, the renowned estate lessees were Shmuel, the son of Chaim Tiwalweitcz, Berko Karkowski who leased all the estates of the starostvo, Chaim Shmuel and Shaul Markowitcz. Their businesses were not without conflicts and complaints. The complaints stated that although they properly managed the farms, they did not take care of the buildings, and the entire management practices were for their own benefit. Because of the frequent complaints and law suits, they were despised by the locals who saw them as taking advantage of those under their supervision. However, the starostvo, continued to support them as these lessees continued to provide a steady income. As opposed to the locals' opinion, the starostvo saw the Jews (the lessees) as important economic contributors who provided them with a source of potential income increase.[22]

In the 18th century during the years of the starosta Stanisław Ciołek Poniatowski and his son Kazimierz, one of the main lessees from Stryj was rabbi Shaul Wahl who actually worked the fields with the Polish peasants. He was an expert in farming[23] as well as raising cattle and horses. He had nice income from all these businesses to provide well for his family of ten sons and one daughter. Poniatowski asked him to recommend an expert to purchase fine wines from Hungary. Shaul Wahl recommended the father of Ber Bolechówer who travelled to Hungary and brought back two hundred barrels of Tokaj wine.

Rabbi Shaul realized that the wine trade was profitable. When Poniatowski decided to manage his own estates and refused to lease them, rabbi Shaul lost his source of income, and was unable to pay his debts.[24]

[Page 25]

Ber Bolechówer wrote in his memoirs that his father suggested rabbi Shaul join him in his wine importing business. So he followed Bolechówer to Hungary, bought there fine wine, sold it at a great profit and was able to pay all his debts.

Some of the wealthy Jews engaged in financial businesses as well. In the 17th century, the renowned bankers and lenders were Michal Janelewicz, Moshe Stinawski, and Josef Moszkowicz, who were lending money to merchants, nobles and the clergy.

The most prominent was the doctor Alimelech. He was lending money against securities such as cloth, milk, wine, linens, weapons, instruments, grain, leather etc. It is not known how much if at all he practiced medicine, but he was the wealthiest of all the Stryj Jews.[25]

Another lender against securities was Haim Herszowitz, an owner of a brewery and soap manufacturer.

In the 18th century, there were many renowned Jewish bankers. Among them: Joachim Mendelowitcz, David Kinjochowski, Herscz Wonjarazow, Moshe Wospowitcz, and the merchant Baruch Eljaszwitz. They were lending money to churches, magnets, and nobles. In turn, they, the urbanites and some orders deposited their capital in cash and valuables. Not surprisingly, the town was able to obtain loans only when Jews were guarantors. In 1708, the town received a loan to cover urgent needs for 3,000 zloty from the noble Helena Maleska, guaranteed by Jews. In spite of the guarantee, the loan and the interest were never paid off, and the trial for this case lasted for years.

At the end of the 18th century, just prior to Poland's partition, several bankers were active in town: Herszko Jankilewicz, Feiwel Isaac, Herszko Wolfowicz, Isaac Fiszel, Herszel Leibowicz, and Jacob Moskowicz. They loaned money at interest rates that sometimes reached up to 100%.[26] These bankers were homeowners in Stryj and Lvov, and some of them invested money in purchasing and leasing estates. At the beginning of the 18th century, Mark Lejzerowicz bought a dwelling (dworek) from the noble woman Wojhowska and in the middle of the 18th century the lessee David Konjochowski bought and sold estates and large farms. In 1754, he sold his farms that were on the town edges and behind the Stryj river.[27]

In the business of lending and banking, there were many complaints, and law suits that lasted for years. The customers accused the lenders of fraud and deceit. On the backdrop of false accusations, law suits, monetary demands, and requisitioning, conflicts and attacks arose between Jews and their Christian clients – nobles and Ruthenian clergy. The Jews showed courage, did not back down even when they were threatened by weapons.[28]

The trade in town was mostly in Jewish hands. A list of the damages from a fire in 1743 shows the extent of the Jewish businesses: Hersch Woroclawski – 18,000 zloty, Leib, a silk merchant - 20,000 zloty, Haim – 10,000 zloty, and the grocer Heszil – 9,000 zloty.[29]

A small number of Jews were craftsmen, mostly dealing with Jewish clients, except for goldsmiths/silversmiths who had also Christian customers. There is no information about unions of Jewish craftsmen in town, or about conflicts between such unions and Christian unions. However, there was always tension between the urbanites and the Jews. The urbanites'complaints centered round the fact that the starosta supported the Jews, thus causing economic hardship to them. As in other towns, the locals saw the Jews as formidable competitors to be attacked at any opportunity.

In addition, with the support of the local clergy, methodical incitement against the Jews continued. In 1722, a priest representing the Przemyśl cardinal who was in charge of the Catholic church in Stryj wrote in his report: "civitas Stryj olim per catholicos fere tota per infedeles Iudacos possessa"[29a] (the city of Stryj once occupied by Catholics is now nearly entirely occupied by Jewish Infidels). In 1746, the cardinal Siarkowski visited Stryj for the first time and reported the number of Jews exceeds the number of Catholics and Ruthenians. He also reported that the Jews do not honor the chrisitan holidays, sell spirits during Sunday services and keep Christian servants against the law.[30]

[Page 26]

These tensions caused sometimes conflicts or even attacks. One such case was during the Sunday funeral of Hershel Aleksandrowicz, which passed by the Ruthenian church during services. Members of the Christian union who were armed, did not allow the funeral procession to pass thru the gate, threw the deceased body on the ground, and did not let it be picked until the end of the services.

Chapter 3
The Kehila (Commuity)

The Stryj Jewish community evolved similarly to the other communities in the Reissin territories. The kehila had mainly administrative, educational and judicial authorities. The kehila was headed by three to five "parnasim" (wardens) or "heads" responsible for all matters concerning the community and representing it towards the authorities. After their election, the members of the board had to swear their loyalty to king and country. In Stryj, they had to be approved by the starosta or his deputy.

The parnasim rotated in their function every month and the head was called the "parnas of the month". In addition there were "good men", a function similar to "boni viri" in the municipalities, and a "congregation committee". The number of members in the congregation committee changed based on needs. The committees were responsible for charity, accounts, the markets, cleaning of the Jewish quarter, security, kashrut supervision, supervision of weights and measurements, education institutions, synagogues and houses of study.

The administrative structure included a rabbi and head of the religious court (beit din) who was the head and the spiritual leader of the community, religious judges and the administrative clerk of the kehila who in most cases was also the lobbyist (syndicus). The kehila was responsible for all the economic, social, religious, and educational matters. It determined the budget and collected all the taxes required for running the kehila, paying the government, the municipality, the schools, the clergy and all other taxes that the Jews were obligated to pay. For the budget, they used direct and indirect income such as maintenance, payments for weddings and funerals, dowries, and from titles bestowed on those deserving.

Stryj was part of the Przemyśl district. The district committee was responsible for electing representatives to the Council of Four Lands (Va'ad

Arba' Aratzot), dividing the taxes and resolve conflicts among the different communities.

From the beginning of the 18th century, Stryj was one of the most important communities in the district with the following affiliated communities: Dynów, Lisiatycze, Uhersko, Bratkowska, Rozhorcze, Ruda, Sokołów, and Holobotów.

The influence of Stryj grew due to the economic standing of the community. In time there were conflicts with the various affiliates who felt that the taxation imposed by Stryj was unjust.

The conflict with the Dynów community reached the council of the four lands, protesting the Stryj authority.[31] Other conflicts erupted between Stryj and the communities of Ruda and Sokołów. Physically, they belonged to the treasury of Przemyśl and did not want to participate in the Stryj expenses. The head of the Stryj kehila, Abraham Ben Michael protested to the Reisin district and emphasized that the members of the kehila paid all the taxes, even more than their fair share. However, the branches were supported by their squires.

[Page 27]

The Jews of Ruda were protected by the squire Wartzel.

In 1697 there was a libel against the Jews of Stryj. Valuable silver religious items inlaid with diamonds and pearls estimated at 12,000 zloty were stolen from the Three Kings church. The Christians suspected the Jews, the head of the kehila was accused, but refused to confess. The trial lasted several years, and in 1708, the priest Michael Torobitski accused the court of leading the trial in the wrong direction. He claimed that the Jewish silversmith who was suspected of the theft was released and the trial for the rest of the suspects was held in a public place. When the Jews were brought out to be tortured, beer was poured onto the fire that was prepared for this purpose, the hangman was bribed and the Jews were freed.

* * *

Among the leaders who shaped the kehila life in the 18th century were Aaron ben Mordechai who had many important roles in the Jewish autonomy institutions, rabbi Zvi Hirsch Mordechis, rabbi Shaul Wahl, and Shmuel Chaimowitcz.

Among the famous rabbis in Stryj during that period of time were:

Rabbi Simcha, the son of the renowned Gaon Leib Cunz[31a], the rabbi of Pińczów. Rabbi Simcha lived in Stryj for a short period of time, then moved to Lvov, became the head of the yeshiva and one of the leaders of the community there;

Rabbi Berish, the son of the Gaon rabbi Moshe Hariff;

Rabbi Zeev Wolf who was the head of the rabbinic court from 1632;

Rabbi Israel bar Dov Ber who gave his agreement in 1759 for the book by Peretz, son of rabbi Moshe, Maggid Mesharim in Brody, "Beit Peretz", Zholkeva, 1759.

In 1700 the Stryj community was represented in the Reissin district by Shmuel. In 1720, its representative participated in the Kulików convention. In 1723, the Styrj lobbyist rabbi Mordechai Ben Bezalel (from Satnislawow) and the lobbyist from Brody were dispatched to Warsaw to take part in the discussions about poll taxes and gave them 2,500 zloty.[32]

Aaron Ben Mordechai was one of the community leaders who represented Stryj during that time in the district committee. In 1753 a representative of the Stryj community participated in the committee meeting in Bóbrka. From that time on, Stryj was represented regularly in all district committee meetings.[33]

In 1724, Aaron Ben Mordechai from Stryj participated as an arbitrator from the Lvov district for the Council of Four Lands (Va'ad Arba' Aratzot).[34]

In 1713 – 1714, the Jews of Stryj paid 2,000 zloty in poll taxes. In 1717, the Jews of Stryj paid 1,010 zloty out of 33,587 zloty in poll taxes that were imposed on Reissin Jews.[34a] In 1727, a tax of 1,950 was imposed by the district committee, but only 1,200 zloty were paid after the owner of the town Sianewska intervened. The treasury agreed to this discount.[35]

During this period of time, the community life was pretty stable. Most of the Jews made their living in retail, peddling, sales of spirits, crafts and only some had businesses such as wholesale, wine trade, grains, and trade in horses and cattle.

A census was held in 1765 and it listed 1727 Jews in Stryj and its kehila branches.[36]

In the final years of the Polish rule, the economic situation deteriorated especially because the decline in wholesale agricultural products trading, which of course impacted the Jewish population.

The kehila needed loans, as they were unable to cover all the expenses. They obtained loans from the nobles, the various orders and churches.

The amounts of the loans are unknown except one for 3,000 zloty that the kehila received as a mortgage from the noblewoman Theophilia Sapiaha.[36a]

2. During the Austrian Rule
Chapter 1: 1772 – 1867

Galicia was annexed to Austria[36b] and the first partition of Poland occurred in 1772 and had a major impact on the life of the Jews. The empress Maria Theresa published a "Jewish Constitution" in 1776. Galitzian Jews were organized in a special body with a hierarchical central board (Generaldirektion) comprised of communities with 6 to 12 leaders each. Galicia had six districts with" head of district" (Besirkshauptmann) in each. All communities in a district were organized under the leader of the district (Kreislandesältester) supervised by the leaders appointed by the state (Landesälteste). There was also one leader appointed by the state name Fishel.

[Page 28]

The six district leaders with the Chief state rabbi assembled the board of Galicia Jews (Galizische General–Juden–Direktion).

The administrative six districts were disbanded on March 22nd, 1782 and were replaced by eighteen districts. Stryj, which originally belonged to the district of Sambor, became an independent district with a few smaller towns and villages.

In 1875, the organization of the Jewish communities based on the "Jewish Constitution" from 1776 was cancelled, and there was no new state supervised body. The new constitution left only the community leaders in charge. Except for Lvov and Brody that had 7 community leaders each, the rest of the communities had only 3 leaders. Their functions included the representation of the community before the authorities, taking care of the poor, supervise the registration of births, marriages and deaths, collection of community taxes, collection of Jewish taxes and handling all the community matters. The local leaders were under the supervision of the district.

One of the initial objectives of the Austrian rulers was to eliminate the sales of spirits, a branch of commerce that was seen by the authorities as hampering the development of the peasants. This impacted greatly the Jews, many of whom made their living in spirits sales. In 1772 and 1774 there were fires in town that burnt Christian and Jewish homes. After the 1774 fire, the kehila appealed for help from the communities of Lvov, Brody and Kraków and indeed they received monetary assistance.

The Stryj municipality requested to waive the debt in the amount of 1,094 florins, and the government agreed to this request.[37] The kehila also requested waiving of its debts.

The gubernia who requested the waiver reported the assistance the kehila received from other communities, emphasizing that the money came from donations and not from these communities' funds.[38] The gubernia's opinion was that there is no basis to waive the debt for the Jews impacted by the fire since they received funds from Lvov, Brody and Kraków.

On November 17th, 1776, and inquiry from Vienna came asking if the money from other communities was for homes and taxes payments. After it was clarified that the money did not come from the other communities' funds, the emperor announced that he decided to waive the debt.[39]

The Austrian authorities continued to collect the poll tax based on the Polish lists. The kehila appealed this practice in March 1776 stating that many Jews were expelled during the Polish confederacy and the Russian invasions, and many left town after the fires. In addition they requested to be put on a payment plan for three years.[40]

A struggle between the city and its owner Pontiakowski ensued due to the municipal privilege. The municipality leased the privilege to the city owner and used the proceeds for fortifications, repairs to the city walls and roads and to purchase arms and equipment. Due to the difficult situation caused by the Russian invasions and the fires, the town was heavily in debt. On September 18th, 1782, the city decided to take back the privilege with the hopes to increase income. This decision was opposed by the two city counsellors who claimed that based on the agreement with the Jews of March 12th, 1783 stating that once the privilege was received they would sell spirits together with the Christians. For the trial against the city owner, the Jews agreed to pay 1,000 zloty and also agreed to pay half of the trail expenses in case it will last for a long time. The agreement was signed by the mayors and ten commissioned members and by the heads of the Jewish community. The mayor Andrzej Saszoniawicz and Konstantin Hladisz originally supported the agreement, but later backed out claiming that knowing the Jews' cunning and their intent to cheat the Christians they demanded from Pontiakowski a larger amount for the lease and then joined the appeal against the agreement which was against the city privilege.

The other side claimed that in the presence of 57 council members on March 7th, 1783 it was decided not to lease the spirit sales, so it can be used by the town itself.

[Page 29]

It was agreed with the Jews that after the return of the privilege, each spirits' seller whether Jewish or Christian will pay the municipality. The trial with Pontiakowski was held in Lvov and the verdict was not known.

In the meanwhile, the starostvo was returned to the municipality and the leasing of spirits' sales were given to the city.[41]

In 1785 the city announced an open contract. It was decided that only four Jews will participate. In a secret meeting it was further decided that no other Jews will try to win the contract and whoever tried will be excommunicated.[42] Still one Jew, Batisz (?) tried to win against the other four, and he was excommunicated. When the authorities found out, they ordered to punish those that excommunicated.[43]

In the meanwhile, the authorities systematically started to eliminate all Jewish spirits sellers, an action that impacted greatly the economic situation including in Stryj.

In addition to the heavy taxation already in place, new taxes were imposed. Among them was a tax on marriages. Those with income had to pay between 3 and 30 ducats for the marriages of their sons. Those marrying their children without a permit were punished and their property was subject to confiscation, and even those participating in illegal marriages were subject to heavy fines.

In 1785, the communities' autonomies were eliminated and the judgmental and national privileges were cancelled. The rabbinical courts were eliminated and the Jews were under the municipal jurisdiction. The kehila taxes were cancelled and individual taxes were imposed instead.

The emperor Joseph II wanted to solve the Jewish problem in Galicia by turning them into farmers. In 1782, it was decided that Jewish farmers would pay only half of the marriage tax and after a while they will be completely relieved of this tax. However, the emperor ordered to create a Jewish farming village on July 6th, 1785. In the spring of 1786 the first farming village was established in the village Dombrowka near Nowy Sacz. Later, another farm called "New Babylon" was established near Bolechów. More, smaller farms were established, but they did not last long. The government programs determined that out of the 1410 Jewish families in Galicia, nine families from Stryj had to be assigned to the farms. Until the end of 1794[44], nine families from Stryj became farmers. They received 4 houses, 4 barns and cow-sheds, 48 parcels of land, 4 agricultural tools, 6 horses, 8 oxen and 4 cows.

At the beginning of the 19th century, one of the families passed away, 5 families left their lands, which were transferred to the landlord.

The plan was to settle 42 families from the Stryj region, but in reality only 40 families did on 334 parcels of land. They received 23 houses, 23 barns and cow–sheds, 23 agricultural tools, 30 horses, 46 oxen and 25 cows.

The families that came outside of Stryj were from the following localities:

Place	Number of Families
Skole	2
Bolechów	8
Żurawno	4
Żydaczów	3
Halicz	3
Wojniłów	2
Bukaczowce	2
Kałusz	3
Rożniatów	2
Dolina	4

The authorities in Vienna were very pleased with the results of the program and ordered the gubernia to praise the regional office for the successful completion.[44a]

However, the status in 1804 was as follows:

Place	Status
Bolechów	8 families were removed due to incompetence
Żurawno	1 of the settlers passed away
Skole	1 family abandoned the farm
Bukaczowce	2 families passed away
Dolina	The community was forced in an order dated September 1798[45] to meet the original quota of 4 families originally only 2 families were settled).

The budget had to be met by the Jewish communities and the expense was calculated to be 250 florins per a settler family.

In 1822, only 25 settler families remained on the farms. 23 of them were self–sufficient financially and the other 2 were supported by the community.

Like in all of Galicia, the Stryj community was heavily burdened by various taxes. In addition to the "tolerance tax", the Jews were forced to pay others. Between the years 1517 – 1790, Jewish families paid 1,790 florins for the "tolerance tax" and 424 administration fees. From time to time, the community had to request a postponement of payments due to inability to pay all the taxes. In 1789, the Jews in the Stryj district still owed 2,002 florins for the "tolerance tax" and 477 florins for administration fees and that was after they already paid 1,946 florins. In 1790, they paid 1,947 tolerance tax and 486 administration fees and they still owed 6,068 florins for tolerance tax and 1,517 florins administration fees.

[Page 30]

The 1795 census showed 225 houses in Stryj and 470 houses in the surrounding areas. There were 641 Christian families and 444 Jewish families in town and 9 in the surrounding areas.

Based on the edict of Emperor Joseph II from March 20th, 1785, the Jews had many obligations. Among them was to establish elementary Jewish schools (Juedische Normalschule). In 1788 such schools were established in Stryj and Dolina.

In 1792, schools were established in Skole, Bolechów, Żurawno, Żydaczów and Kałusz. In Halicz, Wojniłów and Bukaczowce such schools did not exist.

The following were the headmasters of the schools and their salaries:

Town	Name	Annual Salary (Florins)
Stryj	Hersch Wahlmut	200
Skole	Moshe Tadesko	200
Bolechów	Yaakov Bloch	200
Żurawno	Wolf Mittelhon	200
Żydaczów	Moshe Turnebach	150
Dolina	Moshe Meisels	200
Kałusz	Manela Zonnenstein	150

In 1760, the expenses for the schools in the Stryj district were 1,266 florins[46]. In 1783, a general elementary school was opened by the Austrian authorities in Stryj with 4 classes. The Jewish children were allowed to attend the general elementary school, but none of them did.

On February 17th, 1788 a new and harsh edict was ordered for army draft. The Jews tried to avoid this new decree by all means. After two years the law was cancelled, however a draft tax of 30 zloty was imposed on anyone who was supposed to be drafted, a situation that continued until 1804. That year, the Jews had the same obligation to be drafted as the Christian population and the draft tax was eliminated.

With that, the limitation of drafting the Jewish recruits for transport units was lifted[47], and thus the mandatory draft in all districts was enacted. There were some exemptions from service: those eligible for citizenship, craftsmen, merchants and concession owners. Upon learning that the emperor and his advisors decided to "teach the Jews the army work", the Hebrew poet Zeev Wolf Buchner (he was the secretary of the Brody community)[48] appealed to the head of the Stryj community to go to Vienna and try to convince the emperor and his council to cancel.

The "candles tax" that was imposed on November 11th, 1797 started a period of oppression of the masses, robbery, seizure, and inhumane cruelty that lasted until the revolution of 1848.

During the period discussed above two legal issues for Stryj Jews arose. In most Galician towns, the Jews had active and passive voting rights for city council, but not in Stryj. Based on the Josephinism laws, Jews were eligible to be elected as heads of their place of residence, thus having a civil rights. The urbanites were of course opposed to this.

In 1790, the Jew Lonberg wanted to build a house in the town center. The municipality objected and they were supported by the authorities. The municipality took advantage of the situation to bring–up again the question if

Jews should be allowed to lease the municipal privilege. The authorities in Vienna decreed that if the lease is not for spirits sales, then the Jews were allowed to participate.[49]

The authorities really cracked-down on those who leased pubs to Jews.

[Page 31]

In November 1793, the Polish landowner Ignatz Von Kowalski was fined 650 florins because he leased to the Jew Moshe Hertzing from Stryj the pub and pasture in the village of Stankow.[50]

The tax burden increased from year to year to the point where in 1810 – 1812 large debts were accumulated from the meat tax and the candles tax and also from municipal bonds that were imposed on the Jews.

In 1814 there were complaints against the heads of the kehila that they were dishonest in managing the funds. There was a demand to remove them and to conduct new elections.

Instead, the authorities disbanded the council and appointed new heads of the kehila among them Kalman Robinson who was elected chairman. The complaints against him stated that he did not pay the candles tax and therefore was ineligible.

Based on the constitution, the kehila was headed by three "parnasim" (wardens). Each head of a family who paid tax for 7 candles in the year prior to the elections was eligible to vote. Passive voting rights in Stryj were given to those who could read and write in German and who paid the tax for 10 candles in the year prior to the elections. Those complaining about Robinsons' election stated that he did not pay for the required number of candles, but the authorities overruled and determined that he could pay a global sum after his election.[50a]

The protestant priest from Lvov Samuel Bardecki wrote in his book "Travels in Galicia and Hungary" of his impression of Stryj in 1809.[50b] He wrote that the approach to town was by a long road with nice homes and gardens. About the Jewish section he wrote that the small wooden houses were built around a square with dirt and filth around the homes.

Census numbers:

Year	Number of families	Number of residents
1800	465	4,658
1808		5,474

Year	Number of Christians in the District	Number of Jews in the District
1826	190,436	12,347
1827	205,920	12,760

Year	Number of Jewish Families in the Entire Stryj District	Number of Jewish Men	Number of Jewish Women	Total	Number of Jewish Families in Stryj	Number of Jewish Men in Stryj	Number of Jewish Women in Stryj	Total number of Jews in Stryj
1812	2,560	5,490	5,345	10,835	516	1,008	1,058	2,066[51]
1819	2,373[52]							

In 1820 the Jews made their living mainly by trading in grains and other agricultural products, foods, cattle, horses, wines, and production of spirits. Among the craftsmen, the Jews were in tailoring, furs and other clothing, bakers, carpenters, tinsmiths, and fabric printers.[53]

In 1820 in the entire Stryj district there were: 43 cattle traders, 12 lumber traders, 32 brandy traders (out of 63 traders in the entire Galicia), 15 pots traders, 16 shoes and boots traders (out of 23 traders in the entire Galicia).

The Jews who leased the sales of spirits and beer suffered during this period since the authorities cancelled the licenses and were strict about it, although it was admitted that it is difficult to implement as "spirits sales is the preferred occupation by Galician Jews".[53a]

In 1826 there were 44 registered companies, 43 out of them Jewish.[54] That indicated that all the wholesale business was in Jewish hands. The community was established. There were houses of study (beit midrash), hospital, large synagogue, bath–house, and a rest home.

* * *

Stryj was the district capital and its rabbi was responsible for the other communities in the district. His salary was 300 florins. In other towns in the district: Skole, Bolechów, Kałusz. Dolina, Bukaczowce, Żurawno, Żydaczów, Wojniłów and Rozdół the rabbis had a title of "teacher". Their salaries were not uniform. The Skola rabbi earned 400 florins and received an apartment. The Bolechów rabbi earned 400 florins.

[Page 32]

In Wojniłów, the salary was 160 florins and in Bukaczowce 60 florins. In Żydaczów the rabbi was paid 30 kreuzers for each slaughtered animal and in Żurawno 3 florins for each slaughtered bull. In Rożniatów and Kałusz they were supported by the wealthy and engaged in retail. In Dolina, the community paid the rabbi's taxes of 40 florins and in Rozdół the rabbi was a rich man.[54a]

The Stryj rabbi, being a district rabbi received his salary not only from his community, but the other towns in the district had to contribute to his pay. In addition to his salary he was paid for certificates for cantors, for registering births, marriages and deaths 7 and ½, 15 and 30 kreuzers respectively. The rabbi was exempt from paying taxes, but in case his wife or other family members were conducting businesses, the normal taxes had to be paid. By law, the rabbi was not permitted to receive gifts or payments for marriages or divorces.

Rabbi Aryeh Leib HaCohen Heller[55] was the chief rabbi of Stryj In the years 1788 – 1813. He was born in 1745 in Kałusz and was a student of rabbi Meshullam Igra of Tyśmienica. He was recognized as a prodigy and held in high esteem by his contemporaries. He was the head of the rabbinic court in Rożniatów and then a famous teacher in Lvov.

In 1810 his daughter married Solomon (Shi'r) Rapoport, who was a researcher and an intellectual. Although rabbi Heller knew that his son in law was fluent in foreign languages and knowledgeable in secular studies he held him in high esteem due to his expertise and proficiency in the Torah and Talmudic literature. He saw his involvement in the secular studies as a "youth action". In his famous book "Ketzot HaChoshen" ("Ends of the Breastplate") he referred to notes by his son in law. The chief rabbi of Stryj position was offered to him when he was still in Lvov and he was well liked by the members of the community. In 1796 he had a conflict with the authorities due to an unlawful divorce and was imprisoned for 24 hours by an order from Vienna.

In Stryj he published:

Ketzot HaChoshen ("Ends of the Breastplate"), a halachic work which explains difficult passages in the Shulchan Aruch, Choshen Mishpat (which deals mainly with business and financial laws such as contracts, witnesses etc.) with novel ideas proposed by Rabbi Aryeh Leib (part 1 – published in Lvov in 1788; part 2 – published in 1796).

Avnei Milluim ("Filling Stones") a halachic work which explains difficult passages in the Shulchan Aruch, Even HaEzer (which deals mainly with marital issues) with novel ideas proposed by rabbi Aryeh Leib (part 1– published in Lvov in 1816; part 2 – published in 1826). This book was published together with a pamphlet "Moshovev Netivot", rabbi's HacCohen Heller's response to the rabbi from Lissa rabbi Yaakov Lorberbaum who was very critical of the Ketzot HaChoshen.

He passed away in Stryj in 1815. After his death, his son David published his work Shev Shema'tata ("7 passages").

His second son, Joseph David Ber was a rabbi in Wodzisław and his third son, Hirsch was a rabbi in Ungvir.

In 1830, rabbi Yaakov from Lissa passed in Stryj on his way to Opiná (in Hungary) to take a position as chief rabbi there. He was delayed in Stryj awaiting travel papers. When it was became known he was in town, the community leaders including rabbi Enzil Cuzmer decided to offer him to become the chief rabbi of Stryj. He accepted the offer and settled in Stryj for a few years where he also served as the district rabbi.

The Gaon Yaakov ben Yaakov Moshe Lorberbaum[56] was born in Zbaraż where his father Yaakov Moshe (the son of rabbi Nathan Ashkenazi and the grandson of Chacham Tzvi) was a rabbi. After his parents passed away, he was taken into the house of his relative rabbi Yosef Teomim (who was the son-in-law of his uncle rabbi Zvi Hirsch Ashkenazi), the rabbi of Bursztyn, and brought-up there. He studied under Rabbi Meshulam Igra from Tyśmienica.

From 1801 to 1809 he was the head of the rabbinical court in Kalisz. In 1809, he agreed to become the rabbi of Lissa where he enlarged his Yeshiva's enrollment. He was well known and respected as an authority in halachic matters and well-liked by the members of his community. Hundreds of scholars came to study there in the years of his leadership. He left the post in Lissa and returned to Kalisz for unknown reasons and in 1830 he settled in Stryj where he passed away on May 25th, 1832.

  a. Rabbi Yaakov was one of the most influential and knowledgeable teachers of his generation. His works include:
  b. Mekor Chayim (Source of Life), commentary on Shulchan Aruch, Orach Chayim and following, with notes on the commentaries Turei Zahav and Magen Avraham (Żółkiew, 1807);
  c. Torat Gittin (the Study of Gets (divorces)), commentary on Shulchan Aruch, Even HaEzer (Żółkiew, 1807);
  d. Chavat Daat (Epression of Opinion), commentary on Shulchan Aruch, Yoreh Deah (Lvov, 1799);
  e. Netivot HaMishpat (the Ways of Judgement) (Żółkiew, 1800);
  f. Kehilat Yaakov (The Community of Yaakov) (Lvov, 1831);

g. Beit Yaakov (The house of Yaakov) (1823)

He also wrote interpretations of the Torah and towards the end of his life he published Derech Chayim (way of life) on the daily life of the Jewish person. This compendium was very popular and was frequently reprinted and attached to prayer books. After his passing, his grandchildren printed his work Nachalat Yaakov (Yaakov's estate) (Breslau, 1849) comprising of sermons on the Torah Portion, halachic decisions, responsa, and his last will. In this famous ethical will he asked that his sons devote time every day to learn at least one page of Gemara and not become rabbis.

In 1821, the authorities decided to tackle the issue of Jewish clothing.

[Page 33]

During the reign of Joseph II, the order was issued for Galicia Jews to drop their traditional clothing to be completed by the year 1794. The traditional clothing were allowed only for rabbis.

However, because of stern objections, the order was cancelled on May 28th, 1790.

In the years 1816 – 1820, the government was working on a new "Jewish constitution", and the question arose if the traditional dress should be forbidden by law.

The Galician gubernium which was headed by baron Hauer recommended adding explicit prohibition of the traditional dress, which was also supported by some in the Jewish intellectuals' circles. When the rumor about this intention became known, a strong opposition arose.

The Stryj community was one of the first to appear before the authorities with well-stated arguments against the potential new laws:

a. Changing of the dress will cause the Jews great expenses
b. These expenses will impact the meat tax
c. Stores with large supplies of Jewish clothing will suffer damages
d. The price of the fabric for German clothing will go up

    e. The dress of the Galician Jews matches the dress of the rest of the population

The official response from the government was written by Von Widman on April 14th, 1821. It stated that reason b (regarding the meat tax) was not correct, and the proof could be seen in Moravia. The other arguments should be taken into consideration in case the proposal became a law.[57]

Other communities as well as furriers, merchants and others also sent letters regarding the impact that changing the dress would have on both the Jewish and non–Jewish population. It is interesting to note that merchants from the intellectual circles opposed this change (of clothing) stating that no benefit for the government and the treasury would be gained by these measures, but there would be economical hardships. Only a group of intellectuals from Brody sent a letter stating that a change in clothing would be desirable as it would enhance the Europeisation of Galician Jews.[58]

However, all these fears were not necessary, as the central government in Vienna rejected the gubernium's request regarding the Jewish clothing due to more pressing Galician Jewish issues.

[Page 33]

The History of the Jews of Stryj (cont.)
Chapter 1
During the Emancipation
1

The period before 1848 was marked for Galician Jews by harsh struggles between the orthodox Hassidim and the Maskilim (the intellectuals of the Jewish enlightenment movement).

Stryj was not in the center of this struggle. The Haskalah spread here late and slowly and Stryj did not produce any renowned intellectuals like those of Brody, Lvov, Tarnopol, Tyśmienica and Bolechów.

The important merchants were not eager to establish the Haskalah movement in town and did not establish schools and other institutions to promote it.

Stryj was absent during these cultural wars that were prominent in the above communities. The status of the orthodox was strong to prevent the spread of the Haskalah.

The Hassidic movement spread during the 1820's when Tzvi Hirsh Eichenstein was the rabbi of Żydaczów. The rabbi was investigated numerous times by the district high official Musbacher and was even jailed once.

[Page 34]

The authorities were investigating the Hassidic movement, but on March 31st, 1827 the district high official Hibbel wrote in his report that there were no Hassidim in the entire district. With the famous and influential rabbi of Żydaczów this report is hard to believe. It is interesting to learn about the conclusions Hibbel came to: The Hassidim were Talmudic Jews but not as strict as others especially for the poor if the restrictions were going to impact their livelihood. He thought that the name Hassidim meant that their desire was to help the poor and the wretched. However, in regards to Christianity, the Hassidim were the same as the rest of the Talmudic Jews. In his opinion, it was not true that the Hassidim called to act against the government. On the contrary, because their religion was more "ceremonial" they were less dangerous than the Talmudic Jews. It was true in his opinion that if the number of Hassidim would increase, there could be damages to the government due to the fact that they were not so strict about meat and candles and the taxes from those may decrease.

Obviously, these opinions did not reflect the reality of the day as we know that in those years, the Hassidic movement started to flourish in Stryj.

During this period, the chief rabbi of Stryj and the district was rabbi Asher Enzil Cuzmer. He was a distinct student of rabbi Aryeh Leib HaCohen Heller. While still studying under rabbi Heller, rabbi Cuzmer proof-read the works of his mentor and teacher Avnei Milluim ("Filling Stones"). Following his death, rabbi Cuzmer edited the hand written notes of his teacher and mentor and published the second part of the work in Żółkiew in 1826. He supported the opinions of his teacher, who preferred the simple and basic instruction opposing the argumentation of the Polish rabbis. This approach was based on the Sephardic teachings as reported by rabbi Zvi Hirsch Hayot (rabbi of Żółkiew) to the renowned historian Dr. M. Yost.[59] He did not allow the Hassidic influence in his community.

Enzil Cuzmer was a son of a wealthy family and the son-in-law of rabbi Joseph Asher of Przemyśl. Rabbi Mordecai Ziskind Landa was the head of the rabbinic court during his tenure.

Cuzmer was a renowned merchant who continued in his business even after becoming a chief rabbi of Stryj.

The law prohibited excommunication. However, based on the authorities' requirements, the rabbis were committed to excommunicate in the area of meat and candles taxation in cases of criminal activity, embezzlement or non-payments. Committees of all the district rabbis were assembled to discuss these cases. Between 1810 and 1830, six such committees were assembled. In the presence of the authorities, the rabbis would declare the excommunication of the sinners. In addition, the local rabbis declared excommunications which were posted in each synagogue.[60]

In the 1830 convention the following rabbis participated: Yaakov Lorberbaum, rabbi Orenstein from Lvov, rabbi Zvi Hirsch Hayot of Żółkiew, rabbi Enzil Cuzmer of Stryj, and rabbi Tzvi Hirsh Eichenstein of Żydaczów. The Stryj district office conducted investigations against him in 1817 in connection with "collection money for Jerusalem", and once he was arrested for holding a minyan without permission. As a district rabbi, he was obligated to fulfill all authorities' requirements.

During his tenure, he was forced in 1840 to cancel the excommunication that was imposed without permission by rabbi Mendel Hurwitz of Bolechów[60a] on the lessees of meat and candles taxes demanding to reduce the tax amount. He was expelled from Bolechów to his birth place of Stryj[61] after being stripped of his rabbinical position.

The head of the district Igor Golochowski gave his permission to collect money for Eretz Israel (that was conducted by the Kolel in Jerusalem emissary rabbi Israel Abramowicz) on the condition that it will be all collected by an authorized person in each district. Rabbi Cuzmer was selected to be the supervisor in the Stryj district.[61a]

Rabbi Shmuel Deutch of Sambor made some significant proposals to improve the social situation of Galician Jews. His proposals to the authorities included: cancellation of the traditional Jewish clothing, reforms in the communities, suppression of the Hassidic movement which was preventing the spread of the enlightenment, and engaging the Jewish population in agriculture. Rabbi Cuzmer was not interested in any of these recommendations.

Rabbi Cuzmer was not a supporter of the intellectuals. On the contrary, he ensured that they would not have any key positions in the community.

[Page 35]

In spite of his opposition to the enlightenment, he understood that all the Jews have to hold a unified front towards the authorities. In the 1840's, when the Jews felt that the Habsburgs were planning liberal changes, influenced by the intellectuals they started lobbying the authorities to cancel the special Jewish taxes.

In 1847 the Lvov kehila who was already headed by intellectuals took the initiative to organize a convention of all the large Jewish communities, Stryj among them. It was decided to petition the authorities outlining the dismal Jewish situation. As it was prohibited to submit a joint petition of all the communities, it was decided that each community would submit their own petition.

The petitions to Vienna were sent as follows:

Lvov	August 22nd, 1847
Brody	September 19th, 1847
Stanisławów, Sambor and Stryj	September 25th, 1847

The Stryj petition was signed by rabbi Cuzmer and detailed the heavy burden of the taxes. In Stryj, where 650 Jewish families lived, 400 of them were in such poverty that they did not know how they would make a living and feed their families the next day. In spite of this great poverty only 92 families were exempt from taxes and 156 received a discount. The poor families were obligated to pay 10,000 florins to the tax lessee who was not deterred by their situation, and in cases of non-payment would even confiscate their clothing or bed linens. The meat tax caused rising prices, and so only the rich could afford meat. This situation weakened the population as they were unable to buy the food to sustain them. 300,000 Galician Jews suffered various forms of prejudice, thus in addition to the heavy burden of taxes, there were various laws to make their lives difficult and impede their livelihood. In addition, the tax burden was heavier on the Jews than on the Christians as the Jews were the majority in the cities.

The Stryj petition emphasized the difficult situation the Jews were in because of the heavy taxes and the limitations and therefore they had to find various methods and tricks to survive and feed their families – most of them lived in conditions of poverty and starvation that were hard to imagine.

In December 1847, the summary of the petitions was brought before the emperor with the conclusion that Galician Jews were demanding the cancellation of the candles tax following the same cancellation in Bohemia.[62]

The response to the petitions came after the constitution was published on April 25th, 1848. It stated that these matters were forwarded to the parliament for further decision.

In Stanisławów Abraham Halpern was elected as a representative to the first Austrian parliament. He was the son–in–law of rabbi Enzil Cuzmer (the husband of the rabbi's daughter Nechama). Stryj elected the land owner count Alexander Dzidoszicki.

In spite of the changes brought after 1848, most of the Jews of Stryj remained observant and did not aspire for changes and reforms in the kehila that was governed by the orthodox.

The community did not participate in the political actions that were carried out by the communities of Lvov and Brody during these years to improve the political and social standing of the Jews. The Lvov community tried to repeal the limitations on ownership that were imposed on October 2nd 1853 reversing the allowances given to them in 1848. Another law from 1803 that was cancelled in 1848 and reversed in 1853 was to not allow Jews to employ Christian domestic and apprentice help. The Brody, Lvov, Stanisławów and Przemyśl communities made unsuccessful efforts to repeal the reversal, but the Stryj community did not participate in these efforts. On

July 19th, 1852, thirty nine domestic workers were arrested because they did not leave their employment in Jewish homes.[63]

[Page 36]

In 1860, a new law passed allowing Jews to buy real estate – land, homes and estates. However in the years 1862 – 1866 only five applications from Stryj were approved: Yeshayahu Meir Herman[64], Berish Koppler[65] (both wardens of synagogues), L. Halpern[66] (merchant of liquors and grain), S. Garlenter[67] (merchant of fruits) and Shenberg.[68]

A large fire in the army warehouses broke in 1856 and there was a looming danger of the city's destruction. The quick actions by the commander who rushed troops to the area saved the city.

Rabbi Enzil Cuzmer passed away on the 21st of Nisan (April 5th) 1858 and a search for an heir caused much worries and struggles in the community.

The intellectuals whose influence strengthened saw an opportunity for change and modernization in the community, to which rabbi Cuzmer strongly opposed. Their goal was to bring order to the neglected community and organize an efficient administration.

The intellectuals circle was quite strong in those days and among them were some leaders of the community: Menachem Mendel Friedlander, Dov Joel Friedlander, Nathan Samueli, and the physician Dr. Hirsch Herman who was very popular among the Jewish population. The intellectuals had a majority in the community council and they wanted a rabbi academically educated in spite of the orthodox' objections. However, no such candidate was found and therefore they settled on the son–in–law of rabbi Cuzmer – rabbi Eliyahu Meir Ben Yaakov HaCohen Rosenblum.[69]

Rabbi Rosenblum was born in 1797 and was a distinguished student of his father–in–law. Immediately after rabbi's Cuzmer passing, the orthodox demanded his appointment, a struggle that lasted for a year and a half. He was the rabbi of Stryj for nineteen years until his death on the 28th of Nisan (April 11th) 1877. Rabbi Rosenblum was a dedicated to Torah study and charity, distanced himself from any struggles with the orthodox and was highly regarded and respected by members of the community because of his practice of tolerance.

In the 1860s, the Jews of Stryj progressed economically, culturally and educationally. Charitable and educational institutions were established and the existing institutions were improved and extended. The educated Jewish population cooperated with the Lvov intellectuals' circle who established the Jewish political organization "Shomer Israel" (the keeper of Israel). This organization leaned towards the centralistic ideology that did not support the Polish autonomy aspirations.

The young Stryj born Hebrew author Neta Samueli wrote a strong essay objecting the Polish tactics that called for a coup and promised freedom for the Jews. "On the one hand they promise freedom and on the other the Galician Sejm objected Jewish emancipation", he wrote.[70]

A political awakening followed the new Austrian constitution laws of 1860 – 1861. National councils (Landtage) were established in some countries and in Galicia a Sejm was established. The Poles claimed that the Jews did not have active or passive voting rights. After much lobbying by Jewish representatives, the central government in Vienna issued a ruling on March 1st, 1861 stating clearly that all citizens including the Jews would have full and equal civil rights.

The Galician Sejm assembled in 1861 with 141 delegates four of them Jewish: Dr. Liva Shimon Samelson from Kraków, Mark Dobbs from Lvov, Meir Kalir from Brody and Eliezer Dobbs from Kołomyja, who was succeeded after his passing by Dr. Maximilian Landsberger.

When the first Sejm convened, the Jewish delegates submitted a bill supported by the Polish delegates Ziamalkowski and count Igor Golochowski – to give Jews full and equal rights. However, based on the recommendations of the chief Ruthenian delegate, the priest Gushalwitz, the bill was passed to the administrative committee and never came up for discussion.

The Jewish question came up in the Sejm discussions during the years 1862 – 1866 in conjunction with the cities' regulations. There were no limitations based on any religious or ethnic orientations and the Jews were recognized as equal. This bill was strongly opposed in the Sejm by the Poles who wanted to impose various limitation and restrictions on the Jews.

[Page 37]

The Jews protested against these restrictions and organized political actions. All the communities submitted protests against the restrictions, specifically those stating that mayors could be only Christians and council members had to speak Polish.[71] The Stryj protest was submitted in January 1866.

Following long discussions in the Sejm on September 30th and October 8th, 1868[72] the approved cities' regulations bill had no restrictions whatsoever on the Jews. In addition, the Sejm decided to petition the central government to remove all Jewish restrictions.

Based on the cities' regulations the Stryj council was comprised of 36 members: 11 Catholics (Poles), 6 Greek–Catholics (Ruthenians), 3 Evangelic and other religions and 16 Jews.

In nine cities the Jews were the majority in the town councils and only in Stryj they had a relative majority.

The achievement of full and equal rights, the Jews saw the "light of freedom". However, as pointed by the Stryj Jewish intellectual Moshe David Balabban, these changes created much worries among the ultra–orthodox as no one could get married until completion of military service.[73]

The young Stryj author Samueli[74] reported about an interesting case. In 1866, a court house Christian clerk, Adam Miller, told rabbi Josef Zvi Garlanter that he wanted to convert to Judaism. Out of concern, the community refused his request. After the new constitution in 1868, Miller expressed his desire again to rabbi Rosenblum, and again he was refused. Following this refusal, Miller approached the community leaders Berish

Koppler and Josef Garlanter. They referred him to the circumciser Moshe Zecharyahu Schiff who agreed. Together with Neta Samueli they traveled outside of town and warned Miller again, but he did not change his mind. After the circumcision, Miller's name became Abraham Ger–Tzedek (righteous convert to Judaism). This case made a strong impression in Stryj and in the entire Galicia.

In the community, the influence of the intellectuals and the academically educated kept growing.

2

Among the early-enlightened intellectuals in Stryj was Yehosua Levenzohn. He was in contact on a regular basis with the renowned intellectual from Stanislawow Yechiel Meller[75] regarding public matters (by letters).

In one of the letters to Meller (December 16th, 1846)[76] he stated his opinion against the Chasidic dominance in the Jewish education. Although Levenzohn was observant, he understood the dismal cultural situation of Galician Jews. The older generation favored the Chasidim who objected any progress and change, whereas the younger generation was distancing itself from the Jewish values.

Among the Stryj intellectuals who participated in "Kochavei Isaac" (stars of Isaac) was David Moshe Balaban (1841 – 1895) who was born in Lvov. In his youth he was the student of rabbi Josef Shaul Nathanson, but later joined the enlightenment circles.

In 1867 – 1868 he published his first poems in "Kochavei Isaac" (volume 34 p. 33, volume 35 p. 89 – 90). Later he published German poems translations in David Gordon's "Hamagid" (The messenger), Fine's "HaCarmel" (The Carmel) and in Moshe Shulboim's "HaEt" (The time). After his marriage he settled in Stryj, was popular and cooperated with the authorities.

The enlightened poet Moshe Hirsch Enser lived in Stryj for a few years. He was born in Lvov in 1804. He had broad education and knew Greek, German and French. Starting in 1845 he published poems in "Kochavei Isaac".[77] He was well educated in the Torah and in 1854 published a Hebrew grammar book. He was in close contact with Shir (Solomon Judah Löb Rapoport), S. Bloch, and Dr. Arter. In addition to the printed material, there were other manuscripts left by him: "Igrot El Asaf (Letters to Asaf – about the Hebrew language), "HaNoten Zmirot" (The giver of hymns – about the cantillation), interpretations for "Sefer HaNefesh" (Book of the soul) by Shem–Tov ben Joseph ibn Falaquera (1224 – 1290) and a collection of poems "Zera Kodesh" (Seed of holiness). He passed away in Lvov in 1871.

Mordechai Druker was born in Stryj in 1854 and was the nephew of Enser, educated and influenced by him greatly, leaning towards the enlightenment. He was a significant scholar of the Torah and an excellent reader of scriptures. He started his literary career as a writer for the publication "Ivri Anochi" (I am a Hebrew) in Brody. He dedicated himself to the study and research of the Hebrew grammar. He published a book "Safa Lane'emanim" (Language for the Faithful) and later a publication on the Hebrew verbs.

[Page 38]

He later published "Techelet Mordechai", a commentary on the Pentateuch (Lvov 1894); "Tovim Meorot" (The Good Luminaries), sanctification for the sun and moon (first edition Lvov 1897, second edition Lvov 1928); "Ateret Mordechai" (The crown of Mordechai), a commentary on Midrash Rabba using the approach of Hebrew linguistics; "Divrei Hachamim Ve'Hidoteyhem" (The words and riddles of the sages) on the Torah portions.

Druker was an orthodox Jew and he served as "Magid meisharim" in town from 1891.

Other intellectuals in town during this period were Menachem Mendel Friedlander (died 1875), Dan Cohen who translated Lessing's "Freigeist" (Free thinker) (Drohobycz 1886), Haim Mendrochowicz, D. Apfelgreen and Leo Druker.

In the 1860's a new and promising literary came into the limelight in Galicia. Nathan Neta Samueli was born February 28th, 1846 to a renowned family in Stryj. He was educated and familiar with the old Hebrew literature as well as the enlightenment literature. In 1864 – 1865 he published his first stories in the periodical "Ivri Anochi" (I am Hebrew) in Brody – "Seven Saturdays" and "Language of the Faithful" as well as poems in the "HaShahar" (The dawn) and "Kochavei Isaac". In 1868 he published the Neo–Hebrew poetry book"Kenaf Renanim" (The wing of chanting) which was received enthusiastically by the readers. Even Peretz Smolenskin saw in his poems the birth of a new star.

Samueli wrote in Hebrew and German, publishing highly acclaimed poems and short stories[77a] depicting the Jewish life in Galicia. His stories were poetic, although showed also satirical and humoristic elements. His first stories in German were published in the weekly "Lemberger Yiddishe Presse", which he published together with the renowned poet Dr. Mauritz Rappaport.

He introduced to the German reading Jew a new world full of depression and sadness, but also a world full of happiness and rejoicing, a world full of spiritual adventures. In his stories, Samueli described the various Jewish movements – the Chasidim, the intellectuals and enlightened and those who strived to advance with the new European wave – but not in the style of the intellectuals of the early nineteenth century. His characters such as rabbi Haim Resenband, his granddaughter Esther, and Dr. Gustav Ahrenbart – all from small and obscure villages in Galicia – all their ambition was to help people come out of the mental and spiritual depression, to free them from their superstitions and the rabbis, to help them obtain culture and education all that without assimilation.

Samueli's aspirations at the time of his writings were actually in contrast to those he described in his stories. He opposed Chassidism which he saw as a force trying to distance the people from the European culture. However, he managed to describe a colorful picture of the Chasidim so they seemed to be life-like characters. In 48 stories, with a psychological backdrop, he described his contemporaries, characters from all walks of life of Jewish Galicia. These served as a source to understand the traditional Galician life. His German books "Shylock und Nathan" and "Kulturbilder" were received very favorably and were described as the most authentic depiction of Jewish life in Galicia. The anthology of his Hebrew stories that were published in three volumes "From Life" (Warsaw 1891) and two volumes "Faces" (Warsaw 1897 – 1898) were an important contribution to understanding the Jewish life in Galicia.

Samueli was one of the admirers of Peretz Smolenskin and was sharply criticized about it by Yehoshua Heshel Schorr, the owner of "HeHalutz".

In 1882 Samueli published in Sacher-Masoch's Austrian monthly "Auf der Höhe" an assay praising the stories of Smolenskin. Yehoshua Heshel Schorr, who was Smolenskin's adversary, published an article in Brody's "HaIvri", mocking him (Smolenskin).[78] Samueli played an active role in the public life in Stryj and represented his town in the "Day of the communities" in July 1878 in Lvov. Later, he settled in Lvov and lived there until the start of World War I when he escaped to Vienna as a refugee. He later moved to Baden where he passed away on March 26th, 1921.

3

These intellectuals established a club called …. where they gathered to read papers and books and listen to lectures. This club influenced greatly the community life. The fast economic growth in 1860 – 1870 was a major factor in stabilizing the Jewish population. The town and the surrounding areas saw the establishment of factories for metal works, lumber saw-mills, plaster manufacturing, water-mills, alcohol distilleries, soap manufacturing, starch and matches. Much of these industries were Jewish-owned. The economic activity increased even more after the railroad line was opened in 1886.

[Page 39]

The improved economic conditions contributed greatly to the increase in charitable activities headed mainly by the leaders Mordechai Markusohn, Moshe Lifszitz, Lippa Halpern, and Yeshayahu Meir Herman.[79] A Jewish hospital was established which was maintained by donations and also by an allocation from the community. Due to Stryj's location, the commerce with Hungary expended mainly in cattle, agricultural products and lumber.

Politically the influence of Jews grew in public life, mainly in the city council.

The first direct elections for the Austrian parliament were held in 1873. The Poles in the Galician Sejm did not consider the Jewish interests and no (Jewish) representatives were elected for the years 1870 – 1873. In Lvov, the organization "Shomer Israel" (the keeper of Israel) came-up with their own independent list of Jewish candidates. A Jewish elections committee was established on May 28th, 1873 with representatives of the communities headed by Dr. Juliusz Kaliszer as the chair-person and Dr. Emil Byk as secretary. The leadership of the Stryj community supported the "Shomer Israel" political aspirations.[80]

In November 1873 elections were held for both the Austrian parliament and the Galician Sejm. The Jewish candidate Dr. Philip Fruchtmann ran against the Polish candidate Dr. Zygmont Zatwarnicki, won (296 to 199 votes)[81] and was elected to the Sejm, representing Stryj until 1909 – for thirty six consecutive years.

Elections for the town council were held in April 1874. Dr. Fructmann won 31 to 2[82] and was elected mayor and served also in this position for a few years. In the Vienna parliament, Stryj was represented by Christian delegates. In 1890, after the death of the Stryj delegate Otto Hoyzer, Dr. Fruchtmann was offered the position, but he refused.

Dr. Fruchtmann joined "Shomer Israel" because of its ideology and slogans of Polish assimilation. He saw himself as a Pole of the Jewish religion and was not supportive of the Jewish national aspirations. His home and his children's education were Polish. In the Galician Sejm, he cared more for the Polish interests than the Jewish ones.

As a mayor he worked hard to improve and develop the town. The kehila was at the time headed by the enlightened intellectuals and they desired reforms based on those stated by the "Shomer Israel" in Lvov which brought about many changes in the political life of Galician Jews. Mainly they demanded that the communities become more modern and adjust to the new era. Based on the organization's initiative, the authorities demanded reorganization based on uniform regulations for all the communities. "Shomer Israel" made efforts to stabilize and unify all the communities based on regulations approved by the authorities and all communities were required to participate in a conference on June 18th – 20th in Lvov.

The Stryj community was represented by the author Neta Nathan Samueli who participated in the discussions and was instrumental in coming-up with a set of uniform regulations.

As a result of this conference, the orthodox struggled to object any changes in the communities as proposed by "Shomer Israel" and came up with their own organization "Mahzikei HaDat" (Keepers of the religion) led by Shimon Schrieber from Krakow and the Belz rabbi.

These differences in opinions caused many conflicts in Stryj between "Shomer Israel" and their supporters and the orthodox. The district official who supported the orthodox, refused to approve the regulations reasoning that the clause dealing with appointing rabbis stated that the candidate must have general (secular) education and fluency in the state languages.

The district official disbanded the existing kehila committee and appointed a temporary committee comprised of the orthodox. The committee appealed to the authorities, the regulations were approved and elections for the kehila committee were scheduled to be held on October 29th, 1880. The district official tried to postpone the elections but the authorities objected any delays. The elections took place and the "Shomer Israel" candidates won by a large margin.

[Page 40]

One of the reasons for the conflicts between "Shomer Israel" and the orthodox was the issue of electing a new rabbi after the passing of rabbi Eliyahu Meir Rosenblum in 1877. "Shomer Israel" wanted to appoint his son that was orthodox, but also had secular education and was fluent in German. The orthodox objected mainly because he conducted his sermons in German.[83]

After long negotiations, all agreed to appoint rabbi Aryeh Leibush (1848 – 1909). He was the son of rabbi Isaac the son of rabbi Meshulam Yissachar Horowitz of Stanisławów. He was the rabbi of Zilozitz (Założce) between 1871 and 1874 and then the rabbi of Seret (in Bukovina) between 1874 and 1878. He served as the rabbi of Stryj until 1906 when he moved to Stanisławów to take his father's position.

Rabbi Horowitz was a great Talmudic scholar. He published his book of Q&A's "Harei Besamim", in two volumes (First volume was published in Lvov in 1882, and the second volume in 1897). He was a very good lecturer and orator and was fluent in German. He was well regarded and liked by his community and was tactful and well-mannered.

He was supported by the orthodox because of his leanings towards Hassidism and he occasionally visited rabbi David Moshe of Czortków. He tried unsuccessfully to build a bridge between the various factions of the community.

He assisted in the founding the "General Cheder" to the dismay of the orthodox who harassed him until he left town in 1906 to become the rabbi of Stanisławów.

After the orthodox gained control of the kehila, the committee chair stopped paying the rabbi's salary for a few months, but was overruled by the community who supported the rabbi and disliked the orthodox tactics.

A fire erupted in town on April 17th, 1886. Because of the high winds, the flames soon engulfed the entire town. Shops, churches, the old synagogue (circa 1677), houses of study burned to the ground. 970 homes burned at an estimated value of 2.4 million florins and the estimated value of merchandise lost was 2.6 million florins. Many people lost their lives and in the rabbi's house, a fifty thousand florins orphans' fund was lost. More than seven thousand people became homeless.[84]

However, the authorities and the public stepped-in and the town was rebuilt quickly. The Jewish population was assisted greatly by donations from baron Maurice von Hirsch.

An author from town documented Stryj as a "town not big and not small"[85] where many opposites exist – some characteristics were of a big town and some of small, such in clothing, transportation, medicine, wealth, etc.

He also described how the Chasidic interfered with anything and everything objecting the proper management of the community life, but slowly the enlightened gained more support and influence and were able to break the walls of ignorance and did greatly for the advancement of their people.

Influenced by the enlightened, a more modern kehila was established after the orthodox lost the elections. In addition to establishing welfare and charity institutions, they also rebuilt the club that burnt and other cultural establishments. The purpose was to advance the science, Torah and general knowledge and also to raise the Jewish social life and distance the population from the superstitions and ignorance that were very prevalent.

On March 12th, 1887 a "Beit Mikra" was opened. Its function was public readings and lectures. Students under the guidance of Shmuel Weizman got lectures assignments calling for "knowledge, understanding, unity, strengthening of the national spirit, improving the communities, because these were the reasons for Israel's redemption".[86]

[Page 41]

They established a Jewish hospital, women's help societies, charity lodging, and charity tea-house.*

The orthodox, who noticed the national leanings of the more enlightened and educated, pressured the district official to appoint a temporary community committee comprised of their people, but were not successful.

Shortly after the 1886 fire, the town developed quickly, the economy improved and the number of Jews grew.

Census numbers:

	1880	1890	1900	1910
Number of Christians in the district	67,623	78,398	96,194	
Number of Jews in the district	10,382	12,774	15,859	
Number of Christians in cities and townships	7,525 (11.1%)	10,429 (13.3%)	15,239 (15.8%)	
Number of Jews in cities and townships	6,583 (63.4%)	8,241 (64.5%)	10,742 (67.7%)	
Number of Jews in villages	2,537 (24.4%) in 101 villages	3,224 (25.3%) in 100 villages	4,295 (27%) in 99 villages	
Number of inhabitants in Stryj	12,625	16,515	23,205	30,942
Number of Jews in Stryj	5,245 (41.5%)	6,572 (39.8%)	8,647 (37.2%)	10,718 (34%)

Population growth in Stryj between 1881 and 1910:

Poles	260.3%
Ruthenians	130.5%
Other nationalities	31.8%
Jews	104.3%

Jewish real estate holdings as recorded in the district registry:

	Hectares	
1889	55,963	63.8%
1902	16,279	20.3%

Changes took place in education as well starting in the 1860's. Most of the Jews sent their children to public schools – both elementary and high. In 1885 there were 600 Jewish students in the public schools (both elementary and high).[87a]

In 1910 out of 1192 students there were 447 Jewish students[88] in the two high schools in town. There were 10 Jewish high school teachers. Due to the large number of students from out of town, and those without means, a committee led by Dr. Fruchtmann was established to build a hostel (Bursa zydowska). Donations were collected between the years 1908 and 1910. The nice building housed up to 30 students between 1910 and the start of the First World War.

In the late 1880's the spread of Anti–Semitism, the events in Russia, the awakening of the minorities in the Austrian empire and the unfavorable response of certain Poles and Germans to the Jewish assimilation, showed some of the enlightened that the right way was to return to Jewish nationalism. In 1884 – 1885, the high school Jewish youth established Zionist activities to learn about Jewish history, Hebrew, and discussion circles on Zionist–national subjects. The organizer was Gershon Zipper[89] who came to Stryj in 1883 from his town of Tarnopol after failing school there. He communicated with Zionist circles in Lvov and corresponded with Mordecai Ehrenpreis, Dr. Itzhak Feld the author of the Zionist anthem "Dort wo die Zeder" and Abraham Korkis and saw himself as their emissary in Stryj. In the Stryj high school, Jewish religious studies were not taught. The community leaders were completely indifferent to this, although it was actually against the law. Zipper organized a protest of the Jewish students who appeared before the leadership forcing them to appeal to the national education council to appoint a teacher for Jewish religious studies. Due to this action that was also supported by a petition signed by the parents, the council appointed the Hebrew author Yitzhak Aharon Bernfeld (1854 – 1930) (he was the brother of the renowned author and scholar Dr. Shimon Bernfeld) to teach Jewish religious studies in the Stryj schools.

[Page 42]

Zipper continued his activities also among those who were not high school students until he left in June of 1890 to study law at the University of Lvov.

The Zionist activities of the youth encouraged the enlightened and the educated to turn to the national revival movement.

In 1887 a group of maskilim, headed by Dan Hacohen and Meir Abraham Stern, established the "Shoharei Tushia" society for the purpose of spreading the national ideal, supporting the new settlements in Eretz Israel and fostering the Hebrew language and literature.

This society, which was joined by 100 members, was headed by the intellectual Moshe Stern, who was a community activist and a member of the town council, who worked tirelessly for the Jewish population, David Goldberg and Patrach. Three years later all activities were suspended, and in 1891 a number of young men who were not satisfied with the leadership of the "Shoharei Tushia" founded another group called "Hayahadut", for the purpose of promoting the study of Hebrew literature.[90] Because of this split, the general meeting of "Shoharei Tushia" which was held on November 28th, 1890, resolved to change its name to "Haleumi". In its rules and regulations it stated that "its chief purpose was to strengthen and disseminate the Jewish national consciousness among the Jews".

The Stryj Zionists were in constant contact with the Lvov Zionists and held constructive discussions.[90a][91]

The "Admat Israel" society, was founded in March 1891 by Avigdor Mermelstein of Przemysl, with the purpose of popularizing the idea of settlement in Eretz Israel, and collecting money to support the farmers there. Fifty persons joined and Moshe Lipschitz[92] was elected chairperson. A year later another 150 members joined the Society. In November, 1891 the society sent its secretary, Meir Abraham Stern, to Eretz Israel in order to investigate the conditions of the Jewish settlements and "to seek a place there" for setting up a colony of Galician Jews. "Admat Israel" was the first society in Galicia to send its own representative to Eretz Israel. After a visit which lasted a year, Stern came home and gave a detailed report.

On July 24th, 1894 Stern passed away following a long illness, and "Shoharei Tushia" and "Admat Israel" societies lost one of their most active and dedicated members.

In May 1892, Dr. Nathan Birnbaum made a propaganda tour of Galician towns, in the course of which he visited Stryj on May 24th. There he proposed that members of the "Admat Israel" society join the "Zion association" of societies in Vienna. During the meeting Moshe Lipschitz and Moshe Schoenfeld declared that the general assembly which was to be held after the return of Meir Abraham Stem from Eretz Israel would undoubtedly adopt the resolution.

The resolution was adopted and "Admat Israel", whose original purpose was to be a Galician center of societies for settlement of Eretz Israel became a branch of "Zion" in Vienna, and continued its activities on a smaller scale.

Rabbi L. M. Landau and Adolf Stand spoke at the general meeting of the society in November 1894 and encouraged the members.

The establishment of the new Societies[93] led the "Shoharei Tushia", and in particular its chairman Moshe Stern, to renew and stabilize its own activities. A general meeting was held in 1892, and a new committee was elected with Abraham Goldberg as chairman, Michael Hornstein as vice chairman, Mattityahu Patrach – secretary, A.J. Kris – treasurer, Itzhak Reisner, and A. Scheinfeld – librarian. The society started to hold regular meetings and lectures which were addressed by speakers from Lvov, among them Dr. Gershon Zipper, who was already known to and very popular from the time that he studied in Stryj. During the general meeting of March 24th, 1894 the following were elected: Moshe Stern as chairman, David Goldberg as vice chairman, M. Kerner as treasurer, Yaakov Ringel as librarian. The following were elected as committee members: S. Stern, L. Walker, Abraham Scheinfeld, P. Ringel, Michael Rapp, Hirsch Scheinfeld, W. Last and H. Pepperkorn. During the meeting it was decided to modify the regulations and characteristics of the society from a "general Jewish" into a national Zionist body and join the Jewish national party which already existed in Galicia and was centered in Lvov.[94]

[Page 43]

The socialist movement started its activities among the masses during the same period.

Polish workers had begun to organize in Galicia starting in 1870. Bolesław Limanowski and Boleslaw Czerwienski author of the labor poem "Czerwony sztandar" (the red flag), were the first organizers and preachers of the socialist movement among the Polish public. They were mostly supported by Polish political emigrants. Socialist organizations also began to appear among the Ukrainians established by the students of the Ukrainian writer and scholar A. Drahomanov. Ivan Franko and Mykhailo Pavlyk were the first pioneers.

Professionally organized Jewish workers appeared on the scene only at the beginning of the 1890's not as independent organizations, but within the framework of the Polish social democratic movement.

In 1891 Jewish workers were organized in the Polish Sila society of Lvov, but soon after independent societies of Jewish workers were established. Among them were "Yad Hazaka" in Lvov, "Brüderlichkeit" (brotherhood) in Kraków, "Freiheit" (liberty and political freedom) in Stanisławów and a society in Kołomyja.

On September 1st, 1893, the social democratic organization in Galicia published the bi-weekly "Der Arbeiter" in Yiddish (more accurately in German with Hebrew characters) which was edited by Karl Naker. From this journal we can learn about the agitation among the workers in Stryj at the Lipschitz matches factory where the workday was 15 – 17 hours.

The first Jewish workers' society was established in Stryj in 1893 under the name "Brüderlichkeit". Officially it was a society for the dissemination of culture (Bildungsverein).[95] However, it had little real impact on the Jewish public and declined even more following the establishment of the "Poalei Zion" movement.

The Zionist movement gained the most supporters among both the intellectuals and the Jewish masses. Since Zionist societies were established in most towns of Galicia, the question of a common framework for them soon arose. In March 1891, during a convention of "Zion" members in Lvov, Dr. Abraham Salz of Tarnow proposed to unite all the local societies in one organization for the entire Galicia to ensure uniformity. He suggested a convention to be held by the end of 1891 with the participation of all the local societies. To prepare for the convention a special committee was appointed, consisting of representatives of Lvov, Drobobycz and with Gershon Zipper from Stryj. This committee also prepared the convention which, in 1892 united all Zionist societies in Galicia into a single national organization. A plan was prepared and organizational and publicity methods were decided on. The first national conference was held on April 23rd –24th 1893 with the participation of representatives of all the societies. The second national conference was held on September 2nd – 4th 1894 where the organizational ideas were discussed. Theses conferences were attended by M. Patrach, and by Abraham Stern who was elected to be committee president – both from Stryj.

The Zionist societies were a major contributor to raising Jewish national awareness among the younger generation, who organized in secret societies to study Hebrew and Jewish history.

High-school graduates and University students in Stryj established their own society, whose representative participated in the first students' conference held on July 25th – 26th 1899 in Lvov. Juliusz Wurzel was the Stryj representative.

In 1903 the academic society "Veritas" (later became "Emuna") joined the association of academic societies that were not corporations in Austria and had major impact on the Jewish youth. In 1912 it joined the Zionist academic organization which was established earlier at a convention held in Drohobycz on September 15th 1912.

"Bnei Zion" (sons of Zion) organization of high school student existed in Stryj from the end of the 19th century as part of the national "Ze'irei Zion" (youth of Zion) association headed by Nathan Czaczkes (J. Kirton) and Moshe Frostig.

[Page 44]

The process of differentiation first began among the Zionist youth in 1908. The students who supported the "Poalei Zion" ideology began to establish their own societies within national "Herut" (freedom) organization.

In 1911 Stryj had, a "Bnei Zion" circle containing 6 "Ze'irei Zion" branches, with 80 members and 5 Hebrew study courses attended by 40 students. The "Safa Brura" Hebrew school and Club had been established in 1902.

An organization of Zionist workers and laborers called "The commercial associates club" was established in 1901 and was the foundation for the "Poalei Zion" movement in Stryj. In June 1903 it joined the national organization established by the "Ahva" (fraternity/brotherhood) society of Lvov.

Moshe Wundermann established a branch of the "Mizrahi" society following the spread of this movement in Galicia.

Following the visit of Rosa Pomeranz in 1898, a women's Zionist society was established in Stryj led by Dr. Helena Rosenman and Rachel Katz. In 1910 the chapter joined the national organization of Zionist women. The first conference was held in Lvov on February 27th 1910 and was dedicated to the issue of preschools/kindergartens and was addressed by the Stryj representative Dr. Helena Rosenman. She was also elected to the national committee of the association.

Between 1903 and 1906 the Stryj Zionist societies were under the jurisdiction of the Lvov district. From 1902 all Zionist activities in Stryj were led by Dr. Juliusz Wurzel, a lawyer who lived in town until the outbreak of the first world war. In the 1907 Austrian parliament elections Dr. Abraham Salz of Tarnow was the Zionist candidate. The 1907 elections created a wave of Jewish enthusiasm in Galicia (Stryj included). Nobody who saw it could ever forget the devotion and support which the Jewish masses displayed for the Zionist movement.

The Zionist movement at the time was led by Dr. Shlomo Goldberg, Dr. Heinrich Byk, Dr. Wolf Schmorak, and Dr. Michael Ringel.

The election activities were directed by Dr. Wurzel, who was arrested and had his home searched which was quite unusual in those days.

In the 1911 elections the Zionist candidate, Dr. Leon Reich, was among the finalists together with the P.P.S. candidate Moraczewsky in spite of the efforts of assimilationists to have him defeated in the primaries. However, Dr. Reich was not elected because the assimilationists and their orthodox followers voted for the P.P.S. candidate Moraczewsky.

In 1907 Dr. Salz received 1722 votes in Stryj, while in 1911 Dr. Reich received 1541 votes.[96]

Significant changes took place in community life in 1896. The academic intellectual group grew, and they were holding the key positions in public life. In 1896 there were three Jewish lawyers: Dr. Altman, Dr. Fink, and Dr. Fruchtmann. In 1911 there were 16 Jewish lawyers, 2 Jewish surgeons[97] and eight physician specialists.[98]

After Dr. Fruchtmann completed his term as Mayor, four Christian mayors were elected in succession: Dr. Zygmont Zatwarnicki, Ludwig Gettinger, Rettinger, and Alexander Stojalowski. Then, the Jewish lawyer Dr. Juliusz Falk was elected and served a number of years.[98a]

During that time the community was led by Lippa Halperin, David Halperin, Dr. Enzil Goldstein all of them descendants of rabbi Enzil Cuzmer,

Joseph Zvi Gelernter. Dr. Wiesenberg led the community between the years 1911 and 1914. After Rabbi Hurwitz was appointed chief rabbi of Stanisławów no one was appointed to fill the position in Stryj. Following his departure rabbi Feivel Hertz of Głogów and rabbi Jolles (son of rabbi Uri of Sambor) of Mosciska were appointed members of the Beth–Din (rabbinical court). This led to many years of controversy within the community. In 1917 the step–nephew of rabbi Hurwitz, rabbi Eliezer ben Shlomo Ladier (1874–1932) from Seret (Bukovina), was appointed to be the chief rabbi in Stryj. He was a scholar who wrote many works on Talmudic subjects. However he also published poems in Hebrew and German expressing his love for Zion, for the revival of the Jewish people and for the beauty of Nature. His poems were published in various journals and were never collected during his lifetime. In 1933 after his death his son published a volume of his German poems in Vienna under the title"Gedichte". The plans to publish his Hebrew poems never materialized.

During the years 1908 to 1914 there were many activities in the area of Hebrew education and spreading the knowledge of the Hebrew language. Dr. Max Bienenstock, Dr. Zvi Diesendruk and Jonah Gelernter organized the younger generation. They set up classes for Hebrew study and established the"Ivriya" Club. The main private Hebrew school was established by Moshe Wundermann. Active Hebrew teachers before the first world war included Hutriansky and Fuks, a refugee from Russia who was one of the first members of the Jewish self–defense during the pogroms in Homel, M. A. Tennenblatt, Kuhn, and Naphthali Siegel.

[Page 45]

Chapter 3
Personalities

A number of Stryj born Jews made valuable literary, cultural and scholarly contributions to the press, Jewish studies and public affairs during the second part of the 19th century and the beginning of the 20th century.

Ephraim Frisch, a noted Jewish author who wrote in German, was born in Stryj on March 1st 1873 and spent his early years there. In the 1880's he moved to Brody, where he attended the German high–school and joined the Zionist student group.

In 1892 the programmatic brochure of the Zionist students was published in Lvov under the Polish title: "Jaki być powinien program młodzieży żydowskiej" (What should be the Jewish youth program) which centered the Zionist activities around work for Eretz Israel. Frisch then published an essay in Dr. Nathan Birnbaum's "Selbstemanzipation" (self emancipation) in which he attacked the "phraseology" of the brochure – which spoke so much of settlement in Eretz Israel, Zion, etc. without recognizing the prospect of redemption and settlement as the final goal cannot be achieved without making far–reaching reforms within the communities. In his opinion it was necessary to understand the fact that steps must first be taken to improve the social condition of the Jewish workers which was growing steadily in Galicia. Because of the growing influence of the orthodox and the assimilationists it was necessary to disseminate education, knowledge and culture among the masses. Despite his opposition to the very approach of the brochure he could not ignore the basic assumption of the plan that was based on scientific and moral foundations and drew the necessary conclusions from the degraded and impoverished conditions of Galicia's Jews. At the end of his essay he emphasized the brochure's positive aspects.

From Brody Frisch moved to Vienna and shortly afterwards to Berlin. He achieved a reputation as a writer and literary critic. In spite of being active as a German writer he always regarded himself as a Jewish nationalist and supported the Zionist movement. In 1902 he published his novel"Das Verlöbnis" (the engagement) about Jewish life in Galicia. In 1905 he worked for Max Reinhardt as a dramaturge. In 1910, he published"Von der Kunst des Theaters" (From the art of theater). In his 1914 story"Die Kantine" (the canteen) he again described the Jews of Galicia. From 1911 until 1925 he published a political–literary monthly"Der Neue Merkur" (the new mercury) in Munich.

In 1921 he published an article titled"Jüdische Aufzeichnungen" (Jewish records). In 1927 he published the novel"Zenobi" depicting Austrian life in the days before the World War one. His wife, Feiga Frisch (1878–?), who was born in Russia, was also a renowned writer. She translated many works from Russian into German of such authors as Goncharov, Turgenev, Saltykov-Shchedrin, Chekhov, Alexander Pushkin, Leo Tolstoy and others.

The well–known Hebrew writer and educator Eliezer Meir Lipschitz was also a native of Stryj. He was born on November 5th 1879, the son of Yom Tov Lipschitz, one of the first "Lovers of Zion" (Hovevei Zion) in Galicia and the owner of a match factory in Skole. He was educated in both traditional Jewish studies as well as general secular studies. When his parents moved to Lvov he studied under rabbis Isaac Schmelkes and Shlomo Buber. In Lvov he joined the maskilim and Zionist youth circles under the leadership of Mordecai Ehrenpreis, Joshua Tahun, Mordechai Braude and Shlomo Schiller. He was one of the first Hebrew speakers and formed a circle of youth who spoke the language in the Sephardic diction.

After his marriage to Dina Reitzes, who was also fluent in Hebrew he became a merchant. Only Hebrew was spoken in their home and it became one of the centers of the Hebrew movement in Galicia.

With Zvi Karl he established a Hebrew teachers' seminary in Lvov and thanks to his initiative "Ivriya" clubs were established in Lvov and the surrounding towns. He had a major impact in introducing Hebrew as a spoken language, disseminating Hebrew literature and improving its style. In 1904 he published his research on Yaakov Shmuel Buch in the literary calendar "Hermon" which appeared in Lvov and was edited by Gershom Bader. He later published studies on the history of Hebrew culture and literature in the Hebrew monthly "Ha'Shiloah". His true passion, however, was for pedagogical and literary work. He therefore accepted in 1910 the proposal of the "Ezra" society in Berlin to become a teacher in their Hebrew teachers' seminary in Jerusalem.

In Jerusalem he was active in public life and scientific research, publishing essays in "Hatekufa" and in other journals which appeared in Eretz Israel. He called for the establishment of Hebrew educational institutions based on the traditional "Heder", centering on Torah learning with secular studies as well.

During World War one he was arrested by the Turks and exiled to Damascus, but was released as an Austrian subject and forced to leave the country for Berlin. There he published his work "Vom Lebendigen Hebräisch" (From the Living Hebrew) in 1923.

In 1919 he returned to Eretz Israel, and was appointed the head of the teachers' seminary of the Mizrahi educational network. The institution expanded under his leadership. He established a model elementary school for training the students and graduates of the seminary. Later he also established a high-school.

[Page 46]

For a few years he acted as an inspector/supervisor of the orthodox educational system. He was active in developing the educational side of the orthodox system. The essays he published in the press were noteworthy for their sleek style. His better-known works include: A monograph on Rashi

(Warsaw 1912); The Mishna (Jaffa 1922), which also appeared in German in Berlin (1919); a study of the "Heder" ("Hatekufa" – Vol. 7);"Conversations" on religious issues under the pseudonym Azariah Ibn Bezalel; essays on educational questions (Ha'Shiloah 22, 37); and on Agnon (Ha'Shiloah, Vol. 22), which was published in 1920 in Berlin as a separate book.

All his life he worked towards unifying the general education based on the Torah. He passed away in Jerusalem on the 24th of Tammuz 5706 (July 23rd, 1946).

Dr. Abraham Jacob Braver, the noted historian and geographer, was born in Stryj on the 4th of Nissan 5644 (march 30th 1884), and completed his high-school education in town. He received a Ph.D. from the Vienna University, and taught at the Tarnopol high-school in 1910–1911. He came to Eretz Israel in 1912 and became a teacher at the teachers' seminary founded by the Ezra society of Berlin (1912–1914). In the years 1914–1918 he taught in Salonika and Constantinople (Istanbul), and in 1920 he returned to Eretz Israel again to teach at the teachers' seminary.

His first research work was on Fergen, the first Polish commissioner of Galicia and was published in the quarterly"Kwartalnik Historyczny" in 1907. In 1910 he published a work in Vienna on"Galizien wie es an Österreich kam" (How Galicia came to Austria) which was received enthusiastically by historical scientists in Austria. He also published a valuable Hebrew study in"Ha'Shiloah" (Vol. 23) on"The Emperor Joseph the second and the Jews of Galicia". While in Tarnopol, he found a manuscript in the "Perl" Library by Dov Birkental of Bolechów (1723 – 1805) entitled"Divrei Bina" (words of wisdom), about Jacob Frank and the famous dispute between the Frankists and representatives of the Jewish community in Lvov in 1759. He published the manuscript in"Ha'Shiloah" under the title"A new Hebrew Source on the Frankists".

In Eretz Israel he devoted himself to the geography of the country, and published many studies in this field. His renowned work "Haaretz" (The Land) was published in many editions. He also published a geographic atlas.

His father Michael ben Moshe Braver (1862 – 1949), who was a well-known writer on rabbinical subjects, lived in Stryj between 1882 and 1902 and took an active part in the community life. While in Stryj he contributed to "Ivri Anochi", "Hamizpeh" and "Mahazikei Hadat".

---

* The charity tea–house provided the city's poor tea, sugar and a large roll for one kruezer and large families for free. Officially this was opened for all the city's poor, but practically only Jews benefited.

[Page 45]

A number of Stryj born Jews made valuable literary, cultural and scholarly contributions to the press, Jewish studies and public affairs during the second part of the 19th century and the beginning of the 20th century.

Ephraim Frisch, a noted Jewish author who wrote in German, was born in Stryj on March 1st 1873 and spent his early years there. In the 1880's he moved to Brody, where he attended the German high-school and joined the Zionist student group.

In 1892 the programmatic brochure of the Zionist students was published in Lvov under the Polish title: "Jaki być powinien program młodzieży żydowskiej" (What should be the Jewish youth program) which centered the Zionist activities around work for Eretz Israel. Frisch then published an essay in Dr. Nathan Birnbaum's " Selbstemanzipation (self emancipation) in which he attacked the "phraseology" of the brochure - which spoke so much of settlement in Eretz Israel, Zion, etc. without recognizing the prospect of redemption and settlement as the final goal cannot be achieved without making far-reaching reforms within the communities. In his opinion it was necessary to understand the fact that steps must first be taken to improve the social condition of the Jewish workers which was growing steadily in Galicia. Because of the growing influence of the orthodox and the assimilationists it was necessary to disseminate education, knowledge and culture among the masses. Despite his opposition to the very approach of the brochure he could not ignore the basic assumption of the plan that was based on scientific and moral foundations and drew the necessary conclusions from the degraded and impoverished conditions of Galicia's Jews. At the end of his essay he emphasized the brochure's positive aspects.

From Brody Frisch moved to Vienna and shortly afterwards to Berlin. He achieved a reputation as a writer and literary critic. In spite of being active as a German writer he always regarded himself as a Jewish nationalist and supported the Zionist movement. In 1902 he published his novel "Das Verlöbnis" (the engagement) about Jewish life in Galicia. In 1905 he worked for Max Reinhardt as a dramaturge. In 1910, he published "Von der Kunst des Theaters" (From the art of theater). In his 1914 story "Die Kantine" (the canteen) he again described the Jews of Galicia. From 1911 until 1925 he published a political-literary monthly "Der Neue Merkur" (the new mercury) in Munich.

In 1921 he published an article titled "Jüdische Aufzeichnungen" (Jewish records). In 1927 he published the novel "Zenobi" depicting Austrian life in the days before the World War one. His wife, Feiga Frisch (1878-?), who was born in Russia, was also a renowned writer. She translated many works from Russian into German of such authors as Goncharov, Turgenev, Saltykov-Shchedrin, Chekhov, Alexander Pushkin, Leo Tolstoy and others.

The well-known Hebrew writer and educator Eliezer Meir Lipschitz was also a native of Stryj. He was born on November 5th 1879, the son of Yom Tov Lipschitz, one of the first "Lovers of Zion" (Hovevei Zion) in Galicia and the owner of a match factory in Skole. He was educated in both traditional Jewish studies as well as general secular studies. When his parents moved to Lvov he studied under rabbis Isaac Schmelkes and Shlomo Buber. In Lvov he joined the maskilim and Zionist youth circles under the leadership of Mordecai Ehrenpreis, Joshua Tahun, Mordechai Braude and Shlomo Schiller. He was one of the first Hebrew speakers and formed a circle of youth who spoke the language in the Sephardic diction.

After his marriage to Dina Reitzes, who was also fluent in Hebrew he became a merchant. Only Hebrew was spoken in their home and it became one of the centers of the Hebrew movement in Galicia.

With Zvi Karl he established a Hebrew teachers' seminary in Lvov and thanks to his initiative "Ivriya" clubs were established in Lvov and the surrounding towns. He had a major impact in introducing Hebrew as a spoken language, disseminating Hebrew literature and improving its style. In 1904 he published his research on Yaakov Shmuel Buch in the literary calendar "Hermon" which appeared in Lvov and was edited by Gershom Bader. He later published studies on the history of Hebrew culture and literature in the Hebrew monthly "Ha'Shiloah". His true passion, however, was for pedagogical and literary work. He therefore accepted in 1910 the proposal of the "Ezra" society in Berlin to become a teacher in their Hebrew teachers' seminary in Jerusalem.

In Jerusalem he was active in public life and scientific research, publishing essays in "Hatekufa" and in other journals which appeared in Eretz Israel. He called for the establishment of Hebrew educational institutions based on the traditional "Heder", centering on Torah learning with secular studies as well.

During World War one he was arrested by the Turks and exiled to Damascus, but was released as an Austrian subject and forced to leave the country for Berlin. There he published his work "Vom Lebendigen Hebräisch" (From the Living Hebrew) in 1923.

In 1919 he returned to Eretz Israel, and was appointed the head of the teachers' seminary of the Mizrahi educational network. The institution expanded under his leadership. He established a model elementary school for training the students and graduates of the seminary. Later he also established a high school.

[Page 46]

For a few years he acted as an inspector/supervisor of the orthodox educational system. He was active in developing the educational side of the orthodox system. The essays he published in the press were noteworthy for their sleek style. His better-known works include: A monograph on Rashi (Warsaw 1912); The Mishna (Jaffa 1922), which also appeared in German in Berlin (1919); a study of the "Heder" ("Hatekufa" - Vol. 7); "Conversations" on religious issues under the pseudonym Azariah Ibn Bezalel; essays on educational questions (Ha'Shiloah 22, 37); and on Agnon (Ha'Shiloah, Vol. 22), which was published in 1920 in Berlin as a separate book.

All his life he worked towards unifying the general education based on the Torah. He passed away in Jerusalem on the 24th of Tammuz 5706 (July 23rd, 1946).

Dr. Abraham Jacob Braver, the noted historian and geographer, was born in Stryj on the 4th of Nissan 5644 (march 30th 1884), and completed his high-school education in town. He received a Ph.D. from the Vienna University, and taught at the Tarnopol high-school in 1910-1911. He came to Eretz Israel in 1912 and became a teacher at the teachers' seminary founded by the Ezra society of Berlin (1912-1914). In the years 1914-1918 he taught in Salonika and Constantinople (Istanbul), and in 1920 he returned to Eretz Israel again to teach at the teachers' seminary.

His first research work was on Fergen, the first Polish commissioner of Galicia and was published in the quarterly "Kwartalnik Historyczny" in 1907. In 1910 he published a work in Vienna on "Galizien wie es an Österreich kam" (How Galicia came to Austria) which was received enthusiastically by historical scientists in Austria. He also published a valuable Hebrew study in "Ha'Shiloah" (Vol. 23) on "The Emperor Joseph the second and the Jews of

Galicia". While in Tarnopol, he found a manuscript in the "Perl" Library by Dov Birkental of Bolechów (1723 – 1805) entitled "Divrei Bina" (words of wisdom), about Jacob Frank and the famous dispute between the Frankists and representatives of the Jewish community in Lvov in 1759. He published the manuscript in "Ha'Shiloah" under the title "A new Hebrew Source on the Frankists".

In Eretz Israel he devoted himself to the geography of the country, and published many studies in this field. His renowned work "Haaretz" (The Land) was published in many editions. He also published a geographic atlas.

His father Michael ben Moshe Braver (1862 - 1949), who was a well-known writer on rabbinical subjects, lived in Stryj between 1882 and 1902 and took an active part in the community life. While in Stryj he contributed to "Ivri Anochi", "Hamizpeh" and "Mahazikei Hadat".

Notes:

1 In 1467 his heirs were appointed to the starostvo:
Chidorowski, Andrzej Ossoliński, Felix Oktus Panjowski, who gave it to his brother Jerzy Panjowski in 1524. The starostvo was then passed to Jan Tarnowski. His heir was his son Jan Krzysztof Tarnowski until his death in 1567. In 1570 it was passed to Mikolai Miniwski and Hieronim Filipowski. After his death in 1587, the starostvo was awarded by king Zygmunt III to Andrzej Tęczyński in 1588. He was succeeded by his son Gabriel Tęczyński . In 1605 the starostvo passed to Adam Stadnicki and then to Krzysztof Koniecpolski and from 1660 Jan Sobieski. In 1701 the starosta was Andrzej Mikołaj Zborowski and in 1710 Adam Mikołaj Sieniawski. In 1728, the starosta was Stanisław Ciołek Poniatowski, the king's father. His son, Kazimierz Poniatowski was the last starosta under the Polish rule.

The starostvo owned the city of Stryj and three suburbs and 20 villages. The Stryj starostvo brought a nice income to the owners. In 1785, the income from 20 villages was 72,365 zloty and the tax they had to pay to the royalty was 18,341 zloty. From the city Stryj and its suburbs the income was 1,061 zloty and the taxes were 265 zloty.

2 The palace had 61 rooms, 3 kitchens, a bakery, a hall with 9 windows and 2 rooms with 8 windows each. The rest of the rooms had 4 windows each. The palace was surrounded by a moat. There was a farm, a brewery,

stables and living quarters for the service personnel.

3 Wilhelm Sommerfeld: Rozwój m. Stryja (development of the town of Stryj) 1874 – 1924.

4 Antoni Prohaska: Historja miasta Stryja (history of the town of Stryj) Lvov 1926. Dodatki Nr. 6 p. 204

4a. Quote: Latin text (Prohaska l.c. Dodatki Nr. 5 p. 203)

5 Latin text(Prohaska, Dodatki Nr. 11 p. 263)

6 Prohaska 1. c. p. 104.

7 Prohaska 1. c. p. 125.

8 Prohaska 1. c. p. 105.

9 The entire verdict was printed in Prohaska 1. c. p. 1662 there were 1,466 inhabitants in Stryj: 328 Poles, 1,050 Ruthenians, 70 Jews, and 29 palace people.

[Pg 47]

10 Mathias Berson: Parlamentarjusz dotyczący Żydów w dawnej Polsce p. 165 Nr. 294.

10a. Stryj had a small population of Karaites who appealed to the authorities to be treated better than the Jews.

11 Prohaska l.c. Dodatki Nr. 20 p. 227 – 278.

11a. Prohaska Dodatki Nr. 18 p. 224 – 225.

11b. Prohaska l.c. Nr. 22 p. 229

11c. Bolechower, p. 84.

12 Prohaska l.c. p. 109.

13 Prohaska l.c. p. 136.

14 Dr. Majer Balaban: Żydzi Lwowscy na przełomie XVI i XVII wieku" (Jews of Lvov at the break of the 16th and 17th centuries) Lvov, 1906 p. 40.

15 Prohaska l.c. p. 110.

16 Dr. Ignacy Schipper: Dzieje handlu żydowskiego na ziemiach polskich (History of Jewish Commerce in Polish Territories), Warsaw 1937, p. 44

17 Ber Birkental Bolechower – Memoirs. Published by Dr. M. Wiznitzer, Berlin 1924, p. 73.

18 Bolechower, p. 56.

19 Bolechower, p. 31 – 32.

20 Bolechower, p. 29.

21 800 oaks were cut in 1680 in the Stryj forests by the liquor lessee Mark (Mordechai) who removed them "in modo furtive" (Google translate: "on the sly"). Prohaska l.c. p. 113.

22 The renowned Polish historian of Stryj, Antoni Prohaska shows examples

in his book "History of Stryj" (p. 112 – 114) of exploitation and oppression by Jewish lessees (based on documents he found in grad Żydaczów. However, his tone is distinctly Anti-Semitic, comparable to that common in the Polish political journalism after world one and not as expected from an objective researcher.

23 Bolechower: Memoirs, p. 38.
24 Bolechower: Memoirs, p. 39.
25 Prohaska l.c. p. 19.
26 Prohaska l.c. p. 111 - 112.
27 Prohaska l.c. p. 148.
28 In 1683, Stanislaw Ochanski who had a debt was attacked, his property was requisitioned and he was arrested in the Stryj palace. In 1714, after a land owner Wytabicki was attacked, a bloody conflict erupted and one Jew was killed. The Jews armed themselves, chased the attackers and caught-up with them in Korczyna, confiscated the cash and brought them to jail. Stryj's Jews were pretty aggressive, as can be gleaned from the agreement signed with the Christian butcher's union: Polish text
29 Prohaska l.c. p. 245.
29a. Prohaska l.c. p. 116.
30 Prohaska l.c. p.
31 Israel Halperin: Pinkas Va'ad Arba Aratzot (Council of Four Lands), Jerusalem 1945, p.480
31a. Prohaska l.c. p. 117.
32 Prohaska l.c. p. 116.
33 Dr. J. Schipper: German/Yiddish text M.G.W. d.J., 1912 H 7 – 8, p. 467
34 Pinkas Va'ad Arba Aratzot (Council of Four Lands), p. 229
34a. Ossolińskich Library in Lvov, hand written manuscript 279.II
35 Prohaska l.c. p. 917
36 Józef Kleczyński and Fr. Kulczycki: Polish text
36a. Protokolle Galizien 1785 p. 5 ex. June p.12
36b. At the time of Galicia's annexation Stryj was a small town. From a report about the sanitary conditions to the authorities in Vienna one can glean the dismal ad poor conditions in Galicia at the time. In the entire region there were 13 medical specialists, 6 of them without academic certifications. There were 19 Christian surgeons and 34 Jewish doctors, 16 pharmacies and 29 hospitals – 5 of them in Lvov. Stryj itself had no doctors, and the sick were treated by a number of Jewish barbers. Sambor had one Christian surgeon (Krzysztof Wauchter). The pharmacy was owned by the protestant Waulenburg, who was forced to sell it to a catholic. The closest hospital was in Przemyśl.
Władysław Szumowski: Galicia Polish text, Lvov 1907, p. 62, 70

37	Archive German text (Vienna) A.M.J. Protokolle Galizien 1776, 74, ddo 25. X
38	Protokolle 1775, 81, 31/I
39	Protokolle 1776, 81, 14/VIII
	Protokolle 1776, Nr. 49, March
40	Prohaska 1.c. Dodatki Nr. 28, p. 237 □ 239
41	Prohaska 1.c. P. 70 – 73 Dodatki Nr. 28, p. 237 – 239
42	Protokolle 1785 185, July
43	Protokolle 1785 106, August
44	Protokolle 1792 19, July
44a.	On March 2nd, 1788, the commissioner Graff Brigido reported to Vienna that the list contain 41 families from the Stryj district out of 572 families in entire Galicia
45	Protokolle 1788 194, April.
	M.J. IV Nr. 201 ex. June 1804 *German text* October 1803
	The authorities brought (German) settlers from Germany and German Bohemia. In 1783 the settlement Brigado was established followed by Olkszica Nova in 1786, Stryj in 1800, Grabowiec Srtryjeski in 1830, and Angaberg, Plociantal, and Karlsdorf in 1835.
	The other 7 settlement were established in later years.
46	A.M.J IV T11 Carton 2658 (1786 – 1792) ad. Nr. 13
47	ex May 1791 Galizien.
	Stoeger: Lemberg 1833, Bd. II, p. 70 – 72
48	The letter was published in " Tzachut Ha'melitza" ("Purity of Metaphor") of Zeev Wolf Buchner, Berlin 1810, p. 55 – 70
49	Protokolle 1790 33, January
50	Protokolle 1793 21, November
50a.	IV T. 10 Carton 2658 (1786 – 1792) 164, January 1815
50b.	Stanisław Schnür-Pepłowski: Galiciana, Lvov 1896, p. 149, 155
51	IV T2 2582 (1811 – 1818) Nr. 14 ex October 1812
52	A.M.J IV T8 Carton 2632 (1819 – 1820) Nr. 4357
53	Dr. M. Stoeger 1.c., p.204 par. 127, par. 161 in the Brozany district, 4 in the Sambor district
53a.	A.M.J IV T1 ad 14688, 1832
54	Dr. M. Stoeger 1.c I, p. 285
54a.	Dr. M. Stoeger 1.c I, p. 79 – 81, 85

[Pg 48]

55 Szimon Moshe Chanes , Warsaw, 1929, p. 511; A. Walden, Warsaw, 1879, p. 79
Dr. S, Bernfeld: The history of Shir, Berlin 1899, p. 7; Dr. Lois Lewin: Geschichte der Juden in Lissa (History of the Jews in Lissa)

56 P. 168 – 169 p. 61, Chanes, p. 100

57 The application and the response A.M.J IV T1 Carton 2583 (1819 – 1827) 113, April 1821

58 The Gubernium report, the communities' and Brody's enlightened memos A.M.J IV T1 Carton 2583 Nr. 192 April, Nr. 162, May 1821

59 Reform der Judentracht (Reform of the Jewish costume) Dr. J. M. Jost: Neuere Geschichte der Israeliten (Modern History of the Israelites); See also Dr. Refael Mahler: The battle between haskala and Chassidut in Galicia, p. 114 – 115 (1810 – 1848), Berlin 1846 III p. 91

60 Koscherfleisch ein patent c.a. 1810 par. 24, 1824 par. 26, Lichtergeffale patent c.a. 1810 par. 30

60a. Menachem Mendel ben Yisrael Yakov Yukel Horowitz (1804 – 1864) was born in Stryj. After his father's passing in 1832, he was selected as a rabbi in Bolechów. He wrote "Shoshanat Yaakov" (about the Shulhan Aruch), parts 1 & 2 (1838, 1859); Pat 3 (Żółkiew, 1863). After 1848, he left Stryj and returned to Bolechów to become the rabbi

61 Archiv des Kultusministeriums Wien 1840 ad 33, 183

61a. See my book: Aus zwei Jahrhunderten Wien 1924 p. 104

62 Statthaltereiarchiv Lemberg (Archivum pañstwowe): Fasz 1. Allgem. Sachen Juden 1948 Nr. 48 122

63 A. M. J. 1848 – 1854 Fasz 28

64 IV T2 1863, 15711, 1222

65 IV T2 1862, 22266, 1781

66 IV T2 1864, 7369, 688

67 IV T2 1864, 11569, 765

68 IV T2 1866, 16166, 2108

69 Article in: Allgemeine Zeitung des Judentums, 1859, Nr. 7, (7/II) p. 97

70 Hamevaser, Lvov 1863, an article dated February 13th, number 7, page 41

71 Allgem. Ztg. des Judentums, 1866, (15/II) p. 65

72 The protocols of these two yeshivas were published by the Lvov community under the name: Debatten ueber die Judenfrage in der Session des galizschen Landtages vom Jahere 1868. Lemberg 1868 (120pp.)

73 "Hamagid" 1869, vol. 2, addendum from January 13th. It is interesting to note that in 1852 there were 93 Jews among the 777 recruits in the Stryj district.

74 "Hamagid" 1868, addendum to vol. 40 from October 14th

75 Yechiel Meller (1822 – 1893) was a wine merchant from Stnisławów, a

typical "maskil" (enlightened) fighting for the haskala ideals especially as it related to radical changes in the education of the young generation.
He published poems, novellas and reviews in "Kochavei Itzhak" and a famous monography about Samson (Shimshon) Ha-Levi Bloch the author of "Shevile 'lam" (Paths of the World). Most of his literary work was dedicated to fighting the Hasidic movement. He translated and edited poems by Friedrich Schiller, Karl Heinrich, Heidenreich and Jean Paul. His work was published in "Nitei Neemanim" (Lvov 1883).

76 Published in "Kochavei Itzhak" volume 21 (1856) pages 80 -81
77 In volumes 2, 11, 13, 22, 26, 27, 33, 34, and the last poem in 36 (pages 53 – 54)
77a. Samueli also wrote under the pseudonym "Varitas"
78 Ha'Ivri 1882, volume 21, page 221
79 Hamagid 1871, volume 4 page 19
80 Allgem. Ztg. des Jdtums. 1873 p. 636
81 Allgem. Ztg. des Jdtums. 1873 p. 808
82 Der Israelit (Lemberg) 1874 Nr. 9, p. 1
83 Neuzeit (Wien) 1880 Nr. 43, p. 350
84 Neuzeit 1886 p. 299
85 Ephraim Ha'Levi in an article about Stryj in "Ivri Anochi" (Brody) 1887, vol. 24, pages 189, 190 (18.3)
86 "Ivri Anochi" 1887, vol. 37 (24.6) page 288
87 Dr. Stanislaw Gruninski - Materiały do kwestji żydowskiej w Galicji. Lvov 1919, pp. 17, 23, 26. Dr. Ignacy Weinfeld: Ludnoœć miejska Galicji I jej skład wyznaniowy (1881 – 1910) Lvov 1912, p. 36
87a. Neuzeit 1885 Nr. 38
88 In high school number 1 out of 710 students, 217 were Jewish; In high school number 2 out of 472 students, 230 were Jewish. There are no numbers for elementary schools before 1914.
The students were enrolled in eight schools in 1924 – 1677 were Poles, 448 Ruthenians and 1211 Jews.
89 Dr. Gershon Zipper was born July 23rd, 1868 in Monasterzyska and spent his childhood in Podwołoczyska where he was traditionally educated. His father Chaim Ber was an important grain merchant and young Gershon met merchants from Russia who introduced him to the "Hibat Zion" (Lovers of Zion) movement. His father passed away in Mran in 1877 and his mother moved with him to Tarnopol where he was enrolled in the high school. In spite of his talents he was not a hard-working student and had to repeat both the eighth and tenth grades. His teachers predicted a bright future provided he would graduate from high school. From Tarnopol, his mother moved to Stryj where he excelled in his studies
90 Hamaggid 1891, volume 28, page 225

90a. Dr. Mordechai Eherenpreis: "Between east and west" Tel Aviv, 1953, page 30. He wrote about Hornstein: "This was an original fellow and we called him 'Pythagoras from Stryj'. Although his occupation was forests, as a typical yeshiva student he could not limit himself to one area of interest and was involved in mathematics. He used Euklides in Hebrew. His studies and business eventually combined when he invented a measuring instrument (to measure the height and width of a tree). This invention was patented in Vienna as it was very valuable in the lumber business. Eventually he became more and more involved in geometric problems. One day, when we were already close friends, he came by and told us about an important geometrical discovery. The square of the hypotenuse of the right triangle is equal to the sum of the squares of the other two sides. We felt sorry and embarrassed for the waste of time and had to inform him that although his geometrical discovery is correct, it has already been discovered in 500 BC bt a fellow named Pythagoras".

91 Hamaggid 1891, volume 2 (1.8.1891), page 15, volume 12 (19.3) page 95

92 Hamaggid 1892, volume 5

93 Hamaggid 1893, volume 13, page 104

94 Przyszłoœć 1894, Nr. 15, p. 177 – 178

95 Yiddish Text

96 In the first Polish Sejm elections in 1922, the Zionist list received 25,308 votes. Dr. Emil Zomerstein and Karl Eisenstein were elected.

97 1. Dr. Julius Falk, 2. Dr. Ludwig Lidenberg, 3. Dr. Markus Heinrich, 4. Dr. Abraham Firestein, 5. Dr. Nathan Fichner, 6. Dr. Filip Fruchtman, 7. Dr. Emil Polturak,

[Pg 49]

Dr. Zygmont Abend, 9. Dr. Heinrich Byk, 10. Dr. Yaakov Rabinowitcz, 11. Dr.Israel Rsenmann, 12. Dr. S. Sternhal, 13. Dr. Nachman Schindler, 14. Dr. Shlomo Goldberg, 15. Dr. Heinrich Goldstern, 16. Dr. Julius Wartzel

98 Surgeons: 1. Isidor Kenig, 2. Nachman Rosenberg. Physicians: 1. Dr. Filip Hertz, 2. Dr. Aharon Low, 3. Dr. Yaakov Lissel, 4. Dr. leon Pacnik, 5. Dr. Israel Frei, 6. Dr. Josef Kiczales, 7. Dr. Itzhak Schindler, 8. Dr. Shmuel Schechter.

98a. My thanks to Mr. Eliyahu Katz in Tel-Aviv who provided me with these details.

Addendum

Cardinal Jan Dembski's approval to build the synagogue in 1669

Polish text

Agreement by the Town to changes market days and king's approval

A.

Polish text

B.

Polish text

[Page 50]

Polish text continues

Agreement of Stryj's Christian urbanites and the Jews to take away the province from the starosta

Polish text

[Page 51]

At the End of the Nineteenth Century
by Tamar Buchstab – Avi–Yona
Translated by Susan Rosin

I still have pleasant childhood and early teens memories from the nice and tranquil town of Stryj. My family moved in 1883 from Lemberg (Lvov) to Stryj. My father, a government employee was appointed the manager of the railway warehouse in Stryj.

My first memories are probably from age three or four…remembering the area, our first house on the green "Koliovka" avenue near the large bustling train station. Stryj was an important center of the railway network connecting Galicia and Hungary and had great economic value.

The Stryj River was a source of great joy to the children of town, its pure and clear waters flowing slowly among green fields and shrubbery. We played and rested on the banks of the river. A special train took the railway employees and their families to the river in the summer months. Sometimes we swam near the flower mill "Malinovka", which was powered by a fast flowing mountain spring. This pastoral and idyllic picture stayed with me for a very long time.

At the edge of the open scenery were the Carpathian mountains. I can still recall fondly the beautiful and manicured "Olshina" grove and the public park. My maternal grandfather, Shimshon Goldfarb from Lemberg who loved the outdoors walked with me in that grove. He loved to hear the birds singing and amused me with his broken Polish. In this grove I saw for the first time in my life a public park celebration. A lighted fountain left a deep impression on me. Near the lake was a memorial for the Austrian soldiers who died in Solferino, Italy. The statue of a soldier holding a fluttering flag was my first artistic exposure.

As a scared four year–old I still remember the great fire of 1886, the fire that turned our city into a heap of rubble.

Today, almost seventy years later, I still remember the red flames undulating from the Bencher factory and the thousands exploding windows. Our house was miraculously spared. Fortunately, this catastrophe gave the town a push for quick and planned redevelopment. Donations of money, clothing and building materials poured from all over the Austrian empire. I remember how my mother and her friends of the assistance committee gave out pillows, blankets and clothing to those in need.

The life of my family was different from that of many of the Jewish families in town. Unlike the wealthy families in town, my parents did not go to such health resorts as Karlsbad (Karloy Vary) or Marienbad (Mariánské Lázně). Instead, my mother took her children to resorts in Galicia such as Krynica (Krynica–Zdrój) or Iwonicz. My father, who loved the outdoors, took us on long and tiring hikes. We ventured to the Carpathian mountains, hiking the Hoverla, the Tatra mountains and passed through the Carpathians to Hungary. Hiking was not popular among the Jews in town in those days.

My father, Isser (Isidor) Weinbaum Hacohen was the son of an estate lessee in Podolia. Against his Hasidic parents' wishes he was able to study in the technical school in Lvov with the support of some rich relatives. As much of the University youths in his time, he distanced himself from the Jewish tradition and became part of the assimilated educated crowd.

As a railway engineer in Stryj, he was in contact with the Polish educated and became part of the Polish social democratic camp, the P.P.S.

Because of his position as a government employee, my father became friendly with the merchants and exporters in town. Among them: The Shenfelds, owners of the mills, the Sterns who had the monopoly on liquor sales in town, the Ungers who were travel agents, Mondsheins, the owners of saw–mills and traders of lumber, Maneleses, lessees of the tobacco factory. The banker Mintz employed my father as an accountant – a second job at night to increase his income. Our friend was Miller, the brother of professor David Heinrich Miller, the famous orient scholar from the Vienna University.

[Page 52]

We borrowed books from his bookstore.

In elementary school and later in the girls' lycée (there was no high school for girls at the time), my friends were the daughters of these families. Some of these friendships lasted a very long time especially with Regina Schiff and Dvora Katz.

The adolescent girls became friendly with the Stryj high school students. The high school was highly regarded and drew students from out of town as well. There I met Dr. Michael Ringel who became later a senator in Poland. My mother was a close friend of his large family. Dr. Emil Schmorak from Szczerzec who became one of the Zionist leaders in eastern Galicia, and the lawyer and author Mark Scherlag from, Wygoda who for a while was the secretary of Dr. Theodor Herzl and later settled in Haifa. Dr. Gershon Zipper, one of the founders of the Zionist movement in Galicia was also a talented student of the Stryj high school.

As family members of a railway employee we enjoyed free travel. We used this perk to increase our education and knowledge. We visited Italy and Switzerland. My father managed to get even to Egypt, but not to Eretz Israel. Almost every year we traveled to the Alps. Sometimes we went through Worochta in the eastern Carpathians and even reached Trieste on the Adriatic.

The way my family lived, distanced us from the traditional Jewish families. We eagerly read literature and as art lovers we visited Lemberg, where my mother's family lived, to see plays and listen to concerts.

In 1897 we moved to Lemberg. We lost the simplicity and friendliness of our lives in the small city of Stryj, but our horizons broadened.

The "Provincial" Life

I would like to describe the special atmosphere of life in the Austro-Hungarian province as reflected in the enlightened circles and in my parents' house in Stryj.

Two factors determined our social standing in town: My father's status as a government employee, a rarity among the Jews in those days, and the tendency of the enlightened and educated Jews to get closer to the educated non-Jews. The language spoken in our house was Polish. My parents spoke German when they did not want the children to understand. Although both my parents came from orthodox and traditional families, both had a complete secular outlook and rejected the Jewish holidays and traditions. My parents preferred to decorate a Christmas tree rather than light the Hanukah candles. We used to participate in Christmas parties and other Christian celebrations.

An interesting and surprising fact was that an orthodox Jew in traditional clothing supplied our family with the ultimate non-kosher foods such as rabbit meat, lobster etc. Because all items could be easily found in Stryj in those days, our cuisine was a combination of Viennese style baked goods and French menus.

We were not impartial to traditional Jewish dishes. We always participated in the Purim parties given by the Mondsheins and enjoyed the delicious hamantashen as well as nuts in honey (makagigi). These parties were a special yearly event. The wealthy did not give public parties or receptions. They lived in large houses surrounded by large yards with fruit trees. They lived there with the children, their sons and daughters in law, their grandchildren and their servants just like royalty in their palaces.

The weddings were very lavish and the invited guests were served various types of wine and liquor and large amounts of food (beef, chicken and goose) and desserts. Klezmer music both joyous and sad was played alternately and the comedian was there to add to the festive mood.

[Page 53]

All this reminded me of a painting in a Rabelais style but with a Jewish character...We, the Weinbaums were unusual among the crowd at the Mondsheins. Good neighborly and friendly relations existed between the rich but likable Mondsheins and the "educated and enlightened" Weinbaums.

When I turned fourteen I was invited to the parties and balls as well. Although I was a happy and outgoing girl I did not dance. My friends thought I was different. At masquerade balls we teased and hinted in good humor, but also discussed matters of art and literature.

Sometimes we had guests from among my father's friends at our house. The railway workers' band played for the guests. Most of the social life was to meet at a small patisserie in the center of town. The center of all social life in Stryj was the restaurant at the railway station which was active all day and night. This restaurant was popular with my mother and her circle of friends. I remember this restaurant as a reason for fights between my parents. My father had to work frequently until late and could to join my mother at the restaurant. However, my mother who grew–up in the big city of Lemberg could not give–up on listening to the music and the romanticism of the small town. So many evenings ended with fights between my parents scaring me, the little girl.

My parents were very interested in the socialist circles that started to appear in those years in Stryj. Lectures on social issues were held in town by some outstanding personalities from Lemberg, increasing the knowledge and awareness of the participants.

We had much free time for reading. Our house had a large library, so all family members were avid readers. We read many works in the German language which had a great impact on my education.

By age fourteen I read all of Shakespeare, Schiller, Heine and works by Goethe. I read (in German) the great Russian novels, Zola, de Maupassant, and Victor Hugo. I also became knowledgeable in the Greek mythology thus becoming interested in Greek art.

———

Beginning of Zionism (Memoirs)
by Eliyahu Katz
Translated by Susan Rosin

Before the "official" appearance of Zionism in the first congress in Basel in 1897, Jewish intellectuals in Stryj founded a Zionist society called "Agudat Achim" (Society of Brothers) sometime between 1888 and 1890. The first presidents were the banker Dov–Berish Kopler and Moshe Stern (father of Shlomo and Avner Stern) who served as deputy mayor of Stryj for many years. Other members of the society were: Dr. Maximilian Shenfeld (who later was the Lvov community leader), Dr. Norbert Schiff, Dr. Altman and the intellectual book seller Joseph Gross.

Moshe Stern was the first Zionist of Stryj who traveled to Eretz Israel on behalf of the society. An article in the publication "Ha'Am" (the nation) from 17th, of Adar 5652 (March 16th, 1892) stated that: "The "Admat Yeshurun" delegate, Mr. Moshe Stern, visited Eretz Israel to look at our brothers' settlements there and to bring forth his impressions…he wrote his first letter from the holy land on the 13th, of Tevet (January 13th,) saying that: Today I visited the agricultural school 'Mikve Israel' near Jaffa and I will describe what I saw".

[Page 54]

The Awakening after the First Zionist Congress

In the first congress, Styj's Zionists were represented by Dr. Shlomo Goldberg. Dr. Goldberg became the first Zionist kehila leader after it was won over from the assimilators in 1918.

Dr. Karl Lippa from Stanislawów (who resided in Yassi, Romania) stopped in Stryj on his way from the first congress and brought materials such as protocols, booklets, musical notes, the "HaTikvah" text, etc., a visit that caused much excitement among the residents.

After the first congress, the Zionist society in Stryj was registered as a branch of the "Zion" society in Vienna, a step that eased the harassment by the authorities. Among the first in the Zionist societies were: The fabric merchant Leib Ekart, Mordechai Hochberger, Moshe Schur, Avner and Eliyahu Katz, Berl Stern and Aharon Hauptman.

"Veritas", a Jewish academic society was established at the beginning of the twentieth century and it contributed greatly to the strengthening of Zionism in town. The founders of the society were: The student Michael Ringel, Avraham Ringel, Dr. Rosenzweig, the author Mark Scherlag, Norbert Schiff and his brother. Michael Ringel left Stryj and moved to Lvov. His cousin Avraham was a medical student in Vienna where he met Dr. Herzl and corresponded with him for years and was active in the Zionist movement there. He had a deep understanding of literature and was also a violin player. He returned to Stryj without completing his studies and with the influence of the Shenfeld – Ringel families obtained a high position as a consultant at the Stryj municipality. Because of his official position he was unable to take part in the Jewish national life in town.

The year 1906 saw another Zionist awakening when Dr. Julius Wurtzel and Dr. Byk (the son–in–law of Avraham Luft) came to town.

Dr. Gershon Zipper came to town at about the same time and he helped to resolve a Jewish–Zionist issue. In 1906 after the Russia – Japan war and after the revolution, many refugees passed through Galicia on their way to western Europe, England and the united states.

For the first time, help for the refugees was organized by the entire Jewish community (and not just by the wealthy families – Shenfeld, Hurwitz, Halpern etc.) proving the compassion and national awareness of the Jewish population. Most of the activities were coordinated by the Zionist youths. A dispute about the wording of the public appeal erupted between the Zionists and the assimilators headed by Dr. Fruchtman and the lawyer Dr. Markus. The Zionists suggested: "To our brothers and sisters" whereas the assimilators wanted the appeal to read: "To members of our faith". Dr. Zipper was invited to weigh in on the dispute and he lectured at a large gathering at the "dom narodny". He explained that it was so strange that this question was even raised. No doubt that Israel was a nation and all Jews are responsible for each other. He explained that his opinion was based on historical facts: The Spanish Jews helped the Jews that were expelled from Germany and France. In turn, the Italian and Turkish Jews helped the expelled Spanish Jews. And he added, who knew if these refuges who were helped in Galicia would not help the Galician Jews one day...

The revival of the Hebrew language also started during that period. The first Hebrew speakers were mostly from among the Beit Hamidrash students and many of them were the students of rabbi Shraga Feivel Hertz (Der Glogover). They were: Zvi Diesendruck, Yona Garlanter, Haim David Korn, Avraham Schwartzberg, Menachem Mendel Profest, and the brothers Moshe, Pinchas and Eliyahu Katz.

The Jewish Economy 1880 – 1914 in Stryj and the Surrounding Areas

The 1910 census showed that most of the commerce and crafts were in Jewish hands. In 1890 there were two Jewish lawyers (Dr. P. Fruchtmann and Dr. Altman) as compared to ten non-Jewish lawyers. These numbers did not include judges and other official legal professionals who were all non-Jewish. In the following twenty years Jews gained access to many other branches of commerce and manufacturing and their numbers grew in the professions.

[Page 55]

The number of Jews in agriculture (estate owners), clerical positions and those who provided supplies to the city, government and army (specifically to the three regiments stationed in town) grew significantly.

They supplied meat, hay, oats, bread and other items. The Jews leased the collection of road taxes, and pubs for wholesale of spirits. These were owned in

Stryj by the Aberdam family, Moshe Goldberg, Delikatisz, Jekele Shor, and Haim Stern. They employed about eighty families.

During elections, the pub owners were a reactionary force pressured by the owners and the government. The labor P.P.S. party opposed the owners and the pubs lessees who were used by the government against the labor movement.

About 16% of Galician Jews were in agriculture as estate owners, lessees, and laborers. When the Polish and Ukrainian cooperatives (Torhowla Kolko Rolnicze) started marketing the agricultural products and compete with the Jews, many of the villages' Jewish residents became farmers.

The building industry was mostly owned by Jews. Interestingly, Jewish women played a major role in this industry. Hizelkorn built the street next to the court house, Luft built Potocki street and Schiff built the post office and many homes in the town center. Moshe Goldberg built the entire neighborhood from the Ukrainian church to the Stryj river.

The Jews in this field employed Jewish engineers, builders and craftsmen. All building, paving roads and river improvement projects were done by Jewish contractors.

The trade in fruits (Melons, grapes, water melons, etc.) from Hungary increased with the opening of the Ławoczne – Lvov railway. In Stryj, the traders of fruit were the Samet, Win and Bleiberg families. The Rothschild and baron von Offenberg groups that built the Ławoczne – Lvov – Sambor – Sianki – Stryj – Chodorów – Tarnopol railway employed many Jews as sub-contractors. The Jews of Stryj and other locations where the railways and roads were built supplied gravel, sills etc. for the projects.

After the railway became operational, the wagon drivers lost much of their livelihood and many became transportation companies' agents with international connections such as the Weinbach – Engelman, Radler – Leibowitz families and others. The brothers Kaz had a monopoly on the transportation of goods and passengers by buses for the routes Stryj – Lvov and Stryj – Morszyn.

Of the main merchants and manufacturers of note were: Flour mills: Stejerman – Borak; Saw mills: Zelig Borak, Munshein; Matches manufacturing: Lifshitz; Casting: Benczer; Chemicals (export to Russia and Romania): Michael Katz; Furniture manufacturing: the brothers Zalman, Shimshon and Joseph Steiner; Large scale eggs exporting: Insler – Heiber.

Moshe Wunderman

Moshe Wunderman was the son of a cheder teacher from Nadwórna. He arrived in Stryj at about 1904 or 1905 as a Hebrew teacher. At the beginning he wore the traditional clothing and his manner was that of an orthodox Jew.

After hearing that a high–school student failed an exam in the Greek language, he offered his help. Later he tutored additional high school students in Roman, math and other subjects. When the clerk who worked for the Insler – Heiber egg exporters to England fell ill, Wunderman filled–in, proving that he was learned in many areas. But foremost he was a Hebrew teacher. In addition he also conducted classes in commerce in his apartment at the Rynek (Central square).

His house was a gathering place for the well educated and intellectuals of Stryj. He also hosted Zionist delegates and lecturers. His wife was an intellectual as well, participated in the dramatic circles in town and always played the part of the mother.

At the beginning of World War I, he moved to Vienna, studied for the matriculation exams and later received a Ph.D. in philosophy. In Vienna he was a rabbi and a preacher in a synagogue for Jewish emissaries (Dienstmanner) and later he started a prep school for matriculation. When he was asked by a person from his town how he was making a living in Vienna, he responded by saying: If the non-Jew wants to pass the matriculation exams in German, he has to study with the son of a teacher from Nadwórna...

[Page 56]

From the Book "Voices in the Darkness"
by Julian Stryjkowski

This is a part from the book by the Stryj born Jewish-Polish author Julian Stryjkowski "Voices in the Dark". The book describes Jewish life in Stryj before World War one.

Martin Heiber leaned on the windowsill, watching the guests without even noticing the short and bold Borek who stood next to him and talked. Heiber nodded his head occasionally while smiling mechanically.

"I am not complaining" continued Borek, "no one will declare bankruptcy if they have a solid foundation. Every month someone declares bankruptcy. But that is not the case with Borek's firm. If you ask me, Luft, Heidelkorn, and even baron Gerdel are prone to bankruptcy."

Martin Heiber was not listening. He was looking at the new arrivals. A beautiful woman wearing a tight-fitting black velvet dress was helping an old stooping woman who was leaning on a cane. The old woman was supported on the other side by a young girl with a white ribbon in her braid. A heavy set man wearing a black coat and striped pants walked behind them.

"This is old Heidelkorn" whispered Borek, "now we will be able to start. This is her daughter, and he is her son in law, the lawyer Rosenberg".

The old woman took off her silk wrap. The beautiful woman sat at the table and started removing her long purple gloves. Then she glanced at the window and smiled. Suddenly, Heiber noticed that the girl with the white ribbon was standing in front of him. She bowed lightly and handed him three white roses. She looked at him, not understanding why he was not taking the roses from her hand. Then she bowed again and said: "A gift from grandmother".

This time Heiber heard the girl and took the flowers and gazed in the direction of the beautiful woman. She nodded and Martin Heiber approached her, leaned over and told her his name and then took his place at the table.

Mrs. Rosenberg tried to look for friends. She nodded to Kitczels, then to Miriam who did not acknowledge her. Conversations were heard everywhere from the guests who were gathering in groups.

Baruch jumped on the table and with a long match lighted the gas lamp which spread a greenish light. Clara paled and tightened her lips. Baruch laughed, jumped off the table and embraced his wife, but she stepped away.

"Clara dear are you mad again?" laughed Baruch.

"You know I don't like it" Clara answered angrily.

"Herr Doctor" Baruch turned to Dr. Kitczels who was busy talking to the older and shorter pharmacist Shternbach, "Do you think that gas can harm the child? My wife prefers kerosene lamp".

The doctor did not respond and continued telling the pharmacist about a sick Jewish patient. "I told him: 'There is no need to over-eat on Saturday and then fast for the entire week'. And he said: 'That's what God commanded'. I asked him: 'Then why did you come to me?' And he answered: 'Where should I go? The shoemaker or the head of the kehila?"

The head of the kehila, Meirson, tall, thin and a little stooped coughed and said: "Oh! Heretics".

Baruch continued to run between the rooms. Sweat drops appeared on his forehead and his yarmulke fell and covered his right ear. He apologized to Mrs. Heidelkorn as he had to extend the table to accommodate more guests.

[Page 57]

There were only eight armchairs and the rest were chairs set by the table. Baruch blew and put out the kerosene lamp and moved it to the children's room. He then appeared carrying a box with an attached trumpet similar to a large flower.

"Gramophone" cried Mrs. Rosenberg's daughter and clapped her hands. "Mom gramophone, grandma gramophone!"

"Elsa. Come sit here next to me" said Mrs. Rosenberg pointing to an empty seat near her armchair. When Elsa sat down, she whispered: "Don't be silly. So much excitement because of a gramophone?"

Elsa sat with her eyelashes downcast.

Grandma Heidelkorn was listening to old Mr. Goldman nodding her head from time to time. A black lace scarf was fastened to her reddish wig with a large diamond brooch and covered her forehead. She was wearing large earrings and a pearl necklace.

"Why is he not getting married?" she asked pulling up her lower lip and tapped her cane on the floor. "Don't you understand? A thirty year old bachelor? If my Alter Heidelkorn had a son...he has to get married, even to Lusia Borek".

Goldman looked at Baruch who was sitting to his left and murmured something, but Mrs. Heidelkorn tapped her cane again and continued:

"I would not let Borek into my family. Martin is well educated but still a very observant Jew. That is a good person! In Vienna every stone is non-kosher and the air is tempting to sin".

"Yes. He is a great scholar. He is a philosopher whose articles are published". Mr. Goldman coughed. "He even knows Dr. Herzl".

"Herzl, Shmerzl, but he does not denounce his Judaism. Not so my son in law. His father is so orthodox that he does not even speak on Saturday. The worst are those from orthodox families who denounce their faith".

Baruch was attending to the gramophone at the time and announced: "Shall we listen for the first time to a Jewish singer?"

A scratch, a buzz and a rustle were heard and then screaming sounds came out of the trumpet.

Miriam was sitting at the table's edge next to Olga and Helena. In spite of the heat her face was pale. She wet her lips and drops of perspiration showed on her dark eye lids.

Olga turned to Lorka's father: "Do you know what is playing Mr. Scheiner?" Mr. Scheiner, a middle aged person wearing the same silk yarmulke as Mr. Goldman and Baruch with a well-trimmed beard motioned with his hands that he did not know who the singer was.

He turned to the jewelry store owner sitting next to him: "Do you know who the singer is Mr. Waldman?" Waldman stopped waving his hard edged hat and put it in his lap. Accidentally he touched Mrs. Findling's elbow. He apologized and put the hat on his head. He did not know the singer either.

It is [1] "דאָס פּינטעלע ייִד" explained Helena, but Olga was not paying attention as she was watching Heiber who was standing behind Clara's chair still holding the three roses and following Mrs. Rosenberg's gaze who was looking indifferently at the turning player.

"What do you think about this free concert?" asked her husband loudly.

The lawyer's wife looked at him and answered: [2] "מיר געפעלט עס גאַנץ גוט".

Screeching noises sounded when the song ended. Baruch jumped and started looking through the various records. Clara, who was amused by Kitczels' stories, became serious and coughed lightly. Baruch got the message and moved the gramophone into the children's bedroom.

He returned with the servant and started setting the table with sparkling water bottles and fruit baskets.

"Can we get started?" said Goldman to Martin who was standing all this time.

"What are we waiting for? For the Messiah? Let's get started".

"Say what may" sounded a thick voice, "Gramophone in a small town is still a very important invention".

[Page 58]

Olga's face turned red.

She hid behind Helena's back and said: "Dad, please stop. He always says stupid things".

However, the thick voice continued: "If people were shown this kind of box a few years ago, they would think it was a miracle. But today – it is nothing. God willing he will sell the restaurant and its concession that his grandfather obtained from the emperor in 1848. With this money he can turn the town upside down."

"They invented a ball that in addition to rising in the air can also take people with it. However, electricity is better than gas. With the gas, the entire city can burn down. Yes. Some are inventing, and others get rich. Not everyone can be as smart as Edison. But in order to invest, you should be able to distinguish between the truth and the fraud and sometimes you need to take risks. In the middle of the square they already placed a pole. This is the first electrical light in town. From Boryslaw they are already pulling wires. He is waiting for it. He will sell everything".

Olga's father stopped talking and the room fell silent. He sat comfortably in the arm chair and eyed with contempt the Findlings – a young couple that just arrived from Germany. Mr. Findling held a fat cigar between his lips and his wife with a large diamond on her finger was sipping sparkling water and looking at the sparkling crystal glass. Without moving her eyes she reached and took an apple.

Old Mrs. Heidelkorn asked Goldman: "I don't like it that he is not talking. What's his name? Is he one of the Pferbaums? Which branch?"

"The undistinguished branch. The very undistinguished" answered Goldman.

Mrs. Heidelkorn raised her voice: "Listen Pferbaum, I did not understand all of it, but I am sure that Mrs. Findling understood everything". Pferbaum winked agreeably.

Mrs. Findling looked up and asked her husband: [3] "פון מענש דיזער וויל וואס מיר?"

Findling removed his cigar and said: "Mr. Pferbaum, I did not get it and I don't understand what is common to you and us" and he added a shoulder gesture indicating "I don't know".

"A nice question! Our common interest? Photographer. Do you think you are so great with your photographs? Let the first electric street light go on in the square. That will be sufficient for me! Then you will see if we have a common interest or not! You will see the first ad on the street: 'The first Kinomatograph in town or Kino Theater "Edison". The owner of the Kino Theater – Mr. Pferbaum. The first time admission – free for everyone. And then, you will see – people will fight each other to watch the moving pictures. And who will look at your dead pictures, a peasant from a village [4] "איין געבירגס-באור"

Fildling's narrow face twisted and he laughed.

"You can laugh sir. Do you think I don't know what happens in your business?"

"Mrs. Dora is a smart and shrewd woman. Before the pole was erected in the square, she told you to buy all kinds of wires. And I am asking you – why does a photographer need wires? Crates full of jars? What is this? I asked Mrs. Dora. These are batteries. And why does a photographer need batteries? How did you take pictures before there was electricity? Now the pictures will look more alive Mrs. Dora told me. I set my mind a long time ago on the Kinomatograph. Why would one person swallow everything? One will have live pictures and the other dead pictures. Am I not right?"

"Beautiful story" said Kitczels and pounded on his knees, turning to the pharmacist Shternbach and repeated "beautiful story. It should be published in 'Puchingel'. *Mr. Pferbaum, when are you selling the restaurant? Mr. Meirson, as the head of the kehila you must help him".

"What restaurant?" yelled Findling. "It is but a small pub in Targowica".

Pferbaum jumped up and screamed in Yiddish: "A pub? So what? You don't like it? You sell in a pub just like in a store and for the same kind of money!" and he banged his fist on the table.

* A popular satirical weekly published in those days in Lvov.

[Page 59]

The bottles and the glasses clinked on the table. "Is a pub a brothel?"

"Quiet" said old Goldman, "In my house"

"Be quiet" yelled Findling.

Heidelkorn tapped her cane.

"Quiet? Why quiet? Why does the Jew have to be quiet? If he cannot talk, how is a Jew going to cry out about oppression? Let him talk".

Old Mr. Goldman pulled Baruch's sleeve and whispered in his ear. Baruch approached Pferbaum carefully, but he stopped him with his outstretched hand.

"OK. OK. I knew this ahead of time. Respect? I spit on this respect. Aristocracy". With that, he pushed the chair with his foot and left the room slamming the door behind him.

The chair to the left of Miriam was vacated and now she was seen by everyone. She glanced in Olga's direction, but that chair was empty too. When did she leave? Perhaps before her father?

How would she leave the gathering without people noticing her?

Martin Heiber was still standing behind Clara's chair and wiped his forehead. He looked at the lawyer's wife who was just gazing in front of her holding a lace handkerchief.

Her husband stroked her arm. "Don't get too excited Tonia. This is a Jewish wedding and things cannot be different in a Jewish wedding."

Old Goldman sighed. "I can't understand how this happened. It cannot be reversed. I cannot understand how Pferbaum was among the guests. I did not invite him and neither did anyone in my family. Since he was an uninvited guest, we can look at his behavior as rude and vulgar and imposing on the celebration. This can happen anywhere, not just in my house. This is a rude person and he is not welcome."

"Uninvited?" screamed Findling, "Pferbaum sat here and he was uninvited? Unbelievable."

Goldman tapped lightly on the table, as was the custom in synagogue and turned to the guests with a trembling voice: "Let's all listen to Martin Heiber, my late wife's brother."

Heiber stood between Clara's and Baruch's chair, put the white roses on the table, wiped his forehead and started his speech.

His speech was mellow. Occasionally his voice trembled and he covered his eyes. Then, his voice intensified. The faces of those present were blurred by the cigarette smoke that was rising against the green glow of the gas light.

At first, what he said sounded like Shabbat songs, bringing back memories of forgotten childhood, shining melodies of the past. Miriam recovered. This is not a talk, but a stream of pure water.

"The yearnings are carried for thousands of years. My homeland! Zion! You are the prettiest of them all. The coyotes' howl sounds in your deserted vineyards. Your tents are empty. In our forefathers' skies, the sun is covered with smoke. Our palm trees are on fire, the green Jordan River is dying. The drinking stone crumbled, the stone of Judea became so black. Jerusalem, carved from the rock is gloomy."

Like a flying bird, his voice rose and dived bringing the fresh longings of the audience to a hilly country with palm trees, wide clear skies, our skies, shepherd's tents, sheep herds roaming around covered in white wool.

Miriam covered her ears and closed her eyes. When she opened her eyes, she was shocked to see Heiber's face. His hands were pale and his eyes burning. In one gulp he drank a glass of water.

"The Zionism is the most-noble form of our national pride. This is our protest against the injustice and wrong doings of history and the world."

"געטו יודישע דאס אונד אלטר-מיטל דאס געגען קאמף דער איסט דאס" [5].

"Zion is our star". (or from the Latin – From the East comes light)

"Streams of blood and fires did not conquer this nation. Wrapped in their prayer shawls saying the 'Shema Israel' they jumped into the fire.

[Page 60]

This is a great nation. The bible and the prophets are the inspiration and treasure of humanity. Will this nation be lost? Surrounded by a wall of hatred we are still pure and splendid forever. Today, this is a nation of shopkeepers. We need to cleanse our souls, get them out of the bags of the peddlers like the goblet of Benjamin. Cleanse them from the exile, from the humiliation, from the fear, from the depression, from the corruption of the soul, from the everyday worries.

We will raise the nation. We will bring to the world the new truth. On Mount Sinai, this nation gave the world thru Moses the Ten Commandments and on mount Zion the nation will bring the world the messiah. One law for the entire humanity. The Jewish nation that gave the world God and soul will give the world the justice. We will give the world a new generation of prophets. The Jewish nation had so much pain and suffering. When the enemy set fire to the temple, the angel raised the house keys to the heavens and kept them there for the nation that was tortured by the inquisition, expulsions, slaughter and pogroms.

These keys will initiate the golden age. This is the idea of Judaism. This is the spark from the burning bush spreading the warmth on nursing babies, giving strength to those wandering with their bags. This is the flame lighting the faces of rabbis and their mortified students. These are the kabbalists rising to the upper spheres building worlds out of numbers. This is the devotion dancing of the Chassidim uniting with their God in the fields. The Israel spirit is scattered all over the world."

Heiber emptied another glass of water.

"The philosophy of Judaism is the monotheism. We never believed in God and Satan. Our ideal is the completeness in the unity. Therefore, our ancient bible is an inspiration for the world. Our prophets – the justice army, believed that their country is the cradle of the good and eternity and they had the world's rage in their bones."

Tell me, are you Jewish? Miriam had difficulty breathing. She wanted to reach for a drink of water, but did not dare move her hand. She felt like being in a trance.

In Eretz Israel he saw rocky soil and new settlements surrounded by orchards, Yemenite Jews – dark and short of stature, Caucasus natives – sturdy and charming, and Russian natives born after the Kishinev pogroms. All found their homeland there. He was in the new city of Tel Aviv, saw the first Hebrew high school "Herzliya", listened to the language of the prophets, listened to the songs of revival.

Rocky soil is reborn. Eucalyptus trees are sucking the malaria out of the swamps. Trees and forests are taking roots. Pioneers like these have never been seen before. One hand holds a rifle and the other works the fields. They are building the homeland in spite of the Turkish opposition. In spite of its desolation, they are building their old-new homeland, just as Herzl predicted in "Altneuland".

Heiber breathed. The guests seemed awake. "Zionism is the renaissance of Judaism. Israel's soil is so dear. It is being conquered by sweat and small coins. This is a very small country. This is the only country where land is not measured by hectares but by meters, every piece of land is bought for gold. We have never gotten anything for free. We, who are seen by the gentiles as the bankers of the world, are a poor nation, and all our lives are a collection of donations. Even in funerals, we walk behind the coffin with a collection box "charity may save life" (ממוות תציל צדקה). But the Zionist collection box is an elixir. Its color is blue like the skies of Israel, like the flag of Israel. "

The white roses wilted.

Heiber talked about the founder of Zionism, Theodor Herzl, who did not see his dream come-true. Just like Moses who did not enter the promised-land. The ten year anniversary of his passing will be in two years. When he passed away in 1904, it was decided to immortalize him by building a living monument – the Herzl Forest, which requires money.

Heiber slowly removed his glasses. He seemed tired and announced that he completed his speech. He took a seat behind Clara's chair and leaned forward.

The guests, who were listening quietly, started clearing their throats and improving their sitting positions. Some lit cigarettes.

The first to ask a question was Borek.

[Page 61]

"So, how much would it cost to plant such a tree?"

Heiber raised his head and seemed to be deep in thought.

Mrs. Heidelkorn tapped her cane.

"My husband Alter Heidelkorn always said: If you desire something (an item), don't ask for the price. The more you give this item will be more worthy for you".

Kitczels remarked: "This is phantasmagoria."

Heiber smiled sadly. "To those that don't have faith, this is phantasmagoria. What can you do? You are either born with the ability to believe or not. It is not something that money can buy."

Kitczels cleared his throat: "But you sir, have faith. And you have plenty of it. And you want to sell it for money. Look, sir, for the price of one tree I can buy faith from you. Seriously, I don't believe in anything. Everyone here can attest to it, even the head of the kehila. The content is gone. Religion filled the lives of our forefathers and we need to honor them for it."

The lawyer Rosenberg clapped his hands: "Bravo!"

Mrs. Heidelkorn dropped her cane and said: "Kitczels. Why is this doctor talking? I can pay for him too.

Then she turned to her son-in-law, the lawyer Rosenberg and said: "And you, Kuba, I can pay for you too. It's not the first time I am paying for you."

She put her cane between her knees, took a ring off her finger and dropped it on the table. "I can afford to donate it. Why are you pale, my dear son-in-law? Ask him how much of my money he lost in card games. He can stop playing!" And with that, she banged her fist on the table.

Mrs. Rosenberg covered her face with her handkerchief and whispered: "Mother..."

The old woman moved the ring closer to the roses and the diamond surrounded by sapphires sparkled.

"Borek, how much are you donating?" she asked.

"I think that twenty Krones is a not a little contribution."

"Too little!"

"OK. Five more Krones" said Borek, laughing uneasily.

"Too little!"

"Mrs. Heidelkorn. I will go bankrupt. Thirty Krones."

"Two hundred Krones. Do you hear Heiber? Not a penny less from him. And you, Borek, I wish you long life! And now, you can ask for the price of the tree."

Goldman said: "Everyone will give as much as they can. Nobody is forced. Although we the old Jews believe in God and not in Herzl."

Heidelkorn said: "Oh, old man that you are. How do you always avoid everything because of God? Do you want to wait for the messiah? Nobody is stopping you. But Martin does not want to wait. If I had a son, I would be the first one to tell him not to wait. We, the old folks did not get the privilege. And we have been waiting for generations. How much longer? The messiah's honor will not be offended if someone preceded him."

Borek sighed. "Yes, of course. The parents always sacrifice for their children."

Kitczels crushed his cigarette in the silver ashtray.

"I remember when I was a little boy I learned in the cheder about the golden calf that the Jews built in the desert. I could never understand why the women would part with their jewelry. And the teacher said: You are silly. They could not buy anything valuable in the desert anyway."

Rosenberg laughed.

Kitczels handed the ring to Waldman. "I am sure that this is a valuable ring. If we knew its price, we would know its value which is the main content of the Heidelkorn-Heiber deal. Will you agree Mr. Meirson? In Eretz Israel, they will plant good smelling trees and here, the Jews will continue to live in their stench. So, instead of disinfecting the bathhouse, they will build a golden calf. Do you think that with money you can bring back the dead? Play with ideas, children, play with ideas. What do you want, Mr. Heiber to prolong the rotting process? We are rotting, whether we know it or not and we can't see the end. Is not this enough, sir? Whoever can, runs away from here as far away as they can. And you, sir, want to catch them. Why? What for? And you, sir, and people like you. Since religion will not help, you invented some Palestine."

Translator's footnotes

1. This is wordplay on the word Yid meaning Jew and the name of the 10th letter of the Hebrew alphabet, Yod or Yud (or the Yiddish pronunciation Yid). The literal translation is "the dot Yud" since the letter Yod is very small, looking like a mere dot on the paper (פינטעלע means "little dot"). The meaning of the idiomatic expression is that whatever happens and whatever the circumstances, the Jewish soul is still awake somewhere inside. I think it should be translated "the Jewish spark." A detailed explanation is at http://forward.com/articles/9020/an-essential-point/.
2. I quite like that.
3. What does this man want from me?
4. A hillbilly, lit. "a peasant from the mountains"
5. This is the struggle against the Middle Ages and the Jewish Ghetto.

[Page 65]

The First World War (1914-1918)

During the Russian Invasion (1914 – 1915)
Translated by Susan Rosin

The First World War erupted at the beginning of August 1914 and Stryj was conquered by the Russians a month later. Thousands of Galician Jews escaped west to Czechoslovakia, Austria and mainly to Vienna. Some of the Stryj Jews joined the refugees, but most stayed in town and some of the refugees from the eastern parts of Galicia remained in Stryj.

The first days after the invasion were chaotic with kidnappings for slave labor, rape, looting and plunder. A few days into the occupation the town was put under military authority and the civilian institutions were banned. A special committee was formed to represent the Jewish population before the authorities and to prevent further attacks.

The members of the committee were: Abraham Appfelgreen, Zvi (Hersh Wolf) Wizalteer, Yehezkel Lerrer, Shlomo Hertz, the son of rabbi Feivel Hertz from Glogow, Zvi (Hershel) Pferbaum, Leibish Pikholtz, Yeshayahu (Shaya) Weinrab, Samuel Klein, Joseph Shapira. The main function of the committee was to supply workers for the military. Actually this was slave labor without pay and the committee was paying the workers from donations that were collected among Stryj Jews.

The renowned author S. Ansky whose most famous play is The Dybbuk visited Professor J. Bernfeld during the Russian occupation and donated 500 rubles for Passover. Before their retreat in 1915, the Russians, under threats of rape (as in Drohobycz) demanded 200 workers for digs in the Carpathian Mountains. The workers were selected by the committee.

The Russians took hostages upon retreating from the city in 1915. They kept them in jail for three months and then they were deported east into Russia. The names of the hostages were: Professor Bernfeld, Feivel Hertz from Glogow, the religious judge rabbi Yeshaya Yolles, the cantor David Nussbaum, Abraham Appfelgreen, Leibish Pikholtz, Leon Buch, Isaac Ingber, Leiser Unger, the pharmacist Baruch Shur, Elisha Appfelgreen, Chaim Wizalteer, the police chief Reif, Isaac Pikholtz.

All hostages except for the police chief Reif and Elisha Appfelgreen returned to Stryj in March 1918.

The Russian Occupation in Stryj (1914 – 1915)
Naphtali Ziegel
Translated by Susan Rosin

I.

At the beginning of the war in 1914 I was stuck in Stryj. Anyone that was able to, escaped west.

Stryj was overcrowded with refugees that came from the towns and villages bordering Russia in eastern Galicia. They left their homes and everything they owned and came west with the few belongings they could carry and the little bit of money in their pockets. Their fate scared us and we decided to stay.

Without any organization the Jewish homes opened to the refugees and whole families were taken in. The refugees kept telling us about their travels from the east and we were getting even more depressed and concerned.

There were some funny stories due the gullibility of some refugees such as: "We were told there is not going to be fighting in Stryj. The warring governments decided that all hospitals will be in Stryj".

In the meanwhile the Russians continued their advance to the west and terrible rumors were spreading from the neighboring town. Those who were able to, packed their belongings and moved west. Others who had no means stayed behind. My fiancé L.L. and I decided to leave. We packed our belongings in two large trunks and stored them in the train station warehouse for two days. Then we were told our trunks cannot go on the train. We stayed.

[Page 66]

We understood we have "new owners" when the Cossacks who rode into town turned their weapons towards the people. We opened our trunks and waited anxiously for what comes next. Slowly the town's people started coming out of their hiding places and gradually life was getting back to normal.

The Russians' first step was to check the abandoned apartments. In the first few weeks we had a very "active" low-level soldier in our house. He started by removing linens, furs, clothing, and any household items that could be easily moved. He packed all of those in crates and sent them to his home in Russia. After he "cleaned" the apartments he invited various officers and administrators who were partying and drinking at night. When they were cold and could not find fire wood for heating, they would break furniture and even a piano to burn in the stove. The soldiers were rotating from time to time as they were sent to the front.

One day, while standing on the sidewalk by my home, a heavy object fell on my head and caused me to fall. When I came to I realized that this was a Gmara book (Sahs Vilna) bound in leather. I saw that many pages were cut out with a knife. I went upstairs to that apartment and found soldiers that were busy cutting out and tearing pages from Jewish books. I scolded and reprimanded them and even threatened that I would complain to the civil authorities and they will be punished for desecrating holy books. They stopped and even helped me move the remaining books to Beit Hamidrash.

II.

One day I was travelling in a wagon with my father-in-law Abraham Levin Z"L from Lviv to Stryj. Not far from Mykolaiv (Polish: Mikołajów) we noticed a man of about 30 years old who was following us. We asked the driver to stop and the man approached us. After he found out that we were on our way to Stryj he asked if he could come with us. He told us that he was an escaped Austrian prisoner of war and wanted to re-join the army. We provided him with food and clothing and pointed him in the direction of the border. When the Austrians returned to Stryj we received a picture of him in uniform signed "Onofri from the Rawa Ruska area". Did he remember our help when his brethren were murdering and looting our people during Hitler's time?

Another time we transported two Austrian Jewish officers from Lviv to Stryj. They were the renowned Zionist Dr. Loeb from Vienna and Dr. Szerbstein who was employed in a branch of a large Austrian bank in Lviv. Both stayed in Stryj during the Russian occupation and lived in a special room at Salka Szperling's apartment on Botorego Street. She had two rooms and the entrance to the back room was thru the front. By placing a cabinet at the entrance to the second room they were able to conceal it. They left the room only at night.

III.

With time we got used to the new reality. During the day we traded and the nights were spent with the family. The relatives and neighbors gathered in my father-in-law's apartment where I read Shalom Aleichem stories. Everybody laughed and so we forgot our daily troubles.

We kept all our valuables in trunks in the cellar and took turns in guarding them from the looters.

For a while we even spent time in the evenings at Mark Bakka's café and some of the officers became friendly with us. However, we decided it would be safer to stay home.

The fighting got closer to town at one point and the Austrian army occupied the city for one day. Many Jews holding Torah books and led by rabbi Shalom Yolles came out to greet the soldiers. However, the next day, the Russian re-captured the city again. The rabbi managed to escape, but many Jews were punished.

During the Russian occupation the town was neglected and extremely dirty. The officers and soldiers were only interested in liquor and looting.

[Page 67]

The Jewish Defense 1918
Shimon Rosenberg
Translated by Susan Rosin

In the winter of 1817 – 1818 during the fourth year of the First World War, the law and order of the Austro-Hungarian Empire started to collapse in spite of the state of emergency that existed due to the war. Thousands of deserters were wondering in the Carpathain and Sudeten mountains. A strike erupted in the munitions factory in Wiener Neustadt. Demonstrations were held in many places to protest the food rations, its quantity and quality. With the return of POWs after the Russian revolution in 1917, the military discipline started to crumble. They started to rebel against the officers and the military in general. The authorities reacted with restrain to the civilian demonstrations as not to increase the people's exasperation.

The hunger increased in the spring of 1918. It was hard to eat the meager stale bread, the rationing was not administered properly. The black market was not able to supply the demand in spite of the sky-rocketing prices which were out of reach for many. Spontaneous hunger demonstrations erupted in many places. At the beginning the demonstrations were targeting the government offices responsible for the food distribution, but then they turned their anger against the bakeries and especially the food markets openly displaying highly priced delicacies and luxuries while most could not afford the basic staples. The army did not intervene even when the demonstrators looted stores and smashed windows.

The demonstrations and riots did not skip Galicia. In many cases these demonstrations were incited by Anti-Semitic elements who were emboldened by the fact that many food distributors and grocers were Jewish.

During a demonstration on April 16th 1918 in Krakow that was organized by railway workers, Polish legionnaires and the mob, Jewish stores were looted and their owners beaten. The police were nowhere to be seen. A Jewish merchant from Stryj that happened to be in Krakow for business, Petahia Muller was fatally beaten and died that same day.

Petahia Muller's death caused a lot of fear in our city. Rumors abounded that riots were about to start in Stryj as well. Knowing the Ukrainian and Polish mob, the Jews had reasons to fear that they will be the target.

In a meeting of the Poalei Zion council it was decided that pre-emptive action is needed "just in case". A group of 3 was elected to organize the defense and to meet and discuss the situation with the Z.P.S (Zydowska Partia Socjalystczna – Jewish Socialist Party (SR)). A secret meeting was held in an apartment of the Academic Society and a committee to organize the 40 person defense force (20 from Poalei Zion, 10 from the Z.P.S and 10 from the Academic society) was formed consisting of the following members: Shlomo Rosenberg, Leib Tepper, Monderer, Shimon Rosenberg, and Nathan Wunderleich. A "headquarter" was established and the various groups started to prepare. The hunger demonstration in Stryj was held a few weeks after Passover. Among the "organizers" of the demonstration were many from the mob. Demonstrators started congregating in front of Isaac Sheinfeld's house on Potocki street who had a flour warehouse guarded by the military police.

The crowd grew to 500 people and there were cries and slogans for bread. The demonstrators moved towards the plaza (rynek – market), on their way destroyed and looted two kiosks and continued towards Golochowski Street.

[Page 68]

Mickewicz. On the street corner was a café owned by (the Ukrainian) Markipka displaying cakes and other baked goods. The demonstrators were turning towards the stairs and it seemed as if they were going to attack the café. At that moment, the owner Markipka approached the lead demonstrators and seemed to whisper something. The demonstrators retreated and turned into the avenue leading to the train station. The demonstrators did not touch any of the Christian shops they passed, but when they reached the avenue they attacked the Jewish kiosk owned by Jacob Reinhartz. With their intentions clear, the sticks of the Jewish self-defense men came down on their heads. The brave actions of the defense startled the rioters and some of them promptly retreated. The street was full of people including soldiers all taking in the scene. Some of the demonstrators recovered from the shock and started to fight back by hurling stones at the defense members. Luckily a blood shed was averted as one of the stones hit a soldier and he started bleeding. On seeing their wounded comrade the angry soldiers attacked the demonstrators and they dispersed in a few minutes. Undoubtedly the soldiers' intervention prevented casualties among the members.

The Jewish Militia in 1918
Translated by Susan Rosin

With the collapse of the Austro-Hungarian Empire at the end of the war Stryj was included within Ukraine. Without any civilian institutions there was much chaos at the beginning. All facets of civilian life had to be restored including the police. The population was without any protection during these first days. The town was full of soldiers coming back from the front and trying to reach their homes. Many carried weapons and some took advantage of the confusion to rob and loot. Worrying about the security situation, the Jewish parties sent a delegation to the Ukrainian authorities and got an approval to establish a volunteer Jewish militia and were given some rifles.

Each party was supposed to send a number of volunteers that were taking turns in patrolling the streets at night. Only the veteran officers from the Austrian army were paid for their service in the militia. The headquarters was at the "Talmud Torah" building across the street from the Great Synagogue. Before leaving for their patrols at night, the volunteers gathered at the academic society "avoda" on the corner of Botorego and Potocki streets. The commanders of the militia were receiving reports and updates throughout the night from the patrolling volunteers. A fund was created to cover the few expenses of the militia.

The patrol consisted of 4 – 10 people and they had the authority to stop, conduct a search and bring any suspect to headquarters. Sometimes they stopped thieves but in most cases they stopped ex-military personnel carrying weapons that were disarmed but not prosecuted.

The streets were very dark at night and sometimes the Jewish patrols encountered the Ukrainian patrols that were guarding the streets from possible Polish actions of sabotage. These encounters in the middle of the night could be very dangerous as both militias were still wearing the Austrian uniforms and there was always a danger of being fired upon. Luckily, this did not happen.

Once the Ukrainian secured their control of the city, the "Talmud Torah" building was surrounded without warning by soldiers and the Jewish militia was disarmed.

* * *

The members of the defense group were instructed to intervene only if it was clear beyond a doubt that the demonstrations were Anti-Semitic. More than 30 members from the Jewish defense, armed with sticks and other nonlethal weapons followed the demonstrators. A Jewish store was looted on Golochowski street. However, since there were only Jewish stores on that street, this could not be proven to be an Anti-Semitic act. From Golochowski street the demonstration turned into Mickewicz. On the street corner was a café owned by (the Ukrainian) Markipka displaying cakes and other baked goods. The demonstrators were turning towards the stairs and it seemed as if they were going to attack the café. At that moment, the owner Markipka approached the lead demonstrators and seemed to whisper something. The demonstrators retreated and turned into the avenue leading to the train station. The demonstrators did not touch any of the Christian shops they passed, but when they reached the avenue they attacked the Jewish kiosk owned by Jacob Reinhartz. With their intentions clear, the sticks of the Jewish self-defense men came down on their heads. The brave actions of the defense startled the rioters and some of them promptly retreated. The street was full of people including soldiers all taking in the scene. Some of the demonstrators recovered from the shock and started to fight back by hurling stones at the defense members. Luckily a blood shed was averted as one of the stones hit a soldier and he started bleeding. On seeing their wounded comrade the angry soldiers attacked the demonstrators and they dispersed in a few minutes. Undoubtedly the soldiers' intervention prevented casualties among the members.

[Page 68]

The Jewish Militia in 1918

With the collapse of the Austro-Hungarian Empire at the end of the war Stryj was included within Ukraine. Without any civilian institutions there was much chaos at the beginning. All facets of civilian life had to be restored including the police. The population was without any protection during these first days. The town was full of soldiers coming back from the front and trying to reach their homes. Many carried weapons and some took advantage of the confusion to rob and loot. Worrying about the security situation, the Jewish parties sent a delegation to the Ukrainian authorities and got an approval to establish a volunteer Jewish militia and were given some rifles.

Each party was supposed to send a number of volunteers that were taking turns in patrolling the streets at night. Only the veteran officers from the Austrian army were paid for their service in the militia. The headquarters was at the "Talmud Torah" building across the street from the Great Synagogue. Before leaving for their patrols at night, the volunteers gathered at the academic society "avoda" on the corner of Botorego and Potocki streets. The commanders of the militia were receiving reports and updates throughout the night from the patrolling volunteers. A fund was created to cover the few expenses of the militia.

The patrol consisted of 4 – 10 people and they had the authority to stop, conduct a search and bring any suspect to headquarters. Sometimes they stopped thieves but in most cases they stopped ex-military personnel carrying weapons that were disarmed but not prosecuted.

The streets were very dark at night and sometimes the Jewish patrols encountered the Ukrainian patrols that were guarding the streets from possible Polish actions of sabotage. These encounters in the middle of the night could be very dangerous as both militias were still wearing the Austrian uniforms and there was always a danger of being fired upon. Luckily, this did not happen.

Once the Ukrainian secured their control of the city, the "Talmud Torah" building was surrounded without warning by soldiers and the Jewish militia was disarmed.

[Page 69]

The Ukrainian Rule (1918)
by Naphtali Ziegel
Translated by Susan Rosin

I.

My army company was stationed in Stryj during the last days of the Austro-Hungarian Empire. The collapse of the empire was felt by everyone. My commander, the ober-lieutenant Ivanitzki (a Ukrainian from Stryj) summoned me and told me that I was free to go as the empire no longer existed and the area was under Ukrainians rule. He added happily that one of his Jewish acquaintances proclaimed: "From now I am a Ukrainian Jew".

TheWest-Ukrainian People Republic government was set-up In Stanisławów(today Ivano-Frankivsk in Ukraine (SR)), and a proclamation recognizing the Jewish identity was published in Ukrainian, Polish and Yiddish. The renowned Zionist leader Dr. Israel Waldman from Ternopilbecame the minister for Jewish affairs. He established a press service and was in touch with world Jewry that supported the Jewish neutrality and viewed favorably the Ukrainian promise for Jewish autonomy.

There was a debate whether the Jewish soldiers and officers who returned from the war should join the Ukrainian army. The Zionist organization made a decision that the Jews should remain neutral in the struggle between the Ukrainians and Poles. However, the various units should not disperse, but should organize into a Jewish militia to be ready 'just in case'.

The militias and the various parties decided to establish a local national council in every town. All these local councils congregated in Stanisławów to establish a central national council. A 12 person committee was elected headed by Dr. Carl Halpern who was a wealthy landlord non-partisan and non-assimilated and Dr. Jonas Rubin one of the leading Zionists in Stanisławów. The convention speakers were the most active Zionists: Engineer

Israel Reich, Dr. Jonas Rubin, Dr. Hillel Zusman, Dr. Ordober, Dr. Alexander Riterman, Dr. Anzelm Halpern, LeibShusheim and the engineer Naphtali Landau.

The council's had two main objectives: To organize the Jewish life and identity and to fulfill the Zionist dream in Eretz Israel. The council was coordinating it activities with the leaders of the Zionist movement in Vienna.

The Ukrainians with the help of Dr. Waldman tried to take political advantage of their promise for Jewish autonomy and the difference between them and their Polish adversaries: "They are organizing pogroms and we are giving the Jews autonomy rights".

II.

The first action of the council was to organize a memorial service for the Lviv pogrom victims. The memorial took place in the Great Synagogue and was attended by a high level official. The speakers were rabbi Shalom Yolles (Yiddish), rabbi Ladier (German), and myself (Naphtali Ziegel) (Hebrew).

The Stryj Jewish militia had a priority to transfer the Kehila administration matters from the assimilationists led by Dr. Wiesenberg. A delegation of about 50 people marched on his office, and demanded his resignation, which he did under protest. The delegation members were elated and sang the "Hatikvah". Among the delegation members were Dr. Naphtali (Tulo)Nussenblatt, Dr. Borak, the lawyer Dr. Gross and his officer brother, Oper Levi (one of the founders of Poale Zion), Shalom Reich and many many more. One person from the Z.P.S took over the office management and others took over the rest of the Kehila affairs.

The Jewish National Councilwas set up with representatives from all political parties. Dr. Heinrich Bykwas elected chairman, Dr. Max Bienenstock vice-chairman and Naphtali Ziegel secretary. The parties' differences dominated every discussion.

We were isolated from the world and rumors were rampant such as: A Jewish government was established in Eretz Israel with Chaim Weizmann – the president, Max Nordau – secretary of state, baron Edmond de Rothschild – secretary of finance, etc.

[Page 70]

We published a weekly newspaper called Yidishes Folk-Stimme [Jewish People's-Voice] with articles by Dr. Bienenstock (signed "bee house") about Jewish organization in the diaspora and by N. Ziegel about Hebrew education and culture. We published for 18 issues. Some other notable newspapers published in neighboring towns were: Der Yidisher Arbeiter [The Jewish Worker] (Stanisławów), Yidishe Stimme [Jewish Voice], Dos Freie Vort [The Free Word] (Zlotshov – present day Zolochiv), Die Neie Tzeit [The New Time] (Kolomea).

III.

Those were days of high spirits and realization for national and spiritual unity and integration, energizing the Jews who were not paying attention to the restrictions, the edicts, the humiliations and the poverty. The council delegates were busy with their public activism with discussions lasting well into the nights. The Jews united in spite of their political differences to lay a foundation for a brighter future.

A movement for the Hebrew language was established which was also aided by external factors. The youth who were brought-up with Polish stopped using that language fearing the Ukrainians. Those who did not speak Yiddish started to learn Hebrew and its sounds were heard on city streets.

The council sent a memorandum to the secretary of education and cultural affairs Dr. Artimowicz demanding to establish autonomous Jewish schools to be funded by the government. The secretary agreed to the idea in principal but was doubtful if the Hebrew language could be used for basic teaching. A convention of the Hebrew teachers was organized with full agenda in Stanisławówon January 19th – 20th, 1919 to discuss this issue in detail.

Professor D. Horowitz'slecture on "The nationalization of Jewish schools" caused a public discussion that lasted almost the entire convention. The problem was that the accredited teachers could not teach in Hebrew due to their lack of knowledge of the language. On the other hand, those who had the Hebrew knowledge did not have the accreditation.

The discussion was attended by the engineer Reich, a representative of the central council.

The decisions were as follows:

The Jewish school is a national school;

The teachers are employed by the government which also pays their salaries;

All teachers must be accredited.

After a heated argument the convention participants agreed to a compromise suggested by Naphtali Ziegel representing the Hebrew teachers:

Many teachers who were qualified to teach Hebrew but lacking the formal certification would enroll in a program that will provide them with accreditation within five years and take the matriculation exams. In addition, those teaching secular studies would need to be tested in Hebrew. In the meanwhile, the authorities will be asked to provide temporary teaching permits only to teachers recommended by the "teachers union". A central council for education comprising of seven members, among them Dr. M. Bienenstock and N. Ziegel from Stryj was elected.

The heated discussions lasted two days – on thestreet, in the hotel and the restaurant between the "Yiddishists", the assimilationists and the Hebrew teachers. When the "Hebrews" won the public discussion I was asked to give the convention closing address. To this day I can remember one sentence I said from the podium: "Today we lifted the diaspora disgrace"...The excitement was electrifying. We were sure our redemption was near.

IV.

Upon our return to Stryj we started preparing for the upcoming school year. Only one high-school teacher in Stryj knew Hebrew. The rest, even the religious teachers did not know the language. I was the tutor in the training class that was set-up by the council and was attended by all the eleentary and high school teachers. I recall a few names of the participants: Dr. M. Bienenstock and his wife, Dr. Szeft, Tauber, HellaPreis, Deliktish. They were all dedicated students and made great progress. They were proud in their achievements and were able to convince the new council chairman and renowned Zionist Dr. Shlomo Goldberg to join.

[Page 71]

There was a feeling of great national purpose.

Once I traveled to Stanisławów with Dr. Bienenstock for a meeting with the secretary of education and cultural affairs (a former high school teacher). His office was located in a private home that was confiscated by the government and was sparsely furnished. He was very accommodating and promised to fulfill our requests. "I would like to help the poor Jewish people." We left the meeting happy but upon reaching the street we were attacked by soldiers who began removing Dr. Bienenstock's shoes. I started screaming and a passing officer slapped the soldier and made him return the shoes.

The Russians in their time also used to stop people on the street asking them for the time and when a watch was pulled out of the pocket they would grab it and run. The Ukrainians were in rags and used to attack Poles and Jews and remove their shoes. I witnessed Petliura himself riding a horse on the streets of Stanisławów and whipping soldiers who were looting shops and homes.

On our way home as I recalled our conversation with the minister and his promise to help us.I was amused that he, who had barely a desk and two chairs in his office would help the "Jewish millionaires". Not much longer after that I regretted those thoughts. One little pogrom and all our worldly possessions would be gone and we would be left with nothing. The imminent danger of our destruction is constant. But they, the Ukrainians are on their land and it would never be taken away from them.

"And the land was given to people" – Are we people too?

[Page 75]

Institutions and Associations

The Stryj Community (Kehila) Between the Wars
Translated by Susan Rosin

Until the end of world war one, the Kehila leadership in Stryj was not elected democratically and Jewish Community affairs were conducted by parnasim (synagogue and congregational presidents) and local notables.

From the Mid-Nineteenth century the heads of the community were: Lippa Halpern, Anzel Goldstern, David Halpren (a descendant of rabbi Haim Halpern, one of the wealthiest Jews in eastern Galicia in the 19th century), Zelik Borak, Isaac (Itshi) Sheinfeld, Abraham Luft, Dr. Fichner and Dr. Wiesenberg.

During the war years (1914 – 1918) the Kehila was not very influential due to the state of emergency. After the downfall of Austria, the Ukrainians declared the "West Ukrainian State" with its capital in Satnislawow with Stryj included within the new state. The new Government proclaimed national equal rights for all minorities and published a memorandum to that effect in three languages – Ukrainian, Polish and Yiddish. Based on this declaration, representatives of western Galician Jewry congregated in Stanisławów to establish a Jewish National Council (Jüdischer Nationalrat). Most of the representatives were from the nationalist stream. The council goals were to strengthen the national life of Galician Jews, to realize the Zionist ideas of building the Jewish state in Eretz Israel, to energize the masses and communities for the greater good of the people in the diaspora and Zion.

The Jews of Stryj joined in that effort and decided to take over the community matters out of the hands of the assimilationists and the strongmen and make it a democratic institution representing the population and serving its needs.

In the early days of November 1918, during the last days of the Austro-Hungarian Empire, the Jews of Stryj congregated for a meeting that was called by all the parties. Following the meeting, a procession marched through the city streets to the Kehila offices. A delegation of 50 people comprised of all political parties, soldiers, officers and militia members walked into the offices and demanded that Dr. Wiesenberg surrender the keys, the books and leave the premises. The assimilated community leader left under protest and the elated delegation sang the "Hatikvah" marking their victory. A "temporary national council" was established representing all parties, various religious movements, the labor, professional and economic organizations. The 48 member council was comprised as follows: Zionist: Dr. Shlomo Goldberg, Dr. Zeev Presser, Dr. Mordechai Kaufman, Dr. S. Wandell, Dr. Rosmann, Professor Max Bienenstock, Professor Spät, Dr. Norbert Schiff, Shalom Reich, Naphtali Ziegel, Magister Sternberg, the teacher Tauber, Rachel Katz, Abraham Apfelgreen, M. Wohlmut, Berel Stern, Ben-Zion Radler, Jacob Buksbaum, Shmuel Shenbach, Leibush Pickholz, Shmuel Ginsburg. Poalei Zion: Levi Opper, Abraham Hoyftmann, Berel Friedman, Shlomo Rossler, Professor Ekser. Economic organizations: Herman Krempner, Isaac Reich, Leo Teller, Moerdechai Wagner. Professional organizations: and societies: Abraham Levin, Israel Klieger, Davidman. Religious bodies (synagogues): Haim Redler, Shalom Stern, Shmuel Klein, Shlomo Garfunkel, Abraham Egid, Moidel Fritsch, Zvi Fefferbaum. The Bund: Israel Dornfeld, Isaiah Rossler, Moshe Wagman, Nathan Welker, Vove Kenigsberg, Benjamin Ber, and others.

The city was occupied by the Poles in the summer of 1919 and elections for the National Council were held immediately thereafter. The composition of the National Council was almost identical to that elected during the period of Ukrainian rule proving the stability and the aspirations of the Jews of Stryj in the struggle for their national rights through changing governments. However, the Polish authorities did not favor the rise of the Jewish National Movement and their desire for national rights. Supporting those that never joined the

National Movement and the assimilationists they arbitrarily appointed P. Begleiter as head of the Community. The Zionist organizations protested this appointment and felt they were entitled to make their suggestions about elections for the community.

In 1922 after two years under his leadership and based on an agreement, the leadership of the community passed to representatives of the Zionist parties. The community council had 16 members: Dr. Shlomo Goldberg, Dr. Zeev Presser, Dr. Mordechai Kaufmann, Professor Isaac Bernfeld, Magister Abba Sternberg, Zvi Krampner, Abraham Apfelgreen, Leibush Pickholz, Shalom Stern, Abraham Levin, Zeev (Wolf) Spiegel, Joseph Leibowitz, Shalom Schwartz, Shlomo Garfunkel, Israel Dornfeld and Nathan Welker.

[Page 76]

Due to public pressure, the authorities approved elections for the Kehila on November 5th, 1924. A voters' list of 1,200 was published. The authorities disqualified many of the Zionist voters, but the activists did not stop their efforts and 200 voters were added to the list. Dr. Abraham Insler spoke at a large gathering and emphasized the Zionism closeness to religious and traditional values. The Zionists and orthodox created a joint list of candidates and only Agudat Israel boycotted the elections. The elections led to victory for the Zionist lists who won about 80% of the votes. Dr. Insler was elected as the Kehila head but could not officiate due to his other political and public commitments. In January 1925 the Polish authorities surprisingly cancelled the legal elections, and new ones were announced. In May the same year the Zionist list triumphed once again in spite of the authorities objections. Dr. Shlomo Goldberg was elected as the head of the kehila, and Mordechai Kaufmann, Prof. Isaac Bernfeld, Dr. Z. Presser, Magister Abba Sternberg, Dr. Norbert Schiff, Zvi Krampner, Aryeh (Leibush) Pickholtz, Eliezer Apfelgreen, Abraham Levin, Shlomo Gurfunkel, Mendel Horowitz, Shmuel Klein, Israel Dornfeld and Shalom Stern. Agudat Israel was defeated again. Proportional elections to the Kehila were held for the first time in July 1928. Five "parties" presented their candidates to the voters. The national list received 800 votes, Agudat Israel – 386 votes, Yad Harutzim (Diligent Hand) (craftsmen) – 192 votes, Poalei Zion – 148 votes and a private party – 276 votes. The private party candidates represented only their private interests and not the greater good.

In November that year elections were held for the leadership of the Kehila. The ten-member leadership was elected from the three streams Zionists, joint list of Zionists and Poalei Zion and Agudat Israel with some smaller political factions. The Zionists and Poalei Zion gained 6 spots guaranteeing a majority for the national parties.

The Zionist and national parties gained a majority again in the July 23rd, 1929 elections. The Zionist organization got 9 representatives out of the 15 council leadership positions and the craftsmen 1. Agudat Israel again appealed the elections results to the authorities thus delaying the important work of the council for the good of the Jews of Stryj. The members of the national movement offered to work with Agudat Israel but the latter preferred that the authorities appoint an administrator. This situation continued until 1932 when a new election law was enacted. The following members were elected: Zionists - Dr. Mordechai Kaufmann, Moshe Aaron Wohlmut, Zvi Krampner, Shimshon Steiner, Shalom Stern, Shlomo Gurfunkel; Hamizrahi - Selig Zwilling, Zeev Spiegel and Jecheskiel Lehrer; "Hitahdut" (Union) Party - Dr. Azriel Eisenstein, Haim Neuman, Leib Schwamer; Agudat Israel - Shammai Gertner, Shimon Weiss, Mendel Horowitz, H. M. Neubauer, and Moshe Zechariah Goldberg; Yad Harutzim (diligent hand) – Abraham Levin, Michel Hammerschlag; Unaffiliated – Leibush Pferbaum, Mordechai Lorberbaum, Prof. Bernfeld and after his passing Nathan Welker.

The new council's main role was to recover the kehila financially and to provide the social and religious needs of the community. It was also decided to allocate a budget for the national funds for Eretz Israel.

In 1932 the kehila budget was 189,179 zloty. The following funds were allocated: education and culture - 10,600 zloty, social programs – 36,350 zloty, investments – 15,000 zloty. The budget for that year grew by 20,000 zloty. The kehila took over the management of Chevra kadisha, the Jewish hospital and the Talmud Torah.

[Page 77]

In 1936 the community was headed by Dr. Presser, with Dr. Mishel as vice-chairman, Benjamin Klein as Council Chairman and Israel Zeidman as vice-chairman. In 1938 the kehila opened the Dr. Bernfeld public library and was headed by Baruch Neumann.

There were differences of opinion with regard to the choice of a new rabbi after the death of Rabbi Ladier. Certain elements wanted to undermine the work done by the Kehila and its head Dr. Presser that was supported and well liked by the community. The authorities took advantage of the conflict and entrusted the kehila to the non-Zionist "Jewish Economical Society". The Jewish public opposed this arbitrary appointment and demonstrated its support of the kehila executives led by Dr. Presser. It needs to be noted that a delegation of Hamizrahi, Agudat Israel and the Belz chassidim visited the local commissioner and expressed their support of the kehila leadership under Dr. Presser.

This was the last Community Council of Stryj Jewry. The red army occupation ended the Jewish autonomy.

[Page 77]

Synagogues
Translated by Susan Rosin

The Great Synagogue
(Die Große Schul)

Rising in splendor above the low and run-down houses surrounding it was the Great Synagogue built in the oldest Jewish Quarter. Wide steps led to a tall and wide gateway with the inscription in Hebrew: "This is the gate for G-d the righteous will pass thru it".

The building was erected during the time of Reb Enzel Cuzmer at the beginning of the 19th century near the very old cemetery whose remains could still be seen at the end of the 19th century. The women's prayer area was built in two levels which was unusual and caused opposition from some Hassidim prompting them to appeal to the rabbi of Belz. He responded saying that rabbi's Cuzmer's righteousness is so great that no one should second guess him.

Most congregants were everyday folk, and the Ashkenazi prayer style was followed. Until 1905 the honorary first officer (gabbai) was Moshe Stern, and his assistants were Isaac Jerich and Moshe Waldmann. Other public figures were Israel Nussenblatt, Zvi Hirsch Friedlander the shammash (beadle) and Nissan May, the cantor. During 1914-1918 the first honorary officer was Isaac (Itshe) Hauptmann. Until the holocaust the first honorary officer was Shalom Stern (the son of Moshe Stern) and his assistants were Zeev (Wolf) Waldmann and Shimon Halpern (a silversmith and candlestick maker), and the shamash was Abraham Tadanier. The cantors were David Nussbaum and Sender Kessler. Rabbi Eliezer Ladier prayed in the Great Synagogue for years. To the side there was a small room ("polush") used by many of the carriage owners in town.

The Great Beit Hamidrash

To the right of the Great Synagogue stood the Large Beit Hamidrash (House of Study). Its tall windows gave the impression of a two story building. Here too most of the congregants were also everyday folk and the prayer style was Ashkenazi. This was the only synagogue in which the congregation put on their tefillin during the middle days (Hol Hamo'ed) of Passover and Sukkot. The first honorary officer of the Great Beit Hamidrash was Zalman Schwartzberg (a grain merchant) and his assistant who was also his brother-in-law David Schorr. The shammash was Leib Kurtzer. The officers who followed them were Mendel Liebermann and after his passing Abraham Egid.

The learned Abba Hirszhorn used to pray in this Beit Midrash. There was also a minyan in the "polush" in Beit Hamidrash and the gabbaim were Zvi Apfelgreen and Eingenmachtes.

[Page 78]

The Ziditchev Synagogue
(known as the "Blechene Kloiz")
Menachem son of Rabbi Yeshaia Leib Falk

I remember with great sorrow the people of the "Blechene Kloiz" one of the most significant synagogues in town and the place where the soul of Jewish Stryj was molded. They were the last generation of suffering and torture that were not redeemed and only few of them passed away before the holocaust. But, most of them died at the hand of the Nazis. It is them I mourn – the martyrs, the righteous that were put to death with great suffering without a memorial, without a headstone.

May my words be their memorial and may God avenge them.

Rabbi Yekele Schorr was the head of the Kloiz. He sat at a table to the right of the ark (known as the "golden table") near the eastern wall. His face was that of an ancient noble patriarch with a very long silver beard. In his later days when walking was hard for him, he came down to the Kloiz only on special Saturdays and on holidays for morning prayer. On other days a minyan was gathered in his house. He was well liked and respected by the Kloiz community.

To the right of rabbi Yekele sat his son in law rabbi Mendele Horowitz, who was also respected thanks to his admired father in law. Later he was the gabbai of the Klioz and acted with forcefulness. Rabbi Itshe Shohet was the permanent blower of the shofar ("ba'al tfila") during the high holidays (Rosh Hashanah and Yom Kippur) in the Kloiz. After his death, rabbi Shalom Shohet took his place in the additional prayers ("musaffim") and rabbi Mendele in the morning prayers ("shaharit"). Rabbi Mendele was known in town as a public figure, one of the leaders of the Kehila. Even after he lost his fortune, he still acted like a rich man and people still treated him with respect.

To the left of rabbi Yekele, leaning on the prayer pillar stood rabbi Velvele Haftel. He was the student of the rabbi of Dolina (Dolyna) and when he had the means, he would bring his admired teacher to our town. He hosted the rabbi and his entourage of Hassidim in his house. During the stay of the rabbi of Dolina, the house of rabbi Velvele was opened to all who came to greet the rabbi and ask for his blessings. During the visits of the rabbi of Dolina there was a general happiness and spirituality in the Kloiz aided by the "Dolinner Gabbaim" who accompanied him and where known for their musical talents and abilities. With every visit they brought new tunes for familiar prayers and rabbi Velvele tried to learn those so he can share them with the rest of the Kloiz.

Rabbi Velvele himself was praying in the warm Dolina style and for many years he was the one to chant the "Lcha Dodi" (Hebrew: דודי לכה) on Friday nights.

When rabbi Velvele was prosperous he was hospitable and on Friday nights he stayed at the Kloiz until late and brought to his home all those that had no other place to go for the Shabbat meal. Even after he lost his fortune he was still a happy and righteous man and the people respected him.

Across the table sat rabbi Kalman Schorr, the son of rabbi Yekele. He resembled his father in his appearance. He had a long reddish beard and was praying quietly and talking little and responding calmly. He was not a public figure and made his livelihood together with his wife and sons in the oil business. He was lucky to pass away before holocaust.

Several years after the First World War, the second son of rabbi Yekele settled in town. Rabbi Shmelke Schorr married the daughter of the wealthy rabbi Strizower from Rzeszów (Yiddish: רײַשע-rayshe).

[Page 79]

When he lost his fortune in Rzeszów he moved with his family to our town and opened a business of tobacco and newspapers/magazines. After he contracted polio, his wife and three sons worked in the store. Two of his sons became fanatic Belz Hassidim and spent most of their time with the rebbe there. The youngest son, Meir was dedicated to the business, but passed away at a young age.

To his right was rabbi Dov (Berrish) Rotfeld, a learned man whose advice was sought by many. He made a good living and was generous to those less fortunate. He was the follower of the rabbi of Czortków (Chortkiv). His sons are in Israel.

Next to him sat rabbi Azriel Kleinmann, one of the Hassidim of the rabbi of Żydaczów (Zhydachiv). He was a learned man with musical talents. He always chanted during the "three meals" and in the absence of rabbi Velvele Haftel, he chanted the "Lcha Dodi". When he was able to, he was studying in the Kloiz and his sons followed his ways of Torah and piety.

Next to him sat rabbi Shimon Igra, also one of the Żydaczów Hassidim. He was very orthodox and was hopeful that his sons would follow the same path.

His eldest son was one of the prodigies of the Kloiz in his youth. However, after the First World War, when the Haskala movement reached Stryj, he as did many other young people, left the Kloiz to pursue a general education to the dismay of his father. In rabbi Shimon's later days, his son brought him to Israel, treated him with respect and provided all his needs while he (rabbi Shimon) was studying with rabbi Mendele Rand in Jerusalem until the day he died.

Rabbi Nuty Sheinfeld the son of rabbi itshe Sheinfeld one of the most respected people of the Kloiz before World War I was not a frequent prayer there. Like his father before him he was wealthy and a philanthropist. On the anniversary of his father's death he was in the Kloiz after the evening prayers and giving charity to the town's poor as well as providing a ceremonial meal to all in the Kloiz.

The list will not be complete without mentioning one of the most righteous elders of the Kloiz who would have surely occupied an important spot at this table if not for his humility and modesty. Rabbi Koppele Seman, a modest, righteous and God fearing, pious man set his praying spot behind the great stove in the Kloiz.

Rabbi Koppele was praying with great spirituality and reverence. Once, he slid on the ice outside and broke his leg, but he continued praying behind the stove until his strength failed.

This stove which was selected by rabbi Koppele for his prayers was very unique. The front was made of one part, but the back was separated into two by an alcove. In the winter both parts of the stove were lit and its heat spread throughout the entire Kloiz. In the winter, the Kloiz people as well as passers-by congregated by the stove to warm themselves away from the elements.

It seemed like this stove was special and made people feel close to the creator and whenever rabbi Koppele was not there someone else took his place while praying the "Shmoneh Esreh" (the Amidah – in Hebrew: תפילת העמידה, Tefilat HaAmidah "The Standing Prayer").

This stove that absorbed so many prayers was eventually replaced by a more modern one covered in shining tiles. In spite of its new look, the modern stove could not heat the entire Kloiz like its predecessor. The elders did not like the new stove and a rumor was circulating that rabbi's Koppele death soon after the installation of the new stove was due to the demolition of the old one.

Another unique stove was standing in the second corridor of the Kloiz. Throughout the year, prayer shawls (tallit) and books unfit for use (or blemished) were placed inside. Before Passover, the stove was thoroughly cleaned and used to bake the Matzah Shmurah.

There was much excitement before baking the matzah in the Kloiz. On the Saturday before Passover (Shabbat Hagadol), the planks were smoothed with a special plane to remove any hametz that accumulated throughout the year. The rolling pins were scraped and the tools to punch the dough so it would not rise were all made kosher for Passover.

[Page 80]

The following day, Sunday, men from the various Kloiz gathered to bake the matzah, each bringing their own flour. This was the matzah they ate throughout the Passover. The matzah that was bought in market, although kosher for Passover was given to family members.

Rabbi Koppele Seman was kneading the dough with the help of rabbi Kalman Schorr who was pouring the water as needed. Then, the dough was divided among the people standing around the tables. Most of the work was done by the youth from the Kloiz – some of them were successful in creating round matzah while others created squares. Then the matzah was punched and placed in the oven with cries of "a matzah to the puncher" and "a matzah into the oven" the smell of fresh baking matzah in the air.

Same actions took place on Passover eve even more ceremoniously.

At the table to the left of the ark sat rabbi Itshe Shohet who was one of the most popular prayer leaders in town. He was one of the finest Masters of

Prayer and singers in our city, being blessed with a very musical ear and a power of original melody. He used to act as cantor during the Morning, Sabbath and Festival Additional prayers without receiving any pay. Even during his illness and after his passing the chanting and prayers he composed were still heard. The Kloiz youth gathered on Yom Kippur eve after the regular prayers and sang rabbi's Itshe Shohet melodies until after midnight. Then they returned either to their homes or back to the Kloiz to take a nap and get up early to say Tehilim (Psalms).

At the same table sat rabbi Haskele Horowitz a righteous and humble man who regretted all his life the fact that his sons did not follow the Torah ways. Later in life when his sons assumed the burden of making a living for the family, he spent his days in the Kloiz studying and praying. He mostly studied the "simple Gmara" without interpretations. It was said that he studied the six books of the Mishnah seven times. His prayer was spiritual without any self-praise and only for the glory of God.

Across from him sat rabbi Eizik Hubel. He was a learned and wealthy man who owned a factory for cement pipes. For a while he served as the gabbai of the Kloiz. During his tenure he expanded the gas lamps system so the use of the candles for the students could be decreased. He provided wood for the stove in the Kloiz to make sure everybody was warm.

Rabbi Sender Rothenberg sat next to him and for a period of time served as a gabbai, was involved with the students and provided for them. His youngest son became a Belz Hassid, and since then rabbi Sender was a supporter of the Belz students and claimed their "citizenship" in the Kloiz.

His son Kalman was educated traditionally and in his youth was a student.

Rabbi Moshe Kudisch was another participant at this table. He was a man learned in the Torah, member of the community and involved in education for many years. After World War I with the growing interest in the Zionist national movement, rabbi Moshe became involved in the religious Zionist movement the "Mizrahi" and sent his eldest son to Eretz Israel.

Rabbi Leib Krieger was one of the most prominent Torah educators. With the reopening of the Talmud Torah after the World War I, he became one of its activists and directors. He was involved with the students, their progress and their well-being. On Saturdays he tested the students to follow-up on their progress, praised those that excelled and encouraged those that needed improvement and financially supported those in need. All of his deeds were only for the glory of God.

He was at once strict and lenient with the students and treated them as if he was their father. The cheder boys who came to the Kloiz for study liked him and feared him at the same time. He allowed them to be mischievous in their time off and viewed favorably their happiness during the holidays, but was strict with them during the rest of the year. And insisted on study and pray.

He did not expect these young students to be involved in complicated interpretations or discussions. All he demanded from them was to have a simple understanding based on common sense. He himself studied the simple gmara all his life.

The Hebrew School "Safa Brura" (Clear Language) – 1936
Seated in the front row from right to left: Hubel, Shapira (a teacher), J. Garlenter (teacher), Glatstein, and H. David Korn.

Kindergarten adjoining the Hebrew School "Safa Brura" – 1936

Standing in the back: The teacher Frieda Byk and H. David Korn a member of the school board.

A class in the Ber Borochov night school – 1923

Last Row: J. Hass, S. Melpin, David Seltzer, A. Shayke, Shlomo Rosenberg, J. Becher.

Local members of the Zionist Organiation (General Zionists)

Council of the Stryj Kehila – 1925

Standing right to left: Abraham Levin, K. Mayer, L. Apfelgreen, Zvi Krampner, Shlomo Garfunkel, Leibush Pickholz

Seated: Dr. Zeev Presser, Dr. M. Kaufmann, Abraham Apfelgreen, Shalom Goldberg, J. Bernfeld, D. Schiff, Abba Sternberg

The Jewish representatives in the Stryj municipality – 1936

Standing from right to left: Dr. Mishel, Dr. Azriel Eisenstein, A. Apfelgreen, L. Szwammer, Benjamin Klein, Moshe Aaron Wohlmut

Seated: Z. Norbert Schiff, Dr. S. Wendel, Dr. M. Kaufmann, Rachel Katz, Dr. B. Milbauer

The Keren Kayemet L'Israel (Jewish National Fund) Activists – 1913

The Keren Kayemet L'Israel (Jewish National Fund) Activists – 1929

[Page 81]

Rabbi Leib Krieger was a "Lover of Zion" by those days' standards and all his life he aspired to immigrate to Israel, which he was able to realize in his later days with his family. Here too, he continued to be active in public life among the Galicia community.

He died at an old age and was mourned by his many friends in Israel and eulogized as was proper for a God fearing Jew whose deeds were dedicated to God and the good of the community.

Rabbi Haim Brand a regular worhiper in the Kloiz was seated at the end of this table. On weekdays he got-up early to study before prayers. He did not have any sons to continue in his footsteps and therefore he treated affectionately all young people studying in the Kloiz.

Also at the table were seated rabbi Yankele Rosmarin, rabbi Rotbard, rabbi Abner Katz and his brother rabbi Aaron Katz.

Rabbi Abner Katz was a learned and educated man and also gained notoriety thanks to his wife Mrs. Rachel Katz, an educated woman who was a well-known public figure active in many charities in town and many turned to her in their time of need.

His brother rabbi Aaron had the privilege to immigrate to Israel before the war and died at an old age.

On the south side of the Kloiz was the "long table" which almost reached the western wall.

At the head of the table sat rabbi Shalom Shohet. Stryj was blessed with many "Shubs" (Shin Vav Beit are the initials of "Shohet Ubodek", Slaughterer and Inspector).

The first of them was rabbi Sender Shohet followed by his son rabbi Shalom Shohet, rabbi Itshe Shohet and his son-in-law rabbi David, rabbi Nethaneli Shohet and his son-in-law rabbi Shlomo Shohet. All of them were activists and popular with the people.

After rabbi Itshe Shohet became ill rabbi Shalom Shohet became the prayer leader of the additional High Holidays prayers (musafim). He was a man learned in the Torah and had much influence in the Kloiz. He traveled often to the rabbi of Belz, but was considered a Żydaczów Hasid. His eldest son Herzeli who became later the rabbi of Lubicz (Lubitsch) near Belz was considered in his youth a prodigy in the Kloiz. He was considered an expert in Shas (the six books of the Mishnah) and rabbinic Literature. He was a modest and righteous and was famous in the entire area and thepride of rabbi Shalom Shohet's family.

On the south side at the same table sat rabbi Israel Zeidmann who was a regular since he settled in our town after World War One. He was well versed in the Torah as well as general knowledge. He was calm and composed and sound judgment as was the custom in the town of his origin Skala (Skala Podolskaya) where most of the people were Chertkov Hasidim. He spoke several languages and had connections overseas. He did not normally study in the Kloiz, but scheduled lessons at his home. He used to discuss questions of faith and opinions with the senior students of the Kloiz. He did not engage in any public matters of the kehila or the town although he was highly qualified. His eldest son David was a complete opposite of his father. As a young man he joined his father's business and worked hard at it. He had a highly developed sense of community and become a central figure in the public and national affairs of our city. He was an enthusiastic Zionist and later a leader of the Revisionist youth movement. He was a gifted speaker appearing in various gatherings and represented the town's people with the Zionist establishment. He was always ready to help those in need whether with advice or lobbying. Whenever he showed-up at the Kloiz for a quick prayer, people always gathered around him to hear news and updates from the town and from around the world.

Across from rabbi Israel was rabbi Leiser Weiss a Żydaczów Hasid and an in-law of rabbi Itshe Shohet. His sons are in Israel.

Rabbi Aaron Czysez, the brother-in-law of rabbi Shalom Shohet, a Stratyn (Stratin) Hasid was himself slaughterer and inspector, but after settling in Stryj he became a merchant. His son-in-law rabbi Eli Isakawer was also one of the regulars in the Kloiz and friendly with the other scholars there.

Rabbi Shmuel Friedler was a merchant who was a supporter of Torah scholars, a generous, righteous and a philanthropist. After his youngest son Pinni became an enthusiastic Belz Hasid, he supported the Belz students in the Kloiz, and was frequently visiting the rabbi there.

Rabbi Aryeh Fruchter and his brother sat at the other side of this table near the western wall. Unlike the other butchers in town they wore a silk Kapota and shtreimel on Saturdays. They were decent and honest people strict keepers of kashrut as required by their profession.

Rabbi Eli Meir sat at the north table. He taught at the Talmud Torah for many years and many of the Kloiz student were educated by him. He guided his students how to self-study which helped them to further their knowledge.

[Page 82]

Across from him sat rabbi Abraham Shuster, who was a learned man both in the Torah and general studies and was considered a "maskil" (a follower of the enlightenment movement) in those days terms. He was fluent in Hebrew and therefore was frequently asked to be the reader of the scriptures on Saturdays. Next to him sat rabbi Aaron Reiter, a glazier who studied mostly Maimonides (RaMBaM רמב"ם – Hebrew acronym for "Rabbi Mosheh Ben Maimon"). In his later days he published "Moshe and Aaron" a book containing selections of Maimonides commentaries. Waking up early in the morning and staying up late he worked on this book for twenty years collecting material from all Maimonides books.

Rabbi Haim Brickenstein sat at a small and narrow table that was placed next to "the table". He was a Żydaczów Hasid and learned in the Torah diligently studying every day. The Kloiz students were asking for his assistance when they encountered difficulties in their Gmara studies. He had the ability to explain and clarify matters in a simple, understandable and logical way. He was weak physically and used to wear something to keep him warm during the month of Tamuz and he prohibited the Kloiz students from opening windows during summer due to his fear of draft. His eldest son Issachar was a traditionalist and followed in his father's footsteps.

Rabbi Yekele Jerich stood next to "the table" during prayers. He was a tailor by profession, a simple God fearing man, respectful of those learned in the Torah who loved the Kloiz's students. He never missed an opportunity to pray and study, frequently joining any group discussing the Gmara. He frequented the mikva, always participated in the public prayers and believed in the Tzadikim (spiritual masters). His son Isaac did join his father's business as was customary but studied first in the heder and later in the Kloiz.

His neighbor at the Kloiz was rabbi Shimon Shlatiner a brooms and brushes maker whose sons were all educated in the spirit of the Torah, tradition and Hasidism. His eldest son, Mendel was one of the Kloiz's prodigies. His second son Moshe became an enthusiastic Belz follower.

Rabbi Haim Wolff and his brother Nuta Wolff were among the long-standing attendees of the Kloiz. Rabbi Haim, a Dolina Hasid was a respectful landlord in town. He was generous and charitable and helped those in need many times in secret. Haim and Nuta were the sons of rabbi Sender Wolff and their maternal grandfather was rabbi Isaiah Igra (his daughter Mrs. Chaya was the mother of the two brothers).

Rabbi Yessele Boimel stood during prayers at the table, a scholar and a God fearing man. When the shamash (beadle) passed away, rabbi Yessele was asked to take this position with explicit promises from the leaders such as rabbi Yekele Schorr that he would be able to manage the Kloiz affairs as he saw fit without any intervention from the gabbaim (honorary officers of the Kloiz). He carried out his job with fairness and without favoritism, giving the honor of "aliyot" (calling of a member of the congregation to the bimah for a segment of reading from the Torah) equally to the wealthy and the common folk and therefore was well liked and respected by all. He passed away after about ten years during the typhoid epidemic in our town after World War I.

Rabbi Eliezer Melamed was a respected teacher for forty years. There was not a youth in town that did not study under rabbi Eliezer for a period of time. He rose early every morning and prayed reverently. In his later years when he could no longer teach, he requested financial relief from the kehila, but was turned-down. He then requested the same from the prime minister of Poland,

Piłsudski, an act that raised many brows in our town. I cannot remember if eventually his request was granted by the kehila.

The western table also accommodated many regulars as well as passers-by. During summer days the hallways were also full with worshipers mainly "young grooms" and those who were distancing themselves from tradition and spent most of their time in discussions and conversations after a short prayer, the "amidah" and the Shema.

On weekdays there were additional worshipers in the Kloiz that came there because it was close to their residences.

Rabbi Mottel Rathaus one of the two Husiatyn Hasidim prayed on Saturdays and Holidays at the Chortkiv Kloiz but during the week he prayed at the Kloiz close to his house. His regular spot was at the long table near the south wall.

[Page 83]

Like the early Hasidim he came every morning an hour before start of prayers and prepared himself by studying Gmara, reading psalms and studying the "law" for that day. Then he prayed with the third minyan. He was a God fearing man and strictly observed the trivial commandments with as much care as the weighty ones. He had a business of hides in his house but was studying in his free time.

He was normally quiet and spoke little. But when he was at ease on Saturday or holidays with his circle of the first Hasidim he uttered pearls of wisdom telling Hasidic stories and Torah studies.

His sons followed in his footsteps, were students of Torah, God fearing and well educated. Some of the town's people hid in a cellar of a building that was demolished during the first air-raid of Stryj before the holocaust. Rabbi Mottel perished there with his eldest son Shmuel and grandson Yosel (his daughter's son). It took a few days for the rescuers to dig through the heap of ruins and bring the dead for proper Jewish burial.

Among the worshipers in Kloiz during weekdays was my father. He was the second Husiatyn Hasid in town. On Saturdays he prayed with the rabbi of Mosczick (Mościska or Mostyska) with whom he was friendly from the time we lived there. When the rabbi moved to Stryj, my father continued the friendship and was a frequent visitor to his house.

We lived near the Kloiz (in the house of Shaye Samet) and my father used to pray there on weekdays, usually later in the morning during the fourth minyan or on his own. Then he stayed and talked to the students.

He was a sociable person and carried out conversations about Hasidim, Torah and just plain talk while holding the strap of the hand tefillin. He was a Hasid and a God fearing person. However he detested the exaggeration in prayer of the Belz Hasidim as well as their way of dressing with a sash tied low on their stomachs and the showing of the skullcap under their brimmed hats, traditions that do not add to glory of God. My father was popular with the "modern Hasidim" in town (Ruzhin Hasidim) but was harassed by the Belz Hasidim. When the Belz Hasidim gained influence in town, my father left the Kloiz and started worshiping on weekdays at "Shaye Samet's small synagogue".

These weekday worshipers were accompanied by their sons-in-law. Rabbi Itshe Herscz Ehrenkranz was the son-in-law of rabbi Mottel Rathaus and was a prodigy in his youth who could have been easily appointed a rabbi in one of the small towns in Poland. But he preferred to make a meager living in his grocery store and study in his free time for the pure glory of God.

My father's son-in-law rabbi Moshe Kupfer was a student of the rabbi of Mosczick. He married my sister when he was 18 years old and was burdened with making a living and had no time for studying. He was one of the first one thousand Jews in town arrested by the Nazis and murdered in jail.

All morning the Kloiz was full of worshipers and on market days peasants from the neighboring villages joined in.

The last of the minyanim was that of the rabbi of Strelisk. He was from a dynasty of rabbis, but did not have a Hasidic following and was supported by his friends and family. In late morning he gathered some stragglers, those late for prayer and barely could make a minyan or he would "kidnap" passers-by so he can say the prayers that required tem men in attendance. In spite of this there was always some brandy and wafers for "snacks". The money for these came from "blackmailing" the people in his minyan to say a prayer on the anniversary of the passing of some tzadik (righteous one).

*

The religious study system in Galicia was unlike that in Poland and Lithuania, where famous Torah scholars headed the yeshiva and students from all over came to hear their lessons. These students were under constant supervision and their progress closely monitored.

In Galicia, a youth at the "bar mitzvah" age who completed his study in the heder, entered the Kloiz for mostly unsupervised self-study. The more senior students felt it was their duty and privilege to guide these young boys in self-study and advice. This was done without any prompt and without any pay.

[Page 84]

So, these students attended the Kloiz instead of a yeshiva and many prodigies grew that way to serve in the small towns and villages in Galicia. The older students supervised the younger ones and those in turn supervised the little ones.

The "Blechene Kloiz" had a special draw and many of the town's youth studied there. Perhaps it was because of the light and warmth of the Kloiz or perhaps because of the connection and support that the more wealthy and senior members showed these students.

A large bookcase was placed along the western wall and it was full of books: Various editions of the six books of the Mishnah (Vilnius, Zhitomir (Zhytomyr), Lwow and Vienna), the Shulchan Aruch (Hebrew: שֻׁלחָן עָרוּךְ) (Code of Jewish Law), books of rabbinic authority, as well as kabbalah and Hasidic books all used by the Kloiz students.

Most of the Kloiz students were supported by their parents and even those without means spared whatever they could so their sons will study not necessarily to become rabbis but for them not to be uneducated ("Am Ha'aretz") which was considered a disgrace in those days.

As they became older and married, the previous Kloiz students became burdened with making a living and no longer were able to study, but still found some time to stop by for a quick prayer, browse one of the books or just to chat.

Itshe Haftel was a student at the Kloiz in his youth. After his marriage he became a merchant and traveled around Galicia for his business. Upon returning to town he always brought news from "the world" and stories about the other Jewish communities.

Shmuel Rathaus a newlywed, a decent and a gentle soul came often to the Kloiz to learn a page of Gmara.

Shalom Leib Rathaus was one of the more senior students of the Kloiz. Diligent and sharp he studied and taught the Gmara. He was also well versed in general studies and matters. He studied the apocrypha (secret, or non-canonical books), but was not impacted. In his ideology he was close to the Mizrahi movement although he never joined. Like his father, he admired the Husiatyn rabbi. When the rabbi Moshe'le of Żydaczów visited, he was a frequent visitor to his house and became friends with his son Sender Lippale. He was always in discussions with students who happened to stop in town, and was considered a "politician" of the Kloiz, and everyone came to hear from him about events in the "world".

Second to him was Yekel Buk, from the Shalom Shohet family. He was a scholar, studying day and night, supported by his mother who was a merchant. He scheduled learning sessions for the younger students. At the beginning he was leaning towards Hasidism and traveled many times to Belz.

Later, although still very orthodox, he began to consider aliya to Eretz Israel. His plans never materialized. It was rumored that he was shot by a Ukrainian militant on a ghetto street and left to bleed to death.

The third one in this group was Moshe Kleinman who was studying the simple Gmara. He had no plans of turning his studies into a source of income or become a religious official, but only study Torah for the glory of God. He never took part in the "religious wars" that erupted between the Belz students and the "Epicorsim" ("Heretics") and therefore was respected by the more senior members of the Kloiz.

Normally when the Kloiz students matured they acquired some general education and tried to find "purpose" in life. Some even went further and distanced themselves from tradition, turned their back on their past and acted in contempt to anything held dear to an orthodox Jew. Some returned later to their "Jewish traditions" although not to the same degree as in their youth. They became "tradition friendly" eating gefilte fish on Fridays, "fasting" on Yom Kippur talked about their Hasidic past and stopped at the Kloiz occasionally for a chat.

[Page 85]

The opposite happened to Moshe Buk the son of rabbi Shalom Shohet who was the same age as Moshe Kleinman. In his youth he left the Kloiz and distanced himself from all commandments, dressed in a fashionable way and walked around town and in parks on Saturdays as a non-traditional person.

When the rabbi of Belz returned from his exile in Hungary and passed through our town on his way to his temporary home in Oleszyce (Oleshychi), Moshe Buk joined the Hasidic voyage. He spent a few months there with the other "yoshvim" (literally translated "the sitting ones" - a program in Belz which encouraged married and unmarried men to spend all day learning Torah in local shtiebels while supported by local businessmen) and came back a "changed man". He dressed as a most orthodox Hasid and behaved as a "yoshev". His piety was excessive compared to the Kloiz students in those days. He studied all day long and everyone in the Kloiz wondered about his changed behavior.

In time he was joined by Shayke Zeidmann that also became a devout and enthusiastic Belz Hasid. He left his home that he considered not orthodox enough and went to "sit" in Belz for long periods at a time.

When the two returned from Belz, they started to organize young men to join them. They did not necessarily select the most orthodox, but anyone who was willing to join them, even secular, took them to Belz and made them join the "yoshvim". In a short time they created a movement of young men who traveled to Belz. Some went once or twice, but others remained fanatic Hasidim that even exceeded their rabbi s in their orthodoxy and their hatred to the "heretics" that did not join this movement.

Among those that remained Belz Hasidim were: Mottel and Herzel Schorr the sons of Shmelke Schorr who came from a relatively "modern" home became zealous in their behavior and dress; Moshe Shlatiner the son of rabbi Shimon Shlatiner became more learned and orthodox than his father; Israel'ke Rothenberg, the son of rabbi Sender Rothenberg who was unhappy at the beginning about the change in his son's behavior, but later became a supporter of this movement; Pinni Friedler the son of rabbi Shmuel Friedler and others.

Among the younger students of the Kloiz were:

Yerahmiel Rathaus, was an outstanding student since his days in the heder. He was studious and diligent and even as a young boy he prayed with his face to the wall and his prayer book placed on the bench in front of him and when he became older he dedicated himself to studying day and night. After his bar mitzvah he was sent to study with the rabbi of Mosczick and was his star student until the rabbi made aliya to Eretz Israel where he passed away. Yerahmiel was considered a prodigy and was famous even in other Galician towns. After his marriage he became a rabbi in the town, was considered one of the best young rabbis in the area and had many students both young and old.

Matye Zeidmann was also a student of the rabbi of Mosczick and then continued studying in the Kloiz. He joined his father's business, but still continued studying in his free time. He was a gentleman and highly intellectual and even when he could not study on a regular basis, he continued to follow tradition.

Valtshe Buk rabbi Shalom Shohet's youngest son was one of the most important students at the heder of rabbi Meir and studied for a while at the Kloiz under the tutelage of the more senior students. For a while he lived with his brother Herzeli in Lubicz (Lubitsch) and frequented Belz, befriended the less orthodox, and was never considered a part of that sect.

Among those who paid frequent visits to the rabbi of Glogow who was the adversary of the rabbi of Mosczick were:

Mendel Shlatiner, rabbi Shimon Shlatiner's son who studied in the Kloiz and a merchant;

Chaim Cirglass studied for a while under the rabbi of Glogow, then joined his father's business and stopped his studies altogether.

There were others who frequented the Kloiz:

Abraham Lauberboim was very studious and sharp and at the age of 14 received a teaching permit from the rabbi of Mosczick.

[Page 86]

He was knowledgeable in non-religious matters. For a time he was a student in the Lublin yeshiva, then tutoring the Kloiz students and was "splitting hairs" about Talmudic issues and its commentators with the learned people in town. His behavior and clothing were sloppy, but he was a very interesting conversationalist and people were drawn to him.

His first wife was the daughter of the rabbi of Moișei (in Romania) and they divorced due to "irreconcilable differences". He then "fell in love" with the much younger daughter of rabbi Meir'l Garlanter, an affair that became the "talk of the town".

Avner Shapira who was a follower of the rabbi of Glogow was studying in the evenings at the Kloiz. He was an honest and righteous just like his father. He was a God-fearing Jew although he was not a Hasid and did not travel to the rabbi.

There were others who came to the Kloiz, not necessarily to study but to socialize.

Lolly Garlanter was not drawn to the sturdy of the Gmara. He spent his time browsing the Hasidic and kabala books and writing poems in a beautiful Hebrew style.

To the disappointment of his parents he refused to become a rabbi. Many of the young Kloiz students enjoyed spending time with him, listening to his interesting conversations and his witty jokes. He dreamed of becoming a Hebrew poet, but was not able to fulfill it.

Others in the Kloiz included Wolf Ehrenstein a student of the rabbi of Mosczick and his brother Yashe one of the promising young Yiddish writers. Ahara'le, the grandson of rabbi Yehoshua Dayan, a prodigy, an outstanding student of the rabbi of Mosczick and then a student at the Lublin yeshiva. He demanded to become a religious judge (dayan) . Duddy Rabin, an outstanding student of rabbi Eli Meir and Yosele Prastak who discontinued his studies.

Others were drawn to our Kloiz from elsewhere: Leib Peinholz, Duddy Millard and Joel Seif.

Differences of opinions were common among the Kloiz students mainly in matters of "high politics" and the rabbinical institutions in town. Some of the students were followers of the "modern rabbi" Ladier, but most were followers of the various Hasidic streams (Glogow, Mosczick, Chortkiv, Belz, Zhidachov, etc.) causing many disagreements.

With the return of the Belz rabbi to Poland, Moshe Buk and Shayke Zeidmann started to arrange trips for Kloiz students to go and "sit" there (in

Belz) months at a time. Upon their return they became fanatic Belz followers. This "movement" grew every year.

This group entrenched themselves in the Kloiz and disapproved of those who did not join their "movement". Although among those that did not join the "movement" were followers of other Hasidic streams, they were seen as "Epicorsim". They ostracized Shalom Leib Rathaus, who was leaning towards the "Mizrahi" and he became their main target and later Yekel Buk who discontinued his travels to Belz and became friendly with Shalom Leib. They also found supporters among the Kloiz people and in time started to see it as their "Belz Kloiz".

The most "impure" in their opinion was Lolly Garlanter, who knew Hebrew, wrote poetry and discussed matters of religion and faith with the Kloiz students.

The Belz followers occupied the long table where they could watch the "epicorsim". Things heated-up when one winter night a towel was thrown from the Belz side and hit one of the students on the other side which retaliated by throwing an old tallit to the Belz camp. A fist fight erupted and it was a true "war of brothers" where Herzel Schorr was fighting on the Belz side and his brother Meir Schorr fighting on the other side. The fight lasted for a while until the others were able to break it up.

[Page 87]

Following this incident, those who did not belong to the Belz movement left and moved to the synagogue of Wolf Ber known as "die Yevonische Kloiz". This Kloiz had a special advantage because the entrance was in a narrow alley and the interior was dark, thus allowing the students to spend more time reading papers, chatting and even playing chess and cards without the elders watching them.

The "Blechene Kloiz" became empty in time. With the travelling to Blez for "sitting" and the move of others to Wolf Ber there was no need to keep the Kloiz open during day time.

This is the history of our Kloiz between the two world wars. The Stryj community was destroyed, and the people who worked and dreamed some for redemption by the messiah and some looking towards Zion were annihilated and did not live to see the establishment of the state of Israel. May God remember them and avenge them.

...

The Synagogue of Meir Shalom (Meir Shalom's Kloiz)

This was the prayer center of many groups of Hassidim. The Hassidic rabbis of Stratyn, Strelisk, and Sassov prayed there on their visits to Stryj. In 1910 the Vizhnitz rabbi came to town and prayed there. The gabbaim (wardens) were Haim Garfunkel and his son Shlomo Garfunkel, Shimon Weiss and Shmuel Wagner. For years the prayer leader was Israel Glazer, the grandfather of Dr. Zvi Heller a Zionist activist and a delegate to the Polish Sejm. Other worshipers were the mohel Moshe Zechariah Goldberg, the family of Abraham Apfelgreen and Fishel Shenbach.

The Synagogue of Wolf Ber

Was built in the form of a Greek letter, and was therefore known as "die Yevonische Kloiz". The congregation consisted of well-to-do householders, who followed the Sephardic usage (like the Hassidim). An outstanding member of the congregation was rabbi Shlomo Finger, who was warden and also acted as cantor during the High Holidays.

A special tradition was observed in this synagogue to pray without tallit on Yom Kippur eve. This was based on a legend by which a rabbi Leib Saras prayed there on Yom Kippur eve on his way to see Emperor Joseph. All worshipers wore tallitot when suddenly there was great crowding in the room because the dead came to pray as well. Rabbi Saras told the worshipers to remove their tallitot for relief, and that is how this custom came into being.

The Synagogue of the Boyanov Hassidim (Boyanover Kloiz)

The outstanding members of the congregation were rabbi Shammai Gertner, David Ornstein (slaughterer), Shlomo Seif (slaughterer), Leiser and Shlomo Mihlrad.

There were additional houses of prayer (Kloiz) and minyans in our town such as the Kloiz of the Chortkiv Hasidim (also known as "Die Patikker Kloiz"), the Gelle Kloiz where Shmuel Klein was the gabbai, the Kloiz of Moshe Zechariah established by the grandfather of Haim Schiff and Moshe Zechariah Goldberg.

The various minyanim or small prayer groups in our town

The minyan of the rabbi Eliezer Ladier;
The minyan of the Rabbi of Mosczick;
The minyan of the Rabbi of Glogow;
The minyan of the Rabbi of Stretin;
The minyan of the Rabbi of Strelisk;
The minyan of Reb Pinhasel;
The minyan of Motel Drucker;
The minyan of Rabbi Horowitz;

[Page 88]

The minyan of rabbi Eliyahu Labin;
The minyan of Israel Yekels;
The minyan of Yad Harutzim Society;
The minyan of "di Lanys";
The minyan of Moshe Kurzer of "di Szymianszczyzny";
The minyan of Yankele Glezer;
The minyan of the tailors;
The minyan of the butchers

The Talmud Torah

Before the First World War the Orthodox Jews of Stryj had established an institution for educating the younger generation in the spirit of the Holy Torah.

The two story building of the Talmud Torah was built in the shape of the Hebrew letter "dalet" in the Jewish Quarter near the Great Synagogue and "Beit Hamidrash".

The inside of the building was in the form of a school house with long corridors and many large class rooms. There, hundreds of children pursued their Jewish studies all the way from the Hebrew alphabet to Talmud, Gmara and commentaries. Children were moved from the dark and small rooms in the homes of the poor teachers and study in rooms filledwith light and air. The initiators of the 1905 (or 1906) institution were rabbi Haim Meyerson, Yekele Ettinger, Eliyahu Zeldovitch, Moshe Kudisch, and Israel Judah Nussenblatt, who were joined by the communal activists rabbi Shmuel Friedler and Haim Kramer.

The most known teachers in the Talmud Torah were: The teacher "Rozler", Eliezer Melamed, Yehoshua "Behelfer" (Assistant). Teachers of Gmara and commentaries were: Eliyahu Meir Pessburg (known as "Flick") and Yossele Lindner (known as "Skipky").

The "Safa Brura" Hebrew School

The national and cultural movement of the 19th and the beginning of the 20th centuries strongly influenced the educated and the Zionists of Stryj who felt the need to provide a Hebrew education and teach the "live" Hebrew language to the children.

The first teachers in Stryj instructed in the Ashkenazi and later in the Sephardi pronunciations giving private lessons or in small gatherings. The first teachers were Axelrod, B. Fuks, a member of the Jewish Defense in Gomel Russia who arrived in 1904, Sapirstein, Hofenbartel, Chotrinsky (who arrived from Russia in 1906), M. Wundermann, M.A. Tennenblatt and Naphtali Siegel.

Hebrew classes were offered even before World War I, creating the foundation for the Hebrew school. Moshe Aaron Wohlmut, a Hebrew scholar and lover of the Torah, was devoted to Hebrew education and the spread of Hebrew culture initiated the idea. The start was in two rooms on Slowacki street where a play in Hebrew called the "Magical Rose" was staged. Abraham Hauptmann, the son of rabbi Isaac Hauptmann (the slaughterer) was the composer and producer and among the students that performed in Hebrew were Miriam (Mania) Hauptmann, Genia Fischel, Sheva Diemenstein.

Following the victory of the Zionist Movement after the First World War, a framework of Hebrew School system was set up all over Poland and the "Safa Brura" school in Stryj became part of it. In 1923, the number of students grew to 300. A decision was made to open a pre-school and kindergarten for 3 – 6 years olds. The first and only teacher was Frieda Byk the granddaughter of Sender Shochet the slaughterer. The teachers' salaries were made comparable to that of public school teachers.

After a few years of growth and thriving came a period of struggle to survive. The number of students declined partly because parents moved their children elsewhere and the kehilla cancelled the financial support for the school. The school board chairperson for the year 1928 was Moshe Spiegel. Baruch Neumann, a lover of Hebrew language was one of the school activists.

Youth Movements Activists of the Keren Kayemet L'Israel (the National Fund)

The orphanage in Stryj (the Bourse) and its management 1934

Doctors of the Jewish Hospital in Stryj 1934 the year 1928 was Moshe Spiegel. Baruch Neumann, a lover of Hebrew language was one of the school activists.

The management of "TOZ" (Jewish public health organization)

[Page 89]

After a few years of relatively steady progress, the school started to decline in spite of the great interest in Eretz Israel by the people of Stryj. Only the dedication of the teachers M. Helfgott, Shapira and Haim David Kom kept the school opened. In 1937 the school underwent administrative and pedagogical changes to improve the education standards. A new board was elected with Dr. S. Wandel as chair, Dr. Brauner as vice chair, Mrs. Roth the secretary and treasurer Apfelgreen.

The changes were approved by the "Tarbut" center in Lviv and had a positive impact. The school moved to a new location and thanks to the efforts of a group of dedicated and accredited teachers the number of enrolled student grew.

That was the "golden age" of the school in all of its forty years. The school was a source of pride and a symbol of the national revival which was destroyed in the holocaust.

[Page 89]

The Ivriya Society
by Dr. Nathan Kudish
Translated by Susan Rosin

At the house of the grocer Benjamin Stern locatd in the "Rynek" (the square plaza surrounded by houses) a sign on one of the doors read: "The Ivriya Society".

On both sides of the room were two long tables and a shorter table at one end of the room designated for the society's chair and the lecturers. The walls were covered with photos of Herzl, Ahad Ha'am (the pen name of Asher Zvi Hirsch Ginsberg - literally "one of the people"), and other leaders of the national revival. There was a book case with the sign "The library". The first impression might have been of a prayer room or a minyan, but the books were in the "Holy Language" and this was the first Hebrew library in Stryj.

Young people who came to borrow books or for a Hebrew conversation were the most frequent visitors. The idea of the revival of the Hebrew language was spreading and brought many to the modest room of the "Ivriya" society.

They came from many different backgrounds and levels of society: The young "Hashomer Hatzair" girl who came to borrow a book or the girl from an orthodox family would borrow a book and read it secretly away from the watchful eye of her fanatic father or a young man, a member of the Hehalutz movement seeking tutoring in the Hebrew language. From time to time, some of the Beit Hamidrash students would stop by with great hesitation, borrow a book, listen to a lecture and leave without drawing attention. They were still attending Beit Hamidrash, studying the Gmara, but secretly reading Abraham

Mapu, Peretz Smolenskin, Ahad Ha'am, Haim Nachman Bialik, and others. High school and college students attending state schools, but longing for the beauty of the bible and the new Hebrew literature, trying to combine Judaism and humanism.

Some young scholars were among those frequenting the society. During the day they attended to their businesses without much enthusiasm as they were yearning for the world of the new literature and the beautiful sounds of Hebrew that was hears on the streets of Stryj. The intellectuals as well as the young scholars became the driving forces of the society.

All of them helped establish the revival of the Hebrew language in the twenties. Those were the years after the end of the World War I after the foundation was laid for the building of Israel and the start of the third Aliyah. The national awakening was wide spread in Poland and many young people left for Israel. The spiritual expression of this movement was the renewed Hebrew language.

[Page 90]

Although there were many disagreements between the various political parties, the efforts to revive the Hebrew language united them all.

The original founders of the "Ivriya" society were Jewish intellectuals, many among them were graduates of the Batei HaMidrash. The winds of the enlightenment made them look outside of the Beit Hamidrash and into the Hebrew culture. Some even went as far as leaving Judaism altogether, but most remained true to their heritage and established this non-political, quiet and modest society which contributed so much to the revival of the Hebrew language. Their efforts must be remembered in this Stryj Yizkor book.

The "Ivriya" society in Stryj was established in 1910 by Dr. Zvi Diesendruk and Haim David Korn. At that time, only few were familiar with the spoken Hebrew. World War I destroyed those humble beginnings. The Balfour declaration in 1917 awakened many hopes in the Jewish communities everywhere and the national revival activists started organizing.

On a cold January 5th, 1918 Saturday night, 35 young men and women gathered at the "HaShomrim" room with the goal to establish a society to spread the Hebrew language. The meeting was the idea of a young intellectual, Naphtali Ziegel who was joined by other enthusiasts: Levi Teitler, Isaac Sturmlauf and others. The name of the new society was "Agudat Haivriya" (The Hebrew Society). The first committee was: Naphtali Ziegel – chair, Levi Teitler – vice chair, Isaac Sturmlauf – secretary, Rachel Altbauer – treasurer, Yocheved Goldberg – librarian, Sarah Neubauer, Ben-David Schwartz, Aryeh Derfler, and Shalom Reich. This first meeting ended in high spirits and the singing of HaTikvah. The members were very active and the society made its mark in Stryj.

Lectures on biblical subjects and the Modern Hebrew literature were given in Hebrew. The Stryj born author Dr. Zvi Diesendruk was an activist for a short while. The society's activists taught Hebrew to members of youth movements. The library was established and parties were organized. The society supported the Hebrew school "Safa Brura". The "Ivriya" society became a magnet to the national-cultural redemption seeking youth.

Throughout the years, idealistic youths, intellectuals and Batei Hamidrash graduates joined the society.

A new committee was elected in 1920 with the teacher Zvi Gelernter as chair. The other members were: Ben-David Schwartz, Dr. Joseph Schuster (Shilo), Yehoshua Oberlander, Dr. Nathan Kudish, , Jonah Friedler, Haim David Korn, Isaac Schorr, Abraham Shwartzberg, Meir Wieseltier, Ben-Zion Garfunkel, Elimelech Frisch, Aryeh Sachar, Joseph Richter, Aharon Weiss, and Esther Zeif.

The new committee expanded the activities of the society to spread the Hebrew language and culture. Among the other notables of the society: Yehoshua Tileman (an author and teacher), Jacob Stark, Naphtali Gelernter, Moshe Meller, Aharon Meller, Moshe Eisenstein, Isaac Zilberschlag (an author and poet), Jacob Zeman, Moshe Steiner, Isaac Nussenblatt, and Pesach Stark.

Guest lecturers included: Abba Hushi, Meir Ya'ari, Dov Sadan (Stock), Dr. Joseph Schuster (Shilo). The last "Ivriya" committee was: Jonah Friedler – chair, Meisels, and Avigdor Rotfeld.

[Page 91]

The dedicated "Ivriya" activists did their work without much fanfare, but the seeds they planted bore splendid fruits. Those who studied Hebrew at the society brought it back to their youth movements. Many of the activists were able to fulfill their dreams and become poets, authors, well known scientists, cultural activists and educators in the diaspora and in Israel.

Not everyone was fortunate enough to see the Hebrew language flourish and the redemption of the Hebrew culture in the state of Israel. They perished in the hands of the Nazi murderers and their helpers.

May their memory be inscribed in the hearts of those from Stryj and kept forever with the lovers of the Hebrew language and culture and all the dreamers of the Hebrew revival.

[Page 91]

A Town and its charm [1]
(Impressions by a visitor)
by Prof. Dov Sadan
Translated by Susan Rosin
Edited by Yocheved Klausner

A.

It seems like there is no evidence to the charm of a town like that of a "memory error"– you know you visited in the fall, but the memories brought back are of a visit during a glorious summer day and you keep imagining instead of remembering. Indeed, the more I think about those few days I spent in Stryj during my first visit, I imagine the town during the heat of Tamuz (the

10th Hebrew month), the market tiles shining in the sunlight, the streets and alleys bright and the whole town relaxed and calm. These differences between the memories and the actual way things were are curious and can probably be only explained by the mood of the visitor and the charm of the town. I cannot deny that my mood probably contributed to these impressions during this first visit – I was young and was asked to go to a distant town to speak publicly before I made a name for myself. At the time my claim to fame were a few unpublished poems and a few translations of Hebrew authors (G. Shoffmann, D. Shimonowitz and M. Ben Eliezer) into Polish that were published in Lviv and two poems in Yiddish that were published in Warsaw. My younger brother Nissan, who graduated from the Merchant Academy and was employed by the renowned firm of Zelig Borak in Stryj introduced me to Joshua Oberlander, one of the Hebrew activists in town. He invited me to come and speak in front of a group. The invitation was issued on the 4th day of Elul 1922 (August 28th, 1922) by the local Zionist council in Stryj signed by the president and the secretary scheduling the lecture date for Sunday, September 3rd, 1922. The topic of the lecture was praise for the writer David Frishman on the 30th day after his passing (the Shloshim). On the road to Stryj I read about the passing of ShaiIsh Hurwitz (Sha'ul Israel Hurwitz), so I decided to include an obituary for him in my lecture as well. Before my lecture, I had the opportunity to get to know some of the young Zionists in town. On Saturday, there was a lecture by a left leaning Poalei Zion visitor, B. Winogura (Yedidia) who attacked the Zionist movement, its organization and especially its leadership. A debate following the lecture included Israel Igra and two pioneers from Russia, Rabinowitz and Joseph Salvan (now Se–Lavan) and I joined in as well. I can no longer remember the arguments of the lecturer except their forcefulness. All I can remember is that the lecturer argued that Dr. Chaim Weizman is only a pawn in the imperialistic plans of England in the middle–east and called him a "politician behind the stove". I acted surprised and argued as to how it was possible that the shrewd and sly Britain with such grandiose plans would only find a "politician behind the stove." That same evening I went to the Halutzim organization – the meeting took place in a hall that was neither a living room or a meeting room. In the center was a long table stained with ink and it had many nicks created by pocket knives. The atmosphere here was so different from the one in the hall of the previous meeting. In spite of the uproar caused by the lecturer, it was still calm and composed, whereas here, in spite of the intimacy there was an air of fury, and a bohemian atmosphere. This was not the style of the town's halutzim but of those that came from across the border and settled here temporarily. They were the "effervescent" material, and I especially remember Sula, which was either his name or his nickname and who was the embodiment of naughtiness.

[Page 92]

The local halutzim were different from those who came from Russia. The locals had their center in Lviv whereas the Russians had their center in Rovna and then in Lviv. The main person there was Yehuda Raznicenko (Erez) who was visiting and lecturing regularly. The Russians were mostly Socialist Zionists whereas the locals belonged mostly to the Hashomer Hatzair or radical democrats. The locals lived with their parents whereas the Russian lived in communes. But these differences actually brought the two groups closer together, with the locals trying to imitate the Russians. Their adventures in Russia in addition to them staying illegally in Poland gave them a bohemian and secular aura (some of them returned to Russia to help smuggle their friends), which became an object of imitation.

I was asked to deliver a lecture whose topic I can no longer recall. What made it difficult was that I felt this group can educate me more than I can educate them. Some of the halutzim were about to emigrate for Israel. I was introduced by Zippora Byk (later Kahana), the young Wald and Rappaport (called the red carpenter).

Only the darkening room allowed me not to meet the eyes of the audience (among them the very beautiful Lea Pickholtz) and not be embarrassed.

B.

In the meantime I met some of the younger and older generations. I met Rabbi Eliezer Ladier after Shabbat services and his appearance was a surprise to me. A rabbi of an orthodox Galician congregation wearing a modern top hat, who spoke fluent German and published his poems in both German and Hebrew. On Sunday, while having breakfast with my brother at a garden restaurant, I saw a person whose face I recalled from postcards and pamphlets. Before I had a chance to introduce myself, he approached me and said: "You are mistaken. I am his brother." Turns out, this was Aaron Bernfeld, whose brother Shimon's face I knew. Our conversation turned to a discussion of the publication "Hamazkir" (the reminder) which he edited some years earlier. I asked if it was not enough that the assimilationist publications "Shomer Israel" and "Agudat Ahim" published articles in foreign language, so that the "Hamazkir" had to be added to the list and in Hebrew. His answer was short: Sir, if you read the "Hamazkir" you would know that all this assimilation was in just one short article that I named October (in Polish). I was concerned that both the rabbi and the author will come to my lecture at the "Ivriya Society". Fortunately I was not aware that Mandachowitz, the author of "Sparkling Mirror" and the grandson of the famous rabbi Ensel Zusmer was in town.

[Page 93]

My anxiety grew as I was concerned that perhaps Dr. Zvi Diesendruck was in town for the high holidays and he might want to come to the lecture as well. In addition there were the Ivriya society members Jacob Zeman and Isaac Silber whose erudition amazed me, and I requested to deliver my lecture in Yiddish. But, immediately I retracted my request not to mock the goals of the

Ivriya. God was on my side. My lecture went very smoothly and now looking at it after all these years I wonder if I could have done it again. I guess youth, its certainties and the lack of doubts must have helped and I received many congratulations of a "job well done".

I must have done well, because I received another letter on January 27th, 1923 signed by Jacob Zeman and Jonah Friedler inviting me to the Bialik assembly (must have been his 50th birthday) and requesting me to talk about "current events that will be the most important portion of the festivities". I would have probably accepted if not for my lengthy bout with polio. In spite of my illness I knew what was happening in the circles of the halutzim and the "Hebrews" through correspondence not only with my brother but also with others in town. From these I knew about the going–away parties for halutzim leaving for Palestine (among the names mentioned were Chaim Yash, Sula, Weinberg, Rabinowitz, Chayka, Dolek, Faiga, Malia), events in town (such as the "Emuna" Hanukkah party and costume parties), a Maccabi evening with the singer Lehrman, amateur theatre performances such as "God, Man and Devil" where my brother played Leiser the jester, as well as "The inheritance" and "Uriel Acosta". Also I knew about the establishment of a "spiritual/intellectual center" by the General Zionists where at the opening among the distinguished guests were three delegates from the Sejm: Einsler, Sommerstein and Eisenstein. But mainly I remember a nice and lovely town whose charm I can still see (years later in Tel Aviv when I reminded one of the town's people the sign: "He who drinks soda water at Wolf's will live a long life" he responded seriously: "Believe me, I am still alive because of this soda water").

As an added benefit I made many friends among the nice young men and women of the town. The more I read about the town and its people the more I recalled the memories of my visits and these lovely memories just grew within me throughout the years.

C.

My father was very friendly in his youth with Abraham Robinson who was an activist of the Zionist movement and later became the secretary of David Wolfsohn and Efraim Frisch from Stryj who came to study in the high school in our town. The high school in my town of Brody was a magnet for students from near and far. It was closed on Saturdays and the instruction language was German. Among its students were Judah Leib Landau from Lviv who later became the chief rabbi of South Africa, Benjamin Wolf Siegel from Zbaraz who later became the editor of "Ost und West" (East and West), Michal Berkowitz from Stryj who became later Herzl's secretary and translated his writings, and last but not least Efraim Frisch from Stryj who became a renown German author (and friend of Micha Josef Berdiczewski and Jakob Klatzkin) and an editor in the famous Fischer publishing house. This group established sort of an "Ivriya" group and with a couple of young ladies produced a Hebrew play "There is Hope". The extent to which Frisch loved Brody can be gleaned from his first novel "Das Verlöbnis" (The betrothal) published in 1902. The descriptions of his home town are intertwined with those of the town of his studies. On the one hand, there is valley scenery of the Bug River and on the other hand a mountain and a slope better describing the Carpathian mountains. There are descriptions where these two sceneries are completely combined. It is possible this was an early experiment in describing an eastern–Galician shtetl done by a Jewish author in a foreign language, something that was later common to authors from that area writing in our two languages. Anyone studying either the romantics or the short stories written by authors from eastern Galicia has to start with the works of this author. He was a bridge to what we read later in the books of Shai Agnon, A.M. Fuchs, Asher Barash, Rachel Korn and Itzik Metzker. A wave of controversy erupted immediately after the publication of his work by A. Stand (was later translated into Hebrew by Dov Sadan), as well as criticism about him in an article by

Tamar Bockshtav–Evyona, a Stryj native, in the "Voskhod" publication. Stryj natives may have a special interest in this novel – since the characters, the scenes, descriptions and the scenery all resemble Stryj.

[Page 94]

D.

My father reminded me that the little romance between myself, a Brody native and the town of Stryj was preceded by a much bigger romance between Efraim Frisch, a Stryj native and Brody before he left for Germany and did all his writing in German. Similarly, Rabbi Eliezer Ladier, a chief rabbi in Stryj wrote poems in German. Whoever would like to find more about Rabbi Ladier should review the excellent article by Rabbi Eliezer Meir Lifshitz. Two small books are in front of me. The first of them is titled: "A sermon for Saturday by rabbi Ladier from the Stryj district" (1933).

[Page 95]

The other was a book of poems: El. Ladier / Gedichte / Verlag Dr. Heinrich Glanz, Wien (1933) and the opening poem has to do with the life of the poet: "I sing as the jailed bird that cannot hear the voices of the forest and cannot see the light, a bird that will not sit on a branch and will not rule the tree top; I sing a song as a jailed bird."

I am glancing from book to book and am having a hard time believing that it was the same hand that wrote both. On the one hand a serious discussion of religious matters and on the other the lyric poetry. How could these two worlds not collide within him? Perhaps he himself gave an explanation to this conflict in his poem "Memories of My Childhood," which is based on a mystical legend that he heard from his mother, which weaved in his mind dreams of gold during Saturday at dusk and he could hear his grandfather singing during the meal and his mother's voice that was as pure as silver. It seemed as if the Rabbi/Poet exposed his secret and showed us his torn soul between his mother's legend that brought–up his poetic side and the scolding of his grandfather that brought–up his religious law side. And the two cannot merge.

E.

I visited Stryj one more time with the outstanding person, the father of the halutzim Dr. Henrik Sterner, to deal with two important matters and did not get to look around town. The first matter was to complete the negotiation with Mr. Klein regarding the workshops and the second was the Aliya of some brave women pioneers – Rachel Meller, Ratza Rosenberg, Rivka Reinherz and Rivka Feldhorn. These women struggled to get immigration permits not by fictitious marriages, but on their own accord. At the end they were successful and their struggle opened the way for the 4th Aliya.

From Mr. Klein I learnt that Stryj had a long history of practical Zionism. In the 1890's the Admat Israel (the "land of Israel") association sent a special emissary, Mr. Stern to Eretz Israel to check the settling possibilities. He returned bearing good news, but the plans were cancelled due to his sudden death. Years later I saw a pamphlet describing the activity of Admat Israel: Admath Israel, Selbstverlag des Vereines Admat Israel in Stryj, Druck v. A.H. Zupnik in Drohobycz [self–publication, printed in Drohobycz].

[Page 96]

After the main points of the dispute between them are discussed, the matter of the renewal of Eretz Israel is brought–up.

F.

To end this article, I would like to go back to my first visit in Stryj as I remembered a detail during the 3rd Jewish Studies convention in Jerusalem. It had to do with my discussion with the Hebrew elders in Stryj mulling over the famous saying by Ahad Ha'am: What would have happened if the translation of the bible into Greek would coincide in time with the translation of Plato into Hebrew. Rabbi Isaac Aaron Bernfeld said he would be satisfied with the translation of Philo of Alexandria. Rabbi Eliezer Ladier remarked that under these balanced exchanges, the place of the Jewish people may have been eliminated God forbid. And me, jokingly, I remarked that if I lived during those times I would prefer the translation of Aristophanes. If I was pressured, I am doubtful if I would know a comedy written in Hebrew, although my father had among his books a translation into Hebrew of Lessing's comedy "Der Freigeist" by Dan Kohn. Dan Kohn's daughter married Reuven–Asher Broides. But, I could not have imagined that two Stryj natives will translate into Hebrew two Greek works: Plato – translated by Zvi Diesendruk and Aristophanes – translated by Isaac Silberschlag.

Jerusalem, Hanukah 1962

Editor's Footnote

For editorial reasons, direct quotations from the books mentioned in the article have been omitted.

The Students' Organizations in Stryj
by Naphtali Teller, atty.
Translated by Susan Rosin

Since the beginning of the 20th century the Jews in Stryj started sending their children to high–schools and universities, just like Jews in other big cities in Galicia. The large number of boys and girls who were studying in the high schools and universities were instrumental and a major factor in establishing the public and national life of Stryj's Jewry.

Important and renowned figures in the Zionist movement such as Dr. Gershon Zipper, Senator Michael Ringel, Dr. Abraham Insler and Dr. Emil Schmorak were previously students in the high schools of Stryj. While in (the Polish) high schools they were also active in the Zionist circles, activity that was banned by the Polish authorities. They later became leaders of the revival movement.

After World War I and following the Balfour declaration, the Zionist ideas started spreading among the youth studying in high schools and universities in Galicia. Most of the high school students joined "Hashomer Hatzair" (the young guard/watchman) and the universities students joined "Emuna" (faith).

Many of these youths discontinued their studies during the years of the third Aliya (1928 – 1925), emigrated as halutzim (pioneers) to Eretz Israel, and many of them became members of kibbutzim.

In addition to "Emuna" other academic societies were established after the First World War: Hebronia, Kadima, Maccabia and Z.A.S.S (Zionist Socialist Student Association). Most of the Jewish young people who had higher education belonged to one of these organizations.

A group of Betar and Revisionist pioneers (1931):

Standing right to left: I. Pickholz, Geller, Manfeld, H. Zoldan, M. Kaz

Seated: Sishel, Millard, I. Waldman, D. Zeidman, S. Gartenberg, I. Gartenberg

"Ivriya Society" Committee:

Seated from right to left: Hendel, Aron Weiss (Tzahor), Jonah Friedler , Dr. Joseph Schuster (Shilo), Jonah Gelernter, Joshua Tileman, Joseph Richter;

Standing from right to left: Jacob Stark, Naphtali Gelernter, Isaac Schorr, Ben–David Schwartz, Dr. Nathan Kudisch, Joshua Oberländer, Aryeh Sachar

Leadership of the Zionist Labor Party "Hitahdut" 1925:

Seated from right to left: Eisenstein, David Weiss, Leib Schwamer, David Zeidman, Elimelech Frisch, I. Gertner, and L. Garfunkel

Standing: Avigdor Rotfeld, M. Patrach, Robinson, David Tadanir, Mordechai Klar, I. Fruchter, Ben–Zion Garfunkel

WIZO (Women's International Zionist Organization) Circle:

Seated right to left: Mishal, Eisenberg, Kaufman, Rachel Katz, Seinfeld

Second Row: Lerer, Sapir, Zoldan, Knoler, Krebs, Lautman, Wolfinger

Third Row: Gelert, Apfelgreen, Arnold, Osteryung, Erhrlich, Apfelgreen, Hendel

[Page 97]

Due to the close proximity of the universities of Lvov and the economic situation, most of the students lived at home with their parents in Stryj and commuted to school. That was the reason so many students attending higher education institutions were always in town which allowed the activities in the academic societies. Except for "Emuna" the other societies were more like the Viennese "Kadima" whose member was Dr. Herzl.

The Jewish students' societies in Stryj admitted also female students and thus were different from the ones in Western Europe who admitted only men.

It is worth noting that each society had a "junior society" for high–school students from age 12 and on. These youngsters received Zionist instructions by the older university students which included Hebrew language, Jewish and Zionist history and geography. The older students organized parties with lectures and discussions.

An important part of the academic societies' activities was dedicated to developing discipline, the feeling of national pride, brotherhood, mutual assistance, respect for elders, taking care of the younger members, sports, fencing, etc. All these activities were to strengthen the youngsters physically and mentally. When the Anti–Semitic riots broke–out at the universities, these students were ready with a counter attack and protected their brothers' and sisters' honor.

Stryj did not have anti–Zionist academic societies, a fact that can be attributed to the efforts for national education.

The academic societies in Stryj were in close contact with societies in Lvov, Krakow, Warsaw and the El–Al society at the university in Jerusalem. The first world convention of the academic societies took place in Vienna and the Stryj societies were represented.

The members of the societies were active in all the public and Zionist organizations in town such as the Jewish National Fund (KK"L), Foundation Fund (Keren Hayesod), and "Hehalutz" organization. After 1933, the members were at the ready to protect the Jewish population against the provocations by the Polish Anti-Semitic groups and were active in organizing the ban on German products.

The societies were mostly apolitical, although the members themselves belonged to various political parties. The distribution of immigration certificates by political parties made it necessary to be organized more along party lines. And thus Z.A.S.S (Zionist Socialist Student Association) and H.A.Z (Academic Zionist Organization) were established.

The Academic Society "Emuna"
by Arie Hobel
Translated by Susan Rosin

The "Veritas" society was established in 1903 with the awakening of the national awareness at the end of the 19th century. The founders were Dr. Michael Ringel, Dr. Abraham Insler, Dr. Rosenzweig, the writer Mark Scherlag, and Dr. Norbert Schiff.

A few years later, the name of the society was changed to "Emuna" based on the prayer verse: "I faithfully believe ..." ("emuna" is faith in Hebrew). The members fully believed in the immortal values of the Jewish Nationalism, the revival of the Jewish nation and the glory of Israel.

"Emuna" was the first society to attract the academic youth and the high school students and the members were from all political streams "Hashomer Hatzair", "Poalei Zion", "General Zionists", "Hitahdut", "Revisionists" and others. The society had wide spread effect on the life of Stryj's Jewish community both the orthodox and the secular due to the various areas of activity such as education, cultural and national. The activities lasted all day and continued well into the night. The members participated in all public and political activities in town (Town hall elections and Kehila activities) and the country (election for the Polish Sejm) in addition to all the Zionist organizations and institutions. The society became an academic corporation in 1926 – 1927. The society's emblem was a shield with (three) stripes in blue, white and yellow on which the Star of David, surrounded by seven stars was embedded. As was the custom, the members referred to each other as brothers and sisters. The corporation was headed by a Senior, three co–Seniors, librarian, treasurer and various committees. High school graduates were accepted to the society in festive ceremonies. Members meetings and conventions were held in the various circles, but for important matters the entire membership of the corporations gathered. The presidents of the society were: Senator Michael Ringel, Dr. Abraham Insler who was a representative to the Polish Sejm, Dr. Mishel, Dr. Norbert Schiff, Dr. Morclechai Kaufman, Dr. I. Reich, Magister K. Einhorn, Mgr. Selinger, Mgr. Ingber and others. For many years seniors and co–seniors were: Mark Hurwitz, Leon Sternberg, Isaac Feller, Israel Weidenfeld, Joseph Ehrman, Shmuel Spiegel, Moshe Nagler, Judah Wiesenfeld, Leon Hubel, Henryk Wolfinger, Lila Grossmann, Minna Marbach, Frieda Reich, Lucia Bermann, Leib Pilz, Adolf Zehngebot, Asher Zehngebot, Otto Friedlander, Jacob Friedlander, Rena Lindner, Aaron Hoffmann, Reuben Hoffmann, David Hubel, Abraham and Shmuel Marbach, Isaac Nussenblatt, Meir Borer, Joseph Friedlander. Honorary members of the society were: Ze'ev Jabotinsky, Dr. K. Sommerstein, Dr. Rosmarin, Dr. Leon Reich, Senator Dr. Michael Ringel, Dr. Norbert Schiff, and Dr. Tzelermayer (from the Lvov "Emuna").

[Page 98]

"Kadima"
by Mark Wieseltier
Translated by Susan Rosin

The number of Jewish students in the universities increased between the two world wars. Many Jewish academic societies were established and although in general they were in the format of the European corporations their members were brought up and educated on Zionist and national revival values and were very idealistic. This was the golden age for the Jewish youth of higher education in Poland.

In spite of spending twelve years in a Polish high school, the students were not absorbed in the gentile environment. The atmosphere of discrimination against the Jewish national and human rights by the various anti–Semitic Polish governments and the aspirations for redemption and freedom were the motives for establishing "Kadima" in our town.

"Kadima" was founded in 1922, and its membership increased from year to year. The "seniors", "co–seniors" and "fuchs majors" taught and guided the younger members and prepared them for the future with such activities as lectures, songs, physical training in order to deepen the national and Zionist awareness.

"Kadima" participated in all the Zionist activities in our town and had a deep belief in the revival and our bright future in Eretz Israel.

Unfortunately many of those who dreamed and worked so hard to realize the Zionist vision did not live to see splendor of Israel's revival. For them we feel great sadness and deep pain.

Special mention should be made of the active members of the society who were martyred, and also those who were saved and have survived. Kadima's Seniors were Dunek Sander, Bernard Baumann, Srulik Kudisch, Wolff Koppel, Juzek Ber, Filko Redler. Co–senior M. Lerik (Lerikstein). The "Fuchs majors" were Juzek Ekert, Mark Wieseltier, Dr. Hugo Bonum, and Henek Hammermann.

[Page 99]

In 1937 "Kadima" merged with the general Zionist section of "Hebronia" to create a new corporation the "Maccabiah". The seniors were: Norbert Teller, Filco Radler, Salek Hendel, Mark Wieseltier and Dunek Hazelnuss.

The destruction of Jewish Stryj put an end to the "Maccabiah" society as well.

The Academic Society "Hebronia"
by Mgr. Meir Borer
Translated by Susan Rosin

The number of Jewish students from Stryj that attended high-schools and universities grew in the 1930s and there was a need for organizational framework for their activities. Long-standing "Emuna" was a model for other organizations. The students were divided in their ideological/political affiliations and that was the background for establishing additional student organizations. All the societies followed the same organizational structure, behavior, traditions and identifying traits and were corporations. Ideologically each of the corporations followed a certain political-Zionist stream. "Hebronia" was established to organize the youth in a Zionist movement, to attract those who were on their way to assimilation to join the struggle for national recognition and rights and the right to our own country, instilling national pride and, educating the youth in history of the Jews and Zionism.

During the initial period of 1925 – 1929 many high-school students joined the society in spite of the threat of expulsion from school, as belonging to a Jewish youth organization was prohibited by the authorities. The members spread the Zionist ideology among the students and were active in Jewish institutions such as the Jewish National Fund, WIZO, etc. The active members during this period were: Joseph Friedlander, First Senior, Joshua Hazelnuss, Secretary and "Fuchs major", Ephraim Fromm, Emmanuel Zoldan, Alexander Zoldan, Meir Borer, co–Senior, Klemens Lustig (the last two immigrated to Israel). The most active and inspirational member was Joshua Hazelnuss who worked tirelessly to realize the Zionist dream. He discontinued his medical studies at the Prague University, immigrated to Israel and died here at an early age in 1958.

Due to the large number of girls in the society another chapter was established and the active members were: Clara Bleiberg, Mina Wechsler, Henia Nagler, Malka Rudik, Rosa Neumann, Rosa Lentz, and Genia Gerstmann, (the last four immigrated to Israel).

During 1929 – 1933 the society thrived. The students graduated from high schools and enrolled in universities. The central figures during this period were: Joshua Hazelnuss, Shalom Goldberg, Michael Garfunkel, Karol Einhorn, Isaac Nussenblatt (who immigrated to Israel), Leon Arnold and Moshe Steiner. During this period of time, ties with other ideologically close societies in town were tightened. The members were active in all the Kehila institutions, elections for city council and the Polish Sejm. The members were especially active in organizing the ban on German products before the war.

Among the most important guests to visit the society were such Zionist leaders as Ze'ev Jabotinsky, Yitzhak Gruenbaum, Meir Grossman and Emil Sommerstein.

During 1933 – 1939 following the struggle in the Zionist organizations and Jabotinsky's quitting the mainstream Zionist organization, the society split into revisionist "Hebronia" and General Zionists "Hebronia", the latter merged with the "Kadima" society to form "Maccabiah". The two Teller brothers were the leaders of the two societies.

[Page 100]

Academic Socialist Zionist Society – Z.A.S.S.
Translated by Susan Rosin

The influence of the labor movement and the workers' organization (Histadrut) in Eretz Israel increased in the 30th among the studying youth in the diaspora. Many of the more socialist and the liberal leaning students did not feel they fit into the general Zionist and revisionist societies. They saw themselves closer to the labor movement and identified with the ideology of the Poalei Eretz Israel party.

That was the background for the founding for an academic socialist Zionist Society within the framework of the "Hitahdut" party. In 1931 the Z.A.S.S was established in Stryj by Dr. Azriel Eisenstein, Dr. Ada Bar-Lev (Klein), and Dr. Moshe Bar-Lev-Reinhartz.

The active members of the society were: Dr. Azriel Eisenstein, Dr. Ada Bar-Lev (in Israel), Dr. Moshe Bar-Lev (in Israel), Klara Zeidman, Henek Mager, Zvi Wohlmut (in Israel), Loncia Wolf-Rotfeld (in Israel), Moshe Hauptmann (in Israel), Liora Meltzer-Hauptmann (in Israel), Anda Buchman, Jacob Rosler, Mundek Pritzhand, Milek Weisbart (in Israel), Salka Wohlmann, Ruzka Neimann (in Israel), Belka Fogel, Regina Goldman, Rosenzweig, and Mania Polack-Tadanir (in Israel).

Friends of the Hebrew University Society

The local institutions of the Jewish national spiritual revival included the Friends of the Hebrew University in Jerusalem Society. Dr. Lechman from the Hebrew university participated in the opening ceremonies of the society.

The society was headed by Dr. Z. Presser, Dr. Shitzer and Zvi Wohlmut. It should be noted that Stryj was the first provincial city in Galicia to establish such a society and its activities were very successful.

Toynbee Hall

A branch of the Education Movement that spread culture and knowledge in lecture halls known as "Toynbee Hall" was active in our town and was located in the Zionist Casino. It served as a center for the dissemination of national education, Zionist theory, Jewish and Eretz Israel knowledge. Training courses also took place at the same location.

Dr. Byk was the founder of "Toynbee Hall" and the first president of the national council in 1918.

The Amateur Theatre

The cultural revival of the Hebrew and Yiddish languages reached its peak at the beginning of the twentieth century. Yiddish playwrights were very popular. Dramatic groups of young men and women, lovers of the Yiddish Theatre, were set up in every large and small town in Poland and Russia.

The dramatic group in Stryj was founded in 1907 by Aaron Hauptmann, the son of rabbi Isaac (Shohet) Hauptmann who was also the producer of the plays that were staged by the original group. The amateur actors were: Mordechai Wagner, Adler, Eliyahu Hauptmann, Shimon Eckstein (in Belgium), Hannah Leibowitz, Etka Wagner, Salka Sperling, Chippe Wundermann, Salek Waldman-Schwalb, Haya Behr (Tennenblatt). The stage design artist was Berl (Dov) Stern and the stage prompter was Moshe Katz.

The program was based almost exclusively on plays by Jacob Gordin: "Got, Mentsh un Tayvl" (God, Man, and Devil), "Khasye di yetoyme" (Khasye the orphan) and others.

The First World War interrupted the circle's activities, which were renewed in 1917 when new members joined: Miriam (Mania) Hauptmann-Bertshnider (in Israel), Salka Leibowitz, Rachel Altshuler, Tinka Rosenkranz (Monderer), Mania Igra (in Israel), Monderer, Seidenfrau, Buszko Apfelgreen, Dr. Meller (in Israel), Dr. Liebsman, Dr. Singer. The producers were Professor Max Bienenstock and his wife.

[Page 101]

Beit Ha'am
Translated by Susan Rosin

Beit Ha'am (Community Center; literally translated: People's Home) was set-up in 1930. During the founding meeting, Dr. Presser discussed the report prepared by the committee and the rules and regulations of the Beit Ha'am society. Members of the first committee were: Tzeler, Apfelgreen, Diamant, the pharmacist Kindler, Dr. Kohn, Kreisberg, Klueger, Haim Meyersohn, M. Spiegel, S. Stern, Weinreb, and Wohlmut.

The philanthropist Adolf Auerbach donated a plot of land on the corner of Slowacki and Czernicki streets to the society and it was decided to house the offices of the Kehila, the merchants union and the library and reading hall in this building.

The Orphanage
Translated by Susan Rosin

One of the aid and charitable institutions which Stryj Jewry established was the handsome Orphanage. The beginning of this undertaking was a Beit Machse (Home) for poor Jewish students that came from the small surrounding towns and villages to attend the high schools in Stryj. A committee headed by Dr. Philip Fruchtmann (he was one of the most influential personalities in that period and a delegate to the Austrian parliament) was established for this purpose in 1908. The building project was started in 1910 and was completed in 1913 and was financed by donations and housed 30 students.

In 1917, the building was turned into an orphanage and was headed by Dr. Rappaport, Professor Spaet, and Zalman Steiner. In the first few years following the war and until 1923, the home was supported by the Joint. The Stryj Jewish community had to assume the responsibility for the orphans.

Dr. Fichner, one of the founders of the orphanage, a philanthropist whose efforts were channeled to the orphanage passed away in 1929. Following his death a new committee was elected with Professor Resport as the chair person.

The orphanage was moved to a new, more spacious building which was the pride of Stryj's Jewry. Following Professor Resport's tenure, the orphanage was headed by the teacher Tauber, his deputy Mondschein and the secretary A. Lautman.

Due to the difficult economic conditions of Stryj's Jews, the donations to the orphanage dwindled, and the city hall allowance was cut by 50%. However, the Kehila still paid the committed amount. Due to the dedication of the staff, working under very difficult conditions, there was no deficit. Dr. Rappaport and Mr. Weissglass were the heads of this institution during the last years of its existence. 80% of the budget was spent on clothing, food and tuition for those children enrolled in the high schools. The remaining 20% were used to pay the mortgage on the building.

The Jewish Hospital
Translated by Susan Rosin

Across the street from the Great Synagogue on the south side of the square was a rectangular one story building surrounded by a garden that housed the Jewish hospital. Near the entrance were two rooms -one for the physician and one for the management. Along the hallway were the patients' rooms.

This institution symbolized the brotherly love, mutual assistance and mercy feelings of Stryj's Jewry.

The hospital was one of the more important social institutions of the community, helping those Jews who required public health assistance.

The Hospital began as a "Hekdesh" a poor house that was used as a shelter for poor travelers, the homeless and used for hospitalization for those without means. The "Hekdesh" was going through a difficult period at the end of the 19th century and was about to shut-down.

Only very few Jews went to the municipal hospital. Therefore Moshe Stern, the vice-Mayor, Michael Auerbach, Joseph Horowitz, Isaac Sheinfeld, and Dov Pollack appealed to the city to receive a budget equal to the expense for a Jewish patient if accepted at the municipal hospital. Their efforts were successful to strengthen the hospital. The Kehila paid for Jewish patients from outside of Stryj. A council was established to strengthen and remodel the hospital. The members were: Rabbi Haim Mayersohn, rabbi Isaac Hauptmann (the slaughterer), Isaac Sheinfeld, Moshe Zechariah Goldberg. The first physicians who worked at the hospital until 1911 without pay were, Dr. Kiczales and Dr. Lippel.

During the First World War and a few years after, a period of political and social crises and unrest, revolutions and changing authorities, the hospital was closed.

The hospital reopened in 1921. The Jewish population preferred to maintain their own hospital with donations although it was not as well equipped as the government hospital due to the anti-Semitism there. A clinic was always opened next to the hospital staffed by volunteer Jewish doctors who treated the poor. We should mention the doctors who worked there: Dr. Brauner, Dr. Lucia Bienenstock, Dr. Koenig, Dr. Schleiffer, Dr. Shnitzer, Dr. Malka Leibowitz and Dr. Ada Klein. Eliyahu Waldman was the hospital's secretary from 1929 until its liquidation during the holocaust.

[Page 102]

"Yad Harutzim", the craftsmen union contributed an ambulance in 1938. In the last few years before the holocaust, the hospital capacity increased to 60 beds and was instrumental in providing healthcare to Stryj's Jewry. A major improvement in 1939 added a well-equipped delivery room donated by Dr. Brauner in memory of his father rabbi David Brauner.

A class of 25 female nurses and 3 male nurses graduated a month before the start of the war. The ceremony was attended by government representatives, the mayor, the Kehila representative and the hospital's leadership of Dr. Schiff and B. Diamant.

The growing anti-Semitic sentiments before the war caused Jewish populations everywhere to try and develop their own institutions to the extent it was allowed by the authorities.

The hospital, which served loyally the Stryj community, was destroyed in the Shoah. Some of the doctors committed suicide by swallowing cyanide during the last aktion, thus breathing their last breath in purity.

TOZ
(The Jewish Health Organization)
Translated by Susan Rosin

In addition to the efforts by the Jewish hospital in the field of public health, the local branch of the Jewish Health Society "TOZ" made a major contribution, especially concentrating on the health of Jewish children and their proper nutrition. They organized camps out of town. In 1937, 94 children attended the TOZ camps. The active figures of TOZ were Dr. Malka Leibowitz and Dr. Begleiter who visited the camps without receiving any pay.

The Jewish Vocational School
Translated by Susan Rosin

In 1919 the Joint founded a workshop for Jewish youth. The purpose was to train Jewish youth as craftsmen and tradesmen who can support themselves and their families and to prepare them as halutzim – immigrating to Eretz Israel.

When the school opened there were four departments: carpentry, ironwork, lathework and mechanics with up-to-date machines donated by the Joint Distribution committee. Three years later, a dormitory was opened for students from the outlying small towns and villages. The first principal of the school was Dr. M. Kaufman.

In 1922, Mr. Leib Horowitz donated two houses for the school in the name of the Horowitz family. In 1926, the school became accredited by the education ministry of the Polish government as a vocational school.

After the official accreditation, a committee was elected headed by Dr. Schindler and Dr. Schiff.

In 1927, only two departments were operational – ironwork and lathework and the number of students was 32. The income for school operations came from selling the products and aid from Jewish help organizations. JDC budgeted 5,700 zloty, the city 1,000 zloty, the Kehila 800 zloty and Dr. Schindler donated 1,500 zloty from his own money. The property of the school was estimated at 120,000 zloty.

The curriculum was both theoretical and practical. The tuition was 30 – 60 zloty per month. The dormitory housed 20 students. The Joint provided two state-of-the-art machines that were estimated at $1,500. A new committee was elected with: Dr. Schindler – chair, Dr. M. Kaufman, Sommerfeld, A. Levin, Shimshon Steiner, Dr. Hausmann and B. Diamant.

The graduates of the first class passed the government exams in Lvov and found employment. The employers praised their knowledge and professionalism. The yearly JDC report stated that the school operated successfully.

In 1931 at the school committee meeting, Dr. Schindler and Mr. Schwargold reported on the school status. It was estimated that the cost per student was 650 zloty per year. All students passed successfully the government exams and all budgetary commitments were received.

[Page 103]

The school went through a tremendous growth as shown by the 1939 report. The number of students grew to 85. New machines and instruments were added. The school employed 13 full time teachers and 4 foremen under the supervision of the engineer Neustein. The head of the school support society continued to be Dr. Schindler.

Throughout its existence the school trained hundreds of students and many of them immigrated to Eretz Israel to join the builders of the homeland.

With the destruction of Jewish Stryj came also an end to this institution that symbolized the dreams of parents to bring-up their children to be productive members of society.

The Soup Kitchen
Translated by Susan Rosin

As another expression of the Jewish compassion and concern for the poor, a teahouse was opened at the end of the 19th century to help the Jewish (and also non-Jewish) peddlers during the cold days of winter. For one "kreutzer", they could get a cup of hot tea and a large roll. For a long time, the teahouse was housed in rabbi Rafael Wynn's home and was supported by the Kehila and the city. The teahouse was opened from the beginning of fall until Pesach. This meagre meal helped many families who might have suffered starvation otherwise. The teahouse was the initiative of the charitable Mrs. Mahla Katz and rabbi Hirsch Etinger, the son of rabbi Isaac Etinger from Lvov.

In 1932, after years that the teahouse was not in operation, a soup kitchen was opened to meet the new and growing demands. The numbers of Jews who needed public relief due to the financial crisis/depression grew. As a result, the Jewish representatives demanded that the city assist in opening a kosher soup kitchen for the city's poor and the unemployed. At the beginning, the soup kitchen provided 200 meals every day.

Due to the increasing unemployment, the number of meals was increased to 250 per day. Both the city and the Kehila increased their contributions to meet the increaseing needs. The head of the soup kitchen committee, Professor Seinfeld, worked tirelessly to continue and maintain this important institution.

Ezrat Nashim
(Women's help organization)
Translated by Susan Rosin

This organization was founded in the 1880th. The charitable and the kind-hearts of the Jewish women in Stryj found expression in this society whose mission was to pay rents for 6 months for the needy, so that the landlords could pay the mortgages. This assistance was needed in Stryj more than in other towns because many houses were built after the great fire of 1886.

The organization provided medical services for the sick, and sometimes sent them to convalescent centers. Aid was given in secret so as not to affect the credit status of those who were helped. Members took turns in spending the night in the homes of the sick taking care of them. They also paid for doctor visits.

The organization was funded by member donations and budgeted allocations from the city and the Kehila.

The head of the organization for many years was the wife of rabbi Levi Ish-Hurwitz. Malka, the wife of Moshe Goldberg served after her. Other active members were: Chayczi, the daughter of the religious judge rabbi Yeshaia Jacob, Mira'le, the wife of the religious judge rabbi Abraham, Sobele, wife of the religious judge rabbi Karnele Shenbach, Sarah Hammer, the daughter of rabbi Vavi of Bołszowce, Sarah Schiff, Mahla Katz and Mahla Hurwitz. Many other women from Stryj also participated in this charitable organization. The major duty of the members was spending the night with the sick and taking care of them.

The incidence of disease in the Stryj-Sambor district was very high due to the muddy and turbid ground water. The sanitation conditions were poor due to the crowding, even for the more affluent. Infectious diseases were rampant. Not too many nurses were available and the Jewish hospital took care of the most needy only. Therefore the organization had a tremendous impact on saving lives. The members gained much experience in treating various diseases and were trusted and respected by the Jewish doctors (Dr. Meisels, Dr. Pachenick, Dr. Lip, and Dr. Shechter). Mrs. Mahla Hurwitz, a righteous woman, who was dedicated to caring for the needy donated a house on Potocki street for a public purpose.

[Page 104]

Kreuzer Verein Society
Translated by Susan Rosin

The "Kreuzer Verein" society was named so because of the weekly two Kreuzer donation by each member. The main purpose of the society was to assist women who gave birth by providing diapers, sheets, etc., together with three gulden.

The more affluent families were not receiving this assistance, but instead helped with donations on the occasion of childbirth.

Active members included: Helena Rosenman, Rachel Katz, the wife of the lawyer Dr. Byk, and the wife of the lawyer Dr. Norbert Schiff as well as those who were active in "Ezrat Nashim".

The "Gemilut Hesed" (Benevolence) Fund
Translated by Susan Rosin

The "Gemilut Hesed Fund Charitable institution" was founded in 1927, an institution that is well rooted in the Jewish morality and tradition. The institution was a very important factor in easing the financial difficulties of the needy in every community.

In our town, the fund stood on 18,000 gulden (zloty), with part of it contributed by the Joint. In the first year of operation, 600 interest free loans were provided in sums ranging from 50 to 150 guldens. These loans were instrumental in helping the small merchants, craftsmen and artisans in their struggle to survive.

Under the management of M.A. Wohlmut, the fund grew to 33,000 zloty in 1928 with 80% of the loans paid-back on time.

A new committee was elected in 1929 with Dr. B. Milbauer as chair. The annual report of 1931-1932 showed the major impact of the fund in town. Some of the loans were considered a loss because the borrowers were unable to pay them back even in small installments. The society tried to collect, but without imposing additional financial burden on the borrowers.

Due to the economic crisis of 1933 that impacted mostly the lower strata, a fundraising week was announced to help those in need. People and institutions participated and donated generously: The Kehila, the rabbinate, the Zionist parties, Agudat Israel, the craftsmen society, Yad harutzim, the merchants' society, the civil club, and the Jewish economic society.

The pamphlet in Yiddish, Hebrew and Polish that was published on the 10th anniversary, described the importance of the society in helping those whose economic positions were endangered by the growing anti-Semitic forces. The final years were very difficult economically and the public was called to support the efforts of the fund that was managed by rabbi Moshe Kudisch until the holocaust.

Yad Harutzim Society
Translated by Susan Rosin

Literally translated – "Diligent Hand" Society started in a small minyan (prayer quorum) of artisans in 1908. Davidman, an apartment ovens builder (a special profession due to the Polish climate) was the first head. He was followed by the house-painter I. Klieger. In the course of time the minyan became a vocational society of artisans called "Yad Harutzim".

Abraham Levin, an active member was elected chairman in 1920 with I. Klieger as the vice-chairman. The organization had many branches in Galician towns.

Leaders of Hashomer Hatzair groups

Standing from right to left: Gertler, M. Fishbein, Horshowska, M. Opper, Marzand, Tzila Haas, Joseph Haas, A. Lustig, Hana Fruchter, S. Rosenberg, H. Rappoprt.

Seated from right to left: Wexler, D. Kammerman, Zlata Borer, A. Hauptmann, Hella Borer, S. Rosler, Ruth Rosenberg.

Seated in front row: Rosenberg, L. Lipman, M. Polack, I. Opper.

Activists of Poalei Zion 1919

[Page 105]

Ideologically the society members were close to the national Zionist camp. Socially, the members belonged to the working class and were a "trade union" looking out for the economic interests of the members.

Under Abraham Levin, the society grew to 200 members and many of its members belonged to the Zionist parties and were active in the society as emissaries of the popular Zionist organizations.

In 1931, the society split due to differences of opinions regarding the elections to the Polish Sejm (Parliament). The members who left established a new society called "Ihud Baalei Melacha" (Craftsmen Union). A new assembly hall was dedicated during the opening ceremony and the chairman A. Levin announced that the union will cooperate with the national groups. Moshe Weiss was elected secretary and acted in that capacity until his immigration to Eretz Israel in 1934. Shlomo Schwartz was the vice-chairman.

The union members followed a tradition of helping sick members. Taking turns, the members fulfilled the mitzvah of visiting the sick and spending the night in their homes.

Rabbi Meir Garlenter, the father-in-law of the rabbi of Glogow taught the members the weekly parasha (portion of the Torah), and chapters of the Mishnah. During the high-holidays he led the services. The children of the union members were gathering in the evenings in the union rooms to study Torah.

The "Oseh Tov" Merchants Society
Translated by Susan Rosin

The "Oseh Tov" ("Doing Good") society played an important part in Stryj. The members were the large and mid-size merchants, importers, exporters, wholesalers, owners of warehouses and stores. The main goals of the society were mutual assistance, preserving the position of merchants in town and protecting them from discrimination in taxation and the effects of the growing anti-Semitism in Poland.

The society was established after World War I. A few years after the establishment of the Polish state, the authorities started to increase the taxation on the Jewish merchants to undermine their economic positions. Among the most active members were: Kinder, Eli Hauptmann, Moshe Spiegel, Dr. Schiff, D. Reich, and Benjamin Klein. The 62nd meeting of the society was held in 1939 and it was the last meeting of "Oseh Tov". There was also a minyan called "Oseh Tov" where the members attended services. Of note was also the lending facility called Kasa Zaliczkowa established with a grant from IKA. The fund was managed by Dr. Weisenberg and the assimilators and was almost bankrupt in 1922. Dr. Weisenberg was forced to assemble the 48 most prominent public figures including 12 Zionists. In 1928, after the recovery of the fund, the management was transferred to Dr. Presser.

Committee for the Rescue of German Jews
Translated by Susan Rosin

In 1939 a committee was established to help German Jews of Polish citizenship who were cruelly expelled by the Nazis. The destitute refugees were forced to cross the border and arrived in Stryj where they were helped by the local community. The committee worked with the Kehila and helped a few dozens of refugees.

WIZO
Translated by Susan Rosin

The local Stryj chapter of WIZO (Women's International Zionist Organization) opened in 1929 with the talented and devoted Mrs. Rachel Katz as chairperson. Women from all walks of life joined the chapter and were active in Zionist activities, fundraising for the various funds and causes, educating young girls and spreading knowledge about Eretz Israel, the history of the Jewish people and Hebrew and Jewish literature.

When Mrs. Katz resigned, the chapter fell on hard times and only recovered when she returned with her dedicated assistants Mrs. Rosmarin and Mrs. Kaufman.

In 1938, a new meeting hall, in the house of A. Apflegreen at Rynek 6 was dedicated.

[Page 106]

The Jewish Economic Society
by Mgr. Jacob Waldman
Translated by Susan Rosin

A non-Zionist Jewish Economic society was established in 1935. The society was supported by the Jewish representatives to the Polish Sejm Wiszlitzki and Yager and received active help from the Polish authorities. The society was housed in a narrow alley off Zamkowy street.

The society's goal was to cooperate with those who were unaffiliated with any party and with the Polish authorities and was comprised of a number of local and government officials, some merchants and craftsmen from the Bund and some of the more educated. The society was an artificial creation, had no ideological direction, and enjoyed no support from the local Jewry. Dr. Rappaport, once a member of the Bund, was appointed the head of the society.

Although this society did not represent Stryj's Jewry, the authorities entrusted the community to it.

At that time, the various parties and factions struggled with the issue of selecting a new rabbi after the death of rabbi Eliezer Ladier. In spite of the opposition by most Jews in town, the board appointed rabbi Jolles as chief rabbi of Stryj.

The small budget of the Kehila was barely sufficient to cover the expenses of the religious, health and social institutions. It needs to be noted that in spite of the economic difficulties, the non-Zionist board still supported the pioneers immigrating to Eretz Israel.

The Jewish Economic Society did not rule for long. After the elections, the Kehila came again under the leadership of the Zionist parties, and the society and Agudat Israel were forced into the opposition. The issue of electing a new rabbi remained unresolved and the plans of the new leadership for a financial overhaul discontinued when the red army occupied the city in the fall of 1939. The new authorities disbanded this important institution.

The Jewish Civic Casino
by Mgr. Jacob Waldman
Translated by Susan Rosin

The Casino was a meeting-place for the intellectuals of our town, and it was a club without any political affiliation. The rooms were nicely decorated. The members belonged to different parties - from radical Zionists to members of the Bund and the PPS (Polish Socialist Party). Here meetings, conversations and debates were conducted on current affairs especially during the cold winter months. Dr. Milbauer talked about his trip to Eretz Israel and the 1935 maccabiah. The women spent the evenings, playing cards and the men had conversations around the bar. The beautiful rooms and the good company brought even some liberal Poles to the casino. The Presidents of the Club were Dr. Hoffner, Dr. Brauner, Dr. Weiss and Dr. Schindler. The Club Committee supported the Jewish Orphanage and the Jewish Hospital.

The Jewish Sport in Stryj
by Mgr. Jacob Waldman
Translated by Susan Rosin

The first signs of Jewish sport were seen at the beginning of the 20th century. Herzl's and Nordau's slogans of "Muscular Judaism" (Muskeljudentum), awakened the youth of our town into physical awareness in the atmosphere of the national revival.

Polish and Ukrainian sport societies were established in Galicia with support from national athletic organizations such as the Polish "Sokol". The first soccer teams started playing in the fields.

The Jewish youth in Stryj watched with envy their gentile neighbors and followed the Polish soccer team "Pogoń" and the Ukrainian team "Skala".

Although the public park "Yordan" was set-up for sporting events with the support of wealthy Jewish families such as Borak, Shenfeld and Halpern and with help from the Jewish mayor of Stryj Dr. Falik, Jews were banned from it.

[Page 107]

In spite of the ban, a group of Jewish youth entered the park and "played soccer" without knowing the rules, without a coach and with no suitable gear.

The foundations of Jewish sport in the town were laid by a group of Jewish high school students. The first soccer ball was purchased at Shenfeld's and the training practices were held on a field near the barracks of the 33rd Austrian regiment. Borak's sawmill provided the materials to build the goals. This created much enthusiasm among the youth who found a way to gain strength and expend their energy. The initial training was held without sport shoes or uniforms. The first group called itself "Hasmonea" (Hashmonaim חַשְׁאָמוֹנָאִים) the same name used by the sports club in Lviv. After spending time in practice, the groups could play against "Pogoń" and "Skala".

After much effort in convincing the authorities, the Jewish athletes were given a spot to practice in the "Yordan" park, although it was not suitable for proper games. In time, proper relations between the Polish teams and the Jewish group developed and the groups played in friendly competitions.

The dedication and the enthusiasm of the Jewish athletes finally opened the hearts and pocket books of the Jewish population and with that help the first uniforms were purchased: A white shirt with blue stripes and black shorts.

The announcements about the first game between "Hasmonea" and "Pogoń" created much excitement among the Jewish population in town.

Although the Jewish team lost this first game, it was a deeply moving experience for all, and really accelerated the development of Jewish sport in town. The following competitions brought in many spectators who followed breathlessly the efforts of the athletes in blue and white.

The Jews of Stryj understood that it was their duty to support the Jewish sporting societies in order for them to gain strength and be able to compete. Due to these efforts, Stryj already had two trained teams at the level of B league before World War One in 1914.

Following the high school students who established "Hasmonea" came also youth not attending high school and even some attending cheder. These could be seen kicking balls in various areas in towns such as "Targowica" and "Bentszruwka". We need to note that some great players came out of these efforts, and some were later hired by Polish teams.

The first players were mostly students of the upper grades in high school who became the future doctors and lawyers of Stryj: Dr. Allerhand, Dr. Ende, Dr. Fink, Dr. Frenkel, Shlomo Borak, Dr. Wilhelm Hausmann, Dr. Leon Hausmann, Marceli Fogel, Eigenmachtes and even the two Christian evangelical brothers Manjia.

The "Hasmonea" did not operate in accordance with any rules or regulation and was comprised of a number of teams headed by a "Captain". World War one ended the first chapter of the Jewish sport in Stryj.

HaKoach (Strength) Society

The first Jewish sport society HaKoach was established after World War one. Its first president was Dr. Plesser, who contributed his own money for sports shoes for the entire team. Committee members were: B. Apfelgreen, Shlomo Borak, Mgr. Jacob (Tafko) Waldman, Dr. Berlass, the Brothers Henryk and Isidor Wolowski, Dr. Schutzer, Zussman and others.

The members of the first team were: Zygo Weiss, Shlomo Borak, Dr. Houssmann, P. Feuerstein, Benio Haber, Gottesmann, Graubart, Mundek Gritz, Nolek Apfelgreen and M. Redler.

In 1920 a second soccer team was organized as Hakoach II. The members were: Meniu Halpern, Jacob Wien, Filko Meller, Joseph Ber, Israel (Srulik) Kudisch, Benju Larch, Hochmann, Fruchter, Mannes Fefferbaum, Alexander Weiss, Max Hurwitz, Landes, and Joseph Rap. In addition to soccer, the society members also played, tennis and ping pong, conducted exercises, fencing, etc. The society acquired one of the best tennis courts in town and it was also used by Polish and the Stryj garrison tennis players. In tennis the society had great achievements and the outstanding players were: Maciek Stern, Benczer Rab and Dr. Wilhelm Hausmann. Three referees were appointed from among the society members: Mgr. Jacob Waldman, Isaac Katz and Mannes Halpern and they were asked to participate in important matches of Polish teams. Outstanding players were asked sometimes to join Polish teams and the "Hasmonea" team of Lviv.

[Page 108]

In the winters, the members practiced skiing in the sorrounding mountains. The rooms of the society were used as a gathering place and for parties. All profits were used to enhance Jewish sport life in Stryj, soccer being the main sport. In 1924 the best players of the team Halpern, Fefferbaum and Radler left, and the team deteriorated and ceased to exist shortly afterwards.

Dror (Liberty/Freedom)

Shortly after Hakoach ceased to exist a new society, "Dror" was established. Most of the members were from the general public and youth: Knittel, L. Rotstein, Strassmann, Haber, Moshe Filko, Heiber, Moshe Wilff, Rottstein, Rap, Redler, and Mottek Meller. The society was located in the house of Weintraub on Botorego street. The first president was Nathan Welker, and the Committee included: Gleicher, Hammerschlag, Leah Brand, Sabina Binder, Taub, Berger, Weller, Garfunkel and Monderer.

A few years before the war, another team "Hapoel" was established and played with a team from Eretz Israel.

The decision to have the second Maccabiah games in Eretz Israel (despite official opposition by the British Mandatory government) was received with great enthusiasm in the Jewish world and especially in Poland. A headquarters office was established in Lviv with a branch in Stryj to handle the participation of the Jewish athletes, as many saw it as an opportunity for Aliyah and establishing themselves in Eretz Israel.

Dr. D. Lindenbaum headed the Stryj branch for the maccabiah.

[Page 111]

Personalities and Public Figures

Rabbi Arie Leib HaKohen Heller
Author of "Ketzot Hachoshen" ("Ends of the Breastplate")
Translated by Susan Rosin

Rabbi Arie Leib HaKohen (1745 – 1813) was the third son of rabbi Yosef HaKohen of Kalush (Kałusz) and studied under the outstanding authority Rabbi Meshullam Igra of Tyśmienica. He was the head of the rabbinical court in Rozhniativ (Rożniatów) and then became a renowned teacher in Lvov for a number of years. The famous rabbi Shlomo Yehuda Rappaport (SHY"R) was his son in law.

While the head of the rabbinical court in Rozhniativ he lived in poverty. When the famous rabbi Zalman Margaliot honored him with a visit, rabbi Arie Leib remarked that if the visitor was not such a learned figure he would most likely not stop in to visit him in his humble home.

Rabbi Arie Leib became the chief rabbi of Stryj in 1788 after publishing his work "Ketzot Hachoshen". He served in that position until 1813 and had many outstanding students in town. Among the most famous were rabbi Arie Leib Lipshitz who became the head of the rabbinical court in Vyzhnytsia (Yiddish: וויזשניץ Vizhnitz) and rabbi Asher Enzel Cuzmer.

Rabbi Heller was a prominent critic of the Hasidic movement, but was still admired by the community. His famous works are a testament to his deep knowledge and expertise: 1. Ketzot HaChoshen ("Ends of the Breastplate") (Lvov – Part one: 1788; Part two: 1826) is a halachic work which explains difficult passages in the Shulchan Aruch, "Choshen Mishpat"; 2. Avnei Milluim ("Filling Stones") (Lvov – Part one: 1816; Part two: 1826) is a halachic work which explains difficult passages in the Shulchan Aruch, "Even HaEzer". Both famous works proposed novel ideas by rabbi Heller. The second book was accompanied by a pamphlet "Meshovev Netivot" which was a rebuttal to the rabbi from Lissa (rabbi Lorberbaum) about his criticism of "Ketzot HaChoshen"; 3. Shev Shema'tata, innovations to seven Talmudic methods. With his logical and clear reasoning he had a major impact on the learning methods in yeshivas especially in Lithuania. He passed away in Stryj in 1813.

Rabbi Asher Enzel Cuzmer
Translated by Susan Rosin

After rabbi's Heller passing, his student, rabbi Asher Enzel Cuzmer became the head rabbi of Stryj and served in that position for forty years with a two year interval. He was born in Rozdół. While still a student under rabbi HaKohen Heller he proof read his teacher's work "Avnei Milluim" and then published in 1826 his notes in Żółkiew.

Rabbi Enzel Cuzmer came from a wealthy family and was the son in law of rabbi Yoseph Aher who was the head of the rabbinical court in Przemyśl. Being a wealthy man as well as a renowned scholar he continued in his business and was not paid for his work as a rabbi. He was well respected among the scholars in town and the authorities gave him the title of Kreisrabbiner – District Rabbi. He was instrumental in building the Great Synagogue, a project he supported financially. He passed away on 21st of Nissan 5618 (April 5th, 1858).

M. Falk

The Rabbi of Lissa,

Author of "Havat Da'at" (The Opinion)

Translated by Susan Rosin

Among the 30 plus places of worship and study in our town, there was one small out-of-the-way synagogue located in an alley between Lvovska and Botorego streets. This was a special synagogue, located in one of the most dilapidated homes in the alley and had an air of by gone times. I happened to be there for the first time in 1921 or 1922 when some Kloiz students were establishing a new group for Gmara studies by the name of "Tiferet Bahurim" and they selected this location – the shul of the rabbi of Lissa.

The rabbi of Lissa was one of the most renowned Torah scholars of his time and our town was very proud and fortunate to have him as a rabbi. Rabbi Yaakov son of Yaakov Moshe Lorberbaum, known as the rabbi of Lissa, became the chief rabbi of Stryj in 1930, and passed away on May 25th, 1932 leaving a large family. Among his descendants were the brothers rabbi Yokel and rabbi Mordechai Lorberbaum who were murdered in the holocaust.

[Page 112]

History

Rabbi Lorberbaum was the great-grandson of the Chacham Zvi, Rabbi Zvi Ashkenazi head of the rabbinical court of Lvov and Amsterdam and the grandson of rabbi Nathan Ashkenazi, one of the great scholars of Brod (Boród) and the author of the book "Imrei Noam". His father, rabbi Yaakov Moshe was the head of the rabbinical court in Zborów, but passed away at a young age in 1770 before his son was born. The exact year of his birth is unknown. His mother was the daughter of the famous righteous and wealthy rabbi Elyakum Getz from Lubartów. When he was still young he was taken to the house of his relative, the chief religious judge of Bursztyn rabbi Yosef Teomim (he was the son in law of his uncle Zvi Ashkenazi), who brought him up. When he came of age he was married to the daughter of rabbi Herzl of Stanisławów and started working in the wine business there. From time to time he left the business with his wife and went to study under rabbi Meshullam Igra of Tyśmienica.

While in Stanisławów he started working on his book "Havat Da'at" a commentary on the "Yoreh Deah". When he lost his fortune in a bad business deal, he was forced to take a rabbi position in the small town of Monasterzyska. He became a qualified teacher and after a while he was recommended by rabbi Igra for the position of head of the rabbinical court in Kalush (Kałusz).

Most of his works were written in Kalush. In 1799 he published anonymously in Lviv his work "Havat Da'at". This book was disseminated quickly and in 1805 a second edition was published in Poland, followed by a third edition in Austria.

In 1801 he published his book "Ma'ase Nissim" about the Passover Haggadah which was re–published in 1807. In 1804 he published in Lvov "Imrei Yosher" and in 1809 "Mkor Haim".

At that time, rabbi HaKohen Heller was a rabbi in Stryj and when he published his famous work "Ketzot Hachoshen", rabbi Lorberbaum disagreed with him and published his opposition in "Netivot Hamishpat", which was answered by rabbi HaKohen Heller in a rebuttal pamphlet "Meshovev Netivot".

In spite of their disagreements on halachic matters the two rabbis were friendly and used to visit each other on occasion. When rabbi's HaKohen Heller wife passed away he asked to have a marriage arranged between him and the daughter of rabbi Lorberbaum. When the surprised matchmaker commented on the rivalry between the two, rabbi HaKohen Heller answered that just like in the case of Joseph and Osnat the daughter of Potiphar, if rabbi Lorberbaum "would give me his daughter for a wife he would stop hating me and there would be peace between us".

At the preface of his book "Havat Da'at", rabbi Lorberbaum wrote that he meant only to express an opinion and not to teach Halacha (Jewish law). In spite of the fact that the book was published anonymously, he became famous and respected and was asked to become the rabbi of Lissa (Leszno), a position that was vacant for 19 years since the passing of rabbi David Tebbelle in 1792. At the time of rabbi Tebbelle's passing the community was in serious trouble due to the fire in the Jewish quarter, and they did not have the means to hire a rabbi. The religious court judge, rabbi Tebbelle's son, Zacharia Mendel officiated. Slowly the situation improved and they started considering hiring a rabbi for their town, which always had renowned scholars. They heard about rabbi Lorberbaum, but did not know where he lived. Therefore they asked two of the merchants who were on their way to Brod to ask around. When they found that the famous rabbi lived in Kalush (Kałusz) they offered him the position of chief rabbi in Lissa, which he accepted.

[Page 113]

Shortly after his arrival in town, many became his students, among them rabbi Eliyahu Guttmacher, the tsadik of Graetz (Grodziec), and rabbi Zvi Hirsch Kalisher, both famous for their love of Zion.

Although he was not a Hasid, rabbi Loberbaum vehemently fought against the maskilim, the reformers of the Jewish Enlightenment in Germany along with rabbi Akiva Eiger of Poznan and the "Chatam Sofer", the rabbi of Pressburg (present day Bratislava). In spite of his opposition, the community started to introduce changes that were to his dissatisfaction, and he decided to go back to Kalush in 1822 where he was received with open arms. He brought his entire family from Lissa, established a large synagogue and dedicated himself to study and publishing of his books. In 1823 he published his book "Beit Ya'akov", a commentary on Shulchan Aruch, Even HaEzer. In 1828 he published a prayer book (siddur) "Derech Haim" in Zolkiev (Złoczów).

This prayer book became very popular, and four editions were published in his life time.

He served in Kalush for eight years until a man who felt he was wronged in judgment informed the authorities and the rabbi was forced to leave town.

At that time an invitation was extended to him to come and serve as the chief rabbi of Budapest. On his way there, he stopped in Stryj for the night and to get a travel permit. However, the town's people including rabbi Cuzmer decided to offer him the position of chief rabbi and not let him leave town. In the morning, instead of bringing him the travel documents, they brought him a chief rabbi appointment document and urged him to accept the position. Thus he became the chief rabbi of Stryj in 1830.

The rabbi was very famous in all of Poland, but always acted with humility. It is said that once he needed to pass through the town of Sochaczew (Sochatshev), but did not want a special reception by the town's people. Therefore, he got out of the carriage and started walking through the town. When asked by people if he saw a carriage with the famous rabbi in it he said that he did see a carriage and the people continued walking. He then stopped at a tobacco store, but the store keeper said she cannot sell him any because she had to close to go meet the famous rabbi. And so he was able to slip away with the town's people following him.

His cleverness, sharpness and wittiness were famous.

It was told that once he was travelling on a very cold winter day in a matter related to publishing one his books. He stopped at an inn to rest. At the same time, the shohet from one of the neighboring villages came in to slaughter a cow for the innkeeper. Instead of the warm milk offered to him by the innkeeper, the shohet drank several glasses of brandy and then went out to do his deed. He was followed by the distinguished rabbi who told him that although the cow is destined to be slaughtered his sin is that he did it after drinking four glasses (referring to the Chad Gadia in the Passover Haggadah: The angel of death came, and slew the slaughterer who killed the ox) . The shohet understood his meaning and was very embarrassed, asked for his forgiveness and promised to be careful in the future.

[Page 114]

When he accompanied his grandson (his daughter's son), rabbi Abraham Teomim to become the rabbi of Zborów, his grandfather told him that in order to be a rabbi he needs two qualifications: he needs to know the calendar to always know the date of the new moon and he needs to be able to swallow needles pointed downwards without moaning or complaining.

This is the list of books he saw in print during his lifetime:

1. "Chavat Da'at" commentary on "Yoreh De'ah", nine editions;
2. "Masei Nissim", a commentary on the Passover Haggadah, seven editions;
3. "Imrei Yosher", an inclusive commentary for the Five Megillot;
4. "Mekor Haim", commentary on Shulchan Aruch, Orach Chayim, and Passover traditions;
5. "Netivot HaMishpat" on "Choshen Mishpat", in two parts;
6. "Torat Gittin", innovations on the Talmudic tractate Gittin;
7. "Beit Ya'akov", commentary on Shulchan Aruch, Even HaEzer, and on the Talmudic tractate Ketubot;
8. Prayer book "Derech HaChaim";
9. "Kehillat Ya'akov", a collection of discussions and notes on several legal points in the "Even HaEzer" and Shulchan Aruch.

The following scripts were found and published after his death:

1. "Nachalat Ya'akov" sermons on the Torah Portion, and halachic decisions;
2. "Emet L'Ya'akov" on Talmudic lore (Agaddah – a compendium of rabbinic homilies that incorporates folklore, historical anecdotes, moral exhortations, and practical advice in various spheres, from business to medicine);

3. "Milei D'agaggatah" with sermons and innovations on the Talmudic lore.

He passed away on the 25th day of Iyar 5592 (May 25th, 1832).

His headstone said "Keter Torah" (the crown of Torah) and all his works were listed. The other side indicated how much space should be left around his grave per his instructions.

His will, consisting of twenty nine paragraphs, reflected his moral and spiritual character. The will was fist printed in Warsaw in 1872 together with the will of rabbi Akiva Eiger.

Rabbi Eliyahu Meir Ben Yaakov HaKohen Rosenblum
Translated by Susan Rosin

He was the student and son-in-law of rabbi Asher Enzel Cuzmer and inherited the position after the passing of his father in law with the support of the ultra-orthodox. He avoided the disputes between the orthodox, the maskilim, and the assimilated and devoted himself to the study or Torah and to works of charity. He was the Stryj rabbi for 19 years and passed away on the 28th of Nissan 5657 (April 11th, 1877).

Rabbi Arie Leibish Horowitz
Translated by Susan Rosin

Rabbi Arie Leibish Horowitz was born on the 15th of Av 5607 (July 28th, 1847). In his youth he studied Torah with his father rabbi Isaac and his grandfather rabbi Meshulam Issachar.

At the age of eighteen he married the daughter of the wealthy rabbi Moshe Wax from Seret (Siret). In 1831, when he was 24 years old, he became the rabbi and head of the rabbinical court in his father's hometown of Załoźce (Zaliztsi). In 1879 he was nominated as the chief rabbi of Stryj and was considered one of the town's most prominent.

At the beginning of his term, there was much anger and bitterness towards him from the family of the previous rabbi. But because of his character and his Torah knowledge he soon became liked by all. He was a peaceful and people loving man and eventually endeared himself to the family of the previous rabbi.

[Page 115]

His advice and opinion were sought by rabbis from near and far. His answers were accepted as definitive statements on points of the Halacha. He had a brilliant style which enchanted his listeners. He was a brilliant orator, fluent in the German language and therefore appeared as a delegate in front of the authorities. He was well respected by the Austrian authorities and received a medal from the emperor himself, an honor not given to any rabbi before him.

He published his book of responsa "Harei Besamim", in two volumes. The first volume was published in Lvov in 1882 and the second volume in 1897. He also published the booklet called "Haga Arie" which included his first sermon before the community of Stanisławów after he was appointed as rabbi and head of the rabbinical court there. His third book "Arie Noam" dealing with portions of the scripture burnt in the big Stryj fire of 1886.

He was famous not only as a genius, but also as a righteous man. He leaned towards the Hassidic movement and traveled to the Tzadik Rabbi David Moshe of Czortków. He always prayed passionately and with enthusiasm. He avoided the disputes between the parties and did not even participate in the rabbis' meetings. He donated much money to charity. On market days the famous rabbi could be found talking to the merchants trying to solicit donations.

In Stryj he was one of the founders of the "General Cheder" arousing the anger of the ultra-orthodox. Although he was already a famous rabbi who was respected and admired by his community, there were some who were against this step and he was harassed. The head of the kehilla was even so brazen as to withhold payment of his salary for a period of time.

Rabbi Leibish was sympathetic to Zionism although he was not a Zionist. After the death of Dr. Herzl, rabbi Leibish eulogized him as was appropriate for the visionary of the state of Israel.

In 1904, after the passing of his father, rabbi Isaac Horowitz of Stanisławów, rabbi Arie Leibish was invited to become the chief rabbi there (in Stanisławów) as was the tradition to continue the rabbinical dynasty. Although he liked Stryj, he accepted the new position and moved to Stanisławów in 1904.

Many followed him on his journey to Stanisławów, where he was a chief rabbi until his death on the 21st of Sivan 5669 (June 10th, 1909).

Rabbi Shalom HaKohen Yolles
(Der Mościsker)
Translated by Susan Rosin

Rabbi Shalom HaKohen Yolles was born in 1866. His father was rabbi Uri of Sambor and his grandfather was rabbi Isaac Charif, the head of the rabbinical court in Sambor and the author of the work "Pnei Isaac". Rabbi Shalom was the student and later ordained by rabbi Yoseph Shmuel Nathansohn of Lvov, the author of "Sho'el u-Meshiv". In 1884 he was accepted as the rabbi of Neistat (Nowe Miasto) where he had many students. In 1897 he became the head of the rabbinical court in Mościska and in 1904 he was appointed to the rabbinical court in Stryj (as a deputy chief judge).

Rabbi Yolles was considered one of the most outstanding and respected religious figures of his time. In 1903 he was one of the ten most important rabbis who attended a conference in Sądowa Wisznia to reorganize the financial matters of the Austrian kollel (an institute for full-time, advanced study of the Talmud and rabbinic literature) in Eretz Israel. In 1908 he was among the six greatest rabbis who were summoned before the authorities as the representatives of all Galicia rabbis. Thanks to his efforts a Yeshiva was established in Stryj where students learnt Talmud, Rashi and Tossafot under the outstanding guidance of the rabbi Raphael Kitaigorodsky.

The sons of rabbi Yolles were rabbis Ephraim Eliezer and Yeshayahu Asher; His sons in law were the rabbis Gdalyahu Halevi Gottlieb (son of the rabbi of Ludmir and the grandson of rabbi Shlomo of Karlin), rabbi Haim Abraham Klinghoyft (the son of the rabbi of Strelisk), and rabbi Israel Moskowitz (the son of the head of the rabbinical court in Turka). Rabbi Yolles immigrated to Israel and settled in Jerusalem where he passed away on the 9th of Av 5685 (July 30th, 1925). His son, Yeshayahu Asher was elected as a religious judge in Stryj.

[Page 116]

Rabbi Shraga Feivel Hertz (Der Glogover)
Translated by Susan Rosin

Rabbi Shraga Feivel Hertz was the head of the rabbinical court in Głogów, and was appointed to the same position in Stryj following the departure of Rabbi Horowitz to become the chief rabbi of Stanisławów. Since it became clear to the Jewish community in Stryj that replacing rabbi Horowitz with someone of the same stature will not be easy, they took their time and after much deliberation decided to appoint two religious judges: Rabbi Yolles from Mościska and rabbi Hertz from Głogów. Rabbi Hertz was very wise and shrewd and was aware of the events in the Jewish world, followed the trends and grasped the changing attitudes. He found many supporters among the most learned in Torah. His method of studying Talmud resembled that of the Lithuanian Yeshivot – explanation of the topic with the Rashi commentary and then he introduced his students to the argumentations by the early and later authorities.

He was able to show how each Talmudic problem and concept can be adopted to contemporary times. In a short time he gathered around him the young Talmud students who later joined the Jewish national revival movement. His son Shlomo was a genius who studied with Jewish students: they instructed him in secular studies and he taught them Jewish studies. He became the rabbi of Borszczów and perished in the holocaust.

From a historical perspective, the dispute between the rabbis of Mościska and Głogów was futile. The two were two authorities complementing each other. "Both speak the words of the living God", though they found support among different groups of Jews in Stryj.

As told by Eliyahu Katz

Rabbi Eliezer Ben Shlomo Ladier
Translated by Susan Rosin

Rabbi Ladier was born on the 3rd of Adar 5634 (February 20th, 1874) in Seret, Bukovina and passed away on the 7th of Tishrei 7 5693 (October 7th, 1932). He was a dignified figure and was one of the greatest rabbis to occupy the rabbinical seat in Stryj. His talmudic research and halachic argumentation dwelt in harmony in his poetic soul.

His arguments were intellectual in nature, he was thorough in analyzing serious topics, yet he was open to seeing the beauty of nature and outpoured his soul in poems in the Hebrew and German languages. His poems were published in various periodicals, but never collected into an anthology.

In his research he sought scientific and historical truth, while in his poems he expressed the love of Zion, the national awakening, and the glory and elation of humanity.

[Page 117]

Midnight
by Eliezer ben Shlomo Ladir
Translated by Yocheved Klausner

Stillness unfolds all over the world,
Shrouded in mystery and secrets of night.
From the eyes of stars, wondrous eyes,
Shining beads are dropping like tears.
A cloak of silence spreads on earth –
Even the wings of the wind are asleep.
All sounds and whispers died with a kiss,
A mute kiss of silence.
The birds have forgotten their singing
And the wild flowers have bent their heads.
In the arms of eternity Creation is dreaming,
And a silent elegy flows from the depths of night.
The elegy reaches the ear of the soul,
And paves a road through the sea of silence,
Reaching the heights of Heaven,
Weeping for the light destroyed,
For the Divine Presence in exile.

From 1917 until his death he served as chief rabbi of Stryj, the same position that was occupied previously by his uncle and teacher, the author of "Harei Besamim". He dedicated himself to serving his community and worked tirelessly to increase its glory and greatness.

———

The Dayanim
Translated by Susan Rosin

(Dayan is a "Judge" or rabbinical assessor who aided the rabbi in the Bet Din or Rabbinical Court)

One of the greatest dayanim was rabbi Isaiah Yaakov Igra who served during the tenure of rabbis Enzel Cuzmer and Eliyahu Meir in the mid nineteenth century.

Rabbi Isaiah Yaakov was a descendant of rabbi Meshullam Igra known as rabbi Meshullam from Tyśmienica, one of the great authorities of his generation, the author of "Igra Rama", frequently asked questions about the Mishnah (Shas - an acronym for Shisha Sedarim – the "six orders" of the Mishnah), who was also the teacher of the Rabbi from Lissa and rabbi Arie Leibish Horowitz (the first).

The daughter of rabbi Isaiah Yaakov, Haychi, was the mother of rabbis Haim and Nuta Wolff who frequented the Ziditchev Kloiz and who both perished in the Shoah.

Between the two world wars the dayanim were rabbi Isaiah Asher Jolles, son of rabbi Shalom HaKohen Jolles and rabbi Shaul son of rabbi Yaakov Joseph Lusthaus. Both perished with their community in the Shoah.

Rabbi Asher Yeshayahu Frankel
(Known as the Rabbi of Strelisk)
Translated by Susan Rosin

He was the son of rabbi Israel Leib of Przemyślany, the grandson of rabbi Meir'l of Przemyślany, rabbi Naphtali of Ropshits (Ropczyce) and the Baal Shem Tov. His wife, the rebbetzin Bat Sheva was the daughter of rabbi Levi Isaac of Strelisk, the son rabbi Shlomo, the only son of Rabi Uri 'ha-Saraf' from Strelisk.

In 1914, at the start of the war, rabbi Frankel who was 35 at the time and the father of four daughters and two sons moved his family from Sterlisk to Stryj. People flocked to study with him and to listen to his enthusiastic prayers. His son Levi Isaac was a journalist in an orthodox newspaper in Poland. Rabbi Isaac Levi Klinghoyft, the head of the rabbinical court in Otinya (Ottynia) was his son-in-law. The entire family perished in the Holocaust except for one son – Rabbi Dr. Israel Frankel, the author of "Peshat (Plain Exegesis) In Talmudic and Midrashic Literature" and was later the executive director of the Toronto Jewish Public Library.

Rabbi Mordechai (Motel) Druker
Translated by Susan Rosin

Rabbi Mordechai Druker was the student of his uncle rabbi Moshe Enser, an outstanding scholar, intellectual and learned in the Torah. Like his uncle and teacher, rabbi Mordechai Druker was a significant scholar of the Torah, excellent reader (of scriptures) and an expert with regard to Agada, Midrashim and Hebrew grammar.

He started his literary and scientific work by publishing articles in the "Ivri Anochi" (I am a Hebrew) in Brody, "Yehudi" (Jewish) in Pressburg and the "Tor" in Sighet. Later he published a book "Safa Laneemanim" (Language for the Faithful) on the Hebrew verbs (Drohobycz 1883); "Techelet Mordechai", a commentary on the Pentateuch (Lviv 1894); "Tovim Meorot" (The Good Luminaries), sanctification for the sun and moon (first edition Lviv 1897, second edition Lviv 1928); "Ateret Mordechai" (The crown of Mordechai), a commentary on Midrash Rabba using the approach of Hebrew linguistics; "Divrei Hachamim Ve'Hidoteyhem" (The words and riddles of the sages) on the Torah portions. In addition he participated in writing "Ohel Moed" with rabbi Byk.

From 1891 he was a preacher in Stryj, doing so without pay. He was admired and respected by

[Page 118]

all in Stryj. To enable him teach, he was offered the synagogue minyan "Yad Harutzim" as a permanent location and became the spiritual leader of the worshipers there, who were mostly craftsmen and common folks. The synagogue was called later "The Motel Druker Shul".

The Zionist youth, interested in the Hebrew language found him to be an excellent teacher of grammar and the bible.

His wife, mother and grandmother were all famous midwives. After the Stryj fire, his mother Esther was able to reconstruct from memory the births books for an entire generation.

Rabbi Isaac Hauptman
(Rabbi Itshe Shub)
Translated by Susan Rosin

Rabbi Isaac ben Eliyahu Nathan Hauptman was one of the outstanding personalities of our community and talented in many areas. He was very active in all religious matters in our town, head of the Chevra Kadisha, honorary officer of the great synagogue and the Ziditchev Synagogue (the "Blechene Kloiz") and a devotee of the Ziditchev. He had the privilege to visit with the famous rabbi Yitzchak Isaac the founder of the Ziditchev Eichenstein dynasty.

He was a "Shub" (the initials of "Shohet Ubodek", Slaughterer and Inspector) and a circumsizer and was considered an authority in these professions. After his father passed away, rabbi Isaac was appointed a Shub in Stryj at an early age although there were others who were more experienced than him. Because of his expertise in slaughtering many butchers preferred to work with him, a situation that caused jealousy and hard feelings among the rest of the Shubs. To alleviate the problem it was decided by the Kehila board to set forth "daily slaughtering turns". Sometimes there was a shortage of meat because the butchers were waiting for rabbi Itshe's turn.

Rabbi Itshe was a prayer leader, a cantor, musically talented whose singing was delightful. Unlike other cantors at his time, he was proficient in musical notes. He was in touch with other renowned cantors and received from them the melodies which he expertly matched for various prayers. He even used secular and popular melodies for prayers. He worshiped in many synagogues during the morning and evening prayers.

Although he never studied in a secular or technical school, rabbi Itshe was an engineer. He was able to create structural and architectural plans for homes and buildings as well as any certified engineer would.

His talent in this area was so great that the Stryj city engineer Postempski instructed the technical department to immediately send him any plans submitted by rabbi Itshe for approval, whereas plans submitted by certified engineers were many times sent back for revisions.

His character was a combination of the holy and the secular, an orthodox Jew and a Jew who saw national revival in Zionism. Shortly before his death he was nominated as the head of the "Mizrahi" association in Stryj. After the approval of the British mandate in Palestine and after the Balfour declaration in San-Remo by the League of Nations, it was suggested during Saturday prayers to take a collection for the Jewish National Fund. The most orthodox objected, but rabbi Itshe declared that he will call the worshipers for Aliyah (An Aliyah, Hebrew עליה is the calling of a member of a Jewish congregation to the bimah for a segment of reading from the Torah) and elicited donations from them for the JNF. His children, sons Aharon, Eliyahu, Yaakov, Abraham, Menachem, and daughters, Haya Branchi, Fruma, Esther and Sara were all dedicated Zionists and members of Poalei Zion and were active in all areas of Jewish national and communal life.

[Page 119]

Dr. Isaac (Isidor) Aaron Bernfeld
Translated by Susan Rosin

Dr. Isaac Aaron Bernfeld (1854 – 1930) was born in Tyśmienica, was a Hebrew author and taught Jewish studies in Stryj for 44 years.

His father, Moshe was one of the first intellectuals in Tyśmienica and Stanisławów and both sons Dr. Isaac and Dr. Shimon received traditional and secular education. Their father instilled in them love for the Hebrew language. In his opinions, Dr. Isaac Bernfeld leaned towards Polish assimilation although not to the extreme.

He believed that Jews should learn the Polish language, although he saw Hebrew as an only asset that will sustain the Jewish people and their culture.

During 1881 – 1885 he was the editor of "Hamazkir", the Hebrew part of the periodical "Ojczyzna" (The Fatherland), published in Lvov by the assimilators Alfred Nossig and Bernhard Goldman.

While editing the "Hamazkir", he also wrote articles for the "Hamagid" (the Preacher), "Hakol" (the Voice), "Hamelitz" (the Advocate), "Hazefirah" (the

Siren) about Galician Jews and their issues. He also wrote a Yiddish article demanding the establishment of modern Jewish schools suited for the times.

He translated into Hebrew the research book of Abraham Berliner "The Jewish Life in Germany in the Middle Ages" (Ahiasaf Publication, Warsaw 1900). His main scientific interest was the research of Hebrew language. He published a Hebrew-Polish dictionary in 1926, and wrote (in Polish) about the Hebrew grammar. He also translated the Mishnah into Polish, but did not publish it.

Dr. Zvi Diesendruk
(1890 – 1941)
Translated by Susan Rosin

He was one of the shining stars in science and Hebrew literature of our time. He came from a well-to-do family, and his father Yehuda Leib, a Czortków Hassid, educated him in the spirit of tradition and Hassidism at the kloiz of Stryj's famous scholar rabbi Hirsch-Wolff. However, young Zvi who was a prodigy gradually became less religious, and at night he would conceal secular works under the large books of Talmud. Zionist students helped him prepare for the high school entrance examinations.

When still in Stryj he took part in the activities of the Galician Hebrew Movement, and together with his friend Jonah Gelernter he established the "Ivriya" society. In 1909 he left Stryj and moved to Vienna, where he successfully took the matriculation exams and then studied philosophy and classical languages at the University. He was the student of the two well-known professors of philosophy, Shteher and Jodl. In 1912 he went to Eretz Israel where he spent a year as a teacher. From 1913 until 1916 he taught in Berlin, and then served in the Austrian army. After the end of the war he settled in Vienna, where he became a teacher of philosophy and Hebrew literature at the Hebrew Pedagogical Institute headed by Professor Dr. Zvi Peretz Chajes (Zvi-Peretz Hayot). In 1922 he received his Ph.D. in philosophy. From 1925 until 1927 he taught at the Rabbinical Seminary of Dr. Stephen Wise in New York. In 1927 he was invited to be lecturer of Jewish philosophy at the Hebrew University. However, he left Eretz Israel after two years because he was appointed a Professor at the Hebrew Union College in Cincinnati, to replace Professor Dr. David Neumark. He was also the vice-chairman of the American Academy of Jewish Research, and editor of the Hebrew Union College Annual.

[Page 120]

He had started his literary work before the First World War. His first essay was published in Gershom Bader's journal "Ha'et" (the Time) (Lviv 1906). He contributed to "Hashiloah", where he published his first philosophical study. He was active in "Revivim" edited by J. H. Brenner and G. Shoffmann in Lviv, as well as "Haolam" (the World), and "Hatekufa" (the Era). In 1918-1919 he published the monthly "Gevulot" (Borders) in Vienna with G. Shoffmann.

He translated into Hebrew Plato's Phaedrus, Gorgias, Crito and Republic (Shtibel Publishing Company).

In German he published Struktur und Charakter des Platonischen Phaidros (Vienna, 1927). In the Israel Abrahams' Memorial Volume he published Die Teleologie bei Maimonides, Maimonideslehre von der Prophetie (New York 1927). In the 1928 yearbook of the Hebrew Union College - Samuel and Moses Tibbon on Maimonides' theory of providence, The philosophy of Maimonides' theory of negation of privation (proceeding t. VI 1934-1935).

Diesendruk excelled in his deep understanding of philosophical issues and his Hebrew lectures were clear and precise. He was one of the prominent researches of our new literature.

Dr. Naphtali (Tulo) Nussenblatt
Translated by Susan Rosin

Dr. Naphtali (Tulo) Nussenblatt was a member of the "Bnei Zion" Gymnasium Zionist circle founded by Dr. Insler. He later joined "Hashomer", which after the First World War became "Hashomer Hatza'ir". During the war he was an officer in the Austrian army, was wounded in action and received a medal.

After the War he settled in Vienna, studied law and obtained a Ph.D. He never practiced as a lawyer, but devoted himself to literary and political journalism. He specialized in the period and personal history of Dr. Theodore Herzl. He collected much material and published essays and studies in the Zionist press and other anthologies. In 1929 he published his first book: Zeitgenossen ueber Herzl (Brun) a collection of memoirs by Herzl's contemporaries. In his book, Ein Volk unterwegs zum Frieden (Vienna 1933) he collected valuable archival material regarding the political activities of Dr. Herzl, particularly at the time of the Hague Peace Conference in 1899.

In 1937 he began to publish an annual in Vienna, which was devoted to the study of the history of Herzl and the Zionist Movement, under the title,

Theodor Herzl Jahrbuch. However, he was able to publish only the first issue which contained unknown material and historical essays on Dr. Herzl and the early days of the Zionist Movement.

After the Nazis invasion of Austria he escaped to Poland, settling in Dąbrowa Górnicza near Będzin, where his father-in-law lived. During the war he moved to Warsaw and took an active part in Ghetto life and underground activities. In September 1942 he was kidnapped by the Germans, deported to Maidanek where he was murdered.

Dr. Nussenblatt, who was a collector, gathered a large collection of letters and manuscripts by Dr. Herzl. All this material was lost in the Warsaw Ghetto.

Dr. Nathan Ek (Ekron) wrote in his book "Hatoim Bedarchei Ha'et" ("The Lost in the Ways of Time") (Yad Vashem publication, Jerusalem 1960) about his meeting with Dr. Nussenblatt in 1931 when they sat in the Prückel coffeehouse in Vienna, Nussenblatt told him about the conversations he had with people in Vienna to collect information and memoirs about Herzl. One of them was an older Jew, a Herzl contemporary with whom Nussenblatt spoke at the same coffeehouse. Like many of his generation, this man treated Herzl's ideas with perplexity. He tried to convince Herzl to stop his dreams and to devote himself to more material things to promote his career.

The man remembered that Herzl stopped and told him: "After my passing, a generation of young enthusiastic and patriotic people will arise and they will want to research everything I said and wrote".

[Page 121]

And here you are, said the man to Nussenblatt, one of these young enthusiastic people who is a Herzl researcher.

When Nussenblatt heard this, he jumped from his seat as did Archimedes in his time and cried "eureka". "Up until that time, when asked about my profession, I would say:

"historian" or "journalist" or "author". But now I know – I am a Herzl Researcher. This is a new scientific discipline, my profession..."

Jonah Gelernter
Translated by Susan Rosin

Jonah Gelernter was born in Stryj in 1890. He worked together with dr. Zvi Diesendruk in Stryj and later was active in the Zionist movement in Vienna. He wrote stories and essays for the Hebrew publications ("Hamitzpeh" and "Hayom"). In Vienna he dedicated himself to teaching the Hebrew language. Between 1923 and 1938 he taught Hebrew language and literature at the Zvi Peretz Chajes (Zvi–Peretz Hayot) institute in Vienna. He published a monthly in Vienna called "Devarenu" (Our Word). After the Nazis occupied Vienna he escaped to Paris, but was murdered there in 1944.

Memorial for Yehoshua
by Dr. Moshe Mikam
Translated by Susan Rosin

He was restrained in his behavior. He was more a listener than a talker and he hid more than he revealed. He had sadness in him which was largely a hidden world within him. He had dreamy eyes that were sometimes smiling, sometimes sad and sometimes penetrating. This dreamer became sometimes a sarcastic mocker – but his sarcasm was more of a defense than an intentional disrespect.

He was a believer, but refrained from discussing God and religion. He was observant, but not to the extreme. He hated publicity and exaggeration. He was a soldier during the first World War and was deeply affected by the horrors he was exposed to. However, these experiences deepened his religious beliefs and made him closer to God.

The believer in him was not pushed aside by the intellectual in him, and because of that his outlook on life was true and deep and so was his understanding of literature. He was very familiar with the European literature and its many languages. This familiarity was not dry, but clear and fresh and he was able to combine the Jewish culture with that of the world. In his soul Shakespeare and rabbi Akiva, Plato and the Maimonides lived in harmony.

He was a homebody, but was always willing to join others and to help with advice and assistance. People were drawn to him because of his charming personality. Anyone who had conversations with him never regretted it.

[Page 122]

He was a combination of a child's naiveté and a man learnt in the torah who loathed being prominent and avoided being popular and famous.

He was a very prolific writer, but chose not to write unless he was asked to do so. That was how he came produce the excellent translation into Polish of Shai Agnon's famous work "Vehaya Ha'akov Lemishor" ("And the Crooked Shall Be Made Straight"). In the same way he wrote his brilliant essays about the New Hebrew literature.

He was a unique teacher. He taught with all his being and his radiant personality. He knew how to influence by not conforming to the usual teaching methods, but by his inspired spirit, by the remarks and illustrations, his deep scientific understanding and by insisting on attention to detail. His students adored and admired him because they felt he gave his entire being to educating them.

He was proficient in all high school subjects. If a teacher was absent, he was always a substitute. He could teach math, physics, history, geography and satisfy even the most demanding students.

And last but not least was his relationship with his mother. Once when I stayed at her house I saw the radiant stillness, the serenity and tranquility in her and I realized he had those too. Here I saw the flowing love from a son to the woman most dear to him and I understood that love like this can feed a love of Torah, people and God.

My memories are so precious, but painful as well. I can see the dear and admired close friend, but the pain is so great because this wonderful person did not die a normal death, but was murdered by criminals. And I cannot even go to his grave and say "may you rest in peace", but I'll pray for you with pain in my heart "may your pure soul rest with the rest of Israel martyrs. Amen".

Dr. Max Bienenstock (1881 – 1923)
Translated by Susan Rosin

The teacher and author Dr. Max Bienenstock was one of the most outstanding Zionist activists in Stryj between 1912 and 1919.

He was born in Tarnów and completed his studies in Kraków. He joined the Zionist movement in his youth and was active since 1902 in spite of being a government employee. Because of his position he was frequently transferred. In 1912 he was appointed as a German language and literature teacher at the high school in Stryj. In the years before the war he dedicated himself mostly to literary work.

When the Austro–Hungarian Empire crumbled and the establishment of the Western Ukrainian republic in the eastern part of Galicia, hopes were high for establishing a Jewish autonomy Dr. Bienenstock joined the Zionist movement in Stryj and became one of its activists. He was one of the organizers of the Jewish council that was established in Stryj. As an educator he was one of the architects of the national education and one of the founders of national schools in eastern Galicia. In 1919 he was a delegate together with Naphtali Siegel to the Stanislawow convention of Jewish communities in eastern Galicia to establish a network of Jewish schools. He was the editor of the newspaper "Volkstimme" published in Stryj which dealt mainly with issues of Jewish education and the self-governing of the Jewish institutions. He signed the articles "Kaveret" (beehive). He identified with the Zionist-Socialist movement and was one of the founders of "Poalei Zion" and later "Hitahadut". After the Polish invasion of Stryj he was fired from his position but in 1920 became the principal of the Jewish high school in Lviv.

[Page 123]

In 1922 he was elected to the Polish senate as a delegate of the Jewish National party. However, he passed away shortly afterwards in 1923.

He was a very prolific author and journalist who wrote many articles in the Zionist-Socialist media. Later in life he learnt to write Yiddish and published articles about the Yiddish literature and theater in "Togblatt", "Ringen" and "Milgroim". He also published research articles in Polish and German such as "The Effect of German literature on the Romantic Poems of Juliusz Słowacki" (Warsaw 1909), on Lessing and Hubell (1913). The most famous is his book "Das Judentum in Heines Dichnungen". He translated into German "Nie Boska komedia" (Non-Divine Comedy) by Zygmunt Krasinski and the "Yizkor" book for the "Shomrim" (The Jewish Watchmen's Organization in Palestine). He also published an article on Henrik Ibsen's artistic opinions.

Dr. Abraham Insler
Translated by Susan Rosin

Dr. Abraham Insler was born in Stryj on November 2nd, 1893, the son of Benjamin Insler. He received a secular education at home. In high school he joined the Zionist group and learnt Hebrew, Yiddish, and the history of the Jewish people. He was very talented and represented the Jewish youth in the national conventions of "Zeirei Zion" (Youth of Zion) that were held in secret every year in Lviv.

After graduating from high school he studied law at the universities of Lviv and Vienna where he participated in Zionist activities. He was one of the organizers of the "Emuna" Academic Society and later became its chairperson. He published many articles in Polish about current affairs in the Zionist monthlies "Moriah" and "Hashahar".

At the start of the First World War he returned to Vienna and was one of Dr. Nathan Birnbaum's assistants at the periodical "Juedisches Kriegararchiv". Upon his return to Stryj in 1918 he joined "Poalei Zion". After three months he helped to organize the Jewish National Council.

In 1921 after the establishment of the daily Polish Zionist journal "Chwila" in Lviv he joined the editorial staff and was also elected as a member of the Zionist board in western Galicia. In 1922 he was elected for the Polish Sejm as a delegate from the Stanisławów– Kołomyja district. He excelled in his brilliant speeches at the Sejm and was especially interested in local city government issues, was a member of the committee of legal and internal affairs and was one of the seven members of the "human rights league". He joined the faction of Isaac Greenbaum which caused a conflict with the Zionist board in Lviv.

In 1925 he was elected the head of the Kehila in Stryj, but resigned because he moved to Lviv. In 1928 he established together with dr. Michael Ringel and dr. Fishel Rotenstreich the newspaper "Der Morgen" and was its chief editor. He was elected for a second term as a delegate for the Polish Sejm and served until its dispersal in 1930.

[Page 124]

In 1931 – 1932 he was the chief editor of the "Nowe Słowo" (New Word) Zionist daily in Warsaw. Because of disagreements with the management, he left Warsaw and returned to Lviv where he published the distinguished weekly "Opinia" (Opinion). In 1937 he published a pamphlet "False Documents" (Dokumenty Fałszywe) and "Legend and Facts" (Legendy i Fakty) refuting the Anti–Semitic libels and exposing the part played by the Polish army in the 1918 Lviv pogrom. He also published a dr. Gershon Zipper monograph.

He was in failing health in his last years and passed away at the young age of 45.

May his memory be preserved as one of the leaders of the national revival movements in Stryj and all of Poland.*

*Articles about Isaac Bernfeld, dr. Max Bienenstock, dr. Abraham Insler, dr. Zvi Diesendruk, dr. Naphtali (Tulu) Nussenblatt and Jonah Gelernter were transferred with permission from the article "The History of the Jews of Stryj" by dr. M.N. Gelber.

Dr. Zeev Presser
Translated by Susan Rosin

Dr. Presser was born in Stryj to a progressive family. After graduating from the high school in Stryj, he studied law in Vienna. He married the sister of the renowned Zionist leader dr. Abraham Insler. In addition to his professional education he had extensive general knowledge and lectured and wrote articles about world literature. He was a Zionist from a young age and one of the central figures in communal life and one of the outstanding lawyers in Stryj. He was a pleasant person who was popular in both Jewish and non-Jewish circles. He was elected a deputy mayor of Stryj, head of the Zionist institutions in town and the head of the Kehila. He was a dedicated community leader until its destruction.

Dr. Mordechai Kaufmann
Translated by Susan Rosin

Dr. Mordechai Kaufmann was born in Stryj to a traditional and observant family. He was one of the first Hebrew speakers and after high school in Stryj he studied law in Lviv. During the First World War he served as an officer in the Austrian army. He was one of the commanders of the Jewish self-defense during the Ukrainian rule. In his professional work he contributed to strengthening the status of lawyers in our town. He was an active Zionist from a young age. He played an important part as deputy mayor, head of the community and chairman of the general Zionist party.

He was moderate in his views and had a calming influence on political and public life and was admired and respected by his supporters and even his adversaries. In his approach to issues and his influence he resembled Dr. Presser. He immigrated to Eretz Israel but was sent to Poland on a mission by the JNF and was murdered there with his wife.

[Page 125]

Dr. Shlomo Goldberg
Translated by Susan Rosin

While still in high school, young Shlomo Goldberg was influenced by the Hibbat Zion (The love of Zion) movement that encouraged the studying youth to join Zionist activities. The air of nationalism and progress in the home completed the Zionist environment that young Shlomo was exposed to.

After graduating from high school at the beginning of the twentieth century Shlomo left to study law in Vienna where he joined the Zionist circles. He spent his free time recruiting other students for the Zionist movement.

After the war he returned to Stryj where while practicing law he was one of the most prominent leaders of the Zionist movement. After the ousting of the assimilators in Stryj, Dr. Goldberg was elected the head of the Kehila.

Later he was elected deputy mayor on behalf of the Zionist movement. He was the first one to obtain fund allocations for Jewish national purposes from the local government.

He was a strong willed and principled person and as such was not skilled in political maneuvering. This caused many times friction between him and his friends and cost him even prestigious public positions.

In spite of his "stiffness", Dr. Goldberg was an activist who believed whole heartedly in the Zionist idea and acted upon it in his public work and was always prepared to help his town people in their time of need.

Dr. Benjamin Millbauer
Translated by Susan Rosin

Dr. Benjamin Millbauer was born in Bolechów to a teacher of Jewish religion. He studied medicine in Vienna and Prague and was dedicated to Zionist public service, which was unusual among the physicians. He played an important part in the public and Zionist organizations in town either as a chairperson or an active committee member. He visited Eretz Israel and upon his return he praised Israel and spoke to Stryj's Jewry about his experiences.

Moshe Aaron Wohlmut
by Zvi Wohlmut
Translated by Susan Rosin

Moshe Aaron Wohlmut was a man of the people whose mark was in all areas of public Jewish life. For years he served in the city government and as a member of the Kehila committee. He dedicated his time, energy and resources to all the benevolent institutions in town. But above all he was a dedicated Zionist. In Zionism he found a rest for his soul and his calling. His Zionism was not limited to Eretz Israel only, but encompassed the Jewish tradition with all its humanistic values.

[Page 126]

He was an intellectual and a Hebrew scholar and lover of the Torah. He was devoted to Hebrew education and the spread of Hebrew culture. He was one of the leaders of the various Zionist funds and was a tireless fund raiser. At the same time he was an active member of the "Ivriya" society and aided the "Safa Brura" school.

His happiest days occurred during his visit to Eretz Israel in February 1933. He toured the country visiting its towns, villages, settlements and kibbutzim. His love for Israel could be gleaned from his letters. Upon his return he spoke to Stryj's Jewry about his visit, about the fields in the valley and about the Tzabarim (native–born Israelis) with whom he was able to talk in Hebrew – the only language they knew.

Since his visit he never stopped dreaming about immigrating with his family to Eretz Israel as he felt the danger in Poland. Unfortunately he was not able to fulfill his dream. In the race against time, he and his family were trapped in Poland.

Benjamin Klein
by Dr. Ada Barlev Klein
Translated by Susan Rosin

Benjamin Klein was born in Stryj to an observant and distinguished family, was given an orthodox upbringing and attended Beit Hamidrash. Young Benjamin like others in his generation, among them Zvi Diesendruk, read secular books which he hid under the Gmara. He was influenced by the national Zionist movement at the beginning of the twentieth century, left the "Gele Kloiz" where he studied and showed-up one day at home shaved and wearing a short coat bewildering his entire family.

Like other youth who were unable to study in school he was an autodidact. He showed talents in music, drawing and carving. He was unable to develop any of these due to the lack of understanding of his ultra-orthodox parents.

During the First World War he served in the military orchestra. After the war he worked as a bookkeeper at the bank of Dr. Z. Presser and later at his father's rabbi Shmuel Klein bank. Later he became a merchant.

But first and foremost, Benjamin was a dedicated public servant. He was devoted to the Jewish affairs, the institutions and the Zionist movement. He was one of the leaders, member and chairperson of the Zionist, social and public institutions. In public life he was frank, honest and moderate.

Leaders, lecturers and public activists used to stay in his cultural Jewish home when visiting Stryj.

He was well liked by the people. When he was arrested in 1938 by the Polish Anti-Semitic authorities under false accusations, the community was quick to provide moral and material help. He felt he should leave Poland and immigrate to Eretz Israel. But, like many others he delayed his departure too long and perished in the holocaust with the rest of the community to which he had devoted the greater part of his life.

Dov (Berl) Stern

(Passed away 4th of Tishrei, 5706 – September 11th, 1945)

Translated by Susan Rosin

Dov (Berl) Stern was one of the earliest Zionists in town during the Herzl era, a popular figure who took upon himself any task in the Zionist work. He immigrated to Eretz Israel in 1925 and earned his living as a laborer.

[Page 127]

His home served as a first "inn" for new arrivals from Stryj. He was highly respected and admired by the new arrivals from his town and was always ready to help them with advice and support in their first steps in the new country. He passed away in Eretz Israel at a ripe old age.

Meir Frankel

(Passed away 22nd of Kislev 5714 – November 29th, 1953)

Translated by Susan Rosin

Meir Frankel, a native of Mościska immigrated to Eretz Israel before the First World War but had to return to the diaspora due to an illness. He settled in Stryj and was an active member of the general Zionist organization, "Toynbee Hall", "Zion" association and the Foundation Fund. He joined the "Al Hamishmar" group and in 1932 returned to Eretz Israel. He worked as an official in the community and later in the Tel-Aviv municipality.

He was always ready to assist those in need. He was active in the Stryj organization in Israel. He lived to see the establishment of the State of Israel.

Dr. Moshe Barlev (Reinhartz)
Translated by Susan Rosin

All members of the Reinhartz family joined the pioneer (Halutz) youth movements and prepared themselves for immigration to Eretz Israel during the period of the second (1904 – 1914) and third (1919 – 1923) Aliyah. Young Moshe was brought up in a pioneer–Zionist atmosphere at home and while still in high school joined the Zionist movement.

After graduating from high school he studied economics and eastern studies in Liège, Belgium. After graduation he was a director of a commerce school.

Because he was dedicated to the popular–national movement, he soon joined the "Hitahdut" party – the eastern Galicia Zionist workers' party. He contributed greatly to establishing and then expanding the Socialist Zionist Academic Society (Z.A.S). This society was a different from the other academic societies and was based on democratic principles that helped define the intellectual workers in Eretz Israel.

In 1934 he immigrated to Eretz Israel with his wife Dr. Ada Barlev-Klein, the daughter of rabbi Shmuel Klein. In Israel he was a commander in the "Haganah". In the Second World War he served in the British army. He was a treasurer and a member of the management at the "Hamat" industries. In 1959 he started working in the academic worker section of the Histadrut (the Workers' organization). He was instrumental in establishing the department for the academics and graduates in the humanities. He also served as a judge of the Histadrut Supreme court.

He was instrumental in establishing the Stryj organization in Israel before the war. He was on the board of the organization and initiated the idea of publishing the Stryj "Yizkor" book and dedicated much of his time to realize the dream of the survivors both in Israel and the diaspora to memorialize the holocaust victims of the town.

He died suddenly during a meeting of the Histadrut committee.

[Page 128]

Abraham (Buczi) Apfelgruen
Translated by Susan Rosin

Abraham Apfegruen was one of the most outstanding leaders of the "Mizrahi" in Stryj. He was an active public leader and the chairperson of the "Mizrahi" for many years and the chairperson of the Jewish National Fund for two years. He represented his party in Zionist, public and economic institutions in town. He was a man learned in Torah, pleasant and of dignified appearance. He was a "gabai" in the Meir Shalom synagogue and was well liked because of his pleasant nature.

Rachel Katz
by P. Avineri – Katz
Translated by Susan Rosin

Rachel Katz was born in Stryj in 1877. Her family lineage went back to the middle ages and included such famous persons as the Gaon rabbi Naphtali Katz, who was the rabbi of Posen (Poznań), the "Shelah ha–Kadosh" (Isaiah HaLevi Horovitz 1565 – 1630), "Pene Yehoshua" (Joshua ben Alexander HaCohen Falk Katz 1555–1614).

Generations of Torah and faith made her a God fearing, people loving and bright person – characteristics that guided her in her public work and personal life.

Her father rabbi Joseph Katz was the deputy mayor and head of the kehila of Itzkany (Iţcani) in Bukovina. Her mother was an outstanding righteous woman. Rachel inherited her expression ability, public speaking talent, imagination and sense of humor from her father and the perception of justice and honesty from her mother.

She was a well–educated woman and gained much respect and admiration even outside of Stryj.

She was one of the early graduates of the Polish Liceum in Stryj. Among the other notable graduates of this institution were: Dr. Helena Rosenman, Helena Preis, Dr. Byk and other well educated Stryj women. All her life she continued to learn and inspired other young women in Stryj.

She fought for the emancipation and equal rights for Jewish women. She started her activities in earnest in women's charity organizations such as "Ezrat Nashim" (Women's Aid) and "Kreuzer Verein" which heralded the involvement of Jewish women in public life in Stryj.

In 1897, K. Lippa, a relative of Rachel Katz stopped in Stryj on his way from the first Zionist Congress in Basel to Bukovina and brought the message of national revival. During his stay in town, a group was organized to disseminate the ideas of Zionism and the national culture. The group included: Dr. Maximilian Sheinfeld, Dr. S. Goldberg, Dr. Schiff and Rachel Katz, the only woman.

However, during that period, Rachel mostly dedicated herself to working on restoring the self–respect of the Jewish woman and help for young girls and Jewish orphans. She founded the "Women's Club" (Ognisko Kobiet) and the Jewish Girls' Shelter (Ochronka dla Dziewcząt Zydowskich). The shelter was her favorite charity. Poor girls were helped with their studies, received a hot meal, clothing and sometimes even money for their parents. The shelter was named after Rachel following her death.

Rachel appeared on the political arena first in 1907 and then in 1911. She was a gifted public speaker who campaigned on behalf of the Zionist candidates to the Austrian parliament – Dr. Abraham Salz in 1907 and later Dr. Leon Reich.

[Page 129]

Rachel played a major part in establishing the school "Safa Brura" that was instrumental in spreading the Hebrew language among the town's youth.

She influenced establishing similar schools in other towns. Due to all her Zionist activities she was inscribed in the first "Golden Book" in 1911 before she was 34 years old.

The Balfour declaration in 1917 brought a rise in national pride and hope. Many volunteered for action. In a major gathering, Rachel spoke to the crowd in one of her most brilliant speeches.

In 1918 – 1919 during the short rule of the Ukrainians in eastern Galicia the Jews gained some autonomy. Rachel was one of the initiators and the activists in the national council ("nationalrat") that was established to represent Galician Jews. She was active in the Zionist institutions, philanthropic initiatives and municipal issues concerning the Jewish population. In the municipal election she was placed on the list behind Dr. Presser, but gained the maximum number of votes, a testament to the respect and admiration by the town's people. In the municipality she was well liked and respected even by the Polish and Ukrainian council members. After her death, the Polish mayor in the obituary said: "None of us will ever be able to do what Mrs. Katz did and accomplished".

The number of needy families increased in the first years of the Polish rule (after the war). With funds from "The Joint", Rachel opened a soup kitchen where volunteers took turns. She was elected as the "Joint" representative to travel to the US, but refused to use public funds to travel…

When Zionist women organized WIZO and young WIZO, Rachel joined–in and helped establish branches in eastern Galicia towns. She traveled to lecture and reached even Krakow. Her clear style and ability to influence drew large audiences. She also organized classes for Jewish girls to learn practical skills to be prepared for pioneer life in Eretz Israel. As a fighter for women's rights, she demanded that housekeeping will be recognized as a respectable work. In many regards she was ahead of her times…

She was also a talented writer and her articles were published in the Zionist newspapers "Opinia" (Opinion) and "Chwila" (Moment). She donated her royalties to charity.

Rachel was also active in another area – behind closed doors. Many people came to her discuss their hardships and seek her advice. Rachel was always ready to help away from the public eye.

Stryj was so blessed to have this woman in our town. Her life was full of vision and activity, truly the embodiment of "love thy neighbor" commandment, purity of spirit, honesty, understanding and education all combined in this woman of outstanding character.

Dr. Malka Leibowitz
Translated by Susan Rosin

Dr. Malka Leibowitz was one of the outstanding women of Stryj. She was active between the two World Wars and her talents made her a natural leader from a young age.

Dr. Leibowitz was a person of common sense and clarity of thought, possessing excellent organizational skills, energetic and dynamic public speaker. From an early age she willingly dedicated herself to any public role.

While still in high school, she was a leader of the "Hashomer Hatzair" in Stryj and continued to be active in the movement when she was a medical student. She was a member of the centralized activities of "Hashomer Hatzair" in Warsaw. Those who remember her from that period of time can never forget the endearing, heart-warming and popular figure that was always surrounded by young people who admired and loved their devoted leader.

She was unable to fulfil her dream of immigrating to Eretz Israel with the young people she led, most likely because of her family situation.

[Page 130]

After completing medical school, Malka continued in her public activities. She did much for the health of the poor Jewish population and initiated and established public health institutions for Jewish children. She was well liked and respected by the Jewish population in Stryj. Malka was determined not to be captured by the Nazi murderers and took her own life.

Aryeh (Leib) Schwamer
Translated by Susan Rosin

Aryeh Schwamer was born in Bolechow and raised in a traditional family. Later he was able to acquire general education and was trained in trade and economics. Until 1921 he managed a branch of the Phoenix in Krakow and then he managed a Loan Bank in Stryj until the holocaust.

From an early age he showed much interest in political and public life. Until 1914 he was a member of the Territorialism party. He then joined "Poalei

Zion", and later, when the "Hitahdut" party was established in Stryj he became an active and dedicated member until the holocaust.

He was a chairman of "Hitahdut" and vice-chairman of the "Arbeitsgemeinschaft" for many years, was a delegate to the Zionist Congress and a member of the city council. For many years he was active in the various Zionist and economic organizations such as the Jewish National Fund and the Foundation Fund, the "Merchants Society" and others. He was member of the board for the party conventions in Lvov and a permanent member of the national council of the party.

He was a pleasant person, always considerate and ready with advice for those who came to ask his opinion. He was always prepared to help others and was a model public figure who was popular in all circles.

Dr. Azriel Eisenstein
Translated by Susan Rosin

Dr. Eisenstein was born in a village near Skole, attended high school in Stryj and received his law degree from the Lvov University. He joined the "Hitahdut" party and was one of its outstanding figures. While in Lvov he was a member of the national council of the party. When he moved to Stryj, he represented his party in the municipal council, the kehila, the "Arbeitsgemeinschaft" and the lawyers' organization.

David Zeidman
Translated by Susan Rosin

David Zeidman was born in Skala and moved with his family to Stryj at the beginning of World War one. His family was orthodox and his father, rabbi Israel Zeidman was a merchant who studied Torah in his free time.

David showed interest in politics and public service from a young age. He was worldly-wise and familiar with local municipal issues and the various parties. He helped his father in his business, but his real passion was public service and the greater good. His shrewdness, negotiations skills and his power of persuasion made him one of the most prominent Zionist and national figures in our town. His activism stemmed from his will to help resolve the issues of Jews of his town. He did not act on any party's behalf and did not have an agenda and goals to achieve and had no inclination to become an official with authority. In spite of this he was very influential in town.

[Page 131]

Originally he joined the "Hitahdut" party and was active in the Jewish National Fund, the Founding Fund and "HeHalutz". As a member of "Arbeitsgemeinschaft", he was active in the Kehila, the municipality and the elections for Polish Sejm. His incentive was to achieve results and therefore he mostly dedicated himself to work with the Halutzim (pioneers), those who implemented the Zionist ideology into actuality by immigrating to Eretz Israel.

He was influenced by Ze'ev Jabotinsky to join the revisionist camp. The idea of the immediate establishment of a Jewish state fascinated him. He eventually joined the faction of Meir Grossman.

Even as a member of a specific political party he was not a harsh adversary, a trait that made him liked even by his political opponents.

Eliyahu Waldman
Translated by Susan Rosin

Eliyahu Waldman was a dedicated activist for Aliyah. He endangered himself sometimes in his efforts to obtain certificates for the Halutzim and other immigrants. He was helped by his good friend David Zeidman.

Many of those who left Stryj and live in Israel owe their ability to leave to Eliyahu Waldman.

He was the grandson of rabbi Isaac (Itshe) Hauptman Shub ("Shohet Ubodek", Slaughterer and Inspector) and was the secretary of the Jewish hospital for many years. He visited Eretz Israel.

Aaron Meller
Translated by Susan Rosin

Aaron Meller was born in Stryj to an orthodox family and was a student and scholar of Beit Hamidrash. In his youth he joined the Hebrew movement and was one of the first active members of the "Agudat HaIvriya" (Hebrew Society) and one of the early Hebrew speakers in our town. He was a member of the Hitahdut party from the start and represented it in many institutions. Since he was a Hebrew intellectual, he lectured and conducted many classes for Hebrew literature and Bible. He was a member of the national council of the party, the board in Stryj and a member of the Israeli office of the party in Lvov. He visited Eretz Israel.

Joshua Oberlaender
Translated by Susan Rosin

Joshua Oberlander was born to an orthodox family and was a student and scholar of Beit Hamidrash. In his youth he joined the Hebrew circle which centered at "Agudat HaIvriya" and was a true zealot for modern Hebrew and activist in the society for many years.

He was an active member of the Hitahdut party and in 1925 its chairman in Stryj. He was an active member of Zionist committees, and took part in the public life of the Jewish community in town.

[Page 132]

Ben–Zion Garfunkel
Translated by Susan Rosin

Ben-Zion Garfunkel was born in Stryj, belonged to the "Hashomer Hatzair" and was the librarian of the "Ivriya Society" for many years. He was a clerk by profession and was among the earliest members of the "Hitahdut" party. For many years Ben-Zion was the party secretary, and he was elected as the party's representative to the Danzig convention. He played many roles in the party's youth movement and was a chairperson of the popular youth movement "Kadima". He was dedicated to the education of the young members, lectured on party issues and produced plays for the youth movement.

He was a secretary of the "Toynbee Hall", "Arbeitsgemeinschaft" and the Stryj correspondent of the party's newspaper "Dos Neie Vort" (The New Word). He was arrested on June 22nd, 1941 by the NKVD with other Zionist activists, and shot at the prison yard on Trybunalska street.

Abraham Levin
by Naphtali Siegel
Translated by Susan Rosin

Abraham Levin was born in Pinsk, came to Galicia in his twenties and in 1900 he settled in Stryj. In 1905 he invented a plough which was patented in Vienna. He received many offers to sell his invention, but refused to do so. Together with Abraham Aurebach he opened a workshop where they produced the machinery. For years the ploughs they produced were sold by agents in the many villages of Galicia. Later he was a plumbing contractor. As an honest and charitable person, he was well liked and drawn to public life. He was the chairperson of the "Yad Harutzim" society, member of the Merchants Bank committee, member of the Kehila committee, member of the boarding school committee and others.

During World War one he was able to save many Austrian prisoners and help them connect with their families members abroad. He was a dedicated Zionist and was preparing to immigrate to Eretz Israel in 1914 and establish a factory with the engineer Szwartz from Tarnopol (passed away in Tel Aviv), but was not able to carry out his plans due to the start of the war.

*

All his children were brought-up in a national Zionist atmosphere. His eldest daughter Lubka married Naphtali Siegel and his son Aryeh (Lolek) lived in Israel since 1935. His daughter Chaya was fluent in Hebrew and lectured at "HaShomer". She was planning to immigrate to Eretz Israel after high-school, but passed away during the war when she was a sophomore. Following her passing, Abraham was very depressed and many of Stryj's Jews came to pay respects to the family. His daughter Hannah (Henia) a graduate of the Lvov University was murdered with her husband Jacob Nagler and their daughter Tamara.

*

Between the two wars he was instrumental with other Zionist activists in establishing a vocational school for boys who were planning to immigrate to Eretz Israel.

He was a dedicated public figure and all his actions were for the greater good and immigration to Eretz Israel. He passed away during World War two before the Nazi occupation of Stryj.

[Page 133]

Levi Opper
by A. Reis
Translated by Susan Rosin

The Zionist–Socialist movement struggle in Galicia, for the Jewish worker corresponds to the years of Levi Opper's activism.

The struggle was between the Z.P.S. (Żydowska Partia Robotnicza) – the Galician Bund, the Polish P.P.S and with the "red" and "white" assimilators for the national and socialist rights of the Jewish worker.

Levi Opper was one of the most dedicated activists for national, Zionist and socialist causes.

The "Poalei Zion" movement was active in their efforts to record Yiddish as the first language in the 1910 census and also in the elections for the Austrian parliament. These activities were followed by bloodshed in Drohobycz due to the opposition to the candidacy of Dr. Lewinstein as a delegate for the Austrian parliament. Levi Opper was active even before the Frist World War, but he specifically distinguished himself as the party activist between the wars in independent Poland. He started his work in the party's youth movement "Jugent", moved through the ranks and became eventually a member of the central committee – a dedicated, sensible and talented leader who was trained in "the tranches".

He was dedicated to Zionism, the "Poalei Zion" movement, the Jewish worker and generally all matters of the Jewish nation. He was a good public speaker, able to influence people and explain topics, had an acute intellect, traits that made him influential in the party and with the public in Galicia. He never pursued any honor or influence and always fulfilled happily any assignment he was tasked with. He was instrumental in establishing manufacturing and cooperative stores in Galicia, actions that were needed due to the ousting of Jews from their economic positions by the Polish government.

He possessed outstanding organization skills and was an excellent public speaker. He always looked for the unifying factors and hated divisiveness. He was moderate in his approach and always strived for compromise and mutual understanding and was dedicated to the Jewish workers movement and socialist Zionism.

During the Soviet occupation he was accused for being part of the municipal council, taken to the jail on Trybunalska street and did not return...

Michael (Mechel) Opper
Translated by Susan Rosin

All children of Joesf Opper came from a family of public activists in Stryj. The oldest son was Levi, the oldest daughter was an active member of the Z.P.S. – the Galician Bund, a younger sister was a leader of "HaShomer HaTzair", Itzhak – an activist in the "Poalei Zion" movement mainly as a youth leader and the youngest son was Michael.

In his youth, Michael was dedicated to the "Poalei Zion" movement. In 1918 as an Austrian soldier he renewed his activities, first with the youth movement and then in the organization's leadership.

In the 1920's he dedicated himself to strengthening and expending of "Poalei Zion" in Stryj, to establishing education institutions, vocational and professional unions and the strengthening of Jewish political awareness.

In 1928 he was elected to the Kehila and later became a member of the leadership. It was due to his vote that the Kehila remained under the Zionists.

Due to his talents, he was relocated by the party to Łódź, where for years he headed the tailors' union.

At the outbreak of World War Two, he returned to Stryj. When the Germans attacked the Soviets he was drafted to the anti-aircraft defense and the fire department. He perished with the rest of Jewish Stryj.

Itta Becher
Translated by Susan Rosin

Itta (Yette) Becher joined the "Poalei Zion" movement at a very young age and was an activist until the holocaust. She worked for Mondsein and after a hard day at the office, she spent her free time in public activism. For many years she was responsible for the Borochov pre-school.

[Page 134]

She helped anyone in need whether at their home or place of business. More than once she gave her entire pay to someone in need although her family depended on it.

In 1926 she was elected with another member of "Poalei Zion" to the leadership of the health organization after it was ruled for more than thirty years by the P.P.S.

Itta was active for many years in women's organizations and was the secretary of the council of trade unions that was comprised of unions of Polish, Jewish and Ukrainian workers.

The Rossler Brothers
Translated by Susan Rosin

The Rossler brothers were born to a very poor family. Being industrious and in spite of their difficult economic situation the brothers were able to get educated and join the popular intellectuals circles in our town.

They grew-up in the very poor Jewish neighborhood called "Die Beshike" (Baszuwka). In that environment the brothers learned first-hand about injustice and social inequality.

The parents wanted to see their sons move out of the workers' class and become merchants. However, the brothers objected and remained faithful to their social origins and were active in the workers' movement.

Yehoshua Rossler
Translated by Susan Rosin

Yehoshua Rossler started his social activism in the Jewish section of the Polish Social Democratic Party (P.P.S.D.). He was among the founders of the Independent Jewish Socialist Party (Żydowska Partia Socjalno-Demokratyczna or ŻPS) and was one of the talented activists, especially in the arena of cultural training.

After the First World War he was the leader of the ŻPS (later the "Bund"). He was unable to be a political activist due to livelihood needs. Ideologically he leaned towards the "Bund" in Poland.

Shlomo Rossler
Translated by Susan Rosin

The fate of the Jewish people during World War One and the Balfour declaration impacted Shlomo Rossler and in 1917 he left his brother's party and joined "Poalei Zion".

Until the end of World War One he led the "Poalei Zion" branch in Stryj and in December 1917 he participated in the convention of party in Krakow. He established the theatre lovers circle. After the war he established a cooperative store and was among the founders of the soup kitchen on Botorego Street and organized the Max Rosenfeld pre-school.

After the split in "Poalei Zion" he joined the right-wing faction and was very active during the 1930's in the "Ihud" (Hitahdut – Poalei Zion).

Shlomo Rossler perished with his wife Rivka (also an activist in "Poalei Zion") and his son.

Shlomo Rosenberg
Translated by Susan Rosin

Shlomo Rosenberg started his public work during the First World War. He was a member of the "Poalei Zion" leadership since 1917. He was a founder of the "Small Merchants Union" and devoted himself to improving the economic status of this socio-economic group that was heavily taxed by the Polish authorities.

Throughout the years he played a major role in the general Zionist group and was also active in the "Ihud" (Hitahdut – Poalei Zion) until the start of the war.

He perished with his family in the holocaust.

Leib Tepper
Translated by Susan Rosin

Abraham Tepper was one of the first to join "Poalei Zion" even before World War one and Leib Tepper was active initially in the Z.P.S and then the Bund.

Leib was one of the young intellectuals in Stryj, and while he was an employee in the wholesale garment sector during the years 1910 – 1917 he was one of the organizers of the young workers in this sector. He was one of the most dedicated to the Jewish trade unions and a member of the Z.P.S for many years.

[Page 135]

In 1917, during the war he was instrumental in renewing the activity of his party. In the 1920's he was one of the leaders of the "Bund" and even later when he had his own business he was still active in the party.

Leib Tepper was murdered in one of the most cruel "aktions" in Stryj. More than a 1,000 people were herded into the Great Synagogue, starved and then killed. On one of the walls a "call for revenge" was found with the name Leib Tepper under it.

David Seltzer
Translated by Susan Rosin

David Seltzer joined the organizing committee of "Poalei Zion" in 1917 and later was one of the most active members.

In 1918 he was one of the organizers and leaders of Hebrew language classes for immigration candidates.

In 1919 Seltzer organized groups of pioneers that were trained for three years on a farm just outside of town. These pioneers immigrated to Eretz Israel in small groups during 1920 – 1921.

During the 1920's David Seltzer participated in the leadership of the education institutions of "Poalei Zion" (pre-schools, day and night schools) and he himself was an instructor at the night school.

In the 1930's David Seltzer worked in Lvov mainly in the cultural arena.

Eliyahu Katz
by Fella Avineri–Katz
Translated by Susan Rosin

Rabbi Eliyahu Katz was born in Stryj in 1889 and was descendent of famous rabbis among them the author of "Pene Yehoshua" (Joshua ben Alexander HaCohen Falk Katz 1555–1614). In his youth he attended Beit Hamidrash in town and was learned in the Torah. He was one of the first young people who responded enthusiastically to Dr. Theodor Herzl's message of national revival and he became one of the most active Zionists in town.

A true intellectual, his political speeches made him one of the spokesmen in eastern Galicia and a Zionist activist in Austria.

His personality was a reflection of the historical events that occurred during his time.

He and his family made their way to Israel as "Ma'apilim" (illegal immigrants during the British mandate) on the ships "Pacific" and "Patria" and he was one of the "Patria" survivors and sent to the detention camp in Atlit.

When he arrived in Israel he became an active member of the general Zionists party and the Central Europe immigrants association and was considered an intellectual of the Bne'i Brith organization chapter of "Ya'akov Ehrlich".

Anyone who met him was charmed by his personality, his cleverness, and his pleasant ways. His memory was famous as a trove of knowledge and wisdom. Until his last day he never lost his intellectual and physical vigor.

This special and inspired personality could have come only from the special atmosphere of Beit Hamidrash students and Zionist national youth in Stryj.

Rabbi Eliyahu Katz passed away in Tel Aviv on the 21st Sh'vat 5722 (January 26th, 1962).

[Page 136]

Dr. Joseph Schuster-Shilo (1896 – 1958)
by Dr. Nathan Kudish
Translated by Susan Rosin

Dr. Shilo was born in a village in the Skole area in eastern Galicia. His parents, Abraham and Frimcie were affluent land leasers. Their sons received both traditional and secular education by private tutors. Until he was 15 years old, Joseph took his exams as a private student in the high-school in Sambor (Sambir). He attended grades 10 – 12 as a regular student and graduated high-school with distinction in 1914.

During the First World War, the estate was ransacked and destroyed and the family moved to Stryj. He continued his studies in Vienna attending two higher education institutions simultaneously: The University where he studied the Humanities and received his Ph.D. in 1919 and the rabbinical school where his graduated with distinction in 1918. His instructors at the rabbinical school were the Rector Schwartz, dr. Shmuel Krauss and dr. Apftobitzer.

After he completed his studies he started teaching. In 1919 – 1923 he was a teacher in the Hebrew high-school "Safa Brura" in Bolechów (Bolekhov), in the Hebrew high schools in £ódŸ and Bia³ystok and the principal at the "Tarbut" school in Lida. From 1923 until 1935 he was the principal of the Hebrew high-school in Wilno (Vilnius).

Of note are the years that dr. Shilo spent working as a teacher, principal and supervisor in Poland as this was a period of growth and success for the Hebrew and National education. His contributions to the education of the young generation during those years were immense. He was respected by the Polish authorities that commended him on his many contributions to the network of Jewish schools in Poland.

He spent his vacations in Stryj with his family. As an intellectual, his friends were among the Hebrew speakers in town. He was one of the pillars of the "Ivriya Society" and contributed greatly to the spread of Hebrew among the younger generation at Stryj.

In 1935 he immigrated to Eretz Israel. He worked as a teacher in the youth village Ben-Shemen, was a principal at the "Nordia" and "Shalva" high-schools in Tel-Aviv and "Beit Hinuh" in Kfar Sabba. From 1944 until 1958 he was a teacher at the Municipal School in Tel-Aviv. He was considered one of the most outstanding educators. He was a pleasant person and always created an enjoyable atmosphere around him – with his friends, coworkers and students.

Dr. Shilo was also devoted to public affairs and was active in the teachers union specifically in matters concerning secondary school teachers.

Lastly, he was also very dedicated to the Stryj organization in Israel. For years he spent time to collect material for the Stryj "Yizkor" book which laid the foundation for the publication. It was his and others initiative to erect a monument for Stryj community, but unfortunately he passed away before it was completed.

Students of the Ziditchev Kloiz in Stryj

The amateur theatre club in memory of S. Ash

The Jewish civil casino in Stryj

The "Dror" sports society in Stryj 1930

The Jewish cooperative bank in Stryj

Standing from right to left: A. Arnfeld, J. Friedler, Zwilling, R. Reish, A. Frie

Seated from right to left: E. Hauptmann, Dr. J. Mishel, A. Edelstein, Dr. M Presser, J. Shefler, H. Handel

[Page 139]

Organizations and Parties
General Zionism in Stryj
Translated by Susan Rosin

The national awakening in our town started about 20 years before the official Zionism and the establishment of the Zionist organization by Dr. Herzl.

There were various manifestations of this awakening – the aspirations for education and the blending of the Jewish culture with the general culture, the aspirations to relax the religion from constrains of the ultra–orthodox traditions and the yearning for healthy and normal social life. Shortly afterwards, like a lighthouse seen from the stormy seas of aspirations and ideologies, a clear target was seen – Zion. The echoes of the Hibbat Zion (Lovers of Zion) movement, the establishment of the first settlements in Eretz Israel had a major impact on the Galician, pre–Herzl Zionism and affected the first Zionists in Stryj.

This Zionism was general in nature although it had various forms depending on the circles and circumstances – religious, intellectual – cultural, national or social.

In 1887 a group of Maskilim (belonging to the Haskala movement – the Jewish enlightenment) headed by A. Sheinfeld and Abraham Goldberg established the "Shoharei Tushia" (seekers of resourcefulness) Society. A group from the society later established another society called "Yahadut" ("Judaism"). These names are evidence of the purpose of these societies – spreading the national idea, supporting the new settlements in Eretz Israel and fostering the Hebrew language and literature.

The practical work of Hovevei Zion in Eretz Israel and in the diaspora inspired the establishment of another society in Stryj in 1890 – "Admat Israel" (the land of Israel) whose purpose was to aid the pioneers working the land in Eretz Israel.

In a convention of Zionist societies in Galicia in 1893 all three of these societies were represented. In 1894, "Shoharei Tushia" was represented by a delegate to the national convention in Krakow.

With the establishment of the Zionist organization by Dr. Herzl and in spite of the ban by the Polish authorities, the high-school youth joined secret Zionist societies.

One hundred and nine Zionist societies from Galicia were represented in the second Zionist congress in 1898 among them "Ahdut" from Stryj. The outstanding Zionist activists in Stryj during that period were Dr. Gershon Zipper, Dr. Julius Wurzel and Dr. Michael Ringel (who was elected in Stryj as a delegate for the second Zionist congress).

In Stryj, like in other towns, the Toynbee Hall was established to disseminate the Zionist ideology, where classes in Jewish culture and history were held as well as lectures on Jewish subjects. The first Zionist library was established as well. The first academic society "Veritas" ("Emuna" – Faith) was established in 1903. Its ideology promoted respect for the national pride and help for Zion. In 1912, at the Zionist academic societies' convention in Drohobycz, "Veritas" was represented by Abraham Insler and in 1913 it was represented by Markus (Mordechai) Kaufmann and Abraham Insler. The Polish authorities in Galicia fixed the voting districts to prevent Jewish majority, and therefore in 1907 in the first ever general elections for the Austrian Reichsrat (Imperial Council) the Zionist candidates were not elected. The Zionist candidate was Dr. Abraham Salz, the Polish appointed candidate was the assimilator Dr. Goldhammer, and the Polish workers party candidate was the engineer Moraczewski. In order to win the Polish and Ukrainian votes, the slogan was "Cross or Mogen David".

Stryj Jews were able to take part in the political activities and they showed their support for the Zionist candidate and ideology. 90% of the Jews voted for Dr. Salz. The first elections were not decisive. The socialist Moraczewski was elected as the candidate of "the cross" although he got 2300 votes and Dr. Salz got 2500 votes (Goldhammer got 900 votes). Moraczewski's victory was due to a fraud committed by Diamant who was also a socialist candidate who was elected by Jews in Lvov. The assimilators candidate was Klarsfeld (who converted and changed his name to Szaczarski) and Isaac Housemann. The Zionist campainers in the 1907 elections were: Dr. Adolf Stand, Dr. Gershon Zipper, Dr. Leon Reich, Dr. Shmuel Rappaport, Dr. Fishel Korngreen, Dr. Ephraim Washitz, Dr. Spindel-Manor, Leibel Taubes, Dr. Malz, Dr. Gedaliahu Shmelkes. Four Jewish representatives – Dr. Benno Straucher, Dr. Adolf Stand, Professor Arthur Mahler and Dr. Heinrich Gabel were elected to the Austrian Reichsrat in 1907 as the first ever national Jewish party in the world.

[Page 140]

The Jewish population in the area grew tremendously (45%) between 1907 and 1911 and with that grew the number of nationally aware eligible voters. The Zionist candidate in the 1911 elections was Dr. Leon Reich. Even those who objected to the Zionist candidate in the previous elections (1907) due to their economic interests did not intervene this time. The head of the community was at the time Dr. Enzel Goldstein (from the Halpern family) and in spite of the fact that the kehila committee was headed by the assimilators, they did not dare to object to the Zionist candidate. The enthusiasm was great and more than 1000 Jews participated in the rallies.

Some of the young activists from Stryj were campaigning in town and in the smaller towns and villages in the area. One of the most outstanding campaigners was Mrs. Heizelkorn (Schiff). The assimilators lost much of their appeal and even the Polish circles were forced to admit that their ideology of Jewish assimilation in the Polish culture lost its luster.

Moraczewski was the Polish socialist party candidate again in 1911. The historian Professor Ashkenazi who was the National Polish party candidate and supported by the authorities received only 22% of the votes. The elections were inconclusive again with Dr. Reich and Moraczewski receiving the same number of votes. In the run–off election, Moraczewski was elected due to higher voting by Ukrainians. The Ukrainian and Polish socialists did not hesitate to use Anti–Semitic slogans to defame even the Polish candidate Dr. Ashkenazi.

In spite of the defeat of the Zionist candidates Dr. Salz (in 1907) and Dr. Reich (in 1911) and although the kehila was headed by assimilators, the Zionist movement in Stryj strengthened and encompassed wider circles. The practical manifestations were the establishment of the Hebrew school "Safa Brura", donations to the Jewish National Fund, learning of the Hebrew language and national–cultural activities in the "Zion" society. In the meanwhile a new generation, those educated on the Herzl doctrine came of age. Among them were high school students that were organized under the "Youth of Zion" and university students that were organized in "Emuna". These became the future leaders of the Zionist movement in our town. Among them were: Dr. Zeev Presser, Abraham Insler and Mordechai Kaufman. The general Zionism was the main body to put into effect the decisions of the Zionist congresses, such as the decision to gain control of the communities (kehila). The election of Dr. Byk as the vice chairman of the kehila in Stryj was considered a major Zionist achievement. Although two new Zionist factions appeared during the initial years of the twentieth century ("Hamizrahi" and "Poalei Zion"), the general Zionism still remained the main national public outlet.

The First World War paralyzed the activities of the Zionist movement as many were drafted into the Austrian army and the general state of emergency affected the public Jewish life in town.

The Balfour declaration of 1917 and the nomination of Dr. Weizmann as the president of the World Zionist organization created a wave of excitement and renewed activism in town.

In 1918, the leadership of the kehila was taken over by the Zionists and was considered a big victory and celebrated in town. The San–Remo resolution of April 30th, 1920 was considered an important historical event and was celebrated in large public gatherings, prayers in the synagogues and a special celebratory session of the Zionist committee.

In the 1920s two additional Zionist parties were strengthened – the "Hitahdut" and "Hamizrahi" competing with the General Zionist. However, it has to be noted that all three Zionist parties in Stryj were able to unite and find common ground under one common organization – the "Arbeitsgemeinschaft" (working group) where issues of general national interests were discussed and decided.

[Page 141]

At that time the, General Zionist camp had experienced and intellectual public figures among its leadership such as Dr. Shlomo Goldberg, Dr. Zeev Presser, Dr. Mordechai Kaufman and Dr. Abraham Insler – people who were leading the kehila, representing the Jewish population in the municipality and who were active in the Jewish National Fund and the Founding Fund.

The activities of the Stryj Zionists were guided by the Eastern Galicia executive committee in Lvov.

Among the Zionist activists in our town: Dr. Benjamin Mihlbauer, Benjamin Klein, Dr. Norbert Schiff, Meir Frankel, Dov (Berl) Stern, Moshe Aaron Wohlmut, Moshe Leib Wohlmut, Eli Hauptmann, Jacob Hauptmann, Mordechai Wagner, Dr. Eisenshar, Rachel Katz, Moshe Meller, H. Wieseltier , Leo Teller, Leon Reich, Moshe Spiegel, Milhard, and Shalom Reich.

"Arbeitsgemeinschaft"

(Working Group – Cooperation Committee)

Translated by Susan Rosin

An umbrella organization combining all Zionist parties (General Zionists, "Mizrahi" and "Hitahdut") in town was established in Stryj in 1923 under the name "Cooperation Committee of all the Zionist parties".

The goal of the organization was to coordinate all the social and political events in town as well as organizing and supervising the Zionist organizations in town such as the Jewish National Fund, Funding Fund, assistance in immigration to Eretz Israel, the Hebrew school "Safa Brura", HeHalutz, Toynbee Hall and others. The Stryj Zionists were probably the only ones that carried out the Zionist congress resolution to establish local cooperation organizations, and that was in spite of the opposition of the various parties.

The meeting place of all the parties was the "Jewish Casino" which was housed in the spacious apartment of the Toynbee Hall on 3rd of May street. All activities were based on the approved regulations of the Toynbee Hall. The casino had one large hall and several small rooms and was furnished tastefully by a special committee. The casino was opened to all the Zionists as well as apolitical persons and it had a meeting hall, a reading room with all the newspapers that were published in Poland and an office for all the Zionist funds.

Based on the "Arbeitsgemeinschaft" regulations, any decisions in city or Zionist matters (such as funds, Zionist organizations) had to be made by a majority at the plenum. In political matters, the various parties normally reached an agreement.

The plenum consisted of eight to ten members from each party, one representative from each fund and one from each Zionist institution (such as "Safa Brura", HeHalutz, etc.). The plenum selected twelve members for the executive committee and from those the chairperson, two deputies and a secretary. The leadership consisted of one member from each of the parties – general Zionists, "Hitahdut" and "Mizrahi". The secretary was always from the "Hitahdut" party.

The organization had major impact on national matters in town and in the municipality mostly because all parties thrived to achieve agreements, and because of the stature of the people that headed it over the years. The chairmen of the organization were: Dr. Zeev Presser, Dr. Mordechai

Kaufmann, Dr. Benjamin Mihlbauer, Leib Schwamer, David Zeidman, Abraham Apfelgreen, Dr. Sebastian Wandell and Dr. Azriel Eisenstein.

The general Zionist members were: Moshe Leib Wohlmut and Moshe Aaron Wohlmut; "Hamizrahi"; Leibush Pickholz; "Hitahdut": Aron Meller, Haim Neuman, Ben–Zion Garfunkel, Avigdor Rotfeld and Jonah Friedler.

[Page 142]

The "Mizrahi" Organization
Translated by Susan Rosin

The "Mizrahi" organization was established in Stryj in 1902 after the awakening of Zionism and as a need by Jewish orthodox nationalists. The organization was established in Stryj before the First World War, but as a separate stream within the Zionist Movement, the Mizrahi made its appearance in Stryj only after the War.

The Stryj branch of the Mizrahi was relative small, but there were a number of active members whose dedicated work created a great impact by the religious–Zionist movement. Their representatives participated in all the kehila and municipal institutions, submitted their candidates' lists and cooperated with the other Zionist parties in the "Arbeitsgemeinschaft". Their members were active in the various funds and in the national and public institutions.

Among the most active members were Abraham Apfelgreen that served as a chair–person of the Stryj branch between 1919 and 1925. Abraham Auerbach was elected as chair–person in 1925. Stryj representatives to the executive committee in Lvov were A. Apfelgreen, Leibisb Pickholz and Yecheskel Lehrer. Other notable members included: Shmuel Shenbach, Shmuel Ginsburg, Zelig Zwilling, Zeev Spiegel, Isaac A. Hubel, Moshe Kudish, Lippa Honig, Shmuel Paris, Shmuel Wiesengreen, Zeide Rotbaum, Haim David Korn and others.

Agudat Israel
Translated by Susan Rosin

After the establishment of Agudat Israel organization in Poland in 1913 a number of the extremely orthodox Jews established a branch in Stryj. In accordance with their organization, the Stryj branch held an anti–Zionist and anti–nationalist views. Active members were: Shammai Gertner, Mendel Horowitz, Israel and Shimon Weiss, H. M. Neubauer, Moshe Zechariah Goldberg, Isaac Hubel and Israel Zeidman. A "Young Agudat Israel" existed for a short period of time.

Agudat Israel was the stronghold of the orthodox Jews in town and had a role in keeping the spiritual and practical religious traditions. It has to be noted that many of the younger Agudat Israel members joined the Zionist organizations such as the Mizrahi and general Zionists and some even joined the HaShomer Hatzair.

Poalei Zion
(The Jewish workers movement)
by Shimon Rosenberg
Translated by Susan Rosin

After the destruction of Polish Jewry by the Nazis and the murder of three and a half million Jews, the Stryj community disappeared like many others. Before the war, fourteen thousand Jews lived in Stryj and they were 40% of the general population. Only few hundreds survived the war in bunkers and hiding places, unable to salvage the materials describing the colorful life of the Jewish community.

Therefore, we are forced to use our memories, fading with the passing years, to describe the life and the facts that were.

Stryj was not different from many of the other towns and villages in Eastern Europe. Thousands of Jews lived there for many years, weaving the web of their lives, adding another link to the many vibrant communities. Like millions of their brethren, the Jews in Stryj during the 18th, 19th, and 20th centuries were split among the various movements of Hasidim and Mitnagdim (opponents), Maskilim (belonging to the Haskala movement – the Jewish enlightenment) and assimilators, Orthodox and heretics; All of them later integrated into the various social–political and the national –revival movements. During the struggles between the various parties and movements, they created their ideologies, dreamed and hoped.

Each person could find and foster his and hers own special place in this vibrant environment. The Jewish workers movement had a major part in this community.

The history of the Jewish community in Stryj and the sixty years of the workers movement is not based on actual evidence as the actual materials were burnt and the witnesses were poisoned in the gas chambers and murdered. The materials covering the years 1914 – 1928 are based on the memories of the writer of these lines who was an active participant, and the rest is based on various sources. Some of the facts were confirmed by the survivors.

May the following notes serve as a memorial to those martyrs who perished in the Shoah.

[Page 143]

Before the Frist World War
Translated by Susan Rosin

The first signs of the "Poalei Zion" movement could be seen during 1900 – 1903, during the years of the first Zionist congresses. The original Zionist-Socialists who were influenced by the Russian Zionist-Socialists and who remained active for many years in the "Poalei Zion" organization were: Berl Friedman and his wife Bertha, Shmuel Horszowski and Levi Opper.

In September 1903, the "Poalei Zion" organization was registered and its constitution approved by the Austrian county commissioner. Based on its constitution, the organization was allowed to develop Zionist and cultural activities. Even between the two World Wars, the constitution was the basis for all the legal activities of "Poalei Zion".

The members of "Poalei Zion" were workers in the trade, watchmaking etc. fields as well as popular intellectuals. This was in contrast to the members of the Z.P.S. (Żydowska Partia Socjalistyczna – Jewish Socialist Party) who were mostly intellectual assimilationists and laborers in areas such as shoemaking, carpentry, tailoring, etc.

In the first years of its existence, the "Poalei Zion" organization acted in accordance with other Zionist organizations, but later became an independent organization which concentrated on Yiddish cultural activities. Establishing the first Yiddish library, lectures and classes to disseminate Yiddish literature and extending political propaganda were among the activities of the organization. The lecturers were given by the Stryj activists as well as by invited speakers from the party central committee. Among the most notable leaders of the party that visited and lectured in Stryj were: Zrubavel, Chazanowitcz, Kaplanski, Loker and others. The outstanding authors who visited Stry were: Abraham Reisen, Morris Rosenfeld, Dr. Nathan Birnebaum and others.

In addition to the above mentioned members the other activists during the first years were: Hannah Leibowitz, Shmuel Shenbach, one of the Katz brothers, M. Polak, M. Petrach, Marshal (from Kałusz), Isaac Oper, Birnebaum and others.

The first Austrian "Poalei Zion" convention took place in 1904 in Krakow, and a delegation from Stryj participated and officially joined the party.

In 1905, meetings were called in town demanding voting rights to the Austrian parliament. During 1906-1907, "Poalei Zion" campaigned for the trade workers demanding that stores would close at 8 PM (at that time stores remained opened until 11 PM or midnight). This activity took place in the entire country and caused demonstrations in Stryj. Finally the stores owners were forced to close at 8 PM and a law was passed to that effect.

In the 1907 elections for the Austrian parliament "Poalei Zion" campaigned for the Zionist candidate Dr. Salz and against the P.S.S candidate Moraczewski and the assimilator candidate Dr. Ashkenazi. In 1908 a campaign was established in preparation for the Yiddish language convention in Czernowitz. For the 1910 Austrian census, the authorities demanded that Jews record German as their first language. "Poalei Zion" opposed this demand and campaigned to record Yiddish as the first language. These efforts spread to all the various parties and were successful. In the last few years before the First World War, Poalei Zion carried out an extensive Zionist propaganda among the poor and the working class. Most of the cultural and educational programs such as lectures on literature, art and social, political and Zionist subjects, took place mainly on Friday nights and during the holidays.

Poalei Zion Youth
Translated by Susan Rosin

The Poalei Zion youth organization was part of "Union of young laborers and trade workers – Poalei Zion" whose center was in Krakow. The function of the center was to organize and educate the working youth with the ideology of "Poalei Zion". There were two additional societies in Stryj: "Herut" (freedom) academic society an affiliate of the union of academic societies in Vienna and a women's organization "Yehudit" affiliated with the central committee of" Poalei Zion". The First World War brought to a halt the activities of all the parties. Many of the activists were drafted into the army and followed by the Russian invasion. Even after the Austrian army regained control of Stryj, the activities of the parties did not start again until the summer of 1917.

[Page 144]

The Awakening Behind the Front
Translated by Susan Rosin

The public activism renewed in the summer of 1917 although the war was still being fought and the front was close to Stryj – along the Russian – Galician border. The first groups of "Hashomer Hatzair" became active in Stryj and some saw the need to renew the activities of the "Poalei Zion" in town.

The originators of the renewed activities were Bertha Friedman, David Seltzer, Shlomo Rosenberg, Feivel Miller, Sara Hauptmann, Shlomo Rossler and the writer of these notes. The first meeting took place in the society's room on Botorego street. The "Poalei Zion" books were moved to a bookcase and pictures of notable Jewish authors and socialist thinkers and philosophers were hung on the walls.

The renewed activities drew much interest in Stryj mostly because all cultural life was stopped during the war.

The new committee included the above mentioned members who were joined by Abraham Hauptmann, Hannah Rappaport, Hella Borer, Aron Meller and Wagner. Because of the war, the activities were limited to the cultural-artistic arena. Since "Poalei Zion" was the only cultural game in town, it attracted most of the Jewish population, both friend and foe. There were plays and lectures given by invited speakers and guests and sometimes even military people. Often times the speakers were unknown to the public, but still the lectures were interesting and important cultural activity was taking place. In time an orchestra was established with Joseph (Josel) Altbauer as the conductor as well as classes for the Hebrew language under the student Zalel Lest, and a class for Jewish literature under Shlomo Rossler. A dramatic group was set up, and amateur actors presented many Yiddish plays at the " Dom Narodny" Hall. Among the playwrights presented were: Jacob Gordin ("Di shkhite" - The Slaughter — the title refers to ritual slaughter, "Khasye di yesoyme" - Khasia the orphan, "Der yidisher kenig lir" - The Jewish King Lear, "Der meturef" - The Worthless), Leon Kobrin ("Der Dorfs-Yung " - The Village Youth), Peretz Hirschbein ("Di neveyle" – Carcass), Fishel Bimko (" Ganevim " - Thieves) Mark Arnshteyn ("Der Vilner baal ha-bays'l" - The Little Vilna Householder) and others. The plays had to be performed several times due to their great popularity. The troupe sometimes performed in the smaller surrounding towns and villages. Among the amateur actors were: Mania Hauptmann, Sheindel Lebowitz, Mania Igra, Abraham Monderer, Bumik Seidenfrau, Dolek Apflegreen, and Max Horowitz. One of the most active producers was Shlomo Rossler who also doubled-up as the prompter.

When the original leaders of the movement, Berl Friedman and Levi Opper returned at the end of the war, the activities intensified and they were joined by new leaders Lea Bert, Dr. Akser and others. In 1919 there were 300 members in Stryj.

*

Eastern Galicia saw the establishment of the Western Ukraine Republic. New Jewish national rights were proclaimed as well as the right to self-determination, but because of the war these were never instituted. During that time, Poalei Zion helped win the Kehila from the assimilationists headed by Dr. Weisenberg, who refused to give-up the leadership and had to be forced-out.

A group of pioneers in training, Slabodke 1930

A group of pioneers in training from Lanns (Stryj) with the leadership of "Hitahdut"

A group of "Buselia" members

"Hahalutz Hatzair" group

Seated right to left: ?, N. Pumertz, A. Rotfeld

Standing right to left: Waldman, Rosmarin, Fruchter, Meltz, and S. Weis

[Page 145]

"Poalei Zion members were among the organizers of the "Workers' council", which did not last long. The council was joined by the Z.P.S (Żydowska Partia Socjalistyczna - the Jewish Socialist Party later "the Bund"), the P.P.S.D. (Polish Social Democratic Party of Galicia and Silesia) who refused to cooperate because they could not come to terms with the new Ukrainian government and the U.S. D (the Ukrainian Social Democrats) who were busy with the matters of the new state.

Shortly after its establishment, the Western Ukraine Republic was engaged in a war with Poland, causing even greater political and economic chaos. Among other national services, the education system collapsed, and only a few Ukrainian schools remained in operation, leaving the Polish and Jewish teachers unemployed. "Poalei Zion" seized this opportunity to establish a system of primary schools with Yiddish as the instruction language. Apartments and the party rooms were quickly converted to class rooms. Enthusiastic parents enrolled their children in the new schools and in a few days the eight classes filled completely, leaving many children on the outside. The school encountered many difficulties – lack of teachers, text books and budget. Sara and Abraham Hauptmann worked tirelessly to find teachers and books. The text books situation was very difficult as the teachers had to translate daily their lesson materials from German and Polish text books. The hope of getting financial support from municipal and state sources was not materialized. As the parents were not used to pay tuition and due to the difficult economic situation after the war, collecting money from the families was out of the question. The school closed after three months. The authorities, who were concerned by the success of the Jewish school, quickly re-opened the state primary school and closed the Jewish school.

During the Ukrainian short rule, Stryj's Jews showed political maturity and established the National Council (Jüdischer Nationalrat), replacing the old Kehila. All men and women aged 21 and over had voting rights. The elections were held at the end of 1919. "Poalei Zion" got 500 votes, thus giving them five representatives: Levi Opper, Berl Friedman, Shlomo Rossler, Professor Lasker, and Abraham Hauptmann. The members worked on the constitution of the council which never materialized due to the crumbling of the Ukrainian republic. A strong youth organization existed during the Ukrainian period which also had some students among its members. The organization established a cooperative store and tried unsuccessfully to establish a manufacturing cooperative.

The Polish Period
Translated by Susan Rosin

The new Polish authorities were not sympathetic to the Jews and promoted organized assaults, oppression of the workers, arbitrary administrative decrees, searches and detentions. The public activism that was flourishing during the Ukrainian rule ceased. "Poalei Zion" opened a soup kitchen on Botorego street to ease the suffering of the laborers and also to disguise the party activities thru this legal institution.

The Split
Translated by Susan Rosin

The split that occured in the "Poalei Zion" organization in 1920 did not originally affect the Stryj branch. But the debates and ideological disagreements paralyzed practically all the activities. During the fifth world convention in Vienna in August 1920, the organization split an event that was followed by conventions in all the countries to determine the future direction of the local branches. The Ukrainian-Polish conflict that was brought before the League of Nations was not yet resolved, "Poalei Zion" in eastern Galicia decided not to join the Polish party. The eastern Galicia convention took place in Lvov in 1921 and the Stryj chapter was represented by Abraham Hauptmann – the right wing, Levi Opper – the center wing and Shimon Rosenberg – the left wing. In the convention, it was decided on neutrality, but after three months, the Stryj branch split as well. Due to legal issues, the party constitution and all the property (the store, the library, the soup kitchen and the apartment) remained in the hands of the right wing. The veteran public figures had all the licenses and permits and those who left the party (the left wing) were most of the activists and the youth. Soon the right wing started to show decline, leading to the closure of the store and the soup kitchen (at the end of 1921) and stopping of the public activities. On the other hand, the left wing of the party was able to heal the wounds of the split and to organize as a strong workers' organization in town.

[Page 146]

The Left-wing Poalei Zion was declared illegal and had to disguise itself at the Beit Ber-Borochov Children's Home. The first pre-school opened in a house on 31 Rynek street. Originally, the activities of the party took place in the pre-school to disguise themselves from the authorities. In 1923 the first trade union was allowed to organize and the party moved its operations to an apartment on 18 Lvovska street. That same year an evening school for workers was opened, and the first class in the " Cisza" school network was established. The "Cisza" school closed after one and a half years (1923 – 1924). However, the night school existed until 1929 and the pre-school until 1930 which provided hot meals to the children with the support of the YMHA in the US. The teachers were: Hava Gartenberg (from Stryj), Esther Sheike (from Warsaw, passed away in Canada), Sonia Talpin (from Austria, perished in the Shoah), Judith Sapcze (from Kholo, killed during the war), Lea and Ruchtche Gartenberg (later in Brazil) and Henia Fruchter. New members made their mark, including Joseph Hess, Michael Opper (perished in the Shoah), Itta Becher (passed away in 1935), B. Streifer (left for the communist camp and later became a provocateur), Joseph Maurer (later an active Poalei Zion worker in Rio de Janeiro), Leib Nussenblatt (passed away in Vienna), Haim Shamir (in Israel) Shmuel Schwarzberg (later in Paris), David Seltzer (killed in the Lvov ghetto), and others.

"Poalei Zion" organization was persecuted by the Polish authorities. In order to minimize the income channels, no licenses were given for performances and other activities. The branch was visited frequently by the police who carried out searches and arrests, especially before the May 1st annual celebrations. However, the activities of "Poalei Zion" did not weaken, and in 1923-24 the party drew all the unions away from the influence of the Bund.

Elections
Translated by Susan Rosin

In 1922 the Poalei Zion presented their own list headed Nathan Buxbaum for the Polish Sejm elections and gained 699 votes. In the 1927 elections for the "sick-fund" for the first time there was an independent Jewish workers' list. In addition to the P.P.S., there was a list of "Poalei Zion" and two delegates were elected: Itta Becher and B. Streifer. Municipal elections were held that year following the Austrian Curia system. "Poalei Zion" participated in the fourth curia and their candidate Shimon Rosenberg got 900 votes. In 1928 "Poalei Zion" presented its own list in the Kehila elections and Michael Opper was elected as a representative of the Zionist bloc. "Poalei Zion" got hundreds of votes in the 1928 elections for the Polish Sejm.

*

During the thirties the police increased the pressure on the party which paralyzed all the public activities. In 1932, the police closed the party's offices and prohibited any public activity, charging them maliciously with communist activities.

[Page 147]

This illegal activity lasted until the beginning of the war. The big Jewish Polish library in memory of Ber Borochov, whose establishment and expansion lasted 30 years, was saved for the time being from a confiscation by the Polish authorities by a legal maneuver. By issuing a promissory note to Machik Horowitz, he became the owner of the library. When the Soviets invaded in 1939, the books were moved to the municipal public library which was destroyed later by the Nazis.

The Jewish Professional Movement
by S. Stryjer
Translated by Susan Rosin

The Jewish professional unions were established at the same time as the Jewish labor parties. The first ones to organize were the professional unions of the Z.P.S. (Żydowska Socjaldemokratyczna Partia Robotnicza). Although the purpose of these unions was to achieve better employment and social conditions, most of them were based on party lines similar to the "Bund" in Russia.

The carpenters organized first in the years 1903 – 1906 when the Z.P.S. strikes started and were able to achieve wages gains. The tailors organized soon after followed by the organizations of painters, shoemakers, and barbers. In all the unions, most of the members were Jewish and the Christians were a minority.

The conflicts between the employers and the laborers erupted normally just before a peak season. When the laborers were in demand, they were able to get better wages, mostly just for the season. Following the peak season, the wages went down again. This was mostly followed by the disintegration of the union.

Throughout the years, there were some achievements – such as – shorter work hours, better wages, insurance in case of illness, etc.

The activists of these unions emerged mostly from among the party activists, and most of them were under the influence of the Z.P.S. The commerce workers were under the influence of "Poalei Zion" and also followed party lines. Commerce workers who were members of the Z.P.S. had to accept the decisions made by "Poalei Zion".

"Poalei Zion" tried unsuccessfully to exert their influence on the other unions. This situation continued until after the 1st World War. The laborers were strongly influenced by the anti-Zionist ideology of the Z.P.S.

In the 1920's the situation changed. "Poalei Zion" concentrated their efforts on the younger generation, planning to expand their influence through them to the unions.

In 1922 – 1923, many young (eighteen year olds) "Poalei Zion" members entered the work force. At first, the Z.P.S did not consider this threat from "Poalei Zion". In the summer of 1923, during the general meeting of the carpenters union, candidates affiliated with "Poalei Zion" won a majority in the committee. Fist fights broke between members of "Poalei Zion" and members of the "Bund" because of the decision to move activities from the "Bund" apartment to the "Poalei Zion" apartment. The banner of the carpenters union went up on the balcony of the "Poalei Zion" house, marking the first victory of the professional movement.

Shortly afterwards, "Poalei Zion" won additional unions – the barbers, the tailors, metals and print workers and workers in chemical plants.

After several years, the unions became apolitical and the "Bund" members and communists joined–in. Most of the members were influenced by "Poalei Zion" and the anti–Zionist character disappeared completely. Some of the unions produced groups of pioneers ("halutzim") who gained the full support of the various committees.

Later, the movement became socialistic in character. Two strikes, that lasted three weeks ended with the workers' victory. The tailors' strike ended in defeat.

In the 1930, the unions ceased to exist mainly due to the communists' activities and harassments by the police.

———

[Page 148]

The "Hitahdut"
by A. Rotfeld and Dr. N. Kudish
Translated by Susan Rosin

The Hebrew worker in Eretz Israel became an important national and social factor following the second Aliyah. The ideal of manual labor and the success to "conquest the Jewish labor" by the Halutzim (pioneers) had a major educational impact on the Jewish youth in the diaspora. An organized core of Jewish laborers was established in Eretz Israel based on the teachings and ideologies brought forward by A.D. Gordon and Martin Buber.

The "Hapoel Hatzair" and "Tze'irei Zion" of Eastern Europe united into a single party at a conference held in Prague in 1920. This in turn laid the foundations of the "Hitahdut" Zionist Labor Party, whose main center was in Galicia.

Following the establishment of the new movement, a group of young men, mostly Hebrew-speaking members of the "Ivriya" society left the Zionist organization in Stryj in 1921 to establish a branch of "Hitahdut" that in the years to come became one of the largest, strongest and most active of the Zionist labor movement in Galicia. They were: Jonah Friedler, Joshua Oberländer, Nathan Kudish, Aaron Meller, David Zeidman and Elimelech Frisch, who were joined later by David Fruchter, Avigdor Rotfeld and Ben-Zion and Aryeh (Leibish) Garfunkel. In 1922, following the third world convention of the movement in Berlin, new members joined the party: Aryeh (Leib) Schwamer, Haim Neuman, David Weiss, Meir Byk, Dr. Azriel Eisenstein, Shlomo Rosenberg and Abraham Hauptmann.

The party started an extensive publicity action specifically among the students and the working youth. New members joined from the ranks of the general Zionists and even from the non-affiliated.

The "Hitahdut" grew quickly and became one of the strongest Zionist organizations in town and an autonomous body in the Zionist organization. The party was a faithful extension of the "Hapoel Hatzair" and the "Histadrut" (the workers' organization) and had a major part as an educating body in the spirit of the working Eretz Israel.

The "Hitahdut" members took active part in all Zionist, economic, professional and cultural organizations, the pioneer training/preparation programs (hachshara), Hehalutz, in the kehila and the municipality and held important positions in many of these organizations.

The party expanded its social reach to include students and working youth, workers, artisans and clerks, and took steps towards increasing the productivity of small merchants, shopkeepers, untrained people, etc.

Societies, institutions and organizations were established within its framework of activities for the achievement of Zionist goals. The party had considerable influence on the life of the Jewish community and on local Jewish issues.

The "Hitahdut" started its activities in the rooms of the "Ivriya" society whose members were the core of the new movement. From there it moved to the Toynbee Hall and later to a "Kadima" room on Czernicki street. An apartment was purchased later on Kościuszko street at the home of Sobel. Eventually, the "Hitahdut" was housed together with the "Haoved" organization.

The "Hitahdut" branch in Stryj covered the neighboring towns and villages of Drohobycz, Borysław, Dolina, Schodnica, Bolechów, Żydaczów, Rozdół, and Żurawno. The district secretary was Avigdor Rotfeld and until the union with "Poalei Zion" the active leaders also included Leib Schwamer, David Zeidman, Dr. Azriel Eisenstein, Aaron Meller, Ben-Zion Radler, Avigdor Rotfeld, Elimelech Frisch, Joshua Oberländer, Ben-Zion Garfunkel, Mundek Fritzhand, Moshe Freilich, Leibish Garfunkel, David Weiss, David Tadanir, Petrach, Robinson, Mordechai Klar, David Fruchter, Isaac Gartner, Dr. Ada

Klein–Reinhartz–Barlev, Dr. Moshe Reinhartz–Barlev, Joshua Steiner, Moshe Rotfeld, Judah Lustig, Nathan Weiss, Shalom Blau, Swartz, Frieda Byk, Belka Fogel, Lippa Kronberg and others. After the merge with "Poalei Zion", Levi Oper and Shlomo Rossler joined the leadership. The party established many institutions, organizations and youth movements each of which had a significant impact on the public and Zionist life in our town and on preparing the youth for life in Eretz Israel.

[Page 149]

The party cooperated with the general Zionists, Hamizrahi and in the Cooperation Committee ("Arbeitsgemeinschaft") that was headed by Leib Schwamer. In the kehila, the party was represented by Leib Schwamer, Dr. Azriel Eisenstein, Haim Neuman, and Shlomo Rosenberg. Leib Schwamer and Dr. Azriel Eisenstein were members of the municipal council in 1933.

The pride and joy of the "Hitahdut" party were the youth movements that were established based on the principals and ideology of the labor movement in Eretz Israel.

The Aaron David Gordon Zionist Youth Organization ("Gordonia") was established in 1923. After several years as part of "Hitahdut", "Gordonia" became an independent educational pioneer youth movement with its own organization.

The Stryj branch was established in 1927 where members were mostly students of the local vocational school. Avigdor Rotfeld mentored the local leadership, among them Eliyahu Goldberg, Mordechai Shechter, and Moshe Haliczer.

Students from the higher grades of elementary school, high schools, vocational schools, and the working youth from workshops, stores, etc. joined the movement. The members were organized into three age groups and each of these was organized into sub–groups containing 10 – 15 boys and girls.

Various activities took place within the groups. Those included: Zionism history, history of the labor movement and settlements in Eretz Israel, scouting and the Hebrew language.

The "Gordonia" members participated in all the Zionist activities in town such as Jewish National Fund, the Funding Fund, the league for working Eretz Israel, etc. Much attention was devoted to educational and cultural activities. Performances for the public in town were held to celebrate special memorial days such as Dr. Herzl and A.D. Gordon's and holidays such as Hanukkah, Tu Bishvat, etc. all these under the leadership of Ben-Zion Garfunkel and Professor Maczik Horowitz. The performances took place at the "Bursa" or the P.P.S hall.

In 1929, some of the older youths began to attend the pioneer training/preparation programs (hachshara) in order to prepare themselves for Aliyah. Indeed many of these came to live in Israel in the kibbutzim, settlements, villages and towns in Israel.

Camps out of town were organized during summer vacations. These were held in Zakopane, Wygoda, Tatarów, Rozwadów and others.

The youth movement had about 80 members. In additions to those mentioned above the other active leaders were Mundek Fritzhand, Fredericka Fogel, Aaron Rotfeld and Yehuda Frankel.

The youth movement was first located in the "Ivriya" society hall, then at Lvovska street and finally at the home of Radler on Zamkowa street.

The "Hitahdut" and then "Hitahdut–Poalei Zion" assisted and supported the "Gordonia" in all their activities.

During the Danzig convention of 1931 it was decided to unite "Hitahdut" and "Poalei Zion", but those who opposed the union in Stryj established "Hitahdut Right" and a youth movement called "Vitkinia". The activists of the new movement were Ben-Zion Radler, H. Preis and Goldfisher.

As most of "Hitahdut" agreed to the union and the Danzig political platform, they remained in the "Hitahdut" framework and later established a

Zionist–Socialist youth movement for those who were 18 years old and older "Busselia" in memory of Josef Bussel from Degania who drowned in the Kinneret (Sea of Galilee). "Busselia" had several pioneer training/preparation (hachshara) camps: Bielsko, Dolina, Bolechów, Żydaczów, Żurawno, Tarnopol and Stryj.

[Page 150]

The "Busselia" activists and leaders in Stryj were Yehuda Lustig, Mordechai Schechter, Milek Marbach, Moshe Rotfeld (all in Israel). Others that immigrated to Israel were: Eliyahu Kuk, Shulamit Neuman, Shlomo Flick (in Kiryat Anavim), Yaffa Keller–Haliczer, Shprinza Schprung–Lustig.

"Busselia" also established a collective settlement in Ramat HaSharon. That group later split and part of its members joined Kiryat Anavim.

Another popular youth group was "Kadima" who later joined "Hitahdut". Ben–Zion Garfunkel devoted much of his time to this group.

Due to the party's initiative, and especially David Zeidman, the workshop for Jewish boys was expanded, and new disciplines were added: engraving, blacksmithing, metal–working to become a full–fledged vocational school. In time, this institution became a vocational high–school – one of three of this type in all of Galicia. The study course was of three years, and the graduates received a high school diploma while obtaining vocational and theoretical education. The engineer Wolowski headed the school in the years leading to the war.

Dr. Schindler, a non–partisan lawyer headed the school committee for many years.

Students from all over east Galicia came to this school in order to prepare themselves for Aliyah and constructive life. A boarding house was added for those students whose parents were unable to support them financially. Among the institutions that supported the school was "Ezra" (help/assistance) whose main function was preparing the Halutzim.

Most of the vocational school students were organized in the youth movements of "Gordonia" and "Busselia" and many of them became leaders who contributed greatly to the growth of these movements in our town. Many of the graduates immigrated to Eretz Israel and proudly continued working in the trades they acquired at the school.

The active members of the school board were Haim Neuman and Abraham Levin.

The Unification of "Hitahdut" and "Poalei Zion"
by A. Rotfeld and Dr. N. Kudish
Translated by Susan Rosin

In 1921, the "Poalei Zion" party in Stryj split into right and left wings. In 1930, during the Danzig convention it was decided to unify "Poalei Zion" right wing with the "Hitahdut" party under the name "Ihud" (union). The veteran leaders of the "Poalei Zion" Levi Oper, Shlomo Rosenberg and Shlomo Rossler joined the "Ihud" and became part of the leadership of the new party. The "Ihud" was welcomed and joined by many people belonging to student and working youth circles, craftsmen, clerks, academic youth, etc. The leaders of "Ihud" were Dr. Azriel Eisenstein, Leib Schwamer, Avigdor Rotfeld, Aaron Meller, Haim Neuman, Ben-Zion Garfunkel, Levi Oper, Shlomo Rosenberg, Shlomo Rossler, Moshe Freilich, Meisels, Neta Lindner, Mordechai Reinhartz (Bar –Lev), Leibish Garfunkel, Lippa Kronberg, Robinson, Blau, Rubinstein and Yehoshua Steiner.

The candidates for the 17th congress in 1931 on behalf of the working Eretz Israel were Dr. Azriel Eisenstein, Leib Schwamer, Avigdor Rotfeld, Aaron Meller, and Ben-Zion Garfunkel and the "Ihud" received 425 votes in Stryj. In the elections for the world committee of the "Ihud", the Stryj branch got four mandates. The "Hitahdut" established a cooperative for carpenters, to prepare them for Aliyah. This was a new model for immigration – craftsmen with their equipment not as part of the pioneers' immigration.

1933 was an important year for the "Hitahdut" in our town. A celebration to mark the unification of "Hitahdut – Poalei Zion" took place in March of that year in the "Bursa".

[Page 151]

A regional convention of "Hitahdut – Poalei Zion" encompassing 11 towns was held in October. A regional committee was elected with Avigdor Rotfeld as secretary and Shlomo Rossler, Aaron Meller and Meisels as committee members. A farewell party for pioneers and craftsmen immigrating to Eretz Israel was also held that year.

However the main event and a historic occasion that year was the visit of David Ben-Gurion in Stryj which aroused great enthusiasm among the Jewish population of the city. A celebration in his honor was held in the "Adison" theater. A regional convention was held in the "Dom Narodny" with the participation of 18 towns and villages. The main event was a lecture by David Ben-Gurion. In the 1933 elections for the 19th Zionist congress, the "Ihud" had an absolute majority with 1260 votes.

The "Ihud" expanded its activities by creating a "Jewish Clerks' Association" as part of its trade union activity. Up until that time, most clerks worked in stores, financial and economical institutions and in manufacturing and were not organized. The chairperson was Leib Schwamer and Mordechai Keler the secretary. They were followed by Abraham Hauptman as chairman and Rubinstein as the secretary. The members of the first committee were Abraham Hauptman, Moshe Freilich and Avigdor Rotfeld. The last chairperson was Leib Garfunkel.

The party also established a school for sewing and tailoring. Girls who graduated from elementary school and even those with a high school diploma who wanted to learn a craft and were planning an Aliyah attended the school where the tuition was minimal. There were also classes for embroidery under the supervision of the teacher Wurt.

The "Ihud" had great political power among the Jewish people and played a major role in the immigration of large number of members to Eretz Israel.

[Page 151]

Ha'Oved (the worker)
by A. Rotfeld and Dr. N. Kudish
Translated by Susan Rosin

In 1933, a branch of the "Ha'Oved" was established in Stryj. The purpose of this movement, as part of the "Ihud" party was to organize craftsmen and other workers, to provide vocational education and to prepare them for Aliyah.

A convention of the "Ha'Oved" branches took place in Stryj on August 26th 1933. The participating branches included: Drohobycz, Borysław, Turka, Schodnica, Skole, Chodorów, Bolechów and Dolina. The chairperson of the Stryj branch, Ben-Zion Scherer represented our town. A general convention took place in November 1933 and Dr. Zilberstein and Mr. Herring participated.

The leaders were Ben-Zion Scherer, Malka Tanne (Fruchter), Moshe Zipper, Nathan Walter, and Shalom Blau and they worked tirelessly to strengthen and increase the influence of the movement. The number of members grew to 300. A spacious apartment was acquired by the branch, to allow it to expand the professional and cultural activities. The branch was supported by the "Ihud" party. Member of "Ha'Oved" were active in all the Zionist and Jewish activities such as the various funds, "Gemilut Chasadim", the Jewish hospital and "Yad Harutzim". In 1932, "Haoved" established the "Hapoel" soccer team and its members were active in training the youths in sports. Many of the "Ha'Oved" members immigrated to Eretz Israel and lived to see the establishment of the state of Israel.

Z.A.S.S. (Zionist Socialist Academic Society)
by A. Rotfeld and Dr. N. Kudish
Translated by Susan Rosin

The "Hitahdut" party had a great impact on the Jews in Eastern Europe. The party was the educational and organizational extension of the labor movement and the workers organization in Eretz Israel. The national-socialist ideal of the organized workers in Eretz Israel was captivating to the academic youths who were unable to join the existing corporations due to their political views.

[Page 152]

Those who were looking for an organization matching their democratic outlook found a home in the "Hitahdut" movement.

Academic societies, whose members were affiliated ideologically and socially with the labor movement and the Histadrut (the workers' organization) in Eretz Israel were established in many towns in Galicia.

The "Hitahdut" party activists Dr. Azriel Eisenstein, Dr. Ada Bar Lev – Klein (a physician) and Dr. Mordechai Bar-Lev-Reinhartz, distributed fliers calling the academic youths in Stryj to establish a Zionist-socialist society in town. The flier stated the lack of an organization where the socialist academic can find others of the same views, gain education, and prepare for life in Eretz Israel. By establishing a society in the framework of the party, the Jewish academic would be able to realize his/hers national and social views.

The response to the flier were very positive and many young men and women attended the meeting on January 15th, 1931 in the "Hitahdut" apartment at number 10 Kościuszko street and decided to establish the academic Jewish society Z.A.S.S. They rented an apartment, opened a library and started preparing for Aliyah. Many of the movement activists as well as emissaries from Eretz Israel were among the guest speakers. Among them were Fishel Warber, the secretary general of "Hitahdut" in Galicia, Dr. Kopel

Schwartz, the president of "Hitahdut" in Galicia and Haim Schorer from Eretz Israel.

The activists of the movement were: Dr. Azriel Eisenstein, Dr. Ada Bar Lev – Klein, Dr. Moshe Bar Lev, Klara Zeidman, Henek Mayer, Zvi Wohlmut, Loncia Wolf-Rotfeld, Moshe Hauptmann, Liora Meltzer-Hauptmann, Anda Buchman, Rossler, Mundek Pritzhand, Milek Weissbart, Salka Wohlmann, Ruzka Neimann, Belka Fogel, Goldman and Rosenzweig. Additional Z.A.S.S members were: Haim Zeif, David Schechter, Salek Feldman, Hana Oper, Maciaka Weinbach, Hava Teicher, Rivka Rotbard, Leon Rapp, Izio Korn, Shlomo Resenmann and Litaur.

HeHalutz (The Pioneer)
by A. Rotfeld and Dr. N. Kudish
Translated by Susan Rosin

In 1918 Josef Trumpeldor started a pioneer movement in Russia that quickly spread to Lithuania, Poland and other central European countries. The world "Hehalutz" organization was established in 1921. Many young people made-up their minds to leave the diaspora, become pioneers in Eretz Israel to prepare it for future mass immigration.

Most of the first group of pioneers from Stryj came from "Hashomer Hatzair". Even before the establishment of the world "Hehalutz" organization, a group from Stryj emigrated in 1920. The first one was Eliezer Feis who was followed by Issachar Katz, Shamai Rosenberg, Moshe Oper, Eliezer Altshuler and Mendel Zimmerman. Two groups of women pioneers, also from the "Hashomer Hatzair" emigrated the same year.

The members of these groups were among those who paved the roads and established the foundation for communal life in a kibbutz.

Before their departure, a ceremony was held in town. Among the participants were the leaders of the Zionist movement in tow: Dr. M. Kaufman, Rachel Katz and others. Malka Leibowitz, the head of "Hashomer Hatzair" in town passed the movement's flag to the pioneers Josef Roth and Rivka Zelinger to be placed in the homeland.

After the immigration of the first group a branch of "HeHalutz" was established in Stryj in 1922. The movement required that members realize their Zionist goals by immigrating and working in Eretz Israel.

"HeHalutz" members who came from all walks of life studied the Hebrew language, history of Zionism, history of the Jewish people, geography of Israel and the history of the labor movement.

All activities were directed by the center in Lvov.

Preparation/training (hachshra) camps were established in the villages of Uhersko and Dołhołuka in close proximity to Stryj. The "Hahlutz" center contacted landowners who employed pioneers on their farms. In addition, many pioneers got their training in the vocational school. Other training centers were held in Synowódzko, Nadwórna, Broszniów, Zabłotów, and other locations.

The academic society "Kadima" – Stryj 1931

Standing in first row from right to left: **Schindler, Bergman**

Second row: Pomernaz, Gertenberg, Shenfeld, Roth

Third row: Kerner, Kofman, Diamant, M. Wiesaltir, Berlin, Kogel

Seated: Spinard, Rothenberg

The academic committee of the Grossmanic party:

Standing from right to left: Mgr. L. Sternberg, Friedler, Mgr. I. Weidenfeld, I. Feller, Dr. Rosenman, I. Igra

Seated from right to left: Tilda Hand, Mina Arbach, Dr. Norbert Schiff, Luba Schwalb, Genia Heiber

The Student society "Hebronia" in Stryj

"Poalei Zion" activists – 1926

The leadership of "Hamizrahi" 1933 in Stryj

Committee of the Z.P.S party – 1918

The youth of "Agudat Israel" in Stryj

"The HeHalutz" in Stryj 1923

[Page 153]

Most of the Halutzim who were preparing themselves for Aliyah in the camps were 18 years of age or older.

However, younger working youths from poor families joined the Stryj branch of "HeHalutz". After a day of work, they came to the branch to study Hebrew, history and geography. Parties, dances and singing evenings were organized, so that this group of "HeHalutz Hatzair" (the young pioneer) can familiarize themselves with national and cultural values. This was an enthusiastic group who dreamed of redeeming themselves from the desperate poverty and dreaming of life of labor in Eretz Israel.

The leadership of "HeHalutz" in Stryj included Isaac Gartner (secretary), Jacob Wald, M. Reinhartz, Avigdor Rotfeld (secretary), David Weiss, David

Lustig, Esther Altbauer (secretary), Munish Hubel, Sara Tanne, Hana Eichen (secretary), Rachel Meller, Moshe Wagner, Haim Schefer, and Hana Engelman-Zimmerman.

Starting in 1922, many "HeHalutz" members immigrated to Eretz Israel. Among them: Isaac Glazer, Shapira, Tzippora Byk, Lea Brand, Haya Pikholz, Itta Rosenberg, David Frankel, Kerner, Jacob Wald, Jacob Rappaport, Mendel Genzel, Simcha Davidman, Arie Fruchter, Meir Kez, David Tadanir, Rivka Sokol-Lustig, Neta Lindner, Joshua Steiner, Eliezer Koch, Feiga Feldhorn and others.

In the 1930 whole families immigrated. Among them the families of: Shimshon Steiner, Haim Neuman, Moshe Weiss, Avigdor Rotfeld and others.

Hashomer Hatzair
by Josef Gilat (Gottlieb), Kibbutz Gat
Translated by Susan Rosin

The first years of independent Poland were those of national sensitivity and social turbulence. The Polish youth started uniting in national organizations such as the sporting movement "Sokol", Polish scouts movement "Harcerz" and paramilitary organization. The Ukrainian youth also united in a scouting movement similar to the Baden-Powel scouting movement. Later this organization became the O.O.B. – a fighting organization.

Based on this national awakening among the Poles and Ukrainians and with the influence of other youth movements in the world such as "Wandervogel" and the international scouts organization established by Baden-Powel, I want to describe the establishment and growth of the "Hashomer Hatzair" in Stryj.

The national Zionist revival , the enthusiasm following the Balfour declaration, the first settlements in Eretz Israel and the socialist movements influenced the youth in Europe and the Jewish Youth as well after the First World War.

The wave of progress, openness, enlightenment and the social turbulence affected people from all walks of life – the well-educated, the ultra-religious and the ordinary people alike.

The image of the Jewish youth wearing a gray shirt, blue shorts, wide-brimmed scouting hat, a colorful scouting tie and insignia and a long walking stick were the images of the "Shomer" (guard, watchman, or sentry). Many times we would watch a gathering of these youths, not far from the Stryj river around a large birch tree, that was eventually called the "Shomrim Tree".

Here come the Rechter brothers, the Kudish brothers, the Hochs from Lvovska street; Here are the Findlings, the Fennigs, Kligers from the rynek, the Schlaks from Zamkowa, the Bonoms from the outskirts of town, the Reinhartzs from Drohobyczka and many others; The best of the studying and working youths gathered on weeknights and on Saturdays.

[Page 154]

The people I mentioned were the "third generation", meaning they did not know the founders, the original "shomrim".

Who were the forefathers of the "Hashomer Hatzair" in Stryj? It is possible that the beginning of the movement was in 1916 when a small and modest movement named "scout" was established and active on Gerberska street. Others say that the founders were Aryeh Krampner and his friends from the Vienna university who were vacationing in Stryj. Yet others think that the founders were a group of high school students from the neighboring town of Bolechów led by Michael Händell (later the high schools supervisor in Israel), Jacob Seeman (later a Hebrew poet and author in France) and Izio Silberschlag (later a Hebrew poet and author in the US). We remember the energetic and enthusiastic youths: Yuzek Roth, Poldek (Napoleon) Lautman,

Hadassah Dickman, Haya Schlaks, Dzunka Fried, Milek Rechter, Tonka Rechter, Malka Leibowitz, Pnina Freilich, Pnina Reinharz, David Korn (later in the US), and Rivka Selinger. It seems that one of the reasons to establish "Hashmer Hatzair" in our town was the existence of the organized studying youths in secrets Zionist movements even before the First World War, the "Youth of Zion". In time they found their way to the "Shomer" movement and then "Hashomer Hatzair" that at the beginning was a scouting movement. The teachers and lecturers in those days were: Zvi Diesendruck, Naphtali Ziegel, Tulo Nusenblatt, Yehoshua Tilleman, Dr. Salek (Bezalel) Lest, Dr. Aryeh Drefler and Dr. Jacob Laufer.

Thinking young Jews in our town as in other areas of Galicia had reached the conclusion by the years 1918-1920 that there were no prospects for a life of national and social freedom in the diaspora, and wished to fulfil their aspirations in Eretz Israel.

In 1919-1920, with the start of the third Aliyah, two groups of Haluzot (pioneer women) left Stryj for Eretz Israel. They became known as "Bat Sheva", consisting of seven girls and "Ve heheziku" also consisting of seven girls and one young man - Meir Wieseltier (so named in reference to the verse in Isaiah 4, 1, "And seven women shall take hold of one man"). They demanded to pave roads and break gravel. You could still meet these legendary figures in the oldest kibbutzim such as Bet Alpha, Merhavia, Mizra, Mishmar Ha'emek, and others. The "Jugend" and "Hashomer Haoved" organizations joined "Hashomer Hatza'ir" in 1923.

The Stryj branch of "Hashomer Hatzair" expanded and its active members participated in all the conventions and the committees of the movement. Forty Shomrim and Shomrot from Stryj participated in the Shomrim convention held in July 1918 in Tarnowa-Wyzna near Turka. One of the leadership reports stated that the Stryj branch was expanding and 70% of its members were Hebrew speakers.

The leader for many years in Stryj was Malka Leibowitz. She believed that the popular Shomrim would bring more people closer to the ranks of the movement. The branch in Stryj was one of the first in Galicia to have groups of Shomrim from among the laborers and store clerks (Kraków, Tarnów, Jarosław, Stryj). Malka, who became a pediatrician later, did not live to fulfill the movement's ideology, but was completely dedicated to the young Shomrim in thick and thin. She was very active in "Patronat" or "Opayka" which were supporters of the "Hashomer Hatzair" organization in the difficult reality in Poland.

Even during the First World War, uniform wearing Jewish soldiers organized classes, lectured at the "Ivriya" and "Poalei Zion", and the veterans among us remember those who were spreading the Hebrew language among them Naphtali Ziegel.

The organizations that had much influence on the "Hashome Hatzair" members were "Ivriya", who spread the Hebrew language and "Poalei Zion".

[Page 155]

The members were eager to learn the Hebrew language. The most active members at the "Ivriya" were: Naphtali Ziegel, Joseph (Shuster) Shilo, Jonah Friedler, Naphtali Gartner, Aaron Weiss (Tzahor) (later a member of Mishmar Haemek), David Weiss (Tzahor) (later a member of Ein Shemer), the Garfunkel brothers and others. Many at the "Ivriya" were influenced by the idealism and enthusiasm of the pioneers – Shomrim whereas the Shomrim were influenced by the studiousness of the "Ivryia" members and as a result of this interaction many of the pioneer movement members immigrated to Eretz Israel.

"Poalei Zion" and the Borochov library had a part in shaping the Stryj Shomer. This was a period of formulating ideas and concepts and the library aided greatly. The "Poalei Zion" had activists such as Shimon Rosenberg, Ida Becher, Josef Hess, Michael Oper and others.

One of the interesting phenomena was the involvement of the girls in the movement. Starting with the activism of Malka and continued through the immigration of many girls. Two explanations for this phenomenon: it was easier for girls to obtain the necessary papers and many boys left the movement after graduating from high-school.

Many abandoned the movement due to the demands for fulfillment that proved too difficult. Some left the movement quietly, others came-up with excuses, yet others bad-mouthed the movement. These incidents were weapons in the right-wing opposing parties' hands. Malka came to the rescue again to strengthen the movement together with Dr. Ada Klein and other activists from the left – Leib Shwamer and Haim Neuman.

Several pioneer - Zionist movement existed in Stryj during 1927 – 1930. During the third Aliyah, there were always Shomrim from Stryj. Many joined the various "Hashomer Hatzair" kibbutzim Beit Alpha, Merhavia, Mizra, Sarid, Mishmar Ha'emek, Ein Shemer, Ein Hamifratz and Kibbutz Gat.

When I immigrated in 1930's, the Stryj branch of "Hashomer Hatzair" was still active and was headed by Zvi (Honig) Steif, Naphtali Lorberbaum and Libka Szapira; but they never achieved their aspiration and perished with the rest of the community.

The Women of Stryj
by Zvi Livne (Liberman}
Translated by Susan Rosin

In the summer of 1920 the immigration to Eretz Israel strengthened from week to week and most of those were looking to work on the roads and in the quarries.

Seven girls from Stryj, all of them 17 – 18 years old, high school graduates, all of them members of the "Hashomer Hatzair" and Hebrew speakers boarded a ship and upon arrival registered at the "Hapoel Hatzair" immigration center. They requested to be assigned to a work group together.

The work that was available mostly at the time was in paving roads. That was a hard work even for the men. It was not common to send women to work on the roads. The few women who did work on the roads, were part of organized work groups and they mostly worked in the kitchen, doing laundry and cleaning. It was actually forbidden by the leadership to send women to work on the roads.

Every morning these seven women showed-up at my office, and their "representative", Miriam, would step forward and claim: When will you send us to work? Yesterday you sent 20 men, and today you are sending more. When will our turn come? We don't want to wait any longer.

[Page 156]

I tried to send some of them to the other groups, but they refused. They wanted to work together. It was hopeless, and I did not know what to do. I was afraid to send them, as the supervisor had forbidden this.

They showed-up every day, and I kept promising and telling them to be patient.

One morning I gave-up and said: OK. You are leaving tomorrow. Hopefully we will hear good news. They were exuberant, and went to pack their belongings. When they were leaving, I said: I suggest you call your group "Bat Sheva".

I was very uncomfortable about what I did – what if their health will suffer? What if the road management will send them back? Also, the rest of the people in the office criticized me for my "courageous act" and in my heart I agreed with them...

One day, a team leader showed up in the office, and I asked him if by any chance he heard about the group of seven girls from Stryj working on the roads.

"Did you mean the "Bat Sheva" group?" he asked? "How could I not know about them? They are the best workers! All of them are working in the gravel shattering, and their work is outstanding. Their daily quota of gravel equals that of the most experienced men, and many times they even exceed them. Everybody at camp is proud of them and praises the excellence of their work".

I was so happy! After a while, another group of women arrived from Stryj on one of the ships, all of them "Hashomer Hatzair" members. This time, there was one man with them – seven women and one man. When I registered them in the work assignments book, I had to laugh, and told them I'll register them as "Ve heheziku" group.

With the experience of the "Bat Sheva" group, I did not hesitate, and sent them immediately to work on the roads. This group, too, excelled in their work.

Up until today, you can meet in the "Hashomer Hatzair" kibbutzim members of these groups. They distinguish themselves in their work and in the part they take in public life.

In the history of "the conquest of labor" (by Jewish pioneers in Eretz Israel) these two groups from Stryj led the way and broke new grounds.

From "Chapters of the Third Aliyah" by Zvi Livne (Liberman)
"Sifrei Gadish" Publications, Tel Aviv, 1958

The Revisionist Movement
by Zvi Steiner
Translated by Susan Rosin

Towards the end of 1925 a group of young students including Shalom Goldberg, Karol Einhorn and Moshe Steiner started the Revisionist Movement in Stryj. At the beginning many who joined the movement were "deserters" from other parties. In time, the revisionist movement ideology was spread to those that were far from Zionism and even Judaism. The movement got a great boost with the joining of the well-known and energetic Zionist leader David Zeidman. In the elections for the 14,th congress, the revisionist party received 116 votes, more than any other party, an event that generated a congratulatory telegram from Ze'ev Jabotinsky.

[Page 157]

The appearance of the new party with its nationalistic political slogans such as Jewish state, Jewish troops, free immigration, colonizing regime etc. produced interest and enthusiasm among the youth on one side, and reservations and opposition from the old-established parties on the other. In spite of this, the relationships with the other, more traditional parties were good, mostly due to David Zeidman's personality. He worked tirelessly to dull the movement's revolutionary edge and its extremist character. Therefore the movement in Stryj had a special character. Zeidman tried to prevent any political decisions that will impede the relationships with the other Zionist parties and he knew how to handle the attacks by youth who criticized his politics.

The movement grew, establishing the "Betar" youth movement, the Revisionist Hehalutz which was founded under the leadership of Eliyahu Waldman and the joining of the academic corporation "Hebronia".

The party increased its political activities and the members were active in all the national funds, the elections to the town council and the kehila. However, because of the Palestine-centric character of the movement, the members did not take active part in these institutions. Among the active members were Shalom Goldberg, Karol Einhorn, Mgr. Sternberg, Mgr. Rechter, Clara Bleiberg, Dr. Wandel, Mgr. Garfunkel, Mgr. Arnold, Naphtali Rotbaum, and others.

Following the Katowice conference in 1933, the party split. Leaving the Zionist organization and moving away from the ideals we grew-up upon shocked many. It seemed that only in Stryj this decision was not implemented. Under the influence of Zeidman, the split was being postponed until finally, a large portion of the members went over to the Grossman camp which eventually became one of the strongest parties in Poland.

The remaining handful rallied and within a year established the "New Zionist Organization" (H.Z.CH.), known as "Hatzach". The most active members in the new organization were Shalom Goldberg and dr. Shimshon Shertok. In addition to "Betar" and "Hebronia" three additional organizations were established: 1. "Brit HaHayal" (the Soldier Covenant) under the leadership of dr. Gross and dr. Lautman. This was an organization of common people who were joined by porters and coach drivers all strongly believing in the idea of the Jewish state; 2. "Brit Avodah" (Work covenant) was an organization of working students under the leadership of engineer Grieb; 3. "Brit Yeshurun" for the yeshiva students under the leadership of Naphtali Galantner and Josef Friedler. The Tel Hai Fund was also established but it did not achieve its growth goals. Jabotinsky's 1933 propaganda trip and the "evacuation" and state ideas brought new life to the movement.

The state of Israel was established, but the overwhelming majority of those young people, who believed in its establishment, in a Jewish army, Jewish police force and a Jewish rule did not live to see this historical event. They perished in the shoah and were not buried in a Jewish grave.

May their memory be blessed.

The "Betar" Movement
by Berko Igra
Translated by Susan Rosin

At the end of 1926 a young student named Uri Shenberg established a scouting movement that eventually became "Betar" or Brit Josef Trumpeldor. After he left, the leadership passed to Josef Erman. The branch really flourished when the leader became the talented Josef Hauptman assisted by Reuven Hoffman, Miriam Haftel, Zvi Steiner and Berko Igra. From 1928 until 1935, the branch leader was Zvi Steiner after Josef Hauptman left Stryj. Mr. Berko Igra provided the branch with two rooms in his house on Berko Yosilewicz street, rent free. The branch was instructed by the regional commanders in Lvov and Stanisławów and had more than one hundred members. The purpose of this organization was to straighten the backs of Jewish youth, instill statehood values, and prepare them for military service in the impending Jewish State. This scouting movement which had military characteristics and discipline adopted the symbol of the Jewish Legion (Hagdud Ha'ivri), the menorah. The national symbols and slogans attracted boys and girls from all circles: clerks, apprentices and students in spite of the ban by the schools to belong to a Jewish youth movement.

[Page 158]

The branch was structured into three age groups and the transition to the next level was dependent on passing certain tests and on personal behavior. The cultural and educational activities such as Hebrew and Jewish studies, history of Zionism and Israel geography were held in smaller units. The youths were trained in sporting activities, drills, excursions and trips in battalions comprised of three to four groups under the leadership of Zvi Steiner, Reuven Hoffman and Berko Igra.

The movement made efforts to include the Jewish youths into the Polish para–military movements to enable them to train with weapons. It was the first time that Jewish youth marched with rifles in their hands.

With the growth of the branch, additional leaders stood out: Zeev Stein, Isaac Weintraub, and Abba Oster. Among the most active members were Reuven Neubauer, Dov Wisaltier, Hana Open and Yocheved Schechter.

A regional headquarters was established in Stryj in 1930 with responsibility for the following branches: Borysław, Bukaczowce, Dolina, Drohobycz, Wygoda, Żurawno, Żydaczów, Żabie, Medenice, Sokołów, Rożniatów, and Kałusz. The regional headquarters organized meetings and conventions, vocational training and summer camps. The experiences in nature provided a picture of what life would be in the homeland in Eretz Israel.

The head of "Betar", Zeev Jabotinsky visited Stryj in 1933, and his visit provided a deeply felt experience for the members in our town.

Who could imagine that these dedicated youths who swore to die or to conquer the "mountain" would not realize the fulfilment of their dreams.

May their memory be blessed.

"Masada" and the Revisionist HeHalutz
by Meir Kez
Translated by Susan Rosin

As with other movements, soon after the establishment of the general revisionist movement a process of political differentiation and branching began to manifest itself. This was caused by the different attitudes of the members joining the central ideology of the movement. In 1928, two years after the establishment of "Betar", a new society of revisionist youth was established in

Stryj under the name "Masada". Soon about one hundred members joined. The reason for this split was mainly the more moderate approach of the "Masada" members who had reservations about the extremist slogans of "Betar"; they did not like the military discipline and uniforms. In addition they were older than most of the "Betar" members.

The society was located in the house of Kerner at the "rynek". "Masada" was headed by Josef Erman, Lautman and Honig who left "Betar". In 1930, "Masada" became the first revisionist pioneering movement in Stryj, because its members committed themselves to the central ideal of the Zionist movement - fulfillment and immigration to Eretz Israel in addition to activities of education and propaganda. A training camp in Dilove near Stryj was established and members who were planning to immigrate were trained in carpet weaving. The Zionist leader Robert Striker visited the center in 1931. Until the split in the revisionist movement, "Masada" was part of "Betar". After the split between Jabotinsky and Grossman, "Massada" members joined the Grossman camp mainly because of the possibility of immigration to Eretz Israel.

Eli Waldman and Meir Kez participated in the first convention of the "Grossman Revisionists" in Warsaw. The active members of the movement were Eli Waldman and David Zeidman who worked tirelessly for the immigration of the revisionist pioneers. Their memory will never be forgotten by those whom they helped to immigrate. A lot of work went into preparing documents, immigration papers and obtaining funds for those immigrating. The members devoted to these activities were mgr. Sternberg, Eli Waldman and Meir Kez obtaining help from the "Ezra" ("help") fund who supported the immigration. "HeHalutz" was active in Stryj until the holocaust. Tens of members immigrated. A convention in 1934 was held in Eretz Israel and was attended by the leader of the "Statehood Revisionists" Meir Grossman.

Second World War

"HeHalutz" organization 1925

"HeHalutz" organization 1925

"Gordonia" organization 1930

Members of the Revisionist organization in Stryj

The committee of "Poalei Zion" 1917 –1918

From right to left: First row: **L. Mentel, S. Rosenberg**

Second row: D. Seltzer, Hila Borer, Sara Hauptman, S. Rossler, Bertha Friedman, Shlomo Rosenberg

Third row: A. Wagner, H. Rappaport, A. Monderer, Miriam Igra, Rivka Friedman, Mania Hauptman, P. Miller

Toynbee Hall committee

From right to left: Standing: **Eisensher, D. Zeidamn**

Sitting: H. Wizaltier, H. Neumann, M. Wagner, M. Frankel, W. Hauptman, Petrach

The leadership of the united party "Hitahdut – Poalei Zion" 1931

From right to left: Sitting in the first row: I. Lustig, M. Marbach, M. Rotfeld, N. Pomerantz, Meller

Sitting in the second row: Ben Zion Garfunkel, L. Oper, H. Neumann, A. Meller, L. Schwamer, Dr. A. Eisenstein, S. Rossler, S. Rosenberg

Standing in the third row: –?–, Robinson, L. Kronberg, –?–, L. Garfunkel, M. Rinhartz, N. Lindner, I. Meisels, M. Freilich

Standing in the fourth row: Belz, I. Steiner, M. Hubel, –?–, Zukerkendel

The Soviet Occupation (1939 – 1941)
Shimon Rosenberg
Translated by Susan Rosin

During the third week following their invasion of Poland, the Germans occupied Stryj.

Seventeen days after the start of the war, the red army crossed the eastern border with Poland and occupied the eastern parts of the country. At the end of September 1939, the German and red armies faced each other along the Stryj river. Following the negotiations, the German army retreated to the San river. After some tense days, the red army occupied Stryj.

One of the German bombs destroyed the Elner's house in the rynek. Jews that were hiding in the cellar of the house were buried under the rubble. That was the only harm to the Jews inflicted by the Germans – for now.

The Soviet army was received by the population with mixed feelings. The Poles hated the new rulers. The Ukrainians reserved judgment and the Jews felt it was the lesser of two evils.

The new authorities published new rules and regulations. The population was required to relinquish all weapons and open all the stores. Public gatherings and meetings were forbidden.

The Regime

The new instructions and commands did not prevent war time suffering. Within a few days food disappeared off the shelves and prices went up. Long lines formed in front of bakeries, grocery stores, shoe stores and linens stores. Within a few days the stores were emptied out of their merchandise. The merchants amassed large amounts of money and even items that normally had no buyers were snatched. The authorities ensured that the merchants would not hike their prices and hide their merchandise.

It was not the town's people who started this shopping panic, but the soldiers from the garrison. The officers and soldiers were buying anything and everything and sending it to their families back in Russia. Months of starvation and shortage followed and people had to stand in lines for a loaf of bread in the freezing cold. There were instances where hungry people attacked bread deliveries for the army.

In time, the administration in town stabilized. Commissars and their families arrived from the Soviet Ukraine and organized the offices of taxation, commerce, manufacturing, police, cooperation etc. it needs to be noted that the new authorities employed the town's people in their offices without discrimination of religion or nationality. The town's people quickly learnt how to survive with their new authorities and employers. The new relationships were mainly based on "you help me and I'll help you" practice with bribery, corruption and mutual embezzlement...

After the new regime was stabilized, the people started to feel the difference. The Russian goods were not supplied to the people through private trade. Institutions were established to oversee the trade and provide employment. In the first stage, the bakeries, mills, factories and large enterprises were nationalized. In the next stage, the authorities nationalized all homes valued at more than twenty thousand rubles. This rule had wide options for bribery, and many homes that were supposed to be nationalized remained in the hands of the owners as did many apartments. Favoritism and bribery were rampant. Craftsmen were not forced to organize in cooperatives, but because of the taxation they did. Many closed their workshops and organized themselves in cooperatives. Some of the merchants found employment in the national factories, while others made a living from the inventory in their stores. In most cases, the authorities did not single out the Jews, but there were a few arrests.

[Page 162]

The arrest of the renowned lawyer Dr. Wundell caused a stir in town especially because for years he was the defended communists in political trials. Many rumors circulated about the reason for his arrest, none was confirmed and he died in jail. Two "Bund" activists, Benjamin Ber and Fridel Boxer were arrested and they too died in jail. Dr. Hausman was arrested because of a book by Trotsky (that was actually legal during the Polish rule). The truth was that he was arrested because of his lovely apartment that was desired by one of the officers. He too died in jail.

Aside from them, some merchants were arrested due to so–called price gauging. Among them was Kriszer.

In the spring of 1940 a new blow was inflicted on the population. The authorities announced that the Polish currency would no longer be accepted and the only legal currency will be the ruble. Thousands remained penniless. Just a few days before this decree, the authorities paid the workers' wages in the Polish currency, thus leaving many without means.

The Refugees

The Polish–German war created a stream of refuges moving east. Thousands of refugees arrived in Stryj and only a fraction of them found employment whereas the rest continued eastward.

In the summer of 1940, the Soviet authorities decided to "solve" the eastern Poland refugees issue in a brutal act. In Stryj, the authorities descended on the apartments occupied by refugees from western Poland. They allowed 15 –20 minutes for the refugees to gather their belongings and board a train. This decree affected all – men, women, children, old and young, the working and the unemployed. Later it was discovered that this plan was prepared in complete secrecy and for a few weeks large freight cars were prepared at the station for a long journey. They were equipped with sleeping bunks and stoves for heating. For the abductions, specially trained brigades in cooperation with the Soviet militia were used. They performed this task without pity separating families. The trains traveled for many months through the Russian prairie and taiga on their way north. Many perished during this inhumane trip and upon arrival in the polar region, other perished due to the cold conditions.

Many of the expelled had no chance of getting warm clothing and froze in the cold land of exile. Letters of despair and hopelessness were received by relatives of the exiled.

The Relationships Between the Nationalities

The soviets declared eastern Galicia part of the Ukrainian republic and the formal language became Ukrainian. This caused much satisfaction to the Ukrainians and uneasiness to the Polish population. The authorities started in transitioning the administration positions previously held by Poles and Jews to Ukrainians. However, due to the lack of skills among the Ukrainians, not all Jews and Poles could be replaced. For this purpose, the soviets used the most educated Ukrainians although the nationalistic feelings and the hatred towards Russia was strong among this group. This did not cause antagonism between the two nationalities. However, the negative feelings of the three groups towards the occupation forces reduced the tensions among them. The Poles and Ukrainians were more tolerant towards the Jews as compared to the period before the soviet occupation.

[Page 163]

The Jewish Social Life

The soviet occupation brought a complete closure of the Jewish institutions, the various parties and cessation of public life. Some of the institutions such as the orphanage and the children's' home were annexed to Polish and Ukrainian institutions and were administered by the city and lost their Jewish character. Ukrainian was the official language in all institutions.

The authorities opened classes to teach the masses about the bolshevist party and to listen to speeches made by communist leaders. People attended these classes out of fear and in order to keep their jobs.

At first, the authorities did not get involved in the religious life of the Jews, but the religious institutions that were dependent on the kehila encountered difficulties. The Jewish communists that served the authorities did not try to help and on the contrary and as flattery to the authorities promoted the use of the Ukrainian language.

Although eastern Galicia was officially part of soviet Ukraine, the border was closed throughout the occupation. The eastern Galicia civilians that were drafted to the red army were given inferior tasks such as building fortifications.

A week after the German attack on Russia, the soviets left Stryj (on June 22nd, 1941). They abandoned the government offices and institutions taking with them thousands of civilians. A few hundreds of Stryj's Jews took advantage of the situation, joined the transport and escaped to the east.

Immediately after the start of the war with the Germans, the soviets drafted a substantial number of Jews to the red army. Two of Stryj's Jews Israel Pfeffer and Shlomo Segal were executed on grounds of desertion.

Before they left town, the soviets arrested the Jewish activists Benjamin Klein, Ben Garfunkel and Meisels and executed them at the jail yard without trial.

A Refugee Writes about Stryj's Jews
Translated by Susan Rosin

This letter was received in the editorial office of the "Yizkor" book from Mr. Zvi Reps from Dubiecko (Poland).During the war, Mr. Reps arrived in Stryj with other Jewish refugees. In his letter, Mr. Reps who later settled in Tzfat (Israel) described the assistance and kindness of Stryj's Jewry during the cruel expulsion to Siberia by the Soviet authorities.

The Russians arrested us on Friday night. The following day, Saturday we were packed into train cars, and on Sunday we arrived in Stryj. We had no idea where we were being transported to, but Stryj's Jews knew we were being exiled to Siberia. The Russians did not allow any help, but the Jews in Stryj bribed the NKVD. In one day only they bought huge amounts of bread, jam, cheese, butter, herrings, candy, medications and diapers for babies. They even divided a sum of 30,000 rubles among the refugees – a huge amount in those days. It was a well-coordinated effort: a sort of emergency was declared, and the people were asked to give up any luxuries and allocate all resources for the refugees. When the train started moving, a woman handed me a large jar of jam and a bag of sugar saying "it's for all of you".

Hundreds of Jews were at the station when the train left. Many of them were crying. In all of eastern Galicia I did not encounter such warm and humane feelings as we were shown by the Jews of Stryj. For years I was trying to locate a Jew from Stryj, hug him and tell him what it meant for us. Eventually I met someone and told him it is necessary to bring into light what the Jews of Stryj did for their refugee brethren.

[Page 164]

I am confident that those who were with me in Siberia could add much more to what I said about Stryj's Jews.

May their memory be blessed.

(Signed) Zvi Reps, Tzfat

A Stryj Refugee in Russia
Translated by Susan Rosin

The surprise attack of the Germans on Russia on June 22nd 1941was so sudden that people in Stryj could not surmise that the explosions heard that morning had any connection to the war. However, realization set–in with the radio addresses from Moscow that morning.

Stryj was in the danger zone from the first day of the war.

The Russian–German border extended along the San river from Przemyśl in the north through the Carpathian mountains. The mechanized army was able to get from Przemyśl to Stryj in a few hours and the planes reached thetown in a few minutes causing much destruction to the Russian bases.

It is interesting that the people of Stryj were not scared at first and were not aware of the ensuing danger and did not plan an escape.

During the twenty months of the Soviet rule, the army fortified the border, so the general opinion was that the fighting will take a while. However, after two to three days it became apparent that the German army broke through the north–eastern Russian front it became clear that the center front will be next and that Stryj was doomed.

In spite of these facts, it did not seem that the Jews of Stryj were eager to leave. How can this apathy be explained in the face of the danger of German occupation?

Stryj's Jews saw the suffering of the thousands of refugees from western Poland who lived in poverty and suffered hunger during the 20 months of the Soviet rule and were afraid of the same fate;

The Jews were not aware of the Germany's brutal "final solution";

During the Soviet rule many became disillusioned by the corruption, the bribery, the liquidation of all private property and commerce and the general decline in standard of living.

An air of defeatism spread among the Jews and nobody was too eager to leave. Only small groups left Stryj: healthcare workers, communist youths, and men who were drafted to the soviet army and air defense during the initial days of the war. So, only men left town with the retreating soviet army, whereas women and children were left behind.

Anyone who wanted could have left town in the last trains that passed Stryj on their way from Drohobycz – Boryslaw or the trains that left Stryj in the last days before the German invasion. About three hundred of Stryj's Jews left for Russia that way.

In the first few months, the Jews concentrated in the places where they disembarked from the trains, mostly in Ukraine. But because of the rapid progress of the Germans, they spread in the entire European and Asian portions of Russia.

The fate of the few hundred refugees from Stryj was not different from that of the other refugees. They worked in the kolkhozes, in factories and workshops and wandered around Russia, homeless and hungry, dressed in rags. Some engaged in illegal black market commerce.

[Page 165]

Some were sent to prisons and concentration camps, living in filth, contracting diseases and many died. Finally, in 1945/1946, those who remained were returned to Poland. There are no exact numbers for those that returned, but they are estimated to be about two hundred.

Members of the Revisionist organization in Stryj

"HaOved" Organization in Stryj 1934

A group of "Hashomer Hatzair" 1918

A group of "Hashomer Hatzair" 1918

From right to left: Standing: Malka Leibowitz, S. Harshderfer, R. Reinhartz, Weinrab, Kaufman, Shmorack

Seated middle row: P. Kastenbaum, Marbach, R. Lindner, S. Kronberg, Waldman

Seated in first row: S. Lindner, Lindner, L. Reich

The Destruction of the Stryj Community

Holocaust Chapters
by Jonah Friedler
Translated by Susan Rosin

In memory of my parents, brother and their families who perished with the destruction of Polish Jewry

Chapter 1
Our Splendid City

Stryj, on the low laying plain in the south-east of the historical region of Małopolska (Lesser Poland) was a corridor to the mighty Carpathian mountains. Flowing among the green pastures, fields and forests was Stryj river completing the pastoral picture. The river was a blessing to the town's population, as it was moving the wheels of the seven flour mills and also enjoyed as a recreation area during the hot summer months. Geographically, the town is located at a crossroads and during Franz Joseph's days it was an important hub connecting eastern Galicia with Hungary by a railroad line of Stryj-Lawoczne-Budapest to the south, Stanisławów to the south-east and Przemyśl to the north-west.

The neighboring towns and villages of Rozdół, Żydaczów, Mikołajów, Sokołów, Bolechów had sizable Jewish communities. Stryj is close to Drohobycz, Borysław and Schodnica that were rich in oil deposits providing employment to most of the population. Stryj had a population of about forty thousand, divided almost evenly between Jews, Poles and Ukrainians. Economically, the Jews dominated almost all branches of commerce – food, clothing, furniture, building materials, fuel etc. as well as most of the crafts such as leather works, tailoring, tinworks, blacksmithing, glassworks, painting, building, upholstery, fur processing, watchmaking, gold and silver works and works of art. Most stores in town were owned by Jews. Many Jews from the neighboring villages made their living in agriculture. Some owned their land, and others leased large areas of lands from the Polish barons and squires who owned estates. Others leased taverns, based on a tradition where the lease passed as an inheritance from father to son.

The community of Stryj was served by many scholars. Rabbi Arie Leib HaKohen Heller author of "Ketzot Hachoshen" and "Avnei Milluim"; the prodigy rabbi Yaakov from Lissa, the son of the prodigy Rabbi Yaakov Moshe Lorberbaum. He was the author of ten books and Torah interpretations. He passed away on the 25th day of Iyar 5592 (May 25th, 1832); Rabbi Meshullam Igra, the author of "Tshuvut" (answers); rabbi Enzel a son of the distinguished and wealthy Halpern family; Rabbi Arie Leibish Horowitz from Stanisławów, the author of "Harei Besamim" and one of the most prominent scholars of his day. He established the "Or Torah" yeshiva that was headed by the brothers Raphael and Abraham Kitaigorodsky from Lithuania. Before the First World War, rabbi Shalom HaKohen Jolles from Mościska the son of rabbi Uri from Sambor served as the head of the rabbinical court a position he shared with rabbi Shraga Feivel Hertz from Głogów. Then, the chief rabbi was Eliezer Ladier, the stepson of rabbi Horwitz from Stanisławów. The last rabbi was Yeshayahu Asher HaKohen Jolles, who perished in the Shoah, the son of rabbi Shalom, and his brother rabbi Efraim Eliezer HaKohen Jolles that later became the chief rabbi in Philadelphia. A number of famous authors also originated in Stryj. A.M. Lifshitz, the author of the Rashi monograph and later the head of the teachers' academy in Jerusalem; Dr. Zvi Diesendruck, a teacher, philosopher a teacher in Jerusalem and later in Union College in Cincinnati, Ohio; Jonah Garlenter, an author and teacher in the high school in Vienna; Dr. Isaac Silbershlag, an author, a poet and a teacher and the head of the Teachers' academy in Boston; Dr. Nathan Kudish, an educator and a teacher in a high school in Tel Aviv; Dr. Moshe Steiner whose articles were published in Hebrew and English, and others that became famous in the Jewish world.

[Page 170]

Many folkloric stories were interwoven into various literary works among them the story about rabbi Enzel a guest for Saturday in the famous work of Shai Agnon "Vehaya Ha'akov Lemishor" ("The Crooked Shall Be Made Straight").

The kehilla leaders were elected in the spirit of the times. Until the First World War, the kehilla was led by the notary dr. Abraham Wiesenberg, an assimilator who did not understand his people and their needs, but was liked by the district supervisor, a fact that determined the elections outcome. After the war and with the "spring of nations" awakening, the leader was Shlomo Goldberg, who had a traditional Jewish education, a Zionist and a delegate to the first congress in Basel. He was followed by Dr. Zeev Presser (who perished in the Shoah), an intellectual and a man of action, Dr. Mordechai Kaufman (who perished in the Shoah), a dedicated Zionist and well–liked by the community. The last leader was dr. Norbert Schiff (who perished in the Shoah). The last two also served as deputy mayors.

Our town was small, but productive and colorful life was abundant. Most of the Jews in town made their living from trade and the crafts. Even before the first war, the wealthy started to send their children abroad for higher education, mostly because of the "numerous clausus" ("educational quotas" – a practice to limit the number of Jewish students in higher education institutions). Since then, the professional intellectual numbers among the Jews grew in town.

The orthodox Jewry was divided among the various Hasidic groups such as Żydaczów, Czortków, Bojanów, Belz, Bolechów, Stratyń and others. In the initial days of Zionism, there were many struggles between the young Zionists and the orthodox. Between the two world wars, the national conviction grew and the Stryj community became a major force in the national movement in eastern Galicia and made a significant contribution to the building of the homeland in Eretz Israel. Many youths joined "Hashomer Hatzair" and "HeHalutz", growing on the ideals of Haim Brenner and A. D. Gordon. Many of them fulfilled their dream and emigrated during the third Aliyah in the years 1919 – 1923.

These youths who are no longer young contributed much to the building of Israel and they could be found in the kibbutizim, villages and cities. Many from Stryj participated in the fourth Aliya (1924 – 1931), and they could be found in almost every village and town and they too were an integral part in the building of the state of Israel. Stryj pioneers were among the pavers of the Sarafand (Tzrifin) road during the administration of the high commissioner Herbert Samuel.

The Hebrew school "Safa Brura" was founded before the First World War by Moshe Wohlmut (perished in the Shoah) one of the most active Zionists in town. After the war, the school extended its reach and provided Hebrew language training to the Zionist youths. The devoted teachers were: Zvi Garlenter, Moshe Helfgott, Josef Shapira, David Korn, and Yaakov Zeman. These dedicated teachers carried out the dream of reviving the Hebrew language and passing it to the next generation in an environment that was hostile because the orthodox Jewry and the various leftist parties objected to this idea.

Between the two wars, a technical school was established under the leadership of Dr. Schindler. Students were trained in the areas of precision mechanics and metal–works to become productive contributors in the building of the homeland in Eretz Israel and most of them fulfilled their dream.

The "Ivriya" society was established before the first war as a result of the national awakening in Eastern Europe. The purpose of the society was to disseminate the Hebrew language and culture. The activities of the society were interrupted during the war. After the war, the activities were renewed with much energy influenced by the Balfour declaration. The society was headed then by Naphtali Siegel, Levi Teitler, Isaac Sturmlauf, and Arie Derfler. Various literary subjects were discussed led by lecturers from town and outside of town. Among the lecturers were Abba Hushi, Meir Yaari, Dov Sadan (Stock), dr. Josef Schuster-Shilo, Jonah Gelernter, Joshua Tilleman and others. The enthusiasm of these literary discussions was great. The first Hebrew library was established, and spread the knowledge of Hebrew among the student and the working youths. The founders and pioneers of the society were Joshua Oberlander, Dr. Moshe Eisenstein, Naphtali Gernter, Hiam David Korn, Yaakov Zeman, Ben-David Schwartz, Dr. Nathan Kudish, dr. Moshe Steiner, prof. Isaac Nussenblatt, Naphtali Siegel, and Jonah Friedler.

All the various political-national parties were united in the "Arbeitsgemeinschaft".

[Page 171]

The national awakening was strongly felt in the academic societies of "Emuna", "Hevronia" and "Kadima".

The merchant's society "Oseh Tov" was led by dr. Norbert Schiff, Moshe Spiegel and David Zeidman (who perished in Shoah) and was active in the economic-professional sector with national leanings. The craftsmen were united in the "Yad Harutzim" society headed by Abraham Levin (the father-in-law of the author and Hebrew teacher Naphtali Siegel) and Shalom Schwartz.

The great synagogue was a magnificent building decorated by famous artists in biblical motifs. On both sides of the synagogue were two houses of study (batei midrash) and across the street was a Talmud Torah housed in a two story building. It was managed for the glory of God by rabbi Israel Yehuda Nussenblatt, rabbi Eliyahu Zeldowicz, rabbi Shmuel Friedler (my father) and rabbi Shlomo Drimmer. The bath-house was under the supervision of the kehilla and used by all of the town's people. The Jewish hospital was supervised voluntarily by the Jewish doctors.

This was the picture of our town Stryj, the place where our forefathers lived for generations. Simple, Hassidic believers, where they worked, studied, and created an existence unique in their customs, their dress and their language. The religious officials, the wealthy, the educated, the merchants, the peddlers, the shopkeepers, the middlemen, and the loafers. All of them lived strictly by the Shulhan Aruch (the Code of Jewish Law). The center of their being besides making a living was the rabbi and the kloiz. In their spiritual lives they found a reward to their gloomy daily existence. We, the last generation of enslavement and the first generation of redemption and salvation followed them.

On September 1st, 1939 at the outbreak of the war between Poland and Germany, a black curtain dropped on European Jewry ad their fate was sealed on us – the Jews of Stryj.

Chapter 2
The Days of Thunder

The next day, the Messerschmitt aircrafts were already over our town. Like eagles descending on their prey, so did these airplanes dropping their bombs. Sometimes, they shot from automatic weapons. The question on everyone's mind was "where are the Polish defense canons?". One of the bombs was dropped in the city center and destroyed completely the house of Nathan Elner. Twenty six people including women and children took shelter in the cellar of the house and all were killed. Among the victims was rabbi Motel Rothaus who was a much loved and respected scholar and a man of high moral standing. At first we were shocked by the bombings, but soon we got used to them, as there was no relief during the day or night.

Quickly we went into the cellars we thought naively to be safe. The sight of carts with families from Poland and all their belongings that were passing through town on their way from western Galicia to the east depressed us even more. The worries intensified as we saw the Śmigły–Rydz army retreating towards Hungary. The soviet army crossed the border along the Zbrucz river and was getting closer. In the meanwhile, the German army occupied Stryj. They were welcomed by the Ukrainians from the surrounding villages who wore their best clothing for the occasion. They erected a victory arch on Drohobicka street with the banner "we will pave the roads for the German army victory with Jewish skulls".

Festivities took place in town. The Jews were hiding in cellars and attics expecting the worst. Rumors started to circulate about dividing Galicia between the Soviets and the Germans, making us live somewhere between fear and hope. On the third day after the German occupation, the army commanders of the two sides met on the Bolechów bridge of the Stryj river and agreed that the German army will retreat to the river San.

It is hard to describe the joy of the Jewish population seeing the retreat of the German army. On Yom Kippur eve, September 22nd, 1939, the Soviet army entered the city. For the time being we were written in the book of life.

[Page 172]

Chapter 3
Under the Soviet Rule

It is hard to describe the joy of the Jewish population when the red troops entered town. My happiness was great when I was able to speak Yiddish with Jewish officers of the red army. Under the soviets we suffered food shortages compared to the abundance in Poland before the war. But, we were not discriminated against as Jews, and we suffered as the rest of the population. We were "fed" Marxist and Leninist doctrines and were ordered to obey the Stalinist rules: those that don't work do not eat. Although we lost our riches, we rejoiced that our lives were spared. The front moved to the west, and we felt that for us the war was over. One of the reasons for the signing of the non-aggression pact between Germany and the Soviets on August 22nd, 1939 was to prevent dual fronts, thus allowing Hitler to concentrate his efforts in the west, the rest of Europe and Africa without the threat of being attacked from the east. We also saw trains loaded with fine wheat traveling via Stryj from the Ukraine to Germany, which proved the excellent relationships between the two countries…How terrible was our disappointment when on June 22nd, 1941 airplanes appeared in the sky. At first, we were not able to identify if they were our friends' our enemy's, but soon they started dropping bombs. When we asked the Soviet officers about the situation, they tried to calm us down telling us these were military exercises. It is worth mentioning that in the Soviet Union, the people were not privy to any political or diplomatic information – until it was too late. The media was full of success stories of the "Pyatiletka" (5 year) plan thanks to the Stakhanow efficiency method, but no political information was discussed. We could hear the cannons from the direction of Drohobycz – Przemyśl and the planes dropped bombs non-stop. The soviets made preparation to leave town. Trains headed to safety in the east across the Polish – Soviet border were loaded with the families of the military and the party activists. However, many of the trains were destroyed by the German bombers.

Before leaving town, the soviets arrested in the middle of the night several Zionist activists to be exiled to Siberia. I can recall only a few names: Shmuel Klein, his son Benjamin, Ben-Zion Radler, Eliyahu Zeldowicz, Arye Schwamer, H. D. Korn, Ben-Zion Garfunkel, Levi Oper and others. Luckily for me, one of the NKVD people whom I befriended told my wife in secret that I was on the deportation list as well, so I hid with a Polish family, thus avoided the exile.

The bombardment intensified day by day turning the town into wood and stone rubble. Lviv was already occupied by the Germans that attacked from the north-west. We were terrified by the future and prayed for salvation. But, our prayers were not answered. The soviets retreated towards Stanisławów, the Poles were indifferent, the Ukrainians rejoiced and we were heading towards annihilation. It is hard to describe the joy of the Jewish population seeing the retreat of the German army. On Yom Kippur eve, September 22nd, 1939, the Soviet army entered the city. For the time being we were written in the book of life.

[Page 173]

Chapter 4
The Destruction of Jewish Stryj

Now I must begin to describe the liquidation of the Jewish Community and the end of Jewish Stryj. How painful it is to write those words! They include the precious, holy and pure souls of thousands of people, belonging to the families of those who read these lines; souls which were extinguished before their time by suffering and anguish to which nothing can compare since mankind came into being. Neither the legends of the Destruction of the Temple nor the Book of Lamentations, together with the works of the most outstanding and expressive writers, nothing written by mortal hand, could or can express even the least part of what it was my bitter fate to experience and see with my own eyes. The powers of human expression are incapable of recounting the cruelty of the yellow, murderous beast which came forth from its den in order to introduce "a New Order in Europe." "Where is there a Scribe and where one to weigh ?.." And as for me, I am neither a scribe nor the son of a scribe. My hands fail and the pen sticks in the inkwell. O Lord, I beseech you to strengthen and sustain me so that I may be able to tell my brethren in Zion and those who are dispersed throughout the world what the Germans and the Ukrainians did to our brethren and sisters, our children and little ones; in order to ensure that those of our blood are imbued with the duty of vengeance for generation upon generation. And be that my consolation.

The armored units of the Germans came down on the city like a tempest. The earth crumbled away under the tracks of the gigantic steel and iron tanks. They were followed by the S. S. with black skulls and crossbones on their caps; and they brought death with them. Each one was a merciless professional murderer, a bloodthirsty executioner.

When the Nazis arrived the pits in the courtyard of the Municipal prison were opened. Those pits were full of corpses of slain people, covered with flour and rice. The Russians had not had time before leaving to take with them all the political prisoners who were "enemies of the people". Among them were several Jews, but most of them were Ukrainians belonging to the party of Bandera which aspired to establish an Independent Western Ukraine. They had all been shot and flung into these pits. Now the German murderers were astonished to find that anybody contested the monopoly of killing and murdering with them.

Who had killed these people? The Soviets - meaning the Jews! The Jews - the eternal scapegoat, symbolizing the red devil in the eyes of the Germans, and the Bourgeoisie and Wall Street in the eyes of the Russians. Military and civil representatives were summoned together with priests, pressmen and photographers, in order to display Soviet-Jewish cruelty to all. Thousands of townsfolk and others came to see the gruesome sight. The first step to poison the air against the Jews, and incite the population against us, had been successful.

Posters were issued to the effect that war was being waged only against the enemy. "The peaceful urban population, without distinction of race or creed, is our friend. We promise them peace and order. They have only to obey the commands of the Military Command." It was signed by General Von Brauchitz. Further notices appeared requiring the Jews to bring their telephones and radio sets to the Town Council where they would be given a receipt for them. Those who did not do so would be punished in accordance with the Emergency Regulations. It was signed by Haupmann Weide, Military Town Commander.

The German District Officer appointed Oskar Hutterer, the son-in-law of the late Rabbi Eliezer Ladier, chairman, and ordered him to select the members of a Judenrat (Jewish Council). This council had a double task. It was to maintain contact with the German Command, carry out its orders, and handle all the internal affairs of the Jews themselves, who from that day forward would constitute a separate body entirely cut off from the Aryan population. This Jewish Council was chiefly intended to serve as a bridge for passing on the decrees of the Nazi Command to the Jews. The Council was given authority to collect taxes from the Jews, and establish a Jewish police (Ordnungsdienst) which would be under its orders. These Police were composed of young people belonging to all groups and classes. Among them were fine young men belonging to the national and academic youth, and also those from poverty-stricken groups. The Council was provided with food supplies for the Community. The policemen were promised additional rations, and therefore the young people willingly registered for police duties. There was also the attraction of gleaming buttons on uniforms, and the round cap with the dark yellow linen band round it. They were armed with rubber truncheons. The Jewish Council Building was the House of Rabbi Jacob Ettinger at the corner of May 3rd and Potockiego Streets. Departments were set up for taxes, housing, furniture and food, with secretaries, telephones, typewriters, storehouses and shops. A complete state apparatus, one might suppose, down to the last details.

The German officers brought their families with them. The Jewish Council was ordered to provide furniture for their dwellings. The Jewish police set to work with exemplary devotion. They took furniture, household utensils, pillows, quilts and linen first from the homes of the rich Jews and then of the well-to-do and finally average people. Some gave willingly and others unwillingly, but the watchword was: "Better give our goods than our lives." Yet it was a vain slogan. First they gave their property and afterwards their lives as well. For now came the first blow: The Ukrainians gave the police names of ten Jews. Those were people who had spoken badly of Germany under Soviet rule, or who had put pressure on Ukrainian workers in factories where Jews had been appointed foremen. Among them were Ephraim Bucchnbaum, Philip Dunkel, Engineer Schatzker, and the son of the lawyer Kerner. They were executed in the neighboring village of Duliby. The murderers behaved with a certain amount of consideration in these first cases, and permitted the families of the slain men to bring their bodies to Jewish burial.

[Page 174]

The front moved east. Here and there a barber shop or a shop for light refreshments opened. There were no goods because private trading had been forbidden under Soviet rule. A Jewish shop had to be marked by a Star of David and a notice "Jüdischen Geschäfts" (Jewish business). The peasants of the neighborhood began to bring their crops to the market. The Jews were allowed two hours, from ten to twelve to buy food, and woe to anybody who was caught after that time. That person was murderously beaten and flung into prison. During those two hours the Jewish purchasers were received at the market with jeers and curses both by the peasant salesmen and by the crowd, who gnashed their teeth and bitterly cursed the Jews for causing the rise in prices, the war and all the trouble that was coming.

Law and order were supervised by the "Schupo" (Schutzpolizei or civil police), the "Kripo" (Kriegspolizei or wartime police) and the Gestapo, and at the top was the Ukrainian police. Here a few lines must be devoted to our Ukrainian neighbors with their hands steeped in blood, the offspring and descendants of Bogdan Chmielnicki, that nation whose evil deeds are recorded as an everlasting horror in the history of Polish Jewry. They were the axe in the hands of the Gestapo. Their hatred of the Jews led them to savage murders and the robbery and pillage of all that was Jewish. They murdered and robbed. While the Germans shot from automatic rifles the Ukrainians murdered with their own hands. The Ukrainian peasants slaughtered the village Jews like so many sheep with scythes and sickles. They literally cut them to pieces with knives. We had been living in their midst for hundreds of years, both sides had benefited from mutual trade and we had never done them any harm. On the contrary, the Jewish tradesman, peddler and innkeeper had provided them with clothing, footwear, food and drink many times on payments which were often not paid. The Ukrainians had destroyed the basis of our livelihood in Eastern Galicia even before the Second World War. They had organized the village peasantry into Cooperative Societies which supplied all their needs, and thus eliminated the Jews from their economic positions. The priests in church preached in favor of the societies, and forbade all contact and business with the Jews. The Polish Government not only did not prohibit it but looked favorably on this poisonous activity, which diminished Jewish influence in the commercial sphere. Since we were the minority we were always the scapegoat in the political and economic intrigues between the Poles and Ukrainians. Both of them hated us bitterly. Now that the Germans had come the Ukrainians, drunk with joy, regarded them as angels who would deliver them from the Polish-Jewish pressure, and would fulfil their national dream of a free and independent Ukraine built on the ruins of the Jews.

The Ukrainian Police was made up of thieves, murderers, drunkards and scoundrels, and underworld mob. These scoundrels, who had always been dressed in rags and with whom no decent person would come into touch in normal times, now received new army uniforms with gleaming buttons, rifles or revolvers. Now they were given a free hand. Municipal affairs were handed over to the Ukrainians. The Mayor was Engineer Bandera, manager of the Ukrainian Cooperative Society.

On the day after the invasion a German soldier entered my apartment, accompanied by a Ukrainian hoodlum who served him as a guide to Jewish dwellings. I recognized him as the attendant at the bathhouse, where he was always asleep. I was summoned to work and ordered to fetch a pail, broom and rags. On the street I joined other Jews who were taken from their houses. We were led to the town square in order to clean the tanks, collect the bricks from the bombed houses and arrange them in equal-sized squares. The work was not in the least boring, for from time to time the German supervisor brought his whip down murderously over our heads and backs, to the joy of Ukrainian idlers and vagabonds who laughed at our distress. I had the impudence to ask the supervisor why he was beating me if I was working as I had been ordered. Before I had finished my question the German hit me over the face to the accompaniment of unrepeatable curses. The blood began flowing down over my face.

Next day the Jewish police hurried me along to work at the railway station. We carried all kinds of screws, wheels and heavy pieces of metal from place to place on our backs. While I was working I met a young Ukrainian, a high railway official whom I had known from the good old days. "For hundreds of years", he said, "you have been sucking our blood. The Ukrainian peasant sold you the fat poultry and geese while he himself made do with the black bread the Jews sold. The Jews always lived luxuriously. All the houses in town belonged to them. The town is ours, the house yours. Ukrainian hands built them. We were always your servants, your doorkeepers, your boot polishers, your cesspit cleaners. You wore the most expensive clothes, you lived in the finest apartments, you ate our bread and drank our water. Now the time has come to settle your debt. You'll pay with your lives. Now your end has come, the day we have been hoping for, for so long".

[Page 175]

This pained me far more than the whip the day before. When I took off my shirt at home, the skin had peeled from my shoulders and my back was covered with blisters. Yet these two episodes are not even a single drop out of the sea compared to what happened afterwards.

Work was mandatory for every Jew between the ages of 16 and 60. A vast number of institutions were established in the city, including military stores, military laboratories and private German firms. I shall mention some of them: Heeresverpflegungsdepot (Army Supply Depot), Baudienst (Building Service), H.K.P., Wasserwirtschaft (Water Authority), Karpathen Ohl, Altstoff (Old

Clothes), etc., Heeresbarackenwerke (sawmill of Zelig Borak), A.S.A. Clasfabriken (Classworks - in Neubauer's flour mill). The Ukrainians and Poles traded and made money. We were forbidden to leave the town limits. Every morning we went out in our thousands to work at the above places. In return for our work we were given rations of bread and soup. We submitted to this situation humbly, maybe even willingly, for we were still living in our own apartments. This general calm made some innocent ones among us delude themselves with the vain hope that work would save us, since in wartime work is an important factor and the Germans could not permit themselves to kill productive people like us. Who then would work in our places? And on the other hand, they argued, it was impossible that the German nation of poets and philosophers should simple indulge in the mass slaughter of millions of Jews. And what would the world say? But the bitter reality came and proved otherwise. Death is a dreadful thing, but sevenfold more dreadful was the way that led to it.

A few months later the order establishing the Jewish Quarter (Jüdisches Wohnviertel) was published and paved the way for the Ghetto. It meant that the Jews were separated from the Aryan population. The Jewish Quarter began from Kilinskiego Street (the Lachowicz Bookshop) to its end (at the corner of Iwaszkiewicza-Drohobyczka Streets). It continued on the other side along the Stojalowskiego Boulevard, Zamkowa, Rynek, Berka Josselowicze, Kusznierska, Lwówska; Batorego to the Zielona Street. The Jews of the Aryan Quarter were transferred to the Jewish Quarter and crowded into the apartments of the Jews already living there. It was permissible to enter and leave the Jewish Quarter. Jews with work permits were allowed to enter the Aryan Quarter, while Aryans were permitted to enter the Jewish Quarter. And an alternative was promptly provided for those who did not feel comfortable enough in the Jewish Quarter because of overcrowding. At the time the Quarter contained about 12,000 persons. The Jewish Council was ordered to make room for another 11,000 persons who had been expelled from the small towns of the district, which were thus made Judenrein. Beds of two or three levels were made of boards. The overcrowding led to filth and increased diseases. Before long, an additional "easement" came, that was worse than the first. The Actions began. This was the name given to the systematic extermination carried out in accordance with a definite plan, and with precise German order. On this occasion, for example, orders were given to kill 1000 Jews between the hours of 4 and 12. If by chance another Jew came along after twelve, the murderers sent him away until the next Action.

This was in November, 1941, at 5 a.m. before dawn. There was a tremendous downpour. The heavens were weeping for us. Squads of German and Ukrainian police came into the Jewish Quarter. Twelve hundred men were taken out of their beds and led away to prison. After three days of beatings and torture the miserable victims were taken to the Holobotow forest near Stryj. There they dug a common grave for themselves, and were all murdered. Now began the feverish building of bunkers in the houses and courtyards. Jewish intelligence, together with a natural sense of self-preservation, enabled us to invent hiding places which were beyond all human imagination. Blind brick walls were built in cellars, attics, cowsheds, on the ceilings of lavatories, in rubbish bins, in cesspits, in places where the German hounds would never dream of searching. The main difficulty was to hide the entry so that it should remain invisible. For the greater part a few bricks were removed in the corner of the blind wall. We crawled in on all fours through the little hole and afterwards the bricks were cautiously replaced so as not to leave any signs of cement or brick. Sometimes the entries were made through the floors of a room, shop, storage area, or cowshed after some bricks or wooden boards were removed from the floor, and then carefully replaced from within after those who were hiding themselves had entered. One exceptional invention which required special skill was the entry from under a window. The window-sill was removed. The middle bricks were taken out of the wall leaving space for a thin person. The entry to the bunker was through the hollow in the wall that was under the sill. The last to enter put the sill back in place from the inside precisely where it should be, with handles underneath especially made for the purpose. This was done with the utmost precaution, so that there should be no sign of the window-sill having been moved. The danger of death was the mother of strange inventions, of which nobody could have dreamed in normal times. Yet the clever inventions of flesh and blood were not always lucky. There were cases when those who had toiled to hide themselves ten feet underground were discovered, while others who hid themselves in an empty upside-down barrel or behind doors succeeded in escaping, until they fell into the hands of the Germans, that is, in the Actions that followed.

[Page 176]

In December, 1941, in midwinter, Joseph Goebbels of accursed memory, called on the German people to generously donate winter clothing for the German Forces fighting on the Eastern Front in order to liberate the civilized world from the Communist peril. The Aryan population had the choice of doing so or not; but for the Jews it was an order. Notices were published ordering the Jews to bring their furs to the Town Command Office. In order to make sure that this decree was promptly fulfilled, the German and Ukrainian Police did not wait for the Jews to fetch the furs themselves, but went from house to house to collect them. Their energy repaid them. They collected furs were worth thousands of dollars. Some were delivered to the Command Office, but most were sold on the black markets in Lwów and Kraków and the money received was spent on liquor. The drunkenness which then spread among the Aryans, and particularly among the police, is simply indescribable. It expressed their joy at the victories at the front and at the destruction of the Jews. A Ukrainian looking through a window saw the martyred Moshe Goldfischer hiding his fur in the double back of his cupboard, which was so skillfully made that its existence could not be seen. The Ukrainian informed the police about his Jewish neighbor who was hanged by the Gestapo.

The Polish winter descended upon us. The Jewish Council received orders to transfer unproductive families, idlers, and particularly widows and women whose husbands had been taken to the Soviet army, to forsaken hamlets in the heart of the Carpathians, in the direction of Smorze village. The purpose was obvious. Even in normal years the peasants of that dreadful region lived on dry barley bread. Now in wartime there was no doubt that within a few days these people would all perish of starvation. On a cold winter night about 500 souls were loaded on wagons guarded by Ukrainian police on horseback, and taken up to villages that were to be their graves. Very few of them returned some weeks later, bloated with starvation and wrapped in rags and tatters.

Meanwhile the Nazis were preparing public opinion for the idea that Jewish life was worthless. Army cars carried slogans "Death to the Jews". Caricatures were shown in public places displaying fat big-bellied Jews from Europe and America sucking the blood and marrow of the Aryan workers and neighbors through pipes, which brought piles of dollars into their pockets. The Nazis now had the sacred task of purifying Europe from the Jewish monster and eradicating this dangerous international microbe. It was not long before the satanic propaganda had its effect. The ground was prepared for murders and Actions. As we marched in ranks to work in the mornings Ukrainians attacked us and beat us without mercy. In the alleys Ukrainian police regularly stripped off the clothes and boots of Jews, and paid for them with murderous blows.

As remarked, thousands of Jews were engaged in hard labor in all kinds of factories, barracks, mills, stores and military institutions. In addition the Jewish Council sent hundreds of those remaining in the Jewish Quarter to engage in public works every day. But the Nazis did not rest satisfied. From time to time German and Ukrainian police came to the Jewish Quarter in order to kidnap Jews for cleaning cesspits and lavatories. And naturally such kidnappings were always accompanied by blows. Deaths due to these thrashings were numerous. Among the victims was my father-in-law, the martyred Hillel Landau, a God-fearing Jew of exceptional qualities who was widely known for his integrity and charity. The Nazi police caught him in the street, beat him and trampled him underfoot. A few days later, he went to his eternal rest on the 26th of Tevet, 5702.

As usual in times of trouble people yearned for miracles. Maybe Soviet Russia would finally strengthen and proceed to the offensive. Jews were forbidden to buy or sell newspapers. But sometimes we secretly managed to obtain the "Lemberger Zeitung," from a Polish worker while we were working. The news depressed us even more. Despair spread on all sides. At the end of 1941 German submarines sank British warships and aircraft carriers.

[Page 177]

Italian torpedo-ships attacked Alexandria in Egypt and wreaked havoc. We reckoned we were already dead. But what was going to happen to Eretz Israel? Our last hope was that we should rid ourselves of the doubt and fear that the Nazis might reach the Land of Israel. Now the fear that the Nazis will attack the land of Israel was growing stronger. German airplanes sunk the British battleships "Repulse" and "Prince of Wales". On February 12th, 1942, the German battleships "Scharnhorst", "Gneisenau" and "Prinz Eugen" succeeded in crossing the English Channel in spite of the British blockade, and endangered the eastern shores of England. The political horizon was absolutely black. We had the feeling that in a little while the whole of Europe would lie at the feet of the Nazis. Whence would our aid come? Our peril increased a hundred fold. The Germans were preparing to slaughter us.

It was in May 1942, before the Shavuot Festival, that the Jewish Quarter was surrounded on all sides. Anybody who tried to escape was shot and killed on the spot. This time the murderers found empty apartments. Everybody who could had taken shelter inside the bunkers. But the walls were smashed with hammers, pick-axes and hand grenades. When the murderers entered the apartment of the Schor family, an aristocratic Hassidic family who had been

Turkish citizens for generations, the latter showed them their Turkish passports. The Gestapo murderers tore them up on the spot. "Turkey will not go to war with us because of a few dirty Jews!" they proclaimed and added the whole family to the transport. The Jewish Hospital was full of patients. They were all shot in their beds.

After the Action the Jewish Quarter looked like a battlefield. In the hour of danger, when people ran in confusion to hide in the bunkers, many families broke up. Each crawled on his own in to the very closest bunker, for there was no time to choose. After the Action those who were still alive came out of their holes in mourning, bereaved of their dearest ones. Children were orphaned and parents were left bereft. Wives remained without husbands and husbands without wives. At that time a stony indifference resulting from despair and complete hopelessness began to overwhelm the survivors. People wandered gloomily and bowed, without greeting one another. All the civilised politeness of society seemed to have vanished.

After each Action the murderers came to confiscate the property of the victims on behalf of the Nazi institution "Verbreitung des Deutschtums im Generalgouvernement" (Dissemination of Germanizm in the General Government). Stores for Jewish loot were opened in abandoned Jewish homes in Batorego Street. These stores swiftly filled up to the ceiling with the furniture, pillows, quilts, and linen of the victims of the "Uebersiedlung" (resettlement) which was the official name given to the Extermination Operations. The cynicism involved does not call for comment. The furniture of the victims was pillaged and given away to Ukrainians, who came in their thousands with wagons from the villages in order to receive their share of the Jewish inheritance.

As the Jewish population dwindled on account of the Actions the Nazis began to reduce the area of the Jewish Quarter. It started at the House of Adela Katz in the Batorego Street and ended at the house of the martyred Abraham Apfelgruen on the Berka Joselowicza Street.

But the Germans did not permit our tears to dry. They had not yet quenched their thirst for the Jewish blood they were shedding like water. The slaughter of the 3rd of September, 1942 came like a sudden blow. The Action lasted for 3 days and 8,000 persons perished. This time the Gestapo, Schupo, and Kripo together with the Ukrainian Police assailed us with full military equipment. Having learnt from previous experience they now brought with them all kinds of instruments for breaking down the bunkers. Freight cars were waiting at the railway station and the victims were taken to them in groups. It was late summer and hot as a furnace. The victims were flung into the wagons on the heads of those already inside, till they were completely stuffed. Quite apart from the blazing heat outside, a choking heat could be felt in the wagons. It was caused by a chemical powder which produced choking smoke clouds. The Gestapo had put this powder in the cars in order to increase the heat and the airlessness. Nobody paid any attention to those who fainted, for each person felt as though he too were about to faint. Those who shrieked for water through the apertures near the wagon roofs met with the laughter of the Nazis who opened the wagon doors and beat them till they bled. Some tore their clothes off themselves, while others voided themselves for very fear and dread. In one of the wagons was the saintly and martyred Rabbi Mechele, grandson of the Hassidic Rebbe of Stratyń. He ripped his minor talit to little pieces and roared, "Lord of the Universe, I served you all my life with full devotion. Is this the reward of Torah?" After that he fainted and died choking. The earth did not open its mouth and the world was not destroyed.

In the wagon carrying my martyred brother-in-law Shabtai Landau with his wife and child there were a number of brave strong young men who had taken wrenches and various implements for self-defense. From the aperture in the wagon it could be seen that the train was moving towards Lwów.

[Page 178]

This meant that it would cross the bridge across the River Dniester near Mikołajów. Before the train crossed the bridge it usually slowed down. As soon as the train began to move the young men started to use their wrenches. It was hard to shift the bolts and nuts because they had rusted with age. But people become unbelievably strong when they are in danger of death. By the time the train began to slow down on the ascent to the bridge the bolts had been removed. The boards of the door, reinforced with iron bars, were broken and the young fellows began to jump out. But Gestapo men were standing between the wagons and promptly began to shoot. My brother in law Shabtai Landau jumped with his child on his shoulder and was shot. His wife jumped after him. She was saved with a handful more. Those who succeeded in returning to the town had the skin torn off their bodies when they jumped. But what was the use? They were saved only until the next Action. The train went on its way, from which none returned. At Belzec the flesh of the martyrs was ripped from them. Their fat was used for making soap. Yet no matter how the polluted ones try to cleanse themselves their sins stain them forever.

Before we had recovered from this the Nazis planned the last blow against the surviving Jews of the Holy Congregation of Stryj. People began whispering of the establishment of the Ghetto. I shiver at the memory of the word.

The news was received with strange feelings. Some said it was a sign that Stryj was not to be made "Judenrein" for the time being, as had already been done in many cities, nor would we be transferred to a Ghetto somewhere else. The fact that the Ghetto was to be erected made it clear that they did not intend to kill us for the present, since they were establishing a restricted area in order to separate us from the Aryans. And that was all. Maybe deliverance would come meanwhile. But those who did not wish to delude themselves regarded the establishment of the Ghetto as a final step before complete destruction, in accordance with a prearranged plan for the entire Occupied Zone which had been prepared by Hitler, Himmler and Kaltenbrunner. Both groups alike saw that the last Action had been worse than the proceeding ones. In the earlier ones people with work papers had been released, but in the last no distinction at all had been made between workers and idlers. Experience had also proved that the bunkers were "a broken reed". If by some miracle a bunker was not discovered today, it was almost certain to be discovered at the next Action. People with money, which in those days meant gold dollars, found hiding places with avaricious Aryan families eager for Jewish gold. "If somebody was out in the dark, he gave his wallet to a gentile" as the Talmud puts it. First the gentile took his wallet and afterwards his life. Some were compelled to leave their hiding places after only a few days because those who hid them feared that they would be killed themselves. The good gentiles robbed the money and sent the Jews away. But mostly the Jews were murdered and flung out into the streets. Jewish bodies lay rotting on the banks of the River Stryj. They were a regular sight. The Jewish Council was ordered to clear them away. The Jews bore with that impossibly difficult burden called life, life of which they themselves had become weary of until finally they were rid of it.

Large posters consisting of many paragraphs and signed by Hans Frank the Head of the General Government announced the establishment of the Ghetto in Stryj on the 1st of December, 1942. Entry and exit were permitted only to those Jews with work cards stamped by the Gestapo. Those breaking the law were liable to the death penalty. The Aryans were warned not to approach the Ghetto limits. Selling or giving food or offering Jews any kind of help would be punished by hanging. The Ghetto area consisted of the following streets: Berka Joselowicza, Kusznierska, Krawiecka and Lwówska. It had two main entrances, in the Berka Joselowicza and Lwówska streets. Thick wooden posts were set up on both pavements and across them a long pole was placed as a barrier which was raised when necessary. Policemen watched the gates by day and night. Streets that led to the Aryan quarter were blocked with high wooden fences. And now the rope round our necks was tightened to strangle the last of the Jews. The Ghetto was set up with the definite purpose of being destroyed. Its end was inherent with its beginning. Now we were caught like birds in a trap.

Once the Ghetto was established the Jews were divided into two: Those who were working and helping to bring about the Nazi victory, and the idle, weak, aged, women and children. The former wore square patches with the letter "W" meaning "wichtig" (important). This meant that they must be protected, and that the Gestapo must not do them any harm, while the rest were to remain in the Ghetto and wait for their day to come. Day by day thousands of Jews went out into the Aryan Quarter to all kinds of public works, accompanied by Jewish Police. Sometimes lesser ghettoes were set up near the work sites, for those marked with the letter W. Thousands of our finest youth were working there. They were entrusted to the Gestapo so as to be "protected" from any trouble that might befall the main Ghetto, so that these productive workers might be able to work calmly. The Germans said mockingly about them, "These will survive the War". The Jewish workers employed at the Borak sawmill, which was called "Heeresbarrackenwerke", were given the ruins of the barracks opposite Bolechowska Street. The A. S. A. glass factory, the Wasserwirtschaft, the Karpatenöhl, the Altstoff and a number of other German firms placed their Jewish workers in small houses on Franko Street near Bolechowska Street. These houses were emptied of their Jewish inhabitants, who had already been killed in the Actions. Every morning we were lined up like soldiers and went to work under police guard. This was both ridiculous and tragic deceit. In theory the policemen were supposed to protect us, so that the Ukrainians should not beat us on the way to work and the Gestapo should not take us away during an action, but actually the Ukrainians beat us while the Gestapo kidnapped.

[Page 179]

Baking and cooking were prohibited in the Ghetto. Shlomo Sauerbrunn's bakery in Lwówska Street was the only one which baked bread on behalf of the Jewish Council from the coarse flour provided by the Nazis for the Ghetto prisoners. From time to time policemen came to the Ghetto to see whether the chimneys were smoking. A German soldier went patrolling with his dog, which was trained to smell the scent of meat. The cesspits were not cleaned in the ghetto, and it is hard to describe the results. Both electricity and gas were cut off. The water cisterns were stopped up. They left a single pump in the courtyard of Isaac Reich in the Berka Joselowicza Street, and another in Kusznierska Street. People had to get up at five o'clock in the morning and stand in line with their pails, for in case of an Action it was clearly advisable not to enter a bunker without water. Starving people wandered about and lay on the street.Even the healthy looked green and yellow. The bunkers left their mark upon them, as death had cast its shadow over them. All that was left of the wealth of Stryj was a cart and one wizened mare, on which the dead were taken to the cemetery. The burials were handled by the martyred son-in-law of the Dayan Rabbi Saul Lusthaus, and by Mordechai Jungman. Although we were sick of living, conversations in the Ghetto turned chiefly on signs of our end. How many more days would they let us live? How many more Actions would there be, and when? If a mere two German policemen were seen approaching it was enough to start the alarm, "They're coming!" That terrible cry passed through the Ghetto like lightning; and whenever it was heard every living soul vanished from the streets and houses, and we all began crawling into the bunkers. Nor were they always wrong with their fears. From time to time little Actions were carried out by the Jewish police under Nazi orders. Why should the Nazis bother to hunt the despicable Jews if the work could be done by the Jews themselves? It was so easy to set Jews against Jews. How tragic! How low we had fallen! The kidnappers came to the ghetto to find the bunkers of their fellow Jews and hand them over to be killed. The order of the Gestapo required a certain number of Jews to be handed over, and the police had to supply that number. Sometimes there were thrashings and absolute murder when they found a bunker. Those who were caught were first taken to the Great Synagogue and were kept there under police guard until they were handed over to the Gestapo. The well-to-do who could pay a ransom to the Jewish Council were set free, and others were caught in their place. Trade in human Jewish life flourished. But before long all alike found themselves facing the same fate. The Jewish Council imposed a compulsory tax on the population of the Ghetto. Everybody paid whatever was demanded for fear of being caught and taken away at the next Action. The younger people began to feel very bitter with the Council arguing that this money could be used to buy arms for self-defense during Actions. We knew perfectly well that we could not defeat the Nazis. But we wanted to kill as many of them as we could before we were killed ourselves. But the Council carried out the orders of the Nazis like abject slaves. The chairman of the Council thought that all the ghettos would be liquidated but that of Stryj would remain.

New faces began to be seen in the ghetto. They were the remains, the vestiges of communities near and far. All alone, without families or kin, these poor people wandered about as though they were struck insane after their own ghettos had been liquidated. Near me, for example, lived Gerengross, the owner of the largest department store in Vienna, with his Aryan wife who refused to abandon her husband in his distress. During one of the Actions the poor folk pleaded to the Gestapo, "We are Viennese." But their blood mingled with that of our brethren. One young fellow escaped when the camp in the Janowska Street in Lwów was liquidated. He told me that 70,000 Jews have been murdered in a single week on the "Piaski" a suburb of Lwów. My martyred younger brother Joseph succeeded in escaping to Stryj form Stanisławów. There he stood in a long line of thousands of Jews at the cemetery, surrounded by S.S. troops and Gestapo men. The pit was very deep and wide. Those who reached the pit had to strip quickly, put their clothes in order on one side and their shoes on the other, separately. The victims walked over a board and young S.S. men about 18 years old shot them with automatic rifles. The victims fell straight into the Pit. Those who were not killed by the bullets were soon choked to death under the weight of bodies. The crush was dreadful. Everyone wished to be done with their life as soon as possible. The long line moved closer and closer to the board. The people around my brother, and he himself, began to unbutton their clothes and unlace their shoes, to be ready for their turn. To their astonishment the shooting, suddenly ceased. The action was to have been finished at five o'clock, and precisely at five it stopped. "Go away, dirty Jews!" shouted the murderers. "See you at the next Action!". If anyone doubts the German punctuality and order there was the proof.

[Page 180]

Chapter 5
Through the Carpathian Mountains

While the days of the Ghetto were numbered and we were all as pretty much dead, there were Jews living normally only twenty miles away beyond the Carpathian Mountains on the other side of the Hungarian border who knew no ill. A Ukrainian peasant wearing a white band over his arm appeared in the ghetto, bringing a letter to someone or other from his relative in the village near Veretzki, the first little town beyond the Hungarian border. The person receiving the letter was warned to overcome his fear, to risk his life and to cross the border at once by winding paths through the mountains, where the guards did not venture. Following this letter people with relatives beyond the border sent them letters by Ukrainian villagers eager for money, who were paid after bringing an answer back from the relatives. At the same time a rumor spread that the son-in-law of Haim Wolf, the owner of the soda-water factory, had succeeded in crossing the border and reached Budapest safe and sound. People began to whisper about the possibility of escape, and did their best to see that the Jewish police heard nothing. Who could be wise enough at such a time to weigh the pros and the cons? Anybody who put a foot outside the Ghetto was risking his life and was in danger every step of the way, until leaving town. Once outside, there were new perils. These came from both the local police and the German police guarding the bridges along the roads. The Ukrainians knew that whoever tried to escape would be carrying all their money with them. They ambushed in order to kill and rob. If anyone succeeded in crossing the border in spite of all these risks and perils he had to find a place where he could hide on the other side, for the Hungarian police were keeping strict watch all along the border area. If they caught any Jews from Poland they returned them to the Gestapo in Ławoczne. Anyone who found a good hiding-place to stay a few days, he could wait for a suitable opportunity of getting to Munkács (Munkatch) and from there to Budapest.

Yet in spite of the perils and pitfalls, which maybe one in a thousand could evade, it was still worth risking a life that had become worthless. However, the weaklings and cowards in the Ghetto thought otherwise. As long as there were no Actions, they argued, the Ghetto was the sole refuge in which it was possible to live for the present. Leaving the Ghetto was as good as suicide. Why should a Jew go to meet the Angel of Death? Better wait for the Angel of Death to come for him.

The physicians Dr. Shützer and Sobel succeeded in crossing the border and reached the first Jewish house on the soil of Hungary. When they knocked at the window to ask permission to enter, they were met with animosity and contempt. The poor fellows explained that they had just escaped from Poland, and entreated for a place to spend the night. Their pleading and tears were of no avail. It is shameful and painful to have to reveal the reproach of some Hungarian Jews. One even brandished an axe and warned them that they should leave at once otherwise they would be handed over to the border police. They were driven away by force and returned to the hell of the Stryj Ghetto. Hiding a person who escaped from Poland was punishable by up to three days detention. At the time that Polish Jewry was being systematically murdered, Hungarian Jews were afraid of imprisonment.

In spite of everything, people set out to cross the mountains. Hersch Benczer, Moshe Schechter, Manny Kron, Michael Wang, Moshe Kess and others succeeded in reaching Budapest. The delivery of letters to Jews had long ceased. Those happy persons who had reached Budapest wrote letters to Polish addresses in Stryj. The letters were brought to the Ghetto and encouraged people to risk their lives and cross the Hungarian border whatever happened. My three dear martyred brothers Isaac, Joseph and Pinhas, with Ephraim Kramer and his son Saul, engineer Haim Vogel, Leib Risch and David Sobel and their families, Shlomo Ladier, Mendel Meller, the brothers Rosenman and others like them whose names I have simply forgotten in the course of time, these brave people, who decided not to wait for the Nazi murderers and to stand in line by the pit were all shot on the border. The Carpathian ranges, both on the side of Ławoczne and on that of Dolina-Wyschkowo and Perehińsko-Osmoloda, were soaked with the blood of these holy martyrs.

Dozens of people who tried to escape to Hungary were shot on the way at Morszyn or at Synowódzko. A few were wounded and returned to the Ghetto with bullets in their backs and legs, happy that they still had a refuge to which they could return. The Wohlmut, Reiner, Grimm and other families and persons dug bunkers in the Skole district in the Carpathian forest. Soon enough the bunkers were discovered by Ukrainian shepherds who brought the Gestapo there. Moshe Wohlmut was the only one to escape ad he managed to reach Rozdół and Dolina. Ukrainian youngsters searched for Jews in the forests in order to get a reward from the local police. All those who went to the forests and were not discovered returned one by one to the Ghetto or the camps, for they could not face the perils of forest life. Only a handful were saved and survived in these hiding places.

[Page 181]

Chapter 6
Aryan Documents

There was a feeling that the Ghetto was nearing its end; and a drowning man will clutch at a straw. Two well-dressed young fellows, who did not look like Jews entered the Ghetto from the Aryan Quarter. They came from Warsaw and with them they brought the Aryan document plague. They sold birth certificates, documents of the Meldungsamt (Registration Office) and the "Arbeitsamt" (Labor Office) in Warsaw. All the client had to do was to give them any Polish name he chose, two photographs and a down payment. Five days later they brought false Aryan papers from Warsaw. A number of persons particularly those who did not have a Jewish appearance and who spoke Polish well, purchased these bargains, and carefully learned the Christian prayer of "Our God in Heaven" by heart. For if a suspected person was caught, the Police would tell them to recite the Morning Prayer. With these false documents, they hoped to be able to leave for another town before the liquidation of the Ghetto. The Germans discovered this trick as well. Strict watch was kept at the railway station. First they inspected all documents and stared straight in the eyes of the passengers. Afterwards they physically examined those they suspected. Jewish men and women by the hundreds were hung in the railway stations. Only a handful of those who tried to escape from Stryj to Warsaw succeeded in saving themselves with the false documents. Among them were the physicians Schleifer, Hausmann and Kindler, the Brothers Apfelgruen and a few more. Women had a better chance than the men of escaping with the aid of such papers. Is it possible to describe the distress of parents waiting to die in the Ghetto and saying goodbye to their daughter who was going out into a world that was full of peril at every step?

Their parting blessing was, "Listen carefully, daughter, and pay attention. Forget your people and your family".

The Hell in the Ghetto

The murderous situation developed an animal-like instinct within us for feeling the storm before it came. There were clear signs of an approaching action. The kidnapping in the streets stopped. They did not put pressure on us or thrash us at work. The police at the gates did not inspect us, and did not pay attention. Sometimes they even vanished into the neighboring pub. This meant that we were simply not worth guarding any longer. For who guards the dead? Even the Gestapo inspections at the camps, of which we were deadly afraid, stopped. Now the camp was unattended. So when we did not feel the whip and the pressure we knew that this was the calm before the storm, before the last storm that preceded the final everlasting silence, the calm and silence of death. Those who were not prepared to accept the terrible thought that they had to wait with dread for death at the hand of the Nazis, those whose will to live was not yet fully destroyed and who still thought of rescue, had to decide between four alternatives: To hide with non-Jews, to escape to Hungary, to escape to the forests and dig a bunker there or to try to get to another town with false papers. All of these options had a 99.99% probability of death. Those who risked one of these methods of escape had one more temporary option. If the non-Jew did threw him out, or if the conditions in the forests compelled him to return to the town, he could still take shelter in the Ghetto as long as it existed. But after the liquidation of the Ghetto there would no longer be any place for a Jew to hide and could be murdered by anyone as his life is worthless. Those were our thoughts in the spring of 1943.

I will never forget Passover 1943, until the day I die. At the time I was working at the A.S.A. glass factory. Kneeling naked I drew glowing glass vessels out of the furnace. Once a day we got a portion of soup which was not fit for dogs, and a piece of black bread. After work we went to the camp on Bolechówska street at the house of the Nawalnicki sisters. The furniture consisted of two tiers of boards which were infested with lice. Three persons lay side by side on such a bed of boards. The camp was surrounded by tall wooden fence and the gate was guarded by a policeman. The events in other cities made it perfectly clear to us that the Ghettoes would be liquidated first and then the camps in which the productive workers were kept. The Ghetto was generally regarded as a dangerous area, for nobody could guess the day or hour of the next Action which could be sensed in the air.

[Page 182]

On Passover Eve I stole into the Ghetto. My three martyred brothers were no longer alive. They had met their death in the Carpathian Mountains. I, the only survivor, wished to spend the night with my parents, no matter what happened. I had the feeling I would never see them again. Jewish refugees from other towns were staying with my parents who had always been hospitable. They sat around the table, on which burnt a dim candle made of fat that my mother had specially hidden for the purpose. A few black matzas made of coarse meal and hot water had been prepared for the festival. We said the blessing over the matza. When my father asked me to repeat the Four Questions I remembered the Passover Eves of the good years, when we all sat around a table on set with shining dishes of gold, silver, and crystal-ware, and had gaily and cheerfully sung the words of the Haghadah to the traditional tunes.

My tears choked me so that I could not utter a sound. Nor did the eyes of the others remain dry. Suddenly the young fellow who had been watching on the balcony burst into the room. "They're coming", he shouted which cut like a scalpel through the living flesh. In the distance he had seen two shadows approaching the Ghetto, a sign that the Action was impending. Within a moment we were all in the bunkers. This time it was a false alarm. Some people had heart attacks because of such alarms and maneuvers, while others lost their minds.

Next day I saw the martyred rabbi Shlomo Drimmer in the Ghetto. He was a learned Jew, and the secretary of the Talmud Torah. With him he carried a volume of the Mishna text. In answer to my question he told me that he was going to the Czortków kloiz (synagogue), where a minyan (a quorum of ten) Jews met every day. Each of them studied a chapter of the Mishna for the salvation of his own soul, and then said Kaddish after himself. For who would say Kaddish after us if extermination were decreed for our people and not even a memory would survive us? All the synagogues and houses of study were already destroyed. The Ukrainians had smashed, ruined and burnt the Torah scrolls, the books and the furniture. Or else they used them as fuel and for wrapping up goods in the shops. The windows had all been smashed. I stood in front of the "Geyle Kloiz" in Kusznierska Street, the Temple of the God of my youth, my old house of study and I trembled. The holes and spaces of the windows seemed to face me like a man whose eyes were gouged out, humiliated. Should I weep at its destruction, at our own or at both alike?

As I walked in line back from work I entered a Ukrainian shop at the risk of my life in order to buy some tobacco. The shopkeeper wrapped up the leaves in a page of Gemara. Sheets of a Torah Scroll were spread out on the floor. I was shocked and felt my knees and heart shake. Scalding tears suddenly burst from my eyes at the sight of my people's sacred objects being trampled by impure feet.

The tension in the factory increased. People whispered to one another, "They're digging!" a phrase that caused our stomachs to turn. Pits were being dug at the Jewish cemetery in readiness for the day of the impending Action. The terrifying news was brought by Aryan workers from the "Baudienst". That day the men in charge did not drive us hard at work. Such easy-going days always boded evil and catastrophe. Our hands simply did not respond to the work, but seemed to be paralyzed and we stared about like trapped wild animals. Nobody slept at night.

What we feared came about. In May 1943, between the Passover and the Feast of Shavuot, the Ghetto was surrounded. By this time the work of the murderers was far simpler because the area of the Ghetto had been reduced. There was no escape or refuge. Gestapo units were brought from Drohobycz to help the Stryj squads. Those in charge of the slaughter were: Oberleutanant Klarmann, Ebenrecht and Huet of Stryj, and Hildebrandt, Minkus, Josef Gabriel and Gerber of Drohobycz. The murderers and their assistants were all drunk. The echoes of the shots and explosions that reached our ears pierced our souls. It is beyond my powers to describe what went on within us. It is beyond all human comprehension. While we were working for a German victory only a few hundred paces away from the Ghetto, hell was swallowing our families. When the murderers entered cellars or other suspect places, they put their ears to the walls in order to try and distinguish movement or human voices. At such tense moments all those in hiding held their breaths. If anybody coughed or a child began to cry, they all promptly covered him with their clothes and choked him. The children and babies found in the houses on upper floors were not brought downstairs but were dragged from the arms of their mothers and flung from the windows. Their little heads smashed against the pavement, while the little bodies were trampled underfoot by the Nazis and Ukrainians. Bunker walls were smashed open. Those who never heard the yells of the beasts roaring, "Raus! Los!" (Out! Quick!), and those who never heard the weeping and wailing of the babies and little children trampled and murdered in the streets, cannot imagine hell. Hundreds were shot in the streets. Thousands were taken to the Great Synagogue and from there to prison and the cemetery for mass Slaughter. It was obvious to the Nazi murderers that the Jewish Council and Jewish police had to play an active part and help in carrying out the Action. The Jewish police who were called upon to participate received special white jackets. Their task was to take the corpses out of the houses, pile them in heaps on carts and take them to the graveyard. Blood dripped from the carts and the cart-wheels on the Stryj soil. Those Jews who survived this action, and who were not yet done away with by the murderers, washed and scoured the streets of Stryj after the Action, removing the bloodstains left by their brethren. This time the victims were not taken far. Some had prepared cyanide for themselves and committed suicide in prison. They included Dr. Malka Leibowicz and her son, Dr. Schnier, Dr. Kiczales and others. When the victims were sent half-naked out of the prison and climbed on the trucks that took them off to the cemetery, a crowd of Ukrainians gathered at the gateway to see and satisfy their lust for Jewish blood. And let this go into the record: The Ukrainian beasts beat the naked bodies of our brothers and sisters with nail-studded clubs while they were being taken away to be slaughtered. The blood of 8,000 Jews was shed that day at the cemetery. Poles who lived in the Pomiarki suburb next to the Jewish cemetery told me after the Liberation that they went up on the roofs to watch the murder. After the Nazis left the field of slaughter the level of the graves had been raised because of the sea of blood that had been shed. For several days afterwards dogs licked the blood that oozed from the earth.

[Page 183]

After the Action was over the Jewish Council received an account from the Gestapo listing the precise number of bullets used up in carrying it out. The Council was requested to pay for the bullets.

After having cut us limb from limb, the Ghetto was ready to be liquidated. The only bunkers left there were those that had been built by really skilled workmen in hidden places where even the murderers would never dream of searching, and those that had by chance never been discovered. After the last Action, which was on an unheard before scale, the desire of the survivors to keep themselves alive and escape by building bunkers had very definitely weakened. What was the point of saving one's self again if the Ghetto was going to be liquidated anyway? Physical strength was at an end. Some died of starvation and grief or of infectious diseases, while others just committed suicide. Despair spread from the Ghetto to the camps. It was obvious that once the Ghetto was liquidated it would be the turn of the camps. We secretly began building bunkers within the camp itself.

During the middle days of Passover 1943 four young men came to the Ghetto. They had reached Stryj from Warsaw with forged Aryan papers, after running away from the Destruction and crawling to the Aryan part through the sewers. They told of the heroic deeds of the Ghetto fighters who raised the blue-white flag in the burning Ghetto, which was defending itself to the last. The cadaverous faces of the Stryj Ghetto inhabitants grew bright at these tales of bravery. But our joy did not last long. The liquidation of the Ghetto began on 10th July 1943. Ukrainian guards of armed police forces were stationed at all the Ghetto entrances and exits for two weeks. Those who still retained a spark of the will to live left the bunkers, went up to the attics, dug holes between the attics, and paved a way to the Aryan quarter and through the attics reached the house of Fleischer, at Rynek corner of Cerkiewna Street. From there they stole at night to our camp at the Bolechówska Street at the house of the Nawalnicki sisters.

The fires of hell were literally burning in the Ghetto. The murderers went from house to house seeking victims, and completely destroyed the buildings. Where they suspected the existence of bunkers they flung incendiary bombs or flooded the cellars with water. Those who did not drown were buried alive under piles of bricks, stones and dust or else were burnt and choked in the smoke. "Some perished by water and some by fire, some by strangling and some by stoning", as the prayers for the New Year and Day of Atonement put it. Not a single person survived in the last bunkers, which were regarded as unconquered fortresses, at the homes of Moshe Rosenbaum and Ezekiel Reder in Lwówska St. and the home of Moshe Kron in Berka Yoselowicza Street. The sound of bombs and rattle of automatic guns made the town shake to its foundations. We in the camp listened with bated breath to the echo of each bomb and it tore our hearts. A Jew from the Skole District who escaped from the Ghetto hid in the attic of Isaac Reich at the corner of the roof, and through a crack in the wall saw what took place in the courtyard of my parents. He succeeded in making his way through the attic route to the camp, and this is what he told me: My parents left the bunker in sheer exhaustion. As soon as they entered their dwelling the German murderers appeared, accompanied by Ukrainian police. My parents were taken through the outer stairway down to the courtyard. A German knocked my father's skullcap off with his rifle and shot him. Afterwards he shot my mother. May the Lord take vengeance for their shed blood. The murderers emptied my father's pockets, removed a few marks and his watch and chain. Then came the Jewish police and loaded the corpses on a cart.

When the Ghetto was liquidated the Offices of the Jewish Council were burnt and the members were shot, together with the Jewish police. All that was left was the death cart with the skinny mare. She was brought to our camp, whose turn had now come. The last survivors of the Ghetto who had found refuge in our camp hid wizened with starvation in the attics and the cellars. Those who managed to obtain cyanide took their own lives, their final satisfaction being that the Nazis had not touched them. As for the remainder, the last spark of life gradually dimmed in them, and they wandered around like shadows, more dead than alive. The commandant of our camp, A.S.A., August Schmidt of Stuttgart, a glass-factory owner, informed the Gestapo that illegals from the Ghetto had stolen into the camp. One fine morning before sunrise early in July 1943 we were startled to hear sudden shots in the camp itself; shots which flung us off our lice-infested boards. Before we could find out what was going on, we saw through the windows that we were surrounded by Nazi, and Ukrainian forces. The medley of shouts and shots left us highly confused and unnerved. The Jewish police urged us with their rubber truncheons to dress quickly and go down to the courtyard. Through the sound of the shots could be heard the voices of the commanding officers: "A.S.A. workers with the W mark in one row, and the rest in a second row!".

[Page 184]

I stood among the A.S.A. workers and pinned the W badge to my chest; for its absence meant death. My eyes sought my wife and mother-in-law, who had hidden themselves in a bunker under the roof. Shots sounded in the attic. A Schupo and Gestapo men climbed on the roof and shot those who were running away. Their riddled bodies fell into the courtyard beside us. People were dragged out of the chimneys and shot on the spot. Two Jews in an attic defended themselves with knives, and so as a result I saw two bandaged Nazis in the neighboring courtyard. Those who had tried to escape lay weltering in their blood at the camp entrance. This Action was conducted by Oberleutnant Klarmann. His shirt was unbuttoned, his face was red and he looked like a savage and bloodthirsty beast. His head was bare and he had an automatic rifle in his hand. He stood on the steps in the courtyard giving orders. At his side stood Isaac Stark the commander of the Jewish camp police. Through my skull thundered the order: "Count the 165 for the A.S.A. The rest to the second row!" My work card was numbered 164, which meant that I was among the living. When they reached my place I felt my pulse, my muscles and my eyes to see whether I was dreaming or actually awake in this valley of slaughter. I felt that my senses were leaving me. My legs were shaking. Klarmann spoke: "We have taken the Ghetto filth out of your camp, for they dirtied the camp which is intended only for the good workers. It is your duty to work and work, and henceforward let your camp be clean!"

The row of illegals was loaded on trucks with yells and wailings whose echoes still resound in my ears as I write these lines. They were taken to the cemetery to be killed. We, the 165, were led away to work at the factory.

The "Altstoff" and "Wasserwirtschaft" and some other smaller camps were liquidated. The three remaining labor camps in Stryj were those of the A.S.A., Heeresbarackenwerke, and the H.K.P.

There was no longer any doubt that theses would be liquidated too. The question was which would come first. Or maybe they would be liquidated together. Who could guess the plans of the murderers? Those days were just a corridor leading to death. The factory in which I worked was surrounded by grassy areas and trees. Whenever I passed I breathed their scent as deeply as I could, wondering to myself meanwhile whether my feet would be treading this earth tomorrow, or whether I would already be rotting in a common grave. I would be rotting but the grass and trees would continue growing for years to come. And maybe they would even see the downfall of the wicked. In silence and despair we gripped the wooden bars which fenced us in. Any hope and possibility of rescue had vanished. All we could do was to moan in silence and wait for death. Beyond the fence lay the Aryan Quarter, noisy and swarming with life and liberty. How happy were those who had not been sentenced to death like us, and who might come and go as they pleased. Beyond the camp fence people went about their affairs and their work, some smiling, others serious. They looked at us as though we were some kind of show. Thoughts rushed through my head: Why haven't they been sentenced to death like me? Why don't I have freedom of movement like them? Whom have I sinned against?

Underworld types, the scum of the earth, emerged from their dens. Thieves by day and robbers by night, suspect janitors, prostitutes and all kinds of despicable types wandered about by the camp fence. Despite of all the warnings they were not afraid to approach the fence and talk to us. They stood around the camp like crows about to swoop down on corpses, all of them waiting for blood. If anybody still had any article of clothing, a watch, a ring or anything else of value, he exchanged it with them for food. We who were going to die did not need any belongings. The dead are free from needs. Among them were also "rescuers" who came to suggest hiding places and to bargain about it. Some people went with them at night and returned a day or two later, after having been robbed of all they had.

[Page 185]

Some did not return at all. These merciless people took their victims into their cellars and then invited a "friend" disguised as a Gestapo agent to extort a ransom. Wherever you turned there was death, death and death.

The most dramatic night of my life was the night of July 19th, 1943. I clearly felt the footsteps of the angel of death approaching the camp. My heart told me that our hours were numbered. Demoralization and anarchy prevailed in the camp, an atmosphere preceding Action and death. There was no authority. Some drank to intoxication. Some laughed hysterically or wept to ease the terrible tension racking the brains and turning the stomachs. The two stories of the camp and its courtyard had turned to a true madhouse. I could see my own thoughts reflected in the alarmed and confused eyes of those around me. The nervous tension reached its peak. In a little while we must break down. And was it surprising? Hundreds of young men in the prime of their youth, all innocent, had been driven into this filthy unbearably stinking cage. The last drop of blood was being sucked out by exhausting labor, dry bread and a few drops of water. After they extracted the last drop of blood out of the body they were now about to take the souls as well; and we were just waiting for them to come. Each of us could see them in his mind's eye. They were coming, the Germans! They are coming like a storm, in their spick-and-span green uniforms with faces like wild boars. They would surround the camp as usual. They would line-us up in a straight line because they so greatly loved order and discipline even in the face of death. They would take us through the streets of Stryj, through our own streets, straight to the cemetery. People in the prime of their youth, with their vast desire to live, were to be taken alive to the grave like sheep to their slaughter. They would walk to their last resting place on their own feet, direct to the spot where people are carried.

On their legs they would bear their bodies and souls straight to the pit! There we would undress. Undress for the last time. We would walk the plank which crossed the pit like a diving board. We would take our last step. I would ask for only one thing from God, my very last wish - let the bullet hit the brain or the heart directly and be done! For if I fell injured into the pit there was no saying how long it would take to die, until I would be covered over by the heavy weight of corpses, and be choked by them...

All of a sudden I awakened as though from a fever. My thoughts were interrupted by the tune of Tango that came from beyond the fence. Barely ten steps away the rooms were lit up gaily. Cheerful voices and laughter mingled with the melody reaching my ears. Through the windows I could see the dancing couples. The cursed Ukrainian bastards were dancing while death mounted in our windows. Thunder did not smite them from heaven, nor did the earth open her mouth to swallow them up. The pits in the cemeteries were waiting for our bodies. I felt that a critical moment had been reached and a time to make a decision. Either life or death! I did my best to concentrate my thoughts on this single point. No matter what might happen, we had nothing to lose. We had to escape that night. Tomorrow might be too late. My dear wife who had always supported me in times of struggle and bitter stress now stood beside me silent, trembling in despair. She sensed my thoughts and the brewing storm within me in these decisive moments. In answer to my question she replied that she also thought the end had come. We decided to leave the camp that night, no matter what might happen. From nine o'clock on there was a curfew in the town, while a Jew could expect a bullet in the daytime as well if he went beyond the camp fence. But anyone who was thinking of escaping had to put the word danger out of his thoughts. In my mind I weighed the two perils of staying or escaping. The first seemed like the worse of the two. We left the camp at midnight. Our very souls seemed to depart from us, and our breathing stopped at the echo of our own footsteps. When we left the town behind and entered an abandoned cowshed, our clothes were soaked with the cold sweat. I imagine that a person sweats that way only once in his life, when his soul departs from his body. This is not the place to describe the perils and adventures from that night until liberation, on the August 8th, 1944. Indeed, they simply cannot be described.

In the morning of the July 20th, 1943, five hours after we left the camp, the murderers liquidated all the A.S.A. workers who wore the letter W. Most of them were shot in the camp courtyard, the rest at the cemetery. After the Action was completed the Municipal Fire Brigade came to wash the camp courtyard and the neighboring streets clean of Jewish blood. A few days later the Heeresbarackenwerke, the largest camp in town, was also liquidated and many good fellows lost their lives there. The poor fellows had arranged that one of them should give a signal on the way they were being led, and then they would all scatter and flee. As soon as they reached the prison courtyard, Hirsch Finkelstein of Slobótka shouted the signal. Most of them scattered and ran away at once. Many were shot on the spot and the rest at the cemetery. Only a few escaped. The H. K. P. Camp was liquidated the same day. The murderers attacked it in the morning. Those who did not dress quickly enough were shot in their beds. Among them was my dear young brother-in-law Joseph Landau may God avenge him.

The city of Stryj was Judenrein.

[Page 186]

Stryj was occupied by the Red Army on August 8th, 1944. I was one of the first Jews to enter the town. When Ukrainians saw me their eyes bulged out of their heads and they crossed themselves. In their eyes I saw the astonishment of those who witness the rising of the dead. On that great day of liberation, while the thunder of the cannons still shook the town, the few Jews who had escaped went to the graveyard to pay a last visit to their martyred brethren. How dreadful the scene was! The holy ground had become a grazing ground for cattle. It was covered with thorns and thistles. The fence had been broken down. The German barbarians had used the tombstones for road-paving.

Along the paths lay fragments of skulls and scattered bones. We dug a grave for them and gave them a Jewish burial.

My feet led me to the ruins of the Ghetto. The weeping of the stripped and homeless souls hovering round me reaches my ears still as I pen these lines...How great is the pain...

Epilogue

That is the story of the destruction of Stryj, where my mother gave birth to me. During the winter nights of my childhood I walked the streets, a little oil lamp in my hand, when we returned from cheder. I grew up within the walls of the houses of study. There my father hid his head beneath his prayer-shawl when the Priests chanted their blessing. There I became bar-mitzvah. Through its alleys I hastened to the Slichot prayers in the chilly Elul mornings, in order to knock at the heavenly gates and ask for forgiveness for all Israel. That is where I decorated the sukkah, where I recited the Hallel prayer when we prepared Matza shmura for the Passover. On this soil I wove the dreams of my youth, the dreams of a return to Zion. On this soil I grew up and became a man. Stryj! It was my fate to see both the prosperity and the destruction of Stryj, her beauty and her fall; when the enemy set his polluting hand on all her beauty, consumed Jacob and destroyed his home. Those voices of prayer which once tore through to the heavens have grown silent in her synagogues. The sad sweet chant of Torah has departed from her houses of study. No little children recite their verses at the cheder. There are no more disputes between the Hassidim, and no more disagreements between the parties. The Jews have no place in her markets. Her sons have gone and the earth covers the Jews of the Holy Congregation of Stryj forever. The burning bush has been consumed. On her graves and ruins, ruins of wood and stone, scraps of parchment sheets and paper scorched and burnt, I absorbed within myself the holy spirits of the souls which quivered in the empty area of the destroyed ghetto. I absorbed within myself the moan of our brethren and sisters, the death-gasp of tortured and tormented infants and babies who were slain and who call for avengement. Who call to avenge the holy congregation of Stryj, which gave up its collective life to sanctification of the divine name.

When I left the Ghetto ruins I turned my face back and prayed: "Germany! Happy be that repay thee thy recompense for what thou hast done to us. Happy be that seizes and dashes thy babies against the rock. May I yet be one of those. May my feet stand in their blood, and may I wash in their wicked blood as they washed in ours".

We always held dear the memory of the departed. For their sake we used to study Mishna, and particularly that chapter "There are some who rise" in the Tractate "Mikvaot", which was held to aid the souls of the dead to rise aloft. We recited the Kaddish, we drank to the memories of the departed, we lit candles, and we said prayers at the graveside. We gave charity and baked special loaves for distribution to the poor, in order to aid the soul of the dead to mount aloft. All this we did in memory of the single individual. What shall we do to mark the memory of six million of our brethren, including the 12,000 souls of our holy congregation? To mark the memory of men, women and children, all of them slain, burnt, drowned and choked by poison gas and in the furnaces.

May these pages be a soul-light to their memory, and may they be bound up in the bundle of life. Let us pass onto all coming generations their last will and testament calling for vengeance, as a memorial stone to those martyrs who have gone aloft.

Stryj on earth was destroyed by the Nazis in 1943, in the year 5703 of the Jewish era. Stryj on high will live in our memories till our very last day.

Would that my words were written indeed.

Would that they were engraved in a book,

With pen of iron and lead.

Hewn forever in the rock.

For I know that my redeemer lives,

And at the last will rise to avenge on the earth.

(Job XIX).

Brooklyn, Av 5714 (August 1954)
Eleven years after the destruction of the Holy Congregation of Stryj.

[Page 187]

The Destruction of the Stryj Community
by Isaac Nussenblatt
Translated by Susan Rosin

Dedicated to my dear family that perished in Stryj

1

On June 22nd 1941 Nazi Germany launched a surprise attack on Russia. The red army was surprised by the attacks and the bombings and retreated hastily along the German–Russian border. In the first few days, the Germans captured large areas and started moving into the Russian interior.

Stryj was occupied on July 2nd, 1941. A period of horror, fear and persecution started immediately for the Jewish population. Even before the start of the German–Russian war, rumors started circulating about the horrendous atrocities and killings by the Germans of Jews in western Poland which was occupied in September 1939.

Soon after occupying Stryj, the Germans implemented their reign of terror against the Jewish population. In the initial days, the town was managed by the army. The malicious intent to discriminate against the Jews was already evident in the first orders published by the district commander. The Jews were ordered to elect a "Jewish Council" (Judenrat). The council was tasked with registering the Jewish population, opening an employment office to provide workers for forced labor. The council was required to serve the German occupation forces and support its administration. The chairperson of the Judenrat was Oskar Hoterrer and his deputy, the lawyer Mishel.

In addition, a Jewish police – Jüdischer Ordungsdienst which was actually a means by the Germans for Jewish extermination. The Jewish police was required to cooperate with the Nazis, especially during the aktions and to confiscate Jewish property and valuables. Some in this police force treated the population harshly. Because of that it is of note to mention those that were able to use their positions to protect and rescue their brethren. Among them were Heiber, the husband of Mania Stern, the teacher Goldberg and others. The lawyer, Shalom Goldberg who was in Lvov during the Stryj occupation was drafted to the Jewish police there, and acted with other few to help and protect Jews. As time went on, he could no longer bear his role in the police, escaped and hid in the Lvov ghetto. During the liquidation of the Lvov ghetto, the Germans were going to blow–up the bunkers. They were attacked by gun fire from one of the bunkers, where Shalom Goldberg was hiding too. Several Germans were hit and killed. All the fighters in the bunkers were killed and among them Shalom Goldberg.

But the end of the Jewish police was bitter. For their loyalty to the Nazis, they were rewarded with execution on the last day of the Stryj ghetto liquidation on July 3rd, 1943.

2

The military rule in Stryj did not last long. As the Germans progressed in Russia, the military rule was replaced with a "civil" one. New decrees were implemented. All males ages 12 – 60 were required to register in the labor offices for forced labor. In addition, all Jews from age 10 and up were required to wear an arm band with the Star of David. Incompliance carried severe punishment and even death.

Many Jews crowded the labor offices in order to obtain a work certificate, turning them to slaves, that might (that was the belief) save them from death. In the morning hours, large groups of gloomy eyed Jews wearing rags were seen on their way to the forced labor sites.

Some refused to be degraded in body and soul by the forced labor. They did not get the work certificate and instead hid in bunkers and cellars

[Page 188]

and others escaped and joined partisan groups that started to organize and fight the Nazis. Desperation, depression and fear prevailed among the Jews. The streets were empty. Only some children, women rushing to buy groceries and the elderly on their way to the Jewish council clinic were seen.

The Jewish council opened a few stores providing measly rations such as 100 grams (about 3 and Â½ ounces) of bread per day. This of course was not enough and diseases became rampant. The Jewish hospital was full to capacity and there was lack of medications and personnel. After the establishment of the ghetto, when three families had to share one room, the mortality increased dramatically. The dead were buried at night and their family members were not allowed to follow them on their final journey.

The Jews lost all their civil rights. Anyone who abused, robbed or even murdered a Jew was not prosecuted. The Jews were humiliated in any possible way. Their businesses were taken away, their stores were closed and the merchandise looted, schools were closed and the students dispersed, factories were confiscated and the workers dismissed, and the activities of the public institutions were discontinued.

The Ukrainians received the Nazi occupiers enthusiastically. They saw them as their redeemers from the Soviet occupier and they were promised an independent state in east Ukraine ("Zapadnaya Ukraina"). The Ukrainian nationalists that were persecuted during the Soviet occupation of eastern Galicia turned against the Jews since they viewed them as Soviet sympathizers.

The Ukrainians started a massacre of Jews in villages and Jewish farm owners around Stryj. All these atrocities were done with the agreement and encouragement of the German authorities. Few of those who managed to escape arrived in town and brought the news about the massacre by the Ukrainian peasants.

Since the surprise attack by the Germans and the hasty retreat of the red army, many who were out of town were not able to return home. Some walked home, many were caught, brutally tortured and murdered by the Ukrainian hooligans.

3

After they were allowed to brutalize the Jews, the Nazis decided to tame down the Ukrainians, and they were ordered to act only as ordered by the authorities.

After the murder of the Jews in the villages and Jewish and passers-by, the Nazis started their bloody rule. It was not difficult to causes for mass murder. After the retreat of the Soviet army, bodies of prisoners were found in a ditch near the prison. Among them were Ukrainians, Poles and Jewish activists. It was rumored that the atrocities were committed by the NKVD (the Russian secret police). As a result of finding the bodies, the Ukrainians organized a mass demonstration, protesting the atrocities of the Soviet authorities. Thousands from the town as well as multitudes of peasants from the surrounding areas participated.

A mass funeral was held for the murdered. That day turned out to be a disaster for the Jews of Stryj.

Since early morning, Ukrainian thugs started rioting in the streets. They broke into Jewish homes, beat brutally the people, then led them to the Christian cemetery and ordered them to dig graves for the mass funeral victims. The Jews were beaten savagely and there was fear that they will be buried alive, as such things did occur in those days.

I too was in the group that was led to the Christian cemetery that was located about three kilometers (about two miles) from town. When we got to the cemetery, we were placed

The central committee of Stryj immigrants in Israel 1960 – 1961

Seated from right to left: M. Kaz, S. Weis, Dr. N. Kudish, A. Rotfeld, S. Rosenberg, Dr. Ada Bar–Lev, L. Pickholtz

Standing from right to left: J. Lustig, Mgr. J. Nussenblatt, M. Weis, M. Wagner, S. Preiss, Mgr. J. Waldman, J. gartenberg, J. Pickholtz, Dr. M. Bar-Lev, Kugel, J. Boymel

The committee for publishing the Book of Stryj

Dr. Nathan Kudish

Avigdor Rotfeld

Shimon Rosenberg

Moshe Kaz

Dr. Ada Bar–Lev (Klein)

[Page 189]

along the fence. Most of us were certain we will be shot. Scared to death we waited for that final moment. When the nightmare lasted forever, it became clear to me that we were brought to the cemetery to dig graves. We relaxed a little and were ordered to grab tools and dig a grave that measured five meters long, three meters wide and one meter deep (approximately 16.5 feet long, 10 feet wide and 3 feet deep).

It was a hot July day. We were sweating profusely, and were ordered to dig for hours without any breaks. Anybody who stopped or slowed down was beaten with rifle butts and nailed whips. We were released in the evening, exhausted and broken, but feeling we were saved from a certain death. We were ordered to return the next day, but no one from the group obeyed.

We were happy to return home and find our families alive as well. However, quickly we sank into fear and depression with the thoughts of: what would tomorrow bring?

4

After several incidents of murder and abuse more tragic events were not far behind. Rumors spread in July 1941 that the gestapo was preparing a list of communist party members to be executed. Twelve Jews were captured and executed in the Grabowiec village outside of town. These murders were supposed to be a warning for Jews not to support the communist party. In addition, the gestapo picked a group of Jews, led them to Grabowiec in order to dig graves for those to be executed.

My brother David may his memory be blessed was among the grave diggers and told us about the horrors. The grave diggers were beaten savagely with whips and rifle butts. Once the digging was complete, they were ordered to lay flat on the ground and not look back. A few minutes later, machine gun shots were heard and then silence. The diggers then were ordered to get-up and bury the dead. The burying Jews were trying to bury their brethren according to tradition as much as possible. Among the murdered were Freiman from Lvovska street; Dunkel, a renowned merchant in our town; Szatzker (the husband of Kronstein); the engineer Szteirmark; Ringel, a senior official from city hall; Szaczerski (a convert to Christianity) also a city hall official. Only Freiman was actually suspected in belonging to the communist party. The others were never involved with the communists. I was a laborer paving roads and happened by Rilov. I talked to the peasants who confirmed the brutal murders by the Ukrainian police. I wanted to see the burial place of my poor brethren, but was warned that anyone approaching the grave will be executed.

Mass massacre of a thousand Stryj Jews

After barbaric violence and murders of singles and groups came another stage in the extermination of Stryj's Jewry – a mass murder of a thousand Jews. It was on a night of horrors of September 1st, 1941. No one could have imagined that the Germans and their helpers could carry out such a barbaric murder of innocent men, women and children.

On that night of horrors, hundreds of armed German and Ukrainian police and gestapo operatives burst into homes dragging men, women and children out of their beds. All this was planned ahead and done with great brutality. The Jews still did not understand that they have to prepare bunkers and hiding places. Before their incarceration in the prison on Tribunalska street, the prisoners were held in the Ukrainian police yard on Batorego street, undergoing torture. The prisoners were guarded mainly by Ukrainian policemen. Some of the prisoners were able to bribe the guards and upon their return, they told us about terrible torture in the prison cells. During the night, the Ukrainian police burst into the cells and beat the prisoners mercilessly. Many died from their injuries, as no medical help was given and were buried in the prison area. After seven days of brutal abuse, the Jews were led to an undisclosed location. Later it was revealed by the Ukrainian policemen that the Jews were led to a forest near the village Rilov (Holobotov) about 5 kilometers out of town. They talked about horrendous and shocking scenes during the murders. Among the victims of this massacre were: the lawyers Rosenberg and Milek Spiegel, Isaac Hubel, the brothers Zeisler (Josef and Heshiu), Donek Zandenberg, Irka Elner, Shmuel Brauner, Sonia Reichman, David Nussenblatt, Moshe Karon, Yaakov Bar, Mania Welker, Herman Zoldan, Oskar Reiner.

[Page 190]

I was a laborer paving roads and happened by Rilov. I talked to the peasants who confirmed the brutal murders by the Ukrainian police. I wanted to see the burial place of my poor brethren, but was warned that anyone approaching the grave will be executed.

Setting Boundaries of the Jewish Quarter

The times were very hard for the Jews after the night of horrors on September 1st,, 1941 and until September 1st,, 1942. Ostensibly there was relative calm in the city. The Jews were still allowed to live in all parts of town and were able to move around with limited freedom. In October–November 1941, the Jews were ordered to leave the main streets and to crowd into the Jewish quarter. Two or three families were crowded in one room in inhumane conditions. That was a sign of the impending disaster. All the Jewish stores and businesses were closed and confiscated. The Jews were ordered to hand over their furs or risk execution. Most people were afraid and complied. Some, though, decided to defy the "Berlin order" and hid their furs. I recall one case where a woman by the name of Kerner was executed because she did not hand over her fur. I too faced execution due to this "crime", but was saved at the last moment.

After the furs' decree came the furniture decree. Any Jew who had usable furniture was ordered to hand them over to the Nazi authorities, who sent the nicest furniture to their families in Germany. Those who refused to comply were beaten savagely.

The Aktions

All the theft and plunder, persecution and oppression by the Nazis still did not bring the Jews to despair and did not dim the hope of salvation. They handed over all their possessions and their money to save themselves. However their hopes did not materialize and what happened, brought disaster, and most of them died as martyrs.

In September 1942, the Nazis started a systematic and planned extermination of the Jewish population of Stryj. This was done with rigor, precision and brutality that brought the destruction of Stryj's Jewry. At the beginning the Jews knew about every upcoming aktion. Before every aktion, the gestapo showed up and gave orders to the Jewish council and others who were supposed to participate. The rumors about an upcoming aktion spread very quickly and people hid in bunkers and cellars. There were rare instances where the Jewish council was able to postpone the next aktion for large sums of bribes.

The First Aktion

On the evening of August 31st,, 1942 rumors spread that the Germans and their helpers were planning an aktion in town the next day. The Jewish quarter emptied. Many fled to their Christian acquaintances who agreed to hide them for the duration of the "operation". Others hid in bunkers, cellars and attics. At midnight, the Jewish quarter (the ghetto was established later) was surrounded by all kinds of official murderers: the gestapo, the Schupo (Schutzpolizei), Ukrainian police, and Ukrainian youth organizations. The Jewish police was tasked with guarding the area during the aktion. Armed with bayoneted rifles and grenades and wearing helmets, and with bloodhounds they were about to attack the defenseless Jews. In the morning some shots were fired to signal the beginning of the aktion. The wild, blood thirsty murderers emerged from their positions, broke the gates of the quarter and started demolishing the apartments and furniture. The old and the sick were shot in their beds. The murderers searched under the floors and then descended to the bunkers and cellars. Shouting "Juden raus", they took out those hiding, who were scared to death. Those who were found were brought to the market street. Some were executed in a forest near town some in the Jewish cemetery, and the rest were taken by train to the gas chambers in the Belzec death camp.

This aktion, called the first by the Stryj Jews lasted three days from September 1st, to September 3rd,. Five thousand Jews were murdered. Eye witnesses said that many died from thirst and heat on the trains. The Poles and Ukrainians watched from their windows as the Jews were being led to the death cars clearly rejoicing in the Jews misfortune although many of them were their neighbors. They even took advantage of the Jews' tragedy by robbing and stealing whatever was left in the empty apartments. I saw this shameful behavior with my own eyes.

[Page 191]

Here is the list of names of the victims that were murdered in the first aktion based on what I remember and was told by others: Zeyde Schuster, Dr. Nathan Schechter and his family, the Osterjung family, Abraham (Buczi) Apfelgreen and his family, the lawyer Mark Hurwitz, the lawyer Zelinger, prof. Seinfeld, Benjamin Nussenblatt, Pesja Josefberg and her daughter Yetta, Genia Reichman with her daughter Chaja and her two children, Apfelgreen (a shoe merchant) and his family, Israel Nussenblatt with his son Mordechai, the widow Apfelgreen and her daughter Tilda, the wife of lawyer Fichman and their eldest son Lolek, Moshe Bar and his family of four, Lawyer Sheinfeld with his wife, the brothers Robinson, Kremer with his engineer son, Chajka Klinger and her mother, dr. Dora Herstein with her parents, the lawyer Weis, Feivel Rosenberg and his family of five, Handel Fruchter with her son Aharon, Buchwalter with his family of three, Isaac Fruchter with his family, the layer Piltz with his wife and his parents, Max Hurwitz (teacher), Lerner (teacher) and his family of three, his brother in law, Rosenzweig (teacher), dr. Herman Unger and his wife (teachers), Kuba Hirshenhorn (teacher), Babko Unger (teacher), Chawa Wisaltier (teacher).

The Second Aktion

The second aktion followed six weeks later, on October 17th, and 18th, 1942. In between the two aktions the Jews were wondering who will be transported to Belzec and when. All the aktions followed the same pattern. In the evening of October 16th, 1942, the regional gestapo people from Lvov arrived and visited the offices of the Jewish council. There were rumors that something was going to happen. The streets emptied, and the terrified people went into hiding.

At 4 AM, shots were fired, and bands of Jews' "hunters" burst into homes. We were hiding in the attic. We were very quiet and even the children and babies felt that something was happening and did not cry. After sunrise, I could see through the cracks, bands of German police, Ukrainians, Ukrainian youth and a few Jewish policemen who were assisting in finding the Jews. From time to time our hiding place was approached by a group of policemen who were searching every corner. They climbed the roof, and hit it with various demolition tools. When they did not find anything they left. These nerve wrecking searches lasted for two days. We hoped that we were saved. My mother, who was hiding with us prayed constantly and read psalms and encouraged us to hope and not give–up.

For two days and nights we held–up under awful conditions, and we were certain that we were saved. At 5 PM almost at the end of the aktion another group of German and Ukrainian policemen entered the yard and resumed their search. Suddenly we heard loud banging and the boards under which we were hiding from the murderers fell on top of us. The murderers shouted "Juden raus", and they started dragging us and kicking us. My mother of blessed memory, who was sick and her legs were swollen could not walk on her own. My brother Abraham of blessed memory and I picked her up and tried to bring her down the stairs. But, one of the policemen pushed me and my 75 years old mother fell. In spite of the pain, she did not utter a word. We picked her up and brought her to the yard. Before they led us to the gathering place, my nephew Pinchas (the son of my brother Abraham), managed to sneak away and hide. The policemen noticed his disappearance and tried to search for him, but could not find him. He survived and later served in the IDF (Israel Defense Forces).

Broken and decrepit we arrived at the gathering location of the wretched victims. The gestapo praised the Ukrainians for their success. Two thousand Jews were brought to the square. After two hours, we were ordered to line–up in rows of five and march to the train station. When we passed on the streets we could see that the Ukrainians and Poles were rejoicing in our misfortune. I carried my mother, because I was afraid that she would be shot in front of me. The policemen guarding the prisoners used to shoot the sick and the frail who were unable to move at the required pace. With great difficulty I brought my mother to the train station and laid her on the ground. We sat for two hours, while additional groups of Jews were being brought. Then we were put in the train cars. I saw how four Jews helped my mom into the car, and I never saw her again...

[Page 192]

Rudely they squeezed us into the train cars that were intended for cattle transport. The doors and windows were boarded up and barbed wire was placed on top. They placed 100 – 120 people into each car. The crowding was unbearable, forming a lump of human bodies. The younger among us hoped to be assigned for work details and to be saved for the time being. We were not given any food or drink. The train moved after midnight. Immediately, people took out all kinds of tools and started prying the window and the door to jump off the death transport. We all knew that the train was taking us to the gas chambers in Belzec, so there was nothing to lose. I decided to jump. I threw my belongings and then jumped. I fell into the ditch alongside the rails and luckily was just scratched. Many of those who jumped were killed either from the fall or by shots from the gestapo. Others were seriously wounded. A heavy and cold rain started falling and the night was very dark. I had no idea where I was and I did not look for my belongings. I decided to walk in the opposite direction. I walked along the rail in the Stryj direction. In front of me and behind me, people who jumped from the trains were running, and nobody was paying any attention to anyone else. After about ten minutes I heard moaning and I noticed a person who was lying on the wet ground. When I approached I noticed this was a woman. Her face was covered in blood and she could barely talk. When she noticed me she asked who I was and where we were. I told her that I jumped from the death train and I was from Stryj. Then I realized that this woman was the wife of my friend Rosenberg who was a teacher in Lvov. I cleaned her face, and stood her up. Suddenly we heard voices and whistles coming from the nearby forest. We ran into the forest, and there we found another group of people that jumped from the train. There we met Wolowski, a lawyer from Stryj who had a serious leg injury. We did not leave him, and together we moved deeper into the forest. We sat there in the dark on a pile of haystack and decided to wait until morning. Additional escapees joined us. The rain was heavy and cold. We were hungry and scared and did not know what morning will bring. We huddled together for warmth.

In the morning, after a short discussion we decided to proceed to Stryj. The road back was not easy and we entered the nearest village to ask for shelter for a few hours, hoping that someone will feel sorry for us and would give us something to drink and eat. When we approached the first house in the village, we saw a peasant standing at the doorway. I asked him if we can stay in his house for a little while and told him that the axle broke on wagon we traveled in and we could not continue on our way. He looked at us with suspicion. The group that stood in front of him, wounded, scraped, dirty and wearing rags, but we were very pleasantly surprised when he invited us into his house. I am sure he knew we were Jews. Harboring a Jew even for a few hours carried the death penalty. Pleasant warmth enveloped us in the house. We asked him for some milk. The peasant's wife and daughter were still asleep, but he woke them up, and the wife put a large pot of milk on the stove. In the meanwhile, we took off our wet clothing, our socks and shoes and let them dry. Once we got dressed again, we asked the peasant to take us back to Stryj, but he refused telling us that the horses were in the forest and he could not get them. We thanked him and his family and left hoping to find shelter for a few hours in another house, as walking in the day during an aktion was very dangerous. We tried several houses, but no one agreed to help us. They told us to leave the village at once, because a police station was close by. We returned to the forest, and tried to proceed towards town. After walking for about an hour, we left the forest and started walking on the road which was full of German vehicles. Luckily, they did not pay attention to us. We separated into small groups. Mrs. Rosenberg walked some distance in front of the groups and she was supposed to warn us in case of danger. I was in the last group helping Wolowski. Suddenly, Mrs. Rosenberg signaled for us to hide because a Ukrainian unit was checking the papers of passers–by.

[Page 193]

We started running towards the forest, and suddenly hear a shout: "Stop or I'll shoot". Behind us were two Ukrainian policemen, their bayoneted rifles directed at us. We were caught! They hit us savagely with the rifle butts, robbed us of our meager possessions and led us to the nearest police station. In the station we met others from our transport who told us that many of those who jumped from the train were killed in the forest. There was no doubt in our minds that this time we were condemned. I thought to myself that we need to accept our fate. Were we any better than those who were sent to the gas chambers in Belzec?

We were kept in a grain storehouse and got some watery and sour soup. The police searched us and confiscated our papers and letters. I asked the chief to return my university diploma and my personal letters. He looked at me and said that they were useless for me as I would not be able to use them anyway...

In spite of being dead tired we could not sleep. I thought to myself that soon I would be digging a grave for myself and be tortured to death. Suddenly I felt a push, and I was told that I was part of a group that was organized to bring the bodies of those who were shot in the forest. We collected a large number of victims, some of them were still alive, but we could not help them.

We were told to load both the dead and those that were still alive on carts. The carts were placed in a locked warehouse. In the morning, they were all dead. They were all buried in a mass grave, and we whispered "Yitgadal Ve Yitkadash"...

Later that day we were transferred to the jailhouse in Stryj on Tribunalska street. Some from the group were released probably by bribing the gestapo and also due to the intervention of Hoterrer, the head of the Jewish council. After a few tense days, we were told to line–up. We were certain we would be executed. Suddenly, some of the Jewish policemen came in (among them some that I knew) and we were told we would be put on the second transport to Belzec. I noticed that some of the prisoners were directed to the other side of the corridor and let go. I assumed that the gestapo received bribe for them and they were being set free. I did not envy them. I felt I had nothing to live for. My parents, brothers and my entire family were murdered. Suddenly, one of the Jewish policemen said to the Kripo (Kriminalpolizei): "Please release Nussenblatt. He is a high school teacher" and I joined the group that was about to be set free. We were led to the offices of the Jewish council. The Kripo demanded bribe for each released person. I had no money, and asked a young man from Przemyśl for a loan. He was able to give me 500 zloty. The policeman said it was too little money, but agreed to release me after I promised I'll try to get him 500 more.

I found a dreadful scene when I got home. The windows and doors and all furniture were broken, the pillows and quilts all torn. All was deserted, and I could not find anyone from my family.

Establishment of the ghetto in Stryj

After the second aktion, the Germans reduced the area of the Jewish quarter and it became an enclosed area. The ghetto included the streets Batorego, Zielona, Targowica, Krzymirza, Cerkiwna, the eastern part of the

Rynek and Potockiego. The Jews were forced to leave certain streets and to crowd in only a number of streets. The gates to the Aryan quarter were locked and leaving the ghetto area was prohibited.

All Jews, young, old and even women became slave laborers working for the German war machinery. Only a few were assigned to offices, as there was no one else that could do that work. A small portion of the craftsmen were employed by German factories. They earned so little that they could not even feed their families.

The hunger was great. Only a few smuggled food from the Aryan area into the ghetto.

Stryj community memorial tablet in the Chamber of the Holocaust[1]

Nazis abuse rabbi Meir'l, the son in law of the rabbi of Głogów

The organizing committee of the memorial convention for Stryj Jewry in Haifa 1956

[Page 194]

Most survived by selling their clothing, their valuables, furniture etc. The peasants sold food to the Jews at staggering prices. The Jewish council had a soup kitchen that provided meager portions for the hungry. Due to the hunger and diseases many died every day. The doctors tried their best to help the sick. I want to mention the doctors of our town who were devoted to treating their brethren until the last moment and they too were murdered by the Nazis: Dr. Ingber, Dr. Koenig, Dr. Gwirtz, Dr. Brauner and his wife, Dr. B. Milabauer, Dr. Sznir, Dr. Nobbes, Dr. Roth, Dr. Kitczels (committed suicide on November 17th, 1942), Dr. M. Leibowitz (committed suicide) and others.

The Nazis used also to carry-out "special" aktions such as: against the sick (they were shot in bed), against prisoners, against children and against outsiders (those who came to Stryj from neighboring towns and villages). The orphanage and the old folks-home were liquidated by the Nazis. Under these conditions all cultural life disappeared. The schools were shut-down. The parents had no ability or patience to take care of the children. As young as twelve years olds were working hard with the adults. Some of the children traded secretly in cigarettes and candy.

The Jewish council imposed heavy dues on the Jewish population in order to meet the demands of the Nazis who extorted huge amounts of money. The Jews saw in these "contributions" a possible way to save themselves.

The Third Aktion

The ghetto in Stryj was established in November – December 1942. It is hard to estimate the number of Jews that were crowded into the ghetto confines. Before the war the Jewish population in Stryj was 14,000. With the murders and the first two aktions 8,000 Jews perished in the forests around Stryj and the gas chambers of Belzec. Five to six thousand Jews were still alive, and they were joined by another 2,000 – 3,000 of Jews from the neighboring villages, then the number of Jews before the third aktion can be estimated to be around 7,000 – 8,000.

All of them were crowded into the small area of the ghetto. The overcrowding was unbearable and there was no way of maintaining any minimal sanitary conditions. Filth and dirt were all around.

Even before the establishment of the ghetto, many Jews prepared bunkers in their homes which saved them during the first two aktions. Once they were squeezed into the ghetto, many bunkers remained outside of the confined area. Building new bunkers in unfamiliar homes was not easy. A feeling of despair was felt by all. It was hard to tell what could save them. Some started creating bunkers in the homes others escaped into the forest and built bunkers there or joined the partisans. Unfortunately there was no communication between the partisans and the Jews in the ghetto otherwise many would have joined the partisans. Some tried to cross the border into Hungary. Many were captured by German or Ukrainian police and were shot on the spot. Among those killed on the border were S. Ladier (the son of rabbi Ladier) and his fiancé and Dr. Gwirtz. Some hid with Polish or Ukrainian families paying a heavy price. Many were saved that way, but others were betrayed, robbed and then killed by the very people that were supposed to save them. But, the majority just stayed in the ghetto and waited for the inevitable.

In February – March of 1943 another aktion took place and about 2,000 Jews were murdered. Prior to the previous aktions, the Jews knew what was going to happen and were able to hide in the various bunkers and hiding places.

However, after the Jews were enclosed in the ghetto, no rumors from the outside reached them. This made the "work" of the murderers easier and the aktions came as a surprise and there were many victims.

The aktion started on February 28th, at 3 AM and lasted until March 1st, 1943. The guardsmen in the ghetto noticed suspicious movements, but before they were able to warn the people, the gates of the ghetto were broken open, and the armed murderers started their hunt. This aktion came as a surprise, and people did not have time to get dressed and hide in the bunkers. As was their usual practice, the murderers took out about two thousand men, women and children and led them to the death cars at the train station. I can recall a few names of the murdered in this aktion: Henia Sztoltz (Heller) and her daughter Hadassah, Shlomo Rossler with his wife and daughter, Leib Schatz, the policeman Sasha Heller (who was shot by an Ukrainian policeman), the teacher Hella Preis, the Hitachdut activist Aharon Meller.

[Page 195]

There were a few cases in Stryj of active resistance, some with weapons, some of attacking policemen during aktions, and also instances of sabotage in the work camps. However, all these instances of resistance were crushed mercilessly.

The Fourth Aktion

More than a thousand people were captured in the fourth aktion that took place on May 22nd, 1943. Before they were killed, they were held for a few days inside the great synagogue without any food or water. Dreadful things that cannot be written happened in the synagogue. With their bare hands, the condemned, scratched messages into the walls demanding revenge.

On the night before the aktion, my brother–in–law of blessed memory noticed suspicious movement in the ghetto streets. He immediately alerted those in our house and the nearby homes. The bunker in our home could hold no more than fifteen people, but because of the sudden panic about fifty of those from our house escaped and crowded there. We could not breathe or move a limb because people were lying on top of each other. A woman with a baby was one of those who ran into the bunker. Shots and wild voices were heard signaling the beginning of the "hunt". All of a sudden the baby started to cry and the mother who forgot take a bottle with her could not quiet her down. We thought we were condemned and begged the woman to leave otherwise we will all be killed including she and her baby, but she would not budge. The despair was so great among the people that I thought someone was going to choke the mother and her baby in order to save themselves and their families. A miracle happened and the baby stopped crying as the murderers shouting "Juden raus" neared our hiding place. They tried to climb on the walls and the piles of boards that were used as camouflage. But, because the climbing was difficult they gave up and we heard them saying in German: "There are no Jews in here. Let's go". They moved away from our bunker and started looking for others. Across from our bunker was another one which was not camouflaged sufficiently and it was discovered. Suddenly we heard the shouts of "Juden raus" again and we knew they were discovered. I could even hear the voice of the policeman who counted the victims: "one, two, three, ...fifteen". The murderers and their victims left the cellar and we all thought that we were saved. However it was too dangerous to come out at this time. We heard the rumors that the victims were held at the synagogue. So, while they were still in town, it was too dangerous to venture out, as the murderers could always add more victims to those they already had. But, we knew our end was close. Even those in the work camps told us that the Nazis guarding them were hinting that the end of all the Jews was coming.

The Fifth and Final Aktion

The final aktion was more brutal than all those preceding it. This time, the Nazis threw grenades and fire bombs into the bunkers. The people had no chance to leave the bunkers and they were buried and burned alive under the rubble. The sadists also used bloodhounds and set them against those that were found. This aktion, unlike the others lasted a whole month. It was obvious that the Germans decided to destroy the last Jews that still remained in the ghetto.

Instinctively, on the night of June 2nd, groups of Jews escaped from the ghetto – some to the Aryan side to Christian acquaintances, some into the forests and others into the work camps. They hid in attics and cellars, until they too were uncovered by the Nazis.

[Page 196]

The Nazis started this final aktion by first liquidating the Jewish police. In the previous aktions, the Nazis were assisted by the Jewish police, and now it was their turn as well. On June 3rd, the Jewish policemen came to "work" as usual. However, on their arrival, they were captured and led to where the other victims were gathered. Their caps and belts were taken away from them and they were executed on the same day. The head of the Jewish council, Hoterrer was killed on the first day of the aktion near his office.

The victims of the final aktion were shot and buried in mass graves in the Jewish cemetery and in the Rilow – Holobotow forest.

The bravery of the high school teacher Liza Schauder should be noted here. She was captured and was among the prisoners. Suddenly, she started shouting approximately this: "Murderers of my poor people! Robbers! Who gave you the permission to kill and rob the Jewish people? Who gave you the permission to murder millions of innocent Jews, just because they are Jews?! You are laughing and mock us because you have the power! But you will see who will laugh last! I despise you and your crazy leader Hitler. You can kill me right now. I don't care. Revenge! Revenge! The spilled blood of the millions will find its revenge not only in you, but in all your next generations, and you will never find peace. I despise forever the Nazi murderers!".

Upon hearing these brave words, other prisoners started to yell as well. The gestapo officers and the Nazi policemen were stunned at first to hear these brave words. But soon they started using their whips and their rifle butts. Liza

Schauder was removed from the line, her clothes were torn and her fate was like the fate of all the others.

*

The Jewish doctors were murdered together with the remnants of the ghetto. The doctors lived in the house of rabbi Ladier on Potocki street outside of the ghetto and they were allowed a free movement around the house.

On June 3rd, they prepared to go to their work as always and did not realize the lurking danger. Dr. Nobbes and Dr. Sznir were on the balcony of the house and noticed the approaching gestapo, but they thought nothing will happen to them just like in the previous aktions. All those in the house, the doctors and pharmacists were transferred to the prison on Tribunalska street and then to the Holobotow forest where they were killed and buried. Drs. Nobbes, Sznir and Leibowitz, poisoned their family members and then themselves on the way from the prison to the forest. Only a few of the doctors and pharmacists and their families were saved because they hid in the cellar when the others were taken away.

Here are some of the names I remember of those who were murdered (in addition to the doctors) in the final aktion: The religious judge Yeshaya Asher Julles, David Zeidmann, A. Eisenstein, lawyer Shlomo Tauber with his wife and their daughter, Hoterrer's wife, Fela Ladier and her mother (the rabbi's wife), Kuba Nagler, the family of Josef Bar, Karon with his wife and their three daughters and their granddaughters, Rozia Karon and her husband, Yetta Karon and her two sons, Shimon Schtolz, teacher Mania Heiber (Stern) and her mother, Rachel Brauner with her three children, Malcia Schteif, Shmuel Fruchter , his wife, their daughter and his parents and sisters, Munia Pomerantz, Henia Schtolz, Regina Schmorak, the clinic manager Anden with his wife, Zaurbrun, Mrs. Zobel with her daughter in law (wife of her son Nathan), dr. Josef Roht, dr. Ingbar and his wife, dr. Mantel, his wife and sister in law, pharmacist Lonek Stenrberg and his mother, and pharmacist Dicker.

Many Jews tried to save themselves in any way possible. Among them were a number of Jews from Stryj that moved to places far away from the town using Aryan papers. Most of them moved to Warsaw and worked there as Poles, as Volksdeutsche and even as Germans.

Some of the people who chose this route were: Dr. Kindler and his wife, Mrs. Wiesaltier (Meir's wife), Steirmark (later was murdered in Warsaw), Lea Huser (wife of Dr. Gwirtz), Henia Nagler (Levin) and her daughter (they were captured by the schupo and murdered in the Przemyśl prison), Mrs. Finkler (whose husband was a post office clerk) and her daughter, Henia Apfelgreen (Kudish) (was later murdered in Lvov), Kronstein and his wife, Alex Findling and his wife, Theo Findling and his wife. The Aryan papers and the Aryan appearance that many acquired did not always help save their lives and many were captured and murdered.

A gathering of Stryj members of "Hitachut–Poalei Zion" in Israel, 1935

Committee of Stryj organization in Haifa

Standing from right to left: **M. Akert, M. Klieger, M. Honig, J. Glicher, Hobbel**

Seated right to left: M. Walter, Goldring, Dr. Lindenbaum, J. Engelman, J. Pruchter

Gathering of immigrants from Stryj in Tel Aviv, Purim 1935

[Page 197]

Some children who were given by their parents to Poles and Ukrainian were saved. At the end of the war many Christian families refused to give back the children to their surviving parents or relatives. Some parents had to abduct their own children and others had to work through the courts.

A group of Stryj's Jews were saved either in the ghetto or by hiding in the Aryan section, by hiding in bunkers or with Christian families. Here is the partial list: the Wolfinger family (Herman, Clara, Henrik, Josef, Shulamit, Regina), Isaac Nussenblatt and his wife Hela, Belka Schtoltz and her daughter Heda, Mrs. Mina Fried (Wolf), her husband and daughter, M. Selinger, his wife, son and his sister, Yona Friedler and his wife Sara, the lawyer Eisenszar, Roth and his daughter Belka, Rozia Lentz, Schuster, Glantz, Rozia Sak, Mrs. Meller and her two daughters, Robinson, his wife and niece, Freilich and his wife, lawyer Nathan Teller and his wife, Yekel and his wife, Dr. Begleiter , his wife and son, Yanka Wundel, Moshe Kaz, Dora Mantel, her husband and her sister in law (Goldreich), Mrs. Weis and her son, Mrs. Walker and her granddaughter, lawyer Weidenfeld and his wife, Halfgut (teacher's daughter), Eda Adelheid, Bella Zeisler.

Only a few survived out of the 14,000 Jews of Stryj. Some immigrated to Israel and some to other places in the world.

May these things be a memorial forever to our holy community of Stryj which was destroyed by the Nazis and their helpers together with the rest of the holy communities of six million Jews.

Translator's footnote

The Chamber of Holocaust was established in 1949 as the State of Israel's original Holocaust museum and memorial

List of Holocaust Victims
Transliterated by Israel Pickholtz

Notes: Title MG"R means magister, an advanced university degree; initial N seems to signify first name unknown.

The surnames in this list are in alphabetical order in Hebrew. To proceed to a particular letter, click on its name, or scroll down.

Sefer Stryj also has a list of names that appears in English. That list was compiled for overseas survivors and is organized by contributor. It is reasonable to assume that all the names on that list are included in the much larger list here.

א

Alef Index	
AGID	Eliezer, Yetti, Avraham, Hirsch Zvi, Somek, Shmuel
EDELSTEIN	Aharon, Hela, Yehudah, Fischel, Shalom, Shlomo, Shiko, Sheindel
AHARONZWEIG	Beila
OVERLANDER	Yehoshua
AUGUST	Avigdor
UNGER	Dr. Chaim, Chaya, Yoel, Izha
UNIKEL-WALDMAN	Selka
OSTRIUG	MG"R, N.
OFER	Getzel, Golda (Lindner - bat Yosef)
URBACH	Meir
ORENSTEIN	Brendel (bat Yitzhak), David (ben Zeev), Zeev (ben David), Yosef, Yosha, Motel, Nehama
IBNER	Eng.
IGRA	Isidor (ben Yosef), Yosef (ben Ozer), Beila (bat Yosef), Yosef, Finkel (ben Israel Dov), Izio, Bela, P.
EISENBRUCH	Eter, Yetta, Mulo
EISMAN	David
EISENSTEIN	Dr. Isidor, Chana Gitel (bat Yitzhak Dov), David (ben Mechel), Leopold (ben Isidor), Flora (bat Isidor), Cecilia (bat Yosef)
EISENSHER	Dr. Yitzhak, Binyamin, Leizer, Sofia, Hinda (bat Yitzhak Buchalter), Berl (ben Hinda)

EICHEN	Avigdor Moshe (ben Shmuel), Avigdor, Taube, Yonah (Feldhorn), Leah (Lichter - bat Shmuel), Shprinze (Altschiller - bat Shmuel)
EICHENBOIM	Benzion (ben Chaim Mordechai), Zalman (ben Benzion), Yosef (ben Benzion), Rivka (bat Zalman)
EICHHORN	Adolph, Rosa
EICHENHEIM	
EICHENSTEIN	Pinchas
EINER	Julia
ALTBACH	Yosef, Sender
ALTBAUER	Mordechai, Etel
ALTSCHILLER	Yaakov, Hadassah (bat Yaakov)
ELLERHAND	Dr. Ignatz (ben Israel), Irna (bat Ignatz), Dora (bat Leizer)
ENGLEMAN	Henia Itta, Yitzhak Manho Mannes, Sarah, Leizer (ben Simha), Simha (ben Leizer)
APTOVITZER	Shelkes Clara, Irit
AS	Sarah
APPEL	Esther, Yosef
OHEL	Monio
APPELGRIN	Zigmund
APPELSCHMID	Bela
OFER	Yitzhak, Sonia, Pela (bat Yitzhak), Penina/Pepka (bat Zvi Erster)
AXELBERG	(Scher), Bluma, Dov, Hillel, Yosef (ben Moshe), Chaim (ben Avraham), Freida, Zvi (ben Moshe), Rosa
ECKERT	Golda (bat Yosef), Yosef

ב

Bet Index

BAUMGARTEN	Avraham, Leon, Mathilda, Shimik
BAUMAN	Yitzhak, Yitka
BEGLEITER	Ida, Herman, Zelda, Yaakov, Leah, Miriam, Shimon
BUCH	Yaakov

BUCHALTER	Heshiu (ben Avraham), Avraham (ben Yitzhak), Zlata (bat Lipa), Chava (bat Yitzhak), Chana (bat Lipa), Israel (ben Lipa), Lipa (ben Yitzhak), Shmuel (ben Lipa), Sarah (bat Israel)
BUCHENBAUM	Moshe
BOIMEL	Avraham (ben Yosef Moshe), Aryeh, Yerachmiel (ben Eliezer), Suma (bat Berish), Rivka
BUNUM	Avraham (ben Azriel), Beila, Mirka, Frimat
BOKOVSKY	Sender, Rivka
BORGMAN	Yitzhak, Barnard (ben Yitzhak), Pepe
BURGER	Nusia
BORNSTEIN	Jerzy (ben Zeev) - says "Shofet" - may have been a judge?
BORK	Zelig, Adolph, Valentina (bat Zelig), Dr. Jonas, Yaakov, Fani, Shlomo
BORER	David (ben Noah), Dorothy (bat Mir), Dorothy (bat Meir), Cyla (bat Herman Friedlander), Rachel (bat David)
BATALION	Abush, Devorah, Herman, Meir, Manya (bat Abush), Finka (Hovel), Regina, Rozia (bat Abush), Shmuel Mordechai, Shimon (ben Abush)
BINSTOCK-ROSENBERG	Lula
BINSTOCK	Malka
BIRGER	MG"R N., MG"R Polia
BIRNBAUM	Adolph, Golda (bat Yaakov), Chaim, Yaakov (ben Chaim), Sonia (bat Chaim), Regina (bat Israel - Miner)
BIRNBAUM-FRANKEL	M.
BACH	Isaac, Sonia
BACHLER	Laura (Steinbach)
BLUMENSTEIN	Rena, Gedalyahu
BLOCH-WEISS	Pepe
BLUSTEIN	Danuta, Heinrich, Zisha, Chaya (bat Aharon - Hovel), Miriam (bat Moshe), Malvina
BLAUSTEIN	Markus, Moshe, Cecilia, Renata
BLAIBERG	Moshe
BLITNER	Genia (bat Feivel), Mina (bat Feivel), Feivel (ben Zvi), Freida (bat Feivel), Rivka (bat Yitzhak)
BLAM	Musia (Hovel)
BLANKIS	Shalom

BENCHER	Herman (ben Mordechai), Chaya Sarah (bat Mordechai), Chana (bat Mordechai), Julian, Yosef (ben Mordechai), Malka (bat Eliyahu), Mordechai (ben Alexander), Sender (ben Zvi), Fania, Zvi (ben Mordechai), Rivka (bat Zvi)
BANKENDORF	Binyamin (ben Yitzhak), Bronka (bat Yitzhak), Chaim (ben Yitzhak), Tonka (bat Yitzhak), Yitzhak (ben Binyamin), Fania (bat Yitzhak), Raizel (bat Yitzhak), Rachel (bat Yitzhak), Sarah (bat Gudel)
BECHER	Dr. N.
BECKENROT	Meir
BAR	Ida, Avraham, Artur, Binyamin, Binyamin (ben Yitzhak Wolf), Dora, Herman, Tova (bat Yitzhak Wolf), Yaakov, Yaakov (ben Yitzhak Wolf), Yitzhak (ben Isaac), Yitzhak Wolf, Lusia, Munik, Malka (bat Yitzhak Wolf), Machla, Marila, Marek, Moshe, Moshe (ben Yitzhak Wolf)
BRAUNER	Adolph, Berta, Dr. Helena, Yoel, Felix, Dr. Feivel
BRAUNER-FUCHS	Ida
BERGER	Benzion (ben Shmuel), Malka (bat Benzion), Yishayahu Benzion, Leah (bat Reuven), Gitel Miriam, Hela (bat Benzion), Yosef (ben Benzion), Yaakov, Issachar, Lucia, Rachel (Sobol), Shmuel
BARDACH	Berta (bat Shmuel), Helena (bat Mendel), Yaakov (ben Mendel), Mendel (ben Kalman), Karol (ben Mendel), Rachel (bat Avraham - Korn)
BRONSTEIN	Yoel (ben Zvi), Natan (ben Zvi), Pinchas, Zvi (ben Pinchas), Rachel (bat Natan)
BERTLER	Nachman (ben Aryeh)
BRICKENSTEIN	Blumka, Chaim, Yishayahu, Leibush, Noah, Azriel, Pearl, Rivka
BERLS	Betka, Michael
BERMAN	Lusia (Hovel)
BRONKA	Tova Gitel
BRENNER	Gebia, Helena, Malka, Kalman, Shmuel

ג
Gimel Index

GEVA	Israel
GABINSKI	Dr. Hippolite
GUDINGER	Moshe

GODHERZ	Herman, Leibish (ben Tuvia), Tuvia (ben Victor), Ninka, Sofia, Pela, Pessel, Pepe
GOTTESMAN	Yosef (ben Leon), Antonia (bat Leon), Berta, Golda, Zlata (bat Yosef), Chaya (bat Israel), Tova (bat Israel), Israel, Shlomo (ben Israel), Dr. Leon (ben Meshullam), Moshe Yosef, Pesia (bat Israel), Pepe, Rosa
GOTFRIED	Bronia, Dr. Rosa
GOLDBERG	Isaac (ben Yaakov), Hirsch (ben Isaac), Fischel (ben Isaac)
GOLDENBERG	Dr.
GOLDNER	Isaac (ben David), Golda
GOLDFISHER	Bela, Devorah, Yetti (bat Alexander Bencher), Zadok, Sarah (bat Yetti)
GORGEL	Yosef (ben Moshe), Yeroham, Mina, Pepe (bat Mendel)
GEISLER	Eige (bat Eliezer), Chaim (ben Yosef)
GETREI	Mordechai, Rachel (bat Moshe - Seif)
GINSBERG	Chaya (bat Shmuel), Shmuel (ben Zvi), Shlomo (ben Zvi), Chana (bat Shmuel), Chana (bat Shlomo), Miriam (bat Shlomo), Moshe (ben Shlomo), Yetta (bat Yitzhak), Rivka (bat David), Sarah (bat Shmuel), Shraga (ben Shlomo)
GEIST	Dr. Marzli
GAIER	Kopel
GELBARD	Pepe (Korn)
GLASBERG	Etka (bat Herzl), Zelda, Tusia (bat Shimon), Meir, Leon (ben Meir), Shimon (ben Meir), Clara (bat Moshe)
GLAZER	genia, Yitzhak (ben Yehezkel), Markus (ben Yehezkel), Nusik
GLATSTEIN	Adele
GLANTZ	Renata
GALERT	Chaya (Eck), Shoshana/Rosa (bat Michael), Yenta (bat Michael), Leah, Michael
GELLES	Chana, Tolza, Leib, Mela
GELLER	Etel, Adele, Gedalyahu (ben Avraham), Fania (bat Gedalyahu), Bronka (bat Gedalyahu), Mina (Hindler), Lusia (Hindler), Leon (ben Shlomo)
GELERNTER	Chaya Rachel (bat Nissan), Anna/Chana (bat Yosef), Chasia (bat Yoel), Yosef (ben Menahem), Israel/Luli (ben Meir)
GRABERT	Zigmundt
GRUB	Regina (bat Leib Zelinger)

GRUBER	MG"R Leon
GROIBERG	Zigmundt, Esther
GRUL	Israel, Miriam
GRUNDORFER	Yosef, Melia
GRONZALT	Izik, Benzion, Dov, Vitka, Yehoshua, Yosef, Yaakov, Leib, Moshe, Sela, Sarah
GROSS	Eliezer, Helena, Henrietta, Dr. Wolf (ben Aharon), Chaya, Israel (ben Eliezer), Mondek, Nella (bat Wolf), Cyla, Clara, Rozia, Shmuel, Sarah (bat Moshe)
GROSSMAN	Avraham, Yaakov, Pepe, MG"R Lula
GRIMINGER	Esther, Mathilda, Max, Pearl
GRESE	Minder (ben Aharon), Ruth (bat Minder), Rosa (bat Yitzhak)
GERTENBERG	Avraham (ben Fischel), Chaim (ben Avraham), Tonia (bat Yitzhak), Sima (bat Yitzhak), Beila (bat Yitzhak), Berta (Derfer), Chana (bat Yaakov), Yosef (ben Shimon), Sarah (bat Yosef), Mindel (bat Yosef), Rusha (bat Yosef), Mordechai (ben Yosef), Yitzhak, Lili (bat Yitzhak), Marek, Riva (Stern), Retza
GERTNER	Naftali (ben Shammai), Shammai (ben Naftali), Yitzhak, Chaya, Chana (bat Melech), Tonka, Yeroham, Zvi, Cyza, David, Beryl
GARFINKEL	Leibish, MG"R Michel, Tonka (bat Avraham - Teicher), Benzion

ד

Dalet Index

DUDMAN	Lipa, Rachel/Nuna (bat Lipa), Alexander/Zigo (ben Lipa), Gusta
DORNFELD	Alter Israel, Freida (bat Hirsch)
DETNER	Bashe
DIAMENT	Bernard, Dr. Hela, Mischa (ben Baruch), Moshe, Dr. Naomi, Fanka, Shaiko
DIM	Freida (bat Miriam)
DIAMOND	Etel, Brancia, Cipora, Simha
DIMENSTEIN	Hanan (ben Yaakov), Miriam (bat Alexander Bencher)
DICKMAN	Elka, Alter, Yaakov
DICKER	Avraham (ben Yosef), Roiza (bat Yaakov), MG"R Salo, Shlomo (ben Avraham)

DANCIGER	Zeev, Shmuel (ben Zeev), Yosef (ben Zeev), Yaakov, Manya
DACHS	Chana (bat Nahum), Yitzhak (ben Shalom), Leah, Ada (bat Nahum), Reuven (ben Nahum)
DERFLER	Leah (bat Shlomo)
DEROR	Avraham, Sonia, Chaya, Leibish

ה

Heh Index

HAUSMAN	Dr. Isidore, Wilhelm
	Oscar, Helena
HAUPT	Lonek, Mondek (ben Meir)
HAUPTMAN	Yaakov (ben Yitzhak), Avraham (ben Yitzhak), Adele (bat David), Aharon (ben Eliyahu), Eliyahu/Linek (ben Aharon), Eliyahu (ben Yitzhak), Nehama, Eliezer (ben Eliyahu), Shlomo Hersch (ben Belci), Beila Gitel (bat Sender), David (ben Avraham), Chana (bat Eliezer), Yosef, Pearl (bat Fischel), Reuven, Shprinza (bat Eliezer)
HOVEL	Aharon (ben David Hersch), Meir (ben Aharon), Yitzhak (ben Aharon), Belka (bat Aharon), Cipora (bat Aharon), Aharon (ben Moshe), Mordechai (ben Isaac), Ida (bat Isaac), Golda (bat Isaac), MG"R Bronia (bat Isaac), Esther Etel (bat Meir), Golda (bat Israel), Gitel (bat Israel Leib), Tova (bat Zeev - Danciger), Tonia, Yitzhak Isaac (ben David Hersch), Israel (ben Zvi), Israel Leib (ben Moshe), Hinda (bat Israel Leib), Rivka (bat Israel Leib), Moshe (ben David), Moshe (ben Pinka), Cherna (bat Meir), Rosa, Rizi (bat Michael)
HOCHGEBORN	Rivka (bat Moshe), Yehudit (bat Moshe), Leib (ben Moshe), Moshe (ben Shmuel), Freida (bat Isaac), Freida (bat Isaac)
HOLZ	Solomon, Tonka, Max, Freida
HOLZER	Zigmundt, Mina, Salomon, Cyla, Regina
HONIG	Penina (bat Meir Lipa), Cyla, Mordechai, Sarah (bat Avraham David)
HOFNER	Berta, Loda (bat Marek), Dr. Marek, michael (ben Marek), Dr. Clara (bat Shimshon)
HOFFEN	Dr. N.

HOROVITZ	Maya, Elka, Esther, Genia, Hersch, Zalman, Charna, Yaakov, Yehezkel (ben Yaakov), Yehezkel, Yehudit (bat Yehezkel), Mendel, Meir (ben Mendel), MG"R Mordechai ben Mendel), Yitzhak (ben Mendel), Bronia (bat Mendel), Israel (ben Mendel), Mordechai (ben Yehezkel), Feige (bat Yehezkel), Miriam (bat Yehezkel), Natan, Pua, Rachel, Raizel, Shlomo, Shmuel
HORODENKER	Rachel (bat Avraham Schwarzbard)
HOROSHOWSKI	Moshe, Feige, Feivel
HEIBER	Elisha (ben Yosef), Feivel, Genia (bat Feivel), Janka (bat Lazar), Yati, Lusia, Miriam (bat Shalom Stern), Sela, Regina
HEISLER	Shlomo (ben Zeida)
HILZENRAT	Henik, Yomak, Shalom, Selka, Avraham, Blima, Wolf, Yaakov, Leib
HIRSCHHAUT	Eliyahu, Pela (bat Eliyahu), Yaakov (ben Eliyahu), Esther
HIRSCHHORN	Aharon Isser, Esther, Benzion, Hasio (ben Kova), Lincia, Kova, Zvi/Heshu (ben Kova), Rivka, Rechil, Shoshannah, Shprinza (bat Yaakov Rotbard)
HEFLGOT	Fruma (bat Yitzhak), Moshe (ben Yitzhak), Ephraim (ben Yitzhak), Shimon (ben Ephraim), Gisela (bat Ephraim), Tova (bat Aryeh), Miriam (bat Moshe - Pfeffer), Fischel (ben Moshe) [the last two appear twice]
HALPERN	Avraham, Golda, Osiash, Markus, Rozi, Betka, Belka (bat Getzel), Bendit (ben Elimelech), Bernard (ben Samuel), Gershon (ben Chaya), Helena, Chaya (Kleiner), Yitzhak (ben Chaya), Moshe (ben Zvi), David (ben Moshe), Samuel, Natan (ben Samuel), Chesia (bat Yokel - Klahr)
HAMMER	Shmuel (ben Asher), Blima (bat Shmuel), Henia (bat David), Rachel
HAMMERMAN	Henek, Yosef (ben Feivel)
HENDEL	Avraham, Amelia, Henia (bat Yosef), Wolf, Yosef, Leah, Sima, Clara
HENDLER	Gitel, Chaya (bat Moshe), Lisa (bat Heller), Markus (ben Isser), Cipcia (bat Markus), Frima (bat Markus), Shmerl (ben Alexander), Dr. Shmuel (ben Shmerl)
HANEL	Leib (ben Tova), David (ben Leib), Mina (bat Leib), Leah (bat Leib), Yehudit (bat Leib)
HAFTEL	Wolf, Shmuel
HAFTLER	Beila Yetta (bat Yishayahu), Avigdor (ben Moshe), Moshe (ben Avigdor), Shindel (bat Avigdor)

HEFNER-LEV	Mina
HEFNER	Miriam (bat Binyamin Stern)
HERMAN	Leib, Leah (Yekel), Salo, Nuta
HERZ	Gitel, Genia (bat Israel), Chana, Israel, Karola
HERSCHDERFER	N., Izak, Zigmundt, Henio, Yosef, Monio, Sabina, Rozia
HERSCHDERFER-WALDMAN	Tonka
HERSCHDERFER-WOLMAN	Tonka

ו

Vav <u>Index</u>

WAGNER	Esther (bat Naftali - Zoiberg), Sheva (bat Shmuel - Sela), Leon (ben Shmuel), Leah (bat Shmuel), Bernard (ben Shmuel), Tonka (bat Yekutiel), Yaakov (ben Mordechai), Mordechai (ben Zvi), Rivka (bat Mordechai), Moshe (ben Benzion), Rachel (bat Moshe), Rivka (bat Yosef), Shmuel (ben Nahum)
VOLOVSKY	Izio, Henio
WOLMAN	Tuvia (ben Yosef), Penina (bat Tuvia), Amalia (bat Pinchas)
WOLF	Natan-Neta, Beila, Alexander, Atka, Esther, Bashe, Gedalia, Golda, Hillel (ben Yehiel), Chaim Zeev, Chaika, Yehudah, Yitzhak (ben Yehiel), Yeshaya, Malka, Mendel (ben Sender), Feige, Freida, Korn (ben Avraham), Sarah Chana
WOLFINGER	Clara (bat Mendel)
WEIDHOFF	Yosef (ben Bat-Sheva), Shoshannah (bat Yosef)
WEIDHOFF-KATZ	Emma (bat Michael)
WIESELTIER	Salamon, Otilia, Freida, Osiash, Meir, Chava, Yanush (ben Meir), Sonia (bat Meir), Rozia, Moshe, Sima, Ozer, Rachmiel, Yehoshua, Tova, Chana, Zelig, Hersch Wolf, Bashe, Beryl
WEISENFELD	MG"R Yehudah
WEISER	Shlomo

WYLER	Chana (bat Chaim Yitzhak), Yaakov (ben Mendel), Meir (ben Nahum), Rachel (bat Nahum), Mendel (ben Yaakov), Malka (bat Berl), Shoshannah (bat Meir), Aryeh, Chana Miriam, Ita
WEIN	Anjee (bat Yitzhak), Yitzhak, Clara
WEINBACH	Aharon (ben Meir), Zisel (bat Aharon), Zusia (ben Meir), Basia, Yonah, Yehiel ben Yonah), Jonas, Sofia, Meir, Eli (ben Meir), Shlomo (ben Meir), Sarah (bat Meir), Salo (b. Yonah)
WEINBERG	brother
WEINTRAUB	Dina
WEISS	Eliezer (ben Leib), MG"R Eliak, Asher, Bruno, Barzi (ben Eliezer), Regina, Hinda/Helena (bat Beryl), Henio, Yitzhak (ben Yehezkel), Gitel Leah (bat Yitzhak), Dov (ben Yitzhak), Shia (ben Yitzhak), Bernard (ben Yitzhak), Dr. Macio, Polia, Pela, Rivka (bat Shia), Rachela, Rachel (bat Yishayahu - Tabak), Moshe, Aharon (ben Rachel), Sarah (bat Moshe), Nusia (bat Moshe), Yitzhak (ben Moshe)
WEISSBLUM	Dr.
WEISSBERG	Dr. Fred
WEISSBARD	Berta, Zelig, Mordechai, Natan, Sonia, Etzia
WEISSMAN	Avraham (ben Mendel), Moshe (ben Mendel), Hinda (bat Mendel), Mendel (ben Moshe), Charna (bat Avraham)
WEITZ	Avi (ben Shlomo), Rachel (bat Abbe - Eva?), Henia (bat Kalman)
WEINSNER	Gustav
WEISNER	Henka, Yaakov, Etil, Shmuel
WALDINGER	Moshe
WALDMAN	Avraham (ben Aharon), MG"R Olga, Eliyahu, Dr. Artur, David (ben Moshe), Yosef David (ben Leib Jonas), Wolf, Monio, Moshe, Seril, Salka, Panka, Kopel, Clara
VALIK	Esther (bat Moshe), David (ben Sender), Toni (bat Sender), Malka (bat Sender), Shmuel (ben Sender), Sender (ben Isaac)
VALICH	Chana (bat Bendit - Tanne), Shmuel (ben Yitzi Meir)
VALKER	Shlomo (ben Moshe), Jonah (ben Moshe), Aharon (ben Moshe), Dora, Hela, Mela (bat Abush), Moshe (ben Abush), Natan (ben Abush)
VENDEL	Dr. Sebastian

WENDER	Yetka (bat Meir), Yaakov (ben Meir), Meir (ben Yitzhak), Sarah (bat Shlomo - Eisner)
VARDINGER	Chaya (bat Shmuel - Wagner), Stella (bat Moshe)
VARZGER	Yitzhak Dov (ben Naftali), Feige Rachel (bat Yitzhak Dov), Pepe (bat Nahum - Wagner), Sheindel (bat Yitzhak Dov)
WERNER	Etel, Devorah (bat Moshe), David, Zlata, Chava, Israel, Mendel (ben Zalman), Miriam, Sheindel

ז
Zayin   Index

ZOIRBRUN	Shlomo
ZOIRBERG	Shalom (ben Naftali), Esther (bat Naftali), Malka (bat Naftali), Naftali (ben David), Reri (bat Kalman - Robinson)
ZOMMERFELD	N.
ZIGMAN	Tova (bat Yaakov), Yaakov (ben Tova), Zivia (bat Tova), Keila (bat Tova), Shmuel (ben Tova), Shlomo (ben Matityahu)
ZIGER	Yosel, Raisel
ZEIDMAN	Israel, David, Mordechai (ben Israel), Clara, Sarah
SEIF	Moshe (ben Shmuel), Tonia (bat Moshe), Mendel (ben Moshe), Mordechai (ben Moshe) Feige (bat Moshe), Yirmiyahu, Chana (bat Shabtai)
SILBER	Shiya, Ruti (bat Shiya)
SILBERSTEIN	Norbert
ZISSER	Henia
ZELINGER	Emalia, Leib, Genia (bat Leib), Yitzhak (ben Leib), Rosa (bat Leib), Shimon (ben Leib), Herman, Mondek, Wilhelm (ben David), Yoka, Israel, Leah (bat Getzel Shuster), Lulek, Stella (bat Eliyahu), Feivel, Freida, Kreindel, Regina (bat Shimon), Shprinza, Sarah, Charlotte
SELCER	David
ZEMEL	Emalia (bat Menashe), Shmuel
ZEMAN	Tova (bat Chaya - Talenfeld)
ZANDMAN	Wolf, Chana (bat David)
ZANDNER	Chana (bat David)
ZANFAT (?)	Feige (bat Yitzhak - Weiss), Shlomo

	ZACK-GLANTZ	Branislawa
	ZACK	Dora, Mauricio, Regina
ח **Het** Index		
	HAYOT	N.
ט **Tet** Index		
	TAUB	Veba
	TAUBER	Irena
	TEVISL	Binyamin, Lina, Meir, Melicia
	TEVEL	Cherna (bay Aharon)
	TABAK	Yeshayahu (ben Shlomo), Shlomo, Etel (bat Shlomo)
	TAUB / TOJB	Pinchas, Shlomo
	TURKELTAUB	Beila, Chana, Yosef, Natan, Fancia, Rachel
	TIGERMAN	Bernard, Regina, Moshe
	TILLMAN	Dr. Aharon, Yehoshua/Aziash, Dr. Sebastian
	TISHENKEL	Gudel (ben Isaac), Henia (bat David)
	TIRSCH	Maya, Susia
	TEICHER	Avraham (ben Isaac), Devorah (bat Avraham)
	TISHLER	Beryl, Henia (bat Yitzhak Buchalter), Vilo (bat Beryl), Chana (bat Beryl)
	TALBER	Dr. Avraham
	TELLER	Gitel, Leon (ben Naftali), Adele (bat Naftali), Freida (bat Naftali), Chaya (bat Naftali), Mina (ben Moshe Leib)
	TANNE	Chaya (Rotenfeld), Leah (bat Chaim), Moshe (ben Bendit), Cyla (bat Moshe), Bendit (ben Moshe), Bendit (ben Shimshon)
	TENNENBAUM	Genia, Chana, Yosef, Yehezkel, Lorka, Freida
	TEPFER	Chaim, Avraham, Beryl, Henia, Tova, Leib, Malvina, Cyla, Sarah
	TANCIAR	Avraham, Freida

ל **Yod** Index	
JOSEFSBERG	Chaya, Yosef, Yitzhak, Lipa
JUNGERMAN	Batya, Breindel, Berish, Zygmund, Shlomo, Chana
YAAKOV	Bronia, Gershon (ben Avraham David), David (ben Gershon), Hillel (ben Gershon)
YAKEL	Isaac, Shmuel (ben Isaac), Shmuel, Nahum (ben Shmuel), bernard (ben Shmuel), Rikel, Etel, Mendel, Marci, Malka, Israel Leib, Eliyahu Jonah, Alexander (ben Zeev), Breinci, Batya (bat Hani), Veba, Zeev, Shlomo, Natan
כ **Kaf** Index	
COHEN	Yaakov (ben Shmuel - Nadler), Israel (ben Shmuel)
KATZ	Avner (ben Michael), Adele, Chaya, Michael (ben Moshe), Moshe (ben Michael), Pinchas (ben Moshe), Freida (bat Moshe), Mina (bat Aryeh), Herman, Max (ben Herman)
KATZ-GLAZER	Genia
ל KATZ-WALDMAN	Melcia
Lamed Index	
LAUTMAN	..., Adele
LAUFER	Pepe (bat David), Cyla (bat David), Shoshannah (bat David), Rivka (bat David), Roisa (bat David), Rachel (bat Rachel), Sheindel (bat Yosef)
LANDAU	Hillel, Gitel, Chaya/Helen, Yehudah, Yosef, Jancio, Yaakov, Moshe, Shabtai
LEV	Adele, Dr. Albert, Sarah (bat Moshe Spinard)
LEVENTAL	Pela, Zygmund, Israel
LEUTER (or LEVITER)	Edward, Erika (bat Edward), Toncia (bat Pesach)
LEVIN	Berish (Lustik), Chaya (Lustik)
LOFT	Tuli, Esther, Tonia (bat Zelig), Naftali, Fanni, Shalom
LOPSTEIN	Zaida, Chana, Tartal, Yaakov, Rivka
LETMAN	N.

LUSTIK	Yaakov (ben Elkana), Chancia (bat Elkana), Esther (bat Elkana), Alexander (ben Elkana), Alter, Beila, Chana Feige (bat Shlomo Rosenbaum), Leah, Lucia (bat Yaakov Moshe), Leib (ben Yaakov Moshe), Rosa (bat Shaul), Yaakov Zvi (ben Shaul)
LIEBMAN	Chana, Feivel, Regina
LIEBS	Karol, Yaakov (ben Karol)
LIEBSHITZ	Dr. Libshe
LIEBERMAN	Meir (ben Shmuel), Menahem (ben Meir), Sofia (bat Motti), Salka, Shmuel
LITAUER	Mathilda (bat Leib), Orna (bat Leib), Chaya (Spinard), Leib
LITOVITCH	
LEITER	Avraham, Izak (ben Avraham), Hersch (ben Avraham), Chava (bat Avraham), Sarah R. (bat Avraham)
LEIBOVITCH	Pesel, Yosef
LICHTER	Sender, Sonia (bat Sender)
LIMHARD	Clara (bat Israel)
LINDENBAUM	Abbe, Henrika, Yurik
LINDER	Esther, Gusta, Reuven
LINDNER	Mordechai, Chaim Hersch, Ratze, Avraham, Rozia (bat Avraham), Rivka (bat Avraham), Chana (bat Avraham), Chaim/Karol (ben Avraham), Bronka (bat Avraham), Golda Miriam, Gitel, David (ben Leib), Chaya, Yaakov (ben Yosef), Yosef, Yaakov (ben Mordechai), Leo (ben Mordechai), Miriam
LINDER	Mendel (may be a misprint, as this appears in the midst of the Lindners)
LERNER	Sarah (may be a misprint, as this appears in the midst of the Lindners)
LINHARD	Chana, Yosel, Yankel, Max, Ratze
LIPPE	Sabina
LIPPEL	Boleslaw (ben Josef), Dr. Yaakov, Mathilda (bat Yaakov), Emalia (bat Yaakov - Libbes), Slomea, Stephania (Bencher)
LIFSCHITZ	Chaim Mordechai (ben Nahum), Sima (bat Yekutiel - Verzger), Mendel
LEMEL	Chantze (bat Elimelech - Halpern), Paula, Zvi (ben Israel)
LEMPEL	Esther, Chana (bat Meir - Lieberman), Hersch, Leon, Sarah

LAN	N.
LANGERMAN	Bina (bat Chana), Chana (bat Esther), Mina (bat Chana), Shmuel
LANDA	Herman (ben Aharon), Zofia (bat Zvi), Cyla (bat Herman)
LANDSMAN	Henia (bat Moshe), Zelig (ben Shimon Leib), Yaakov (ben Shimon), Moshe (ben Shimon), Zalman (ben Zelig), Chaya (bat Zelig), Tova (bat Zelig), Feige (bat Zelig), Raisel (bat Zelig), Shimon (ben Zelig), Yosef (ben Tuvia), Moshe (ben Tuvia), Sarah (bat Zalman)
LANC	Alter (ben Shraga), Rachel (bat Michael)
LAST	Charna (bat Mechel), Liba (bat Chaim), Mechel (ben Avraham), Raisel (bat Yashe)
LEPMAN	David, Chaya, Leah, Shmuel
LARIKSTEIN	Lusia, Edgia, Fuldak
LERNER	N., Avraham Zvi, Beila, Hencia, Moshe, Rivka, Shosha

מ

Mem Index

MEYER	Golda (bat Kalman), Liba, Manka (bat Zeev), Penina, Kalman, Sarah (bat Kalman)
MAGAR	Avraham, Henech
MAGAR-ZEIDMAN	Clara
MOLDAUER	Hanan
MOND	Yaakov
MONDERER	Abush, Sabina (bat Moshe)
MONDSCHEIN	Genia, Dr. David, Herman, Erika, Rivka
MOSKOVITCH	Gitel Chana, Samuel
MILBAUER	Dr. Binyamin
MOLDAUER	Dr. Isidore
MODAUER	Dr. Natan
MILLER	Yehoshua (ben Moshe Zvi), Shraga (ben Yehoshua), Machla (bat Yehoshua), Rachel (bat Chaim), Pepe (bat Chaim), Zygmund (ben Chaim), Israel Yosef (ben Yitzhak), Leah (bat Shraga)
MILLARD	Yaakov (ben Eliezer), Fischel (ben Eliezer)
MINDEL	Sarah (Krohn), Yitzhak

MINER	Ida (bat Shlomo - Birnbaum)
MELZ	Pearl (Kleiner), Yenta (bat Serl), Yaakov (ben Serl), Tova
MELZER	Feivel (ben Natan), Shmuel (ben Feivel), Leibel (ben Feivel), Avraham (ben Feivel), Genia (bat Feivel), Dora (bat Jonah Chaim), Andjia (ben Jonah Chaim), Berna (bat Avraham), Herman (ben Moshe), Chana (bat Moshe), Mendel (ben Moshe), Natan (ben Jonah Chaim), Jonah Chaim, Moshe (ben Hersch), Rosa, Slova
MELLER	Aharon, Bela (bat Shmuel), Hinda Rachel (bat David Yitzhak), Chana (bat Yaakov), Yaakov Shiya (ben Shmuel), Mordechai (ben Yaakov Shiya), Keila (bat Yaakov Shiya), Shmuel Hersch (ben Yaakov Shiya), Rochche, Shmuel, Shlomo, Frimat
MANSBERG	Bernard, Zissel
MESSINGER	Toiba, Yosef
MARBACH	Aharon, Dora, Israel, Mina MG"R, Raizel
MARZANT	Leib
MARKZAMMER	Beracha (bat David), Dov (ben Cherni)
MARK	Rachel
MESHER	Chana (bat Eliezer), Shlomo

Nun   Index

NAGLER	Adele (bat Avraham), Golda (bat Shimon - Robinson), Risho (bat Shimon), David (ben Shimon), Sarah (bat Hersch), Shimon (ben Hersch), Tova (bat Hersch), Meir Shalom (ben Hersch), Nachman (ben Hersch), Yehoshua (ben Nachman), Tonka (bat Yehoshua Zvi), Meir ben Yehoshua Zvi), Natan (ben Yehoshua Zvi), Salka (bat Yehoshua Zvi), Shimon (ben Yehoshua Zvi), Yehoshua Zvi (ben Nachman)
NAGAR	Pika
NIEBAUER	Aharon Leib (ben Reuven), Yoel Reuven (ben Aharon Leib), Chaya Tila (bat Aharon Leib - Rin.), David Eli (ben Chaim Mordechai), Hersch Leib (ben Chaim Mordechai), Chaim, David (ben Chaim), Yitzhak, Chaya, Mondek (ben David), Mordechai Hersch, Naftali, Etel, Frimat, Reuven (ben David), Regina (bat David), Rivka, Bluma (bat Bezalel Neta), Chaim Mordechai
NIEBEUR	Gitel

NEUMAN	Baruch (ben Shmuel), Chana (bat Baruch), Sarah (bat Baruch), Ema (bat Shraga)
NUSSBAUM	Avraham, Vema, Sarah
NUSSENBLATT	Dr. Naftali, Dr. Aharon Yitzhak, Irena (bat Aharon Yitzhak), Elsa (bat Aharon Yitzhak), Shammai, David (ben Shammai), Rivka, Avraham (ben Shammai), Israel (ben Shammai), Meir (ben Shammai), Mordechai (ben Israel), Ruth (bat Israel), Tonka (bat Israel), Yaakov (ben Avraham), Mondek (ben Avraham), Mondek (ben Feivel), Dora (bat Pinchas), Henzia, Chana (Feder), Chaya (bat Hersch Ber), Snak, Feivel (ben Aryeh), Feige, Pesia, Freida (bat Leon), Esther, Binyamin, Batya (bat Herman), Golda (bat Shlomo), Baruch
NUSSBLATT	Adele (bat David) [may be a misprint, as this appears in the midst of the Nussenblatts]
NATANSON	Shaul (ben Abbe), Sarah
NIVES	Helena (bat Henrik - Sternberg), Alonia, Dr. Henrik
NIESTEIN	Dr. Maurici (ben Michael)
NIMIROV	Katriel, David (ben Katriel), Zissel (bat Katriel), Chana, Yetka (bat Katriel), Nahum (ben Katriel), Rosa, Marek
NIRTAL	Aryeh (ben Yosef)

ס
Samech Index

SEGAL	Eliezer, Zaide, Sonia (bat Zaide), Yehudit, Mina (bat Getzel Schuster), Marek, Paula (bat Baruch)
SOBOL	Leib (ben Yaakov), Zygmund (ben Yaakov), Shenka (bat Yaakov), David (ben Yaakov), Bernard (ben Yaakov), Belka (bat Yaakov), Etka (Last), Genia, Daizia, Zuzia,
	Yosef, Yitzhak, Lotka (Hornick), Dr. ...(ben Leib), Wolf (ben Leib), Zalel (ben Leib), Leib (ben David), Leopold, Leizer, Chana (bat Pinchas), Raizel, Cyla
SONFELD	Chaya, Shiya
SOKL	Yishayahu (ben Ovadiah), Nahum (ben Ovadiah), Ovadiah (ben Yishayahu)
SACHER	Benyo, Rosia
SPRING	Berta, Daniel, Herman, Minka

ע **Ayin** Index	
EDELTEIN	Yehudah
EDELSTEIN	Liba, Simka, Fischel, Shiya
ENDA	Max
ECK	Chaya (bat Michael - Gellert)
ERENBERG	Blima, Yosef Asher, Ya'kel, Mendel, Natan
ERSTER	(Hersch)

פ **Peh** Index	
FOGEL	Avraham, Chaya
POLLACK	Yitzhak David, Freida (bat Pinchas)
POMERANZ	Hersch, Rachel Leah, Pepe, Genia, Moshe Eli, Rivka (bat Avraham), Rachel (bat Avraham), Leah (bat Avraham), Rachel (bat Shalom), Wolf (ben Shalom), Leah (bat Wolf - Shtulbach), Monia (ben Shmuel), Shimon
POSANT	Regina
POPPER	family
FUCHS	Bernard (ben Mordechai), Chana (bat Beryl), Mordechai, Pela, Frania
FIEDLER	Gitel (bat Leib Stein)
FEITLEZACK	Elkana, Aharon (ben Elkana), Helena (bat Avner), Lunik/Leizer (ben Elkana), Nahum (ben Elkana)
PILTAGE	MG"R Leib
PILZ	Leib
PILCI	Leah (bat Mendel)
PINELES	Michael
FINK	Chaya (bat Avraham), Chana (bat Shlomo), Malka (bat Shlomo), Meshullam (ben Shalom), Yosef
FINKLESTEIN	N., Lili

PICKHOLZ	Sarah (bat Baruch), Shimshon (ben Baruch), Fischel (ben Baruch), Chaim (ben Baruch), Livka (bat Matityahu), Yitzhak (ben Matityahu), Gita (ben Matityahu), Hirschel (ben David Shmuel), Sarah, Sarah (bat David Shmuel), Sheindel (bet David Shmuel), Yetta (bat David Shmuel), Moshe (ben Yitzhak), Baruch (ben Yitzhak), Keila (bat Yitzhak Isaac), Meir Shimon (ben Yitzhak Isaac), Pinchas (ben Yitzhak Isaac), Yehudah (ben Yitzhak Isaac), Pinchas (ben David), Wolf (ben David), Machla (bat David), Malka (bat David), Moshe (ben David), Leibish, Chaya, Sarah, Cipora (bat Leibish), Feige (bat Leibish), Hinda (bat Leibish), Miriam (bat Leibish), Hersch, Gitel, Binyamin, Zusia, Cyla, Yehoshua, Leache, Lusia, Cirl, Sarah (Sneiberg), Markus, Yocheved (bat Bendit), Golda (bat Chaim Mordechai), Devorah (bat Avraham Leib)
PACH	Chava, Israel, Frimka (bat Israel)
FALVER	Dr. Avraham
FELDHORN	Wolf
FELDMAN	Eliezer, Esther (bat Samuel), Bina, Chaya, Yosef Hersch (ben Samuel), Yaakov, Yaakov Mendel, Leah, Leib, Lica, Mina, Masia, Miriam, Freidka (bat Samuel), Cyla
FELDMAN-SHEFER	Samuel, Miriam
FELDSTEIN	Yulik, Hela
FALIK	Aharon, David Yonah, Chana, Yehudit, Yaakov, Leah, MG"R Lusia, Lipa, Cipora
FLEISHER	Yenta (bat Feivel), Yitzhak (ben Zvi), Pepe (bat Yitzhak)
PELSER	Dr. N.
PELLACH	Moshe
FALK	Chaya (Feldman)
FELLER	Esther, Hersch, MG"R Yitzhak, Tsasha
PFEFFER	Sucher (ben Markus), Wolf (ben Markus), Yitzhak (ben Wolf), Pepka, Rina (bat Sucher)
PFEFFERBAUM	Berta (bat Leibush), Lina (bat Leibush), ...(ben Yishayahu), Miriam (bat Hersch)
PATCHNIK	MG"R Nela

FRUCHTER	Aharon (ben Dov), Aharon (ben Feivel), Izak (ben Yosef), Ephraim, Aryeh (ben Izak), Bina (bat Moshe), Blima (bat David Meshullam), Bernard, Golda, Golda (bat Hersch), Genia, Donia (bat Feivel), Herman (ben Aharon), Leah (bat Samuel), Yenta (bat Aharon), Yaakov (ben Aharon), Helena (bat Aharon), Helena (bat Shmuel), Hersch/Zvi, Hendel, Chaya (bat Chune), Chana, Toiba, Yosef (ben Wolf), Yosef Yaakov (ben Isaac), Yitzhak Isaac, Sima (bat Isaac), Sarah (bat Yosef), Shlomo (ben Yosef), Leah (bat Yosef Stoltz), Chune (ben Yosef), Nehemia (ben Yosef), Moshe (ben Yosef), Leib (ben Yosef), Malka, Max (ben Feivel), Markus (ben Feivel), Ezra, Pinchas (ben Aryeh), Freida, Rivka, Rosa, Shmuel, Shlomo (ben Feivel), Sarah, Henia (bat Baruch)
PROSTAK	Yosef, Kalman, Sarah (bat Aler)
FRIED	Genia, Devorah (bat Yitzhak Tevel), Yaakov (ben Lipa), Yitzhak (ben Yaakov), Israel
FRIEDLANDER	Adolph (ben Zygmund), Otek, Emalia, Bruno, Bronia, Gusta, Hersch (ben Yehezkel), Yosef (ben Herman), Eli (ben Herman), Yaakov (ben Herman), Chana, Chana (bat Aharon), Yeda, Yosef, Miriam, Yehezkel, Yosef (ben Yehezkel), Yaakov (ben Yehezkel), Feige (ben Yehezkel), Moshe (ben A.), Israel (ben Zvi), Fania (bat Zvi), Freida (bat Zvi), Rivka (bat Zvi), Moshe, Cyla (bat Moshe), Felicia (bat Adolph), Malka
FRIEDLER	Shmuel, Chaya, Yitzhak, Yosef, Hersch, Pinchas
FRIEDMAN	Esther, Babonia (bat Yosef David - Waldman), Bernard, Philip
FRIEDENHEIM	Yaakov, Max, Felix, Motti
PRIZENT	Regina (bat Avraham Bunem)
FROELICH	Isaac, Motel, Chana (bat David), Moshe, Philip (ben David)
PRICE	David (ben Chana), Hela, Chaim (ben Chana), Chana, Yitzhak (ben Chana)
PRIM	Max (ben Reuven), Rubin (ben Max), Liza (bat Max), Koba, Clara (bat Cherna)
FRIMAN	Beti, Lili, Rosa, Shmuel (ben David)
PRINTZ	Chana (bat Leizer), Tova (bat Leizer), Rachel (bat Leizer)
PERLMUTTER	Alter, Mindel, Rivka, Rosa

FRANKEL	Isaac (ben Avraham), Yaakov (ben Avraham), Baruch (ben Yosef Mechel), David (ben Yosef Mechel), Yitzhak Moshe (ben Yosef Mechel), Yetti (bat Yitzhak Moshe), Sabina (bat Yitzhak Moshe), Shoshannah (bat Yitzhak Moshe), Zvi Aryeh (ben Sender), Devorah, Bela (bat Zalman)

Tsadik Index

TSAUM	Noah, Sabina, Salamon, Cherna, Reuven
TSHENGBUT	Adolph, Asher
TSOBEL	MG"R Dora
ZWILLING	Emalia (bat Wolf), Andjia (bat Jonas), Gideon (ben Jonas), Zelig (ben Meir), Sprinza (bat Meir), Jonas, Malka (bat Mendel)
ZWILLINGER	Eliyahu, Benzion, Shoshannah, Sarah, Belka (bat Motel)
ZUCKERBERG	David, Hersch (ben Motel), Chaika (bat Motel), Motel, Mondek (ben Motel), Rachil
ZEISLER	Yosef
ZIMMERMAN	MG"R N., Etel, Regina (bat Mordechai - Fruchter), Baruch
ZIRGLASS	Meshullam (Normot), Fruma (bat Yaakov Moshe - Lustik)

Kof Index

KAUFMAN	Zelda (bat Moshe - Spinard)
KUGEL	Eliezer
KUDISH	Moshe (ben Alexander), Cirl, Miriam (bat Moshe - Yekel), Chana (bat Moshe - Appelgrin), Kreindel, Rivka, Shiko
KON	Leib
KOHN	Yulka (bat Yitzhak), Fencia (bat Zelig), Ruta (bat Yitzhak)
KOCH	Zindel, Chaya beila (bat Zvi), Mechel (ben Zindel), Machla
KOLM	Dr. N.

KOPLER	Dr. Yosef, Yetti, Leah, Leizer, Mali, Markus, Clara, Sheva, Sarah
KORN	Elka, Elta (bat Shlomo), Hasik, Hersch (ben Shlomo), Chaim David (ben Avraham), Dora (bat Avraham), Mina (bat Avraham - Hovel), Elia (bat Shlomo), Rivka, Shlomo (ben Moshe)
KORNBLIT	Gershon, Esther (Shp.) Devorah, Moshe, Freida, Cipora, Reuven
KORNER	Eugenia, Yaakov, Leon, Markus, Marek, Regina
KURZER-EIGENMACHT	Mina (bat Rosa)
KURZER-SILBERSHLAG	Adele (bat Leon), Leah (bat David), Sarah (bat David)
KAZ	Samuel (ben Yosef), Cyla (bat Yosef), Jonah (ben Yosef), Simha (ben Yitzhak), Yehudah (ben Yitzhak), Hinda (bat Yitzhak), Israel (ben Yehudah), Yitzhak (ben Israel), Yosef (ben Israel), Eta (bat Simha), Etka (bat Hersch - Teicher), Elka (Kerner), Tonka

[Page 225]

Memories from the Old Home
by Sara Weiss-Hauptman
Translated by Susannah Juni

Stryy was my birth town. There I lived with my parents and with the entire Hauptman family. There in Stryy I spent my childhood years. There I dreamed and fantasized of a brighter, greater world – childish dreams from a time happily spent.

I remember yet well that big Zionist Folk-Fest in the park, "Olshina." The sensations from the Fest were 12 cutters from the Land of Israel fields. I was one of them. In white clothes, white head-scarves, white-blue sandals on our feet, scythes in our hands and grasses gathered up in our aprons, we went around the great park, raising our scythes high and sang in Hebrew: "How loved and dear you are to us, our earth in Zion."

In the avenues of the park were standing small tables, where we sold various things and onzikhts - kortlakh [?] from the Land of Israel. People called these avenues "Jerusalem Avenues." the money went for the K. K. L.

The initiators of the Folk-Fest were Berl Stern, Aron Hauptman, Benyamin Klein, Chaim Dovid Korn, M. Wagner, of blessed memory.

A second event from that time:

A well known woman from Stryy came to my father and recounted to him the following:

A Ukrainian neighbor had accused her husband in court, of spitting on him and his sacred pictures in his home, for not punctually paying his apartment rent. The Christian lived by them [were renters] and didn't want to pay for the apartment. He had devised a frame-up lie on them. His 8 year old boy testified that the "Zshid" had expressed to his father: "I spit on you and your god." The second day a home-agent came and arrested her husband for insulting the Christian religion. The woman cried before my father and asked him to help her.

My father was out to the Jewish Court Counsel, Yanas, whom he personally knew and asked him to be personally interested with the matter.

"It's bad," said the Court Counsel, Yanas, 'here we're dealing with problems of people who are religious feeling offended, when it comes to this, some of our Christians are inventive, especially when it's a matter of a Jew. But I am sure and believe that it is a frame-up lie, and I will see about something to do about this thing.

[Page 226]

The Jewish Militia in Stryj
Translated by Daniella Heller

Chaos ensued after the end of the First World War, when Stryj came under the Ukrainian rule. The new rulers had no organized administration and no functioning police. During the first days after the war, the town was a lawless no-man's land. Day and night demobilized armed and unarmed soldiers wondered the streets, trying to get back to their homes.

[Page 227]

Various Jewish parties took initiative and approached the Ukrainian authorities asking for permission to create a Jewish militia in order to protect the Jewish population.

According to the agreement each party had to supply certain number of people for armed patrols in the streets.

Some officers took it upon themselves to organize and implement the project. The headquarters of the militia was established near the synagogue, where the weapons' store room was also located. The patrols assembled in the Academic Union hall, where the night duty officer was stationed. A small fund was established in order to cover the expenses of the militia.

The patrols consisted of four men for each one hour shift. They had the authority to detain and interrogate any suspicious person wondering the streets at night. If they caught a thief they had the authority to arrest him. Often they found weapons which they confiscated as most of the thieves were demobilized soldiers.

Sometimes there were violent encounters in the dark streets. As there were no street lights some clashes occurred with Ukrainian military patrols, but luckily no one was hurt.

One day the Ukrainians attacked the headquarters of the Jewish militia and took all their weapons.

The First Self Defense in Stryj
Translated by Daniella Heller

During the last winter of the First World War 1917-1918, the discipline in the Austro-Hungarian army started to deteriorate. Thousands of deserters were wondering around. Hunger spread everywhere and demonstrations and riots occurred due to the situation. The war prisoners started to return from Russia after the revolution.

[Page 228]

In the spring of 1918 the food shortages increased and hunger was felt everywhere. As the food became scarce the black market flourished. Hunger demonstrations were held in various places against delicatessen stores. Polish organizations took advantage of these demonstrations to inflame their anti-Semitic talk and action.

On April 16th, 1918 a demonstration took place in Krakow during which Jews were beaten and robbed. A man from Stryj who happened to be in Krakow on business was killed in the riots. The murder of Mahler made a big impact on the Jewish community in Stryj. The committee of Poalei Zion decided to prepare for future dangers and appointed people to organize a self defense. A secret meeting was held in which five men were elected to the committee: Shlomo Rosenberg, Leib Teper, Avraham Menderer, Shimon Rosenberg, and Nathan Wunderlicht. It was decided to deploy forty men on the roofs to protect the Jewish population.

Some weeks after Passover it became known that an Austro-Hungarian demonstration was going to take place in Stryj in cooperation with local criminals.

[Page 229]

A crowd started to gather before noon in front of the house of Itche Sheinfeld on Potocki Street. The entrance to the yard was guarded by the police. The crowd of about five hundred people was shouting slogans about hunger and bread and marched towards the market square.

The Jewish self defense groups were ordered not to interfere unless there was a specific anti-Semitic action. The self defense groups were armed with sticks and other cold weapons and deployed around the demonstrators.

As the crowd approached a coffee house owned by gentiles, the leaders went up the stairs but stopped and left after the owner came out and said quietly something to them. They went on to a Jewish owned kiosk which was closed and started to break the doors. When it became clear that Jewish shops were the target, it was decided to act and the members of the self defense group attacked the hooligans. The rioting mob started to escape as many passersbys, Jews and gentiles were watching. As stones were thrown by the hooligans, one of them wounded a soldier. The army attacked the mob and they dispersed.

This was the first, and probably the only public action of the Jewish self-defense in Stryj.

———

[Page 230]

Béla Kun in Stryj

By S. Rosenberg

Translated from Yiddish by Ganit Eiron

Translated from Hebrew by Susan Rosin

The Stryj railway station was an important transportation hub of the Hapsburg Empire's provinces with the east. There were north-south and east-west connections in Stryj. At the end of the First World War, Stryj was an important hub for the Empire's trains transporting soldiers from the east and the west back to their homes. This line also transported returning prisoners of war from both sides of the conflict. Since the Przemyœl – Lvov line did not operate due to the hostilities between Poland and Ukraine, Stryj became a major hub. The multitudes on the trains were a heart breaking sight: Frozen, dirty and hungry people travelling in a variety of cars: first, second and third class cars without the windows' glass, without heat and without any basic conveniences, as well as in open freight cars. Bodies of those who died because of the cold, hunger, and diseases were constantly removed from the open cars. Slowly the town's people got used to these difficult sights.

A well-armed Ukrainian unit was present at the station at all times. They used to stop and search each and every car and disarm those who were inside. Only then, they allowed the trains to proceed. That was the agreement that was put in place for all areas of the crumbling Austro-Hungarian Empire.

An incident caused much worry and stress in town. A train carrying many Hungarian prisoners of war returning from their captivity in Russia in overflowing cars was stopped in town. The train "commander" refused to let the Ukrainians inspect the cars and disarm the occupants. The Ukrainians brought machine guns and threatened to shoot at the train and its occupants. Instead of white flags, the occupants pulled out their weapons, gun barrels appeared in the windows and they threatened to open fire as well. The town commander brought reinforcements from the barracks and the station was closed. The news spread fast and the more daring young people came to the station to watch the dangerous game.

A negotiation between the two sides did not yield results. The Ukrainians threatened that they would not release the train move. The rebels responded with a threat of their own - they would take the train station by force. The atmosphere became charged. The Ukrainians did not want to get into an armed confrontation with the rebels that numbered about two thousand. In the end, the Ukrainians relented and let the train continue to Munkács (Mukacheve).

Later it became known that Béla Kun, the future leader of the Hungarian communist revolution was on the train with his bodyguards.

First Train with Petliura Forces in Stryj

In the summer of 1919, the Ukrainian army started to retreat due to the pressure from the Poles. The front line lay in a great curve from the San and Bug rivers to Stryj. The fiercest battles took place in the Przemyœl region and the Polish army threatened the Boryslaw oil area. Whereas Poland won the support of almost all the western countries, the Ukrainians had to rely only on themselves. Petliura's great Ukraine was torn apart in the civil war, and his gangs had to retreat towards the Galician border under pressure from the Red Army. In order to gain some ground, Petliura agreed to send some of his forces to the Boryslaw front. These forces, who took part in the pogroms, were corrupt and spoiled and had a thirst for Jewish blood. They had poor morale and barbaric behavior because of the defeats on the various fronts. The Eastern Galicia Ukrainian regime was very careful to prevent pogroms because it needed the recognition and support of the League of Nations, which was supposed to convene and discuss their case. For that reason, the Petliura people were transported unarmed by trains. At the transit stations in the cities, they were not allowed to get off the trains in order to prevent anti-Jewish outbursts. As the Petliura units had to pass through the Stryj station, the local military authorities tried very hard not to let these "heroes" roam the city until the train's departure. Incidentally, delegations of Jewish representatives warned the local authorities against this danger.

[Page 231]

On one occasion, the railway to Boryslaw was blocked due to other trains, and the Petliura units had to stay in Stryj for a few hours. Several hundred of them burst into the streets of the city and began to rob local shops. There was a danger of a pogrom. The local military unit was called and with arms in hand surrounded the train station and forced the savage people of Petliura to return to the cars. Fortunately for the Jewish population, the Petliura people were not armed.

Bloody Wednesday in Stryj
By S. Rosenberg
Translated from Yiddish by Ganit Eiron
Translated from Hebrew by Susan Rosin

Stryj was a typical Polish provincial town. Life was mostly peaceful and quiet. There were no particularly interesting places in town that might have made life there more exciting. It was not famous in terms of social diversity or industry. In its industry, such as wood, metal, and matches there was not much agitation. If there were wage struggles or strikes, they were mostly peaceful.

Just like in neighboring Drohobycz during the 1911 elections it was the fate of Stryj to record a bloody chapter in its history. In Stryj, it was bloody Wednesday in March 1926.

This was a year of great economic crisis and high unemployment in Poland. Masses of workers in Poland suffered through a severe winter of unemployment and distress. There was no sign of an improvement in the economic situation. On the contrary, the number of unemployed people only rose to hundreds of thousands in the country. The crisis also affected Jewish professions. The Jewish workers' parties and labor unions convened a conference in Warsaw under the slogan "The right to work."

[Page 232]

From the Polish Sejm, and in meetings in the cities, the workers' representatives demanded work and assistance for the unemployed. Under public pressure from the workers, the reactionary government of Chjeno-Piast agreed to grant limited funds to the unemployed. However, the local authorities did not rush to distribute the money.

During the 1925-1926 winter several sawmills ceased operations in Stryj. Other sectors of the economic spectrum saw major cuts as well. The Council of Professional Organizations (Rada Zwi¹zków Zawodowych) that included most sectors (except for the railway workers) and was under communist influence organized rallies and sent representatives to the mayor's office demanding assistance.

The authorities finally agreed for the professional organizations to register the unemployed and be provided with the lists. Since the government ruled that only the unemployed who worked in a factories or workshops with at least five workers would be eligible for assistance, the council refused to recognize most of the Jewish unemployed who were previously employed in smaller workshops. Because of this rule, a conflict arose with the representatives of the Jewish professional organizations that were represented by the Poalei Zion party. The Jewish representatives left the Joint Council and established an independent committee of the unemployed. A delegation from this association visited the mayor's office and informed him that the Jewish representatives would create their independent lists and send them separately.

Many weeks passed but there was still no support for the unemployed. In mid-March, before Passover, the council started to organize a demonstration with the purpose of appealing to the mayor. The demonstrators gathered on Wednesday, March 31st, (second day of Passover) near the trade union building. About 500 workers, including a small number of Jews who belonged to the Communist Party, marched through the streets. Prior to their arrival, the city hall was fortified with an army unit ready for battle. The demonstrators approached the building peacefully, but the entrance was blocked by the police. The police allowed only a delegation to enter the building and they remained in there for a relatively a long time. The people on the street grew impatient and were incensed by the various propagandists. Later there was a speculation that among the crowds were political agitators sent by the authorities. At one point the demonstrators tried to break into the building. The police retreated upstairs. The demonstrators were encouraged and began to climb the stairs. At this point the bloodbath began. The police commander ordered his men to shoot after getting an agreement from the mayor. The barrage of bullets started without warning. The shots were fired into the crowd and many were killed and many more injured. On the street there was a horrifying sight: the echo of the shots created a terrible panic. In a sense of mortal fear, the people fled in every possible direction. Some fell dying on the street; Bloodied people, sought first aid. Soon the size of the massacre became known: Eleven dead and several dozens wounded. Among thedead was the nineteen year old Jewish man Krigger.

This event took place during the noon hours. The shocking news
[Page 233]
spread fast and the streets emptied except for the brave and curious few. Armed policemen patrolled the streets. Afraid of riots, the Stryj army unit was placed under the highest alert.

The news of the unscrupulous massacre spread throughout the country. The next day, the newspapers were filled with the news of the bloody Wednesday in Stryj. The city was full of journalists looking for sensational material. The workers' parties in the Sejm strongly condemned the attack and it was decided to establish an inquiry commission. As a result of the investigation, the mayor was removed and the police officer was found guilty.

The funeral of the Jewish victim was conducted by the police. To avoid possible demonstration it was held in secrecy with only the family present.

The other funerals were held three days later, during Passover and were attended by workers and delegations from all three nationalities. The police and the army were prepared to prevent possible disturbances. Policemen and soldiers stood guard during the entire funeral procession of the ten coffins. The victims were eulogized by representatives of all the workers' parties: P.P.S., the communist faction of the Sejm – by members of the Sejm Pasztaszok and Pristopa, the Jewish workers and Po'alei Zion – by Shimon Rosenberg. In spite of the anger and the tense atmosphere, the funerals passed peacefully.

With these events, some members of the workers' council were arrested, among them the Jewish communist activist Moshe Wagman, who later was sentenced to a year in prison.

The authorities were still very concerned about the workers' possible reaction to the bloodshed that had taken place earlier. To prevent this, they arrested all activists from the left-wing parties on the eve of May 1st, including Shimon Rosenberg of Poalei Zion.

The Jewish Labor–Movement in Stryj
By S. Rosenberg
Translated by Yocheved Klausner

After the great destruction that Hitlerism has brought upon our people, the town Stryj remained one of the innumerable white stains on the great map of the Jewish communities – the three–and–a–half million Jews of the Jewish settlement in pre–war Poland. Of the 16 thousand Jewish souls – some 40% of the Stryj population – only a few hundred survived Hitler's sword and can give testimony about the years of occupation. However, none of those remnants from the hiding places and bunkers managed to save materials and documents, which would enable to construct a picture of the multi-colored mosaic of the social life of the Jewish population in town.

Thus we have to follow the traces of the years and events, based only on our own memory, on which time has probably wiped out details and facts; we must be aware of the fact that we will not be able to create a full picture of the life that existed and does not exist any more.

*

[Page 234]

Among the towns of its size in Austria and later Poland, Stryj was one of the regular, non-specific towns. In the life of the simple and quiet Jewish community in Stryj one cannot find out-of-the-ordinary qualities. For generations, thousands of Jews lived here, weaved their colorful lives and contributed their part, like a ring to the chain of the great and lively Jewish settlement in Eastern Europe. Like their thousands of brethren, they experienced the years of ramification of Hassidim and Mitnagdim, enlightenment [haskala] and assimilation, religiosity and atheism during the period of the 18th, 19th and 20th centuries, and entered the times of social-political conflicts brought about by national and political awakening. Through this struggle, they still weaved their ideals, dreamt their dreams, advanced their hopes and found their Tikun [correction, amendment]. In this wonderful rainbow of a pulsating Jewish life, each part, each layer, each individual managed to find his corner, which he nurtured and enriched, cared for and protected. In this colorful reality, the Jewish labor-movement found its place as well.

The history of the Stryj Jewish community, as well as of its working sector, will never be written. Its registries were burned, its witnesses gassed, shot and exterminated. What I am describing here are only fragments and pieces of the sixty years' Jewish labor movement in Stryj. The material from the years 1914–1928 is based on my own direct participation and experience, the rest on tradition. Some of the facts were verified by survivors, who have been members of the movement.

May these notes serve as a memorial for those who died and those who perished in Hitler's hell.

Po'alei–Zion in Stryj (1900–1914)
By S. Rosenberg
Translated by Yocheved Klausner

The first buds of the Po'alei–Zion in Stryj appeared in the years 1900–1903, in the time of the first Zionist Congresses. Among the first Zionist Socialists, who were later active in Poalei Zion, we find: Berl Friedman, his wife Berta, Shmuel Horoshovski, Eli Katz, Avraham Tepper, Kirshner Yosef, Saltche Sperling, Lola Imber, Dr. Yoni, Pinye Bloch, Gladstein, Eli and Leibush Katz, Moshe Weiss, Levi Opper and others. From the memories that were related in later years, we learn that the first circles of Poalei Zion in Stryj were influenced by Zionist–socialist movements like "SS", "Sejmists" and Poalei-Zion, who, in those years became active in Russia. Later, from these circles the Association Po'alei Zion was formed.

In September 1903, the decree concerning the "Association of Po'alei Zion in Stryj" was issued by the authorities, giving it the right of cultural and Zionist activity. Later, in the period between the two World Wars, this decree remained the legal basis for the Po'alei Zion activity in town.

The people who, in those years, were members of Po'alei Zion were very different from those who belonged to the Z.P.S. [Jewish Socialist Party, later the "Bund"]. To Po'alei Zion belonged workers and employees in professions like merchants, watchmakers, etc. as well as circles of the Jewish intelligentsia, while the Z.P.S. contained the assimilated intelligentsia in various professions of physical work, as: carpenters, tailors, shoemakers and others.

During the first years, the Po'alei Zion Association worked in co-ordination with the other Zionist groups, later it stepped out and became independent. It devoted special attention to cultural activity in the Yiddish language, founded the first library of Yiddish books, organized lectures and courses of Yiddish literature and led a broad political instruction activity. As teachers and speakers served local people, as well as lecturers sent by the Party Center. Some of the lecturers who visited Stryj, later became leaders of the Po'alei Zion, among them: Zerubavel, Chazanowitz, Kaplanski, Loker, Dr. Schieffer and others. By the initiative of Po'alei Zion, some Yiddish writers visited Stryj as well, among them: Avraham Reisen, Maurice Rosenfeld, Dr. Nathan Birenbaum, Y. L. Peretz, S. Ash, Ch. D. Nomberg and others.

[Page 235]

In addition to those mentioned above, the following were active in Po'alei Zion during its first years: Chone Leibowitz, Shmuel Schoenbach, Mendel Polack, Mathias Patrach, Marshal (came from Kalish), Yitzhak Opper, Birenbaum, Yitzhak Rosenberg and others.

*

In May 1904, the founding-assembly of Po'alei Zion in Austria took place. A delegation from the Stryj organization participated as well, and joined the newly formed party.

In 1905, Po'alei Zion organized in town a series of mass-assemblies, demanding the right to vote for the Austrian Parliament.

In 1906–1907, Po'alei Zion, together with the commerce employees, led the "close at 8" campaign, demanding that the stores be closed at 8 p.m. At that time, the employees worked in the shops until 11 or 12 at night. This campaign, which was led all over the country, in Stryj was accompanied by stormy street-demonstrations. The demonstrators would stop near each store and take out the employees who were still at work. If the owner refused to let them go, the demonstrators would begin breaking doors and windows and then mass-arrests were made. Later, they began using as demonstrators minors, who were not in danger of being punished by the police. A short time later a new law was issued, forcing the stores to close at eight in the evening.

In 1907, Po'alei Zion in Stryj took an active part in the election campaign to the Austrian Parliament, in favor of the candidate Dr. Avraham Saltz. It was the first time that the Zionists acted against the PPS candidate Andrey Moratchevski and the assimilated Jew Ashkenazi.

In 1908, Po'alei Zion led agitations and propaganda activity during the preparations of the Czernowitz "Language-Conference."

During the 1910 referendum, the Austrian government expressed its desire that the Galicia Jews declare that their mother-tongue was Yiddish. On the other hand, the local government threatened to punish those who did so. Po'alei Zion was very active in the effort to convince the Jewish population to give Yiddish as their mother-tongue. This activity turned into a mass-movement, which encompassed all parties, and ended in a great success. During the last years before the war, until August 1914, the Po'alei Zion organization devoted time and attention to the Zionist activity among the poor and working population and carried out an intensive cultural and educational work. On Friday evenings, as well as on Saturdays and holidays lectures were given constantly, on literature, art, political questions, social problems, Zionism etc. Particularly active in these projects were Messrs. Eli Katz, Avraham Hauptman, Kevi Opper, Moshe Weiss and others.

In the professional realm, Po'alei Zion supported the struggle of the professional unions, especially the clerks' union.

The *Po'alei Zion* Youth

Under the influence of Po'alei Zion, a youth organization was active in town. Its central offices, "The association of young workers and commerce practitioners Po'alei Zion," were located in Krakow. This organization conducted a ramified educational work and raised young members in the spirit of Po'alei Zion.

[Page 236]

*

Other two groups in the Po'alei Zion organization were active in Stryj, doing special work, each in its area: the group of university students, named Herut [freedom], connected to the central offices in Vienna, and a women's circle, named Yehudit, whose management was at the party's central offices.

* * *

With the outbreak of WWI, the activity of all parties, as well as of Po'alei Zion stopped suddenly. Most of the management was recruited to the army, and later the Russian occupation came. When in 1915 the Austrian–German armies reoccupied Stryj, there was no person who could resume the work. The place where Po'alei Zion used to meet remained locked until the summer of 1917.

* * *

Awakening Behind the Front Line

In 1917, the Jewish Street experienced a beginning of social awakening. The first groups of Hashomer Hatza'ir began their activity. Among one of the groups of Po'alei Zion the idea arose to renew the activity of the organization. Those were days when the fire of war burned in the entire world, and the front–line stretched along the old Russian–Galician border.

The initiators of the renewed organizational activity were: Berta Friedman, David Seltzer, Shlomo Rosenberg, Feivel Miller, Sara Hauptmann, Shlomo Rossler and the writer of these lines. After a short preparation, the first assembly was called. The assembly took place in the hall on Batorega Street, which was rented in partnership with the Hashomer Hatza'ir and remained, however, the meeting place and "home" of the Po'alei Zion organization until the end of the war. The library, which had been stored in boxes in the attic of the craftsmen's association Yad Harutzim was unpacked and arranged, the pictures of Jewish writers and socialist theoreticians were hung on the walls and work was renewed.

After a tree-year-silence, when he Jewish population has remained without any social leadership, meetings or theater performances, the renewed activity of Po'alei Zion aroused great interest in town. To the newly elected committee belonged, in addition to the founding group mentioned above: Chana Rappaport, Hella Bohrer, Aharon Wegner and Aharon Meller. Due to the war, the activity was limited to literary, art and cultural work. Since the Po'alei Zion Club was for a long time the only social corner where people could meet, the activities were visited by people from all layers of life – allies and opponents, workers, simple people and intelligentsia. The weekly lectures had great success. People of all levels who happened to pass through town were asked to serve as lecturers: artists, occasional guests in town and members of the military. Since in most cases these were people not known in town, curiosities occurred: For example, it was announced that a lecture will be given on the subject: "God the socialist, Moses the socialist and the socialist Jews." The lecturer was a military man, a Jew from Budapest. He began the lecture, said a few sentences and stopped. Apparently he learned his speech by heart and forgot it. After such an event, jokes were repeated for weeks. But there were also very interesting and serious lectures, and it can be said that in general, great cultural work was done.

[Page 237]

Later, other areas of activity were added: a choir was established, under the direction of Yosl Altbaumer; courses of the Hebrew language were organized, led by Shlomo Rossler; a drama club was formed, in partnership with the academic association Emuna [faith], which led a very successful activity. This non-professional drama club systematically performed on stage plays from the "Narodni" theater, among them: The slaughter – I. Gordin, The village youth – Kobrin, Thieves – Bimka, King Lear – Gordin, The mute – Weiter, The mad one, Chasye the orphan – Gordin, The Vilner balebossel, Moshe Maimon and others. Masses came to the performances, which often had to be repeated. Sometimes they performed in the neighboring towns as well (Kalush, Skale, Daline).

Permanent members of the drama group were: Mania Hauptman, Sheindl Leibowitz, Mania Igra, Munye Monderer, Avraham (Bumik) Seidenfrau, Boshke Apfelgreen, Max Horowitz, Tania Rosenkranz, Mordechai Bergstein, Rochtche Schiller-Tzengebatt. The director was most of the times Shlomo Rossler.

On 1 May 1918, after a 3-year pause, First-of-May festivities were allowed again. An assembly of Polish, Ukrainian and Jewish workers took place in the Ringplatz, and a Po'alei Zion delegate was one of the speakers.

On that day, the town looked as if under siege, all the streets were occupied by the 6th Graz Regiment ready for action.

The end of the war, November 1918, brought new life to the organization. The former leaders returned: Berl Friedman and Levi Opper, and with them the entire executive committee. New members joined, among them: Lea Bard (now in Israel), Dr. Ochser and others. In the beginning of 1919 the number of members reached 300.

* * *

In Eastern Galicia, the "Western Ukraine Republic" was established. New ideas spread. The right of national and personal autonomy of the Jewish population was proclaimed, although, due to the war, it was never realized.

In those days, Po'alei Zion conducted intensive and ramified work; it took an active part in the leadership of the community, where the old president, the assimilated Wiesenberg has not agreed to step down peacefully. He was one of the initiators of the Workers' Council, which, however, did not last long, because only Po'alei Zion and Z.P.S joined; other organizations declined, either because they were in dispute with the Ukrainian authorities or because they were busy with other matters.

During the first months of the Ukrainian rule, the Po'alei Zion organization made a great step forward:

Soon after its establishment, the Ukrainian power was involved in a war with the Polish Republic, which considered East–Galicia as an integral part of Poland. The political–social chaos of the post–war period deepened. School education stopped functioning; apart from a small number of Ukrainian schools, inherited from the Monarchy, the other schools, where the teachers were mostly Poles and Jews, closed. Po'alei Zion used this moment and opened an elementary school for Jewish children, where the language of instruction was Yiddish. Several party halls and some apartments were transformed into school classes.

The parents welcomed this activity and registered the children.

[Page 238]

In just a few days, all four elementary classes were filled, and many children could not be accepted for lack of space. The school was challenged by a series of difficulties, as: lack of teachers, lack of schoolbooks and, naturally, budget. The problem of teachers was soon solved. Great devotion and energy was invested in this area by Sara and Avraham Hauptman. They worked tirelessly as teachers and mobilized for this work a number of teachers from the former government schools, as well as students. More difficult was the problem of books: the teachers had to prepare the lessons every day, translating from Polish and German books. But most difficult was, naturally, the problem of the budget: the hopes of receiving support from government sources ended in nothing; the Jewish community was not organized for such an endeavor; tuition was out of the question, because Galicia was not accustomed to that, as well as because of the great economic crisis. So we had to resort to taxes and money collected at various assemblies, to cover a minimal part of the needs.

On the third month, however, the schools closed for another reason entirely: under the pressure of the agreement, the Ukrainians opened their elementary schools and closed the Jewish school.

During the short, but stormy Ukrainian rule, the Jewish population managed to create a national leadership – the "National Council" – which replaced the old Community. Elections to the National Council were held, right to vote given to men and women over 21 years old. The elections took place in winter 1919. Po'alei Zion led an intensive election campaign on a wide platform and received close to 500 votes and 5 mandates out of 50. The elected persons were: Levi Opper, Berl Friedman, Avraham Hauptman, Shlomo Rossler and Prof. Dr. Achser. Later, the party took an active part in in preparing the work program, which, however, remained on paper due to the fall of the Ukrainian Republic.

During the Ukrainian period, a strong youth organization and an influential circle of students numbering several tens of members were active in Po'alei Zion. The organization established its own consumer cooperative, and made several unsuccessful attempts to create a production cooperative.

The Polish Period

After the Polish army occupied Stryj in the fall of 1919, the new regime began its rule with new anti–Jewish decrees and sharp persecutions of the Jewish labor parties, expressed in administrative harassment, revisions and arrests. The social work in the Jewish Street lost its impetus that was present during the Ukrainian times. Po'alei Zion opened a worker's kitchen on the Batorega Street with the aim to meet the needs of the workers, and also to serve as cover for the persecuted party activity.

The Split

The split of the Po'alei Zion movement in the summer of 1920, reached Stryj about a year later. The ideological differences of opinion and the heated discussions paralyzed all activity.

After the split of Po'alei Zion at the 5th World–Conference in august 1920 in Vienna, local conferences took place in all countries, where the fates of the local parties were decided. The dispute between the Poles and Ukrainians about Eastern Galicia had not been settled yet, and the Eastern Galicia Po'alei Zion took a neutral stand in this question, guarded its independence and did not join he Polish Party. The party conference in Eastern Galicia took place in March 1921 in Lemberg. Stryj was represented by three delegates, of three positions: Avraham Hauptman – right, Levi Opper – center and S. Rosenberg – left. The Conference decided, on a small majority, to remain neutral, not to join any of the fractions and attempt to attain a reunification. However, two months later, the Eastern Galicia Po'alei Zion was divided as well. In Stryj, due to legal reasons, the party as well as its property – the consumer cooperative, the library, the meeting hall, the workers' kitchen and all legal documentation – remained in the hands of the Elder Right activists. On the other hand, the young people and the majority of the activist cadre turned to the left, and this fact decided the fate of the Po'alei Zion in Stryj: the right lost power gradually, leading to the liquidation of the consumers cooperative and the kitchen (end of 1921), and the end of all open activity. The left, however, needed only a very short time to heal the wounds of the split and rise to be the strongest workers' group in town.

[Page 239]

The Po'alei Zion Left organization was still illegal at the time, yet it obtained legalization for a children's home, named "Children's Home in the name of B. Borochov." They founded the home on Ringplatz 31 and it served also as camouflage for the party activity. The activity of the home and the professional work was carried out at first in the same hall, the cover vis-à-vis the authorities being as mentioned above. Only in 1923, the first professional unions were recognized by law, Po'alei Zion rented a place on Lemberger Street 18 and part of the party activity relocated there. In 1923, an evening school for workers and a day school were founded. Due to the special conditions in Galicia, which had a tradition of public government schools from the time of the Austrians, the day-school functioned only one school-year (1923-1924) and in the middle of the second year it closed. The evening school, on the other hand, existed until 1929 and the children's home until 1930. During the first years of its existence, the children's home met the needs of food for the children with the support of the American "YMCA."

The following teachers worked in the Po'alei Zion schools: Chana Gartenberg (from Stryj), perished during the German occupation; Esther Shayko (from Warsaw), died in Canada; Sonia Salfin (from Austria), perished during the German occupation; Yehudit Toptche (from Kolo), perished in Paris during the war; Chana Guttman (from Luck), lives in Israel; Yenna Lamm (from Polaw), perished during the war; Gartenberg Lea and Gartenberg Rutche from Stryj, now in Brazil, Henia Fruchter and Frieda Haber.

During that period, an entirely new group of people rose as activists in Po'alei Zion, among them: Yosef Hass (now in Israel), Michael Opper (perished during the German occupation in Stryj), Yite Bekher (died in 1935), Dolek Baktrag (today a doctor near Paris, B. Streifer (later joined the communists and became a provocateur), Yosef Mauerer (today a Po'alei Zion activist in Rio-de-Janeiro and leader of the Brazilian Magbit [collection campaign] for Israel), Leib Nussenblatt (died in Vienna), Shmuel Schwarzberg (a member in Paris), David Seltzer (perished in the Lemberg Ghetto), Yechezkel Laufer (in Israel), Avraham Grossman (in Israel), Chone Seiff (perished in the Lemberg Ghetto), Sender Derfler (in Israel), Hersch Meyer, Leib Lipman (perished in the Stryj Ghetto), Lasst (perished in Stryj), Fruchter Israel (in

Brazil), Morbach Yitzhak (died in 1927), Toyb Israel (perished in Stryj), Katz Shmuel (in Israel), Altbauer Shlomo (in Israel) and others.

[Page 240]

The activity of the organization was subject to constant police persecution. In order to suppress the financial activity, the authorities removed all permits of the institutions that provided some income. Often Police visited the places of assembly and arrested the active leaders, especially before the 1st of May. All this, however, has not weakened the intensive activity, and the work in the professional areas developed in particular. During the years 1923–1924 Po'alei Zion controlled all Jewish professional unions, entirely stopping the influence of the "Bund."

Political and Cultural Activity

In the course of that period, the Stryj organization – in most difficult conditions – led a very intense and open political and cultural activity. Open lectures and meetings, which dealt with and reacted to actual happenings in the Jewish life in the country and outside it, were held in the largest meeting-places in town, with speakers who have visited Stryj in the course of the years: I. Zerubavel (several times), Nathan Buchsbaum (many times), Shekhna Zogan, Yakov Kenner, N. Nier, Yosef Rosen, Yakov Peterseil and others.

In the Po'alei Zion locale (Ringplatz 31, Lemberger 18 and Batorego), weekly lectures were given, on various subjects. In order to enable political lectures, fake subjects were invented (astronomy, geography, mathematics and the like). When Police made a "blitz–attack" on such a lecture, the lecturer would change the subject from politics to astronomy. The audience was accustomed to this and would continue to sit quietly and never give away the "hocus–pocus".

An active part of the organization was the section of trips and study of the land. A good drama club was also active for many years, as well as a registered choir, and evening performances were given often.

In April 1926, the Po'alei Zion Right organization ceased to exist and merged with Po'alei Zion Left. The two libraries were united and the locale on Batorego Street was turned into a meeting place for Po'alei Zion young members.

In the course of the years, the Stryj Po'alei Zion organization led a very successful campaign for the Eretz-Israel Workers Fund and a series of activities for the workers in Eretz-Israel.

Voting Activity

In 1922, the Po'alei Zion in Stryj appeared for the first time as an independent party in a public political activity – the elections to the Sejm. The first place on the list was occupied by Nathan Buchsbaum (Lemberg).

In 1927, elections for the health-insurance organization were held, where an independent Jewish workers' list appeared for the first time. Two councilmen were elected – Yite Bekher and B. Streifer.

The same year, elections for the municipal council were held as well, according to the old Austrian system. Po'alei Zion presented a list and the first candidate (Shimon Rosenberg) received 900 votes.

[Page 241]

In the beginning of 1928, a list of Po'alei Zion participated in the elections to the community for the first time. The person elected was Mechl Opper, who later was elected to the executive committee on the Zionist Block list.

In the elections to the Sejm in 1928 the Po'alei Zion participated as well, and it received hundreds of votes.

During the first years after WWII, groups formed in the organization with the intention to make Aliya; later these groups became independent. With the active support of Dr. Malka Leibowitz, Dr. Ada Klein and others, these groups instructed pioneer groups, who, in various stages, made Aliya in great numbers. In 1919, another group of members of Po'alei Zion, under the leadership of David Seltzer, founded a training camp for several tens of pioneers [halutzim] who worked in agriculture and carpentry. Most of the members of this group made Aliya. Later, after the split in the party, when Po'alei Zion Left severed the contact with the world Zionist organization, Po'alei Zion Left did not receive "certificates." Due to this situation, only numbered members succeeded to make Aliya, by various means.

In the thirties, repressions and police persecutions against Po'alei Zion began, which paralyzed any legal public activity. This situation lasted until 1932, when, under the pretext of communist activity the police closed the locale and forbade any activity of Po'alei Zion. The illegal period lasted until the outbreak of WWII. The great Yiddish–Polish Borochov Library, which had functioned 30 years, was confiscated by the authorities, with certificates given to Matchek Horowitz. Based on this, the library remained in his possession until the Russian occupation at the end of 1939. Then the books were transferred to the possession of the town library and were destroyed during the German occupation.

The Association Jugend [Youth]

During the years of the Po'alei Zion activity in Stryj, a large organization of young people, recruited from among workers, clerks and students up to the age of 18 was active in town. This organization followed the ideology of Po'alei Zion. Education–wise, however, it led an intensive, ramified and independent activity.

The leaders during the first years were: Shimon Rosenberg, Mordechai Bergstein and Yitzhak Opper. In later years: Yitzhak Vinik, Leib Nussenblatt, Streifer and others.

Thanks to the strong youth–organization, in particular in the years 1918–1821, hundreds of new members, educated in the spirit of Zionism joined the professional unions. As a result, in 1922–1924 Po'alei Zion managed to pull out all professional unions from under the influence of the Bund.

In the beginning of the thirties, the "Jugend" shared the fate of their older friends and were forced by the ruling power to keep an underground existence.

Z.P.S. – BUND
By S. Rosenberg
Translated by Yocheved Klausner

By the end of the 19th century, a considerable number of Jews were members of the social–democratic parties in the Austro–Hungarian Empire; most of them belonged to the assimilated Jewish intelligentsia. This was true also in Galicia, where the Polish social–democratic party (PPSD) was active. In those years, the socialist idea began to penetrate more and more the Jewish working street. It happened due to the influence of the Bund activity in Russia, as well as to the changes of the Jewish social structure among the Jewish masses in Galicia itself.

[Page 242]

Jewish workers – the more conscious among them – began joining the P.P.S.D. At the beginning of the (20th) century, large groups of Jews were members, and their number grew constantly. The Jewish membership in P.P.S.D. began to be a problem – it was not comfortable for the party to absorb such a large number of Jews, whom the Polish members did not accept with a great deal of sympathy. The Jewish members, as well, did not feel "at home" in the Party. One of the great obstacles was the language. Very few of the Jews spoke good Polish, and in the corners they began "sinning" by speaking Yiddish. But then the Jewish members found a way out of the problem: they began establishing Jewish Sections, and in some cases they met in a different place. The pretext was that this way more Jewish members would be attracted and join. Several years later, these sections formed a new party, by the name: Jewish Social–Democratic Party, later known by the initials "Z.P S." Only the openly assimilated elements remained in the P.P.S.D., known by the nickname "sectionists." Ideologically, the new Jewish party crystallized under the influence of the Bund in Russia. Language and cultural matters were the only Jewish recognizable quality, which marked the difference between the Z.P.S. and P.P.S.D.

During the years 1901–1902 a Z.P.S. organization in Stryj was established – stemming mainly from the Jewish section of P.P.S.D. The organization became legal by the name of the "Progress" Union and led a broad activity in the cultural, professional and propaganda areas. In the years before WWI, Z.P.S. in Stryj was a strong organization, with a relatively great influence in town. During the two elections to the Austrian Parliament – 1904 and 1911 – Z.P.S. led an energetic campaign for the P.P.S.D. candidate Andrei Moratchevski and fought against the Zionist candidates Dr. Salz and Dr. Reich. In 1907, Salz lost due to a few hundred Jewish voters, who, following the activity and influence of Z.P.S. voted for Moratchevski.

In the professional area, the Stryj Z.P.S. could mark significant achievements in organizing the Jewish workers in Workers' Unions – carpenters, cobblers, house–painters, barbers, tailors and others. For many years, these unions identified themselves ideologically with Z.P.S.

Among the founders and activists of Z.P.S., until WWI, were: Wove Koenigsberg, perished in the Lemberg ghetto; Leib Freilich, perished in the Stryj ghetto; Israel Dornfeld, died before WWII; Rosmarin, Rosenbaum, perished in ghetto Stryj; Binyamin Ber, arrested by the Soviet authorities and died in jail; Fania Horowitz, perished in ghetto Stryj; Yakov Wunderlich, lives in America; the brothers Shiye and Shlomo Rossler, perished in ghetto Stryj; Leib Tepper, perished in ghetto Stryj; Yosef Leibowitz, died before the war; Gitl Tirkel, perished in ghetto Stryj; Friedl Boxer, arrested by the Soviet authorities and died in jail and Moshe Wagman, perished in the Soviet Union.

A sister–organization of Z.P.S. – a women's union, was also active in Stryj, by the name of "Zvyanzek Kobyet." This union was established in the time of the "sectionists" as a competition to the Zionist women's union "Ognisko Kobyet". "Zvyanzek Kobyet" was intended to be a mixed Polish–Jewish union, but Polish women did not join, except very few, among them the wife of the member of Parliament Moratchevski. To this Union belonged also the "sectionists" who had remained in the P.P.S.D. This way the union became sort of a bridge between the two parts of the former friends. Most of the union identified ideologically with Z.P.S.

[Page 243]

The World War cut off, for some time, the activity of Z.P.S. and only in 1917 a group of members tried to bring back to life the association "Progress," but without much success. It remained weak and was not recognized in town. This situation lasted until the end of the World War.

After the war, the old active members of Z.P.S. returned and the organization was revived with eagerness. The happenings in Russia, Germany and Austria strengthened the feelings for Z.P.S. The old members were joined and helped by the Jewish "sectionists" from P.P.S.D., which was inactive in the times of the Ukrainian rule. "Progress" took over one floor of the building on Ringplatz 37 and the work of a series of professional unions was renewed. At the beginning of the Ukrainian rule, the Stryj Z.P.S. issued a weekly paper, edited by Moshe Wagman – Di Roite Fon [The red flag]. Together with Po'alei Zion, Z.P.S. organized the workers' council. At the elections to the Jewish National Council, Z.P.S. received over 700 votes and 9 mandates.

*

After the Poles occupied Stryj, Z.P.S. lost many of its members and much of its influence. The consumer–cooperative closed, the production–cooperative became a private enterprise, the "sectionists" returned to the P.P.S. and a decline in all areas could be observed.

A year later, the Z.P.S. dissolved and merged with the Polish Bund. But the organization lost its old brilliance: the youth joined Po'alei Zion, many members became independent craftsmen and due to their new social situation they became passive. The downward movement lasted until 1939.

In November 1922, during the elections to the Sejm, the bund in Stryj obtained almost an equal number of votes as Po'alei Zion. At the elections to the health–insurance fund, summer 1927, the Bund list was disqualified, because it had not obtained the necessary number of signatures.

In 1928, at the elections to the community, the Bund did not present a list; one of its candidates figured on the list of Po'alei Zion.

At the elections to the Sejm in 1928, the Bund withdrew its list and called to vote for the P.P.S.

The last 10 years before WWII, the Bund in Stryj was almost inactive in public. The remaining group of Bund members kept in contact with the party organs and published a small number of issues of the Bund daily newspaper.

[Page 244]

The Jewish Professional Movement
By S. Stryjer
Translated by Yocheved Klausner

The Jewish professional labor associations in Stryj began functioning almost at the same time that the Jewish labor parties were founded. The first who created a Jewish professional organization was ZPS, the Jewish Socialist Party. Although the official aim was social improvement, the associations were formed according to party lines, by the model of the Bund professional movement in Russia.

The first to organize were the carpenters, and the first strikes in that profession occurred in 1903-1904, led by the ZPS. Since the strike brought some improvement in life conditions, it didn't take long and the tailors formed their own organization, then the house-painters, the shoemakers and the barbers. With very few exceptions, the dominant leaders of all these occupations were Jews. The conflicts would begin at the start of the season: the workers would go on strike, usually achieving some raises in salary; but he raises lasted only during the height of the season, and were later cancelled. Some organizations, for example the house-painters, would dissolve when the season ended.

Still, in the course of the years, better working conditions were achieved: higher salaries, shorter working-hours, sick insurance etc. The activists were usually the same people who were active in the various political parties.

The influential people in the above-mentioned occupations were mostly ZPS people. The commercial employees, on the other hand, were closer to the Po'alei Zion, and managed their organizations according to party lines. And although there were a considerable number of ZPS members among the employees, they suffered the fate of the few Po'alei Zion members in the other associations – they had to obey the decisions of the majority. The Po'alei Zion tried hard to enter the Workers' Unions, but without success.

This situation continued until WWI and a few years after that. In this way, hundreds of workers were educated in the exclusive spirit of ZPS – with an anti-Zionist inclination.

The situation changed radically only at the beginning of the twenties. The reason of the change was the great influence that Po'alei Zion had on the young workers. In truth, the aim of Po'alei Zion after the War was to gain influence in the workers' unions, with the help of the young generation of workers. This gave fruit in the years 1922-1923, when masses of young members of Po'alei Zion, who by that time reached the age of 18, began joining the existing occupations. At the beginning, the ZPS people did not pay much attention to that; it was felt the first time in the summer of 1923, at the general assembly of the carpenters' union – the largest and strongest Jewish union – when the candidates of Po'alei Zion were elected to the management by a large majority. This assembly witnessed a great fist fight between Bundists and Po'alei Zion members concerning the decision that the activity of the Union will be transferred from the locale of the Bundists to the Po'alei Zion hall. The sign of the carpenters' union on the wall of Po'alei Zion symbolized their first victory in the professional field. During a quite short period, Po'alei Zion reached a majority of votes in other professional unions as well – tailors, barbers, metal–workers, printing and chemistry workers. In the course of only a few years, the Bund has lost its influence in these areas.

As time passed, the unions changed, but most of the members still were under the influence of Po'alei Zion, and they were joined by Bundists and Communists. Yet, the anti–Zionist spirit which had reigned in the past was over. In some of the Unions, groups of Hechalutz movement were formed and they enjoyed the full sympathy of the Union management.

[Page 245]

The continuing professional activity was expressed by a struggle of social character. Two strikes of the barbers, after two weeks ended in victory; and a strike of the tailors was lost. In the thirties, Unions were destroyed thanks to the communists' dividing activity and Police harassment.

The Borochov Library
By Avraham Grossman
Translated by Yocheved Klausner

Among the various Jewish cultural institutions that were active in Stryj, the large library named after B. Borochov must be mentioned. It had a special educational significance among the Jewish population in Stryj.

The library was founded in 1922 by Po'alei Zion left, and its first organizer and manager was Shimon Rosenberg. He devoted much energy to this institution and thanks to him in 1926 it already was the largest and most beautiful public library in Eastern Galicia.

At first it was located on Ringplatz 31, later it relocated to Lemberger Street 18, in the house of the bakery owned by Sauerbrunn.

It must be noted that the Borochov Library was actually a continuation of the Po'alei Zion library, which was founded before the First World War and for a while, before the split, it remained in the possession of Po'alei Zionright, and in 1926 it became again the property of the Borochov llibrary.

Due to its aesthetic arrangement, professional management and rich variety of books, the library attracted hundreds of readers from all walks of life: workers, office employees, students, merchants, young people and also a considerable number of Yeshiva students.

In 1927, a Polish section was opened as well, of about 2,000 books.

The library had a great educational significance for the young workers, who had, usually, only a few years of elementary schooling, or only Cheder education. These workers continued their self-education with the help of the Borochov Library.

The rich section of drama and theater literature helped developing the Drama Circles in Stryj, beginning with the Amateur Drama Club in 1917. Later there were: the Shalom Ash Club, the Y.L. Peretz Club, the A. Goldfaden

Club and other Drama Circles affiliated with the Zionist organizations. All were inspired by the unforgettable director Prof. Matchek Horowitz.

A characteristic fact, which at the time shook the Jewish as well as the non–Jewish population in town should be mentioned here:

Just like other Jewish cultural institutions in Poland, the Borochov Library struggled for its material existence, and was always several months late paying the rent. The landlord, owner of the property, was interested to exploit this situation, to get rid of the library and free the apartment and make a nice profit. He hired a band of hooligans and, with the silent approval of the Police, in the middle of the night they threw out on the street the library with all its contents. The Police was interested to help liquidate one of the most beautiful Jewish Institutions in town.

[Page 246]

The library management had to make a choice: to enter a long judicial process with the risk of meanwhile losing the institution, or immediately react with force. It chose the second way. The Jewish workers were called, through Po'alei Zion, to assemble right after work on the street of the library. The Polish and Ukrainian workers were also instructed to come after work to help the Jewish cultural institution. On 4:39 p.m. the street was full of Jewish and non–Jewish workers. They closed all entrances, so that the police would not interfere. In only a few minutes the hired hooligans retreated and the library was soon back in its place. For a long time after that, workers patrolled around the place in order to defend ii.

The Borochov Library later moved back to its first locale on Ring–Platz 31 and was active many years, until it fell prey to Police persecution.

In the course of the years, the following were especially active and helping: Sender Derfler (now in Israel), Yosef Meuerer (now in Brazil), Michael Last, Chaim Shamir (now in Israel), Israel Fruchter (now in Brazil), and the writer of these lines.

The Soviet Occupation in Stryj
By S. Hirschorn
Translated by Yocheved Klausner

Transition

In the third week after the invasion of Poland, 17 September 1939, the Germans occupied the town. On the 17th day after the outbreak of the war the Soviet Armies crossed the Eastern border of Poland and began occupying the Eastern regions and on 29 September 1939 the two armies – the German and the Russian – met at the River Stryj. At the time, discussions concerning a demarcation line were conducted between the two Powers: the Russians demanded a borderline, and after a number of arguments and a few days of war of nerves the Germans retreated from our Eastern Galicia corner and the town was occupied by the Red Army.

The Germans have not done much damage to the Jewish population, apart from one bomb on Elner's house, on the Ringplatz, which killed some 50 people.

The Russian occupation was received by the inhabitants of Stryj with mixed feelings: by the Poles with absolute hate, by the Ukrainians with reserve and by the Jews with lesser anger compared to the reception of the Germans.

The Regime

At first, the new Power was content with issuing various administrative regulations, as the order to return all weapons, the order to open the shops and the prohibition to raise prices.

[Page 247]

Little by little, the new order gained stability. However, it didn't help much. All consequences of wartime began to be felt: food disappeared from the market, prices rose to new heights, lines formed in front of the bakeries.

Textile shops, shoes, haberdashery and sweets – in a few days all stores were empty. The merchants took home bags full of money. Even all cheap merchandise that had remained for months on the shelves was taken. The inspectors watched that the prices will not rise too much and that the merchandise will not be hidden.

The panic was not caused by the town population. On the contrary – the inhabitants showed considerable restraint. The buying panic and "catch-as-catch-can" atmosphere was caused by the Soviet military in town. The officers began buying whatever came into their hands, without limit. Only later the "secret" was revealed: the land of the occupants had been, for long years, hungry for everything. The merchandise that they bought was sent as gifts home, to the families. Thus began a period of months of hunger. There were cases when the population, after standing in line for a whole night in the bitter frost in order to obtain a bread, would lose its patience and begin to rob passing military cars full of bread and other baked things, on their way to the army barracks.

Meanwhile, the new authorities stabilized their power and all offices were occupied by Commissars from Ukraine, who came with their families. They managed the town municipality, taxes, commerce, industry, co-operation, militia etc. It must be said, that all were employed – of any nation, social class, or affiliation with a party in the past, apart from very few exceptions, following the activity of informers, who were local communists or plain charlatans. The local population learned very fast how to live with the new rulers and the new bosses at work, mostly by the principle of "live and let live," with the help of bribe, corruption and common needs.

After the stabilization – more or less – of the new regime, changes were gradually felt: merchandise that came from Russia was not handled by private hands anymore; central authorities took over the management of commerce and labor; mills, bakeries and other big enterprises were nationalized, and later also houses estimated as worth more than 20,000 Rubles. All this provided a large area for bribes, thanks to which a large part of the houses remained private ownership. In the area of rented dwellings, bribe and nepotism reigned. In the field of handiwork and craftsmanship there were no restrictions about opening workshops; however, such high taxes were imposed upon the private craftsmen, that they were forced to close their shops and work with the co–operation. A considerable number of former merchants adapted themselves during the first days and went to work with the government enterprises. The rest lived for a while from the money obtained by selling the shops.

In general, there was not much persecution. But a series of arrests was made, as for example Levi Oper, a leader of Po'alei Zion. For some time he was in the local jail, then he was sent away and did not survive. To everyone's surprise, two Jewish long–time communists were arrested as well: Shabetay Ketz and Mechl Ketz. The official reasons for the arrests were never disclosed; about the last two it was later discovered in the Polish Archives that they had been "provocateurs." The arrest of the Stryj attorney Dr. Wandel became a sensation, since for many years he had been the defending attorney in trials of communists. Several assumptions were expressed concerning the reasons for this arrest – but the truth was never discovered. Wandel died in prison. The two former Bund activists, Binyamin Ber and Friedl Bakster were arrested as well; both perished in prison. A while later Dr. Hoizman was arrested, under the pretext that a book by Trotzki was found in his library [by the way, this was legal in Poland]. The real reason for his arrest was that one of the new Soviet officers coveted Hoizman's beautiful apartment and this way he got rid of him. Hoizman perished as well. Several merchants were also arrested and sent to prison, allegedly for hiding merchandise, among them: Krischer, Kostman and others.

[Page 248]

On 22 February 1940, the new regime unexpectedly hit the entire population: a sudden regulation was issued – that the Polish currency was out of circulation and only the Ruble remained the legal tender. Ninety percent of the money that was in circulation became thus valueless and thousands of households found themselves without money. Interestingly, several days earlier the government institutions paid their employees the salaries in Polish currency, and so thousands of workers remained without means of sustenance.

Refugees

The war and the German occupation of Poland were followed by a great stream of refugees, who, at the beginning fled from the Germans to the East and there they fell under the Soviet occupation. In Stryj there were thousands of them; only a few managed to settle there, the rest continued eastward.

In the summer of 1940, there was an unexpected Aktzia, which cruelly "solved" the refugee problem on all territories of the former Polish Eastern Provinces. In Stryj the Aktzia looked thus: one night they attacked all quarters where Jewish refugees from Congress Poland lived, gave them 15–20 minutes to pack the most needed things and took them to the train. This encompassed young and old, men, women and children, workers and non–employed. As it became known later, this Aktzia was prepared secretly. During weeks they prepared in the station a number of freight cars for long trips. In the cars they arranged cots for sleeping and stoves to keep warm. For the purpose of "catching" or kidnapping the people they organized in advance, secretly, several brigades of their own trustworthy people who, together with the militia carried out the work rigorously; they took women without the men, if the men were by chance away from home, and men without the women. They also took parents without some of their children if they were not at home at the moment. These refugees traveled for months through the Russian Taiga and Steppe, in the direction of the Northern regions. On the way, there were many victims due to the inhuman and unsanitary conditions. Later, arriving to the

Polar region, the number of the victims increased. The letters that arrived to family and friends were full of cries for help: some of them did not have warm clothes when they arrived in the areas of fearful frosty climate. The food was scarce and they became ill with scurvy and other Polar diseases; also the living and working conditions were difficult.

[Page 249]

The Relationship between various National Groups

As is known, Eastern Galicia was declared part of the Ukrainian Soviet Republic, realized through a so–called Referendum. Following this decision, the Ukrainian language became the official language. Naturally, this flattered the Ukrainian population and hurt very much the national feelings of the Polish people. The occupation authorities also made every effort to replace Poles and Jews in leading positions with Ukrainians. This, however, was accomplished with difficulty and was realized only to a small measure, since it was hard to find a sufficient number of qualified Ukrainians for the jobs. Because of the tendency of Ukrainization, all members of the Ukrainian intelligentsia, who were known nationalists and hated the Soviet Union, were employed. There was no antagonism between the two parts of the population mentioned above; the negative attitude toward the occupant has weakened the old national tensions. The relationship between the Poles and Ukrainians and the Jews improved considerably compared to the situation before the war.

Social Life in the Jewish Sreet

The Soviet occupation resulted in a complete liquidation of all political parties and all Jewish social activity. The Jewish charitable, philanthropic, cultural and other institutions ceased to exist. Other institutions, like orphanages, homes for the aged and the like were merged with Christian institutions of the same kind and transferred to the municipal administration. They were emptied of all Jewish content. The official language became Ukrainian. In general, the entire social life turned gray, uninspiring, devoid of any Jewish cultural activity, except some lessons and courses, where the listeners were fed with the history of the Bolshevik Party or the speeches of Soviet officials. Those courses were packed with masses of government officials and employees, who came mainly for fear of the consequences.

The religious life continued without any interruption in all synagogues and Batei Midrash. The religious institutions, however, which before the war were subsidized by the Jewish community did have financial problems. They remained without help and had to resort to self-sustenance.

Notwithstanding the official integration of Eastern Galicia into the Soviet Ukraine, the border between the two parts of the country was closed, until the end of the occupation. The duty of the Eastern Galicia citizens to serve in the Red Army was different as well: the recruited served only in labor battalions and were employed at building fortifications.

[Page 250]

The End of the Soviet Regime

One week after the German attack on the Soviet Union (22 June 1941) the Soviet forces left the town. During that week, the soviet institutions in town – their personnel, many soviet citizens and others – were evacuated by the authorities. Several hundred Jews seized this opportunity and fled to the East.

When the war against the Germans broke out, a great number of Jews was called to serve in the army. If they did not follow the order of mobilization, they were shot for desertion. So was shot Popper and another Jew.

Before leaving town, the Soviets carried out a cruel act: without reason they arrested the Zionist activists: David Seidman, Binyamin Klein, Benye Garfinkel, Yitzhak Meisels and Schwammer Leib.

All, except Seidman, were shot without trial, in the courtyard of the Stryj jail.

The Soviet Occupation in Stryj
By S. Hirschorn
Translated by Yocheved Klausner

The following letter was sent to the editorial board of the Yizkor–Book by our friend Zvi Raps – now in Tzefat [Safed].

During the war, Raps arrived to Stryj as a refugee. In his letter he describes the aid that the Stryj Jews gave the refugees, who, in the summer of 1940 were cruelly loaded by the Soviet occupants onto freight cars and sent away to the far Northern regions of Russia.

The Editorial Board

It was Friday evening when the Russians began the action of sending us to Siberia. On Saturday morning they loaded us onto freight cars and on Sunday morning our transport arrived in Stryj. We did not know where we were taken but the Stryj Jews knew the secret – that we were being sent away to Siberia.

The Russians have not allowed the Stryj Jews to approach the station. So they bribed the NKVD people and received permission. In the course of one day they bought a wagon of bread, challah, cakes, marmalade, butter, herring, sweets – and what not? even diapers and clothes for children. They also brought over thirty thousand Rubles – a considerable sum at the time.

In addition, people brought to the station cooked food, warm and cold. The Community announced that any luxury planned for that day must be devoted to the refugees. A wagon load full of medicines was brought and divided among the train cars; it was of great help during the journey.

This I shall never forget:

As the train already began to move, a woman gave me a jar full of the finest marmalade and a bag of sugar. She shouted through the window: "This is for all!"

As the train left the station, several hundreds of Stryj Jews were standing on the platform, weeping loudly. Such a warm behavior as in Stryj I have never seen. For years I am carrying with me the thought that I must meet at least one Stryjer Jew and kiss him with gratitude. Finally I met one of them in Safed and I told him that what they did must never be forgotten.

I hope that many of the hundreds of Jews who have been with me in Siberia will read my letter in your Yizkor–Book and will add to it more and more. Because what I am writing here is only like a drop in the sea of what the Stryj Jews have done.

May their memory be blessed!

Signed: Raps, Tzefat, Street 19, No. 6

[Page 251]

Stryj Refugees in the Soviet Union
Translated by Yocheved Klausner

The German attack of the Soviet Union, on 22 June 1941, was so unexpected, that in the early morning hours, while the Stryj people were still in their beds, nobody believed that the echoes of bomb explosions and the noise of fire arms had any connection with a real war. Only in the later hours of the morning, after the radio announcements from Moscow, they began to wake up to the situation. They realized that heavy clouds are gathering above the town and a storm in unavoidable.

Stryj was situated in the most dangerous region. The Soviet-German demarcation line extended from the San in Przemysl to Lavochne in the Carpathian Mountains. Hostile mechanized divisions could make the distance Przemysl-Stryj in several hours. The German air force did it in a few minutes and spread destruction over the Soviet military bases in the region.

However, interestingly, the Stryj population did not realize the full meaning of the danger, and never thought of fleeing from the place. The faces of the people showed distress, but not panic.

The Stryj Jews were well aware of the fact that in the course of the last 20 years the Soviets have built strong fortifications along the border. Therefore, during the first two days it was surmised that the border-battles would not last a long time, but, when on the third and fourth days news arrived that in the NE and SE the Germans have broken the lines, it became clear that the fate of the central front in mid-Galicia was sealed and that in a few days Stryj would fall into the hands of the Germans.

Yet, the Jewish population in Stryj was not shaken. No mass-movement of evacuation was observed. How can we explain the relative calm and indifference with which the Jews have met the danger of German occupation? There were three reasons:

a) Twenty months experience of living in Stryj with the few thousand refugees from West Galicia and Congress-Poland, who were most of the time without a roof over their heads and suffered hunger, lack of minimal hygiene and separation of families – all this resulting in a great fear of becoming a refugee.

b) Lack of realization and evaluation of the danger of the brutal German plans of murder and annihilation.

c) Bitterness accumulated among the Jewish middle-class and intelligentsia during the 20 months of Soviet occupation, due to: liquidation of private commerce and private ownership, contempt of the Soviet authorities toward the intelligentsia and disappointment of the working class from the Soviet regime, because of its corruption, bribery, nepotism and low level of life.

For the above reasons, defeatist voices were indeed heard among the Jewish population, yet the will to pick up the "wanderer's staff" was not strong. Therefore, the evacuation from Stryj was limited to a relatively small number of people, of the following categories: personnel of sanitary services, hospitals and other health-care; communist youth; mobilized people during the first days of the war and air defense. In some of the above-mentioned categories only the men left, leaving the women and children behind.

The trains that left Stryj in the direction of the Ukraine during the last days before the Soviet Army left, accepted every one who desired to escape. There was no control or limitation – there were two or three such trains. But there was also a possibility to escape in the direction of Drohobitch-Barislav, by trains which passed through Stryj.

[Page 252]

Some 300 Jewish refugees from Stryj arrived this way to the Soviet Union.

During the first few months, the Stryj refugees concentrated, in larger or smaller groups, in the regions where they were taken off the train, but mainly in the Ukraine. Later, as the Germans marched out, they spread all over the Asian parts of the Soviet Union.

*

The few hundred Stryj refugees in Russia suffered the same fate as their brother-refugees in Congress Poland: they worked in the kolkhoz; were employed in factories and workshops; wandered around the wide Russian areas without a roof over their heads, dirty, naked, barefoot and hungry; traded regularly in the black-market; spent time in jail and in concentration camps; died of typhoid fever and other illnesses as a result of all the troubles and finally, in 1945-46 were re-evacuated to Poland. We do not have exact numbers – neither of those who escaped from Stryj by train nor of those who did not live to return to the "old home." We also do not have the exact number of those who were re-evacuated to Poland. It is estimated to be around 200.

This is the short story of the "last remnant" [*she'erit hapleita*] of the Jews of Stryj, who experienced the "Soviet Chapter." Most of those who survived live now in Israel.

The Annihilation of the Jewish Community in Stryj

The following chronicle is an abbreviated form of the story told by Yona Friedler and Yitzhak Nussenblatt, two well-known Stryj Jews, who in 1941-1944 experienced the Nazi Hell in town, witnessing the ruin of the Jewish Community of Stryj.

Eye-Witnesses Tell the Story

On the 2nd of July 1941 the Nazi hordes occupied the town. 10 days – from 22 June to 2 July – the town was feverish with panic and fear.

The German air force constantly bombarded and terrorized the retreating groups of the Soviet army as well as the civilian population. The Ukrainian Haidamaks, from town and from the neighboring villages, prepared for robbery and murder.

The Soviet Garrison in Stryj evacuated in great panic, and with them went several hundred Jews – families and singles – some of them by force, some of them by their own will. The remaining Jewish population, numbering over 14 thousand souls, was in panic and distress.

On the first day of the invasion, the Germans opened several mass-graves, in the courtyard of the Stryj Tower. Before the Russians left, they shot in a hurry and buried tens of political prisoners: Ukrainians, Poles and Jews, whom they were not able to take with them to the East. Among those killed were several Zionist activists.

The Nazis exploited the situation and proceeded with a poisoning anti-Soviet and anti-Jewish incitement.

[Page 253]

To the exhumation they invited Ukrainians from the villages, priests and people from the press. They began with the anti-Semitic fire: "This was done by the Jewish-Communist regime – take revenge!"

These were the first days of the legalized murderous Ukrainian Bacchanalia. They started beating, murdering and robbing Jews, cursing and humiliating. All doors opened for the Ukrainian underworld. The accumulated Jew-hatred during generations, from the time of Chmielnicki, became overt in his great-grandchildren. It should be mentioned, that they performed the horrible, bloodthirsty work not worse than the Germans.

The first German regulations were:

a. Confiscate all radio and telephone sets of the Jewish population.

b. Organize the Judenrat.

The orders came from the military town commander – Hauptman Weide. The son-in-law of the former rabbi Eliezer Ladir, Oscar Hatterer was charged with arranging a list of people who could serve in the Judenrat. It included the following persons:

Jewish Elder Oscar Hatterer. Members: Dr. Wolf Mishel, Moshe Walmut, Dr. Rechter, Dr. Binyamin Millbauer, Lipe Honig, Yitzhak Reich, Shlomo Sauerbrunn, Michael Wang and others.

The Judenrat was charged with the following duties: the Jews should carry out all orders and regulations of the military and civil authorities; should deal with all Jewish problems in the Jewish Quarter, including imposing taxes for the activity of the Judenrat.

The Judenrat organized a series of activities, for example: Jewish Police service, food, taxes, apartments, furniture, work etc. The Judenrat offices were situated in the house of the Ettinger family, corner of Pototzki and 3 May Streets.

Right from the start, the members of the militia received a series of privileges, also special uniforms and hats with a yellow band, and were armed with rubber sticks.

One of the first regulations of the Judenrat was to arrange furniture for the apartments of the German officers who lived in town. Naturally, it was done by confiscating Jewish furniture.

The offices of the Judenrat were organized and furnished nicely, with telephones, typewriters, secretaries. The Judenrat also owned property and opened stores in the Jewish region.

During the first days, Jews were allowed to move outside the Jewish quarter – formally between 10 a.m. and 12 noon – to do their shopping in the general market, but there they were met with the worst offenses, humiliation and beatings by Ukrainians and Poles. Hatred and incitement grew day by day: the quantity of the produce in the market decreased daily, and the scapegoat were the Jews.

The Regime

In town, the power was in the hands of the "Schupo" [Schutz-Polizei = Protecting Police], the "Kriepo" [Kriegs Polizei = War Police], the Gestapo and the Ukrainian Police. The Ukrainian police served as the right hand of the Gestapo. Their cruelty was often worse than the expectation of those who gave them the orders. Their hands were immersed in rivers of Jewish blood.

The first bloody terror act happened in the first few days. Following the notice of a Ukrainian informer, 12 Jews were caught and accused of communist activity and of harassing Ukrainians during the Soviet occupation. They were taken to the village Dolib and shot.

The entire accusation was no more than an invented lie.

[Page 254]

The murdered people had never in their lives any connection with communism or with the "good deeds" of the German authorities. Among the people who were shot: Efraim Buchenbaum, Feivel Dunkel, Eng. Schatzker, the son of Att. Kerner, Freiman, Steiermark, Ringel, Sterski-Klarsfeld (a convert to Christianity) and others.

On the second day after the invasion, they began taking the Jews to the hardest, dirtiest and mostly senseless work, in order to humiliate them and terrorize them with beatings and hunger. The Ukrainians were the "first violin" of the great orchestra, and made every effort to use all their animal brutality.

Later, the Germans began to introduce "Ordnung" [order], to best exploit the Jewish force-labor for their needs. With the help of the Judenrat, work-service was enforced on all Jews of the ages of 16-60. "Work-Brigades" were organized and living quarters were provided for them, in several small camps outside the Jewish quarter. Those brigades worked in food production, building, water, petrol industry, rags, wood and glass production.

The hope of some of the Jews, that the forced labor will protect them from worse trouble, was later proved false. None of them was spared the fate of the rest of the Jewish Community.

The Jewish Quarter – the Ghetto

The Jewish quarter, which was created in town right at the beginning, was in fact a ghetto, only not yet hermetically locked. It comprised the streets: Klinski Drohobitza, the Ringplatz to Targovitza and the streets between

Batorego and Karzmierska. About 12 thousand Jews were crowded between these borders.

A few months later, the Judenrat received an order to bring to this area another 11 thousand Jews, who were evacuated from the neighboring district.

In December 1942, the size of the Jewish quarter was reduced, cut off from all other parts of town, and locked. Thus it became a real ghetto, crowded in a box between the North of the Ringplatz up to Zhelona-Targovitza and between Batorego and Berka Yoselevitcha.

The First Aktzia

In September 1941, the first Aktzia was carried out, in a most brutal way. Some 1200 Jewish men were pulled out of the Jewish quarter, and after 3 days of torture they were sent to Halabutev, a village not far from town. There they forced them to dig graves, then they were all shot and buried.

The Jewish population panicked and began feeling the danger of death which awaited everyone. In all houses and courtyards they started arranging hiding places – every home was looking for a place to hide on the day of attack. They built bunkers, some of them well camouflaged, which gave protection during the first Aktzias.

The greatest danger, in spite of the hiding places, were the local Ukrainians who, together with the Germans took part in all Aktzias. They knew the town very well – the streets, the courtyards and all the corners. Even more dangerous was the group of outcasts from the Jewish "order-service," who made the Germans' work much easier.

Between the Aktzias there were pauses. And meanwhile, the first winter for the Germans on the Eastern fronts approached, and they needed warm clothing. In December 1941, the order of the fur-Aktzia was issued. Those who did not give up their furs were threatened by death penalty. Moshe Goldfinger was hanged after a Ukrainian neighbor informed the authorities that he hid his fur coat.

In general, the Aktzias of money contributions by Jews and confiscation of Jewish property brought the Christian population to a horrible moral low: corruption, theft, robbery, drunkenness and murder became the habit of their daily life.

[Page 255]

One Aktzia was carried out – of deporting the unproductive, non-working Jews. They were pulled out of the Jewish quarter and deported to Smarze, a far and abandoned place in the Carpathian Mountains. We do not have numbers – but we know that all deportees died of hunger and frost.

The news that came from the front caused worry and fear. On the Eastern front, the Germans marched forward and on the way destroyed every Jewish settlement. The anti-Jewish propaganda increased, the authorities became more severe every day; life became hell: forced labor, beatings, hunger and murder were the daily bread. And the sword of further Aktzias hung over the Jewish community.

The third Aktzia was not a long time away: it came in May 1942, on the eve of the Holiday of Shavuot. The entire Jewish quarter was suddenly filled with German troops and Ukrainian police. They began opening the bunkers and pull out young and old from the hiding places. There were terrible scenes; children were torn away from their parents and parents from children. All sick people in the hospital were shot.

After each Aktzia, the remaining property was assembled, carefully sorted and sent to Germany.

On 3 September 1942, a new Aktzia was organized, one of the biggest. About 8 thousand Jews were taken to the train, loaded onto cattle cars, without food, without water, crowded and dirty. This transport left for Belshetz.

On the way, several Jews managed to make some holes in the car and jumped off the train. Most of them, however, were later caught in the forest by the Ukrainian police. Only very few, who managed to find their way back home, were saved.

In December 1942, the ghetto was closed off, and only with a "work-card" could one step out of the ghetto.

The locked up Jews were in a frightful position. Only one bakery, which belonged to Shlomo Sauerbrunn was working in the ghetto.

Electricity and gas were shut off. The sewage was not cleaned. With the hunger and dirt came death. Diseases spread and the ghetto went into a state of dying.

Yet, even in this situation there were some desperate attempts to pull out of the claws of death. Through round-about ways, some managed to get out from the ghetto and run, risking death, toward the Hungarian border. There was one spark of hope to cross the border to Hungary and save oneself. But the ray of hope soon dispersed, because the roads were full of Ukrainians, with and without uniform, who blocked the roads everywhere. Tired and desperate, all of them fell into the hands of the pursuers and shared the fate of their brethren in the ghetto.

There were attempts to escape by other ways as well, but only few succeeded to escape the sword.

A few people managed to find shelter in the "Arian" part of town, hidden by Christians. The documents were obtained through a messenger from the Warsaw Ghetto.

Very few survived in the forests, fewer still in bunkers, with the help of Christians.

The following perished, among others, in the first Aktzia (to Belzhec):

Schuster Zeide, Dr. Nathan Schaechter and his family, the Esteryung family, the family of Att. Mark Horowitz, Att. Selinger, Prof. Seinfeld, Binyamin Nussenblatt, Pesia Josefsberg and her daughter Yita, Reichman Genia, Chaia and children, the Appelgruen family (shoe merchants), Israel Nussenblatt and son, Mrs. Appelgruen and daughter, Dr. Fikhmann's wife and son, Moshe Beer and family, the Schindler family, the Robinson brothers, the Kraemer family, the Klinger family, the Hartstein family, Att. Weiss, Rosenberg Feivel and family, Fruchter Haendel and family, the Buchwalter family, Fruchter Aizik and family, the Filtz family, Max Horowitz, the Lerner family, Rosenzweig, Ungar, Hirschhorn Kuba and family, Dr. Ungar and wife, Chava Vizeltir.

[Page 256]

In the Aktzia of 28 February 1943 perished, among others: Henia Schatz and daughter, the Shlomo Rassler family, Leib Schatz, Sasha Heller, Hella Preiss, Aharon Meller.

In the Aktzias in 1943, there were cases of active resistance against the police, but they were suppressed with cruelty.

In the camps, there was also some sabotage activity.

In the Aktzia of 22 May 1943, about 1000 people perished. They were caught and locked up for several days in the Great Synagogue, which was situated outside the ghetto. They were kept there without food, without water, without necessary sanitation for their physiological needs.

When they opened the doors of the synagogue, gruesome sights were seen. The Christian neighbors said that their heads turned over and their blood froze in their veins from the horrible sights.

On the walls of the synagogue were found scribbled words, asking for vengeance.

The last liquidation Aktzia started on 22 June 1943 and lasted a month. When they sent away the transport, the teacher Lisa Schwieder addressed the German escort with the following words: "Murderers of my people! Bandits! Who gave you the right to murder millions of people? You are a mockery, a shame, you and your crazy Fuehrer! There will be revenge, not only on you but on your coming generations! The blood of innocent children will beat forever and rob your life. Eternal shame be on you!"

The Germans stopped in wonder and distress, but soon recovered and proceeded with their work.

In June 1943, the Jewish doctors were killed. They were taken to a house on Potocki Street, from there to the Tower and then to Holobotov.

On the way they were poisoned with Kaliumcyanid gas: Dr. Malka Leibowitz, Dr. Shnir and Nives with the family.

In that liquidation Aktzia, the following perished as well, among others:

Rabbi Yeshayahu Asher Yales, Seidman David, Dr. Eisenstein, Shlomo Toyber and family, Hatterer, Mrs. Ladir and daughter, Nagler Kuba, Yosef Ber Kraan and family, Stoltz Shimon, Manya Haber and her mother, Rachel Broyner and family, Malia Steiff, Shmuel Fruchter and family, Mania Pomerantz, Henia Stoltz, Regina Smarak, Enden and family, Sauerbrunn, the Tzobel family, Dr. Yosef Raat, Dr. Ingber and wife, Dr. Mantel and family, Pharmacist Lianek Sternberg and his mother, Pharmacist Dicker.

All those who were hidden in the "Arian" side fell into the hands of the Germans and the Ukrainians and perished.

During the three years of German occupation, approximately 14 thousand Stryj Jews perished, and a similar number from the surrounding province.

In 1944, when the town was liberated, there were in town about twenty Jews, who had been hidden by Christians.

[Page 259]

Organization of Former Stryj Residents in Israel
Translated by Susan Rosin

1

The immigration to Eretz Israel intensified during 1933 – 1934. It also included hundreds of immigrants from Stryj: Pioneers (halutzim), members of youth organizations and middle class families. Many of the Stryj immigrants encountered difficulties in finding work and a place to live when they first arrived. During this period of enhanced immigration it was easier to find a job than finding an apartment or a room. The official Yishuv institutions and various party organizations did all they could, but in many cases the assistance they provided was not sufficient in helping the new immigrants during their initial period in the new country. The Stryj immigrants needed much support and encouragement upon their arrival.

Among the more established Stryj immigrants who arrived earlier were many who were willing and able to assist the newcomers. In Tel–Aviv, Berl Stern was prominent in his willingness to assist the new immigrants. His two room apartment on Maccabi street was a first stop for many of the Stryj new arrivals, where they could stay for a while. This was very meaningful and of great importance in those days. For years his apartment was a meeting place for those from Stryj, both the new arrivals and those who were already established and it served also unofficially as an information and resource center and mutual aid.

In time, when the number of Stryj newcomers grew it became clear there was a need for both moral and material support for them. As a result, the Stryj organization was established to provide a more streamlined and formal assistance.

The first meeting to establish the "The Organization of Former Stryj and Surrounding Areas residents in Israel" took place in November 1934 in Tel–

Aviv. Dr. Emanuel Rechter was elected as the chair person, and the executive committee members were: Meir Frankel, Berl Stern, Yehuda Lustig, Moshe Weiss, and Yaakov Boymel. The tenure of the first executive committee was short, but the assistance for the new arrivals did not stop and was most notably given by those members who were already established in public and financial institutions and were in positions to help with loans and with finding work.

Up until the start of the Second World War the Stryj people used to gather once a year in Tel–Aviv during the Purim holiday to meet, exchange information and take photos.

2

In 1942, when information started to come in about the Stryj refugees in Russia the organization renewed its activity. The committee contacted the Jewish agency in an effort to get the names, addresses, and information about the fate of the Stryj refugees. Immediately after receiving the information, a shipment of clothing and food was organized to the Stryj remaining Jews who were exiled to the Siberian wilderness.

At the same time news started to arrive about the systematic extermination of Europe's Jewry.

World Jewry and the Yishuv in Eretz Israel started to plan rescue missions. However, due to the positions of the main power players and the British, these efforts were very minimal at best.

After the triumph of the allies and Russians, and the retreat of the German army from the territories they occupied, the full scale and the horror of the mass murder of six million Jews by the Nazis and their helpers in Europe was uncovered.

Conditions for an organized and an all–encompassing operation to rescue the survivors returning from Russia to Poland and Germany became feasible only in 1944.

The Yishuv demanded that the British mandate authorities allow the immigration of the survivors in the displaced persons camps in Europe. Despite of the British opposition, the Yishuv's highest institutions made the decision to bring these refugees to Eretz Israel. Thus began the struggle between the Yishuv institutions and the British mandate authorities for the right to bring the surviving refugees to their homeland.

At the same time, organizations of the various Jewish communities in Eretz Israel started to organize as well in order to assist and support their hometown's survivors.

In September 1944 a meeting of the Stryj organization was held. Avigdor Rottfeld in his opening remarks stressed the urgent need to broaden and expand the activity of the organization. The roles of the organization were defined as:

[Page 260]

1. Finding addresses of the Stryj survivors;
2. Sending care packages;
3. Assistance to arriving refugees;
4. Memorializing the community by creating a "Yizkor" book;
5. Handling the property of those who perished.

Dr. Zvi Heller, the representative of the Poland Immigrants organization also spoke during the meeting. Mr. Eliyahu Katz talked about his memories of Stryj and the engineer Pinchas Fried, one of Stryj's survivors described the situation in the diaspora. This meeting was also attended by the organization's delegates from Haifa and Jerusalem. It was decided to elect a small committee and the expanded council included: Avigdor Rottfeld, Eliyahu Katz, Meir Frankel z"l, Ben-David Schwartz, Moshe Weiss, Eliyahu Eisenshar, Zisia Lentz, Meir Kaz, Shmuel Marbach, Chaim Preiss, Yaakov Boymel, Yehuda Lustig, Mordechai Schechter, Nathan Pomerantz, Pinchas Polack, Shlomo Borek z"l and Zvi Wohlmut.

After a lengthy and lively discussion the following action items were decided upon: Fund raising among the former Stryj residents in Israel, an appeal to Stryj residents in the US, fixed monthly dues, establishment of secondary organizations in Haifa and Jerusalem, creating a card catalog of all previous Stryj residents, personal assistance to the needy, scheduling the next full meeting and drafting policies and regulations.

A meeting in Haifa of the former residents of Stryj took place on October 28th, 1944. Dr. Zvi Heller, the representative of Poland's former residents as well as representatives of the Tel-Aviv Stryj chapter participated.

3

Three major goals of the organization were established:
- A. Mutual aid to needy Stryj new comers and other Stryj former residents;
- B. Organizing a yearly gathering to commemorate the Stryj martyrs;
- C. Publishing the Stryj Yizkor book to commemorate the Stryj community that was destroyed in the holocaust.

The organization's funds normally were not sufficient for loans for all those that needed them. It is to be noted that some of the more established former residents continued to financially support their needy brethren.

Starting in 1943 a commemorative gatherings for Stryj martyrs were held in Tel-Aviv and sometimes in Haifa. The community and its martyrs were eulogized by dr. Joseph Shilo (Schuster), Avigdor Rottfeld, dr. Nathan Kudish, Shimon Rosenberg and dr. Mordechai Bar-Lev.

The gatherings were an opportunity to meet former residents from all over the country. Every year, the organization's committee and its chair-person were elected. The committee membership did not changed much in recent years. The members were: Avigdor Rottfeld – chair person, Meir Kaz – treasurer, dr. Joseph Shilo (Schuster) z"l (passed away in 1958), Shimon Rosenberg, dr. Nathan Kudish, dr. Ada Bar-Lev, dr. Mordechai Bar-Lev, mgr.

Yaakov Waldman, mgr. Zisia Lentz, Yehuda Lustig, Israel Pikholtz, Israel Gartenberg, Abraham Stern, mgr. Itzhak Nussenblatt, Moshe Weiss and Chaim Preiss.

Haifa's chapter committee members were: Menachem Walter, Menachem Hobbel, David Honnig, Munia Kliger, dr. Lindbaum, D. Golding, Moshe Agrat, Joseph Gliecher, Itzhak Engelman, Itzhak Fruchter. The Jerusalem's committee members were: Chaim Neiman, Arye Hobel, and Shoshana Carmel.

Two sub-committees were established:

1. Mutual assistance committee whose members were: Meir Kaz, Avigdor Rottfeld, Shimon Rosenberg, and Yehuda Lustig. Meir Frankel z"l who was a member of this committee was very dedicated to the Stryj residents in Israel and devoted much of his time and energy to this cause.
2. Stryj Yizkor book committee members were: Dr. Shilo z"l, Avigdor Rottfeld, dr. Ada Bar-Lev, dr. Nathan Kudish, Shlomo Rosenberg, and Meir Kaz.

These two committees met frequently to discuss current issues and make decisions. The extended committee met every couple of months to get reports from the two committees and to make decisions about general and fundamental matters.

In recent years additional Stryj survivors began arriving in Israel and some of them needed assistance. Due to that reason and to coincide with the publication of the Stryj Yizkor book, the organization revitalized.

The Stryj organization was part of the former Poland Residents organization.

The Stryj organization felt the importance of its public activity and was encouraged by the support of the many former Stryj residents who live in Israel.

[Page 261] **APPENDIX**

List of Stryjers who died in Israel before 1962

Transliterated by Israel Pickholtz

The surnames in this list are more or less in alphabetical order in Hebrew.

EGOZI, Yehoshua	KATZ, Eliyahu	PROPST, Mendel
IGRA, Shimon	KATZ-CIRING, Riva	ZIMMERMAN, Esther
IDLER, Bronka	KATZ, Izio	ZUCKERBERG, Chaim
EISENSHER, Dr. Yitzhak	LUSTIG, David	ZUCKERBERG, Shimon
ALTBAUER, Pesia	LENTNER, Rachel	ZUCKERBERG, Mordecai
BOIMEL, Mendel	MEINER, Shelomo	ZIMMERMAN, Esther
BOK, Feige	MEINER, Sarah	ZAFRONI, Sarah (ALTBAUER)
BORGMAN-BATAT, Chana	MARBACH, Alter	KESTENBAUM, Michael
BARLEV (REINHERZ), Dr. Moshe	NUSENBLATT, Hersch	KESTENBAUM, Esther
BRAND, Leah	NUSENBLATT, Zvi (ALTBAUER)	KISELEVITZ, Miriam (Shiffman)
GOLDBERG, Beracha	NAIMAN, Bluma	KLEIN, Henia
DERFLER, Gita	SEGAL, Leibush	KRIEGER, Leib
DERFLER, Yosef	SEGAL, Sarah	RATHAUZ, Zvi
DERFLER, Chana	SEGAL, Yaakov	ROTBARD, Dr. Mordecai
HAUPTMAN, Yehudah Isidore	FELDHORN, Rachel	REINHERZ, Herz Yaakov
HOVEL, Avraham	FELDHORN, Soveli	REINHERZ, Rachel Malka
HOVEL, Bluma	FELDMAN, Leib	STERN, Beryl
HAMMERSHLAG, Moshe Leib	FLEISCHER, Moshe	STRASSFELD, Moshe
HENIG	PFEFFERBAUM, Yoel Herz	STRASSFELD, Alta Miriam
HAFTAL, Esther	PFEFFERBAUM, Beila	STEINER, Zalman
WOLFINGER, Henrik	PFEFFERBAUM, Mecha	STEINER, Sarah
WALDMAN, Bronka	FRANKEL, Shalom	STEINER, Sonia
WALDMAN, Rachel	FRANKEL, Rivka	STEINER, Shemuel
VORM, Lunek	FRANKEL, Meir	STARK-ROSENMAN, Chana
ZAGER, Shlomo	FRANKEL, Sheva	SCHILLER, (Schuster) Dr. Yosef
KATZ, Aharon	FREI, Liza	SHIFFMAN, Genia
KATZ, Sarah	PRICE, Rachel	SHIFFMAN, Shemuel
KATZ, Issachar	FRUCHTER, Penina	SHIFFMAN, Yachzi
KATZ, Shmuel	FREIDLAND, Rivka	

Name Index
Translated by Susan Rosin

Page numbers are the page numbers of the original book, not this translation.

Family name	First names	Remarks	Page (s)
Alef			
AVNER	Dr. Zygmond		40
AVRAHAM			55
AVRAHAM		"dayan"	103
	Avraham	Son of Michael. Stryj community leader	26
AVRAHAM	Shmuel	Jewish Expoter	23
ABRAMOVICZ	Israel		34
AGID	Avraham		75, 77
AGRAT	Moshe		260
ADELHEIT	Eda		197
ADLER			100
	Ahara'le	Grandson of rabbi Yehoshuale Dayan	86
	Aharon	Son of Mordechai. Stryj community leader	27
EHRENPREIS	Dr. Mordecai		41, 42, 45,

			48
OBERLANDER	Yehoshua		90, 91, 131, 148, 155, 170
UHERSKO		Jewish community in Stryj vicinity	26, 152
OCHANSKI	Stanisław		47
OLKSZICA	Stanisław		47
UNGER	Babko		191
UNGER	Herman		191
UNGER	Leiser		65
UNGER			51
ONOFRI			66
OSSOLINSKI	Andrzej		46
OSTER	Abba		158
OSTERJUNG			191
VON-OFFENBERG	Baron	Business group	55
OPPER	Josef		133
OPPER	Hana		152, 158
OPPER	Itzhak		133, 143
OPPER	Levi		69, 75, 133, 143, 146, 149, 150, 151, 172
OPPER	Michael (Mechel)		133, 146, 155
OPPER	Moshe		152
AUREBACH	Avraham		132, 142

AUREBACH	Adolf		101
AUREBACH	Michael		101
	Uri	Rabbi from Sambor	169
ORDOBER		Doctor	69
ORNSTEIN	David	Slaughterer	87
ORNSTEIN		Rabbi	34
ETINGER	Hirsch		103
ETTINGER	Yekele		88
ETINGER	Isaac		103
IBNITZKI			69
IGRA	Berko		157, 158
IGRA	Josef		157
IGRA	Isaiah Yaakov		82, 117
IGRA	Mania		100, 144
IGRA	Meshullam	rabbi from Tyśmienica	32, 11, 112, 117, 169
IGRA	Shimon		79
IWONICZ		Resort Town in Galicia	51
ISAKOWITCZ	Theodor		23
ISAKAWER	Eli		81
	Isaac	Custom Lessee	23
EISENSTEIN	Moshe		90, 170
EISENSTEIN	Dr. Azriel		76, 92, 100, 130, 141, 148, 149, 150, 152, 196

EISENSTEIN	Karl		48
EISENSHAR	Dr.		141, 197
EISENSHAR	Eliyahu		260
EINHORN	Mgr. K. (Karol)		98, 99, 156, 157
EICHEN	Hana		153
EICHENSTEIN	Rabbi Yitzchak Isaac	Founder of the Ziditchev Dynasty	118
EICHENSTEIN	Rabbi Hersch		33, 34
EINGENMACHTES			77, 107
INGBER	Isaac		65
INGBER	Mgr. L.		98, 194, 196
INSLER	Abraham		76, 92, 96, 97, 98, 120, 123, 124, 139, 140, 141
INSLER-HEIBER			55
Ish-Horowitz		Rabbi	103, 116
ALTBAUER	Esther		153
ALTBAUER	Josef (Josel)		144
ALTBAUER	Rachel		90
ALTMAN		Dr.	44, 53, 54
ALTSHULER	Eliezer		152
ALTSHULER	Rachel		100

ELI	Meir		81, 85, 86
ALIMELECH		Dr.	25
ELIASHOWITZ	Abule		28
ELIEZER		Melamed (teacher of young children)	88
ALEXANDROWITCZ	Yehuda		25
ELNER	Irka		189
ELNER	Nathan		161, 171
ALLERHAND		Dr.	107
ENGELMAN	Itzhak		260
ENGELMAN-ZIMMERMAN	Hana		153
ANDEN			196
ANSKY	S.		65
APPFELGREEN	Abraham (Buczi)		65, 75, 76, 87, 101, 105, 128, 141, 142, 177, 191
APPFELGREEN	Eliezer		76
APPFELGREEN	Elisha		65
APPFELGREEN	Buszko		100, 107
APPFELGREEN	D.		38
APPFELGREEN	Nolek		107, 144
APPFELGREEN	Henia (Kudish)		196
APPFELGREEN	Zvi		77
APPFELGREEN		Widow	191

APPFELGREEN		Shoe merchant	191
AXELROD			88
EKSER		Professor	75, 144
EKERT	Yuzek		99
EKERT	Leib		54
ECKSTEIN	Shimon		100
ARTIMOWICZ			70
	Arye Leib	Ber Bolichower's brother	24
EHRMAN	Joseph		98, 157, 158
ARNOLD	Leon	Mgr.	99, 157
EHRENSTEIN	Wolf		86
EHRENSTEIN	Yashe		86
ASHKENAZI		Professor	143
Bet			
BAUMANN	Bernard		99
BALABAN	Moshe David		37
BASZUWKA		A village near Stryj ("Die Beshike")	134
BEGLEITER	P.		75, 76, 102, 197
BOYMEL	Yaakov		260
BOIMEL	Yessele		82
BOJANOW		Town	170
BUCH	Leon		65
BUCHWALTER			191
BUCHMAN	Anda		100, 152
BUCCHNBAUM	Ephraim		174

BUCHNER	Zeev Wolf		30
BUCHSTAB – AVI-YONA	Tamar		51, 94
BOLECHOW		City (Bolekhiv)	22, 24, 29, 30, 31, 33, 34, 47, 48, 125, 130, 136, 150, 151, 153, 169, 170
BOLICHOWER	Ber		23, 24, 25, 46, 47
BOLSZOWCE		Town (Bilshivtsi)	103
BONUM	Dr. Hugo		99
BONOMS		Family	154
BUK	Herzel	Rabbi in Lubicz (Lubitsch)	81, 85
BUK	Valtshe		85
BUK	Yekel		84, 86
BUK	Meir		148
BUK	Moshe	Son of rabbi Shalom Shohet	84, 85
BYK	Frieda		149
BYK	Tzippora	Later became Kahana	92, 153
BUKACZOWCE		Place	29, 30, 31,

			32, 47*, 158
BUKSBAUM	Jacob		75
BUXBAUM	Nathan		146
BOXER	Fridel		162
BORYSŁAW		Town	93, 148, 151, 158, 164, 169
BORAK		Family	106, 107
BORAK		Dr.	69
BORAK	Zelik		55, 75, 91, 175
BORAK	Shlomo		107
BORER	Hella		144
BORER	Meir		98, 99
BURSZTYN		Place	112
BORSZCZÓW		Place	32, 112
BATORY	King Stefan		17, 19, 20
BATISZ		A Jew	29
BIDLOWSKI	Alexander		21
BIELSKO		Place	150
BINDER	Sabina		108
BIENENENSTOCK	Dr. Lucia		102
BIENENENSTOCK	Prof. Max		44, 69, 70, 71, 75, 100, 122, 124

BYK	Emil		39
BYK	Dr. Heinrich		44, 48, 54 ,69, 100, 104, 128, 140
BIRNBAUM/ BIRNEBAUM	Dr. Nathan		123, 143
BECHER	Itta/Yetta		133, 146, 155
BLAU	Shalom		149, 150, 151
BLOCH	Yaakov		30
BELZ		Town	18, 39, 80, 81, 82, 83, 84, 85, 86, 87, 170
BELZEC		Concentration camp	178, 190, 191, 192, 193
BLEIBERG	Clara		99, 157
BLEIBERG		Family	55
BANDERA	Engineer		174
BENCZER	Hersch		180
BENCZER			55
BENCZER	Rab		108
BER	Wolf		87
BER	Benjamin		75, 162

BEHR (TENNEBLATT)	Haya		100
BER	Juzek		99
BAR	Yaakov		190
BAR	Moshe		191
BRAUDE	Mordechai		45
BRAWER	Dr. Avraham Yaakov		46
BRAWER	Michael Ben Moshe		46
BRAUNER	Dr.		102, 106, 194
BRAUNER	Rachel		196
BRAUNER	Shmuel		189
BRATKOWSKA		Jewish community in Stryj vicinity	26
BERGER			108
BARDECKI	Samuel		31
BRODY		Community	28, 33, 35, 36, 38, 45, 92, 94, 11, 112, 117
BROCHWICZ	Zundel		28
BROSZNIÓW		Place	153
BERT	Lea		144
BRIGIDAU		German settlement	47
BRIGIDAU		Graff, Galician commissioner	47
BRICKENSTEIN	Haim		82

BRICKENSTEIN	Issachar		82
BAR-LEV (KLEIN)	Ada		100, 102, 127, 152
BAR-LEV (REINHARTZ)	Dr. Moshe		100, 127, 149, 152
BERLASS	Dr.		107
BERMANN	Lucia		98
BRAND	Haim		81
BRAND	Leah		108, 153
BERNFELD	Professor J./Issac Aharon		42*, 65, 76, 77, 92, 96, 119, 124
BERNFELD	Dr. Shimon		42*, 48*, 92, 119
BAT-SHEVA		Group	154, 156
Gimmel			
GWIRTZ	Dr.		194, 196
GABEL	Dr. Heinrich		140
GABRIEL	Josef	Nazi	182
GOTTLIEB	Gdalyahu Halevi		115
GUTMAN			42*, 107
GOLDBERG	Abraham		149
GOLDBERG	Eliyahu		
GOLDBERG	David		42, 43*
GOLDBERG	Yocheved		90

GOLDBERG		A teacher	187
GOLDBERG	Malka		103
GOLDBERG	Moshe		55, 103
GOLDBERG	Moshe Zechariah		76, 87, 101, 142
GOLDBERG	Shalom		99, 156, 157, 187
GOLDBERG	Dr. Shlomo		44*, 48*, 53, 70, 75, 76, 125, 128, 141, 170
GOLDHAMMER	Dr.		139
GOLDING	D.		260
GOLDMAN	Bernhard		119*
GOLDMAN	Regina		100, 152*
GOLDFISHER			149, 176
GOLDFARB	Shimshon		51
GOLDREICH		Sister in law of Dora Mantel	197
GOLDSTERN	Anzel		75
GOLDSTEIN	Dr. Enzel		140
GOLDSTERN	Heinrich		44*
GOLUCHOWSKI	Agenor	Galician commisioner	34*, 36*
GORSKI	Samuel		21
GURFUNKEL	Shlomo		75, 76
GETTINGER	Ludwig		44*

GISZAŁEWITCZ			36*
GIARDZIŃSKI	Paweł		21
GINSBURG	Shmuel		65*, 75
GLEZER	Yankele		88
GLAZER	Israel		87
GLAZER	Isaac		153
GŁOGÓW		Rabbi from - Refer to Rabbi Hertz Feiwel (from GLOGOW)	
GLEICHER			108
GLANTZ			197
GARLENTER	Zvi		170
GELERENTER	Zvi		90
GARLANTER	Yona		44*, 54,
GELERENTER	Jonah		119, 121, 124, 170
GARLENTER	Jonah		169
GARLENTER	Josef Zvi		37*, 44*
GARLANTER	Lolly		86
GARLANTER	Rabbi Meir'l		86
GARLENTER	Rabbi Meir		105
GALANTNER	Naphtali		157
GALANTNER	S.		36*
GENZEL	Mendel		153
GETZ	Elyakum		112
GRABOWIEC		A village	18, 47*
GERBER		A Nazi	182
GRÓDEK		Present day Horodok, Ukraine	17

GRAUBART			107
GROSS	Dr.		69, 157
GROSS	Joseph		53
GARTENBERG	Israel		260
GARTENBERG	Hava		146
GARTENBERG	Lea		146
GARTENBERG	Ruchtche		146
GARTNER	Isaac		148, 153
GERTNER	Naphtali		170
GELERENTER	Naphtali		90
GERTNER	Shammai		76, 87, 142
GRIEB	Engineer		157
GRIMM	Family		181
GRITZ	Mundek		107
GERENGROSS			179
GERSTMANN	Genia		99
GARFUNKEL			108
GARFUNKEL		Brothers	155
GARFUNKEL	Mgr.		157
GARFUNKEL	Ben-Zion		90, 132, 141, 148, 149, 160, 163, 172
GARFUNKEL	Haim		87
GARFUNKEL	Shlomo		87
GARFUNKEL	Leibish Aryeh		141, 148, 150, 151
GARFUNKEL	Michael		99
GER-TZEDEK	Abraham		37*

Dalet

DOBBS	Eliezer		36*
DOBBS	Mark		36*
DAVID MOSHE	Rabbi of Czortków		10*, 115
DOLINA		Village	18, 29, 30, 31, 32, 148, 150, 151, 158, 174, 158, 181
DOLEK			93
DĄBROWA GÓRNICZA		Place	120
DOMBROWKA		Village	29
DUNEK	Sander		98
DUNKEL	Philip		174, 189
DORNFELD	Israel		75, 76
DIAMANT			101, 102, 139
DIEMENSTEIN	Sheva		88
DIESENDRUCK	Dr. Zvi		44*, 54, 90, 92, 96, 119, 121, 124, 126, 154, 169
DAITCH	Rabbi Shmuel	from Sambor	34*

DYNÓW		Commuity	26
DICKMAN	Hadassah		154
DICKER		Pharmacist	196
DELIKATISZ			55
DELIKITISH			70
DAMBESKI	Jan	Cardinal	22, 48*
DROHOBYCZ		Town	38*, 43*, 65, 117, 133, 139, 148, 151, 158, 164, 169, 182
DRUKER	Leo		38
DRUKER	Mordechai (Motel)		37*, 38*, 117,
DRUCKER	Motel		87
DRIMMER	Shlomo	Rabbi	171, 182
DERFLER/DREFLER	Arie/Aryeh		90, 154, 170
Hey			
HAUSMAN/ HAUSMANN	Dr. Wilhelm		107, 108, 162
HAUSMANN	Dr. Leon		107
HOUSEMANN	Isaac		140
HAUSMANN	Dr.		102, 181
HAUSER	Otto		39*
HUSER	Lea		196
HAUPTMANN	Abraham		75, 88, 118, 144,

			145, 146, 148, 151
HAUPTMANN	Aharon/Aaron		54, 100, 118
HAUPTMAN	Eliyahu		100, 105, 118, 141
HAUPTMAN	Esther		118
HAUPTMAN	Haya Branchi		118
HAUPTMAN	Josef		157
HAUPTMAN	Yaakov/Jacob		118, 141
HAUPTMAN	Rabbi Isaac	Rabbi Itshe Shub	77, 78, 80, 81, 100, 101, 118, 131
HAUPTMAN	Menachem		118
HAUPTMANN	Miriam (Mania)		88, 100, 144
HAUPTMANN	Moshe		100, 152
HAUPTMAN	Fruma		118
HAUPTMAN	Sara		118, 144, 145
HALICZ		Region	29, 30
HAFTEL	Velvele		78, 79
HAFTEL	Itshe		81, 84
HUBELL			123
HABER			107, 108

HUBEL	Eizik/Isaac A.		80, 142, 189
HUBEL	David		98
HUBEL	Leon		98
HUBEL	Munish		153
HUTTERER/ HOTERRER	Oskar		173, 187, 193, 196
HOCH	Family		153
HOCHBERGER	Mordechai		54
HOCHMANN			107
HOLOBOTOW/ HOLOBOTOV		Community	26, 196
HUNGARY		Country	17, 23, 24, 31, 32, 39*, 51, 55, 169, 180, 194
HONIG			158
HONIG	Lippa		142
HUSIATYN		Town	82, 83, 84
HOFFMAN	Reuven		157, 158
HOFENBARTEL		Hebrew teacher	88
HOFFNER	Dr.		106
HOROWITZ	Haskele		80
HOROWITZ	Rabbi Isaac	Son of rabbi Meshulam Issachar	40*, 114
HOROWITZ	Rabbi Arie Leibish		40*, 44*, 87,

			114, 115, 116, 169
HOROWITZ	Joseph		101
HOROWITZ	Leib		102
HURWITZ	Mahla		103, 104
HOROWITZ	Mendel		76, 78, 142
HOROWITZ/HURWITZ	Max/Maczik/Machik		107, 144, 146, 149, 191
HURWITZ	Mark		98, 191
HOROWITZ	Prof. D.		70
HOROWITZ	Rabbi Mendel	From Bolechow	34*, 48*
HURWITZ		Family	54
HORNSTEIN	Michael		42*
HORNSTEIN	Moshe		42*, 48*
HORSZOWSKI	Shmuel		143
HAZELNUSS	Donek		99
HAZELNUSS	Joshua	Yehoshua Egozi	99
HEIBER			108, 187
HEIBER (STERN)	Mania		196
ISAAC	Feiwel		25
HEIZELKORN	Mrs.		44*, 140
HILDENBRANDT		Nazi	182
HIRSCH	Maurice	Baron	40*
HIRSZHORN	Abba		77
HAMMERSCHLAG			108

HIRSHENHORN	Kuba		191
KOHN	Dan		96
HLADISZ	Konstantin		28
HALEVI	Ephraim		48*
HALICZER	Moshe		149
HELFGOTT	M.		89
HALFGOTT		Teacher's daughter	197
HALPERN	Abraham	Son in law of rabbi Cuzmer	35*
HALPERN	Dr. Anzelm		69
HALPERN	Dr. Carl		69
HALPERN (HALPREN)	David		44*, 75
HALPERN	Lippa		36*, 39*, 44*, 75
HALPERN	Meniu/Mannes		107, 108
HALPERN			54, 106, 140
HALPERN	Nehama	Daughter of rabbi Cuzmer	35*
HALPERN	Shimon		77
HELLER	Rabbi Arie Leib HaKohen		32*, 34*, 111, 112, 169
HELLER	Rabbi Zeinwil		34*
HELLER	Rabbi Yosef HaKohen		111
HELLER	Sasha		195
HELLER	Rabbi Zvi		32*
HELLER	Dr. Zvi		260
HAMMER	Sara	Daughter of Rabbi Vavi of Bolszowce	103

HAMMERMANN	Henek		99
HAMMERSCHLAG	Michel		76
HANDELL	Michael		154
HENDEL	Salek		99
HESS	Josef		146, 155
HAFTEL	Miriam		157
HERRING			151
HERMAN	Hirsch	Physician	*36
HERMAN	Yeshayahu Meir	Parnas	*36, *39
HERTZ	Shraga Feivel	Der Glogover	44*, 54, 65, 85, 86, 87, 105, 116, 169
HERTZ	Shlomo	Son of rabbi Shraga Feivel	65, 116
HERTZ	Dr. Filip		48*
HERTZING	Moshe	Jew	31
HERSZOWITZ	Haim		25
HESZIL		Grocer	25
HERSTEIN	Dr. Dora		191
Vav			
WAGMAN	Moshe		75
WAGNER	Mordechai		75, 100, 141, 144
WAGNER	Moshe		153
WAGNER	Etka		100
WAGNER	Shmuel		87
WEISS	Shimon		87,
VE HEHEZIKU		A group	154, 156

WAUCHTER***	Kszysztof		47*
WUNDERLEICH	Nathan		67
WUNDERMAN	Moshe		44*, 55, 88
WUNDERMANN	Chippe		100
WOJHOWSKA		Noble woman	25
WAHL	Shaul	Wealthy Jew	24, 27
WOLOWSKI	Henryk		107, 192
WOLOWSKI	Isidor		107
WOLOWSKI		Engineer	150
WALTER	Menachem		260
WAHLMUT	Hersch		30
WOHLMUT	Moshe Aaron (M.A.)		75, 76, 101, 104, 125, 141, 170
WOHLMUT	Moshe Leib		141
WOHLMUT		Family	181
WOHLMUT	Zvi		100, 152, 260
WOHLMANN	Salka		100, 152
WOLFF/WOLF	Haim		82, 180
WOLFF	Chaya		82
WOLFF	Nuta		82
WOLFF	Sender		82
WOLF-ROTFELD	Loncia		100, 152
WOLFF	Koppel		99
WOLFOWICZ	Herszko		25
WOLFINGER	Henryk		98

WOLFINGER		Family (Herman, Clara, Henrik, Josef, Shulamit, Regina)	197
WOLFSOHN	David		93
WOSPOWITCZ	Moshe		25
WARTZEL		Squire of Ruda	27
WARTZEL/WURTZEL	Julius		43, 44, 48, 54, 139
WIELHORSKI	Michał		18
WIARSZANOWITCZ			20
WYGODA		Place	52, 149, 158
VON WIDMAN			33
WEIDENFELD	Israel		98
WISALTIER	Dov		158
WIESELTIER/WIZALTEER	Haim		65, 141
WISALTIER	Chawa	Teacher	191
WIESELTIER	Meir		90, 154
WIESELTIER	Mark		99
WIZALTEER	Zvi (Hersh Wolf)		65
WIESELTIER	Mrs.	Meir's wife	196
WIESENBERG/WEISENBERG	Dr. Abraham		44*, 69, 75, 105, 145, 170
WIESENGREEN	Shmuel		142
WIESENFELD	Judah		98
WITBICKI			*47

WEINBAUM HACOHEN	Isser (Isidor)		51
WEINBACH-ENGELMAN		Family	55
WEINBACH	Maciaka		156
WEINTRAUB	Isaac		158
WEINBERG			93
WEIDENFELD		Lawyer	197
WEINREB/WEINRAB	Yeshayahu (Shaya)		65, 101
WEINTRAUB			108
WEISS (Tzahor)	Aharon/Aaron		90, 155
WEISS (Tzahor)	David		148, 155
WEISS	Zygo		107
WEISS	Israel		142
WEISS	Shimon		76, 87, 142
WEISS	Leiser		81
WEISS	Moshe		105, 153, 260
WEISS	Nathan		149
WEISS/WEIS	Dr.	Lawyer	106, 191
WEISBART	Milek		100, 152
WEISSGLASS			101
WEITZMAN	Shmuel		44*
WILANÓW		Place	22
WILNO (VILNIUS)			136
WILFF	Moshe		108
WIEN	Jacob		107
WYNN	Rafael		103
WIN		Family	55
WINOGURA	B. (Yedidia)		91
WONJARAZOW	Herscz		25

WOJNIŁÓW			29, 30, 31, 32
WISZLITSKI			106
WISZNIAWESKI	Jan		23
WISZNICA			11*
WECHSLER	Mina		99
WALD			91
WALD	Jacob		153
WŁADYSŁAW		King, the IV	18, 20, 21
WALDMAN	Eliyahu (Eli)		131, 157, 158
WALDMANN	Zeev (Wolf)		77
WALDMANN	Moshe		77
WALDMAN	Mgr. Jacob (Tafko)		107, 108
WALDMAN-SCHWALB	Salek		100
WALDMAN	Dr. Israel		69
WALTER	Nathan		151
WALKOWSKI	Andrzej		20
WELKER	Mania		190
WELKER	Nathan		75, 76, 108
WALKER		Mrs.	197
WUNDEL	Yanka		197
WANDELL/WENDEL/ WUNDELL	Dr. S.		75, 89, 141, 157, 162
WARBER	Fishel		152
WOROCHTA		Place	52
WOROCLAWSKI	Hersch		25

VERETZKI		Hungarian town	180
WARSAW			27, 38, 91, 97, 114, 119, 120, 123, 124, 129
WASHITZ	Dr. Ephraim		140

Zayin

	Zeev Wolf	Rabbi	27
ZAURBRUN			196
SAUERBRUNN	Shlomo		179
ZATWARNICKI	Dr. Zygmont		39, 44
ZABŁOTÓW		Town	153
ZBOROWSKI	Andrzej Mikołaj		46
ZBARAŻ		Town	32, 93
ZOLDAN	Alexander		99
ZOLDAN	Emmanuel		99
ZOLDAN	Herman		190
ZOLKIEV ZŁOCZÓW		Town	32, 34, 48, 111, 113
SOMMERFELD			102
SOMMERSTEIN	Dr. Emil		48, 92, 99
SOMMERSTEIN	Dr. K.		98
ZONNESTEIN	Manela		30
ZUSSMAN			107
ZUSMAN	Dr. Hillel		69

ŽURWANO		Town	29, 30, 31, 32, 47, 148, 150, 158, 169
SIEGEL	Benjamin Wolf		93
SIEGEL	Naftali		44, 69, 70, 75, 88, 90, 123, 132, 154, 155, 169, 170
	Zygmunt August	King, the II	19
	Zygmunt	King, the III	17, 19, 20, 21, 46
ŻYDACZÓW/ ZHIDACHOV		Town	17, 19, 20, 29, 30, 31, 32, 33, 47, 79, 81, 82, 84, 86, 117, 118, 148, 150,

			158, 169, 170
ŻYDACZÓW	Grad		47
ZEIDMANN/ZEIDMAN	David		81, 130, 141, 148, 150, 156, 157, 196
ZEIDMANN/ZEIDMAN	Israel		77, 81, 130, 142
ZEIDMANN	Shayke		85, 86
ZEIDMANN	Matye		85
ZEIDMAN	Klara		100, 152
SEIDENFRAU	Bumik		100, 144
SEINFELD		Professor	103, 191
ZEIF	Esther		90
ZEIF	Haim		152
SEIF	Joel		86
SILBER	Isaac		93
ZILBERSTEIN		Dr.	151
ZILBERSCLAG/ SILBERSCLAG	Dr. Isaac		90, 96, 154, 169
ZILDOWICZ	Haim		22
SINGER		Dr.	100
ZELDOVITCH/ ZELDOWICZ	Eliyahu		88, 171, 172
ZAŁOŻCE (ZALIZTSI)		Town	114

ZLOTSHOV (ZOLOCHIV)			70
SELINGER	M.		197
ZELINGER/SELINGER		Mgr./Lawyer	98, 191
SELINGER/ZELINGER	Rivka		152, 154
ZALMAN		Brothers	55
STEINER	Shimshon and Joseph	Furniture store owners	55
SALZ	Dr. Abraham		43, 44, 128, 139, 140, 143
SELTZER	David		135, 144, 146
ZEMAN/SEEMAN	Jacob/Yaakov		90, 93, 154, 170
SEMAN	Rabbi Koppele		79
ZANDENBERG	Donek		189
ZAPLATON		Village	17
ZAKOPANE		Resort town	149
ZAKLIKA		Nobleman	17
Chet			
CHODORÓW		Small town	151
CHOTRINSKY		Hebrew teacher	44, 88
CHIDOROWSKI			46
HAYOT - CHAJES	Zvi–Peretz		34, 120, 121
	Haim	A Jew	25
CHAIMOWICZ	Shmuel		22, 24, 27
CHAIM	Shmuel	A Jew	24

	Chayczi/Haychi	The daughter of the religious judge rabbi Yeshaia Jacob/Isaiah Yaakov	103, 117
	Chayka		93
HARIFF	Berish		27

Tet

TAUB			108
TAUBER		Teacher	70, 75, 101
TAUBER	Shlomo		196
TELLER	Norbert		99
TADANIER	Abraham		77
TAHUN	Joshua		45
TAUBES	Leibel		140
TOROBITSKI	Michael	Priest	27
TURNEBACH	Moshe		30
TADESKO	Moshe		30
TURKA		Place	116, 151, 154
TATRA		Mountains	51
TATARÓW		Place	149
TIWALWEITCZ	Shmuel son of Chaim		24
TEITLER	Levi		90, 170
TEICHER	Hava		152
TYŚMIENICA		Place	32, 33, 111, 112, 117, 119
TILEMAN/TILLEMAN	Yehoshua/Joshua		90, 121, 154,

			170
TALPIN	Sonia		146
TELLER	Leo		75, 141
TELLER	Nathan		197
TELLER		Brothers	99
TELLER	Norbert		99
TANNE (FRUCHTER)	Malka		151
TANNE	Sara		153
TENNEBLATT	M.A.		44, 88
TĘCZYŃSKI	Andrzej		46
TĘCZYŃSKI	Gabriel		46
TEPPER	Abraham		134
TEPPER	Leib		67, 134
TARNÓW		Town	44, 122, 154
TARNOWSKI	Jan		17, 19, 46
TARNOWSKI	Jan Krzysztof		17, 19, 46
TARNOWA-WYZNA		Place	154
TARNOPOL		Town	33, 34, 41, 46, 48, 150
TADESKO	Moshe		30

Yod

JAGIŁŁO	King Władysław		17, 20
JAN KAZIMIERZ		King John II Casimir	17, 18, 20, 21

JASTASZEWSKI	Stanisław		21
YASH	Chaim		93
JABŁONOWSKI	Stanisław Jan	wojewoda	18
	Yehoshua	"Behelfer" (Assistant)	88
JOSEFBERG	Pesja		191
JOSEFBERG	Yetta		191
YOLLES/JOLLES	Ephraim Eliezer	Rabbi in Philadelphia	115, 169
YOLLES/JOLLES	Yeshayahu Asher	Religious judge	65, 115, 116, 117, 169
YOLLES/JOLLES	Rabbi Shalom HaKohen	Rabbi from Mościska	44, 66, 69, 83, 85, 86, 87, 106, 115, 116, 117, 169
JUNGMAN	Mordechai		179
	Josef	A Jew in Stryj	22
	Yoseph Aher	head of the rabbinical court in Przemyśl	34, 111
	Joseph II	Austro-Hungarian emperor	29, 30, 33, 87
JANELEWICZ	Michal		25
JANKILEWICZ	Herszko		25
JERICH	Isaac		77, 82
JERICH	Rabbi Yekele		82

YEKEL			197
YEKELS	Israel		88
JAROSŁAW		Place	154
JERUSALEM			45, 97, 116, 120
YESHAIA	Jacob	Religious judge	103
ISRAEL		Rabbi	27
Kaf			
COHEN	Dan		38, 42
KATZ	Avner/Abner		54, 81
KATZ	Aaron		81
KATZ	Eliyahu		54, 135
KATZ	Dvora		52
KATZ	Michael		55
KATZ	Moshe		100
KATZ	Naphtali		128
KATZ	Joseph		128
KATZ	Mahla		103
KATZ	Isaac		108
KATZ	Issachar		152
KATZ	Pinchas		54
KATZ	Rachel		44, 75, 81, 104, 105, 128, 129, 141, 152
CARMEL	Shoshana		260
Lamed			
LAUTMAN	A.		101, 157, 158

LAUTMAN	Poldek (Napoleon)		154
LAUFER	Dr. Jacob		154
LOEB		Dr.	66
LVOV/LVIV		City	18, 19, 24, 25, 27, 28, 29, 31, 32, 33, 35, 36, 38, 39, 42, 43, 44, 45, 46, 47, 48, 51, 52, 53, 69, 91, 97, 98, 103, 107, 108, 111, 112, 114, 115, 117, 119, 120, 123, 124, 130, 131, 140, 141,

			146, 151, 152, 157, 172, 176, 179, 187, 191, 192, 196
LAWOCZNE/ ŁAWOCZNE			169, 180
LABIN	Eliyahu		88
LADIER	Rabbi Eliezer ben Shlomo		69, 77, 86, 87, 92, 94, 95, 96, 106, 116, 117, 169, 173, 194, 196
LADIER	Fela		196
LADIER	Shlomo		180, 194
LUBICZ (LUBITSCH)		Place	81, 85
LUBLIN		Town	19
LEVIN	Lubka	Naphtali Siegel's wife	132
LUBARTÓW		Place	112
LUBARTOWICZ	Fedor		17

LEVIN	Abraham		66, 75, 76, 102, 104, 105, 132, 150, 171
LEVIN	Aryeh (Lolek)		132
LEVIN	Chaya		132
LEWINSTEIN		Dr.	133
LONBERG		A Jew	30
LUSTHAUS	Rabbi Shaul son of rabbi Yaakov Joseph		117, 179
LUSTIG	David		153
LUSTIG	Judah/Yehuda		148
LUSTIG	Klemens		99
LUFT	Avraham		54, 75
LUFT		Mrs.	55
LAUBERBOIM	Abraham		85
LORBERBAUM	Yokel		112
LORBERBAUM	Mordechai		76, 112
LORBERBAUM	Rabbi Yaakov	rabbi of Lissa	32, 111, 112, 169
LORBERBAUM	Naphtali		155
LIEBSMAN		Dr.	100
LIEBERMANN	Mendel		77
LITAUR			152
	LEIB	a silk merchant	25
LEIBOWITZ	Hannah		100, 143

LEIBOWITZ	Dr. Malka		102, 129, 152, 154, 155, 183, 194, 196
LEIBOWITZ	Salka		100
LEBOWITZ	Sheindel		144
LEJZEJEROWICZ	Mark		25
LIDENBERG	Ludwig		48
LINDENBAUM	Dr. D		108
LINDNER	Yossele ("Skipky")		88
LINDNER	Neta		150, 153
LINDNER	Rena		98
LIP		Dr.	104
LIPPA	Dr. Karl		54, 128
LISSEL/LIPPEL	Dr. Yaakov		49, 101
LIFSHITZ/LIPSCHITZ	Eliezer Meir		45, 94, 169
LIPSHITZ	rabbi Arie Leib	Head of the rabbinical court in Vyzhnytsia (Yiddish: וויזשניץ Vizhnitz)	111
LIPSCHITZ	Yom Tov		45
LIFSHITZ		Family	55
LISIATYCZE		Place	26
LECHMAN		Dr.	100
LANDAU	Hillel		176
LANDAU	Judah Leib		93
LANDAU	Shabtai		177, 178

LANDAU	Naphtali		69
LANDES			107
LANDSBERG	Dr. Maximilian		36
LENTZ	Zisia		260
LENTZ	Rosa/Rozia		99, 197
LEST	Dr. Salek (Bezalel/Zalel)		144, 154
LEST	J.		43
LASKER		Professor	145
LOW	Dr. Aharon		49
ŁEKIENSKI	Nikodem		19
KLERIK/LERIKSTEIN	M.		99
LARCH	Benju		107
LERNER		Teacher	191
LERRER/LEHRER	Yehezkel/Jecheskiel/Yecheskel		65, 76, 142
Mem			
MAHLER	Prof. Arthur		140
MAURER	Joseph		146
MAZTNER	Shimon		23
MEYERSON/ MEYERSOHN	Haim		88, 101
	Malia		93
MEDENICE		Place	158
MOJSESZOWITZ	Isaac		23
MONDERER			67, 100, 108
MONDERER	Abraham		144
MONDSCHEIN			101, 133
MONDSCHEIN/ MUNSHEIN		Family	51, 52, 53,

			55
MONASTRZYSKA		Small town	48, 112
MORACZEWSKI			139, 140, 143
MORSZYN		Place	181
MOSKOWICZ	Josef		23, 25
MOSKOWICZ	Jacob		25
MOSKOWICZ	Michal		20
MOSKOWICZ	rabbi Israel		116
MARKOWITCZ	Shaul		24
	Andrzej	Starosta from Tańczyn	19
MAIDANEK		Concentration camp	120
MEISELS			91, 150, 151, 163
MEISELS		Dr.	104
MEISELS	Moshe		30
Mechele	rabbi	grandson of the Hassidic Rebbe of Stratyń	177
MILBAUER/ MILLBAUER/ MILABAUER	Dr. B./Benjamin		104, 106, 125, 141, 194
MITTELHON	Wolf		30
MILLER			51
MILLER	professor David Heinrich		51
MILLER	Feivel		144
MILLARD	Duddy		86
MIHLRAD	Shlomo		87
MIHLRAD	Leiser		87

MIHLRAD			141
MINIWSKI	Mikolai		46
MINTZ		Banker	51
MINKUS		Nazi	182
MYKOLAIV/ MIKOŁAJÓW		Place	66, 169, 178
	Mira'le	Wife of the religious judge rabbi Abraham	103
MISHEL		Dr.	77, 98, 187
MAŁACHOWSKI	Mikołaj		19
MELAMED	Rabbi Eliezer		82
MALZ		Dr.	140
MELTZER-HAUPTMANN	Liora		100, 152
MELLER		Dr.	100
MELLER		Mrs.	197
MELLER	Aharon/Aaron/Aron		90, 131, 141, 144, 148, 150, 151, 195
MELLER	Moshe		90, 141
MELLER	Yechiel	Wine merchant	48
MELLER	Filko		107
MELLER	Mottek		108
MELLER	Mendel		180
MELLER	Rachel		95, 153
MENDELOWITCZ	Joachim		25

MANTEL		Dr.	196
MANTEL	Dora		197
MANELES		Family	51
METZKER	Itzik		94
MARBACH	Minna		98
MARBACH	Shmuel/Milek		98, 150
MARBACH	Abraham		98
MARGALIOT	rabbi Zalman		111
	Mordechai Ben Bezalel		27
	Maria Kazimiera	Sobieski's wife	22
	Maria Theresa	Empress	27
	Miriam	"Bat Sheva" representative	155
	Mark (Mordechai)	liquor lessee	47
MARKUS	Dr. Heinrich		48
MARKIPKA			68
MARSHAL		from Kałusz	143
	Moshe'le	rabbi of Żydaczów	84
Nun			
NAWALNICKI		Sisters	181, 183
NAGLER	Moshe		98
NAGLER	Henia		99, 132, 196
NAGLER	Jacob/Kuba		132, 196
NAGLER	Tamara		132
NADWÓRNA		Town	55, 153
NOWY SACZ		Place	29
NEUBAUER	H.M.		76,

			142
NEUBAUER	Sarah		90
NEUBAUER	Reuven		158
NEUMANN	Baaruch		89
NEUMANN	Haim		76, 141, 148, 149, 150, 153, 155
NEUMANN	Shulamit		150
NEUMANN/NEIMANN	Rosa/Ruzka		99, 100, 152
NUSBAUM	David	Cantor	65, 77
NOSSIG	Dr. Alfred		119
NUSSENBLATT	Abraham		191
NUSSENBLATT	Pinchas		191
NUSSENBLATT	Benjamin		191
NUSSENBLATT	David		189
NUSSENBLATT	Hela		197
NUSSENBLATT	Isaac		90, 98, 99, 170, 193, 197
NUSSENBLATT	Israel Judah/Yehuda		77, 88, 171, 191
NUSSENBLATT	Leib		146
NUSSENBLATT	Mordechai		191
NUSSENBLATT	Dr. Naphtali (Tulo)		69, 120, 124, 154

	Nachman	One of the leaders of the Bolechów congregation	22
NOBBES		Dr.	194, 196
NEW BABYLON		A farm	29
NATHAN	Yehuda		22
NEIMAN	Chaim		260
NEISTAT		Nowe Miasto	115
NATANSOHN	Rabbi Yoseph Shmuel		115

Samech

SAPIAHA	Theophilia	A noblewoman	27
SASZONIAWICZ	Andrzej		28
SEGAL	Shlomo		163
SADAN (STOCK)	Dov		91, 170
SIENIAWSKI	Adam Mikołaj		46
SOBIESKI	Jan Władysław	King	18, 21, 46
SOBEL		Dr.	180
SOBEL	David		148, 180
SUBKULAKTOR	Moshek		23
SULA			92, 93
SĄDOWA WISZNIA		Place	115
SOKOLÓW		Place	26, 158, 169
SOKOL-LUSTIG	Rivka		153
SCHODNICA		Place	148, 151,

			169
SACHAR	Aryeh		90
STADNICKI	Adam		45
STINAWSKI	Moshe		25
STANISŁAWÓW		Town	35, 37, 40, 43, 44, 48, 69, 70, 71, 75, 112, 115, 116, 119, 123, 157, 169, 172, 179
STANKOW		Village	31
STRIZOWER		from Rzesz&#oacute;w (Yiddish: רײשע - Rayshe)	78
STERNER	Dr. Henrik		95
STRATYN/STRATIN/ STRETIN		Town	81, 87, 170
STRELISK		Town	81, 87, 117
STRELISK	Rabbi from		83
SASZONIAWICZ	Andrzej		28
SIANEWSKA		Town	27
SIARKOWSKI		Cardinal	26
SIENIAWSKI	Mikołaj	Starosta	19
SAKOLASKI	Isaac		23
SYNOWÓDZKO			153,

			158, 181
SAMBOR			47, 115, 136
SAMUELI	Nathan Neta		36, 37, 38, 39, 48
SMORZE		Village in the Carpathian mountains	176
SAMET	Shaye		83
SAMET		Family	55
SENDER	Lippale	Son of rabbi Moshe'le of Żydaczów	84
SASOV			87
SAPCZE	Judith		146
SAK	Rozia		197
SKOLA/SKOLE/SKALA		Small town	24, 29, 30, 31, 45, 47, 81, 106, 107, 130, 136, 181
Ayin			
EBENRECHT		Nazi	182
EHRENKRANZ	Rabbi Itshe Herscz		83
ETTINGER	Jacob		123
ENSER	rabbi Moshe		37, 117
Peh			
PANJOWSKI	Jerzy		46

PANJOWSKI	Felix Oktus		46
PFEFFER	Israel		163
FOGEL	Belka		100, 149, 152
FOGEL	Marceli		107
FOGEL	Fredericka		149
PUHACZ	Maritz		18
FIRESTEIN	Dr. Abraham		48
POLTURAK	Dr. Emil		48
FEUERSTEIN	P.		107
POLAK	M.		143
POLACK	Pinchas		260
POLACK-TADANIR	Mania		100
POMIARKI		Stryj suburb	183
POMERANTZ	Munia		196
POMERANTZ	Nathan		260
POMERANTZ	Roza		44
PONTIAKOWSKI		Owner of Stryj	28, 29
PONIATOWSKI	Stanisław August	King	18, 22
PONIATOWSKI	Stanisław Ciołek		24, 46
PONIATOWSKI	Kazimierz		24, 47
POSTEMPSKI		Stryj city engineer	118
POPIAL	Roman		22
FUKS	B.	Hebrew teacher	88
FUCHS	A.M.		94
PETRACH	M.		143, 148
	Faiga		93
FEIS	Eliezer		152
PEINHOLTZ	Leib		86

FINGER	Shlomo		87
FICHMAN		Lawyer	191
FICHMAN	Tilda		191
FICHMAN	Lolek		191
PILTZ/PILZ	Leib	Lawyer	98, 191
FILKO	Moshe		108
FICHNER	Dr. Nathan		48, 75, 101
FILIPOWSKI	Hieronim		46
FINDLING	Alex		197
FINDLING	Theo		197
FINKLER	Mrs.	Wife of post office clerk	197
FINKELSTEIN	Hirsch	From Slob&#oacute;tka	185
PIKHOLTZ/ PICKHOLTZ	Leibish Aryeh		65, 75, 141, 142
PIKHOLTZ	Isaac		65
PIKHOLTZ	Haya		153
PICKHOLTZ	Lea		92
FISCHEL	Genia		88
	Fishel	A Jew	22, 28
PELED	Isaac		41
FELDHORN	Feiga		153
FELDHORN	Rivka		95
FELDMAN	Salek		152
PROHASKA	Antoni		47
FLEISCHER			183
FLICK	Shlomo		150
PLESSER		Dr.	107
FALIK/FALK	Dr. Julius		48, 106
FELLER	Isaac		98

	Rebbi Pinhasel		87
FENNIGS		Family	153
PESSBURG	Eliyahu Meir	known as "Flick"	88
PFERBAUM	Leibush		76
FEFFERBAUM/ PFERBAUM	Zvi (Hershel)		65, 75
FEFFERBAUM	Mannes		107, 108
PACHENICK/PACNIK	Dr. Leon		48, 104
PRASTAK	Yosele		86
FRUCHTMAN	Dr. Filip/Dr. Philip		39, 41, 48, 54, 101
FRUCHTER			107
FRUCHTER	Henia /Handel		146, 191
FRUCHTER	Aharon		191
FRUCHTER	Isaac		191
FRUCHTER	Shmuel		196
FRUCHTER	Rabbi Aryeh /Arie		81, 153
FRUCHTER	David		148
FRUCHTER	Itzhak		260
FROMM	Ephraim		99
FROSTIG	Moshe		44
PROFEST	Menachem Mendel		54
FRIED	Dzunka		154
FRIED (WOLF)	Mina		197
FRIEDLANDER	Otto		98
FRIEDLANDER	Joseph		98
FRIEDLANDER	Jacob		98

FRIEDLANDER	Zvi Hirsch	the shammash of The Great Synagogue	77
FRIEDLANDER	Dov Joel		36
FRIEDLANDER	Menachem Mendel		36, 38
FRIEDLER	Jonah/Yona		90, 91, 93, 141, 148, 152, 197
FRIEDLER	Josef/Joseph		157, 179, 180
FRIEDLER	Isaac		180
FRIEDLER	Pinhas/Pinni		81, 85, 180
FRIEDLER	Shmuel		81, 85, 88, 171
FRIEDMAN	Bertha		143, 144
FRIEDMAN	Berl/Berel		75, 143, 144, 145
PARIS	Shmuel		142
FRITSCH	Moidel		75
FREI	Dr. Israel		49
FREILICH	Moshe		148, 150, 151, 197
FREILICH	Pnina		154
FREIMAN			189
PREISS	Chaim		260
PRITZHAND	Mundek		100, 148, 149,

			152
FRISCH	Elimelech		90, 148
FRISCH	Ephraim/Efraim		45, 93, 94
FRISCH	Feiga	Ephraim's wife	45
	Franz Joseph	The emperor	169
FRENKEL		Dr.	107
FRANKEL	Rabbi Asher Yeshayahu	Known as the rabbi of Strelisk	117
FRANKEL	David		153
FRANKEL	Yehuda		149
FRANKEL	Meir		127, 141
PRESSER	Dr. Zeev		75, 76, 100, 101, 105, 124, 126, 129, 140, 141, 170
PRZEMYŚL		City	19, 22, 25, 26, 39, 47, 111, 164, 169, 193, 196
Tzadik			
ZOBEL		Mrs.	196
	Zvi Hersch	Horse trader	23

	Zvi Hersch	son of the late rabbi Mordechai	23, 24
	Zvi Hirsch Mordechis		27
CUZMER/ZUSMER	rabbi Asher Enzil/Enzel		32, 34, 35, 36, 77, 111, 112, 113, 114, 117
ZWILLING	Selig/Zelig		76, 142
CZORTKÓW		Town, today Chortkiv	79, 82, 86, 170, 182
CZYSEZ	Rabbi Aaron		81
ZEISLER	Bella		197
ZEISLER	Josef		189
ZEISLER	Heshiu		189
ZIMMERMAN	Mendel		152
ZIPPER	Dr. Gershon		41, 42, 48, 52, 54, 96, 124, 139, 140
ZIPPER	Moshe		151
CIRGLASS	Chaim		85
TZELERMAYER		Dr.	98
ZEHNGEBOT	Adolf		98
ZEHNGEBOT	Asher		98

Kof

KAUFMAN		Mrs.	105
KAUFMAN	Dr. Mordechai/Markus		75, 76, 98, 102, 124, 139, 140, 141, 152, 170
VON KOWALSKI	Ignatz		31
KUDISH		Brothers	152
KUDISH/KUDISCH	Moshe		80, 88, 104, 142
KUDISH	Nathan		90, 148, 169, 170
KUDICSH	Srulik Israel		99, 107
KOHN		Dr.	101
KOCH	Eliezer		153
KHOLO		Place	146
KOLOMEA		Town	36, 43, 70
KULIKÓW		Place	27
KONIECPOLSKI	Krzysztof		17, 20, 46
KOPLER	Dov–Berish		36, 37, 53
KUPFER	Rabbi Moshe		83
KOCZINSKI	Alexander		23
KUK	Eliyahu		150
KORNGREEN	Dr. Fishel		140

KORN	Haim David		54, 88, 90, 142, 154, 170, 172
KORN	Izio		152
KORN	David		154, 170
KORN	Rachel		94
KORCZYNA		Place	47
KURTZER	Leib		77
KURZER	Moshe		88
KITAIGRODSKI	Abraham		35
KESS/KAZ	Moshe		180, 197
KEZ	Meir		153, 158
KINDLER		Dr.	101, 181, 196
KINDER			105
KINJOCHOWSKI	David		25
KICZALES/KITCZELS	Dr. Josef		49, 101, 183, 194
KLAR	Mordechai		148
KLARSFELD			140
KAŁUSZ		Town	29, 30, 31, 32, 47, 111, 112, 113, 143, 158
KLIEGER/KLUEGER	Israel		75, 101, 104

KLLIGERs		Family	153
KLEIN	Benjamin		77, 95, 105, 126, 141, 163, 172
KLEIN	Shmuel		75, 76, 87, 126, 127, 172
KLEIN-REINHARTZ-BARLEV	Dr. Ada		149, 155
KLEINMAN	Moshe		84, 85
KLEINMANN	Azriel		79
KLINGHOYFT	rabbi Haim Abraham	Son of the rabbi of Strelisk	115
KLINGER	Chajka		191
KALISHER	Zvi Hirsch		113
KELER	Mordechai		151
KELLER-HALICZER	Yaffa		150
KOENIG		Dr.	102, 194
KENIG	Isidor		48
KENIGSBERG	Vove		75
KNITTEL			108
KESSLER	Sender	Cantor	77
KRAKOWSKI	Andrzej		18
KROGULECKI	Jan		21
KARWAS	David		23
KARON	Yetta		196
KARON	Rozia		196
KARON/KRON	Moshe		183, 190

KRON	Manny		180
KRONBERG	Lippa		149, 150
KRONSTEIN			197
KRONSTEIN		Wife of the engineer Szatzker	189
KROCZEWSKI	Stanisław		19
KRIEGER	Rabbi Leib		80
KREISBERG			101
KRISZER			162
KARLSDORF			47
KRAMPNER	Aryeh		154
KRAMPNER/ KREMPNER	Zvi Herman		75, 76
KRAMER/KREMER	Ephraim		180, 191
KRAMER	Haim		88
KARNELE		Religious judge	103
KERNER			153, 158
KERNER		A woman	190
KARKOWSKI	Berko		24
KRASINSKI	Zygmunt		123
KRAKÓW/ CRACÓW/ KRAKOW			26, 36, 39, 43, 97, 122, 129, 130, 134, 154

Resh

RAB	Benczer		108
RABIN	Duddy		86
RAND	Mendele	In Jerusalem	79

RABINOWTICZ	Dr. Yaakov		49
	Rabbi from Dolina		78
RADLER	Ben-Zion		75, 148, 149, 172
REDLER	Haim		75
RADLER/REDLER	M.		107, 108
REDLER	Filko		99
RADLER-LEIBOWITZ		Family	55
REDER	Ezekiel		183
RUBIN	Dr. Jonas		69
ROBINSON	Kalman		31
ROBINSON			148, 15, 197
ROBINSON		Brothers	191
RUBINSTEIN			150, 151
RUDA			26
RUDIK	Malka		99
RAWA RUSKA			66
ROZWADÓW			149
ROZDÓŁ			31, 32, 47, 111, 148, 169, 181
ROZHORCZE			26
"ROZLER"	The teacher		88
ROSMANN			75
ROSMARIN	Mrs.		105
ROSMARIN	Dr.		98
ROSMARIN	Yankele		81
ROSENBAUM	Moshe		183

ROSENBLUM	Rabbi Eliyahu Meir Ben Yaakov HaKohen		36, 37, 40, 114
ROSENBERG	Itta		153
ROSENBERG	Nachman		49
ROSENBERG	Feivel		191
ROSENBERG		Lawyer	189
ROSENBERG		Mrs.	192
ROSENBERG	Shimon		67, 142, 146, 155, 188
ROSENBERG	Shlomo		67, 134, 144, 146, 148, 149, 150
ROSENBERG	Shamai		152
ROŻNIATÓW		Town	29, 32, 11, 158
ROSENMAN		Brothers	180
RSENMAN	Dr. Israel		49
ROSENMAN	Dr. Helena		104, 128
ROSENMANN	Shlomo		152
ROSENZWEIG			97, 100, 152
ROSENZWEIG		Teacher	191
ROSENKRANZ (MONDERER)	Tinka		100
ROTH		Dr.	194
ROTH			197
ROTH	Belka		197
ROTH		Mrs.	89

ROTH	Josef/Yuzek		152, 154
ROTBAUM	Zeide		142
ROTBARD	Rivka		152
ROTBARD	Naphtali		157
ROTBARD		Rabbi	81
RATHAUS	Yerahmiel		85
RATHAUS	Rabbi Mottel/Motel		82, 83, 171
RATHAUS	Shalom Leib		84, 86
RATHAUS	Shmuel		83, 84
ROTHENBERG	Israel		80, 85
ROTHENBERG	Rabbi Sender		80, 85
ROTHENBERG	Kalman		80
ROTENSTREICH	Fishel		124
ROTFELD	Avigdor		91, 141, 148, 149, 150, 151, 153
ROTFELD	Aaron		148
ROTFELD	Moshe		149, 150
ROTFELD	Dov (Berrish)		79
ROTSTEIN	L.		108
ROTHSCHILD		Group	55
ROSSLER	Yehoshua		134
ROSSLER	Shlomo		75, 134, 144, 145, 149, 150, 151,

			195
ROSSLER	Rivka		134
ROSSLER	Isaiah		75
ROSLER	Jacob		100
ROSSLER			152
ŚMIGŁY-RYDZ			171
RITERMAN	Dr. Alexander		69
REICH	D.		105
REICH	Isaac		75, 179, 183
REICH	Shalom		69, 75, 141
REICH	Israel		69, 70, 98
REICH	Frieda		98
REICH	Dr. Leon		44, 98, 128, 140, 141
REICHMAN	Genia		191
REICHMAN	Sonia		189
REICHMAN	Chaja		191
REINHERTZ	Jacob		68
REINHARTZ	Rivka		95
REINHARTZ-BAR-LEV	Dr. Mordechai		150, 152, 153
REINHARTZ	Pnina		154
"REINHARTZS"		Family	154
REINER	Oskar		190
REINER		Family	180
REISIN		Territory/District	26, 27

REIF		Chief of police	65
REITZES	Dina		45
RICHTER	Joseph		90
RILOV/RILOW (HOLOBOTOV)		A village	189, 190, 196
RINGEL	Avraham		54
RINGEL	Jacob		43
RINGEL	Dr. Michael		52, 54, 96, 97, 98, 124, 139
RINGEL		senior official from city hall	189
RINGEL		Family	54
RISCH	Leib		180
RECHTER	Tonka		154
RECHTER	Milek		154
RECHTER		Mgr.	157
RECHTER		Brothers	153
RAPPAPORT		Dr.	101, 106
RAP/RAPP	Joseph		107, 152
RAP	Michael		44
REPS	Zvi	from Dubiecko (Poland)	163, 164
RAPPAPORT	Hannah		144
RAPPAPORT	Dr. Shmuel		140
RAPPAPORT	Jacob		153
RAPPAPORT		Dr.	101, 106
RAPPAPORT		called the red carpenter	92

RAPPAPORT	rabbi Shlomo Yehuda (SHY"R)		32, 37, 111

Shin

SCHAUDER	Liza		196
SCHATZ	Leib		195
SZERBSTEIN		Dr.	66
SHOHET	rabbi Sender		81
SCHWAMER	Leib Arye		76, 130, 141, 148, 149, 150, 151, 155, 172
SCHWARGOLD			102
SZWARTZ		engineer from Tarnopol	132
SCHWARTZBERG	Zalman	a grain merchant	77
SCHWARTZBERG	Shmuel		146
SHOHET	Nethaneli		81
SHOHET	Shlomo		81
SHOHET	Itshe		78, 80, 81
SHUSHEIM	Leib		69
SCHUSTER			197
SHUSTER/SCHUSTER	Abraham		82, 136
SHUSTER/SCHUSTER	Frimcie		136
SCHUSTER	Zeyde		191
SCHUSTER/SHUSTER (SHILO)	Dr. Joseph		90, 91, 136, 155, 170

SCHORR	Isaac		90
SHUR	Baruch		65
SCHORR	David		77
SCHORR	Yekele		78, 82,
SCHORR	Kalman		78, 80,
SCHORR	Shmelke		78, 85
SCHORR	Herzel		85, 86
SCHORR	Mottel		85
SCHORR	Meir		79, 86
SCHUR	Moshe		54
SCHOR		Family	177
SWARTZ			149
SCHWARTZ	Ben-David		90, 170
SCHWARTZ	Shalom		76, 171
SCHWARTZ	Shlomo		105
SCHWARTZBERG/ SHWARTZBERG	Avraham/Abraham		54, 90
SCHTOLTZ	Belka		197
SCHTOLTZ	Heda		197
SCHTOLTZ	Hadassah		195
SCHTOLTZ (HELLER)	Henia		195, 196
SCHTOLTZ	Shimon		196
SZTEIRMARK/STEIRMARK		Engineer	189, 196
STURMLAUF	Isaac		90, 170
STEIN	Zeev		158
STEINER	Zalman		101
STEINER	Joshua/Yehoshua		149, 150, 153
STEINER	Shimshon		76,

			102, 153
STEINER	Moshe		90, 99, 156, 169, 170
STEINER	Zvi		157, 158
SCHTEIF	Malcia		196
STEJERMAN - BORAK		Owners of floour mills	55
STEIF	Zvi (Honig)		155
STAND	Adolf		42, 94, 140
STRAUCHER	Dr. Benno		140
STREIFER	B.		146
STERN	Berl/Berel/Dov		54, 75, 100, 126, 141
STERN	Haim		55
STERN	Meir Avraham		42, 43, 95
STERN	Abraham		260
STERN	Mania		187
STERN	Maciek		108
STERN	Moshe		42, 43, 51, 53, 77, 101
STERN	Shalom		42, 43, 75, 76, 77, 101
STERN			

STERNBERG	Magister Abba		75, 76, 157
STERNBERG	Lonek		196
STENRBERG	Leon		98
STERNHAL	Dr. S.		49
STRASSMANN			108
STARK	Isaac		194
STARK	Jacob		90
STARK	Pesach		90
STERN	Benjamin		89
SHEIKE	Esther		146
SCHILLER	Shlomo		45
SCHINDLER	Dr. Nachman		49, 102, 103, 106, 150, 170
SCHINDLER	Dr. Itzhak		49, 102, 103, 106, 150, 170
SCHIFF	Regina		52
SCHIFF	Mrs. Sarah		55, 103
SCHIFF	Haim		87
SCHIFF	Moshe Zecharia	Circumciser	37
SCHIFF	Dr. Norbert		53, 75, 76, 97, 98, 102, 104, 105, 128, 141, 170, 171

SHITZER/SCHÜTZER/SCHUTZER	Dr.		100, 107, 180
SCHECHTER	David		152
SCHECHTER	Yocheved		158
SCHECHTER/SHECHTER	Mordechai		149, 150
SCHECHTER	Moshe		180
SCHECHTER	Dr. Nathan		191
SCHECHTER/SHECHTER	Dr. Shmuel		49
SCHECHTER	Mordechai		260
SHLATINER	Mendel		82, 85
SHLATINER	Moshe		82, 85
SHLATINER	Shimon		82, 85
SCHLAKS	Haya		154
SCHLAKS		Family	153
SHOHET	Rabbi Shalom		81, 84, 85
SZLOMOWITCZ	Gershom		23
SCHLEIFFER/SCHLEIFER		Dr.	102, 181
SCHMORAK	Dr. Emil		52, 96
SCHMORAK	Dr. Wolf		44
SCHMORAK	Regina		196
	Simcha, Rabbi	Son of the renowned Gaon Leib Cunz	27
SCHMIDT	August	Nazi, of Stuttgart	184
SHAMIR	Haim		146
SHMELKES	Gedaliahu		140
SCHMELKES	Rabbi Isaac		45
SHENBACH	Sobele		103

SHENBACH	Rabbi Karnele	religious judge	103
SHENBACH	Fishel		87
SHENBACH	Shmuel		75, 142, 143
SHENBERG	Uri		157
SHENBERG			36
SHNITZER	Dr.		102
SCHNIER/SZNIR	Dr.		183, 194, 196
SHEINFELD	A.		43, 139
SHEINFELD	Hirsch		43
SHEINFELD	Isaac (Itshi)		67, 75, 79, 101
SHEINFELD	Nuty		79
SHENFELD		Family, owners ofmills	51, 54, 106
SHENFELD/ SHEINFELD	Dr. Maximilian		53, 128, 191
SHENFELD/ SHEINFELD	Moshe		42
SZEFT/ SPAET	Dr./Professor		70, 75, 101
SPIEGEL	Zeev (Wolf)		76, 142
SPIEGEL	Moshe		101, 105, 141, 171
SPIEGEL	Shmuel (Milek)		98, 189
SPINDEL-MANOR	Dr.		140
SHAPIRA			153
SHAPIRA	Avner		86

SHAPIRA	Josef	Hebrew teacher	89, 170
SHAPIRA	Joseph		65
SZAPIRA	Libka		155
SCHEFER	Haim		153
SCHORER	Haim		152
SCHPRUNG-LUSTIG	Shprinza		150
SZPERLING/ SPERLING	Salka		66, 100
SZCZERZEC		Location	52
SCHATZKER/ SZATZKER		Engineer	174, 189
SZTEIRMARK		Engineer	189
SHERTOK	Shimshon		157
SCHERLAG	Mark	Writer	52, 97
SCHERER	Ben-Zion		151
Tav			
TEOMIM	rabbi Yosef	Bursztyn rabbi	32, 112

English Section

[English page 5]

The Aftermath of Catastrophe
by Marc Wieseltier

The Jew is haunted by the catastrophe of 1939-1945. Six million Jews lost their lives in Europe. The national psychology has been shaken. By nature and tradition an optimist, the Jew has become an easy prey to disillusion.

He cannot forget or forgive this tragic holocaust of our age, except by an impulse of faith unparalleled in history and by a will of greatness.

This book tells of the great deeds of Jews of our hometown Stryj, and this history will live for all time a perpetual monument after our dearest ones. It is a history of noble men who fought and suffered and persist in living so that our Nation might continue in a land of freedom ruled by free men.

This Yizkor Book of our hometown will add a new page, heretofore unwritten, in the history of the Jewish people.

The Benevolent Stryjer Fraternity consists of former Jewish inhabitants of the township of Stryj who arrived in the United States after World War 11. Having miraculously escaped brutal death at the hands of the Nazis, a small remnant of a once flourishing and populous Jewish community, settled in New York City environs banded together and founded in October 1958 the above named Fraternity.

Scattered over the tremendous expanse of the metropolitan area and neighboring cities and states, they felt a need to get together at least for festive occasions to see each other, to exchange news about friends and relatives in distant places, to comfort each other, to assist with advice and material help to those among us who may need it, to establish organized close contact with Irgun Olej Stryi who have settled in the State of Israel.

At the foundation meeting in October 1958, an executive committee was elected to guide the Fraternity.

The committee consists of:

Marc Wieseltier, President
Jonah Friedler, Vice-President
Sam Seliger, Vice-President
Edward Friedlander, Treasurer
David Kron, Secretary

Benevolent Stryjer Fraternity organized in New York City on the 8th of October, 1958.
Standing left to right: Sam Selinger vice pres., Edward Friedlander treas.
Sitting left to right: Marc Wieseltier president, Jonah Friedler vice pres.
David Kron secr.

אגודת יוצאי סטרי שהוקמה בניו־יורק ב־8 באוקטובר 1958

United Stryjer Young Men's Benevolent Association

What sparked lively activity among the membership, and occasioned many meetings and social get-togethers, was the idea of publishing a Yizkor Book in Israel consecrated as a memorial to our fathers and mothers, brothers and sisters, nephews and nieces, who succumbed to ruthless Nazi massacre during World War II, and a history of the Jewish Community of our hometown Stryj since its inception many hundreds of years ago up to its last, dark clays during the Nazi years of extermination.

We have managed to establish relationship with our brotherly organization in Israel, and we hope, if needed, to be a help not only to the organization but to the State of Israel.

United Stryjer young men's Benevolent Association

The United Stryjer Y.M.B.A. was organized on August 16, 1913 by:
Nathan Stark (D) First President

Dave Brumer (D) Former President
Henich Berger (D)
Max Heller (D) Former President
Kalmen Horowitz (D) Former President
Jacob Schachter (D) Former President

Henry Meltzer, Former President
Reuben Horowtiz
Samuel Kleiner
Harry Goldberg
Max Seeman
Samuel Lichteneger
Joseph Lampel

United Stryjer young men's Benevolent Association

In Memoriam

Max Birnbaum	Dr. Leo Rubin
Dave Brummer	Herman Schottenfeld
Joseph Friedler	Oscar Schottenfeld
Leo Flamenbaum	Samuel Schottenfeld
Samuel Goldfisher	Solomon Schwartz
Harry Gottesman	Moe Sherman
Hyman Gross	Joseph Singer
Louis Haber	Nathan Stark
Max Heller	Harry Wachtel
Samuel Lieberman	Daniel Weitz
Dave Mehler	Hyman Ziering
Harry Newirth	Sigmund Ziering
Jack Patrick	Joe Meltzer
Nathan Rothstein	

From its inception the organization has continually come to the assistance of its Stryjer brethren. In 1915 the first Stryjer Relief Committee was founded to raise money to send to European families left destitute by the First World War. In 1933 the Stryjer Matzo Fund was set up by Reuben Fried and Abraham Sieger and for several years it supported the sending of Passover matzos to the poor families of Stryj. The end of the Second World War witnessed the reactivation of the Stryjer Relief Committee dedicated to coordinating the efforts of all Stryjer organizations to assist Stryjer refugees scattered throughout Europe. The Relief Committee, through CARE, sent hundreds of food packages and it also financed the construction of a house in Israel.

The present officers of the United Stryjer Y.M.B.A. are:

President, Abraham Sieger
Vice President, Reuben Fried
Secretary, Abraham Liebowitz
　Trustees:

　Max Zaum
Jack Birnbaum
Louis Ackerman

Treasurer, Joseph Baron
Sergeant-at-Arms, Solomon Lampel

Cemetery Committee:

Chairman, Louis Lichteneger

Hospital Committee:

　Chairman, Joseph Baron
　Member, Reuben Fried

United Stryjer Young Men's Benevolent Association
Front row, left to right:
　Abraham Seiger, President; Reuben Fried, Vice-President
Back row, left to right:
　Abraham Liebowitz, Secretary; Joseph Baron, Treasurer;
　Louis Lichteneger, Chmn., Cementary Committee.

האגודה המאוחדת של יוצאי סטרי הצעירים

[English page 6]

The History of the old Independent Stryjer Society in New York
by Morris Friedlander

Two months after the big fire in Stryj, in the year of 1886 on "Shabath Hagadol", whereby the entire city of Stryj was almost wiped out, a handful of Stryier "landsleit" in New York came together in June 1886, and organized a Stryjer Congregation.

The purpose was to create headquarters for Stryjer people to meet, to hear news from home, to help each other in need and at the same time to have their own place to congregate on Saturdays and Holy days.

The first President they elected was Mr. Gotthoffer, and then down the line to this day have been: "Schwartzer, Wecker, Becher, Chaim I. Eichel, Feldman, Gruber, Wanderer, Fink, Mittler, Judis, Schechter, Nussenblatt, Friedlander, S. Eichel, Lippman, Fairberg, Opper.

This organization was growing rapidly in membership. The first step was to provide the members and their families with burial ground in case of death, therefore a moderate piece of ground was purchased on Washington Cemetery in Brooklyn.

In order to provide the members with burial expense and death benefits, they decided to join up as a branch in the order Brith Abraham, because the capital of the society was too small to carry that burden. Later in years when the capital and membership grew, they decided to withdraw from the Order and become an Independent society.

At that time there was in New York in existence another society by the name of "Chevra Anschei Zedek" of Stryjer people. The two societies came together and decided to merge in one. In that committee was: Gersliom Ast, M.

Abner, Morris Darmstender, Moshe Wolf Fiedler, Berish Last, Louis Opper, Louis Wurstel. The decision was favorable to both sides and so it was created the "Independent Stryjer Benevolent Society with the provision that each member is entitled to: sick and shiva benefit, death benefit to $ 500, and burial ground.

They also did not forget their home town Stryj, and the people left behind, therefore every year before Pesach, a substantial sum of money as Muoth Chitim for Matzoth was sent to Stryj, for the distribution to needy families.

At the end of the World War Two, we organized a Stryjer Relief Committee, from the three Stryjer societies: The Independent Stryjer, The United Stryjer Young Men, and the Stryjer Ladies Society. The following were the members of this committee: Morris Friedlader, Chairman, Dr. Nathan Reichbach, Secretary, later Sam Uchteneger became secretary, Morris Darmstander, Abe Seiger, Charles Opper, Rubin Fried, David Kerner, Samuel Schoen, Max Zaum, Max Kleiner, Minnie Karnell, Gussie Weingarten, Bertha Baer.

This Committee functioned several years and sent thousands of packages of food and clothing and also money to the Stryjer refugees in concentration camps in Europe and in Israel, also to many others that we had information of their whereabouts.

At the same time the President of the Galicianer Verband, Mr. Sussman, went to Warsaw Poland as a delegate from the Joint, he cabled us that Stryjer people were there, naked and starving and that help was needed urgently. We immediately cabled back to him "one thousand dollars" for the distribution to the Stryjer people there. When he came back to America he gave us receipts for the amount of fifteen hundred and fifty dollars with which he had helped our landsleit there. We gave him the balance.

This Stryjer Relief committee also gave $300 for the adoption of a war orphan in the Krakau orphan home, which was taken care then by the Galicianer Verband.

We also gave $ 2,250 to the United Jewish Appeal for a housing unit in Israel, which was built by the "Amidar", in the name of the Stryjer landsleit in New York. When the refugee camps were evacuated this committee was dissolved.

With the birth of Medinat Israel our Independent Stryjer Benevolent Society took an active part in all undertakings that were functioning in New York for the help of Israel. We contribute every year about $500 to the United Jewish Appeal. We have already purchased from our treasury $13,000 Israel Bonds, exclusive of the individual members that buy Israel Bonds.

We also take an interest in local philanthropic organizations and the Yeshiva University in New York, with a yearly contribution.

The present officers of the Independent Stryjer Benevolent Society are as follows: Charles Opper, President, Max S. Lieberman, Vice President, Herman Schein, Treasurer, Morris Friedlander, Financial Secretary, Abraham Kriss, Recording Secretary, Jacob Ginsburg, Comptroller, Max Kleiner, Chairman of Cemetery, The trustees are: Charles Opper, I. Jonas Speciner, Morris Friedlander.

May the Almighty give long life to our society, to all our members, and to the people in Israel.

Old Independet Stryjer Society

Standing from left to right: Jakob Ginsburg, Heiman Schein, Treas;
Abraham Kriss, secr.
Sitting from left to right: Maks S. Lieberman vc. pres.;
Charles Opper pres.; Morris Friedlander secr.;
Max Kleiner Cem. Chairman.

אגודת יוצאי סטרי הותיקה הבלתי תלויה

[English page 8]

The Stryj Community after 1886
by Dr. N. M. Gelber

Within a relatively brief period after the Fire of 1886, there was an increase in the total number of inhabitants and an improvement in the economic situation. The number of Jews in the city also rose.

In the year 1880 the total non-Jewish population in the entire Stryj District had amounted to 67,623, and that of the Jews to 10,382. Of these 7.515(11.1%) of the Christians lived in the towns and larger villages, with 6,383 (63.40/o) of the Jews. In 101 villages there were 2,537 (24.4%) of the Jews.

Ten years later, in 1890, there were 78,398 non-Jews and 12,744 Jews in the entire District. Of these, 10,429 Christians (13.3%) and 8,241 (64.5%) Jews lived in the towns and large villages, while 3,224 (25.3%) of the Jews lived in 100 villages.

In 1900 there were 96,194 Christians and 15,859 Jews, of whom 15,239 (15.8%) Christians and 10,742 (67.7%) Jews lived in the towns and large villages, and 4,295 (27%) Jews in 99 villages.

In the city of Stryj itself there had been in 1880 some 5,245 (41.5%) Jews out of a total population of 12,625. In 1890 the numbers were 6,572 Jews (39.8%) in a population of 16,515. For 1900 the figures were 8,647 Jews (37.2%) out of 23,205; and in 1910 there were 10,718 Jews (34.6%) in a population of 30,942.

Thus proportionately speaking the Jewish population had grown between 1880 and 1910 from 5,245 to 10,718. As compared with the total number of inhabitants, however, it must be remarked that during the period in question the proportion of Jews had declined from 41.5% in 1880 to 34.6% in 1910.

Between 1881 and 1910 the Polish population in Stryj increased by 260.3%, the Ruthenians by 130.5%, other nationalities by 31.8%, and the Jews by no more than 104.3'%,.

Real estate owned by Jews and registered at the Land Registry (Tabula) amounted to 55,963 hectares (63.8%) for the entire district in 1889. By 1902 it amounted to only 16,278 hectares (20.3%). This was a very appreciable reduction, and was clue to the peculiar economic conditions current in the District.

A change had also come about in the field of education. From the 'Sixties' onward there had been a constant increase in the number of Jews attending the general elementary and secondary schools. Most of the Jewish inhabitants used to send their children to school. In 1885 a total of 600 Jewish pupils attended all schools (including both elementary and secondary).

In 1910 the two secondary schools then in the town were attended by 447 Jews, out of a total of 1182 pupils in all. There were then 10 Jewish secondary school teachers, while a large proportion of the Jewish pupils came from out of town. In view of this fact, as well as the number of pupils without the means that would permit them to continue their studies, a special committee under the chairmanship of Dr. Fruchtmann was set up in 1908 for the purpose of building a Jewish Students' Home (Bursa Zydowska). Between 1908 and 1910 contributions were collected and a handsome building was erected, in which an average of 30 Jewish pupils were housed from 1910 until the outbreak of the First World War.

Beginnings of the Zionist Movement in Stryj

By the end of the 'Eighties some of the Jewish intellectuals were beginning to take an interest in Jewish national issues. The spread of Antisemitism, the events in Russia, the awakening of the smaller nationalities within the Austro-Hungarian Empire, and the lack of sympathy shown by certain Polish and

German circles towards Jewish assimilation, made it clear to these Jewish intellectual circles that there was no point in trying to identify themselves with some alien people, and that the only effective step was to return to the bosom of their own people. As early as 1884-1885 a national movement had developed among the Jewish pupils attending the Gymnasiums (Secondary or High Schools). "Zionist" circles (though the term was not yet in use) were established whose members studied Jewish history and Hebrew, and engaged in debates which dealt with Jewish national and Zionist themes.

The vital spirit in all this was a pupil who had come from Tarnopol in 1883 after failing in examinations in the sixth form, and was now continuing his studies at Stryj. This pupil was Gershon Zipper. He established contact with the Zionist students at Lwów (Lemberg) and corresponded with Mordechai Ehrenpreis Feld, the author of the once famous Zionist anthem "Dort wo die Zeder" (Yonder where the Cedars...), and Abraham Korkis; and he regarded himself as their emissary in Stryj. During his period of studies he organised Jewish national activities in Stryj, which made an impression throughout the whole of Galicia.

At the Stryj Gymnasium, Jewish religious studies were not taught, and Jewish pupils were exempted from religious subjects. This state of affairs was actually against the law, but the Community Council treated it with absolutely superb indifference. Zipper organised demonstrations by the Jewish pupils and their parents, who went to the heads of the Community and compelled them to intercede with the National Educational Council for the appointment of a teacher of the Jewish religion. This step was supported by a petition signed by the parents of the pupils, and thanks to it the Council in 1886 appointed the Hebrew writer Isaac Aaron Bernfeld (1854-1930), brother of the famous Hebrew scholar and writer, Dr. Simeon Bernfeld, as teacher of Jewish religion for the schools of Stryj. Zipper also conducted propaganda for the national idea among the young Jews outside the Gymnasium. He continued with this after completing his secondary school studies and until June, 1890, when he went to Lwów University in order to study law.

Zionist work among the youth naturally had a positive effect, awakening an echo among Jewish intellectual circles as well, and first and foremost among the maskilim(readers and writers of the 19th Century Secular Hebrew Enlightenment literature), among whom there was in any case a recognizable turn in the same direction. In the German and Hebrew press these circles read what was taking place in Jewry elsewhere, and were informed about the beginnings of the national revival.

In 1887 a group of maskilim, headed by Dan Hacohen and Meir Abraham Stern, established the "Shoharei Tushia" Society for the purpose of spreading the national idea, supporting the new settlements in Eretz Israel and fostering the Hebrew language and literature.

This society, which was joined by 100 members, was headed by the maskilMoshe Stern, (one of the active communal workers of the city and a member of the Town Council, who achieved a great deal for Stryj and her Jewish population), David Goldberg and Patrach. Three years later all activities were suspended, and in 1891 a number of young men who were not satisfied with the leaders of the "Shoharei Tushia" Society founded another, which they called "Hayahadut", for the purpose of promoting the study of Hebrew literature. Under the impress of this split the General Meeting of "Shoharei Tushia" which had already been held on the 28th of November, 1890, resolved to change its name to "Haleumi". In its rules and regulations it provided that its chief purpose was to strengthen and disseminate the Jewish national consciousness among the Jews.

The Stryj Zionists maintained close contact with those of Lwów, who used to visit them and conduct programmatic debates. Dr. Mordechai Ehrenpreis, who participated in these discussions, relates in his "Recollections": "In the small and pleasant town of Stryj, on the banks of one of the tributaries of the Dniester, we had one of our most decisive victories among the intellectuals and Hebrew-reading youth. We quickly learned that we could rely completely on the support of our comrades there, and on their good will. Among those whom I came to know well personally were Ephraim Frisch who afterwards became a talented German writer, and a young Jewish merchant named Moshe Hornstein."

In addition to these two Societies, another, the "Admat Israel" Society, was founded in March 1891 on the initiative of Avigdor Mermelstein of Przemysl, with the purpose of popularizing the idea of settlement in Eretz Israel, and collecting money to support the tillers of the soil there. Fifty persons joined and Moshe Lipschitz was elected chairman. A year later another 150 members joined the Society. In November, 1891, little more than half a year after its establishment, the Society sent its Secretary, Meir Abraham Stern, to Eretz Israel in order to investigate the condition of the Jewish settlements and "to seek a place there" for setting up a Colony of Galician Jews. "Admat Israel" was the first Society in Galicia to send a representative of its own to Eretz Israel for the said purpose. After a visit which lasted a year, Stern came home and gave a detailed report. On the 24th of July. 1894, he passed away following a protracted illness, and in him died one of the most active members of the "Shoharei Tushia" and "Admat Israel" Societies.

In May 1892, Dr. Nathan Birnbaum made a propaganda tour of Galician towns, in the course of which he visited Stryj on the 24th of May. There he proposed to the members of the "Admat Israel" Society that they should join the Zion Association of Societies in Vienna. Moshe Lipschitz and Moshe Schoenfeld declared in his presence that undoubtedly the General Meeting to be held following the return of Meir Abraham Stem from Eretz Israel would adopt a resolution in that sense. It was actually adopted in due course, and "Admat Israel", which had originally dreamt of becoming a centre of Societies in Galicia for the settlement of Eretz Israel now became a branch of Zion in Vienna, and continued its small-scale activities in that fashion.

In November, 1894 Rabbi L. M. Landau and Adolf Stand spoke at a General Meeting of the Society, encouraging the members. The establishment of the new Societies led the "Shoharei Tushia", and in particular its Chairman Moshe Stern, to renew and regularize its own activities. An extraordinary General Meeting was held in 1892, and elected a new Committee composed of: Abraham Goldberg, Chairman; Michael Hornstein, Vice-Chairman; Mattitiahu Patrach, Secretary; A.J. Kris, Treasurer; Isaac Reissner; and A. Scheinfeld, Librarian. The Society began to conduct meetings and hold lectures which were addressed by speakers from Lwów, including Dr. Gershon Zipper, who was already known to and popular with the Jewish public in Stryj from the time of his nationalist activities while studying there.

The General Meeting held on the 24th of March, 1894 elected Moshe Stern, Chairman; David Goldberg, Vice-Chairman; M. Kerner, Treasurer; Jacob Ringel, Librarian; and S. Stern, L. Welker, Abraham Scheinfeld, P. Ringel, Michael Raff, Hirsch Scheinfeld, W. Last and H. Pfefferkorn as Committee. At this meeting it was resolved to alter the regulations of the Society, the formal character of which was general Jewish only, turn it into a national Zionist body and join the Jewish national party which already existed in Galicia with its centre in Lwów.

At that time the Socialist Movement also began its work among the masses. Polish workers had begun to organise themselves in Galicia from 1870 on. Boleslav Limnanowsky, and Czerbinsky, author of the Labour song "Czerwony Sztandard"', were the first organisers and preachers of the Socialist Movement among the Polish public. They were chiefly supported by Polish political emigress. Socialist organisations also began to appear here and there among the Ukrainians. They were established by the disciples of the Ukrainian writer and scholar A. Dragomanow. Ivan Franko and Michel Pavelo were the first pioneers.

Professionally organised Jewish workers appeared on the scene only at the beginning of the Nineties. Not as independent organisations, however, but within the framework of the Polish Social Democrat Movement. In 1891 Jewish workers were organised in the Polish Sita Society of Lwów, but within a little while independent societies of Jewish workers were being established. Among them were "Yad Hazaka" at Lwów, "Brüderlichkeit" at Cracow, "Freiheit" at Stanislaw and a Society at Kolomea.

On 1st September, 1893, the Social Democrat Organisation in Galicia began to issue a fortnightly, "Der Arbeiter" in Yiddish, or, more correctly, German in Hebrew characters, under the editorship of Karl Nacher. From this journal we learn that a ferment among the workers was also beginning in Stryj at the Lipschitz Match Factory, because they were working there for 15-17 - hours a day.

Little by little Jewish workers in Stryj too began to organise their independent Society. In 1893 the first Society of Jewish workers was established there under the name "Brüderlichkeit". For official purposes it was a Society for the dissemination of culture (Bildungsverein). However, it had little real influence on the Jewish public and declined even more following the rise of the Poalei Zion Movement.

The political movement which gained the largest number of supporters among both the intellectuals and the Jewish masses was the Zionist movement. In virtue of the fact that Zionist societies had been established in most cities of Galicia, there soon arose the question of a common framework for them. In March 1891, at a Convention of "Zion" members in Lwów, Dr. Abraham Salz of Tarnow proposed to unite the societies of the country in a close territorial organisation for the purpose of uniform activity. To this end he suggested that a countrywide convention should be called for the end of 1891, and should be participated in by representatives of all the existent societies. In order to carry out this plan a special Committee was appointed, consisting of representatives of Lwów, Drobobycz and Stryj; the latter being Gershon Zipper. This Committee also prepared the Convention which in 1892 brought about the union of all Zionist Societies in Galicia within a single territorial framework. A programme was also prepared, and organisational and propaganda methods were decided on. The first Territorial Conference was called for 23-24 April 1893 on the initiative of the Lwów Zionists, with the participation of representatives of all then existent societies. The second Territorial Conference was held on 24 September 1894. The organisational foundations were laid down and fixed at these two gatherings. They were attended on behalf of the Stryj Zionists by M. Patrach, and by Abraham Stern who was elected to the Präsidium on both occasions.

The Zionist Societies made a considerable contribution to the increasing Jewish national consciousness of the younger generation, who organised in secret societies in order to master Hebrew and study Jewish history. Gymnasium graduates and University students in Stryj set up their own Society, whose representative participated in the first Students' Conference held on 25-26 July 1899 at Lwów. On this occasion the Stryj representative Juliusz Wurzel took an active part.

In the year 1903 the "Veritas" Academic Society (afterwards called "Emuna") joined the Association of Academic Societies other than Student Corporations in Austria. The Society exerted a considerable influence on the Jewish youth, and in 1912 joined the Zionist Organisation which was established at a Convention held in Drohobycz on 15th September.

An Organisation of Secondary School youngsters, "Bnei Zion", had been in existence at Stryj, from the end of the Nineteenth Century within the framework of the country wide "Ze'irei Zion" Association headed by Nathan Czaczkes (J. Kirton) and Moshe Frostig.

It was in 1908 that the process of differentiation first began to affect the Zionist youth. Under the influence of the Poalei Zion those students who supported the Poalei Zionist ideology began to set up their own societies within the framework of the country wide "Herut' Organisation. In 1911 Stryj had, a "Bnei Zion" circle containing 6 Ze'irei Zion branches, with 80 members and 5 Hebrew courses attended by 40 students. The "Safa Brura" Hebrew School and Club had been established in 1902.

In 1901 the Commercial Assistants Club, an Organisation of Zionist employees and workers, was set up and laid the foundations for the Poalei Zion movement in Stryj. In June 1903 the Club joined the national Organisation established by the "Ahva" Society of Lwów.

After the Mizrahi began to set up its branches in Galicia, a Mizrahi Society was founded in Stryj as well by Moshe Wundermann.

Following the visit of Rosa Pomeranz in 1898, a Women's Zionist Society was established and led by Dr. Helena Rosenman and Rachel Katz, who served as a member of the Stryj Municipal Council for some years. In 1910 the Society joined 'the National Organisation of Zionist Women. Dr. Helena Rosenman, representative of Stryj, spoke at the First Conference which met at Lwów on 27th February, 1910, dealing with the subject of Hebrew Kindergartens. She was also elected to the National Committee of the Association.

Between 1903 and 1906 the Stryj Zionist Societies came under the Lwów District Committee. From 1902 Zionist activities were conducted by Dr. Juliusz Wurzel, a lawyer who lived in the city until the outbreak of the First World War. At the elections to the Austrian Parliament in 1907 the Zionist Candidate was Dr. Abraham Salz of Tarnow. In 1911 Stryj, like all the rest of Galicia, was affected by a wave of Jewish enthusiasm. Nobody who saw it will ever forget the devotion and support which the Jewish masses displayed for the Zionist Movement.

At that time the heads of the Zionist were Dr. Shlomo Goldberg, Dr. Heinrich Buch, Dr. Wolf Schmorak and Dr. Michael Ringel. Election activities were directed by Dr. Wurzel, who was arrested and had his home searched; a very unusual proceeding in those days.

In the 1911 elections the Zionist Candidate, Dr. Leon Reich, got as far as restricted election with the P.P.S. Candidate Moraczewsky, in -spite of all the efforts of assimilationists to have him defeated at the preliminary polls. However, Dr. Reich was not elected because the assimilationists and their religious supporters preferred to vote for the P.P.S. candidate. In 1907 Dr. Salz received 1722 votes in Stryj, while in 1911 Dr. Reich received 1541 votes.

Very considerable changes had taken place in communal life since 1896. The academic intellectual group had grown, and occupied the key positions in public life. In 1896 there had been three Jewish lawyers named respectively Dr. Altman, Dr. Fink and Dr. Fruchtmann. In 1911, however, there were 16 Jewish lawyers, 2 Jewish surgeons and 8 other medical specialists.

After Dr. Fruchtmann completed his term of service as Mayor, four Christian mayors were elected in succession. Then once again came the turn of a Jew, the lawyer Dr. Juliusz Falk, who served for a number of years.

At that time the Community was headed by Lippe Halperin, David Halperin, Dr. Goldstein-Enzl (all of them descendants of Rabbi Enzl Cuzmer), Joseph Zvi Gelernter, and Dr. Wiesenberg between 1911-1914.

After Rabbi Hurwitz was appointed to the rabbinical office at Stanislawow no successor was appointed in Stryj. Following his departure from the city Reb Feivel Hertz of Glogow and Rabbi Jolles (son of the Hassidic rebbe Reb Meir of Sambor), of Moicisko were appointed members of the Beth-Din (Rabbinical Court). This led to many years of dissension within the community. In 1917 the step-nephew of Rabbi Hurwitz, Rabbi Eliezer ben Shlomo Ladier (1874-1932), was appointed rabbi in Stryj. He was a major scholar who wrote works on Talmudic themes, but was also devoted to poetry and published poems in Hebrew and German in which he gave expression to the love of Zion, the revival of the Jewish people and the beauty of Nature. His poems were dispersed in various journals and were never collected during his lifetime. However, his son published a volume of his German poems in Vienna after his death under the title "Gedichte". His Hebrew poems were also to have been published, but nothing came out of this.

Activities in respect of Hebrew eduaction and the spread of the Hebrew language were to be noted in the years 1908-1914. Dr. Max Bienenstock, Dr. Zvi Diesendruk and Jonah Gelernter organised the younger generation, set up courses for Hebrew study and established the "Ivriya" Club, while the main private Hebrew school was established by Moshe Wundermann. Active Hebrew teachers before the First World War included Chutriansky and Fuks, a refugee from Russia who had been one of the first members of the Jewish Self-Defence during the pogroms at Homel; M. A. Tennenblatt; Kuhn and Naphthali Siegel.

Personalities

At the close of the Nineteenth and beginning of the Twentieth Centuries the Jews of Stryj produced a number of individuals who made valuable literary, cultural and scholarly contributions to the press. and in the fields of Jewish. scholarship and public affairs.

Ephraim Frisch, a noted Jewish author who wrote in German, was born in Stryj (1873) and spent his early years there. At the end of the Eighties he moved to Brody, where he studied at the German Gymnasium and joined the Zionist student group.

In 1892 the programmatic brochure of the Zionist students was published in Lwów under the Polish title: Jakim byc powiniem program mlodzieiy zydowskiej. In it work for Eretz Israel was made basic for Zionist activities.

Frisch then published an essay in Dr. Nathan Birnbaum's "Selbstemanzipation" in which he attacked the "phraseology" of the brochure, which spoke so much of settlement in Eretz Israel, Zion, etc. without knowing that it was impossible to begin with settlement as though that were the national idea; and without recognising that as long as no steps were taken to introduce far-reaching reforms within the communities there was no prospect of any kind of improvement.

In his opinion it was necessary to reckon with the fact that steps must first be taken to improve the social condition of the Jewish proletariat which was undergoing a steady numerical increase in Galicia; and in view of the control exerted by the Orthodox and the Assimilationists it was necessary to operate in the field of culture, and disseminate enlightenment among the masses. Despite his opposition to the very approach of the brochure he could not disregard the nature of the internal and external programme, which was based on scientific and moral foundations and drew the necessary conclusions from the degraded and impoverished conditions in which the Jews of Galicia were living. At the end of his essay he went out of his way to stress the brochure's positive aspects.

From Brody Frisch proceeded to Vienna and soon after went to Berlin, where he achieved a reputation as a writer and literary critic. In spite of his activities in the field of German literature he always regarded himself as a full Jewish nationalist and supported the Zionist Movement. In 1902 he published his novel "Das Verlöbnis" (The Engagement) which dealt with Galician Jewish life. In 1905 he worked for Max Reinhardt as a dramaturge. Some years later, in 1910, he became famous through his book "Von der Kunst des Theaters" (1910) and his novel "Die Kantine" dealing with a Jewish theme from Galicia. From 1911 until 1925 he published a political and literary monthly called "Der Neue Merkur" in Munich. In this monthly he published an essay in 1921 entitled "Jüdische Aufzeichnungen" (Jewish Notes) and a novel entitled "Zenobi" in 1927, which dealt with Austria of the days before the First World War.

Feiga Frisch, his wife (1878-?), who was born in Russia, was also a well known writer, and in particular translated from Russian to German such authors as Concharov, Turgenieff, Saltikov-Shchedrin, Chekhov, Alexander Pushkin, Leo Tolstoy, etc.

Of Hebrew writers in Stryj, mention should be made of Isaac Aaron Bernfeld (1854-1930). He was born in Tysmienice, to be sure, but spent most of his life in Stryj. For 44 years he was instructor in religion at the secondary Schools there. His father, Moshe, who had been one of the first maskilim in Tysmienice and Stanislawow, had provided Isaac Aaron and his older brother, the better-known scholar Simeon Bernfeld, with a traditional education at home which, however, also included a thorough secular and general background. Politically speaking Isaac Bernfeld tended towards a mild assimilation among the Polish majority. In his opinion the Jews ought to acquire the Polish language. Nevertheless he regarded the existence of the Hebrew language as the only possession which could preserve the Jewish people and its culture.

In the years 1881-1885 he edited the Hebrew section "Hamazkir" of the Polish journal "Oiczyzna", which was published in Lwów by the Asismilationist Society headed by Dr. Bernhard Goldmann and Dr. Alfred Nossig. After the measures organised by Gershon Zipper for the introduction of the teaching of Jewish religion in the Stryj secondary schools, Isaac Aaron Bernfeld was appointed teacher of the subject and continued to serve in that capacity for the rest of his life. Owing to his external appearance he could never control his pupils. They laughed at him, though he was a considerable scholar and had something to tell the wild young gymnasiasts, if only they had been prepared to listen. While he was still editor of "Hamazkir" he wrote articles in "Hamaggid", "Hakol", "Hamelitz" and "Hatzefira" on the situation and problems of the Jews of Galicia, particularly in respect of education and schools. He also wrote a Yiddish brochure on "Die Kleinstetldige Assefa", in which he demanded the establishment of Jewish schools on modern foundations adapted to the needs of the times.

He prepared a Hebrew translation of Abraham Berliner's work, "Jewish Life in Germany in the Middle Ages" which was published by the Ahiassaf Company in Warsaw in 1898; and "Abot" into Polish (published in Drohobycz, 1898). His main interest lay in the study of the Hebrew language. In 1926 he published a Hebrew-Polish Dictionary to which he devoted much labour. He also wrote a Grammar of the Hebrew Language in Polish, and prepared a Polish translation of the Mishna; which, however, he never saw in print.

When referring to Jewish teachers and writers who worked in Stryj, mention should be made of Dr. Max Bienenstock (1881-1923), who taught at the Gymnasium in 1912 and who, during the period of the West Ukrainian Republic, organised a Hebrew educational network together with Naphtali Siegel. After the Poles took Stryj in 1919 he was arrested because of his Zionist activities and his earlier contacts with the Ukrainian authorities. Following a trial he was released, but was dismissed from his post as teacher in the Government Gymnasium.

Bienenstock was a native of Tarnow, and co mpleted his studies at the Cracow University. From 1902 onwards he was actively engaged in Zionist work, and became known as one of the fathers of the Poalei Zion Movement in Galicia. He wrote essays and articles in the spirit of the Zionist Socialists, and published studies in German and Polish on such literary themes as 'The Influence of German Literature on the poetic works of Slowacki" (1910), "Hebbel and Heine" (1913) and "The artistic Views of Ibsen" (1913). His book "Das Judenthum in Heines Dichtungen" (Judaism in Heine's Literary Works) is particularly well-known. He translated Krasinski's "Nieboska Komedja" into German, and also the "Sefer Yizkor" (Memorial Book) to the Shomrim who fell in Eretz Israel before the First World War. In addition he wrote in Yiddish on the problems of Yiddish Literature, and participated in the miscellanies "Ringen" published in Lwów, and "Milgroim" in Berlin. During his period of educational work in Stryj he continued his Zionist activities in spite of the attitude of the authorities. From 1918 on he directed the Jewish Gymnasium in Lwów, where he headed the Hitahdut Organisation. In 1922 he was elected to the Polish Senate from the Zionist list, but passed away during the following year.

The well-known Hebrew writer and teacher Eliezer Me'ir Lipschitz was also a native of Stryj, where he was born on 5th November 1879 at the home of his father Yom Tov Lipschitz, one of the first Hovevei Zion in Galicia and owner of a match factory at Skole. He received a traditional Jewish upbringing, and acquired a very wide general education besides a lifelong devotion to Jewish studies. When his parents moved to Lwów he studied with the sages Rabbi Isaac Stekeles and Reb Shlomo Buber, the grandfather of Professor Martin Buber. In Lwów he was in contact with the maskilim and Zionist youth who were headed by Mordecbai Ehrenpreis, Joshua Thon, Mordechai Braude and Shlomo Schiller. He was one of the first to begin speaking Hebrew as a living language, and gathered round him a circle of young men who introduced the Sephardic or Eretz Israel pronunciation of the language.

After marrying Dinah Reitzes, who also knew Hebrew, he became a merchant and his home, in which Hebrew only was spoken, became one of the centres of the Hebrew Movement in Galicia.

In Lwów he set up a Hebrew Teachers' Seminary together with Zvi Karl, and thanks to his initiative "Ivriya" Clubs were established in Lwów and the neighbouring towns. His was a major influence in introducing Hebrew as a vernacular, disseminating Hebrew literature and improving Hebrew style. In 1904 he published his study of Jacob Samuel Bock in the "Hermon" Hebrew Almanac, which appeared in Lwów under the editorship of Gershom Bader. He subsequently published studies in the History of Hebrew culture and literature in the Hebrew monthly "Hashiloah". It was his aspiration to devote himself to pedagogical and literary work. He therefore acceded to the proposal of the "Ezra" Society in Berlin and became a teacher at the latter's Hebrew Teachers' Seminary in Jerusalem, to which he proceeded in 1910.

In Jerusalem he was active in public life and devoted himself to his scholarly studies as well, publishing essays in due course in "Hatekufa" and in journals which appeared in Eretz Israel. He called for the establishment of Hebrew educational institutions based on the traditional foundations that characterised the old-fashioned 'Heder", in which sacred studies would be central and secular subjects peripheral.

During the First World War he was arrested by the Turks and exiled to Damascus, but was liberated as an Austrian subject and compelled to leave the country. He proceeded to Berlin, where he published his little work "Vom Lebendigen Hebräisch" (From the Living Hebrew) ' in 1923. In 1919 he returned to Eretz Israel, where he was appointed the head of the Central Teachers' Seminary of the educational network conducted under the auspices of the Mizrahi (Religious Zionist Movement). The institution developed and expanded under his direction, and he established a model elementary school for training the students and graduates of his Seminary. In the course of time he also added a gymnasium.

For some years he likewise acted as Inspector of the schools conducted by the religious current in the Yishuv, and did much to develop the pedagogical side of the religious educational system.

The essays he published in the press were noteworthy for their beautiful style. His better-known works include: A monograph on Rashi (Warsaw 1912); The Mishna (Jaffa 1922), which also appeared in German in Berlin (1919); a study of the Heder (Hatekufa, Vol. 7); "Conversations" on religious themes under the nom de plume Azariah ibn Bezalel; essays on educational questions (Hashiloah, Vols, 22, 37); and on Agnon (Hashiloah, Vol. 22), which also appeared as a separate volume, Berlin 1920.

All his life long he laboured to unify Jewish education on a basis of the Torah and modem general knowledge.

He passed away in Jerusalem on 24th. Tammuz 5706 (1946).

Among Hebrew writers of the more recent generation mention must be made of Dr. Zvi Diesendruck 1890-1941). He came from a well-to-do family, and his father Yehuda Leib, a Czortkow Hassid, educated him in the spirit of tradition and Hassidim at the klois (conventicle) of Stryj's famous scholar Reb Hirsch Wolff. However, his son who was a prodigy gradually became more free in spirit, and at night he would conceal secular works under the large folios of the Talmud. Zionist students at the gymnasium gave him lessons and prepared him for the gymnasium examinations.

While he was still in Stryj he took part in the activities of the Galician Hebrew Movement, and together with his friend Jonah Gelernter he established the Ivriva Club. In 1909 he left Stryj and proceeded to Vienna, where he matriculated and studied philosophy and classical languages at the University. He was the pupil of the two well-known professors of philosophy, Steher and Jodl. In 1912 he went to Eretz Israel where he spent a year as a teacher. From 1913 until 1916 he taught in Berlin, and then served in the Austrian army. After the close of the First World War he settled in Vienna, where he became a teacher of Philosophy and Hebrew literature at the Hebrew Pedagogical Institute headed by Professor Dr. Zvi Peretz Chajes. In 1922 he received the degree of Doctor of Philosophy. From 1925 until 1927 he taught at the Rabbinical Seminary of Dr. Stephen Wise in New York, and was then invited to be lecturer in Jewish philosophy at the Hebrew University. After two years, however, he left Eretz Israel and was appointed Professor at the Hebrew Union College in Cincinnatti, to replace Professor Dr. David Neumark. He was also the vice-chairman of the American Academy of Jewish Research, and editor of the Hebrew Union College Annual.

He had already commenced his research activities before the First World War. His first essay was published in Gershon Bader's journal "Haet" (Lwów 1906). He contributed to "Hashiloah", where he published his first philosophical study, and later to "Revivim" edited by J. H. Brenner and G. Schofmann in Lwów, also to "Haolam", and "Hatekufa". In the years 1918-1919 he issued the monthly "Gevulot" in Vienna together with G. Schoffmann.

He translated Plato's Phaedrus, Gorgias, Crito and Republic from Greek into Hebrew for the Stybel Publishing Company.

His German works included: Struktur und Charakter des Platonischen Phaidros, Vienna, 1927 (Structure and Character of Plato's Phaedrus); and Maimonides Lehre von der Prophetie (Maimonides' Doctrine of Prophecy, New

York, 1927). In the Israel Abrahams Memorial Volume he published: Die Teleologie bei Maimonides (Teleology in Maimonides). In the Hebrew Union College Annual College 1928 he contributed: Samuel and Moses ibn Tibbon on Maimonides' Theory of Providence; and subsequently: The Philosophy of Maimonides' Theory of Negation of Privation (proceedings TVI 1934-1935).

Diesendruck had a deep comprehension of philosophical problems and could handle them in a clear and exact Hebrew style. He was one of the deepest research students of our new literature.

Jonah Gelernter (born in Stryj 1889) worked in the Hebrew Movement of Stryj and Vienna together with Zvi Diesendruck. He published stories and essays in the Hebrew press ("Hamizpeh" and "Hayom"). In Vienna he devoted himself to Hebrew teaching. Between the years 1923 and 1938 he taught Hebrew at the Chajes Jewish Gymnasium. In Vienna he issued a monthly "Devarenu" and headed the Histadrut Ivrit. Following the Nazi invasion of Austria he escaped to Paris, where he was murdered by the Nazis in 1941.

Dr. Abraham Jacob Braver, the noted historian and geographer, was born in Stryj on 4th Nissan 5644 (1884), and studied at the gymnasium there. After completing his studies at the Vienna University and receiving his doctorate there, he taught at the Tarnopol Gymnasium in 1910-1911. He came to Eretz Israel in 1912 and became a teacher at the Teachers' Seminary founded by the Ezra Society of Berlin (1912-1914). In the years 1914-1918 he taught in Salonika and Constantinople, and in 1920 he returned to Eretz Israel again to teach at the Teachers' Seminary. He commenced his scholarly publications with an essay in the "Kwartalnik Historyczny" Quarterly (1907) on Fergen, the first Polish Commissioner for Galicia. In 1910 he published a work in Vienna on "Galizien wie es an Oesterreich kam" (How Galicia came to Austria) which was received with considerable approval by historical circles in Austria. He also published a valuable Hebrew study in "Hashiloah" (Vol. 23) on "The Emperor Joseph 11 and the Jews of Galicia". While in Tarnopol he found a manuscript in the Perl Library by the. well-known eighteenth-century figure

Ber of Bolechow, entitled "Divrei Bina" (Words of Understanding), dealing with Jacob Frank the sectary and the famous debate held between the Frankists and representatives of the Jewish community at Lwów in 1759. This he published in "Hashiloah" under the title "A new Hebrew Source on the Frankists".

In Eretz Israel he devoted himself to the geography of the country, and published many studies in this field. His standard work on this subject, "Haaretz" (The Land) has gone into a large number of editions.

His father Michael ben Moshe Braver 18 62 -1949), who was a well-known writer on rabbinical subjects, lived in Stryj between 1882 and 1902 and took an active part in communal affairs. While in Stryj he contributed to "Ivri Anochi", "Hamizpeh" and "Mahazikei Hadat".

Among the younger communal workers of Stryj mention should be made of Dr. Abraham Insler (1893-1938), who received a non-religious liberal education at his home, but at the Gymnasium joined a Zionist circle and studied Hebrew, Yiddish and Jewish history. He represented the Zionist Gymnasiast youth at the country wide conferences of "Ze'irei Zion" which were held in secret every year at Lwów, and made his mark there with his addresses and lectures. After matriculating he studied law at the Lwów and Vienna Universities and enthusiastically engaged in Zionist activities. He served as chairman of the "Emuna" Academic Society in Stryj, and was one of the founders of the Academic Zionist Federation (HAZ). He published articles on current problems in the Polish Zionist monthlies "Hamoriah" and "Hashahar". At the commencement of the First World War he proceeded to Vienna, where he became an assistant of Dr. Nathan Birnbaum in the "Juedisches Kriegs-Archive" (Jewish War Archives).

On 1918 he returned to Stryj where he led active national workers, organised the National Committee and headed all public activities of the Jewish population.

When the daily "Chwila" was started in Lwów in 1921 he joined the staff. He was elected member of the East Galician Zionist Executive, and was a member of the Polish Sejm (Parliament) 1922-1927. At the Jewish Sejm Members' Club in Warsaw he joined the Isaac Gruenbaum group, which led to differences of opinion between him and the Zionist Executive in Lwów. In 1925 he was elected as Community Chairman in Stryj, but resigned as he then moved to Lwów. In Galicia he established the Radical Zionist Group founded by Isaac Gruenbaum, and disregarded the resolution of the Galician Zionists by supporting the Minorities Bloc of the Polish Sejm in 1928. He was re-elected and remained in the Sejm until 1930, taking an active part in the administrative and legal committees. In 1931-1932 he edited the Warsaw Zionist daily "Nowe Slowo".

Following differences of opinion with the management of the daily he left Warsaw and began to publish the weekly "Opinja" in Lwów. This was followed by "Nasza Opinja". which was marked by its high literary and publicist level and standing.

As a publicist Insler was marked by a high political level and his clear grasp of the problems with which he dealt in his essays.

Two fundamental works by Dr. Insler revealed the anti-Jewish factors and background of the pogrom which took place in Lwów in November 1918, and was organised by the Poles in strictly, military fashion. These works, "Dokumenty" and "Legendy i fakty", Lwów 1937), clearly demonstrated the part played by the Polish army in the pogrom, and were banned by the Polish Government. Dr. Insler also published a monograph in Polish on Dr. Gershon Zipper (1923).

Dr. Tulo Naphtali Nussenblatt was a member of the "Bnei Zion" Gymnasium Zionist circle founded by Dr. Insler. He later joined "Hashomer", from which the "Hashomer Hatza'ir" Movement developed after the First World War, during which he was an officer in the Austrian army, was wounded at the Front and was decorated.

After the War he settled in Vienna, studied law and obtained a doctorate. Instead of devoting himself to his profession he engaged in literary and publicist activities, specialising in the period and personal history of Dr. Theodore Herzl. He collected much material and published essays and studies in the Zionist press and miscellanies. In 1929 he published his first volume: Zeitgenossen ueber Herzl (Bruenn) (Contemporaries on Herzl). He collected the reminiscences of Herzl's contemporaries in his book, "Ein Volk unterwegs zum Frieden" (Vienna 1933) (A Nation en route to peace). He also published valuable material dealing with the political activity of Dr. Herzl, particularly at the time of the Hague Peace Conference of 1899.

In 1937 he began to issue an annual in Vienna, which was devoted to the study of the history of Herzl and the Zionist Movement, under the title, "Theodor Herzl Jahrbuch". However, he succeeded in publishing only the first volume, containing hitherto unknown material and historical essays on Dr. Herzl and the early days of the Zionist Movement.

After the Nazi entry into Austria he escaped to Poland, settling at Dombrowa-Gornice near Bendin, where his son-in-law lived. During the Second World War he moved to Warsaw and took an active part in Ghetto life and also in underground activities.

In September 1942 he was kidnapped by the Germans, who took him to one of the closed camps in the Lublin district where he was murdered.

Dr. Nussenblatt, who was a collector, gathered a large collection of letters and manuscripts by Dr. Herzl. All this material was lost in the Warsaw Ghetto.

[English page 19]

Stryj Between the Two World Wars
by Dr. Natan Kudish

Stryj during the First World War, 1914 – 1918:

During the Tsarist Russian invasion of Galicia, 1914-1915, many Jews fled from Stryj westwards to Czechovakia, Hungary, and in particular – Vienna. However, the great majority stayed in the city, where they suffered greatly at the hands of the Russians. A Committee was set up to represent the population vis-a-vis the military occupation authorities. When the Russians retreated in 1915 they took a number of Jews with them as "hostages".

The Austro-Hungarian Empire began to collapse in Winter 1917 – 1918. Strikes and hunger demonstrations were held throughout the entire Imperial territories. In Stryj the Hunger Demonstration was held after the Passover. The local Jews mobilised a self-defence force of 40 men from various parties and academic societies. The Polish and Ukrainian demonstrators, including many members of the underworld, passed along Potocki Street towards the avenue that leads to the railway station, while the self-defence men kept level with them on the pavements. The demonstrators did not touch any of the Christian shops they passed, but when they reached the avenue they attacked the Jewish kiosk owned by Reinhartz. Thereupon the sticks of the Jewish self-defence men came down on their heads. The startled rioters promptly retreated. The self-defence group also protected the Jews of Stryj during the period of confusion which accompanied the passage of authority from the Austrians to the Ukrainians in 1918.

Institutions and Societies

The Community (Kehilla):

Until 1918 the affairs of the Stryj Community were conducted by pamassim (synagogue and congregational presidents) and local notables. From the Mid-Nineteenth century the heads of the community were: Lippe Halperin, David Halperin, Zelik Borak, Isaac Sheinfeld, Abraham Luft, Dr. Fichner and Dr. Wiesenberg. After the downfall of Austria, Stryj was included within the "West Ukrainian State" the Government of which proclaimed national equal rights for all minorities. The Stryj Zionists then won community control from the Assimilationists, and a Jewish National Council (Jüdischer Nationalrat) was set up containing 48 representatives of all parties. Zionist: Dr. Shlomo Goldberg, Dr. Zeev Presser, Dr. Morclechai Kaufman, Dr. S. Wandell, Dr. Rosmann, Professor Maks Bienenstock, Professor Spät, Dr. Norbert Schiff, Shalom Reich, Naphtali Siegel, Magister Sternberg, the teacher Tauber, Rachel Katz, Evelina Apfelstein, M. Wohlmut, Berel Stern, Ben-Zion Radler, Jacob Buksbaum, Shmuel Shenbach, Leibush Pickholz, Shmuel Ginsburg. Poalei Zion: Levi Opper, Abraham Kaufmann, Berel Friedman, Shlomo Rossler, Betty Friedman. Economic organisations and societies: Abraham Levin, Israel Klieger, Davidman. Religious bodies (synagogues): Haim Redler, Shalom Stern, Shmuel Klein, Shlomo Garfunkel, Abraham Egid, Moidel Fritsch, Zvi Fefferbaum. The Bund: Israel Dornfeld, Isaiah Rossler, Moshe Wagman, Nathan Welker, Vove Kenigsberg, Benjamin Ber, Leib Tepper, Fanny Horowitz, Zvi Akser.

In February 1919 the Poles occupied the city. The composition of the National Council was almost identical with that elected during the period of Ukrainian rule. However, the Polish authorities did not view the rise of the Jewish National Movement with approval, and appointed P. Begleiter as head of the Community. After two years under his leadership all the national parties elected the following Community Council: Dr. Z. Presser, Dr. M. Kaufmann,

Magister Sternberg, Zvi Krampner, Abraham Apfelgruen, Leibush Pickholz, Shalom Stern, Abraham Levin, Wolf Spiegel, Joseph Leibovitz, Shalom Schwartz, Shlomo Garfunkel, Israel Dornfeld and Nathan Welker.

In 1924 the first elections to the Kehilia were held and led to a victory for the Zionist lists. The Kehilla head elected was Dr. Insler; but the Polish authorities cancelled the legal elections, and new ones were announced in 1925. Once again the Zionist list triumphed, with the election of Dr. Z. Presser, Magister Abba Sternberg, Dr. N. Schiff, Zvi Krampner, Leibush Pickhoiz, EleazarApfelgruen, ShmuelKlein, Israel Dornfeld and Shalom Stern. The Agudas Israel was defeated. Proportional elections to the Kehilla were held for the first time in 1928, and as in subsequent ones of 1929 and 1932 the greater part of the Jewish population voted for the Zionist lists and against the Assimilationists and the ultra-religious groups. In 1936 the community was headed by Dr. Presser, with Dr. Mishel as vice-chairman, Benjamin Klein as Council Chairman and Israel Zeidman as vice-chairman. However, there were differences of opinion with regard to the choice of a new rabbi after the death of Rabbi Ladier; and the authorities entrusted the Kehilla to those who were prepared to do what was wanted by the Polish District Commissioner. The Jewish public did not submit to this arbitrary appointment and demonstrated its support of the Kehilla Executive headed by Dr. Presser. This was the last Community Council of Stryj Jewry.

The "Safa Brura" Hebrew School:

One of the signs of the spiritual revival at the beginning of the 20th. century in our town was the opening of a Hebrew School for Jewish children. The first teachers were Axelrod, B. Fuks from Russia, Sapirstein, Hofenbartel, Chotrinsky, M. Wundermann, Tennenblatt and Naftali Siegel. Following the victory of the Zionist Movement after the First World War, the school was fitted into the framework of the Hebrew School system set up all over Poland. The number of pupils increased by hundreds, and the standard of studies also improved. Though the school passed through some critical periods, the devotion of the teachers M. Helfgott, Shapira and David Kom, and the activity of the communal workers Moshe Spiegel, Baruch Neumann, Dr. S. Wandel, Dr. Roth, Jonah Friedler and the treasurer Apfelgruen enabled it to fulfil its educational functions. The Catastrophe brought this source of the national revival to an end as well.

The Ivriya Society:

Hebrew began to be spoken by youngsters of all sections and circles of the community. At the close of the First World War an "Ivriya" Society was founded in Stryj, as in so many other towns of Galicia. The Society met at the home of Benjamin Stern in the "Rynek". Lectures and discussions were held on subjects and problems of old and new Hebrew literature. The first Hebrew Library was established, and spread the knowledge of Hebrew among the student and working youth. The founders and pioneers of the Society were Naphtali Siegel, Levi Teitler, Isaac Sturmlauf, Rachel Altbauer, Yocheved Goldberg, Sarah Neubauer, Ben-David Schwartz, Aryeh Derfler, Shalom Reich, Dr. Zvi Diesendruk, Zvi Gelernter, H. David Korn, Isaac Schorr, Aryeh Sachar, Joseph Richter, Mrs. Seif, Joshua Tileman, Dr. Joseph Schuster, (Shilo), Joshua Oberländer, Dr. Nathan Kudisch, Jonah Friedler, (now vice-president of the Benevolent Stryjer Fraternity, N.Y.), Naphtali Gelernter, Moshe Meller, Aron Meller, Moshe Eisenstein, Isaac Nussenblatt, Isaac Silberschlag, Jacob Stark, Jacob Zeman, Moshe Steiner, Pessah Stark, Meisels, Esther Altbauer and Avigdor Rotfeld.

The Academic Societies

From the commencement of the Twentieth Century an increasing number of boys and girls were sent to the secondary schools and the universities by their parents. Former pupils of the Stryj secondary schools included such outstanding Zionist figures as Dr. Gershon Zipper, Senator Michael Ringel, Dr. Abraham Insler and Dr. Emil Schmorak. With the increasing maturity of the National Movement, Jewish academic student societies were set up in Galicia. Even before the First World War an academic society called "Veritas" had been founded in Stryj. After the War there was set up, in addition to the "Emuna" (formerly "Veritas") Society, the further societies Hebronia, Kadima, Makkabia and Z.A.S.; the latter being a Society of Zionist Socialist Students. Almost all the Jewish academic youth of the town belonged to one or other of these. After 1926 all these societies became Corporations, although girls were also accepted as members. Members acquired Jewish culture in addition to the general education obtained at the Government institutions. Their sense of national consciousness was deepened, their physical strength increased thanks to sports activities, and their sense of national pride and self-respect was fostered. The members of the "Emuna" Society came from all the popular and Zionist parties.

The presidents of the "Emuna" Society and its initial members were Dr. M. Ringel and Dr. A. Insier, who were followed by: Dr. Rosenzweig, the writer Mark Scherlag, Dr. N. Schiff, D. M. Kaufmann, Dr. I. Reich, Magister K. Einhorn, Mag. Selinger, Mag. Ingber and others. The society was headed by the Senior and three co-Seniors, and there were various active committees. Active members and office-holders were Mark Hurwitz, Leon Sternberg, Isaar-Feller, Israel Weidenfeld, Joseph Ehrman, Shmuel Spiegel, Moshe Nagler, Judah Wiesenfelcl, Leon Hubel, Henryk Wolfinger, Lila Grossmann, Minna Marbach, Frieda Reich, Lugia Bermann, Leib Pilz, Adolf Zehngebot, Asher Zehngebot, Otto Friedlander, Jacob Friedlander, Rena Lindner, Aaron Hoffmann, Reuben Hoffmann, David Hubel, Abraham and Shmuel Marbach, lzchak Nussenblatt, Meir Borer, Joseph Friedlaender.

The Hebronia Society was close to the Revisionist Movement in its ideology. When it was founded it was headed by Joseph Friediaender, First Senior, Joshua Hazelnuss, Secretary and "Fuchsmajor" (Chief of New members, who were called "foxes"), M. Borer, co-Senior, Ephraim Fromm, Emmanuel Zoldan, Alexander Zoldan, Klemens Lustig, Clara Bleiberg, Minna Wechsler, Henia Nagler, Malka Rudik, Rosa Neumann, Rosa Lentz, Genia Grossmann, Shalom Goldberg, Michael Garfunkel, Karol Einhorn, Icchak Nussenblatt, Leon Arnold and Moshe Steiner.

Kadima, the second academic society, was founded in 1922, and its membership increased from year to year. This wasthe golden age of the Jewish academic corporations in Poland. Kadima participated in all the activities and aims of Zionist circles in Stryj. Special mention should be made of the active members of the society who were martyred, and also those who were saved and have survived. Kadima's Seniors were Dunek Sander, Bernard Baumann, Srulik Kudisch, Wolff Koppel, Uzek Ber, Filko Redler, Co-seniors were M. Lerik, Hugo Bonum, The "Fuchsmajoren" were Yuzek Ekert, Marek Wieseltier (now President of the Benevolent Stryjer Fraternity N.Y.) and Henek Hammermann.

The Z. A. S. S.:

The year 1931 saw the establishment of the Zionist Socialist Academic Society of the Hitahdut Party. Its members organised and based their activities on the standards of the Israel Labour Movement and the Mifleget Poalei Eretz Israel, or Mapai Party. The initiators were: Dr. Azriel Eisenstein, Dr. Ada Bar-lev-Klein, Dr. Moshe Bar-lev-Reinhartz.

Many members of the Z. A. S. S. proceeded to Eretz Israel in due course. The active members were: Klara Seidman, Henek Mayer, Mandek Pritzhand, Moshe Hauptmann, Anda Buchman, Salka Wohlmann, Ruzka Neimann, Belka Vogel, Lea Meltzer-Hauptmann, Loncia Wolf-Rotfelcl, etc.

Society of Friends of the Hebrew University:

The local institutions of the Jewish national spiritual revival included the Society of Friends of the Hebrew University in Jerusalem. It should be noted that Stryj was the first provincial city in Galicia to establish such a Society; and its activities were crowned with success.

Committee for the Rescue of German Jews:

In 1938, when the Nazis cruelly drove the Jews of Polish origin in the Reich back to Poland, several dozen refugees arrived in Stryj. They were aided by the Committee together with the community.

Toynbee Hall:

A branch of the Education Movement was active in our town, and had lecture halls which were known as "Toynbee Hall" after the centre in East London. These halls served as a centre for the dissemination of national education, Jewish knowledge and scholarship, and Zionist theory among extensive circles in the city.

WIZO:

In 1929 a branch of WIZO (Women's International Zionist Organisation) was established under the chairmanship of the talented and devoted communal worker Mrs. Rachel Katz, and won Jewish women to action for the Zionist idea. During the final years Dr. Rosmarin and Mrs. Kaufmann were also active there.

The Amateur Theatre:

The Yiddish Popular Theatre Movement developed in Poland and Russia early in the Twentieth Century. Dramatic groups of young men and women, lovers of the Yiddish Theatre, were set up in every large and small town.

In Stryj the Dramatic Circle was founded by Aaron Hauptman, the son of Reb ltshe Shohet. The amateur actors were: Mordechai Langer, Adler, Elijah Hauptmann, Shiman Eckstein, Hannah Leibovitch, Etka Wagner, Salka Sperling, Chippe Wunderman, Salka Waldman-Schwalb, Haya Behr. The Producer was Aaron Hauptman, Scenic Painter Berl Stern, and Prompter Moshe Katz.

The First World War interrupted the Circle's activities, which were renewed in 1917 when fresh members joined: Mania Igra, Monderer, Seidenfrau, Buszko Apfelgruen, Dr. Meller, Dr. Lieberman, Dr. Singer. The producers were now Professor Max Bienenstock and his wife.

The Beit Ha'am or People's Forum:

In 1930 a Beit Ha'am or People's Forum was set up in the town in addition to the other charitable and public institutions. It was founded by the outstanding public figure Dr. Presser. The members of the first committee were: Tzeler, Apfelgruen, Diamant, Kindler, Dr. Kohn, Kreisberg, Klueger, Haim Meyersohn, M. Spiegel, Stern, Weinreb, and Wohlmut. The Beit Ha'am Society received a plot of land from the philanthropist Adolf Auerbach and resolved to erect a central building for various institutions.

The Jewish Hospital:

Among the social institutions of the community an important part was played by the Hospital, which did much for those Jews who required public health assistance. The Hospital began as a "Hekdesh" (communally owned, and therefore usually neglected, property) and poor travellers' lodging place. With the assistance of Moshe Stern, the vice-Mayor, Michael Auerbach, Joseph Horowitz, Isaac Sheinfeld, and Dov Pollack, the "Hekdesh" was liquidated and instead a Hospital was erected for Jewish patients, who could not receive medical aid in the Government Hospital on account of the Antisemitism rampant there as in all other Government institutions. The Community supported the Hospital ,which underwent severe crises. Mention should be made of the Jewish communal workers and physicians who gave their services to the Hospital without charge. These were Reb Haim Mayersohn and Reb Isaac Hauptmann (the slaughterer), Moshe Zechariah Goldberg, Dr. Kiczales, Dr. Lippel, Dr. Brauner, Dr. L. Bienenstock, Dr. Kenig, Dr. Shützer, Dr. Schleiffer, Dr. Malka Leibovitz and Dr. Ada Klein.

TOZ (The Jewish Health Organisation):

There was also a branch of the Jewish Health Society "TOZ", which looked afterthe health of Jewish children. The active figures of TOZ were Dr. M. Leibovitz and Dr. Begleiter.

The Orphanage (The Bourse):

One of the aid and charitable institutions which Stryj Jewry established was the handsome Orphanage. To begin with it was a Beit Niachse (Charitable Home') for poor Jewish pupils, and its Committee was headed by Dr. Philip Fruchtmann. In 1917 it was transformed into an Orphanage headed by Dr. Rappaport, Professor Spaet, Zalman Steiner, Dr. Fichner, Professor Resport, Professor Tauber, Mondschein. Towards the end support of the institution dwindled and its economic position deteriorated. The final heads were Dr. Rappaport and Mr. Weissgiass.

The Popular Kitchen:

In Stryj a Jewish charitable institution such as a "Tamhui" or People's Kitchen and restaurant was to be found. As early as the end of the Nineteenth Century the charitable Mrs. Mahla Katz had initiated a kitchen which provided the Jewish hawkers of the market place with hot tea and a roll for one "kreutzer" in Winter. The poverty-stricken Jews always needed the help of such a public institution, particularly during the last years before the Catastrophe. The community therefore kept it up under the devoted care of Professor Seinfeld.

The "Ezrat Nashim" (Women's Aid) and "Kreuzer Verein":

The charity and kind-heartedness of Jewish women in Stryj found expression in the two societies for aid to the needy. The members of these societies paid rent and helped to pay off mortgages; particularly for those who had built houses after the Great Fire of 1886. They provided medical services for the sick, and sometimes sent them to convalescent centres. Aid was given in secret so as not to affect the credit status of those helped. Members took turns in spending the night in the homes of the sick. The "Kreuzer Verein" chiefly assisted women in childbirth by sending them diapers, sheets, etc, together with three gulden. Active members included: Helena Rosenman, Rachel Katz and the wife of Advocate Dr. Byk, also the wife of Advocate Dr. Norbert Schiff.

The "Gemilat Hesed" (Interest-free Loan) Fund:

In 1927 a "Gemilat Hesed Fund Charitable institution" was founded for the purpose of mutual aid within the Jewish community, and assisted the small merchants the craftsman and artisan, etc. with loans without interest. It proved of particular importance after 1933, when the large-scale extrusion of the Jews from their economic positions began. The basis for the Fund was the assistance of the Joint Distribution Committee following the First World War. Time and energy were devoted to the Fund by M. A. Wohlmut and Dr. B. Milbauer. During the final years the Fund was headed by Reb Moshe Kudisch, who was its manager until the Catastrophe.

The Jewish Vocational Training School:

In 1919 the Joint Distribution Committee founded a workshop for Jewish Youthwhich in the course of time developed into a vocational school at a high technical level. During its existence and until the Catastrophe this school trained hundreds of young Jews for working life in the Exile, and provided halutzim with the vocational preparation which proved so useful when they proceeded to Eretz Israel.

There were four sections: carpentry, ironwork, lathework and mechanics. The Joint Distribution Committee provided up-to-date machinery, while the JCA, the Jewish Community, the Municipality and philanthropists (Leib Horowitz and Dr. Schindler) supported the school financially.

The Chairman of the School Society from its establishment until the Catastrophe was Dr. Schindler, who devoted himself entirely to this institution. Other active members were: Dr. M. Kaufman, Sommerfeld, A. Levin, S. Steiner, Dr. Hausmann and B. Diamant.

Yad Harutzim (Diligent Hand) Society:

In 1908 a small minyan (prayer quorum) of artisans was established, thanks to Davidman, the builder of ovens, followed by the house-painter I Klieger. In the course of time the minyan became a vocational society of artisans called "Yad Harutzim". Abraham Levin was elected chairman in 1920. Most of the members were close to the National group. There was a split in the society in 1931 because of the elections to the Polish Sejm (Parliament). Those members who remained faithful to the national group established a new society called "Ihud Baalei Melacha" (United Craftsmen), Their secretary was Moshe Weiss, while Shlomo Schwartz was their vice-chairman.

The "Oseh Tov" (Do Good) Society:

The outstanding economic society was the Jewish Merchants "Oseh Tov" Society, which watched over their interests in the city and tried to counteract the anti-Jewish discrimination of the authorities. Its most active members were: Kindler, Moshe Spiegel, Dr. Schiff, I. Reich, Benjamin Klein, Dr. Z. Presser, David Seidman and others.

The Jewish Economic Society (Zydowskie Zrzeszenie Gospodarcze):

This Society was set up by non-Zionist and other external factors with the aid of the Polish authorities. It was an artificial creation, and enjoyed no support from the local Jewry. In spite of this, the authorities entrusted the community to it, and appointed Dr. Rappaport, once a member of the Bund, as head of the Kehilla. After the elections the community returned to the Zionist parties headed by Dr. Presser.

The Jewish Civic Casino (Zydowskie Kasyno Nueszczanskie):

The Casino was a meeting-place for the intellectuals of our town, a club without any political coloration. Here meetings, conversations and debates were conducted on current affairs. The Presidents of the Club were Dr. Hoffner, Dr. Brauner, Dr. Weiss and Dr. Schindler. The Club Committee supported the Orphanage and Hospital.

Jewish Sport

Sport as a Jewish activity in Stryj went back to the early Twentieth Century. The Jewish National Revival, and Dr. Max Nordau's Zionist slogan of Muscular Judaism brought about a physical revival together with a spiritual and social one. Even before the First World War there were the beginnings of sport activities in our town, though they were not properly organised and merely showed the trend of the youth. The foundations of Jewish sport in the town were laid by a group of Jewish secondary school students who established the first football club called "Hasmonea" (the Maccabeans). They played their first game, wearing blue-and-white, against the Polish. teams "Pogon" and "Skala". The first players were later to be lawyers and physicians in Stryj; among them Drs. Allerhand, Ende Fink and Frenkel.

After the first World War sport developed considerably. The first sport society was established under the name "Hakoah". Its first president was Dr. Plesser, and the Committee members were: B. Apfelgruen, Shlomo Borak, Mgr. Jacob (Tafko) Waldman, Dr. Berlass, the Brothers Henryk and Isidor Wolowski, Dr. Schutzer, Zussman and others. The members of the first team were: Zygo Weiss, Shlomo Borak, Dr. Houssmann, P. Feuerstein, Benio Haber, Gottesmann, Graubart, Mundek Gritz, Nolek Apfelgruen and M. Redler.

In 1920 a second football team was organised as Hakoah II. Its members were: Meniu Halperin, Jacob Wien, Filko Meller, Jósek Ber, Srulek Kudisch, Benju Lerch, Hochmann, Fruchter, Mannes Fefferbaum, Alexander Weiss, Max Horwitz, Landes, Yumck Rap. The society acquired a tennis court of its own, and the outstanding players were : Maciek Stern, Benczer and Dr. Wlhelm Hausmann. Three referees were appointed from among the society members. These were: Mgr. Tafko Waldmann, Isaac Katz and Mannes Halpern. The members engaged in various other games besides football, and established a social club.

In about 1925 another football club was founded under the name of "Dror" (Liberty), consisting of members who came from the ranks of the general public and youth. Its members were : Knittel, Hochstein, Strassmann, Haber, Filko Meller, Moshe Wolff, Heiber, Rotstein, Rap, Redler, Mottek Meller. The first president was Nathan Welker, and the Committee included: Gleicher, Hammerschlag, Leah Brand, Sabina Binder, Taub, Berger, Meller, Garfunkel and Monderer.

The Synagogues

The Great Synagogue (Die Große Schul) rose in splendour in the Old Jewish Quarter. It was a lofty building which had been erected during the time of Reb Enzel Cuzmer in the 19th. century. Most of the congregation were everyday folk, and the Ashkenaz usage was followed. Until 1905 the First Warden was Moshe Stern, the Assistant Wardens were Isaac Jerich and Moshe Waldmann. The Askan (notable) was Israel Nussenblatt and the shamash (beadle) was Zvi Hirsch Friedlander. The cantor was Nissan May. During 1914-1918 the First Warden was Isaac (Itshe) Hauptmann, and until the Catastrophe the First Warden was Shalom Stern while the Assistant Wardens were Zev Waldmann and Simeon Halpern, and the shamash was Abraham Tadanier. The cantors were David Nussbaum and Sender Kessler. Rabbi Eliezer Ladier prayed in the Great Synagogue for years. A special minyan (prayer group) of Jewish cab-drivers of Stryj also prayed there.

To the right of the Great Synagogue stood the Large **Beit Hamidrash** (House of Study), most of the congregation of which were also everyday folk. This was the only synagogue in which the congregation put on their tefillin during the middle days of Passover and Tabernacles. (This is normal among Ashkenazic jewry in general, but Hassidim have introduced what was originally the Sephardic practice of not putting on tefillin during these intermediate days). The wardens of the Large Beit Hamidrash were Zalman Schwartzberg and his brother-in-law David Schorr. The beadle was Leib Kurtzer. The wardens who followed them were Mendel Liebermann and Abraham Egid.

Reb Meir Shalom's Synagogue, known as Meir Shalom's Kloiz, was the prayer centre of many groups of Hassidim. It was used on their visits to town by the Hassidic rabbis of Stretin, Strelisk, Sassov, and the Rabbi Wyiznic. The wardens were Haim Garfunkel and his son Shlomo Garfunkel, Shimon Weiss,

Wagner, the mohel Moshe Zechariah Goldberg, the family of Abraham Apfelgruen and Fishel Shenbach.

The synagogue of Wolf Ber was supposed to be built in the form of a Greek letter, and was therefore known as "die Yevonische Kloiz". The congregation consisted of well-to-do householders, who followed the Sephardic usage (like the Hassidim). An outstanding member of the congregation was Reb Shlomo Finger, who was warden and also acted as cantor during the High Holidays.

The synagogue of the Boyanov Hassidim (Boyanover Kloiz):

The outstanding members of the congregation were Reb Shammai Gertner, David Ornstein (slaughterer, ritual), Shlomo Seif (slaughterer), Leiser and Shlomo Mihlrad.

The Ziditchev Synagogue (known as the "Blechene Kloiz") was one of the important synagogues in the town. The congregation included many town worthies who were both Hassidim and scholars. The synagogue was the spot where the young Talmud students pursued their studies. Outstanding and typical personalities included Reb Yekele Schorr, Itshe Shohet, Mendele Horowitz, Velvele Haftel, Kalman Schorr, Shmelke Schorr, Dov Rotfeld, Azriel Kleinmann, Shimon Igra, Nuty Sheinfeld, Itshe Sheinfeld, Shalom Shohet, Sender Shohet, Haskele Horowitz, Koppele Seman, Eizik Hubel, Sender Rothenberg, Moshe Kudisch, Leib Krieger, Haim Brand, Yankele Rosmarin, Rotbard, Abner and Aaron Katz, Israel Seidmann, Leiser Weiss, Shmuel Friedler, Eli Meir, Abraham Shuster, Aaron Reiter, Haim Brickenstein, Yekele Jerich, Haim Wolff, Nuta Wolff, Yessele Boimel, Eliezer Melamed, Mottel Rathaus, Falik Moshe Kupfer, Shmuel Rathaus, Itshe Haftel, Leib Rathaus and others.

The various minyanim or small prayer groups, included:

The minyanim of the rabbi Reb Eliezer Ladier, of the Rabbi of Mosczick, of the Rabbi of Glogow, of the Rabbi of Stretin, of the Rabbi of Strelisk; the minyanim of Reb Pinhasel, of Reb Eliyahu Labin, of Yankele Glezer, of Israel Yekels, of "di Lanys", the minyan of "di Szymianszczyzny", the minyan of Reb Eli at the Yad Harutzim Society, of Motel Drucker and the minyan of Rabbi Horowitz.

The Talmud Torah:

Before the First World War the Orthodox Jews of Stryj had established an institution for educating the younger generation in the spirit of the Holy Torah. The two-story building which housed this Talmud Torah was set up in the Jewish Quarter near the Great Synagogue and the Batei Hamidrash (Houses of Study).

In the "hedarim" or classes of this Talmud Torah hundreds of children pursued their Jewish studies all the way from the Hebrew alphabet to Talmud and commentaries.

The initiators of the institution were Reb Haim Meyersohn, Yekele Ettinger, Eliyahu Zeldovitch, Moshe Kudisch, and Judah Nussenblatt, who were joined by the communal workers Shmuel Friedler and Haim Kramer.

The teachers in the Talmud Torah were: "Rozler" teacher, Eliezer teacher, Yehoshua "Behelfer" (Assistant). Teachers of Talmud and commentaries were: Ellyahu Meir Pressburg (known as "Flick") and Yossele Lindner (known as "Skipky").

Personalities and Figures

Rabbi Aryeh Leib Hacohen Heller (1745--1813), pupil of Reb Mesliullam Igra of Tysmenic was an outstanding authority. From 1788 till 1813 he was rabbi of Stryj. His works "Ketzot Hahoshen" (Ends of the Breastplate) and

"Avnei Milu'im" (Inset Stones) are commentaries on the Shulhan Aruch. When the rabbi of Lissa criticised "Ketzot Hahoshen" he replied with the pamphlet "Meshovev Netivot".

Rabbi Asher Enzel Cuzmer was the pupil of Reb Aryeh Leib Hacohen and was rabbi in Stryj for forty years. Being a wealthy man as well as a renowned scholar he engaged in business besides acting as rabbi. He was given the rank of Kreisrabbiner (District Rabbi). The Great Synagogue was erected during his term of office and with his support, and was opened on 21st Nissan 5618 (April 1858).

The Rabbi of Lissa author of the work "Havat Daat" (Statement of Opinion) became rabbi of Stryj after Reb Aryeh Leib Hacohen Heller, author of "Ketzot Hahoshen". He was one of the outstanding occupants of the rabbinical chair at Stryj and the pride of the city, besides being a descendant of the renowned sages Hacham Zvi Ashkenazi and Reb Nathan Ashkenazi, who were leading rabbinical scholars in the early part of the eighteenth century. His descendants in Stryj included Reb Yokel and Reb Mordechai Lorberbaum. In his own time he was one of the leading halachic authorities of European Jewry. Evera, student of the sections of the Shulban Aruch entitled "Yoreh Deah" and "Hoshen Hamishpat" is also familiar with his commentary on them entitled, "Havat Daat". After having been rabbi in Lissa and Kalish he was invited to the Rabbinate in Budapest. On his way to Hungary he stayed in Stryj for a while, and the leaders of the Congregation, headed by Reb Enzel Cuzmer offered him the rabbinical office. He agreed to serve as their Rabbi,. until 1832, the year of his death, and left behind him an ethical will reflecting his moral and Spiritual character. He wrote thirteen important works, including commentaries on the Shulchhan Aruch, and his own Novellae on Torah, Agada and various commentators.

Rabbi Elijah Meir ben Yaakov Hacohen Rosenmann was rabbi from 1858 till 1877. He was the pupil and son-in-law of Reb Asher Enzel Cuzmer. Though supported by the ultra-observant, he avoided the disputes between the latter and the maskilim, and devoted himself to the study or Torah and to works of charity. He passed away 28th Nissan 5657 (1897).

Rabbi Arie Leib Horwitz author of "Harei Besamin" (Mountains of Balsam) who belonged to a widely-branching rabbinical family, was appointed Rabbi of Stryj in 1878 and became known as one of the leading rabbinical figures of his generation. His Responsa were accepted as definitive statements on points of the Halacha. Besides having a brilliant Hebrew style he also knew German well. His work "Harei Besamin", a volume of Responsa, gave him a leading reputation among his contemporaries and later scholars. In Stryj he helped to establish a modern Heder, arousing the anger of the ultra-orthodox. He showed his sympathy for Zionism and delivered a memorial address on Dr. Herzl. In 1904 he was summoned to be Rabbi of Stanislawow after the death of his father, Reb Isaac Horwitz.

Rabbi Eliezer Ben Shlomo Ladier of blessed memory , was born on the 3rd of Adar 5634 (1874) at Seret in Bukovina. Blessed with an august presence, he was one of the greatest rabbis to occupy the rabbinical seat in Stryj. His was a poetic soul in which Talmudic research and legal dialectics dwelt in harmony. In his researches he sought scientific and historical truth, while in his German poems he gave expression to the love of Zion and to exalted beauty. From 1917 he served as rabbi of Stryj after his uncle Reb Aryeh Leibush Horwitz, serving his community faithfully and raising the standards of his city.

Rabbi Shalom Hacohen Jolles of blessed memory was one of the outstanding rabbis of the country. Thanks to his efforts a Yeshiva was established in Stryj where students learnt Talmud, Rashi and Tossafot under the outstanding guidance of the Gaon Rabbi Raphael Kitaigorodsky. In 1929 he came to Eretz Israel, where he settled in Jerusalem and passed away there.

Reb Shraga Feivel Hertz was rabbi and head of the Rabbinical Court in Glogow, and was appointed to the same offices in Stryj after Rabbi Horowitz gave up his rabbinical post and returned to Stanislawow. Rabbi Hertz, who was very wise and shrewd, was sensitive to everything that took place in the Jewish world. His method of studying Talmud resembled that of the Lithuanian Yeshivot. Once his students comprehended the problem before them, he would introduce them to the keen dialectic and casuistics of the early and later authorities. He showed how the halacha, the legal principles, could serve contemporary needs. As a result there gathered round him those young Talmud students who later joined the Jewish National Movement. His son became Rabbi of Borszczow and perished in the Catastrophe. Looking back over the decades, the dispute between the rabbis of Mosczisk and of Glogow seems to have been one of the cases of "Both alike speak the words of the living God", though they found support among different groups of Jews in Stryj.

The Dayanim ("Judges" or rabbinical assessors who aided the Rabbi in the Bet Din or Rabbinical Court): Reb Isaiah Igra, a descendant of Reb Meshullam Igra, one of the great authorities of his generation, was a leading dayan in Stryj in the middle of the Nineteenth Century.

Between the two World Wars the Dayan of Stryj was Reb Isaiah Usher, son of Reb Jolles, and Reb Shaul son of Reb Jacob Joseph Lusthaus.

Reb Mordechai (Motel) Drucker, an outstanding scholar, was particularly expert with regard to Agada, Midrashim and Hebrew grammar. He was an excellent cantillator of the Pentateuch, and served as the maggid and darshan (preacher and homilist) of the Stryj community. Highly esteemed by all circles, he published scholarly essays and the works : "Safa Laneemanim" (Speech for the Faithful, on the Hebrew verbs); "Techelet Mordechai' , a commentary on the Pentateuch; "Tovirn Meorot" (the Luminaries are good), giving the prayers for Hallowing the Sun and moon; "Ateret Mordechai" (The Diadem of Mordechai), a commentary on Midrash Rabba. The synagogue in which he prayed was known as Reb Mottel Drucker's Kloiz after him.

Reb Isaac "Show" Hauptmann (Reb Itshele Shohet – "Show" are the initials of "Shohet Ubodek", Slaughterer and Inspector): One of the outstanding personalities of our Orthodox community was the interesting and original Reb Isaac Hauptmann Show, a faithful worker in the observant community and its institutions, Warden of the Great Synagogue and of the Zydyczow Synagogue (Blechene Kloiz). He was an outstanding slaughterer and mohel (circumciser), in which traditional Jewish function he was a very great expert. In addition he was one of the finest Masters of Prayer and singers in our city, being blessed with a very musical ear and a power of original melody. He used to act as cantor during the Morning, Sabbath and Festival Additional prayers without receiving any pay. Reb Itshe Shohet showed his originality by his knowledge of engineering, housebuilding and repairing. The Technical Department of the Stryj Municipality always approved his plans although he was not a qualified engineer. Unlike most of the Orthodox community, he openly declared his belief in Zionism and in the Jewish National Revival.

Dr. Zvi Diesendruck:

One of the most brilliant scholars originating from Stryj, a leading figure in Hebrew learning and literature. Belonging to a Hassidic family, he was an active figure in the Hebrew Movement of Galicia. In 1922 he received his Ph. D. He was a teacher at the Vienna Hebrew Pedagogical Institute headed by Professor Zvi Peretz Chajes. From 1925 to 1927 he taught at the Jewish Religious Seminary established in New York by Dr. Stephen Wise. In 1927-1928 he lectured at the Hebrew University, Jerusalem, then returned to USA and was appointed Professor at the Hebrew Union College in Cincinnati as successor to Professor David Neumark. He became Vice-President of the American Academy of Jewish Research and editor of the Hebrew Union College Yearbook. His essays and studies were published in "Haet", and "Hashiloah", in "Revivim" under the editorship of J. H. Brenner and G. Schoffmann, and in "Haolam" and "Hatekufa". In Vienna he published the monthly "Gvulot" jointly with C. Schoffmann. From Greek Diesendruck translated Plato's Phaedrus, Corgias, Crito and Republic into Hebrew. In German he published a work on

"The Structure and Character of Plato's Phaedrus". In the 1928 issue of the Hebrew Union College Annual he published a study of "Samuel and Moses Ibn Tibbon on Maimonides' Theory of the Negation of Privation", and an essay on Maimonides' Theology in the Israel Abrahams Memorial Volume.

Dr. Naphtali (Tulo) Nussenblatt:

One of the first Zionist students in the youth movements of our city. After the First World War he settled in Vienna where he obtained a Doctorate of Law, but devoted himself to literary activities, and particularly to the study of Dr. Theodore Herzl. He collected very ample material on the Zionist Movement during Herzl's lifetime. and was the leading specialist on Herzl's life and times. In 1929 he issued a volume entitled "Zeitgenossen ueber Herzl" (Contemporaries on Herzl), and in 1933 "Ein Volk unterwegs zum Frieden" (A People en route to Peace). In 1937 he began to issue an annual "Theodor Herzl Jahrbuch". After the Nazi entry into Vienna he fled to Poland where he was active in the Underground of the Warsaw Ghetto during the Second World War. He was murdered in the vicinity of Lublin in 1942, and his collection of Herzl's correspondence and manuscripts was lost with him.

Jonah Gelernter:

was born in Stryj in 1890, and was active together with Dr. Diesendruck in Stryj and Vienna. He wrote stories and essays. Between 1923 and 1938 he taught Hebrew Literature at the Zvi Peretz Chajes Jewish Gymnasium in Vienna, and also published a monthly in that city called "Devarenu" (Our Word). He escaped to Paris from the Nazis, but was murdered in that city in 1944.

Joshua Tilleman was one of the interesting scholars and maskilim of the town, though he rarely displayed himself. He was a Hebrew speaker from his youth up, as well as a literary critic and publicist. A teacher at the Hebrew gymnasium, he intended to proceed to Eretz Israel but did not live to do so.

Dr. Max Bienenstock (1881-1923) was one of the outstanding figures in the field of Zionist activities during a brief period after the First World War. He was one of the organisers of the Nationalrat (Jewish National Council) established in Stryj under Ukrainian rule, and helped to lay the foundations of Jewish national education in Eastern Galicia. He also edited the journal "Volkstimme" (People's Voice) which was published in Stryj in 1919. In 1922 he was elected to the Polish Sejm as a Senator. He contributed to the "Togblatt" (Daily journal) which was published in Lwów, and published books and studies in "belles lettres" in German and Polish.

Dr. Shlomo Goldberg:

One of the Zionist figures of Herzl's generation. He prepared the ground for Zionism in our city before the First World War, together with Dr. Heinrich Byk, Dr. Julius Wurzel, Dr. Michael Ringel, and Dr. Wolf Schmorak. After the War he was elected Head of the Kehilla, and was held in high esteem by the Stryj community.

Dr. Abraham Insler (1893-1938), born in Stryj, received a secular education and while at the gymnasium joined the Zionist group of the "Zeirei Zion". He studied law in Vienna where he participated in Zionist activities, and afterwards became chairman of the "Emuna" Academic Society. Upon his return to Stryj in 1918 he helped to organise the Jewish National Council. From 1921 he was a member of the editorial staff of the Polish Zionist journal "Chwila".

Dr. Zeev Presser, born in Stryj to a progressive family, was possessed of extensive professional and general knowledge and was a central figure in communal life. He was a Zionist leader and a devoted head of the community, a pleasant person who was welcome to all.

Dr. Mordechai Kaufmann, born in Stryj to a traditional and observant family, was one of the first to speak Hebrew and was an active Zionist from his youth. He played an important part as vice-Mayor, head of the Community and Chairman of the General Zionist Party. In his spiritual characteristics, approach to problems and influence he resembled Dr. Presser. After settling in Eretz Israel he returned to Poland on a mission and met his end during the Catastrophe.

Dr. Benjamin Mihlbauer was born in Bolechow to a teacher of Jewish religion, and was a physician. He was devoted to Zionist activities and played an important part in the Zionist Party and numerous committees. He also visited Eretz Israel.

Moshe Aaron Wohlmut, a Hebrew scholar and lover of the Torah, was devoted to Hebrew education and the spread of Hebrew culture. He was an active member of the Ivriya Society and aided the Safa Brura School. A devoted Zionist worker. he was an active member of the Community Council and Municipality, and visited Eretz Israel.

Benjamin Klein came of an observant family and was given an orthodox upbringing. In his youth he joined the Zionist Movement. He was a merchant, but devoted himself to the communal requirements of Stryj Jewry, and to the Zionist Movement. He was a member of the General Zionist Organisation and one of the party's popular workers. He was active himself, led others to participate in the committees of many Zionist and general institutions and organisations, and was moderate, open-hearted and upright in all his public dealings. Like so many others. he was planning to come to Eretz Israel, but delayed too long and met his death during the Catastrophe together with the rest of the community to which he had devoted the greater part of his life.

Dov (Berl) Stern was one of the earliest Zionists in the town in the days of Herzl, and was a popular figure. He went to Eretz Israel in 1925 and made a living by manual labour. His home in Tel Aviv served as a first stopping-place for new arrivals from Stryj. He passed away in Eretz Israel at a ripe old age.

Meir Frankel was a devoted Zionist, who went to Eretz Israel before the First World War but had to return on account of illness. He was an active member of the Stryj General Zionist Organisation. Returning to Eretz Israel in

1932, he worked as an official in the community and municipality, and lived to see the establishment of the State of Israel.

Abraham (Buczi) Apfelgruen:

One of the oldest and most outstanding leaders of the Mizrahi in the city. An active communal worker, he represented his party in Zionist, public and economic institutions. He was a man of fine presence and pleasant to get along with, a true sage and popular on account of his equable temperament and good nature.

Rachel Katz was born in 1877 and was a talented communal worker, who was esteemed and revered by the entire Jewish population of the city. She was a herald of the emancipation of Jewish women, and fought valiantly for equal rights and the restoration of self-respect. She took the initiative in founding the "Women's Club" (Ognisko Kobiet) and the Jewish Girls' Shelter "Ochronka dla Dziewczat Zydowskich". In 1907-1914 she engaged in politics during the election campaigns, played an important part in the National Council in 1918, and afterwards took steps to organise a branch of WIZO. She expressed her life's vision nobly and giftedly both verbally and in writing.

Dr. Malka Leibowitz was one of the outstanding women of Stryi. Between the two World Wars she played a decisive' part in founding and developing the Hashomer and "Hashomer Hatzair" Movements in Stryj. Her qualities made her a natural leader and guide of the youth, who revered and loved her. It would be impossible to think of or mention the Stryi Hashomer Hatzair without its central figure - Malka. As a physician she did much for the health of the poor Jewish population and initiated and established public health institutions for Jewish children.

Aryeh (Leib) Schwamer received a traditional training and gave himself a general education. From 1921 until the Catastrophe he managed a Loan Bank. When the Hitahdut Party was established in Stryj he left the Poalei Zion and joined the new group, to which he was devoted until the community was destroyed. He served as chairman of the Hitahdut and vice-chairman of the "Arbeitsgemeinschaft" and was a delegate to the Zionist Congress. A good-natured person, he was prepared to help others and was a model communal worker who was popular in all circles.

Dr. Azriel Eisenstein, a lawyer, joined the "Hitahdut" Party and was one of its outstanding figures. He represented his party on the Municipal Council and the Community Council on behalf of the Stryi branch of his party.

Levi Oper:

One of the founders of the Poalei Zion Organisation of Stryj in his early youth, and an active worker for it He had outstanding organising capacity and was an excellent public speaker. Thanks to these qualities he headed the Stryj branch and later came to play an important part in the Polish Poalei Zion Movement. Following the split he remained faithful to the Zionist Organisation and joined the right wing of the party, "Hitahdut", in which he continued his dynamic activities.

David Seidmann, born in Skala, came to Stryj with his family at an early age. Blessed with a highly developed community sense, he was at home in communal problems and become a central figure in the public and national affairs of our city. A shrewd public worker with a clear sense of political realities, his field of activities covered both Zionist and local affairs. Though he held no official position he was one of the most influential persons in the town.

He first belonged to the Hitabdut but afterwards joined the Revisionists and finally supported Meir Grossman's Jewish State Party. Practical-minded and with clear objectives, he devoted himself more particularly to aiding halutzim and helping them to proceed to Eretz Israel. He was killed in 1943 during the Catastrophe.

Aaron Meller, a longstanding student and scholar at the Beit Hamidrash, joined the Hebrew Movement in his youth and was one of the first active members of the "Aguclat Ivriya" (Hebrew Society). He participated in many institutions as a representative of the Hitahdut Party.

Joshua Oberlaender received a traditional education and was brought up in the Beit Hamidrash, but while young he became irreligious and joined the Hebrew circle which gathered in the Ivriya Society. He was one of the first zealots for Modern Hebrew in the city. An active member of Zionist committees, he was part and parcel of the public life of the Jewish community.

Ben-Zion and Aryeh (Leibush) Garfunkel were clerks by profession and were among the earliest members of "Hitahdut", faithfully carrying out the duties required of them. For many years Ben-Zion was Party Secretary, Chairman of the Popular Youth Society "Kadima", and Stryj correspondent to "Dos Neie Vort" (The New Word), the party organ.

Dr. Joseph Schuster-Shilo arrived in Stryj with his family at the end of the First World War. His was an extensive Jewish and general culture. As a Hebrew maskil he was one of the central pillars of the Ivriya Society, and contributed greatly to the spread of Hebrew among the younger generation at Stryj. In 1935 he proceeded to Eretz Israel where he worked devotedly as a teacher and headmaster in various secondary schools. He was one of the initiators of the "Yizkor" volume in memory of the Stryj Community, and for many years devoted himself to the collection of material, laying the foundations for publication.

The General Zionists:

In Stryj Zionism preceded the Zionist Movement and Organisation set up by Dr. Herzl. The national revival, indeed, had commenced there some twenty years earlier.

The first specifically Zionist body appeared in Stryj in 1887, when the "Shoharei Tushia" Society was founded, to be followed very soon by the "Yahadut" Society, established by the city's maskilim headed by Moshe Sheinfeld and Abraham Goldberg. The members devoted themselves to the study of the Hebrew language and literature. In 1890 a third society was founded. This was "Admat Israel", which was joined by about 200 young men for the purpose of aiding the land-workers of Eretz Israel.

After the World Zionist Organisation had been founded by Dr. Herzl, Jewish student youth also joined the "Zeirei Zion" Society, which was prohibited by the authorities and therefore illegal. In the elections to the Austrian Parliament and the Galician Sejm the Zionist candidates were Dr. David Salz in 1907 and Dr. Leon Reich in 1911. General Zionism was the dominant Zionist and public force before the First World War, in spite of the presence of two competing groups, the Mizrahi and the Poalei Zion. The new Zionist idea was disseminated among the Jews of Stryj through the establishment of such institutions as the Toynbee Hall, the "Veritas" Jewish Academic Society, the "Zion" Society, the first Hebrew School "Safa Berura", and the Jewish National Fund Committee. But the First World War paralysed all this national and public life within the community.

The Balfour Declaration in 1917, and the appearance on the scene of Dr. Weitzman as the President of the World Zionist Organisation, led to a wave of enthusiasm and renewed the activities of the Zionists of the city. Their greatest victory was the capture of the Community Council from the Assimilationists in 1918. During the Twenties the General Zionists included in their ranks such experienced veterans, of cultural and communal standing, as Dr. Shlomo Goldberg, Dr. Zeev Presser, Dr. Mordechai Kaufmann and Dr. Abraham Insler, who were chairman of the Community, representatives of the Jews on the Municipal Council, chairmen of the various national fund bodies, etc. Their activities were guided by the Executive of the Zionist Organisation for Eastern Galicia, with its headquarters at Lwów.

"Arbeitsgemeinschaft":

Or "Committee for Cooperation between all Zionist Parties". This body was established in 1923 with the purpose of coordinating all Jewish political activities and affairs in the town, as well as organising and supervising the Zionist institutions. The offices of the institution were at the Zionist Casino in the 3rd. of May Street, and activities were conducted on the base of the "Toynbee Hall" Constitution.

For years the Casino was the centre of all Zionists and active party members. Decisions on municipal and Zionist matters were adopted by a majority vote of the plenum. In general the parties reached agreement on matters of principle. Representatives of all Zionist parties, Funds and institutions participated in the plenum. Thanks to this model cooperation between the parties, the Committee exerted a decisive influence in all Zionist and municipal affairs.

Chairmen of the Arbeitsgemeinschaft were Dr. Z. Presser, Dr. M. Kaufman, Dr. S. Wandel, Dr. B. Mihlbauer, Leib Schwamer, David Seidman, Abraham Apfelgruen and Dr. A. Eisenstein.

The Mizrahi Organisation:

Jewish nationalists with an orthodox orientation first organised themselves in Stryj before the First World War, following the establishment of the World Mizrahi Organisation. As a separate stream within the Zionist Movement, however, the Mizrahi made its appearance in Stryj only after the War. Though the local branch was not very numerous, the proportion of active members was exceptional. The Mizrahi cooperated with all the national groups, and its representatives participated in all Zionist, urban and public institutions and organisations. Among the most active members mention should be made of: Abraham Apfelgruen, Abraham Auerbach, Leibisb Pickholz, Samuel Shenbach, Samuel Ginsburg, Jecheskiel Lehrer, Selig Zwilling, Itzchak A. Hubel, Moshe Kuclisch, Z'ev Spiegel and others.

Agudat Israel:

After the Agudat Israel Organisation was established in Poland in 1913 a number of the extremely orthodox Jews established a branch of the new body in Stryj. Active members were: Shammai Gertner, Mendel Horowitz, Israel and Simeon Weiss, H. M. Neubauer and Moshe Zechariah Goldberg. A "Young Agudat Israel" was set up not very long after.

The Poalei Zion Society was registered in 1903 and received permission to engage in cultural and Zionist activities. The members worked in various callings and included members of popular intellectual circles. At first activities were coordinated with those of the Zionist Societies. Later, however, work was conducted in Yiddish and Yiddish literature was fostered. The first active members were : Berl Friedmann and his wife Perele, Shmuel Horshovsky, Levi Opper, Hannah Leibovitch, Shmuel Shenbach, M. Pollak, M. Patrach, Isaac Oper, Birnbaum and others. In 1907 the Poalei Zion took part in the elections to the Austrian Parliament on behalf of the Zionist candidate Dr. A. Salz. In 1908 they supported the Yiddish Language Convention at Czernowitz. During the years before the First World War they maintained their informative work, spreading the Zionist idea among the poverty-stricken and toiling masses.

Thanks to their influence a society for young folk was established in the city under the name "Igud Poalim Tze'irim Ve'ovdei mis'har – Poalei Zion" (Association of Young Workers and Business Employees Poalei Zion). The war suspended the activities of the party.

Those who revived it after the war included David Seltzer, Shlomo Rosenberg, Feivel Miller, Sarah Hauptmann, Shlomo Rossler and Shimon Rosenberg. A dramatic group was set up, and amateur actors presented many Yiddish plays at the "Dom Narodny" Hall.

In 1919 there were 300 members in Stryj. The Poalei Zion helped to win the community from the Assimilationists, and tried to help set up a network of Jewish elementary schools. They had 5 representatives in the National Council set up under Ukrainian rule. The new Polish regime however, suppressed Jewish communal work, and the Poalei Zion had to cloak their activities by assuming the form of aid institutions for the poor.

In 1921 the Poalei Zion Convention for East Galicia was held in Lwów. The delegation from Stryj included : Abraham Hauptmann, representing the Right wing, Levi Oper the Centre and Shimon Rosenberg the Left. The branch in Stryj split. The Left-wing Poalei Zion was proclaimed illegal and had to disguise itself as the Beit Borochov Children's Home. In 1923 the first trade union was allowed to organise, an evening school for workers was opened, and the first class in the "Cisza" school network was established together with a kindergarten. The teachers were: Hava Greenberg and Lea Greenberg, and Ruchtche and Henia Fruchter. New members made their mark, including Joseph Harr, Michael Oper, Otto Becher, S. Streifer, Joseph Maurer (now an active Poalei Zion worker in Rio de Janeiro), Leib Nussenblatt, Shmuel Schwarzberg, Davicl Silber, etc. Although the Poalei Zion were persecuted by the Polish authorities its activities did not weaken, and in 1923-24 the party drew all the unions away from the influence of the Bund.

In 1922 the Poalei Zion presented their own list for the Polish Sejm elections. In 1928 it presented its own list at the Communal elections. During the Thirties the police began putting more and more pressure against the Party which, however, continued to function until the Catastrophe.

The "Hitahdut" Party:

The "Hapoel Hatzair" and "Tze'irei Zion" of Eastern Europe united into a single party at a conference held in Prague in 1920. This in turn laid the foundations of the Hitahdut Zionist Labour Party, whose main centre was in Galicia. A group of young men, mostly Hebrew-speaking members of the "Agudat Ha'ivriya", were the nucleus of the Hitahdut party in Stryj. They were: Jonah Friedler, Joshua Oberländer, Nathan Kudisch, Aaron Meller, David Zeidman and Elimelech Frisch, who were joined by David Fruchter, Avigdor Rotfeld and Ben-Zion Garfunkel. In 1922 the following new members joined: Leib Schwamer, Haim Neuman, David Weiss, Meir Byk, Dr. Azriel Eisenstein, Shlomo Rosenberg and Abraham Hauptmann.

The party expanded its social foundations to include student and working youth, workers, artisans and clerks, and took steps towards the productivisation of young traders, shopkeepers, untrained people, etc. Societies, institutions and organs were set up within its framework of activities for the achievement of Zionist aims; and it exerted a considerable influence on the life of the Jewish community and on local Jewish problems.

The "Hitahdut" branch covered the neighbouring towns and villages, and until the union with the Poalei Zion the active leaders also included Mundek Fritzhand. Moshe Freilich, David Tadanir. Robinson, Mordechai Klar, Dr. Ada Klein-Reinhartz, Dr. Moshe Reinhartz-Barlev, Joshua Steiner, Judah Lustig, Nathan Weiss, Frieda Byk and Moshe Rotfeld.

The pride of the Hitahdut Zionist Labour Party was the pioneer and Zionist youth societies whose roots and sources came from the Eretz Israel Labour Movement. They were: "Gorclonia", "Busselia" and "Vitkinia".

Under the influence of the Party fresh classes were opened at the Jewish Boys School, where vocational training was given to members of the Youth Movements of Stryj and other towns of the neighbourhood. Many former pupils are now living by the fruits of their toil in Israel. The active members in this connection were Haim Neuman and Abraham Levin.

Ihud (Hitahdut Poale-Zion):

In 1930 there was a split in the Poalei Zion Movement, which divided into Right-wing and Left-wing Poalei Zion. The Right Wing joined the Hitahdut, and the "Ihud" (Hitahdut Poalei-Zion) was established. The veteran leaders of the Poalei Zion, Levi Oper, Shlomo Rosenberg and Shlomo Rossler joined the "Ihud", which was welcomed and joined by many people belonging to student and working youth circles, craftsmen, clerks, academic youth, etc. The "Ihud" set up a Carpenters' Cooperative and a large branch of the "Haoved" Movement, headed by Ben-Zion Oper, Malka Tanne, Moshe Zipper, Nathan Walter, and Shalom Blau. "Haoved" established the "Hapoel" Football team.

Many academicians who did not find their place in the old-established academic corporations founded their own academic society within the framework of the "Ihud" under the name "Z.A.S.S." (Zionist Socialist Student Association). The "Ihud" also organised clerks in the Jewish Clerks' Association as part of its trade union activity; and sewing circles were established for girls who were preparing to proceed to Eretz Israel. The visit paid by David Ben-Gurion to Stryj in 1933 was a historic occasion for the Party, and aroused great enthusiasm among the Jewish population of the city.

Hashomer Hatza'ir:

The period of the First World War and the years that followed were a time of nationalist and social ferment in Europe, including Poland. At that period large national and international youth movements came into being. Against this backround, combined with that of the Zionist revival, there came about a Hashomer Youth Movement. This was a scout movement evolving in due course into the Hashomer Hatza'ir Movement which exerted a great influence on the Student and Working Youth of the city. The first Shomrim who founded the Stryj branch were: Arieh Krampner (Amir), Michael Händell Jacob Seeman, Isaac Silberschlag (now a leading Jewish educationalist in U.S.A.), Yuzek Roth, Poldek Lautman, Hadassah Dickman, Haya Schlaks, Dzunka Fried, Mela Rechter, Tonka Rechter, Malka Leibovitch, Pnina Freilich, Pnina Reinharz, David Korn (now Secretary of the Benevolent Stryjer Fraternity in N.Y.) and others.

Leaders of Hashomer Hatza'ir

In 1919-1920 two groups of organised Haluzot proceeded to Eretz Israel from Stryj and became famous under the name "Bat Sheva" consisting of seven girls, and the "Ve heheziku" Group, also of seven girls, so named in reference to the verse in Isaiah 4, 1, "And seven women shall take hold of one man". For with them was one youngster, Meir Wieseltier.

Thinking young Jews had reached the conclusion by the years 1918-1920 that there were no prospects for a life of freedom and honour in the Exile, and wished to fulfil their aspirations in Eretz Israel. The "Jugend" and "Hashomer Haoved" Organisations combined into "Hashomer Hatza'ir". The Hashomer Hatza'ir branch in Stryj was one of the largest in Eastern Galicia and sent 40 Shomrim to the Convention of Shomrim held in July 1918 at Tarnawa-Wyzna.

In writing of this Movement in our city we must pause again to mention the figure of Malka Leibovitz, who was the leader of the local group for many years. This was its most brilliant period.

Many Stryj Shomrim are now veteran members of the oldest Kibbutzim in Israel. They are found in Bet Alpha, Merhavia, Mizra, Sarid, Mishmar Ha'emek, Ein Shemer, Ein Hamifratz and Kibbutz Gat. During the Thirties the Shomer unit in Stryj was headed by Zvi (Honig) Steif, Naphtali Lorberbaum and Libka Szapira; but they never achieved their aspiration and lost their lives with the rest of the community.

The Revisionist Movement:

Towards the end of 1925 a group of young students including Shalom Goldberg, Karol Einhorn and Moshe Steiner organised the nucleus of the Revisionist Movement in Stryj. Many joined the new Organisation, among them the well known communal leader David Seidman. The Revisionist party received 116 votes for the 14th Congress.

The appearance of the new party with its state political slogans produced interest and enthusiasm among the youth on one side, and reservations and opposition from the old-established parties on the other. It soon branched out. The Betar Movement was established and the Revisionist Hehalutz was founded under the leadership of Elijah Waldman. The academic corporation Hebronia joined. Its active figures were: Shalom Goldberg, Karol Einhorn, Magister Sternberg, Magister Rechter, Klara Bleiberg, Dr. Wandel, Magister Garfunkel, Mgr. Arnold, Naphtali Rotbaum, and others. After the Katowice Conference in 1933, which announced that the movement was leaving the Zionist Organisation, there was a split in the Stryj branch and a large proportion of the members went over to the Grossman ramp. The remaining handful rallied. The "New Zionist Organisation" known as "Hatzach" was established with the Organisation "Brit Yeshurun". The Tel Hai Fund was also established.

A Jewish State has come into being, but the overwhelming majority of those young people, who believed in its establishment, in a Jewish army and a. Jewish regime did not live to see the fulfillment of their dreams.

Brit Trumpeldor Or Betar. The purpose of this Organisation was to straighten the backs of Jewish youth, inculcate the values and standards that go with statehood, and prepare them for later military service in the impending Jewish State. The Organisation was joined by boys and girls from all sections of the community. Its leaders and active members were: Zvi Steiner, Uri Shenberg, Joseph Hauptman, Rouven Hauptman, Berko Igra, and Miriam Haftel.

Soon after the appearance of the General Revisionist Movement a process of political differentiation began to be manifest within it. In 1928, two years after the establishment of Betar, a fresh Society of Revisionist youth was established under the name "Massada".

This Organisation adopted an attitude of reserve towards the extremist slogans of Betar. In 1930 Massada became the first Revisionist Halutz Organisation and demanded that its members should proceed to "Hagshama" (Fulfilment), meaning Aliya to Eretz Israel. In Eretz Israel the active members of Massada were Joseph Erman, Lautman, Honig and David Seidman. At the first convention of Grossmanite Revisionists Stryj was represented by Elijah Waldman and Meir Kez. The Revisionist Hehalutz was active until the Catastrophe.

Ezra:

The halutzim preparing to proceed to Eretz Israel needed aid in training and on their journey. Most of them were unable to pay for their fare. Some went there against the wishes of their parents. For these reasons an institution known as "Ezra" (Aid) was founded, with its Central Committee at Lwów. In Stryj "Ezra" operated as a joint Zionist institution participated in by representatives of all the parties, Stryj Jewry contributed generously for this purpose, and the Community Council also allocated part of its budget to it.

[English page 35]

The Death of a Community
by Jonah Friedler

Chapter One: An Established City

Stryj lying in the plains and lowlands at the southeastern corner of Poland Minor, was the city holding the corridor to the Carpathian Mountains, whose summits rise proudly against the mists of the distant horizons on the way to Skole, a small town lying southwards in the direction of the Hungarian frontier. The River Stryj serves as a diadem to the wide-stretching and multi-coloured city, with its embroidery of fields and forest as far as the foothills of the mountains. Twining and murmuring gaily, its waters, clear as crystal, move the wheels of the mills from which the city used to obtain its flour, and beside which the townsfolk bathed in the hot summer. The city lies on a crossroads, and in the days of the Emperor Franz Joseph of Austria it linked Eastern Galicia with Hungary by the railway line that ran from Lemberg and Lawoczne to Budapest in the south, with Stanislawow to the southeast and Prszemyil to the northwest.

There were Jewish communities round and about in all directions, and these included the hamlets of Rozdol, Mikolayow, Zurawno, Sokolow, Zydaczow and Bolechow. Not far away lie Drohobycz, Boryslaw and Schodnica, with their oil-wells, from which most of the population of these towns made their living. This population of approximately 40,000 persons consisted in roughly equal proportions of Jews, Poles, and Ukrainians. The Jews were the vital spirit and dominated the entire economic life. They handled manufactures, trade, food supply, clothing, footwear, furniture, building materials, fuel, drapery, haberdashery and the like. Their handicrafts included harness-making, carpentry, tailoring, tinkering, glaziery, house-painting, building, upholstery, furriery, watchmaking, manufacture of oilcloth, gold and silversmith work, and the handling of all other kinds of metals and skilled mechanics. The Jews reigned supreme in all branches of handicrafts. Almost all the shops in town were in Jewish hands. Many Jews in the surrounding villages made their living directly or indirectly by agriculture. Some lived directly from their farms, while others leased vast stretches of land from Polish barons and noblemen who were estate holders, and cultivated them on behalf of the latter. Or else they leased inns in traditional fashion, the leaseholds passing from father to son for generations.

The Stryj Community is of proud lineage. Its Rabbinical seat had been occupied by Geonim - "Cedars of Lebanon, giants of Torah" as the Hebrew puts it, such as:

Rabbi Aryeh Leib Hacohen Heller author of the work "Ketzot Hahoshen" (published Lwów 1787-1795) and "Avney Miluim" (published Lwów 1815-1825).

Rabbi Yaakov Lorberbaum, called Rabbi Yaakov of Lissa, a great authority in Rabbinical Law in the early nineteenth century, author of ten books in the field of Halacha and Bible commentary. Died 1832.

Rabbi Meshullam igral called Rabbi Meshullam Tismenitzer, a descendant of Rashi, considered as a virtual genius in Rabbinics, author of the works "Igra Ramah", "Teshuvot" (Responsa) and a treatise on Maimonides. Born 1751, died 1801.

Rabbi Ensel Zusmer of the aristocratic and wealthy Halpern family. Rabbi Arych Leibish Ish Hurwitz of Stanislawów, an outstanding personality and one of the leading figures of his generation in the world of Torah, author of the "Harey Besamim". He established the "Or Torah" Yeshiva which was headed by Rabbis Raphael and Abraham Kitaigrodski from Lithuania. Before the First World War the Head of the Rabbinical Court had been the late and great Rabbi Shalom Hacohen Yolles of Moscisk, the son of Rabbi Uri of Sambor, together with Rabbi Shraga Feivel Hertz of Glogow. After that the Rabbinate was occupied by the late Rabbi Eliezer Ladier, the stepson of Rabbi Hurwitz of Stanislawow, while the last Rabbi of all was the martyred Isaiah Asher Yolles may he be avenged, son of Rabbi Shalom Hacohen and brother of the famous and scholarly Rabbi Ephraim Eliezer Hacohen Yolles, Rabbi in Philadelphia may he be granted longevity, who is, happily, still with us. From the school of these rabbis, who established homes for the Torah and raised up an entire generation of scholars and sages, there came forth personalities and writers who have established a very considerable reputation in our literary world. Out of Stryj came the late E. M. Lipschitz, author of the monograph on Rashi and Director of the Mizrachi Teachers Seminary in Jerusalem; Dr. Zvi Diesendruk, the writer, philosopher and teacher at the Hebrew University, who afterwards proceeded to the Hebrew Union College in Cincinnati; Jonah Gelernter, writer and teacher at the Vienna Hebrew Gymnasium; and, happily, still with us, Dr. Isaac Silberschlag, writer, poet and aesthete, one of the leading Hebrew writers in U.S.A. and head of the Boston Hebrew Teachers College; Dr. Nathan Kudish, teacher and headmaster in Tel Aviv, who is widely known for his essays on education and teaching; Dr. Moshe Steiner, writer, scholar and critic, whose works have been published in Hebrew and English; and other learned scholars who are widely known in the Jewish world. Many tales of the Rabbis of Stryj have become part and parcel of Jewish national folklore, and have been interwoven into Hebrew literature. Here I need only mention the tale of Rabbi Haensel and the poor Sabbath guest which S.J. Agnon incorporated in his tale 'Ve'haya He'akov Le'rnishor' (and the Crooked shall become Straight).

The leaders of the Stryj Community changed with the spirit of the times. In the days of the Austro-Hungarian Empire, before the First World War, the Head of the Community was the Notary Dr. Abraham Wiesenberg, an assimilationist who did not know the Jewish people and its needs. But he was a friend of the District Governor, and that was what counted for the Elections in those days. After the First World War, when the "springtime of the nations" came, his place was taken by Dr. Shlomo Goldberg, a Jew who had been educated and grown up in religious surroundings, and an outstanding Zionist who had been a delegate to the First Zionist Congress in Basle. He was followed y Dr. Zeev Presser, may his blood be venged, who was both intellectual and a practical man. He in turn was followed by Dr. Mordechai Kaufmann, may his blood be avenged, a devoted and popular Zionist. The last communal Head was Dr. Norbert Schiff, may his blood be avenged. The two latter also served as vice-mayors.

The city in which we were born was mall but was full of a rich and colourful life. Even before the First World War the well-to-do people had begun to send their children to foreign Universities on account of the numerous clausus. From then on the intellectual Jewish professionals began to be relatively numerous. The observant Jews belonged to various Hassidic sects, and followed their rebbes of Zydaczów, Czort, Bojan, Belz, Bolechow, Stretin, etc. In the early Zionists period there had been considerable conflict between the young Zionists and the Hassidim. During the period between the two world wars, however, national consciousness had become ripe. The Stryj Community was a rich national fount, a vital and active sector in the Jewish National Front of Eastern Galicia, which contributed amply to the upbuilding of Eretz Israel. At the time the best of the youth organised themselves in Hashomer Hatzair and Hehalutz, imbued as they were with pioneer ideas deriving from Brenner and Gordon. They fulfilled the requirements of self-labour in their own lives and proceeded to Eretz Israel during the Third Aliya of 1919-1923, in order to help shape our Homeland. These young people, who have meanwhile grown old, now constitute an important and active element in Kibbutzim, Kvutzot, and the town and country life of Israel.

Stryj also made a generous contribution to the Fourth Aliya of 1924-1931. Townsfolk can be found in almost every town and village of Israel, where they lent a hand in building up the country. In the days when Sir Herbert Samuel was High Commissioner the road to Sarafend was built with the sweat of Stryj Halutzim.

Even before the First World War the "Safa Berura" (Choice Speech) Hebrew School was founded by my friend the martyred Moshe Wohlmut, one of the outstanding Zionists at the time. After the War it expanded and the Zionist and Hehalutz youth received their Hebrew training there. Here mention should be made of the teachers Zvi Gelerter, Moshe Helfgott, Joseph Shapira, Haim David Korn, all of blessed memory and Jacob Seeman, who is still, happily, with us, now in Paris. These pioneer teachers were imbued with the vision of reviving the Hebrew language, in hostile surroundings, when both Orthodox Jewry and the various left-wing groups were bitterly fighting against us.

Between the two World Wars a technical school was established in Stryj and headed by Dr. Schindler. In it young Jews were given a productive education and learnt mechanics and metal work. The pupils of this school mostly went to Eretz Israel as Halutzim, and constituted a productive and fruitful element in the country.

Even before the First World War the national revival in Eastern Europe led to the establishment in Stryj of the Ivriya Society for popularising the Hebrew Language and Culture. It broke up during the war but was renewed when the latter came to an end and enthusiasm spread following the Balfour Declaration. Those who established it were Naphtali Siegel, Levi Teitler, Icchak Sturmlauf from Czechoslovakia, and Arie Doerfler, now in London. Lectures on various literary subjects were given by both local lectures and persons from elsewhere. The lecturers included : Abba Hushi, Meir Yaari, Dov Stock, (Sadan), Dr. Joseph Schuster (Shilo), Jonah Gelernter, Joshua Tilleman, etc.

In its own time the Ivriya Society was a power house of the spirit of national revival among the nationally-minded younger generation. They employed the enthusiasm which in earlier times had gone into the discussion of Talmudic topics and niceties in order to deal with national and literary problems, books and writers. Those were the days immediately after the First

World War, when the Stiebel Publishing House was just commencing its activities. "Hatekufa" was appearing once in three months in Europe, and the monthly "Miklat" in New York. The Hebrew Library of the Ivriya Society was an important factor in the local revival of the Hebrew language and literature. The devoted members and active workers of Ivriya included the martyred Joshua Oberländer, Dr. Moshe Eisenstein, Naphtali Gärtner, the martyred Haim David Korn; and those who are still, happily, with us, Jacob Seeman, Ben-David Schwartz, Dr. Nathan Kudish, Dr. Moshe Steiner, Professor Isaac Nussenblatt and the writer of these lines.

All the national and political schools of thought were to be found represented in the Jewish Community. The various Jewish National Movements were associated in a single 'Arbeitsgemeinschaft" (Working group), in which they were all represented. The young Jewish academicians of Stryj call for special mention. There was ample national spirit in their societies, "Emuna', "Hebronia" and "Kadima". The Merchants' Society "Oseh Tov" (Do Good) was active in economic and professional matters and stood on a firm national ground. Its managers were Dr. Norbert Schiff, Moshe Spiegel and David Seidman, a devoted and diligent Zionist organiser and worker. The craftsmen had their own society, called "Yad Harutzim" (Diligent Hand). It was headed by Abraham Levin, father-in-law of the Hebrew teacher and writer Naphtali Siegel, together with Shalom Schwartz, until the outbreak of the Second World War.

The Jewish Quarter, which was very typical of all towns in Poland, centred on the Great Synagogue, a magnificent building adorned with rare and impressive paintings on Bible themes painted by famous artists. On either side of the Great Synagogue were the two Batei Midrash (houses of study), while facing it was the Talmud Torah building of two stories. Its upkeep was the voluntary concern of Reb Israel Jehuda Nussenblatt, the martyred Reb Eliyahu Seldowicz, my father, Reb Samuel Friedler, and Reb Shlomo Drimer. Near the synagogue was the bath-house under communal supervision which was used by all residents of the town; and also the Jewish Hospital which was looked after, gratis, by the Jewish physicians.

That in miniature was the city of Stryj, on whose soil our heart-whole Hassidic fathers and forefathers lived for generations. They were believers as their own fathers had been. There they worked, studied and fashioned their own modest and self-sustained life. It was a peculiarly Jewish self-sufficiency in faith, custom, garb and language, with its Rabbis and communal officials, householders, intellectuals, merchants, hawkers, shop-keepers, workers, craftsmen, agents and idlers at street corners. They were everyday Jews who made a scanty living, thankful for a dry crust accompanied by tranquillity, faithful to the traditions and sanctities of the Jewish People, who lived in accordance with the Shulhan Aruch and did not deviate from it even by a hair's breadth. Apart from their worries about making a living, the centre of their world was their klois or shtiebel (Hassidic conventicle) and their particular Hassidic wonder-rabbi, the foundation of their universe. In their spiritual world they found compensation for the gray reality. Thence they drew their Hassidic fervor and love of Israel, that fervent devotion for which we so yearn. We followed them, a last generation in bondage and first of redemption. (But "though Redemption will come, yet let me not perceive it" as one of the Talmudic sages said).

On the First day of September 1939, with the outbreak of war between Germany and Poland, a black curtain fell and the fate of European Jewry was sealed; and among them the fate of those who were so clear to us, the Jews of Stryj.

[English page 39]

Chapter Two: In the Throes

The following morning the Messerschmidt aeroplanes were already throbbing overhead. They came sweeping down and dropping their bombs. From time to time they fired from machine guns, with no opposition. Where were the Polish anti-aircraft guns? - was the question everybody was asking. A bomb fell on the house of Nathan Ellner in the town square and smashed it entirely. The twenty-six men, women and children who had taken cover in the cellar were all killed. Among the victims was Reb Motel Rathaus, the modest Hassid and gentle sage.

Yet shaken though as we were by the first bombs, we swiftly grew accustomed to them. We knew no quiet by day or by night. No sooner did we try to rest from the horrors of the day then the throbbing in the skies disturbed us once again. We dashed down into cellars which, in our innocence, we thought might save us.

Long columns of wagons, loaded with families of Poles together with all their belongings, moved through the town from Western Galicia towards the east and depressed our spirits still further. Matters became worse when we saw the Polish forces retreating in confusion to the Hungarian frontier. Masses of Polish families, crazed with fear by the bombing, passed through the town in their panic flight, going from the frying pan into the fire. For the Soviet Army had crossed the Polish frontier along the River Zbrucz and was approaching us.

Meanwhile the German army entered the town. Ukrainian peasants from the surrounding villages came in crowds to greet them, dressed in their finest clothes. The riders wore coloured garments. A triumphal arch was set up in Drohobycka street, with the Proclamation, "We shall pave the way of victory for the German soldiers with Jewish skulls." The city was gay and lively, but the Jews hid in attics and lofts and cellars.

Meanwhile it began to be rumoured that Galicia had been divided between the Soviets and the Germans. We lived between hope and fear. On the third day after the German entry army commanders from both sides met on the Bolechow Bridge crossing the river Stryj. They decided that the Germans should withdraw to the River San, and that Stryj should be included in the Soviet Occupation Zone. The joy of the Jews when they saw the Germans leaving the town was beyond description. On the Eve of the Day of Atonement, 1939, Soviet forces entered the city and for the time being we were inscribed for life.

Chapter Three: Under Soviet Rule

The Jews revived when the first Red Units entered the city. It rejoiced my heart to talk pure Yiddish with Jewish officers. One of them began talking to me, and after we had become friendly he told me in secret : "We have brought you joy and happiness. You'll rejoice at a loaf of bread and be happy if you can obtain a piece of sugar or butter."

His words proved true. Our joy was only an imaginary one. Under the Soviets. to be sure, we suffered from want as compared to the rich and ample living of prewar Poland; but not as Jews. We suffered together with all the other peoples of Soviet Russia during the emergency; but not more than they did. The Soviets fed us on the doctrines of Marx and Lenin, and ordered us to obey the Stalinist Constitution in accordance with which he who does not work shall not eat.

They did not raise the lowly to the heights but they did bring the proud down to the ground so that rich and poor became indistinguishable. Yet though we lost our work and were left impoverished, they did nothing against our lives. So we were happy in our lot, happy that we had been delivered from the fangs of the lions.

The Front moved west and we seemed to be out of it. We thought that we were fortunate to live in peace under the protective wings of the Soviets, and would find shelter in the shadow of the Red Flag until the days of wrath had passed. There seemed to be reason for this supposition. On the 22nd of August, 1939, Stalin had signed a non-aggression pact with Hitler, the chief purpose of which had been to ensure that Germany would not fight on two fronts. The treaty had ensured Hitler freedom of action in the West and the other parts of Europe and Africa, without any fear of being attacked from the East. Then, economically speaking, we could see with our own eyes that great railway trucks of 50 tons each, loaded with first class wheat, were passing through the Stryj railway station on the way from the Ukraine to Germany: An obvious proof of the friendly relations between Germany and Soviet Russia.

Yet things did not come about as we had supposed. On the 22nd of June 1941 aeroplanes suddenly appeared at a great height. We could not recognise whether they were ours or the enemy's. Bombs began to fall from out of the clear sky. We asked the Soviet officers what it meant. Some silenced us by saying, "These are only maneuvers and there is nothing to be afraid of. You should remember that in Soviet Russia the public is not informed what is going on in diplomacy and politics." The facts came and disproved his words. The Soviet press was as usual full of Victorious achievements in accordance with the Five-Year Plan thanks to Stakhanovist methods, while nothing at all was said about politics. The echo of artillery fire reached our ears from the direction of Drohobycz and Przemysl. German aeroplanes began appearing without a break and dropped bombs. There could no longer be any doubt that this was really war. The Government and party officials made their preparations to leave the city. Railway wagons were placed at the disposal of the families of soldiers and party members, to take them to safe places across the Russian frontier. Yet countless such railway wagons were bombed and completely smashed and destroyed by the German planes as they made their way eastward.

Before leaving the city the Soviet authorities took a parting shot at several residents who were suspected of Zionism, including ordinary residents who were perfectly innocent. They were taken out of their beds at midnight and carried away to Siberia. Those I remember include: Samuel Klein, his son Benjamin and son-in-law Ben Zion Radler, Elijah Seldowicz, Aryeh Schwammer, Haim David Korn, Ben Zion Garfunkel, Levy Opper, etc. An acquaintance of mine in the N.K.V.D. told my wife that my name was also on the list of candidates for Siberia. If I had not hidden with a Polish family I would also have been taken away. Hundreds of Jewish refugees who succeeded in escaping from Western Galicia, and in crossing the river San at the risk of their lives into the Soviet paradise, were all carried off to Siberia.

The bombing grew worse from day to day. Houses became heaps of wood and stone within a moment. Lwów was already in the pincers of the Germans who had encircled it from the north and west. The Germans began to approach. We were abandoned with our bitter pain, forsaken and trembling and waiting for the Angel of Death. All we could do was to pray in silence : "Lord of the Universe, give the Russian soldiers the strength to withstand the German beasts, for our lives depend on it. Do not make an end of us."

But the Gates of Mercy were closed. The Soviet Forces left the town in the direction of Stanislawow. The Poles were indifferent. The Ukrainians went wild with joy as our world grew dark about us.

[English page 41]

Chapter Four: The Destruction of Jewish Stryj

Now I must begin to describe the liquidation of the Jewish Community and the end of Jewish Stryj. How painful it is to write those words! They include the precious, holy and pure souls of thousands of people, belonging to the families of those who read these lines; souls which were extinguished before their time by suffering and anguish to which nothing can compare since mankind came into being. Neither the legends of the Destruction of the Temple nor the Book of Lamentations, together with the works of the most outstanding and expressive writers, nothing written by mortal hand, could or can express even the least part of what it was my bitter fate to experience and see with my own eyes. The powers of human expression are incapable of recounting the cruelty of the yellow, murderous beast which came forth from its den in order to introduce "a New Order in Europe." "Where is there a Scribe and where one to weigh ?.." And as for me, I am neither a scribe nor the son of a scribe. My hands fail and the pen sticks in the inkwell. O Lord, I beseech you to strengthen and sustain me so that I may be able to tell my brethren in Zion and those who are dispersed throughout the world what the Germans and the Ukrainians did to our brethren and sisters, our children and little ones; in order to ensure that those of our blood are imbued with the duty of vengeance for generation upon generation. And be that my consolation.

The armoured units of the Germans came down on the city like a tempest. The earth crumbled away under the tracks of the gigantic steel and iron tanks. They were followed by the S. S. with black skulls and crossbones on their caps; and they brought death with them. Each on his own was a merciless professional murderers a bloodthirsty executioner.

When the Nazis arrived the pits in the courtyard of the Municipal prison were opened. Those pits were full of corpses of slain people, covered with flour and rice. The Russians had not had time before leaving to take with them all the political prisoners who were "enemies of the people". Among them were several Jews, but most of them were Ukrainians belonging to the party of Bandera which aspired to establish an Independent Western Ukraine. They had all been shot and flung into these pits. Now the German murderers were astonished to find that anybody contested the monopoly of killing and murdering with them.

Who had killed these people? The Soviets - meaning the Jews! The eternal scapegoat, symbolizing the red devil in the eyes of the Germans, and the

Bourgeoisie and Wall Street in the eyes of the Russians. Military and civil representatives were summoned together with priests, pressmen and photographers, in order to display Soviet-Jewish cruelty to all. Thousands of townsfolk and others came to see the gruesome sight. The first step to poison the air against the Jews, and incite the population against us, had been successful.

Posters were issued to the effect that war was being waged only against the enemy. "The peaceful urban population without distinction of race or creed are our friends. We promise them peace and order. They have only to obey the commands of the Military Command. Signed : General von Brauchitz." Further notices appeared requiring the Jews to bring their telephones and radio sets to the Town Council where they would be given a receipt for them. Those who did not do so would be punished in accordance with the Emergency Regulations. Signed: Haupmann Weide, Military Town Commander.

The German District Officer appointed Oskar Hutterer, the son-in-law of the late Rabbi Eliezer Ladier, chairman, and ordered him to select the members of a Judenrat (Jewish Council). This council bad a double task. It was to maintain contact with the German Command, carry out its orders, and handle all the internal affairs of the Jews themselves, who from that day forward would constitute a separate body entirely cut off from the Aryan population. This Jewish Council was chiefly intended to serve as a bridge for passing on the decrees of the Nazi Command to the Jews. The Council was given authority to collect taxes from the Jews, and establish a Jewish police (Ordnungsdienst) which would be under its orders. These Police were composed of young people belonging to all groups and classes. Among them were fine young men belonging to the national and academic youth, and also those from poverty-stricken groups. The Council was provided with food supplies for the Community. The policemen were promised additional rations, and therefore the young people willingly registered for police duties. There was also the attraction of gleaming buttons on uniforms, and the round cap with the dark yellow linen band round it. They were armed with rubber truncheons. The Jewish Council Building was the House of Reb Jacob Ettinger at the corner of May 3rd and Potockiego Streets. Departments were set up for taxes, housing, furniture and food, with secretaries, telephones, typewriters, storehouses and shops, A complete state apparatus, one might suppose, down to the last details.

The German officers in all kinds of military command offices brought their families with them. The Jewish Council was ordered to provide furniture for their dwellings. The Jewish police set to work with exemplary devotion. From the homes first of rich Jews and then of the well-to-do and average people they took furniture, household utensils, pillows and quilts and linen. Some gave willingly and some unwillingly, but the watchword was : "Better give our goods than our lives." Yet it was a vain slogan. First they gave their property and afterwards their lives as well. For now came the first blow

The Ukrainians denounced ten Jews. Those were people who had spoken badly of Germany under Soviet rule, or who had put pressure on Ukrainian workers in factories where Jews had been appointed foremen. Among them were Ephraim Bucchnbaum, Philip Dunkel, Engineer Schatzker, and the son of Koerner the lawyer. They were executed in the neighbouring village of Duliby. The murderers behaved with a certain amount of consideration in these first cases, and permitted the families of the slain men to bring their bodies to Jewish burial.

The front moved east. Here and there a barber shop or a shop for light refreshments opened. There were no goods because private trading had been forbidden under Soviet rule. A Jewish shop had to be marked by a Shield of David and a notice "Juedisches Geschaeft" (Jewish business). The peasants of the neighbourhood began to bring their crops to the market. The Jews were allowed two hours, from ten to twelve, to buy their food, and woe betide anybody who was caught after that time. He was murderously beaten and flung into prison. During those two hours the Jewish purchasers were received at the market with jeers and curses both by the peasant salesmen and by the crowd, who gnashed their teeth and bitterly cursed the Jews for causing the rise in prices, the war and all the trouble that was coming.

Law and order were supervised by the "Schupo" (Schutzpolizei or civil police), the "Kripo" (Kriegspolizei or wartime police) and the Gestapo. The worst of all the Ukrainian police. Here a few lines must be devoted to our Ukrainian neighbours with their hands steeped in blood, the offspring and descendants of Bogdan Chmelnitzky, that nation whose evil deeds are recorded as an everlasting horror in the history of Polish Jewry. They were the axe in the hands of the Gestapo. Their hatred of the Jews led them to savage murders and the robbery and pillage of all that was Jewish. They murdered and robbed. While the Germans shot from automatic rifles the Ukrainians murdered with their own hands. The Ukrainian peasants slaughtered the village Jews like so many sheep with scythes and sickles. They literally cut them to pieces with knives. We had been living in their midst for hundreds of years, Both sides had benefited from mutual trade and we had never done them any harm. On the contrary, the Jewish tradesman, peddler and innkeeper had provided them with clothing, footwear, food and drink against reasonable payments which were often enough not met. The Ukrainians had destroyed the basis of our livelihood in Eastern Galicia even before the Second World War. They had organised the village peasantry into Cooperative Societies which supplied all their needs, and thus eliminated the Jews from their economic positions. The priests in church preached in favour of the societies, and forbade all contact and business with the Jews. The Polish Government not only did not prohibit it but looked with a favourable eye on this poisonous activity, which diminished Jewish influence in the commercial sphere. Since we were the minority we were always the scapegoat in the political and economic intrigues between the Poles and Ukrainians. Both of them hated us bitterly. Now that the Germans had come the Ukrainians, drunk with joy, regarded them as angels who would deliver them from the

Polish-Jewish pressure, and would fulfil their dream of a free and independent Ukraina built on the ruins of the Jews.

The Ukrainian Police was made up of thieves, murderers, drunkards and scoundrels, a rabble from the underworld of this people. These scoundrels, who had always been dressed in rags and with whom no decent person would come into touch in normal times, now received new army uniforms with gleaming buttons, rifles or revolvers. Now they were given a free hand. Municipal affairs were handed over to the Ukrainians. The Mayor was Engineer Bandera, manager of the Ukrainian Cooperative Society.

On the day after the German Occupation a German soldier entered my apartment, accompanied by a Ukrainian ruffian who served him as a guide to Jewish dwellings. I recognised that he was the attendant at the bathhouse, where he was always asleep. I was summoned to work and ordered to fetch a pail, broom and rags. In the street I joined a group of Jews whose numbers rose from house to house. We were led to the town square in order to clean the tanks, collect the debris from the bombed houses and arrange the bricks in equal-sized squares. The work was not in the least boring, for from time to time the German supervisor brought his whip down murderously over our heads and backs, to the joy of Ukrainian idlers and vagabonds who laughed at our distress. I had the impudence to ask the supervisor why he was beating me if I was working as I had been ordered. Before I had finished my question the German hit me over the face to the accompaniment of unrepeatable curses. The blood began flowing down over my face.

Next day the Jewish police hurried me along to work at the railway station. We carried all kinds of screws, wheels and heavy pieces of metal from place to place on our backs. While I was working I met a young Ukrainian, a high railway official who had known me in bygone days. "For hundreds of years", said he, you have been sucking our blood. The Ukrainian peasant sold you the fat poultry and geese while he himself made do with the rye bread the Jews sold. The Jews always lived luxuriously. All the houses in town belonged to them. The town is ours, the house yours. Ukrainian hands built them. We were always your servants, your doorkeepers, your boot polishers, your cesspit cleaners. You wore the handsome expensive clothes, you lived in the finest apartments, you ate our bread and drank our water. Now the time has come to settle your debt. You'll pay with your lives. Now comes your finish, the day we have been hoping for so long."

This pained me far more than the whip the day before. When I took my shirt off at home, the skin had peeled from my shoulders and my back was covered with blisters. Yet these two episodes are not even a single drop out of the sea compared to what happened afterwards.

Every Jew from the age of 16-60 was compelled to work. In the city a vast number of institutions were established, including military stores, military laboratories and private German firms. I shall mention some of them : Heeresverpflegungsdepot (Army Supply Depot), Baudienst (Building Service), H.K.P., Wasserwirtschaft (Water Authority), Karpathen Ohl, Altstoff (Old Clothes), etc., Heeresbarackenwerke (The sawmill of Zelig Borak), A.S.A. Clasfabriken (Classworks - in Neubauer's flour mill). The Ukrainians and Poles traded and made money. We were forbidden to leave the town limits. Every morning we went out in our thousands to work at the above places. In return for our work we received rations of bread and soup. We submitted to this situation humbly, maybe even willingly, for we were still living in our own apartments. This general calm made some innocent ones among us delude themselves with the vain hope that work would save us, since in wartime work is an important factor and the Germans could not permit themselves to kill productive people like us. Who then would work in our places? And on the other hand, they argued, it was impossible that the German nation of poets and philosophers should simple indulge in the mass slaughter of millions of Jews. And what would the world say?

But the bitter reality came and proved otherwise. Death is a dreadful thing, but sevenfold more dreadful was the way that led to it. A few months later the order establishing the Jewish Quarter (Juedisches Wohnviertel) was published and paved the way for the Ghetto. It meant that the Jews were separated from the Aryan population. The Jewish Quarter began from Kilinskiego Street (the Lachowicz Bookshop) to its end at the corner of Iwaszkiewicza-Drohobycka Streets). It continued on the other side along the Stojalowskiego Boulevard, Zamkowa, Rynek, Berka Josselowicze, Kusznierska, Lwówska; Batorego to the Zielona Street. The Jews of the Aryan Quarter were transferred to the Jewish Quarter and crowded into the apartments of the Jews already living there.

It was permissible to enter and leave the Jewish Quarter. Jews with work papers might enter the Aryan Quarter, while Aryans were permitted to enter the Jewish Quarter. And an alternative was promptly provided for those who did not feel comfortable enough in the Jewish Quarter because of overcrowding. At the time the Quarter contained about 12,000 persons. The Jewish Council was ordered to make room for another 11,000 persons who had been expelled from the small towns of the district, which were thus made Judenrein. Beds of two or three levels were made of boards. The overcrowding led to filth and increased diseases.

Before long an additional "amelioration" came which was worse than the first. The Actions began. This was the name given to the systematic extermination carried out in accordance with a definite plan, and with precise German order. On this occasion, for example, orders were given to kill 1000 Jews between the hours of 4-12. If by chance another Jew came along after twelve, the murderers sent him away until the next Action.

This was in November, 1941, at 5 a.m. before dawn. There was a tremendous downpour of rain. The heavens were weeping at our calamity. Squads of German and Ukrainian police came into the Jewish Quarter. Twelve hundred men were taken out of their beds and led away to prison. After three days of beatings and torture the unhappy victims were carried off to the

Holobotow forest near Stryj. There they dug themselves a common grave with their own hands, and were all murdered.

Now began the feverish building of bunkers in the houses and courtyards. Jewish intelligence, together with a natural sense of self-preservation, enabled us to invent hiding places which were beyond all human imagination. Blind brick walls were built in cellars, attics, cowsheds, on the ceilings of lavatories, in rubbish bins, in cesspits, in places where the German curs would never dream of searching. The chief difficulty was to hide the entry so that it should remain invisible. For the greater part a few bricks were removed in the corner of the blind wall. We crawled in on all fours through the little hole and afterwards the bricks were cautiously replaced so as not to leave any signs of cement or brick. Sometimes the entries were made through the floors of a room, shop, store or cowshed after the course of bricks or the wooden board was removed from the floor, and replaced from within when those who were concealing themselves had entered. One exceptional invention which required special skill was the entry from under a window. The window-sill was removed. The middle bricks were taken out of the wall leaving space for a thin man. The entry to the bunker was through the hollow in the wall that was under the sill. The last to enter put the sill back in place from the inside precisely where it should be, with the aid of handles specially made underneath for the purpose. This was done with the utmost precaution, so that there should be no sign of the window-sill having been moved. The danger of death was the mother of strange inventions, of which nobody could have dreamed in normal times. Yet the clever inventions of flesh and blood were not always lucky. There were cases when those who had toiled to hide themselves ten feet underground were discovered, while others who hid themselves in an empty upside-down barrel or behind doors succeeded in escaping, until they fell into the hands of the Germans, that is, in the Actions that followed.

In December, 1941, in midwinter, Joseph Goebbels of accursed memory, called on the German people to donate winter garments on a generous scale for the German Forces fighting on the Eastern Front in order to liberate the civilised world from the Communist peril. The Aryan population had the choice of doing so or not; but for the Jews it was an order. Notices were published requiring the Jews to bring their furs to the Town Command Office. In order to make sure that this decree was promptly fulfilled, the German and Ukrainian Police did not wait for the Jews to fetch the furs themselves, but went from house to house to collect them. Their energy repaid them. They collected furs which were worth thousands of dollars. Some were delivered to the Command Office, but most were sold on the black markets of Lwów and Cracow and the money received was exchanged for spirits. The drunkenness which then spread among the Aryans, and particularly among the police, is simply indescribable. It expressed their joy at the victories at the Front and at the destruction of the Jews. A Ukrainian looking through a window saw the martyred Moshe Goldfischer hiding his fur in the double back of his cupboard, which was so skillfully made that its existence could not be seen. The Ukrainian denounced his Jewish neighbour who was hanged by the Gestapo.

The full cold of the Polish winter settled down on us. The Jewish Council received orders to transfer unproductive families, idlers, and particularly widows and women whose husbands had been taken to the Soviet army, to forsaken hamlets in the heart of the Carpathians, in the direction of Smorze village. The purpose was obvious. Even in normal years the peasants of that dreadful region lived on dry barley bread. Now in wartime there was no doubt that within a few days these people would all perish of starvation. On a cold winter night about 500 souls were loaded on wagons guarded by Ukrainian police on horseback, and taken up to villages that were to be their graves. A very few of them returned some weeks later, bloated with starvation and wrapped in rags and tatters. Meanwhile the Nazis were preparing public opinion for the idea that Jewish life was worthless. Army cars carried slogans "Death to the Jews". Caricatures were shown in public places displaying fat gross big-paunched Jews from Europe and America sucking the blood and marrow of the Aryan workers and neighbours through pipes, which brought piles of dollars into their pockets. The Nazis now had the sacred task of purifying Europe from the Jewish monster and eradicating this dangerous international microbe. It was not long before the satanic propaganda had its effect. The ground was prepared for murders and Actions. As we marched in ranks to work in the mornings Ukrainians attacked us and beat us without mercy. In the alleys and entry-ways of the town Ukrainian police regularly stripped off the clothes and boots of Jews, and paid for them with murderous blows.

As remarked, thousands of Jews were engaged in hard labour in all kinds of factories, barracks, mills, stores and military institutions. In addition the Jewish Council sent hundreds of those remaining in the Jewish Quarter to engage in public works every day. But the Nazis did not rest satisfied. From time to time German and Ukrainian police came to the Jewish Quarter in order to kidnap Jews for cleaning cesspits and lavatories. And naturally such kidnappings were always accompanied by blows. Deaths due to these thrashings were numerous. Among the victims was my father-in-law, the martyred Hillel Landau, a God-fearing Jew of exceptional qualities who was widely known for his integrity and charity. The Nazi police caught him in the street, beat him and trampled him underfoot. A few days later, he went to his eternal rest on the 26th of Tevet, 5702.

As usual in times of trouble people yearned for miracles. Maybe Soviet Russia would finally strengthen and proceed to the offensive. Jews were forbidden to buy or sell papers. But sometimes we secretly managed to obtain the "Lemberger Zeitun," from a Polish worker while we were working. The news depressed us even more. Despair spread on all sides. At the end of 1941 German submarines sank British warships and aircraft carriers. Italian torpedo-boats were attacking Alexandria in Egypt and wreaking havoc. We reckoned we were already dead. But what was going to happen to Eretz Israel? Our last hope was that we should rid ourselves of the doubt and fear that the

Nazis might reach the Land of Israel. Now that far was growing stronger. German aeroplanes had sunk the British battleships "Repulse" and "Prince of Wales". On 12th February, 1942, the German battleships Scharnhorst, Gneisenau and Prinz Eugen succeeded in passing through the English Channel in spite of the British Blockade, and endangered the eastern shores of England. The political horizon was absolutely black. We had the feeling that in a little while the whole of Europe would lie at the feet of the Nazis. Whence would our aid come? For our peril had increased a hundredfold. The Germans were preparing to slaughter us.

It was in May 1942, before the Shavuot Festival, that the Jewish Quarter was surrounded on every side. Anybody who tried to escape was shot and killed on the spot. This time the murderers found empty apartments. Everybody had taken shelter inside the bunkers. But the walls were smashed with hammers, pick-axes and hand grenades. When the murderers entered the apartment of the Schor family, an aristocratic Hassidic family who had been Turkish citizens for generations, the latter showed them their Turkish passports. The Gestapo murderers tore them up on the spot. 'Turkey will not go to war with us because of a few dirty Jews !" they proclaimed and added the whole family to the transport. The Jewish Hospital was full of patients. They were all shot in their beds.

After the Action the Jewish Quarter looked like a battlefield. In the hour of danger, when people ran in confusion to hide in the Bunkers, many families broke up. Each crawled on his own in to the very closest bunker, for there was no time to choose. After the Action those who were still alive came out of their holes in mourning, bereaved of their dearest ones. Children were orphaned and parents were left bereft. Wives remained without husbands and husbands without wives. At that time a stony indifference resulting from despair and complete hopelessness began to overwhelm the survivors. People wandered gloomily and bowed, without greeting one another. All the civilised politeness of society seemed to have vanished.

After each Action the murderers came to confiscate the property of the victims on behalf of the Nazi institution "Verbreitung das Deuschtums in General Government" (Dissemination of Germanism in the General Government). Stores for Jewish loot were opened in abandoned Jewish homes in Batorego Street. These stores swiftly filled up to the ceiling with the furniture, pillows, quilts, and linen of the victims of the "Uebersiedlung" (resettlement) which was the official name given to the Extermination Operations. The cynicism involved does not call for comment. The furniture of the victims was pillaged. It was given away to the Ukrainians, who came in their thousands with wagons from the villages in order to receive their share of the Jewish inheritance.

As the Jewish population dwindled on account of the Actions the Nazis began to reduce the area of the Jewish Quarter. It started at the House of Adela Katz in the Batorego street and finished at the house of the martyred Abraham Apfelgruen in the Berka Joselowicza Street.

But the Germans did not permit our tears to dry. They had not yet quenched their thirst for the Jewish blood they were shedding like water. The slaughter of the 3rd of September, 1942 came like a sudden blow. The Action lasted for 3 days and in it 8,000 persons met their deaths. This time the Gestapo, Schupo, and Kripo together with the Ukrainian Police assailed us with full military equipment. Having learnt from previous experience they now brought with them all kinds of instruments for breaking down the Bunkers. Goods wagons were stationed at the railway station and the victims were taken to them in groups. It was late summer and hot as a furnace. The victims were flung into the wagons on the heads of those already inside, till they were stuffed chockful. Quite apart from the blazing heat outside, a choking heat could be felt in the waggons. It was caused by a chemical powder which produced choking smoke clouds. The Gestapo had put this powder in the carriages in order to increase the heat and the airlessness. Nobody paid any attention to those who fainted, for each person felt as though he too were about to faint. Those who shrieked for water through the apertures near the wagon roofs met with the laughter of the Nazis who opened the wagon doors and beat them till they bled. Some tore their clothes off themselves, while others voided themselves for very fear and dread. In one of the wagons was the saintly and martyred Rabbi Mechele, grandson of the Hassidic Rebbe of Stretin. He ripped his arba kanfot to little pieces and roared, "Lord of the Universe, I served you all my life with full devotion. Is this the reward of Torah ?" After that he fainted and died choking. The earth did not open its mouth and the world was not destroyed.

In the wagon containing my martyred brother-in-law Shabtai Landau with his wife and child there were a number of brave strong young men who had taken wrenches and various implements for self-defence. From the aperture in the wagon it could be seen that the train was moving towards Lvów. This meant that it would cross the bridge across the River Dniester near Mikolajow. Before the train crossed the bridge it usually slowed down. As soon as the train began to move the young men started to use their wrenches. It was hard to shift the bolts and nuts because they had rusted in with age. But people become unbelievably strong when they are in danger of death. By the time the train began to slow down on the ascent to the bridge the bolts had been removed. The boards of the door, reinforced with iron bars, were broken and the young fellows began to jump out. But Gestapo men were standing between the wagons and promptly began to shoot. My brother in law Shabtai Landau jumped with his children his shoulder and was shot. His wife jumped after him. She was saved with a handful more. Those who succeeded in returning to the town had the skin torn off their bodies when they jumped. But what was the use? They were saved only until the next Action. The train went its way, from which none returned. At Betzec the flesh of the martyrs was ripped from them. Their fat was used for making soap. Yet no matter how the polluted ones try to cleanse themselves their sins stain them forever.

Before we had recovered from this the Nazis planned the last blow against the surviving Jews of the Holy Congregation of Stryj.

People began whispering of the establishment of the Ghetto. I shiver at the memory of the word. The news was received with strange feelings. Some said it was a sign that Stryj was not to be made "Judenrein" for the time being, as had already been done in many cities, nor would we be transferred to a Ghetto somewhere else. The fact that the Ghetto was to be erected made it clear that they did not intend to kill us for the present, since they were establishing a restricted area in order to separate us from the Aryans. And that was all. Maybe deliverance would come meanwhile.

But those who did not wish to delude themselves regarded the establishment of the Ghetto as a final step before complete destruction, in accordance with a prearranged plan for the entire Occupied Zone which had been prepared by Hitler, Himmler and Kaltenbruner. Both groups alike saw that the last Action had been worse than the proceeding ones. In the earlier ones people with labour cards had been released, but in the last no distinction at all had been drawn between workers and idlers.

Experience had also proved that the bunkers were of little service. If by some miracle a bunker was not discovered today, it was almost certain to be laid bare at the next Action. People with money, which in those days meant gold dollars, found hiding places with avaricious Aryan families eager for Jewish gold. "If somebody was out in the dark, he gave his wallet to a gentile" as the Talmud puts it. First the gentile took his wallet and afterwards his life. Some were compelled to leave their hiding places after only a few days because those who concealed them feared that they would be killed themselves. The good gentile rescuers took the money and sent the Jews away, but mostly the Jews were murdered and flung out into the streets. Jewish bodies lay rotting on the banks of the River Stryj. They were a regular sight. The Jewish Council received an order to clear them away. The Jews bore with that impossibly difficult burden called life, life of which they themselves had become weary. They dragged it from one gentile to another till finally they were rid of it.

Large posters consisting of many paragraphs and signed by Hans Frank the Head of the General Gouvernement announced the establishment of the Ghetto in Stryj on the 1st of December, 1942. Ingress and egress were permitted only to Jews with work cards stamped by the Gestapo. Those breaking the law were liable to the death penalty. The Aryans were warned not to approach the Ghetto limits. Selling or giving food or offering Jews any kind of help would be punished by hanging. The Ghetto area consisted of the following streets: Berek Joselowicza, Kugnierska, Krawiecka and Lwówska. It had two main entrances, in the Berka Joselowicza and Lwówska streets. Thick wooden posts were set up on both pavements and across them a long pole was placed as a barrier which was raised when necessary. Policemen watched the gates by day and night. Streets that led to the Aryan quarter were blocked with high wooden fences. And now the rope round our necks was tightened to strangle the last of the Jews. The Ghetto was set up with the definite purpose of being destroyed. Its end was involved in its beginning. Now we were caught like birds in a trap.

Once the Ghetto was established the Jews were divided into two: Those who were working and helping to bring about the Nazi victory, and the idle, weak, aged, women and children. The former wore square patches on which was darned the letter W. meaning "wichtig" (important). This meant that they must be preserved and safeguarded, and that the Getsapo must not do them any harm, while the rest were to remain in the Ghetto and wait for their day to come. Day by day thousands of Jews went out into the Aryan Quarter to all kinds of public works, accompanied by Jewish Police. Sometimes lesser ghettoes were set up near the working places, for those marked with the letter W. There thousands of our finest youth were working. They were entrusted to the Gestapo so as to be "safeguarded" from any trouble that might befall the main Ghetto; in order that the productive workers might be able to work calmly. The Germans said mockingly about them, "These will survive the War". The Jewish workers employed at the Borak sawmill, which was called "Heeresbarrackenwerke", were given the ruins of the barracks opposite Bolechowska Street. The A. S. A. glass factory, the Wasserwirtschaft, the Karpatenöhl, the Altstoff and a number of other German firms placed their Jewish workers in small houses in Iwana Franka Street near Bolechowska Street; houses which had been emptied of the Jewish inhabitants, who had already been killed in the Actions. Every morning we were lined up like soldiers and went to work under police guard. This guard was both ridiculous and tragic deceit. In theory the policemen were supposed to protect us, so that the Ukrainians should not beat us on the way to work and the Gestapo should not take us away during an action, but actually the Ukrainians beat us while the Gestapo kidnapped.

Baking and cooking were prohibited in the Ghetto. Shlomo Sauerbrunn's bakery in Lubowska Street was the only one which baked bread on behalf of the Jewish Council from the coarse flour provided by the Nazis for the Ghetto prisoners. From time to time policemen came to the Ghetto to see whether the chimneys were smoking. A German soldier went patrolling with his dog, which was trained to smell the scent of meat.

The cesspits were not cleaned in the ghetto, and it is hard to describe the results. Both electricity and gas were cut off. The water cisterns were stopped up. They left a single pump in the courtyard of Isaac Reich in the Berka Joselowicza Street, and another in Kugnierska Street. People had to get up at five o'clock in the morning and stand in line with their pails, for in case of an Action it was clearly advisable not to enter a bunker without water. People wandered about and lay about lean and starving. Even the healthy looked green and yellow. The bunkers left their mark upon them, as death had cast its shadow over them. All that was left of the wealth of Stryj was a cart and one wizened mare, on which the dead were taken to the cemetery. The burials were handled by the martyred son-in-law of the Dayan Rabbi Saul Lusthaus, and by Mordechai Jungman. Although we were sick of living, conversations in the Ghetto turned chiefly on signs of our end. How many more days would they permit us to live? How many more Actions would there be, and when? If a mere two German policemen were seen approaching it was enough to start the alarm, "They're coming!" That terrible cry passed through the Ghetto like lightning; and whenever it was heard every living soul vanished from the streets and houses, and we all began crawling into the bunkers. Nor were they always wrong with their fears. From time to time little Actions were carried out by the Jewish police under Nazi orders. Why should the Nazis bother to hunt the contemptible Jews if the work could be done by the Jews themselves ? It was so easy to set Jews against Jews. How tragic! How low we had fallen! The kidnappers came to the ghetto to find the bunkers of their fellow Jews and hand them over to be killed. The order of the Gestapo required a certain number of Jews to be handed over, and the police had to supply that number. Sometimes there were thrashings and absolute murder when they found a bunker. Those who were caught were first taken to the Great Synagogue and were kept there under police guard until they were handed over to the Gestapo. The well-to-do who could pay a ransom to the Jewish Council were set free, and others were caught in their place. Trade in livestock of this kind flourished. But before long all alike found themselves facing the same doom.

The Jewish Council imposed a compulsory tax on the population of the Ghetto. Everybody paid whatever was demanded for fear of being caught and taken away at the forthcoming search. The younger people began to feel very bitter with the Council on this account. if they had any sense, we said, they would use this money to buy arms for self-defence at the time of the Actions. We knew perfectly well that we could not defeat the Nazis. But we wanted to kill as many of them as we could before we were killed ourselves. But the Council carried out the orders of the Nazis like abject slaves. The chairman of the Council thought that all the ghettos would be liquidated but that of Stryj would remain.

New faces began to be seen in the ghetto. They were the remains, the vestiges of communities near and far. All alone, without any kith or kin, the poor people wandered about as though they were moonstruck after their own ghettos had been liquidated. Near me, for example, lived Gerngross, the owner of the largest Department Store in Vienna, with his Aryan wife who refused to abandon her husband in his distress. During one of the Actions the poor folk entreated to the Gestapo, "We are Viennese." But their blood mingled with that of our brethren.

One young fellow escaped when the camp in the Janowska Street in Lwów was liquidated. He told me that on the "Piaski" a suburb of Lwów 70,000 Jews have been murdered in a single week. My martyred younger brother Joseph succeeded in escaping to Stryj form Stanislawow. There he had stood in a long row of thousands of Jews at the cemetery, surrounded by S.S. troops and Gestapo men. The pit was very deep and wide. Those who reached the pit had to strip quickly, put their clothes in order on one side and their shoes on the other, separately. The victims walked over a board and young S.S. men about 18 years old shot them with automatic rifles. The victims fell straight into the Pit. Those who were not killed by the bullets were soon choked to death under the press of bodies. The crush was dreadful. Every one wished to be done with his life as soon as possible. The long file moved closer and closer to the board. The people around my brother, and he himself, began to unbutton their clothes and unlace their shoes, to be ready for their turn. To their astonishment the shooting, suddenly ceased. The action was to have been 'finished at five o'clock, and precisely at five it stopped. "Go away, dirty Jews!" shouted the murderers. "See you at the next Action!" Here is a fact which once for all dispels every doubt as to German punctuality and love of order.

[English page 50]

Chapter Five: Through the Carpathian Mountains

While the days of the Ghetto were numbered and we were all as much dead as alive, there were Jews living normally only twenty miles away beyond the Carpathian Mountains on the other side of the Hungarian frontier who knew no ill. All of a sudden a Ukrainian peasant wearing a white tie over his arm appeared in the ghetto, bringing a letter to someone or other from his kinsfolk in the village near Veretzki, the first little town beyond the Hungarian frontier. The person receiving the letter was warned to overcome his fear, to risk his life and to cross the frontier at once by devious paths through the mountains, where the frontier guards did not venture. Following this letter people with relatives beyond the frontier sent them letters by Ukrainian villagers eager for money, who were paid after bringing an answer back from the relatives. At the same tine a rumour spread that the son-in-law of Haim Wolf, the owner of the soda-water factory, had succeeded in crossing the frontier and had reached Budapest safe and sound.

People began to whisper together about the possibility of escape, and did their best to see that the Jewish police heard nothing. Who could be wise enough at such a time to weigh the pros and the cons? Anybody who put a foot outside the Ghetto was risking his life and in danger of death at every step, until he had left the town behind. Once outside, there were fresh perils. These came from-both the village police and the German police on guard at the bridges along the roads, waiting in ambush in order to murder and pillage. if anyone succeeded in crossing the frontier in spite of all these risks and perils he had to find a place where he could hide when crossing the frontier, for the Hungarian police were keeping strict watch all along the border area. If they caught any Jews from Poland they returned them to the Gestapo at Lawoczne. But if anyone found a good hiding-place where he could stay a few days, he could wait for a suitable opportunity of getting to Munkacz and from there to Budapest. Yet in spite of the perils and pitfalls, which maybe one in a thousand could evade, it was still worth risking a life that had become worthless.

However, the weaklings and cowards in the Ghetto thought otherwise. As long as there were no Actions, they argued, the Ghetto was the sole refuge in which it was possible to live for the present. Leaving the Ghetto was as good as suicide. Why should a Jew go to meet the Angel of Death? Better wait for the Angel of Death to come for him.

The physicians Dr. Shützer and Sobel succeeded in crossing the frontier and reached the first Jewish house on the soil of Hungary. When they knocked at the window to ask permission to enter, they were met with animosity and contempt. The poor fellows explained that they had just escaped from Poland, and entreated for a place to spend the night. Their entreaties and tears were of no avail. It is shameful and painful to have to reveal the reproach of some Hungarian Jews. One even brandished an axe and warned them that they should clear away at once, otherwise they would be handed over to the frontier police. They were driven away by force and returned to the hell of the Stryj Ghetto.

A Hungarian Jew who was caught hiding a person who had run away from Poland was liable to three days' detention. At the time that Polish Jewry was weltering in its blood, Hungarian Jews were afraid of imprisonment.

In spite of everything, people set out to cross the mountains. Hersch Benczer, Moshe Schechter, Kron, Michael Wang, Moshe Kess and others succeeded in reaching Budapest. The delivery of letters to Jews had long ceased. Those happy persons who had reached Budapest wrote letters to Polish addresses in Stryj. The letters were brought to the Ghetto and induced people to risk their lives and cross the Hungarian frontier whatever happened. My three dear martyred brothers Isaac, Joseph and Pinhas, with Ephraim Kramer and his son Saul, engineer Haim Vogel, Leib Risch and David Sobel and their families, Shlomo Ladier, Mendel Meller, the brothers Rosenman and others like them whose names I have simply forgotten in the course of time, - these brave fellows, who did not wish to wait for the Nazi murderers and to stand in line by the pit were all shot on the frontier. The Carpathian ranges, both on the side of Lawoczne and on that of Dolina-Wiszkow and Perehinsko-Osmoloda, absorbed the blood of these holy martyrs.

Dozens of people who tried to escape to Hungary were shot on the way at Morszyn or at Synowódzko. A few were wounded and returned to the Ghetto with bullets in their backs and legs, happy that they still had a refuge to which to return. The Wohlmut, Reiner, Crib and other families and persons dug themselves bunkers in the Skole district in the Carpathian forest. Soon enough the bunkers were discovered by Ukrainian shepherds who brought the Gestapo there. Moshe Wohlmut was the only one to get away. He succeeded in returning to the Ghetto where he died of grief and anguish when he contracted typhoid. Some people dug themselves bunkers in the forests near Rozdol and Dolina. Ukrainian bastards searched for Jews in the forests in order to obtain a reward from the village police. All those who went to the forests and were not discovered returned one by one to the Ghetto or the camps, for they could not face the perils of forest life. Only a bare handful escaped from these hiding places.

Aryan Documents

There was a feeling that the Ghetto was nearing its end; and a drowning man will clutch at a straw. Two well dressed young fellows, who did not look like Jews. entered the Ghetto from the Aryan Quarter. They came from Warsaw and with them they brought the Aryan document plague. They sold birth certificates, documents of the Meldungsamt (Registration Office) and the "Arbeitsamt" Labour Office in Warsaw. All the client had to do was to give them any Polish name he chose, two photographs and a down payment. Five days later they brought false Aryan papers from Warsaw. A number of persons, particularly those who did not have a Jewish appearance and spoke

Polish well, purchased these bargains, and carefully learned the Christian Paternoster by heart. For if they were not certain of anyone they caught, the Police would tell him to say a prayer. With the aid of these forged documents, they hoped to be able to leave for another town before the liquidation of the Ghetto.

The Germans discovered this trick as well. Strict watch was kept at the railway station. First they inspected all documents and stared straight in the eyes of the passengers. Afterwards they physically examined those they suspected. Jews and Jewesses by the hundreds were hung in the railway stations. Only a handful of those who tried to escape from Stryj to Warsaw succeeded in saving themselves with the false documents. Among them were the physicians Schleifer, Hausmann and Kindler, the Brothers Apfelgruen and a few more. Women had a better chance than the men of escaping with the aid of such papers. Is it possible to describe the distress of parents waiting to die in the Ghetto and saying goodbye to their daughter who was going out into a world that was full of peril at every step? Their parting blessing was, "Listen carefully, daughter, and pay attention. Forget your people and your family."

The murderous situation developed an animal-like instinct within us for feeling the storm before it came. There were clear signs of an approaching action. The kidnapping in the streets stopped. They did not put pressure on us or thrash us at work. The Police at the gates did not inspect us, and let things pass. Sometimes they even vanished into the neighbouring inn. This meant that we were simply not worth guarding any longer. For who guards the dead? Even the thoroughgoing Gestapo examinations at the camps stopped; examinations of which we had been in deadly fear. Now the camp was unattended. So when we did not feel the whip and the pressure we knew that this was the calm before the storm, before the last storm that preceded the final everlasting silence, the calm and silence of death. Those who were not prepared to accept the terrible thought that they had to wait tremblingly for death at the hand of the Nazis, those whose will to live was not yet fully destroyed and who still thought of rescue, had to decide between the following four alternatives: To hide with non-Jews, to run away to Hungary, to escape to the forests and dig a bunker there; or to try to get to another town with false papers. All of these alike meant 99.99% sure death. Those who risked one or other of these methods of escape had one more temporary possibility. If the non-Jew flung him out alive, or if the conditions in the forests compelled him to return to the town, he could still take shelter in the Ghetto as long as it existed. But after the liquidation of the Ghetto there would no longer be any place for a Jew to enter if he did happen to be alive. He was simply outlawed and could be killed by the first passerby. Those were our thoughts in Spring 1943.

I shall remember Passover, 1943, in the Ghetto until my eyes close forever. At the time I was working at the A.S.A. glass factory. Kneeling naked I drew glowing glass vessels out of the furnace. Once a day we received a portion of soup which was not fit for dogs, and a piece of black bread. After work we went to a camp in the Belechowska street, at the corner house of the Nawalnicki sisters. The furniture consisted of two tiers of boards which were infested with lice. Three persons lay side by side on such a bed of boards. The camp was surrounded by tall wooden palings, while a policeman stood at the entrance gate. The events in other cities made it perfectly clear to us that first the Ghettoes would be cleared, and afterwards the camps in which the productive workers were kept. The Ghetto was generally regarded as a place which it was dangerous to enter, for nobody could guess the day or hour of the approaching Action which could be sensed in the air.

On Passover Eve I stole into the Ghetto. My three martyred brothers were no longer alive. They had met their end in the Carpathians. On this night I, the only surviving one, wished to be together with my parents, whatever happened. My heart forewarned me that I would never see them again. Jewish refugees from other towns were staying with my parents who had always been hospitable. They sat round the table, on which burnt a dim candle made of fat that my mother had specially hidden for the purpose. A few black matzot made of coarse meal and hot water had been prepared for the festival. We said kiddush over the Matzot. When my father asked me to repeat the Four Questions I remembered the Passover Eves of the good years, when we had sat like olive-shoots round a truly royal table on which shone vessels of gold, silver, and crystal-ware, and had gaily and cheerfully sung the words of the Haggadah to the traditional tunes. My tears choked me so that I could not utter a sound . Nor did the eyes of the others remain dry. Suddenly the young fellow who had been watching on the balcony burst into the room. They're coming", came the cry, cutting like a lancet through the living flesh. In the distance he had seen two shadows approaching the Ghetto, a sign that the Action was impending. Within a moment we were all in the bunkers. This time it was a false alarm. Some people had heart attacks because of such alarms and maneuvers, while there were those who lost their minds.

Next day I met the martyred Reb Shlomo Drimmer in the Ghetto. He was a learned Jew, and the Secretary of the Talmud Torah. With him he carried a volume of the Mishna text. In answer to my question he told me that he was going to the kloiz (synagogue) of the Czortkow Hassidim, where a quorum of ten Jews met every day. Each of them studied a chapter of the Mishna for the salvation of his own soul, and then said Kaddish after himself. For who would say Kaddish after us if extermination were decreed for our people and not even a memory would survive us? All the synagogues and houses of study were already destroyed. In the curse of the actions the Ukrainians had smashed, ruined and burnt the Torah scrolls, the books and the furniture. Or else they used them as fuel and for wrapping up goods in the shops. The windows had all been smashed.

I stood in front of the "Geyle Kloiz" in Kusnierska Street, the Temple of the God of my youth, my old House of Study; and I trembled. The holes and spaces of the windows seemed to face me like a man whose eyes have been put out, and made their demand. Should I weep at its destruction, at our own or at both alike?

As I walked in line back from work I entered a Ukrainian shop at the risk of my life in order to buy some tobacco. The shopkeeper wrapped up the leaves in a page of Gemara. Sheets of a Torah Scroll were spread out on the floor. I was shocked and felt my knees and heart shake. Scalding tears suddenly burst from my eyes at the sight of my people's sacred objects being trampled by impure feet.

The tension in the factory increased. People whispered to one another, "They're digging!" At the sound of the words the bowels within one seemed to turn over. Pits were being dug at the Jewish cemetery in readiness for the day of the impending Action. The terrifying news was brought by Aryan workers belonging to the "Baudienst". That day the men in charge did not drive us hard at work. Such easy-going days always boded evil and catastrophe. Our hands simply did not respond to the work, but seemed to be paralysed. We stared round about us like trapped wild beasts. Nobody slept at night.

What we feared came about. In May 1943, between the Passover and the Feast of Weeks, the Ghetto was surrounded. By this time the work of the murderers was far simpler because the area of the Ghetto had been reduced. There was no escape or refuge. Gestapo units were brought from Drohobycz to help the Stryj squads. Those in charge of the slaughter were: Oberleutnant Klarmann, Ebenrecht and Huet of Stryj, and Hildebrandt, Minkes, Josef Gabriel and Gerber of Drohobycz. The murderers and their assistants were all drunk. The echoes of the shots and explosions that reached our ears pierced to our very vitals. It is beyond my powers to describe what went on within us. It is beyond all human comprehension. While we were working for a German victory only a few hundred paces away from the Ghetto, Hell was opening its maw to swallow our families. When the murderers entered cellars or other suspect places, they put their ears to the walls in order to try and distinguish movement or human voices. At such tense moments all those in hiding held their breaths. if anybody coughed or a child began to cry, they all promptly covered him with their clothes and choked him. The children and babies found in the houses in upper floors were not brought downstairs but were dragged from the arms of their mothers and flung from the windows. Their little heads smashed against the pavement, while the little bodies were trampled underfoot by the Nazis and Ukrainians. Bunker walls were smashed open. Those who never heard the yells of the feral beasts roaring, "Raus! Los!" (Out! Quick!), and those who never heard the weeping and wailing of the babies and sucklings trampled and murdered in the streets, can have no idea of Hell. Hundreds were shot in the streets. Thousands were taken to the Great Synagogue and from there to prison and the cemetery for mass Slaughter.

It was obvious to the Nazi murderers that the Jewish Council and Jewish police had to play an active part and help in carrying out the Action. The Jewish police who were called upon to participate received special white jackets. Their task was to take the corpses out of the houses, pile them in heaps on carts and take them to the graveyard. All the way there blood dripped from the carts and the cart-wheels on the Stryj earth. Those Jews who survived this action, and who were not yet done away with by the murderers, washed and scoured the streets of Stryj after the Action, removing the bloodstains left by their brethren.

This time the victims were not taken far. Some had prepared cyanide of potassium for themselves and committed suicide in prison. They included Dr. Malka Leibowicz and her son, Dr. Schnier, Dr. Kiczales and others. When the victims were sent half-naked out of the prison and climbed on the lorries that took them off to the cemetery, a crowd of Ukrainians gathered at the gateway to see and satisfy their lust for Jewish blood. And let this go into the record: The Ukrainian curs beat the naked bodies of our brothers and sisters with nail-studded clubs while they were being taken away to slaughter.

The blood of 8,000 Jews was shed that day at the cemetery. Poles who lived in the Pomiarki suburb next to the Jewish cemetery told me after the

Liberation that they went up on the roofs to watch the murder. After the Nazis left the field of slaughter the level of the graves had been raised because of the sea of blood that had been shed. For several days afterwards dogs licked the blood that oozed from the earth.

After the Action was over the Jewish Council received an account from the Gestapo listing the precise number of bullets used up in carrying it out. The Council was requested to pay the bill.

After having cut us limb from limb, the Ghetto was ready to be liquidated. The only bunkers left there were those that had been built by really skilled workmen in hidden places where even the murderers would never dream of searching, and those that had by chance never been discovered. After the last Action, which was on a hitherto unprecedented scale, the desire of the survivors to keep themselves alive and escape by building bunkers had very definitely weakened. What was the point of saving one's self again if the Ghetto was going to be liquidated anyway? Physical strength was at an ebb. Some died of starvation and grief or else of infectious diseases, while others just committed suicide. Despair spread from the Ghetto to the camps. It was obvious that once the Ghetto was liquidated it would be the turn of the camps. We secretly began building bunkers within the camp itself.

During the middle days of Passover 1943 four young men came to the Ghetto. They had reached Stryj from Warsaw with forged Aryan papers, after running away from the Destruction and crawling to the Aryan part through the sewers. They told of the heroic deeds of the Ghetto fighters who raised the blue-white flag in the burning Ghetto, which was defending itself to the last. The cadaverous faces of the Stryj Ghetto inhabitants grew bright at these tales of bravery.

But our joy did not last long. The liquidation of the Ghetto began on 10th June 1943. A permanent guard of armed Ukrainian police was stationed at all the Ghetto outlets for a fortnight. Those who still retained a spark of the will to live left the bunkers, went up to the attics, made holes between one attic and the next, fashioned themselves a way to the Aryan Quarter and through the attics reached the house of Fleischer, at Rynek corner of Cerklewna Street. From there they stole at night to our camp at the Nawalnicki Sisters' Building in Bolechowska Street.

The fires of hell were literally burning in the Ghetto. The murderers went from house to house seeking victims, and absolutely destroyed the buildings. Where they suspected the existence of bunkers they flung incendiary bombs or flooded the cellars with water. Those who did not drown were buried alive under piles of bricks, stones and dust or else were burnt and choked in the smoke. "Some perished by water and some by fire, some by strangling and some by stoning", as the prayers for the New Year and Day of Atonement put it. Not a single person survived in the last bunkers, which were regarded as unconquered fortresses, at the homes of Moshe Rosenbaum and Ezekiel Reder in Lwówska St. and the home of Moshe Kron in Berka Yoselowicza Street. The sound of bombs and rattle of automatic guns made the town shake to its foundations. We in the camp listened with bated breath to the echo of each bomb as though a battle were going on.

A Jew from the Skole District who escaped from the Ghetto hid in the attic of Isaac Reich at the corner of the roof, and through a crack in the wall saw what took place in the courtyard of my parents He succeeded in making his way through the attic route to the camp, and this is what he told me: My parents left the bunker in sheer exhaustion. As soon as they entered their dwelling the German murderers appeared, accompanied by Ukrainian police. My parents were taken through the outer stairway down to the courtyard. A German knocked my father's skullcap off with his rifle and shot him. Afterwards he shot my mother. May the Lord take vengeance for their shed blood. The murderers emptied my father's pockets, removed a few marks and his watch and chain. Then came the Jewish police and loaded the corpses on a cart.

When the Ghetto was liquidated the Offices of the Jewish Council were burnt and the members were shot, together with the police. All that was left was the deathcart with the skinny mare. She was brought to our camp, whose turn had now arrived.

The last survivors of the Ghetto who had found refuge in our camp hid wisened with starvation in the attics and the cellars. Those who managed to obtain cyanide of potassium took their own lives, their final satisfaction being that the Nazis had not touched them. As for the remainder, the last spark of life gradually dimmed in them, and they wandered round like shades, more dead than alive. The commandant of our camp, A.S.A., August Schmidt of Stuttgart, a glass-factory owner, informed the Gestapo that illegals from the Ghetto had stolen into the camp. One fine morning before sunrise early in July 1943 we were startled to hear sudden shots in the camp itself; shots which flung us off our lice-infested boards. Before we could find out what was going on, we saw through the windows that we were surrounded by Nazi, and Ukrainian forces. The medley of shouts and shots left us highly confused and unnerved. The Jewish police urged us with their rubber truncheons to dress quickly and go down to the courtyard. Through the sound of the shots could be heard the voices of the commanding officers: "A.S.A. workers with the W mark in one row, and the rest in a second row!"

I stood among the A.S.A. workers and pinned the W badge on my chest; for its absence meant death. My eyes sought my wife and mother-in-law, who had hidden themselves in a bunker under the roof. Shots sounded in the attic. A Schupo and Gestapo men climbed on the roof and shot those who were running away. Their riddled bodies fell into the courtyard beside us. People were dragged out of the chimneys and shot on the spot. Two Jews in an attic defended themselves with knives, and so as a result I saw two bandaged Nazis in the neighbouring courtyard. Those who had tried to escape lay weltering in their blood at the camp gateway.

This Action was conducted by Oberleutnant Klarmann. His shirt was unbuttoned, his face was red and he looked like a savage and bloodthirsty beast. His head was bare and he had an automatic rifle in his hand. He stood on the steps in the courtyard giving orders. At his side stood Isaac Stark, the Commandant of the Jewish Camp Police. Through my skull thundered the order: "Count the 165 for the A.S.A. All the others to the other row!" My work card was numbered 164, which meant that I was among the living. When they reached my place I felt my pulse, my muscles and my eyes to see whether I was dreaming or actually awake in this valley of slaughter. I felt that my senses were leaving me. My legs were shaking. Klarmann spoke: "We have taken the Ghetto filth out of your camp, for they dirtied the camp which is intended only for the good workers. It is your duty to work and work, and henceforward let your camp be clean!"

The row of illegals was loaded on lorries with yells and wailings whose echoes still resound in my ears as I write these lines. They were taken to the cemetery to be killed. We, the 165, were led away to work at the factory.

The Altstoff and Wasserwirtschaft camps were liquidated with other small camps. The three labour camps left at Stryj were those of the A.S.A., Heeresbarackenwerke, and the H.K.P. There was no longer any doubt that they would also be liquidated. The question was which would come first. Or maybe they would be liquidated together. Who could guess the plans of the murderers? Those days were just a corridor leading to death. The factory in which I worked was surrounded by fields and trees. Whenever I passed I breathed their scent as deeply as I could, wondering to myself meanwhile whether my feet would be treading this earth tomorrow, or whether I would already be rotting in a common grave. I would be rotting but the grass and trees would continue growing for years to come. And maybe they would even see the downfall of the wicked.

After our work in silence and despair we gripped the wooden bars which fenced us in, silent and despairing. Every hope and possibility of rescue had vanished. All we could do was to moan in silence and wait for death. Beyond the fence lay the Aryan Quarter, noisy and swarming with life and liberty. How happy were those who had not been sentenced to death like us, and who might come and go as they desired. Beyond the Camp fence people went about their affairs and their work, some smiling, others grrave. They looked at us as though we were some kind of show. In the brain hammered the thought; why haven't they been sentenced to death like me? Why don't I have freedom of movement like them? Against whom have I sinned?

Underworld types, the offscourings of humanity, emerged from their dens. Thieves by day and robbers by night, suspect janitresses, prostitutes and all kinds of scoundrels wandered about by the camp fence and opposite it. In spite of all the warnings they were not afraid to approach the fence posts and talk to us. They stood round the camp like black ravens about to swoop down on corpses, all of them waiting for blood. If anybody still had any article of clothing, a watch, a ring or anything else of value, he exchanged it with them for food. We who were going to die did not require any belongings. The dead are free from needs. Among them were also "rescuers" who came to suggest hiding places and to bargain about it. Some people went with them at night and returned a day or two later, after having been robbed of all they had. Some did not return at all. These merciful people took their victims into their cellars and then invited a "comrade" disguised as a Gestapo agent to extort a ransom. Wherever you turned there was death, death and death.

Then came the most dramatic night in my life, the night of the 19th of July, 1943. I clearly felt the footsteps of the Angel of Death approaching the camp. My heart told me that our hours were numbered. In the camp demoralisation and anarchy prevailed, an atmosphere preceding Action and death. There was no authority. Some drank to intoxication. Some laughed hysterically or wept to ease the terrible tension racking the brains and turning the very bowels over. The two storeys of the camp and its courtyard had turned to a true madhouse.

I could see my own thoughts reflected in the alarmed and confused eyes of those around me. The nervous tension reached its peak. In a little while we must break down. And was it surprising? Hundreds of young men in the bloom of their youth, all innocent, had been driven into this filthy unbearably stinking cage. The last drop of blood was being pressed out in exhausting labour for dry bread and a few drops of water. After they had sucked and pressed the blood out of the body they were now about to take the souls as well; and we were just waiting for them to come.

Each of us could see them in his mind's eye. They were coming, the Germans! Coming like a tempest in their spick-and-span green uniforms with faces like wild boars. They would surround the camp as usual. They would line us up in a straight row because they so greatly loved order and system even in the face of death. They would take us through the streets of Stryj, through our own streets, straight to the cemetery. People in the bloom of youth, with their vast desire to live, were to be taken alive to the grave like sheep to their slaughter. They would walk to their last resting place on their own feet, direct to the spot where people are carried. On their legs they would bear their bodies and souls straight to the pit!

There we would undress. Undress for the last time. We would walk the plank which crossed the pit like a diving board. We would take our last step. I would ask for only one thing from the Lord, my very last entreaty - that the bullet should hit the brain or heart direct and done! For if I fell injured into the pit there was no saying how long it would take to die, until I would be covered over by the heavy weight of corpses, and be choked by them...

All of a sudden I awakened as though from a fever. My thoughts were interrupted by the tune of a Tango that came from beyond the fence. Barely ten paces away the rooms were lit up gaily. Cheerful voices and laughter mingled with the melody reaching my ears. Through the windows I could see the dancing couples. The cursed Ukrainian bastards were dancing while death mounted in our windows. Thunder did not smite them from heaven, nor did the earth open her mouth to swallow them up. The pits in the cemeteries were waiting for our bodies. I felt that a critical moment had been reached in which there was something decisive. Either life or death!

I did my best to concentrate my thoughts on this single point. No matter what might happen, we had nothing to lose. We had to escape that night. Tomorrow might be too late. My dear wife who had always supported me in times of struggle and bitter stress now stood beside me silent, trembling in despair. She sensed my thoughts and the tempest within me in these decisive moments. In answer to my question she replied that she also thought the end had come. We decided to leave the camp that night, no matter what might happen. From nine o'clock on there was a curfew in the town, while a Jew could expect a bullet in the daytime as well if he went beyond the camp fence. But anyone who was thinking of running away and escaping had to blot the word danger out of his thoughts. In my mind I weighed the two perils of remaining or escaping. The former seemed the worse.

We left the camp at midnight. Our very souls seemed to depart from us, and our breathing stopped at the echo of our own footsteps. When we had left the town behind and entered an abandoned cowshed, our clothes soaked with the cold sweat that covered us. I imagine that a man sweats that way only once in his life, when his soul departs from his body.

This is not the place to describe the perils and adventures through which we passed from that night until the Liberation, on the 8th of August, 1944. Indeed, they simply beggar description.

In the morning of the 20th of July, 1943, five hours after we left the camp, the murderers liquidated all the A.S.A. workers who wore the letter W. Most of them were shot in the camp courtyard, the rest at the cemetery. After the Action was completed the Municipal Fire Brigade came to wash the camp courtyard and the neighbouring streets clean of Jewish blood. A few days later the Heeresbarackenwerke, the largest camp in town, was also liquidated and many good fellows lost their lives there. The poor fellows had arranged that one of them should give a signal on the way they were being led, and then they would all scatter and flee. As soon as they reached the prison courtyard, Hirsch Finkelstein of Slobótka shouted the signal. Most of them scattered and ran away at once. Many were shot on the spot and the rest at the cemetery. Only a few escaped.

The H. K. P. Camp was liquidated the same day. The murderers attacked it in the morning. Those who did not dress quickly enough were shot in their beds. Among them was my dear young brother-in-law Joseph Landau, may the Lord avenge him. The city of Stryj was Judenrein.

Stryj was occupied by the Red Army on the 8th of August 1944. I was one of the first Jews to enter the town. When Ukrainians saw me their eyes bulged out of their heads and they crossed themselves. In their eyes I saw the astonishment of those who witness the rising of the dead. On that great day of liberation, while the thunder of the cannons still shook the town, the few Jews who had escaped went to the graveyard to pay a last visit to their martryred brethren. How dreadful the scene was! The holy ground had become a grazing ground for cattle. It was covered with thorns and thistles. The fence had been broken down. The German barbarians had used the tombstones for road-paving. Along the paths lay fragments of skull and scattered bones of skeletons. We dug a grave for them and gave them a Jewish burial.

My feet led me to the ruins of the Ghetto. The weeping of the stripped and homeless souls hovering round me reaches my ears still as I pen these lines...

That is the story of the destruction of Stryj, where my mother gave birth to me. During the winter nights of my childhood I wandered through her streets, a little oil lamp in my hand, when we returned from heder. I grew up within the walls of her houses of study. There my father hid his head beneath his prayer-shawl when the Priests chanted their blessing. There I became bar-mitzva. Through its alleys I hastened to the Selichot Penitential prayers in the chilly Ellul mornings, in order to knock at the heavenly gates and entreat forgiveness for all Israel. There I adorned the sukkah, there I recited the Hallel prayer when we prepared Matza shemura for the Passover. On her soil I wove the dreams of my youth, the dreams of a return to Zion. On her soil I grew up and became a man.

It was my fate to see both the prosperity and the destruction of Stryj, her beauty and her fall; when the enemy set his Polluting hand on all her beauty, consumed Jacob and destroyed his home. Those voices of prayer which once cleft the heavens have grown silent in her synagogues. The sad sweet chant of Torah has departed from her houses of study. No little children recite their verses at the heder. There are no more disputes between the Hassidim, and the quarrels of the parties are at an end. The Jews have no place in her markets. Her sons have gone forth and earth covers the Jews of the Holy Congregation of Stryj forever. The burning bush has been consumed.

On her graves and ruins, ruins of wood and stone, scraps of parchment sheets and paper scorched and burnt, I absorbed within myself the holy spirits of the souls which quivered in the empty area of the destroyed ghetto. I absorbed within myself the moan of our brethren and sisters, the death-gasp of tortured and tormented infants and babies who were slain and who call for avengement; who call for vengeance to be taken for the holy congregation of Stryj, which gave up its collective life to Santification of the divine Name.

When I left the Ghetto ruins I turned my face back and prayed:

"Germany! Happy he that repayeth thee thy recompense for what thou hast done to us. Happy he that seizeth and dasheth thy babies against the rock. May I yet be one of them. May my feet stand in their blood, and may I wash in their wicked blood as they washed in ours."

We always held the memory of the departed dear to us. For their sake we used to study Mishna, and particularly that chapter "There are some who raise" in the Tractate "Mikvaot", which was held to aid the souls of the dead to rise aloft. We recited the Kaddish, we drank to the memories of the departed, we lit candles, we would say prayers at the graveside. We gave charity and baked special loaves for distribution to the poor, in order to aid the soul of the dead to mount aloft. All this we did in memory of the single individual. What shall we do to mark the memory of six million of our brethren, including the 12,000 souls of our holy congregation? To mark the memory of men, women and children, all of them slain, burnt, drowned and choked by poison gas and in the furnaces.

May these pages be a soul-light to their memory, and may they be bound up in the bundle of life. Let us pass onto all coming generations their last will and testament calling for vengeance, as a memorial stone to those martyrs who have gone aloft.

Stryj on earth was destroyed by the Nazis in 1943, in the year 5703 of the Jewish era. Stryj on high will live in our memories till our very last day.

Would that my words were written indeed.
Would that they were engraved in a book,
With pen of iron and lead.
Hewn forever in the rock.
For I know that my redeemer lives,
And at the last will rise to avenge on the earth.
(Job XIX).

Brooklyn, Ab 5714 A. M., August 1954 C. E.
Eleven years after the extermination of the Holy Congregation of Stryj.

[English page 61]

Jews of the Stryjer Community Victims of the Nazi Holocaust as Commemorated by Their Relatives in the United States

BAUMAN, BERNARD commemorates:

BAUMAN, ISAAC (YITZHAK), Father
BAUMAN, YETKA, Mother

BAUMGARTEN, HERMAN commemorates:

BAUMGARTEN, LEON, Father
BAUMGARTEN, MATYLDA Mother
BAUMGARTEN, ABRAHAM, Brother
BAUMGARTEN, SZYMEK, Brother

BATALION, PHILIP commemorates:

BATALION, MAYER, Father
BATALION, REGINA, Mother
BATALION, REBORA, Sister
BATALION, HERMAN, Brother
BATALION, SAMUEL-MORDECHAJ, Brother

BATALION, HELEN commemorates:

SCHIFF, FANNY
SCHIFF, NATAN

BEER, CHASKEL commemorates:

LIPPA, SABINA, Sister and her family

BEER, HERMAN, Brother and his family

BEER, ABRAHAM, Brother and his family

MARK, RACHELA, Sister and her family

BEER, MACHLA, Wife

BEER, AWNER, Son

BEGLEITER-BEGLEY, EDWARD DAVID Dr. commemorates:

BEGLEITER, SIMON, Father

BECLEITER, IDA, Mother

SEINFELD, MATYLDA, Sister

SEINFELD, ELIAS, Brother-in-law

HAUSER, OSCAR & HELENA, Parents in law

SEINFELD, HERBERT, Nephew

BONOM, HUGO commemorates:

BONOM, ABRAHAM, Father

BONOM, FRIMETA, Mother

PUSANT, REGINA, Sister and daughter

SCHEIMAN, ELLA, Aunt

BONOM, MIRKA, Sister-in-law and daughter

BRASELITEN, R. & STEIN SALOMON commemorate:

STEIN, KLARA, Wife and Mother

SPINRAD, MATHILDA, Daughter and Sister

STEIN, SAMUEL, Brother

STEIN, JACOB, Brother

SPINRAD, WILHELM, Brother in law

SPINRAD, MARCUS, Brother in law

EDELSTEIN, SAMUEL & ROSE commemorate:

GROSS, KLARA

GROSS, CHAIM

GROSS, CYLA

GROSS, HENRIETTA

EDELSTEIN, JUDA

EDELSTEIN, LIBA

EDELSTEIN, FISCHEL

EDELSTEIN, SIMKA

EDELSTEIN, SZYJE

FELDSTEIN, HELA

FELDSTEIN, JULEK

ELBER, REGINA commemorates:

KLEINMANN KRESSEL, Mother

KLEINMANN AZRIEL, Father

KLEINMANN MOSES, Brother

KLEINHANN EISIG, Brother

KLEINMANN NUCHIM, Brother

KJLEINMANN JACOB, Brother

FALIK MORRIS commemorates:

FALIK ZIPORA, Mother
ARON, Brother
RIFKA, Sister
CHANA, Sister
JACOB, Brother
LIPA, Brother's children
JUDES, Brother's children
DAWID JANE, Brother's children
LEA, Brother's children
MORDECHAI, Sisters' children
AIJY, Sisters' children
ZALLEL, Sister's children
RACHEL, Sisters' children
HENIA, Sisters' children
JOSEF, Sisters' children

FARBER HELENA commemorates:

BATALION, NATAN
BATALION, FANNY

FELDMAN LOUIS commemorates:

FELDMAN, JACOB MENDEL, Father
KLARA, Sister with husband and 3 children
BINAH, Sister with husband and 1 child
ELIESER, Brother with wife and 3 children
LEAH, Sister with husband and 3 children

FELDMAN MARK commemorates:

FELDMAN–SCHEFFER, SAMUEL, Father
FELDMAN–SCHEFFER, MARJEM, Mother
FELDMAN JACOB, LAIB, Brother
FELDMAN JOSEF, HERSCH, Brother
FELDMAN, FRYDKA, Sister
FELDMAN, ESTERA, Sister

FELLER, ISIDORE commemorates:

FELLER, HERSCH, Father
FELLER, ESTER, Mother
SHONFELD, CHAJE & SHIJE with sons, relatives
LINDNER, RACE & CHAIM HERSH with children, relatives
WEINBACH, JONAS & SOFIE with children, relatives
ROSENBERG, RIZA & SALKE with Mother, relatives
SHUSTER, HERSH & SIMA with children, relatives
FRIEDLANDER, MOSHE & CHANA with CILA, relatives
VOGEL, ABRAHAM & CHAJE with children, relatives

FISCHER, SALOMON commemorates:

STEIF, HERSCH, Father
STEIF, ROSE, Mother
STEIF, HERZEL, Brother
STEIF, MUNCHI, Sister
STEIF, PEPPI, Sister
STEIF, RACHELA BRAUNER, Sister
STEIF, MALKA, Sister
STEIF, PINCHAS, Brother

FLEISCHER, RONALD S. commemorates:

RUBINSOHN, LEON, Father
RUBINSOHN, RACHELA, Mother
RUBINSOHN, TYNIA, Sister

FRIED, RUBIN commemorates:

WEITZNER, HANKA, Sister
WEITZNER, GUSTAW, Brother-in-law
FRIED, ISRAEL Brother
FRIED, GENIA, Sister-in-law
SCHMORAK, GITTEL, Aunt
SCHMORAK, SAMUEL, Uncle

FRIEDLANDER, EDWARD commemorates:

FRIEDLANDER, HERMAN, Father
FRIEDLANDER, AMALIA, Mother
FRIEDLANDER, BRUNO, Son
FRIEDLANDER, IDA, Sister
FRIEDLANDER, GUSTA, Sister
HANDEL, WOLF, Father-in-law
HANDEL, AMALIA, Mother-in-law

FRIEDLER, JONAH commemorates:

FRIEDLER, SAMUEL, Father
FRIEDLER, CHAJA, Mother
FRIEDLER, ISAAC, Brother
FRIEDLER, GUSTA, Sister-in-law
FRIEDLER, EDWARD, Nephew
FRIEDLER, JOSEPH, Brother
FRIEDLER, PEARL, Sister-in-law
FRIEDLER, MORDECHAI, Nephew
FRIEDLER, HERSH, Brother
FRIEDLER, PINCHAS, Brother
FRIEDLER, RYSIA, Sister-in-law

GARTENBERG –TANNENBAUM, BERNARD commemorates:

TANNENBAUM, JOSEF
TANNENBAUM, CHANA
TANNENBAUM, GENIA
TANNENBAUM, FRIDA
TANNENBAUM, JECHESKIEL
TANNENBAUM, LORKA

GELOBTER, NORBERT commemorates:

JAKUBOWICZ, MICHAEL, Friend
JAKUBOWICZ, DUSKA, Friend

GOLDFISCHER, SIMON commemorates:

GOLDFISCHER, CUDIK, Father
GOLDFISCHER, DEBORA, Mother

GOTTESMAN, LEO commemorates:

GOTTESMAN, GOLDE, Mother
GOTTESMAN, MOISZE JOSEF, Brother
GOTTESMAN, ROSA, Wife
GOTTESMAN, PEPA, Daughter

GOTTESMAN, SAM commemorates:

GOTTESMAN, GOLDA, Mother
GOTTESMAN, RYSIA, Wife
GOTTESMAN, TONKA, Daughter
GOTTESMAN, MORITZ, Brother

GROLL, LEON commemorates:

GROLL, ISRAEL, Father
GROLL, MARYAM, Mother
LINHARD, KLARA, Sister
LINHARD, JACOB, Brother-in-law and two daughters
Sister with SHERMAN, REBECA, husband and two daughters

GROSS, ELLA commemorates:

MELZER JOJNE CHAIM, Father
MELZER ROSE, Mother
DORA, Sister
ANDZIA, Sister
NATAN, Brother
KORN, RYFKA, Relative
KORN, SZLOJME, Relative
KORN, ALTA, Relative
KORN, ELKA, Relative
KORN, HESIEK, Relative

GRUNDORFER, MICHEL & BRONIA commemorate:

GRUNDORFER, JOSEF, Father
GRUNDORFER, MALA, Step-Mother
DIAMAND, CYPRA, Sister
DIAMAND, SIMCHY, Nephew
DIAMAND, BRANCIA, Niece
DIAMAND, ETHEL, Niece
ROSEN, JACOB, Brother-in-law
ROSEN, AMALIA, Sister-in-law
ROSEN, ALFRED, Nephew

HALPERN, MANES commemorates:

HALPERN, SAMUEL, Father
HALPERN, HELENA, Mother
NATAN, Brother
BERNARD, Brother

HELLER, W. JACK commemorates:

HELLER, SAMUEL MEDECH, Father
HELLER, ROSE, Mother
HELLER, ISAAC MOSES, Brother
HELLER, ADELA, Sister
HELLER, HENIA, Sister
HEMENFELD, KLARA, Sister
MEHLER, FEIGA. Sister

HOLZER, M. commemorates:

HOLZER, SALOMON, Father
HOLZER, REGINA, Mother
HOLZER, ZYGMUND, Brother
HOLZER, CYLA, Sister
HOLZER, MINA, Sister

HUDYMA, STEPHEN commemorates:

HAENDEL, JOSEPH, Father
HAENDEL, SYMAH, Mother
KLINGS, MOSHE, Brother-in-law
KLINGS, BELA, Sister
KLINGS, CHANAH, Niece
KLINGS, RUTH, Niece
HAENDEL, ABRAHAM, Brother
HAENDEL CLAIRE, Sister in law
HAENDEL, JOSHUA, Nephew
HAENDEL, LEA, Sister
GARTENBERG, MARC, Brother-in-law
GARTENBERG, RACA, Sister

IGRA, S. Dr. commemorates:

IGRA, F., Mother
IGRA, JOSEF, Father
IGRA, BELA, Sister
IGRA, IZIO, Brother

JUBILER, R. commemorates:

MANESBERG, ZISEL, Mother
MANESBERG, BERNARD, Uncle

KATZ, IRA commemorates:

KATZ, JACOB
KATZ, ADELA
KATZ, BERTHA
KATZ, MOSES
KATZ, WOLF
KATZ, RACHELA
KATZ, HERMAN

KAY, CLARE commemorates:

HALPERN, MOZES, Father
HALPERN, BATKA, Mother
HALPERN, DAVID, Brother

KLAU, HARRY commemorates:

KLAU, HERSCH, Father
KLAU, ZISEL, Mother
KLAU, SHAJE LEIB, Brother
FRIEDMAN, ESTHER, Sister

KIEINBART, DAVID J. commemorates:

KLEINBART, BERTHA, Mother
BLAUSTEINI, MIRIAM, Aunt
BLAUSTEIN, MARKUS, Uncle
BLAUSTEIN, MOZES, Cousin
BLAUSTEIN, CECILIA, Cousin
BLAUSTEIN, RENATA, Cousin
RAPP, LEON, Dr., Friend
RAPP, SCHIJUM & PEAL, Parents of the Friend

KILEINHAMMER, JACOB commemorates:

KLEINHAMMER, MAYER, Father
KLEINHAMMER, MOTEL, Brother
KLEINHAMMER, LOLA. Sister
KLEINHAMMER, MECHEL, Brother
KLEINHAMMER, GIZIA, Sister

KOERNER, HERMAN & RENATA SCHIFFER commemorate:

KOERNER, MARCUS, Father
KOERNER, EUGENJA, Mother
KOERNER, LEON, Brother
KOERNER, JACOB, Brother
KOERNER, REGINA, Sister-in-law
KOERNER, MARK, Nephew
HERSCHDORFER, MARCUS

KOFLER, JEHUDA commemorates:

KOFLER, JOSEPH, Brother
KOFLER, JETTI, Sister-in-law
KOFLER, MALI, their child
KOFLER, MARCUS, Brother
KOFLER, SHEVA, Sister-in-law
KOFLER, LEIZER, their child
KOFLER, SARAH, their child
KOFLER, LEAH, their child
KOFLER, CLARA, their child

KORNBLUTH, ABRAHAM commemorates:

KORNBLUTH, RUBIN, Father
KORNBLUTH, FRAJDE, Mother
KORNBLUTH, DEBORA, Wife
KORNBLUTH, RUBIN, Son
KORNBLUTH, MOISHE, Son

KRIEGER, IRWIN commemorates:

KRIEGER, ABISH, Father
KRIEGER, DORA, Mother
KRIEGER, IRO, Brother
KRIEGER, MUNDZIO, Brother
KRIEGER, ICKO, Brother

KRON, DAVID commemorates:

KRON, JOKHEVED, Sister with husband and 3 daughters
KRON, MOSHE, Brother with wife and children
MINKEL, SARA, Sister with husband & children
SECHER, ROSALIE, Sister with husband & children

LAMPEL, JOSEF commemorates:

LAMPEL, ESTER, Step Mother
LAMPEL, HERSH, Brother
LAMPEL, LEON, Brother
LAMPEL, SARA, Sister

LANDAU, NAFTALI commemorates:

LANDAU, HILEL, Father
LANDAU, SZABSE, Brother
LANDAU, JACOB, Brother
LANDAU, JEHIDE, Brother
LANDAU, JOSEPH, Brother
LANDAU, CHAJA (HELEN), Sister-in-law
LANDAU, JANCIO, Nephew

LERNER, SISIE commemorates:

LERNER, MOISZE
LERNER, RYFKA
LERNER, BEILA
LERNER, AVRUM ZVI
LERNER, HENCIE
LERNER, SURE
LERNER, SOSIE
ZIMERMAN, BUROCH
ZIMERMAN, ETEL, with 2 children
ROSENBERG, GECEL
ROSENBERG, SIME, with 4 children

LEREK, AL commemorates:

LERIKSTEIN, F., Mother
SCHWALBENDORF, F., Step-Father
LERIKSTEIN, POLDEK, Brother
LERIKSTEIN, LUSIA, Sister
LERIKSTEIN, EDZIA, Sister

LIEBMAN, FISCHEL commemorates:

LIEBMAN, CHANNA, Wife
LIEBMAN, REGINA, Daughter
LIEBMAN, FEIWEL, Father

LISS, THELMA commemorates:

HILSENRAD, SHOLUM, Brother-in-law
HILSENRAD, SALKA, Sister and sons
ROSENBERG, JACOB, Brother
ROSENBERG, HELA, Sister-in-law and children

LUKOVITCH, TYNIA commemorates:

BIRNBAUM, ADOLF, Father
BIRNBAUM-FRANKEL, MICHAEL, Brother
SCHEER, OTTO, Husband

LUSTIG, JOACHIM commemorates:

LUSTIG, ESTER, Mother
LUSTIG, JEHUDA, Father

MARBACH, ABRAHAM commemorates:

MARBACH, ARON, Father
MARBACH, DRESEL, Mother
MARBACH, DORA, Sister
MARBACH, MINA, Sister
MARBACH ISRAEL, Brother
TABISEL, BENJAMIN, Uncle
TABISEL, MALCIA, Aunt
TABISEL, MAYER, Cousin
TABISEL, LINA, (his wife) & their 3 children

MONDSCHEIN, JACOB Dr. commemorates:

MONDSCHEIN, ERIKA, Daughter
ELNER, JULIA, nee MONDSCHEIN, Sister
TAUBER, IRENA, nee EINER, Niece
MONDSCHEIN, HERMAN, Uncle

MOSKOWITZ, SELIG commemorates:

MOSKOWITZ, SAMUEL, Father
MOSKOWITZ, GITTEL CHANNAH, Mother
RINDER, CHAYITTA, Sister
FRUCHTER, LEAH, Sister
APFELLSCHMITT, BELLA, Sister

NENNER, MURRAY commemorates:

NENNER, FEIGE, Mother
SHINDLER, ISRAEL. Cousin
EISENBRUCH, MULO, Relative
EISENBRUCH, YETTA, Relative
EISENBRUCH, ESTEA, Relative
SHINDLER, SARA, Relative

NIEMIROV, HARRY commemorates:

NIEMIROV, KASRIEL, Father
NIEMIROV, CHANA, Mother
NIEMIROV, DAVID, Brother
NIEMIROV, NUCHIM, Brother
NIEMIROV, SISSEL, Sister
NIEMIROV, JETKA, Sister
NIEMIROV, ROZA, Wife
NIEMIROV, MAREK, Son

PECH, MORRIS J. & PECH, MICHAEL commemorate:

PECH, ISRAEL, Father
PECH, EVA, Mother
RUBIN, ESTHER, Sister
SCHTULBACH, SARA, Sister
PECH, FRIMKA, Sister

PICKHOLZ, SOL & PICKHOLZ, IZAK commemorate:

PICKHOLZ, LEIBISH, Father
PICKHOLZ, CHAJA, Mother
PICKHOLZ, HINDA, Sister
PICKHOLZ, FEIGA, Sister
PICKHOLZ, CIPORA, Sister
PICKHOLZ, SARA R., Sister
PICKHOLZ, MIRYAM, Sister
GAJER, COPEL, Brotherin law
PICKHOLZ, CYLA, Friend
PICKHOLZ, LUSIA, Child
LEITER, ABRAHAM, Brother in law
LEITER, IZAK, Nephew
LEITER, SARA R., Niece
LEITER, CHAVA, Niece
LEITER, HERSCH, Nephew
ZILBER, SHIJE, Brother in law
ZILBER, RUTI, Niece

PICKHOLZ, PINKUS commemorates:

PICKHOLZ, CIRYL, Mother

PICKHOLZ, ZISSIE, Brother with wife and son

PICKHOLZ, GITEL, Sister with husband A. WEINBERGER and children

PICKHOLZ, LAJCIE, Sister with husband A. LADEN and children

PICKHOLZ, BENJAMIN, Brother with wife and children

PICKHOLZ, JEHOSHUAH, Brother with wife Sara and children

PICKHOLZ, HERSCH, Brother

PICKHOLZ, SARAH, Siwith husband and daughter Cipora

PICKHOLZ, JITAH, Sister

NATANSON, SAUL JOSEPH, Brother with wife Sara

POLEWSKI, LEON commemorates:

SACK, MAURYCY, Father

SACK, REGINA, Mother

SACK-GLANZ, BRONILAWA, Wife

GLANZ, RENATA, Daughter

SACK, DORA, Sister

RIECHTER, WILLIAM Dr. commemorates:

RECHTER, PESACH, Father

LEWITER, TONCIA, Sister

ROTHENBERG, JOSEF & CLARA commemorate :

KARNELE, ABRAHAM CHAIM, Father

KARNELE, MARYA, Mother

SHNEEWEISS, SARA CHANA, Children

SHNEEWEISS, ROJZA, Children

SHNEEWEISS, SALOMON DAVID, Children

Sisters and their Husbands:

LANDAU, GITEL & MOSES, & their 3 children

WEISS, USHER & RIWKA. and their 3 children

SPEIER, LIPA & MACHLA & their 2 children

LITOWITZ, WOLF DR. & SARA CHANA, and their daughter

KARNELE, SABINA, Sister

KARNELE, MESHULIM HERSCH, Brother

ROTHENBERG, IZAK MOZES, Father

ROTHENBERG, FREIDA, Mother

ROTHENBERG, FRADEL, Wife

JACOB MEIER, Son

HENIA, Daughter

SCHMIEL, ISSER, Son

Sisters and Brothers:

ROTHFELD, TAUBA, Sisterand 4 children

KLEINER, REIZEL and 3 children

ROTHENBERG, SZIE

ROTHENBERG, MAIER SZULIM

ROSENBERG, MAX commemorates:

HILSENRATH, SALKA, Sister
HILSENRATH, SHULIM, Brotherin law
HILSENRATH, HENIK, Nephew
HILSENRATH, JUMEK, Nephew
ROSENBERG, JAKOB, Brother
ROSENBERG, HENIAH, Sister in law
ROSENBERG, HENIK, Nephew

ROSEMAN, BERTHA (nee KESTENBAUM) commemorates:

LINHARD, RACA, Sister
LINHARD, JANKEL, Brother-in-law
LINHARD, HANNAH, Niece
LINHARD, JOSSEL, Nephew
LINHARD, MAX, Nephew
FINK, JOSEPH, Brother

ROTHBAUM, NORBERT commemorates:

ROTHBAUM, MATES, Father
ROTHBAUM, TAUBE, Mother
ROTHBAUM, MOSES, Brother
ROTHBAUM, SCHEINKU, Brother
ROTHBAUM, JOSEF, Son
ROTHBAUM, LOLU, Son
ROTHBAUM, DORA, Wife
ROTHBAUM, KALMAN, Uncle
ROTHBAUM, HINDA, Aunt
MOLDAUER, DAVID, Relative
MOLDAUER, CHUNA, Relative

ROTHSTEIN, HARRY commemorates:

FREIMAN, SAMUEL

FREIMAN, ROSE

FREIMAN, LILY

FREIMAN, BETTY

SCHIFF, N. Dr. commemorates:

SCHIFF, JACOB, Father

SCHNEELICHT, EMIL commemorates:

SCHEITEL, HELENE, Sister

SCHEITEL, JOSEPH, Brother-in-law & 3 children

SCHNEELICHT, MORRIS, Brother

SCHNEELICHT, ROS, Sister-in-law & 5 children

JAEGER, ESTER, Sister

JAEGER, SAMNET, Brother-in-law and 4 children

SCHNEELICHT, SAUL, Brother, wife & 5 children

SCHNEELICHT, BRUNO, Brother

SCHNEELICHT, SABINA, Sister-in-law

SCHNEID, MOSES commemorates:

NELHEMYE, Father
RYFKA, Mother
CHANA CHAJA, Sister & their 3 children
MEYER, Brother
CHAIM, Brother
WOLF, Brother
SCHNEEWEIS, ELIASH, Uncle
FELDHORN, WOLF, Uncle
DEBORA, Aunt
DRESEL, Aunt
CHANA, Aunt
SIMA, Aunt and 3 children

SCHIVIORAK, EISSIG commemorates:

SCHMORAK, CHANCIA, Sister
SCHMORAK, SOBOLA, Sister
SCHMORAK, SCHURCIA, Sister
SCHMORAK, SCHMEIL, Brother
SCHMORAK, HERSCH, Father
SCHMORAK, GOLDE, Mother

SCHNUR, JOSEPH commemorates:

SCHNUR, WOLF, Father
SCHNUR, HENIA, Mother
SCHNUR, SALA, Sister

SCHWARTZ, NATHAN commemorates:

SCHWARTZ, LEIZER, Cousin

SCHWARTZ, BERIL & AIZ', Cousins

SCHUBERT, LEO commemorates:

SCHUBERT, FEIWEL, Father

SCHUBERT, MALI, Mother

SCHUBERT, JOSEPH, Brother

SCHUBERT, JACOB, Brother

SCHUBERT, POLA, Wife

SCHUBERT, FREDZIO, Son

SEIGER, ABE commemorates:

ROZMARYN, LIBBY & GERSCHEN, Sister and Brother-in-law with 3 children

SEIGER, JOSEL & REISEL Brother and Sister-in-law with 5 children

SCHEITEL, JEUNE, Cousin & wife and family

SCHEITEL, CHAIM. Cousin

SCHEITEL, PESL, Cousin

SCHEITEL, MOISHE HERSH, Cousin & wife and family

SELIGER, BRAUNER MALCIA commemorates:

BRAUNER, JOEL

BRAUNER, BERTHA

BRAUNER, FELIX

BRAUNER, ADOLF

SELIGER, SAM commemorates:

SELIGER, LEIB, Father
SELIGER, LEA, Mother
SCHUSTER, SZYJA, Relative
SCHUSTER, EISIG, Relative
SCHUSTER, KLARA, Relative
SCHUSTER, LEA, Relative
SEGALL, SEIDE, Relative
SEGALL, MIHA, Relative
SEGALL, SIVNIA, Relative
TEPPER, TAUBE, Relative
SCHUSTER, SYMA, Relative

SEEMAN, MAX commemorates:

TURKELTAUB, RACHELA, Sister

SPRING, ISADORE commemorates:

SPRING, DANIEL, Father
SPRING, BERTHA, Mother
SPRING, HERMAN, Brother
SPRING, MINKA, Sister

STERN, M. commemorates:

STERN, AVNER, Father
STERN, GISELA, Mother

TIEGERMAN, SIMON commemorates:

TIEGERMAN, BERNARD, Father
TIEGERMAN, REGINA, Mother
TIEGERMAN, MOSES, Brother

TURKELTAUB, LEON commemorates:

TURKELTAUB, ELIAS, Father
TURKELTAUB, RACHELA, Mother

WANDEL-FRANK, JANINA commemorates:

WANDEL, SEBASTJAN Dr., Father
LINDENBAUM, HENRYKA, Sister
LINDENBAUM, EWA, Daughter
LINDENBAUM, JUREK, Son
GEIST, MARCELI Dr., Husband
BLAUSTEIN, HENRYK, Uncle
BLAUSTEIN, MALWINA, Aunt
BLAUSTEIN, DANUTA, Daughter

WIESELTIER, MARC commemorates:

WIESELTIER, SALOMON, Father
WIESELTIER, OTYLIA, Mother
WIESELTIER, OZJASZ, Brother
WIESELTIER, FRYDA, Sister
WIESELTIER, MAYER, Relative
WIESELTIER, OZJASZ, Relative
WIESELTIER, CHAWA, Relative
HOLZ, SALOMON, Relative
HOLZ, TONKA, Relative
HOLZ, MAX, Relative
HOLZ, FRYDA, Relative
BACKENROTH, MAYER & Family, Relative

ZAUM, MAX commemorates:

ZAUM, SALOMON, Father
ZAUM, CHARNA, Mother
ZAUM, NOAH, Brother
ZAUM, RUBIN, Brother
ZAUM, SABINA, Sister

ZWILLING, DAVID commemorates:

GRIMINGER, ESTERA, Sister
GRIMINGER, MAKS, Brother-in-law
GRIMINGER, MATYLDA, Daughter
GRIMINGER, PERLA, Daughter

Index

This index does not include those on the lists that start on pages 424, 503 and 685.

A

Abend, 80
Aberdam, 91
Abner, 577
Achser, 464
Ackerman, 575
Adelheid, 423
Adler, 187, 608
Agnon, 69, 73, 171, 235, 352, 595, 640
Agrat, 501
Ahad Ha'am, 163, 164, 173
Aher, 210
Ahrenbart, 50
Akser, 289, 602
Aleksandrowicz, 21
Alimelech, 19
Allerhand, 206, 613
Altbauer, 165, 288, 320, 467, 604
Altman, 64, 88, 90, 589
Altschiller, 425
Altshuler, 188, 311
Anden, 419
Ansky, 106
Apfelgreen, 50, 123, 124, 128, 139, 140, 156, 162, 178, 188, 206, 207, 283, 406, 462
Apfelgreen (Kudish), 420
Apfelgruen, xx, 251, 369, 379, 603, 604, 608, 613, 615, 624, 628, 660, 670
Apfelstein, 602
Apflegreen, 202, 289
Apftobitzer, 272
Appelgruen, 495
Appfelgreen, 106, 107
Arbach, 314
Arnfeld, 274
Arnold, 327, 606, 635
Arnshteyn, 289
Arter, 49
Artimowicz, 118
Ash, 274, 458, 476
Ashkenazi, 37, 127, 128, 159, 211, 279, 287, 459, 617
Ashkenazy, 16
Auerbach, 188, 190, 283, 608, 609, 628
Axelrod, 159, 603

B

Bader, 68, 72, 230, 594, 596
Baer, 577
Bakka, 110
Bakster, 480
Baktrag, 466
Balaban, 48, 75
Balabban, 47
Balfour, 164, 175, 227, 254, 267, 280, 321, 354, 627, 642
Bandera, 359, 362, 649, 653
Bar, 403, 406, 419
Bar –Lev, 307
Barash, 171

Book of Stryj Index

Bard, 462

Bardach, viii

Bardach–Oher, viii

Bardecki, 33

Barlev, xx, 246, 249, 250, 304

Bar-Lev, xiii, 186, 310, 311, 399, 401, 500, 501, 606

Bar-Lev – Klein, 310, 311

Bar–Lev (Klein), 401

Bar-Lev-Klein, 606

Bar-Lev-Reinhartz, 310, 606

Baron, 575

Báthory, 3, 7, 9

Batisz, 28

Batory, 3, 11

Baumann, 183, 606

Becher, xx, 137, 266, 298, 299, 323, 576, 631

Beer, 495

Begleiter, 124, 192, 422, 602, 609

Behr, 187, 608

Bekher, 466, 468

Belz, 337

Ben Bezalel, 24, 543

Ben Eliezer, 167

Ben Michael, 23

Ben Mordechai, 24

Bencher, 83, 428, 429, 437

Benczer, 92, 207, 378, 557, 613, 668

Ber, 24, 36, 79, 123, 155, 156, 183, 207, 340, 471, 480, 496, 602, 606, 613, 615

Ber Bolechówer, 17, 18

Ber Bolichower, 16, 508

Ber of Bolechow, 598

Berdiczewski, 171

Berger, 208, 573, 613

Bergstein, 462, 470

Berkowitz, 171

Berlass, 206, 613

Berlin, 313

Berliner, 592

Bermann, 182, 605

Bernfeld, xix, 58, 59, 78, 106, 107, 124, 125, 126, 139, 169, 174, 228, 240, 582, 591, 592

Berson, 75

Bert, 289

Bertshnider, 188

Bialik, 164, 170

Bidlowski, 11

Bienenstock, xix, 65, 117, 118, 119, 120, 123, 188, 191, 236, 237, 240, 590, 593, 602, 608, 609, 622

Binder, 208, 613

Birenbaum, 458

Birkental, 69, 74, 75

Birnbaum, 60, 66, 70, 239, 439, 574, 575, 584, 590, 598, 629

Birnebaum, 286

Blau, 304, 307, 309, 632

Bleiberg, 91, 185, 327, 606, 635

Bloch, 49, 79, 457

Bock, 594

Bockshtav–Evyona, 172

Bohdan, 2

Bohrer, 461

Boimel, 146, 615

Bonom, 321

Bonum, 184, 606

Borak, 92, 117, 122, 167, 205, 206, 207, 364, 373, 602, 613, 654, 664

Borek, 93, 95, 103, 104, 499

Borer, 182, 184, 185, 199, 288, 335, 605, 606

Book of Stryj Index

Borochov, xxii, 137, 266, 298, 299, 323, 465, 469, 476, 477, 631

Boxer, 340, 472

Boymel, 399, 498, 499

Brand, 143, 208, 320, 613, 615

Braude, 67, 72, 594

Brauner, 162, 191, 204, 403, 414, 419, 609, 612

Braver, 69, 70, 73, 74, 597, 598

Brickenstein, 145, 615

Brigido, 77

Broides, 174

Broyner, 496

Brummer, 574

Buber, 67, 71, 302, 594

Bucchnbaum, 361, 651

Buch, 68, 72, 107, 588

Buchenbaum, 491

Buchman, 186, 311, 606

Buchner, 32, 77

Buchsbaum, 467, 468

Buchstab – Avi–Yona, 82

Buchwalter, 406, 495

Buk, 150, 151, 153, 154, 155

Buksbaum, 123, 602

Byk, 52, 64, 80, 89, 136, 159, 168, 187, 196, 224, 253, 280, 302, 304, 320, 610, 622, 631, 632

C

Carmel, 48, 501

Chaimowicz, 14, 17

Chaimowitcz, 17, 24

Chajes, 230, 233, 596, 597, 620, 621

Chanes, 78

Chazanowitcz, 286

Chazanowitz, 458

Chotrinsky, 159, 603

Chutriansky, 590

Cirglass, 153

Cohen, 49

Cuzmer, xix, 37, 41, 42, 43, 44, 45, 64, 127, 209, 210, 214, 216, 223, 522, 589, 614, 617

Czaczkes, 63, 587

Czerbinsky, 585

Czysez, 144

D

Darmstender, 577

Davidman, 123, 197, 320, 602, 611

de Maupassant, 86

de Rothschild, 118

Deliktish, 120

Dembski, 81

Derfer, 429

Derfler, 165, 354, 466, 477, 604

Deutch, 42

Diamant, 188, 191, 193, 279, 313, 608, 611

Dicker, 419, 496

Dickman, 322, 633

Diemenstein, 159

Diesendruck, 90, 169, 322, 351, 595, 597, 620, 621

Diesendruk, xix, 65, 164, 165, 174, 229, 231, 233, 240, 246, 590, 604, 640

Dobbs, 46

Doerfler, 642

Dornfeld, 123, 124, 471, 602, 603

Dragomanow, 585

Drahomanov, 61

Drefler, 322

Drimer, 643

Drimmer, 354, 382, 672

Book of Stryj Index

Drucker, 157, 616, 619

Druker, xix, 49, 50, 224, 225

Dunkel, 361, 402, 491, 651

Dzidoszicki, 44

E

Eckstein, 187, 608

Edelstein, 274

Egid, 123, 128, 602, 614

Eherenpreis, 80

Ehrenkranz, 148

Ehrenpreis, 58, 67, 72, 582, 583, 594

Ehrenstein, 154

Ehrman, 182, 605

Eichel, 576

Eichen, 320

Eichenstein, 40, 42, 226

Eigenmachtes, 206

Eiger, 213, 216

Eingenmachtes, 128

Einhorn, 182, 185, 326, 327, 605, 606, 635

Eisenshar, 281, 499

Eisenstein, xx, 80, 125, 140, 165, 170, 177, 186, 257, 283, 302, 303, 304, 307, 310, 311, 337, 354, 419, 496, 604, 606, 625, 628, 631, 643

Eisenszar, 422

Ek (Ekron), 232

Ekert, 184, 606

Ekser, 123

Eljaszwitz, 19

Elner, 338, 355, 403, 478

emperor Joseph II, 29

empress Maria Theresa, 26

Ende, 206, 613

Enden, 496

Engelman, 91, 320, 421, 501

Enser, 49, 224

Erman, 329, 331, 636

Esteryung, 494

Etinger, 194

Ettinger, 158, 360, 490, 616, 651

F

Fairberg, 576

Falk, 64, 80, 128, 210, 252, 270, 589

Fefferbaum, 123, 207, 602, 613

Feis, 311

Feld, 58, 582

Feldhorn, 173, 320, 425

Feldman, 311, 442, 576

Feller, 182, 314, 605

Fennig, 321

Fergen, 69, 73, 597

Feuerstein, 207, 613

Fichman, 406

Fichner, 80, 122, 189, 602, 609

Fiedler, 577

Fikhmann, 495

Filko, 183, 207

Filtz, 495

Findling, 96, 97, 98, 99, 100, 321, 420

Fine, 48

Finger, 156, 615

Fink, 64, 206, 576, 589, 613

Finkelstein, 391, 682

Finkler, 420

Fischel, 159, 428

Fishbein, 199

Fiszel, 19

Flamenbaum, 574

Fleischer, 385, 676

Flick, 158, 306, 550

Fogel, 186, 206, 304, 305, 311

Frank, 69, 74, 372, 598, 663

Frankel, xx, 223, 224, 248, 249, 281, 305, 320, 336, 498, 499, 501, 623

Franko, 61, 585

Frei, 80

Freilich, 303, 307, 308, 322, 337, 422, 471, 632, 633

Freiman, 402, 491

Frenkel, xix, 206, 613

Fried, 322, 499, 574, 575, 577, 633

Fried (Wolf), 422

Friedlaender, 605

Friedlander, 45, 49, 127, 182, 185, 274, 426, 571, 576, 577, 578, 605, 614

Friedler, xxvii, 144, 152, 158, 165, 166, 170, 177, 274, 283, 302, 314, 323, 328, 350, 354, 422, 488, 571, 574, 604, 615, 616, 631, 638, 643

Friedman, 123, 286, 288, 289, 296, 335, 457, 460, 462, 464, 602

Frisch, 66, 67, 70, 71, 165, 171, 172, 177, 302, 303, 584, 590, 591, 631

Frishman, 167

Fritsch, 123, 602

Fritzhand, 303, 305, 632

Fromm, 185, 606

Frostig, 63, 587

Fruchter, 145, 177, 199, 207, 295, 298, 302, 303, 309, 320, 406, 419, 444, 466, 477, 495, 496, 501, 613, 631

Fruchtman, 80, 89

Fruchtmann, 52, 53, 58, 64, 90, 189, 581, 589, 609

Fuchs, 171, 183, 185

Fuks, 65, 159, 590, 603

G

Gabel, 279

Garfinkel, 484

Garfunkel, xx, 123, 124, 139, 156, 165, 177, 185, 208, 261, 262, 283, 302, 303, 305, 306, 307, 308, 323, 327, 337, 342, 357, 602, 603, 606, 613, 614, 626, 631, 635, 648

Garlanter, 47, 48, 90, 154, 155

Garlenter, 45, 135, 201, 351, 353

Gartenberg, 176, 298, 399, 466, 501

Gartner, 303, 319, 323

Gelernter, xix, 65, 165, 177, 230, 233, 240, 354, 589, 590, 596, 597, 604, 621, 640, 642

Gelerter, 642

Geller, 176

Genzel, 320

Gerengross, 375

Gerngross, 666

Gernter, 354

Gerstmann, 185

Gertenberg, 313

Gertler, 199

Gertner, 125, 157, 177, 284, 615, 629

Ger–Tzedek, 48

Gettinger, 64

Getz, 211

Giardziński, 11

Ginsberg, 163

Ginsburg, 123, 283, 578, 602, 628

Gladstein, 457

Glantz, 422

Glatstein, 135

Glazer, 156, 320

Gleicher, 208, 613

Book of Stryj Index

Glezer, 157, 616

Glicher, 421

Gliecher, 501

Goebbels, 366, 656

Goethe, 86

Goldberg, xix, 59, 60, 64, 80, 88, 91, 120, 123, 124, 125, 139, 156, 157, 165, 185, 190, 195, 242, 243, 253, 277, 281, 284, 304, 326, 327, 328, 352, 396, 573, 583, 585, 588, 602, 604, 606, 609, 615, 622, 626, 627, 629, 635, 641

Goldfaden, 476

Goldfarb, 82

Goldfinger, 492

Goldfisher, 305, 574

Goldhammer, 278, 279

Golding, 501

Goldman, iii, 95, 96, 97, 99, 100, 104, 186, 228, 311

Goldmann, 592

Goldreich, 423

Goldring, 421

Goldstein, 64, 279

Goldstein-Enzl, 589

Goldstern, 80, 122

Golochowski, 42, 46, 112, 114

Gordin, 187, 289, 462

Gordon, xxvi, 48, 302, 304, 305, 353, 641

Gorski, 11

Gottesman, 574

Gottesmann, 207, 613

Gotthoffer, 576

Gottlieb, 219, 320

Graubart, 207, 613

Greenbaum, 239

Greenberg, 631

Grimm, 378

Gritz, 207, 613

Gross, 88, 117, 328, 574

Grossman, 185, 259, 328, 331, 466, 476, 625, 635

Grossmann, 182, 605, 606

Gruber, 576

Gruenbaum, 185, 599

Gruninski, 79

Gurfunkel, 124, 125

Gushalwitz, 46

Guttmacher, 213

Guttman, 466

Gwirtz, 414, 415, 420

H

Haas, 199

Haber, 207, 466, 496, 574, 613

Hacohen, 59, 83, 583, 617

HaCohen, 35, 41, 45, 252, 270

Hacohen Heller, 616, 617, 639

Hacohen Jolles, 618

Hacohen Rosenmann, 617

Hacohen Yolles, 639

Haendel, 495

Haftel, 129, 130, 150, 329, 615, 636

HaKohen, xix, 209, 210, 212, 223, 351, 522, 534, 559

HaKohen Rosenblum, 216

HaKohen Yolles, 218

Halfgut, 423

Halperin, 64, 76, 589, 602, 613

Halpern, 44, 45, 52, 89, 116, 117, 122, 127, 205, 207, 279, 351, 437, 613, 614, 639

Halpren, 122

Hammer, 195

Hammermann, 184, 606

Hammerschlag, 125, 208, 613

Book of Stryj Index

Hand, 314

Handel, 274

Händell, 321, 633

Hariff, 24

Harr, 631

Harshderfer, 349

Hass, 137, 466

Hatterer, 489, 496

Hauptman, xix, 89, 226, 260, 308, 329, 335, 336, 446, 459, 462, 463, 464, 465, 489, 608, 636

Hauptmann, 127, 159, 186, 187, 188, 190, 199, 201, 274, 281, 288, 296, 297, 302, 311, 460, 606, 608, 609, 614, 619, 630, 631

Hausman, 340

Hausmann, 193, 206, 207, 379, 611, 613, 670

Hayot, 41, 42, 230, 233

Hazelnuss, 184, 185, 605

Hebbel, 593

Heiber, 92, 93, 94, 96, 99, 100, 101, 102, 103, 104, 105, 207, 314, 396, 419, 613

Heidelkorn, 93, 94, 95, 97, 99, 103, 104, 105

Heine, 86, 593

Heinrich, 64, 79, 80, 84, 117, 172

Heizelkorn, 279

Helfgott, 162, 353, 604, 642

Heller, iii, xix, 35, 36, 41, 156, 209, 210, 212, 351, 416, 431, 495, 499, 500, 573, 574

Hendel, 177, 178, 184

Herman, 45, 52, 525

Herring, 309

Hersch, 16, 17, 20, 506

Herstein, 406

Herszowitz, 19

Hertz, xix, 65, 80, 90, 106, 107, 219, 351, 589, 618, 640

Hertzing, 33

Herzl, 84, 89, 95, 102, 104, 163, 171, 180, 204, 212, 218, 231, 232, 248, 270, 277, 278, 280, 305, 600, 618, 621, 622, 623, 626, 627

Hess, 298, 323

Hibbel, 40

Hirschbein, 289

Hirschhorn, 495

Hirschorn, 478, 484

Hirshenhorn, 406

Hirszhorn, 128

Hizelkorn, 91

Hladisz, 28

Hobbel, 421, 501

Hobel, 181, 501

Hoch, 321

Hochmann, 207, 613

Hochstein, 613

Hofenbartel, 159, 603

Hoffman, 329

Hoffmann, 182, 605

Hoffner, 204, 612

Hoizman, 480

Honig, 283, 324, 331, 421, 489, 565, 635, 636

Honnig, 501

Hornstein, 60, 80, 584, 585

Horoshovski, 457

Horowitz, xix, 54, 78, 119, 124, 125, 129, 133, 157, 190, 192, 216, 218, 219, 223, 284, 289, 299, 305, 351, 462, 469, 471, 477, 494, 495, 506, 573, 602, 609, 611, 615, 616, 618, 629

Horowtiz, 573

Horshovsky, 629

Horshowska, 199

Horszowski, 286

Book of Stryj Index

Horwitz, 351, 613, 618

Hoterrer, 395, 411, 418, 419

Housemann, 279

Houssmann, 207, 613

Hovel, 426, 427, 445

Hoyftmann, 123

Hoyzer, 52

Hubel, 133, 135, 182, 283, 284, 320, 337, 403, 605, 615, 628

Hurwitz, 42, 65, 89, 167, 182, 195, 196, 207, 406, 589, 605, 639

Huser, 420

Hushi, 166, 354, 642

Hutterer, 359, 650

I

Ibn Bezalel, 69, 73

Igra, 35, 37, 130, 146, 167, 188, 209, 212, 223, 289, 314, 329, 335, 351, 462, 608, 615, 616, 619, 636, 639

Imber, 457

Ingbar, 419

Ingber, 107, 182, 414, 496, 605

Insler, xix, 92, 124, 175, 181, 182, 231, 238, 240, 278, 280, 281, 598, 599, 605, 622, 627

Isaac, 9, 15, 19, 506

Isakawer, 144

Isakowitcz, 15

Ish-Hurwitz, 195

Ivanitzki, 116

J

Jabłonowski, 4

Jabotinsky, 182, 185, 259, 327, 328, 330, 331

Janelewicz, 19

Jankilewicz, 19

Jastaszewski, 11

Jerich, 127, 145, 614, 615

Jodl, 230, 596

Jolles, 65, 203, 223, 351, 589, 619

Josefberg, 406

Josefsberg, 494

Joseph II, 31, 38, 534

Judis, 576

Julles, 419

Jungman, 374, 665

K

Kahana, 168, 509

Kalir, 46

Kalisher, 213

Kaliszer, 52

Kammerman, 199

Kaplanski, 286, 458

Karkowski, 18

Karl, 61, 68, 72, 79, 80, 88, 506, 594

Karnell, 577

Karon, 403, 419

Karwas, 16

Kastenbaum, 349

Katz, xx, 63, 80, 84, 88, 89, 90, 92, 123, 140, 143, 178, 187, 194, 195, 196, 202, 207, 220, 252, 253, 254, 270, 271, 281, 286, 311, 312, 369, 457, 459, 467, 499, 588, 602, 608, 610, 613, 615, 624, 660

Kaufman, 123, 178, 182, 192, 193, 202, 274, 280, 281, 312, 349, 352, 602, 611, 628

Kaufmann, xix, 124, 125, 139, 140, 241, 278, 283, 602, 605, 608, 622, 627, 641

Kaz, 91, 176, 399, 400, 422, 499, 500, 501

Book of Stryj Index

Kazimiera, 13, 543

Kazimierz, 2, 3, 10, 11, 18, 74, 548

Keler, 308

Keller–Haliczer, 306

Kenigsberg, 123, 602

Kenner, 467

Kerner, 60, 313, 320, 331, 361, 404, 445, 491, 577, 585

Kess, 378, 668

Kessler, 127, 614

Ketz, 480

Kez, xiii, 320, 330, 331, 636

Kiczales, 80, 190, 384, 609, 674

Kinder, 201

Kindler, 188, 379, 420, 608, 612, 670

king Władysław IV, 9

king Zygmunt III, 3, 8, 9, 74

Kinjochowski, 19

Kirshner, 457

Kirton, 63, 587

Kitaigorodsky, 219, 351, 618

Kitaigrodski, 639

Kitczels, 94, 96, 98, 103, 104, 105, 414

Klar, 177, 303, 632

Klarsfeld, 279

Klatzkin, 171

Klein, xx, 106, 123, 124, 126, 140, 157, 173, 186, 191, 201, 246, 250, 281, 304, 324, 342, 357, 446, 469, 484, 602, 603, 609, 612, 623, 648

Kleiner, 431, 439, 573, 577, 578

Kleinman, 151

Kleinmann, 130, 615

Klein-Reinhartz, 632

Klemens, 185, 606

Klieger, 123, 197, 198, 421, 602, 611

Kliger, 321, 501

Klinger, 406, 495

Klinghoyft, 219, 224

Klueger, 188, 608

Knittel, 207, 613

Kobrin, 289, 462

Koch, 320

Koenig, 191, 414

Koerner, 651

Kofman, 313

Kogel, 313

Kohn, 174, 188, 608

Kom, 162

Koniecpolski, 2, 9, 10, 74

Konjochowski, 19

Kopel, 310

Koppel, 183, 606

Koppler, 45, 48

Korkis, 58, 582

Korn, 90, 135, 136, 164, 165, 171, 283, 311, 322, 353, 354, 357, 427, 428, 432, 446, 604, 633, 642, 643, 648

Korngreen, 279

Kostman, 480

Kraan, 496

Kraemer, 495

Krakowski, 3

Kramer, 158, 378, 616, 668

Krampner, 124, 125, 139, 321, 603

Krampner (Amir), 633

Krauss, 272

Kreisberg, 188, 608

Kremer, 406

Krempner, 123

Krieger, 134, 142, 615

Book of Stryj Index

Krigger, 454

Kris, 60, 585

Krischer, 480

Kriss, 578

Kriszer, 340

Kroczewski, 8

Krogulecki, 11

Kron, 378, 385, 571, 668, 676

Kronberg, 304, 307, 337, 349

Kronstein, 402, 420

Kudisch, 133, 158, 177, 183, 197, 207, 604, 606, 611, 613, 615, 616, 628, 631

Kudish, i, xiii, xxvii, 163, 165, 271, 283, 302, 307, 309, 310, 311, 321, 352, 354, 399, 400, 500, 501, 507, 601, 640, 643

Kugel, 399

Kuhn, 65, 590

Kuk, 306

Kun, xxi, 450, 451

Kupfer, 148, 615

Kurtzer, 128, 614

Kurzer, 157

L

Labin, 157, 616

Ladier, xix, 65, 117, 126, 127, 154, 157, 169, 172, 174, 203, 221, 351, 359, 378, 415, 419, 589, 603, 614, 616, 618, 640, 650, 668

Ladir, 222, 489, 496

Lamm, 466

Lampel, 573, 575

Landau, 60, 117, 171, 368, 370, 371, 391, 585, 658, 661, 682

Landes, 207, 613

Landsberger, 46

Langer, 608

Larch, 207

Lasker, 296

Lasst, 466

Last, 61, 440, 477, 577, 585

Lauberboim, 153

Laufer, 322, 466

Lautman, 178, 189, 321, 328, 331, 633, 636

Lebowitz, 289

Lechman, 186

Lehrer, 125, 283, 628

Leib, xix, xx, xxvi, 20, 24, 35, 36, 41, 89, 142, 150, 155, 156, 192, 209, 223, 268, 303, 304, 440, 567

Leibovitch, 608, 629, 633

Leibovitz, 603, 609, 635

Leibowicz, 19, 384, 674

Leibowitz, xx, 91, 124, 187, 188, 191, 192, 255, 286, 312, 322, 323, 349, 414, 419, 458, 462, 469, 472, 496, 624

Leibush, 54, 124, 125, 283

Lejzerowicz, 19

Łekieński, 8

Lentz, 185, 422, 499, 501, 606

Lerch, 613

Lerik, 183, 606

Lerik (Lerikstein), 183

Lerner, 406, 495

Lerrer, 106

Lest, 289, 322

Levenzohn, 48

Levi, xx, 79, 117, 123, 297, 307, 631

Levin, iii, xx, 109, 123, 124, 125, 139, 193, 198, 200, 262, 263, 307, 354, 602, 603, 611, 632, 643

Lewinstein, 264

Lichteneger, 573, 575

Book of Stryj Index

Lichter, 425

Lieberman, 437, 574, 578, 608

Liebermann, 128, 614

Liebowitz, 575

Liebsman, 188

Lifshitz, 92, 172, 351

Lifszitz, 52

Limnanowsky, 585

Lindbaum, 501

Lindenbaum, 208, 421

Lindner, 158, 182, 307, 320, 337, 349, 424, 605, 616

Lip, 196

Lipman, 199, 466

Lippa, 52, 64, 88, 122, 253

Lippel, 190, 609

Lippman, 576

Lipschitz, 59, 60, 61, 67, 71, 584, 586, 593, 640

Lipshitz, 209

Litaur, 311

Livne (Liberman), 326

Livne (Liberman}, 324

Loeb, 109

Loker, 286, 458

Lorberbaum, 36, 37, 42, 125, 210, 211, 212, 213, 324, 351, 617, 635, 639

Low, 80

Luft, 89, 91, 93, 122, 602

Lusthaus, 223, 374, 619, 664

Lustig, 185, 199, 304, 306, 320, 337, 399, 498, 499, 501, 606, 632

Lustik, 436, 444

M

Mager, 186

Mahler, 78, 279, 448

Małachowski, 8

Maleska, 19

Malz, 279

Maneles, 83

Manfeld, 176

Manjia, 206

Mantel, 419, 422, 496, 514

Marbach, 182, 306, 337, 349, 499, 605

Margaliot, 209

Markipka, 112, 114

Markowitcz, 18

Markusohn, 52

Marshal, 286, 458

Marzand, 199

Mauerer, 466

Maurer, 298, 631

May, 127, 614

Mayer, 139, 311, 606

Mayersohn, 190, 609

Mazatner, 16

Maztner, 16

Mehler, 574

Meir, 615

Meirson, 94, 98, 105

Meisels, 166, 196, 307, 308, 337, 342, 484, 604

Melamed, 146, 158, 507, 615

Meller, xx, 48, 78, 165, 173, 188, 207, 260, 281, 283, 288, 302, 303, 307, 308, 320, 337, 378, 416, 422, 461, 495, 604, 608, 613, 625, 631, 668

Melpin, 137

Meltz, 295

Meltzer, 186, 311, 573, 574

Meltzer-Hauptmann, 186, 311, 606

Mendelowitcz, 19

Menderer, 449

Book of Stryj Index

Mendrochowicz, 50

Mermelstein, 59, 584

Messrs, 459

Metzker, 171

Meuerer, 477

Meyer, 466

Meyersohn, 188, 608, 616

Meyerson, 158

Mihlbauer, 281, 283, 623, 628

Mihlrad, 157, 615

Mikam, 234

Milabauer, 414

Milbauer, 140, 197, 204, 611

Millard, 154, 176

Millbauer, xix, 243, 489

Miller, 47, 48, 84, 288, 335, 460, 630

Mintz, 83

Mishel, 126, 140, 182, 274, 395, 489, 603

Mittler, 576

Mojseszowitz, 15

Monderer, 111, 188, 208, 289, 335, 462, 608, 613

Mondschein, 189, 609

Mondsein, 266

Mondshein, 83

Mondsheins, 85, 86

Moraczewski, 278, 279, 287

Moraczewsky, 64, 588

Moratchevski, 459, 471, 472

Morbach, 467

Mordechis, 17, 24, 553

Moskowicz, 19

Moskowitcz, 15

Moskowitz, 9, 15, 219

Moszkowicz, 19

Muller, 111

Musbacher, 40

N

Nacher, 586

Nagler, 182, 185, 263, 419, 496, 605, 606

Nagler (Levin), 420

Naker, 61

Nathan, 15, 51

Nathansohn, 218

Nathanson, 48

Neiman, 501

Neimann, 186, 311, 606

Neubauer, 125, 165, 284, 330, 364, 604, 629, 654

Neuman, 125, 283, 302, 304, 306, 307, 320, 324, 631, 632

Neumann, 126, 159, 161, 185, 336, 337, 604, 606

Neumark, 230, 596, 620

Newirth, 574

Nier, 467

Nives, 496

Nobbes, 414, 419

Nomberg, 458

Nordau, 118, 204, 612

Nossig, 228, 592

Nusenblatt, 322

Nussbaum, 107, 127, 614

Nussenblatt, xix, 117, 127, 158, 165, 182, 185, 231, 232, 240, 298, 354, 395, 399, 403, 406, 411, 422, 466, 470, 488, 494, 501, 576, 599, 600, 604, 605, 606, 614, 616, 621, 631, 643

O

Oberlaender, xx, 261, 626

Oberlander, 165, 167, 261, 354

Book of Stryj Index

Oberländer, 177, 302, 303, 604, 631, 643

Ochser, 462

Oper, 117, 286, 304, 307, 311, 323, 337, 357, 480, 625, 629, 631, 632

Opper, xx, 123, 199, 264, 265, 286, 289, 296, 297, 298, 299, 457, 458, 459, 462, 464, 465, 466, 468, 470, 576, 577, 578, 602, 629, 648

Ordober, 117

Orenstein, 42

Ornstein, 157, 615

Oster, 330

Osterjung, 406

P

Pachenick, 196

Pacnik, 80

Paris, 233, 283

Patrach, 59, 60, 62, 177, 458, 583, 585, 587, 629

Patrick, 574

Pavelo, 585

Pavlyk, 61

Peinholz, 154

Pepperkorn, 61

Peretz, 458, 476

Pessburg, 158

Peterseil, 467

Petliura, 120, 451, 452

Petrach, 286, 303, 336

Pfefferkorn, 585

Pferbaum, 97, 98, 99, 100, 106, 125

Pickholtz, iii, 124, 169, 399, 424, 502

Pickholz, 123, 124, 139, 176, 283, 602, 603, 628

Pikholtz, 106, 107, 501

Pikholz, 320

Piltz, 406

Pilz, 182, 605

Plesser, 206, 613

Polack, 186, 199, 458, 499

Polak, 286

Pollack, 190, 609

Pollak, 629

Polturak, 80

Pomerantz, 337, 419, 496, 499

Pomeranz, 63, 588

Pomernaz, 313

Poniatowski, 3, 13, 18, 74

Pontiakowski, 27, 28

Popial, 13

Prastak, 154

Preis, 120, 253, 305, 416

Preiss, 399, 495, 499, 501

Pressburg, 213, 224, 616

Presser, xix, 123, 124, 126, 139, 187, 188, 201, 240, 241, 246, 254, 274, 280, 281, 282, 352, 602, 603, 608, 612, 622, 623, 627, 628, 641

Pritzhand, 186, 311, 606

Prohaska, 75, 76, 77

Pruchter, 421

Puhacz, 4

Pumertz, 294

R

Raat, 496

Rab, 207

Rabbi Berish, 24

Rabbi Mechele, 370

rabbi Nachman, 14

rabbi Yaakov from Lissa, 37, 351

Rabinowitcz, 80

Rabinowitz, 167, 170

Book of Stryj Index

Radler, 91, 123, 184, 207, 303, 305, 357, 602, 648

Raff, 585

Rand, 131

Rap, 207, 613

Rapoport, 36, 49

Rapp, 61, 311

Rappaport, 50, 168, 189, 203, 209, 279, 288, 320, 335, 461, 609, 612

Rappoprt, 199

Raps, 484, 485

Rassler, 495

Rathaus, 147, 148, 150, 152, 155, 615, 645

Raznicenko (Erez), 168

Rechter, 321, 322, 327, 489, 498, 633, 635

Reder, 385, 676

Redler, 123, 183, 207, 602, 606, 613

Reich, 64, 117, 119, 123, 165, 182, 201, 253, 279, 280, 281, 349, 374, 386, 471, 489, 588, 602, 604, 605, 612, 627, 664, 676

Reichbach, 577

Reichman, 403, 406, 494

Reif, 107

Reiner, 378, 403, 669

Reinhartz, xx, 112, 114, 186, 249, 304, 307, 319, 321, 349, 601

Reinhartz-Barlev, 632

Reinhartz–Barlev, 304

Reinharz, 322, 633

Reinherz, 173

Reis, 264

Reisen, 286, 458

Reish, 274

Reisner, 60

Reissner, 585

Reiter, 145, 615

Reitzes, 67, 72, 594

Reps, 342, 343

Resenband, 50

Resenmann, 311

Resport, 189, 609

Rettinger, 64

Richter, 165, 177, 604

Ringel, 60, 61, 64, 84, 89, 175, 181, 182, 239, 278, 402, 491, 585, 588, 605, 622

Rinhartz, 337

Risch, 378, 668

Riterman, 117

Robinson, 33, 171, 177, 303, 307, 337, 406, 422, 434, 439, 495, 632

Roht, 419

Rosen, 467

Rosenbaum, 385, 437, 471, 676

Rosenberg, xiii, xx, 80, 93, 94, 95, 96, 103, 104, 105, 110, 111, 137, 173, 199, 268, 284, 288, 297, 299, 302, 304, 307, 311, 320, 323, 335, 337, 338, 399, 400, 403, 406, 409, 410, 449, 450, 452, 455, 457, 458, 460, 465, 468, 470, 476, 495, 500, 501, 630, 631, 632

Rosenblum, xix, 45, 47, 54

Rosenfeld, 267, 286, 458

Rosenkranz, 188, 462

Rosenman, 63, 196, 253, 314, 378, 588, 610, 668

Rosenzweig, 89, 181, 186, 311, 406, 495, 605

Rosler, 186, 199

Rosmann, 123, 602

Rosmarin, 143, 182, 202, 295, 471, 608, 615

Rossler, xx, 123, 266, 267, 268, 288, 289, 296, 304, 307, 308, 311, 335, 337, 416, 460, 461, 462, 464, 472, 602, 630, 632

Rotbard, 143, 311, 431, 615

Book of Stryj Index

Rotbaum, 283, 327, 635

Rotenstreich, 239

Rotfeld, xiii, 130, 166, 177, 186, 283, 294, 302, 303, 304, 305, 306, 307, 308, 309, 310, 311, 319, 320, 337, 399, 400, 604, 615, 631, 632

Roth, 162, 312, 313, 321, 414, 422, 604, 633

Rothenberg, 133, 152, 313, 615

Rothstein, 574

Rotstein, 207, 613

Rottfeld, 499, 500, 501

Rottstein, 207

Rsenmann, 80

Rubin, 116, 117, 574

Rubinstein, 307, 308

Rudik, 185, 606

S

Sachar, 165, 177, 604

Sadan, 166, 171, 354

Sadan (Stock), 166, 354

Sak, 422

Sakolaski, 15

Salfin, 466

Saltz, 459

Salvan (now Se–Lavan), 167

Salz, 62, 64, 253, 278, 280, 287, 471, 586, 588, 589, 627, 629

Samelson, 46

Samueli, 45, 46, 47, 48, 50, 51, 53, 79

Sander, 183, 606

Sapcze, 298

Sapiaha, 25

Sapirstein, 159, 603

Saszoniawicz, 28

Sauerbrunn, 373, 476, 489, 494, 496, 664

Schachter, 573

Schaechter, 494

Schatz, 416, 495

Schatzker, 361, 491, 651

Schauder, 418, 419

Schechter, 80, 306, 311, 330, 378, 406, 499, 576, 668

Schefer, 320

Schein, 578

Scheinfeld, 60, 61, 585

Scherer, 309

Scherlag, 84, 89, 181, 605

Schieffer, 458

Schiff, 48, 84, 88, 89, 91, 123, 124, 139, 140, 157, 181, 182, 191, 192, 195, 196, 201, 253, 279, 281, 314, 352, 354, 602, 603, 605, 610, 612, 641, 643

Schiller, 67, 72, 79, 86, 594

Schiller–Tzengebatt, 462

Schindler, 80, 192, 193, 204, 306, 313, 353, 495, 611, 612, 642

Schipper, 75, 76

Schlak, 321

Schlaks, 322, 633

Schleifer, 379, 670

Schleiffer, 191, 609

Schmelkes, 67, 71

Schmorak, 64, 84, 175, 419, 588, 605, 622

Schnier, 384, 674

Schnür-Pepłowski, 77

Schoenbach, 458

Schoenfeld, 60, 584

Schorer, 311

Schorr, 51, 128, 129, 130, 132, 146, 152, 155, 165, 177, 604, 614, 615

Schottenfeld, 574

Schprung–Lustig, 306

Book of Stryj Index

Schrieber, 53

Schtoltz, 422

Schtolz, 419

Schuster, xx, 165, 166, 177, 271, 354, 406, 422, 440, 494

Schuster (Shilo), 165, 166, 177, 604, 642

Schuster-Shilo, xx, 271, 626

Schutzer, 206, 613

Schwalb, 187, 314

Schwamer, xx, 125, 177, 256, 283, 302, 303, 304, 307, 308, 337, 357, 624, 628, 631

Schwammer, 484, 648

Schwargold, 193

Schwartz, 124, 165, 177, 200, 272, 311, 354, 499, 574, 603, 604, 612, 643

Schwartzberg, 90, 128, 614

Schwartzer, 576

Schwarzberg, 298, 466, 631

Schwieder, 495

Seeman, 321, 573, 633, 642, 643

Seidenfrau, 188, 289, 462, 608

Seidman, 484, 496, 606, 612, 628, 635, 636, 643

Seidmann, 615, 625

Seif, 154, 157, 428, 604, 615

Seiff, 466

Seiger, 577

Seinfeld, 178, 194, 406, 494, 610

Seldowicz, 643, 648

Seliger, 571

Selinger, 182, 322, 422, 494, 605

Seltzer, xx, 137, 269, 288, 298, 335, 460, 466, 469, 630

Seman, 131, 132, 615

Shalom Aleichem, 109

Shamir, 298, 477

Shammai, 125

Shapira, 106, 135, 154, 162, 320, 353, 604, 642

Shayke, 137

Shayko, 466

Shechter, 196, 304

Shefler, 274

Sheike, 298

Sheinfeld, 111, 122, 131, 190, 253, 277, 406, 449, 602, 609, 615, 626

Shenbach, 123, 156, 195, 283, 286, 602, 615, 628, 629

Shenberg, 45, 329, 636

Shenfeld, 88, 89, 205, 313

Sherman, 574

Shilo, 165, 166, 177, 272, 273, 323, 354, 501, 642

Shilo (Schuster), 500

Shimonowitz, 167

Shitzer, 187

Shlatiner, 146, 152, 153

Shmelkes, 279

Shmorack, 349

Shmuel, 18, 24

Shmuelik, 16

Shnir, 496

Shnitzer, 191

Shochet, 159

Shoffmann, 167, 230

Shohet, 129, 132, 143, 144, 150, 151, 153, 187, 226, 260, 509, 608, 615, 619

Shor, 91

Shteher, 230

Shulboim, 48

Shur, 107

Shusheim, 117

Shuster, 145, 323, 434, 615

Book of Stryj Index

Shützer, vi, 377, 609, 668

Shwamer, 324

Shwartzberg, 165

Siarkowski, 20

Siegel, iii, 65, 159, 171, 237, 262, 263, 354, 537, 590, 593, 602, 603, 604, 642, 643

Sieger, 574, 575

Sieniawski, 7, 74

Silber, 169, 631

Silberschlag, 174, 321, 604, 633, 640

Silbershlag, 351

Singer, 188, 574, 608

Smarak, 496

Smolenskin, xxvi, 50, 51, 164

Sobel, 303, 377, 378, 668

Sobele, 195

Sobieski, 3, 4, 11, 12, 13, 74, 543

Sokol, 205, 320

Sommerfeld, 75, 193, 611

Sommerstein, 170, 182, 185

Spaet, 189, 609

Spät, 123, 602

Speciner, 578

Sperling, 187, 457, 608

Spiegel, 124, 125, 159, 161, 182, 188, 201, 281, 283, 354, 403, 603, 604, 605, 608, 612, 628, 643

Spinard, 313, 436, 437, 444

Spindel–Manor, 279

Stand, 60, 171, 279, 585

Stark, 165, 177, 387, 573, 574, 604, 678

Steher, 596

Steiermark, 491

Steif, 324, 635

Steiff, 496

Stein, 330, 441

Steiner, 92, 125, 165, 185, 189, 193, 304, 307, 320, 326, 329, 337, 352, 354, 604, 606, 609, 611, 632, 635, 636, 640, 643

Steirmark, 420

Stekeles, 594

Stem, 60, 584

Stenrberg, 419

Stern, xx, 59, 60, 61, 62, 83, 88, 89, 91, 123, 124, 125, 127, 163, 173, 187, 188, 190, 207, 247, 248, 281, 396, 419, 429, 431, 432, 446, 497, 498, 501, 583, 584, 585, 587, 602, 603, 604, 608, 609, 613, 614, 623

Sternberg, 123, 124, 139, 182, 314, 327, 331, 440, 496, 602, 603, 605, 635

Sterner, 173

Sternhal, 80

Sterski-Klarsfeld, 491

Stinawski, 19

Stock (Sadan), 642

Stoeger, 77

Stojalowski, 64

Stoltz, 443, 496

Strassmann, 207, 613

Straucher, 279

Streifer, 298, 299, 466, 468, 470, 631

Striker, 331

Strizower, 130

Sturmlauf, 165, 354, 604, 642

Subkulaktor, 15

Sula, 168, 170

Sussman, 577

Swartz, 304

Szaczarski, 279

Szaczerski, 402

Szapira, 324, 635

Book of Stryj Index

Szatzker, 402, 557

Szeft, 120

Szerbstein, 109

Szlomowitcz, 15

Sznir, 414, 419

Szteirmark, 402

Sztoltz (Heller), 416

Szwammer, 140

T

Tadanier, 127, 614

Tadanir, 177, 186, 303, 320, 632

Tahun, 67, 72

Talpin, 298

Tanne, 309, 320, 632

Tarnowski, 2, 7, 74

Taub, 208, 613

Tauber, 120, 123, 189, 419, 602, 609

Taubes, 279

Tebbelle, 213

Teicher, 311, 429, 445

Teitler, 165, 354, 604, 642

Teller, 123, 174, 184, 185, 281, 422

Tennenblatt, 65, 159, 187, 590, 603

Teomim, 37, 211, 215

Teper, 449

Tepper, xx, 111, 268, 269, 457, 472, 602

Thon, 594

Tileman, 165, 177, 604

Tilleman, xix, 322, 354, 621, 642

Tirkel, 472

Tiwalweitcz, 18

Toptche, 466

Torobitski, 23

Toyb, 467

Toyber, 496

Tzahor, 177, 323, 526

Tzeler, 188, 608

Tzelermayer, 182

Tzobel, 496

U

Uchteneger, 577

Ungar, 495

Unger, 83, 107, 406

V

Vinik, 470

Vizeltir, 495

Vogel, 378, 606, 668

von Hirsch, 55

Von Kowalski, 33

W

Wachtel, 574

Wagman, 123, 455, 472, 602

Wagner, 123, 156, 187, 281, 288, 320, 335, 336, 399, 434, 446, 608, 615

Wahl, 18, 24

Wald, 168, 319, 320

Waldman, xiii, xx, 96, 105, 116, 117, 176, 187, 191, 203, 204, 206, 207, 259, 260, 295, 327, 331, 349, 399, 443, 501, 613, 635, 636

Waldmann, 127, 613, 614

Waldman-Schwalb, 608

Walker, 61, 423

Walkowski, 10

Walmut, 489

Walter, 309, 421, 501, 632

Book of Stryj Index

Wandel, 162, 327, 480, 604, 628, 635

Wandell, 123, 283, 602

Wanderer, 576

Wang, 378, 489, 668

Warber, 310

Wartzel, 23, 80

Washitz, 279

Wax, 216

Wechsler, 185, 606

Wecker, 576

Wegner, 461

Weide, 359, 489, 650

Weidenfeld, 182, 314, 423, 605

Weinbach, 91, 311

Weinbaum Hacohen, 83

Weinbaums, 86

Weinfeld, 79

Weingarten, 577

Weinrab, 106, 349

Weinreb, 188, 608

Weintraub, 208, 330

Weis, 295, 399, 406, 423

Weisbart, 186

Weisenberg, 201, 289

Weiss, 125, 144, 156, 165, 177, 200, 204, 207, 284, 302, 303, 319, 320, 323, 434, 446, 457, 459, 495, 498, 499, 501, 612, 613, 614, 615, 629, 631, 632

Weissbart, 311

Weissglass, 189

Weitz, 574

Weizman, 55, 167

Weizmann, 118, 280

Welker, 123, 124, 125, 208, 403, 585, 602, 603, 613

Weller, 208

Wendel, 140

Wexler, 199

Wiarszanowitcz, 9

Wielhorski, 5

Wien, 78, 79, 172, 207, 613

Wiesaltier, 420

Wiesaltir, 313

Wieseltier, 165, 183, 184, 281, 322, 570, 571, 606, 634

Wiesenberg, 65, 117, 122, 123, 352, 462, 589, 602, 640

Wiesenfelcl, 605

Wiesenfeld, 182

Wiesengreen, 283

Wilff, 207

Winogura (Yedidia), 167

Wisaltier, 330, 406

Wiszniaweski, 15

Wizalteer, 106, 107

Wizaltier, 336

Władysław IV, 3, 11

Władysław Jagiełło, 1

Wohlmann, 186, 311, 606

Wohlmut, xx, 123, 125, 140, 159, 186, 187, 188, 197, 244, 281, 283, 311, 353, 378, 499, 602, 608, 611, 623, 642, 669

Wojhowska, 19

Wolf, viii, 24, 32, 64, 77, 186, 311, 376, 427, 489, 577, 667

Wolff, 146, 223, 229, 595, 613, 615

Wolfinger, 178, 182, 422, 605

Wolfowicz, 19

Wolf-Rotfeld, 606

Wolowski, 206, 306, 409, 410, 613

Wonjarazow, 19

Woroclawski, 20

Book of Stryj Index

Wospowitcz, 19
Wundel, 422
Wundell, 340
Wunderleich, 111
Wunderlicht, 449
Wunderman, 92, 608
Wundermann, 63, 65, 159, 187, 588, 590, 603
Wurstel, 577
Wurzel, 62, 64, 278, 587, 588, 622
Wynn, 194

Y

Yaari, 354, 642
Ya'ari, 166
Yales, 496
Yash, 170
Yekel, 422
Yekels, 157, 616
Yolles, xix, 107, 110, 117, 218, 219
Yost, 41

Z

Zaklika, 1
Zandenberg, 403
Zatwarnicki, 52, 64
Zaum, 575, 577
Zaurbrun, 419
Zehngebot, 182, 605
Zeidman, xx, 126, 176, 177, 186, 258, 260, 283, 284, 302, 303, 306, 311, 327, 328, 331, 354, 603, 631
Zeidmann, 144, 152, 153, 154, 419
Zeif, 165, 311
Zeisler, 403, 423
Zeldovitch, 158, 616
Zeldowicz, 354, 357
Zelinger, 312, 406, 428
Zeman, 165, 169, 170, 353, 354, 604
Zerubavel, 458, 467
Ziamalkowski, 46
Ziegel, 107, 116, 117, 118, 119, 123, 165, 322, 323
Ziering, 574
Zilberschlag, 165
Zilberstein, 309
Zildowicz, 13
Zimmerman, 311, 320
Zipper, 58, 59, 60, 62, 79, 84, 89, 90, 175, 239, 278, 279, 309, 582, 585, 586, 592, 599, 605, 632
Ziskind Landa, 41
Zobel, 419
Zogan, 467
Zola, 86
Zoldan, 176, 178, 185, 403, 606
Zomerstein, 80
Zukerkendel, 337
Zusman, 117
Zussman, 206, 613
Zwilling, 125, 274, 283, 628
Zygmunt II, 7, 8

www.ingramcontent.com/pod-product-compliance
Lightning Source LLC
Chambersburg PA
CBHW081421160426
42814CB00039B/272